THE CORRESPONDENCE OF

Alexander Pope

ALEXANDER POPE

Crayon portrait by Jonathan Richardson

THE CORRESPONDENCE OF Alexander Pope

EDITED BY
GEORGE SHERBURN

VOLUME I
1704–1718

OXFORD
AT THE CLARENDON PRESS
1956

Oxford University Press, Amen House, London E.C. 4
GLASGOW NEW YORK TORONTO MELBOURNE WELLINGTON
BOMBAY CALCUTTA MADRAS KARACHI CAPE TOWN IBADAN

PRINTED IN GREAT BRITAIN
AT THE UNIVERSITY PRESS, OXFORD
BY CHARLES BATEY, PRINTER TO THE UNIVERSITY

PREFACE

THIS edition, as all my friends know, has been in progress, intermittently, since about 1934. Academic duties, augmented during the war, and administrative duties rashly assumed after the war have for considerable periods stopped the work almost completely. The results of this prolongation of effort have been to allow time for the accumulation of new letters, and perhaps for some confusions to arise between early footnotes and later ones. It is hoped that the footnotes of 1935 may still sing more or less in the same key with those of 1955.

This is the customary moment for thanking one's friends for assistance. The task is enormous. It is easy to recognize aid given in financial subsidy by the three distinguished universities which I have served during my work on Pope: Chicago, Columbia, and Harvard have all been generous. Thanks to them I have had indispensable assistance from Professors Arthur Friedman, V. A. Dearing, Agnes Sibley, and from Mrs. Ruth Macrae and Miss Elizabeth Cook. For aid in reading the proofs I gratefully acknowledge help from Sir Harold Williams, James M. Osborn, Sava Klima, and Robert Halsband. For the rest I am inclined to imitate Cordelia and refuse to heave my heart into my mouth. If I began with Oxford and continued all the way to the Huntington Library in California, naming the distinguished scholars who have borne with and lightened my ignorance, I might well be accused of insufferable pride. The editors of the Twickenham *Pope* —and especially the late Norman Ault—have all been most helpful. On both sides of the Atlantic I have many friends, and I do not know of one who has not helped me. To name them all would gratify my pride—and in some cases theirs—but would do no more. Many of them will find their aid acknowledged in various footnotes. To owners and especially dealers in autographs acknowledgements are made at the beginning of each letter, as a help to students and as an act of gratitude on my part. Almost without exception dealers have been ready to allow photostats or transcripts to be made—and this in spite of the current tradition that such procedure cuts the money value of a letter. Having watched the prices of Pope letters now for twenty-five years, I should like to register the opinion that publication or other reproduction has far less bearing on the price of a letter than some imagine. If dealers or owners have suffered financial loss through helping me, I am very sorry. They have been generous, and my hope is that interest in Pope, increased through this edition, may eventually reward them.

They have enabled me to present an edition of the correspondence augmented by something like 35 per cent. over the last edition, that of

Elwin and Courthope (1871–89). Some readers, viewing the extensiveness of Pope's epistolary achievements, will be inclined to sigh with a former colleague of mine who does not love Pope, and exclaim, 'Who would have thought the little man had so much ink in him.' To less prejudiced readers the letters here presented will give a portrait of Pope and his mind such as has not been seen before.

G. S.

Middlebury, Vermont

CONTENTS

VOLUME I

VOLUME II

VOLUME III

VOLUME IV

VOLUME V

INTRODUCTION

IN his own century no man did more to further the art of letter-writing than Pope, and no man had a higher reputation as a letter-writer. His fame as a satirist, however, was even higher and more lasting; and by the beginning of the nineteenth century critics had become increasingly ready to assume that a satirist was less a man of austere values than an ill-natured person, whose letters must be either ill-natured or insincerely good-natured. The further assumption that letters should above all else be sincere made it difficult for readers to reconcile the attitudes of Pope in his letters with those in his satires. Swift's opinion that out of Pope's letters 'there might be collected the best system that ever was wrote for the conduct of human life' (iv. 77) seemed simply amusing. And so critics shut their eyes to Pope's moral commonplaces as well as to the obvious kindliness of his friendly instincts and to the graceful and elegant phrasing of which he was capable. Satires, unlike letters, are not written to friends; and Pope in his letters made almost a cult of friendship. By the middle of the nineteenth century, however, when Dilke and Elwin, through the discovery of Pope's letters to John Caryll, found that in publishing his letters Pope had recombined parts of two or three, had omitted passages, and had transferred some letters to correspondents to whom they were never sent, condemnation became extreme. Editors seemed to forget that Pope himself published only a very small part of his correspondence.

Pope's attitude towards individuals in his letters is most interesting. No one, of course, consistently writes letters in order to offend his friends, and Pope writes always as an indefatigably kind person. The variety and the frequency of his kind deeds are astonishing. He corrects the verses of other poets; he even corrects the Latin of his friends—though his own is not impeccable. He writes letters on behalf of servant girls; he is ready to arrange the acquisition of Scots cattle for Lord Bathurst's son; he designs gardens, advises on architecture, on sculpture, or on the choice of pictures, and even on the growing of pine-apples, in which he was expert. He writes to beg Oxford dons to be kind to sons of friends. If a preacher is to be elected at the Charterhouse or a Professor of Poetry at Oxford, Pope is energetic in working for his candidates. Though a Roman Catholic, he more than once exercised influence in the disposal of Anglican livings. He was always busy, even officiously busy. If attacks on himself ate at his heart, as they are said to have done, that fact hardly appears in the letters. His normal position is, You may say what you like of my works: you have no right to attack my personal character if you have no personal acquaintance with me.

The letters vary enormously, but by and large they are hastily and casually written. Some, to be sure, are studiously composed as show pieces. His merry account of his journey to Oxford with Lintot (i. 371–5) is one of those, as are many of the letters that he himself published. Some of these are self-consciously noble and polished. His letters of 1740 to Hugh, Earl of Marchmont, urging public duties upon his lordship (letters not published until 1831) are serious, carefully written examples of moral—and political—eloquence. Most of his letters that he did not publish, however, are the product of a rapid pen, and their innocuous insincerities are simply those of polite social relations: kindness encourages one to tell friends in letters what the friends will like to hear. Many of the unpublished letters are brief notes: nowadays they would be telephone calls; here they serve to show Pope's multifarious activities.

His concept of a good letter was that it was 'talking on paper' to friends. More self-consciously he tells us that 'a letter should be a natural image of the mind of the writer' (i. 94). Thus he flattered himself that his letters to *good men* (i.e. friends) might be as creditable to him as all his verses put together (ii. 419). So the letters became in a sense a part of his works, capable of polish, revision, amalgamation, transfer to correspondents other than the original recipients—capable even, though very seldom, of factual falsification. He wished his letters to be what he said the Duke of Buckingham's *Works* were, 'a monument of his mind and a more perfect image of himself'.

The proper interest of the letters is then chiefly psychological. Under pressure he did write 'news letters' to his friends 'Mrs. Blounts', as he called them collectively; but he protests that he does *not* write such letters, that he is no brother to such newsmen as Dyer and Dawkes (i. 307). He finds little news—even in the days of Sir Robert Walpole's fall—to report to Hugh Bethel, who was in 1742 lonely in Italy. Pope does not picture the times: he does frequently give us thoughtful and severe comment upon them. He does not even talk much concerning a poem in process of composition: he is habitually content to report the momentary states of his mind. If Pope was as great a poet as we have been led to believe, his mind is worth study, and his personal qualities can be more directly seen in his letters than elsewhere. The study is not easy. He speaks more than once of 'the April weather' of his mind, and his concept of 'chaos of thought and passion all confused' was more than a brilliant phrase. For many readers his letters might be more enjoyable if they were more like those of Horace Walpole, less introvert and more given to laughable social detail, more conscious of the pageant of life about him. But he writes of himself and out of himself, not out of his social environment. The study of an artist's personality easily goes to excess; but Pope is a fascinating problem, and if the letters here presented are read without Victorian prejudice, the picture of his mind will be different in some respects from that which in many quarters has been current, and much nearer the truth.

HISTORICAL SURVEY

As early as 19 November 1712 Pope was thinking of the possibility of using his letters for publication. He wrote to Caryll then, requesting the return of letters on the ground that 'several thoughts which I throw out that way in the freedom of my soul . . . may be of use to me in a design I am lately engaged in'. Possibly the design had to do with his agreement to write essays for *The Guardian*; but whatever his project, there is no evidence that he actually did use the letters. His next keen interest in getting letters returned followed the publication in 1726 (under the date of 1727) of his letters to Henry Cromwell, which the disreputable bookseller, Edmund Curll, had purchased from Cromwell's discarded mistress, Elizabeth Thomas. This publication so upset Pope that he attempted, with only partial success, to persuade friends to return all letters not yet destroyed. The letters to Cromwell seem to have had little vogue with readers, but their publication stayed in Pope's mind.

When in 1728 the then reigning Prince of the Dunces, Lewis Theobald, brought out a volume of *Posthumous Works of William Wycherley*, Pope was again annoyed. He had grudges to work off against Theobald, who had scorned his edition of Shakespeare. Now in turn Pope determined to discredit Theobald's editing of Wycherley. Many years earlier Pope had been asked by Wycherley to revise and polish poems for possible publication; and after some rigorous work by Pope, resulting in a period of estrangement, Wycherley seems to have agreed with Pope that it was inadvisable to publish. But on his death-bed Wycherley married, and his widow's next husband, Captain Shrimpton, eventually nominated Theobald to see through the press some of Wycherley's poems, left in manuscript—poems that, as Pope well knew, Wycherley had decided not to publish. Theobald furthermore apparently at times printed phrases or lines formerly inserted by Pope, which were not Wycherley's. Pope had letters from Wycherley that threw light on the matter, letters that would put Wycherley and himself in a good light and Theobald and Shrimpton, by implication, in a bad and mercenary light. Pope had few or none of his letters to Wycherley, but he had preserved at least some of Wycherley's letters to him. One original recently has come into the possession of Harvard University. In November 1729 Pope brought out a second volume of *The Posthumous Works of William Wycherley*, which contained texts of certain poems more authentic than those published by Theobald and (more important) contained Wycherley's correspondence with him concerning the poems.[1] The letters, naturally, put the young poet in a favourable light; it is doubtful if they put him in a falsely favourable light. They showed that the clever youth had a great influence over the old dramatist, and that evidently the dramatist had decided not to publish the poems. Pope's volume was designed to make it clear that only mercenary persons would publish a dozen years after the poet's death poems that were not surely genuine and that in any case would not enhance Wycherley's reputation. Pope's attempt came to nothing, for his volume was suppressed. It may be that Wycherley's heirs objected, but Professor Dearing is probably right in his opinion that Lintot, with whom Pope had quarrelled before 1728, objected to an obvious infringement of *his* copyrights in Pope's reprints of certain poems. In any case the volume was suppressed, and the sheets containing the letters became Pope's property—to be used later in 1735.

The preface 'To the Reader', here reprinted from the volume, shows that Pope did not acknowledge any connexion with the publication, and this fact brings us to his central fixed idea with regard to subsequent publication of his letters. He felt strongly that to be known to publish one's own letters laid one open to charges of reprehensible self-conceit. Three months after the publication of the 'unauthorized' editions of 1735 he talked the matter over with Joseph Spence[2] and spoke of the modesty or 'prudery' involved. Concerning such 'imputation' he wrote to Lord Orrery in 1740 (iv. 286). The feeling was vague, but it was unfortunately strong.

It led to chicanery: for he would publish. One of his most striking traits, seen often in letters, is his ability to persuade others to serve as agents, almost as 'cat's-paws'. The Harleian Library was his great resource.[3] The Wycherley letters, so his preface and certain letters said, were there deposited by consent of Lord Oxford; and from there by consent of his lordship freed for publication—without, as it was falsely avowed, Pope's consent. Lord Oxford, proud of his magnificent library and of his intimacy with Pope, continued, even after Pope's publication of the Wycherley volume, to be hospitable to the making of transcripts of Pope letters, either by his own scribes or by others outside the library, and to the deposit of the transcripts in the library. This work went on for at least some years after 1728, and in the making of transcripts there is doubtless added opportunity for the corruption of texts. But the Harleian transcripts, as they are here to be called, seem

[1] Professor V. A. Dearing has published an admirable account of the volume in *PMLA*, lxviii (1953), 223–36.

[2] The manuscripts of Spence, now in the possession of Mr. James M. Osborn of Yale University, contain this bit. Mr. Osborn numbers the anecdote as Add. Anec. 1320. 13 bottom.

[3] See 'Pope's Letters and the Harleian Library' (by the editor) in *ELH*: *A Journal of English Literary History*, vii (1940), 177–87.

practically always to have been made legitimately and carefully from original letters. Lord Oxford took more interest in some correspondences than in others, but he seems in most cases to have compared the transcripts with the originals, as a proof-reader might; for on occasion he adds an address or a postmark that his scribe had omitted; and addresses often and postmarks always imply originals. He corrected the texts, especially of the Swift letters. Since Swift's hand was difficult for the scribe, his lordship adds words in spaces left blank in such detail as to imply that he was correcting from original letters. These Harleian transcripts are now preserved at Longleat, and the present editor has high confidence in their texts. Footnotes to individual letters will indicate exceptions.

One cannot be certain how far Lord Oxford was in Pope's confidence concerning later projects to get these, or some of these, letters into print. By 1733, however, Pope had invented a neat scheme. Edmund Curll loved to publish opprobrious biography, and in 1733 he advertised more than once for biographical facts and documents for use in a life of Pope. Presently on 11 October 1733 there came a letter to Curll, a letter (iii. 387) signed only with the initials 'P. T.', containing plausible but erroneous information about Pope's family, which might draw in Curll, and which certainly did not underrate the poet's family tree. The intention was to lead Curll to present Pope in a favourable light, which Curll would regret when the information was found to be false. Curll was directed to reply in *The Daily Advertiser* for 18 October, and he said he did, but search discovers no such advertisement. On 15 November, however, P. T. wrote again offering as material for Pope's life 'a large collection of letters' that had fallen into P. T.'s hands. This should have been very tempting to Curll; and the substitution of an epistolary image (self-drawn) for an abusive biography assembled by Curll would immensely please Pope. But Curll, always wary, refused the bait, and nothing happened thereafter for sixteen months.

Then at long last Curll approached Pope directly, sending enclosed the letters of P. T. and asking an alliance. Pope loudly scorned the overture; but P. T. (doubtless, as Curll later said, 'Trickster Pope' himself) again moved into action, and after long, sly, and even melodramatic intrigues, on 12 May 1735 mysterious agents began delivering at the shop of Curll octavo volumes of Pope's printed letters, in various states of completeness. Pope's trickery through P. T. had worked: he himself seemed perfectly concealed, and now his loud, hypocritical outcries of injury, as well as the pre-publication advertisements announcing and denouncing the edition, aroused such interest that the letters were the literary event of the year. Several printings were called for.

Pope's manipulations of his texts were well concealed by the seeming fact that the whole affair was the fraudulent work of unscrupulous persons who had respect neither for authentic texts nor for truth. No objections arose to the factual inconsistencies in the letters. Caryll, some of whose letters had been transferred to Addison, Wycherley, and others—transferred ostensibly by Curll or the thieves of the letters—died in the spring of 1736 and Pope's (or Curll's, as it seemed) chicanery as editor lay hidden for the most part until the Victorians got to work. Curll, however, soon knew that he was the dupe of Pope himself, and he pointed out that the early editions of 1735 used Pope's sheets of the 1729 edition of Wycherley's letters without reprinting But Curll's disrepute was such that he was unheard, and no serious study of the editorial aspects of the printings was made in Pope's day.

Other details of all this intrigue may be found dispersed in the letters of 1733 and 1735 here printed, and in the anonymous, but Pope-inspired, *Narrative of the Method by which Mr. Pope's Private Letters were procured and published by Edmund Curll*, published in June 1735, and here reprinted, iii. 458–67. Further details appear in Curll's preliminary documents in his second volume of *Mr. Pope's Literary Correspondence* (published in July 1735) and, in recent years, more disinterestedly in Professor Griffith's second volume of his Pope *Bibliography* (1927). The intrigue was complex, and not all the details need be repeated here.

The problem of copyright speedily arose. Who owned the copy? The mysterious P. T. and his helper R. S.? Or did Curll? The two agents published initialed denials that they had sold the copyright to Curll. He went to Chancery about it, and Pope on 15 July and thereabouts published advertisements to the effect that the several editions of his letters were stolen and incorrect, and that he felt obliged to bring out an authentic edition, in which spurious letters and passages would be omitted, and errors corrected. Curll's prompt reaction was a threat to reprint any such edition as legally his property. The threat may have halted Pope temporarily.

In the spring of 1736, however, won by the kind and benevolent tone of the letters, the wealthy Ralph Allen of Bath became Pope's admirer and friend. Allen wished Pope to proceed with his authentic edition, and apparently thought it should be done in a large format similar to the editions of the poems in 1717 and 1735. A minute study of the editions involved shows that Pope's intention would have been satisfied by a small octavo edition; but he was persuaded to project a subscription edition in folio and quarto. So he went to work and produced the 'official' or 'authorized' edition of his letters in quarto and folio (1737). The small octavos of the same year were not acknowledged by Pope as his; but it is clear that he was responsible for most of them.

The text of the official edition was frequently 'improved' from a small octavo edition,[1] evidently prepared, most of it, before the official edition, but published as volumes v and vi of Pope's *Works*, with the imprint of J. Roberts, a month after the official edition was out. The texts of later octavo editions in Pope's lifetime all reprint those of Roberts or of succeeding octavos. The official texts of the quarto and folio were largely abandoned by Pope in later reprintings.

The improved official texts illustrate Pope's principles of revision. Trivialities concerning daily life or finances are omitted; so also are small indecorous remarks, either slightly salacious or profane. Personal names also are frequently excised. Perhaps the most common changes are purely stylistic: the letters are made more concise, the sentences more straightforward, the diction more elegant. There is little change in the sense of any letter except such as is due to omissions. By tactful omissions the general tone is made more dignified, more worthy of the gentlefolk for whom these quartos and folios were designed. For later readers, if the aim is to get something like what Pope actually wrote in the original letters, the octavo texts of the trade editions are far superior. In moral and literary quality the revised official texts were to Pope the more satisfactory—were 'a more perfect image of himself'. In making an edition that he called 'authentic', he omitted many letters found in earlier editions and added between sixty and seventy new letters. These changes, first made for the most part in the Roberts octavos, would probably have satisfied Pope's notion of an authorized edition; but the influence of Allen and other very moral persons led him to revise in the quartos and folios.

After the summer of 1737 there were few important changes in editions until the appearance in 1741 of the Swift–Pope letters. There were octavo editions published by T. Cooper in the autumn of 1737 and again in 1739. These make small additions and changes which lead one to believe that Pope was now co-operating with his publisher—though without public acknowledgement of the fact. The chief activity, apart from alarms and excursions by Curll, arose from Pope's persistent desire to publish his correspondence with Swift. This desire was evidently stimulated when, upon the death of John Gay in December 1732, Swift's letters to Gay were returned to Ireland—after Pope or Lord Oxford had had transcripts made. It is fairly certain that from the moment the editions of 1735 appeared Pope began suggesting to

[1] Professor V. A. Dearing establishes these facts in his essay 'The 1737 Editions of Alexander Pope's Letters', published in *Essays Critical and Historical dedicated to Lily B. Campbell*, Berkeley, Calif., 1950, pp. 185–97. Dearing's unpublished Harvard dissertation, *A History of the Publication of Alexander Pope's Letters during his Lifetime* (1949), gives a detailed and helpful account of the matters here briefly presented. See *infra*, pp. xxii–xxiii.

Swift the publication of their letters. On 3 September 1735 Swift answers a suppressed letter from Pope on the subject.[1] As yet there was nothing tortuous in Pope's dealings with Swift concerning their letters. Pope's fear of 'imputation' eventually did him great disservice; for, in his desire to have no apparent connexion with the publication of his letters, he suppressed in 1741 practically all his urgent requests for the return and publication of their correspondence. These passages, if preserved, would doubtless have made it clear that Swift appreciated Pope's desire to have their letters printed. Evidence of such requests still exists in Pope's letters to Lord Orrery, who, when in Ireland, became at times almost Pope's agent in urging the return of the letters. Both Swift and Pope agreed in desiring to erect memorials to their friendship. Swift more than once had repeated to Pope Cicero's plea to a friend, *Orna me*, and, not content with *The Dunciad* as inscribed to him, had hoped for an Epistle. Pope's ambition was to make their letters the memorial, but Swift preferred poetry as more lasting and noble. On 17 August 1736 Pope wrote to Swift, 'You are a very ignorant man; you do not know the figure his [Bolingbroke's] name and yours will make hereafter. I do, and will preserve all the memorials I can that I was of your intimacy.'

Pope, according to this editor's theorizings, now began to use pressure of a doubtfully legitimate sort. Towards the end of 1736 Curll brought out a pamphlet called *New Letters of Mr. Alexander Pope*, which contained a letter from Pope to Swift and another from Bolingbroke to Swift (here placed in August 1723: iii. 123–9). Curll's prefatory address 'To my Subscribers encore' contained a statement perfectly adapted to Pope's purposes: 'Beside what is here represented to you, I have several other very valuable originals in my custody, which, with these, were transmitted to me from *Ireland*.' Similarly, Curll in *The London Evening Post*, 11 November 1736, had advertised that his volume of *New Letters* (it seems to have consisted of sixty pages) printed the letters to Swift from 'original manuscripts transmitted from *Ireland*'. Armed with this evidence that his letters, if they remained in Ireland, were in danger of publication by undesirables, Pope redoubled his efforts to persuade Swift to return them. This does not appear directly in the Swift letters that he printed, but in a letter to Lord Orrery, which Pope did not publish, he wrote (4 March 1737), 'I would have gladly been the recorder of so great a part of it [Swift's merit] as shines in his letters to me' (iv. 60). Orrery transcribed this letter and sent a copy to Swift (iv. 60), who consequently knew Pope's desires. Earlier Pope had expressed to Orrery the wish that Swift would send back 'those letters, and mark over every sentence he would leave out; I would copy, and return them to him' (iv. 53). Swift also

[1] For the best text of this letter see v. 16.

must have had knowledge of this project; for after looking over the letters he makes the highly significant comment: 'I found nothing in any of them to be left out' (iv. 72). One suspects that in printing this comment in the letter of 31 May 1737 Pope omitted a promise by Swift to return the letters. Pope printed no remark that would indicate that the letters were not still in Ireland. At any rate in June (iv. 76) Swift agreed that Orrery might take the letters back to Pope. In view of the remark about 'nothing to be left out', one can be certain that he perfectly understood Pope's intention to publish the letters. On 23 July 1737 Orrery could report to Swift (iv. 81) that Pope had his letters.[1]

Pope has been accused of crooked dealings with Swift in this matter, but up to this time the only suspicious circumstance is the apt behaviour of Curll in printing the two letters said to be 'transmitted from Ireland'. It is even possible, but not probable, that they did come from Ireland—and from Swift. We have no evidence; but Swift as well as Pope delighted in ingenious subterfuge with booksellers. In preparing the correspondence for publication Pope was again obsessed with a desire to conceal his own connexion with the work. By suppressing his appeals for the return of the letters he tried to create the impression that publication was initiated in Ireland. That notion necessitated a belief that the letters were still in Ireland, or that they had been transcribed before being returned to Pope. He chose the former alternative, though at times suggesting the other.

When selection and revision of the correspondence was completed, Pope printed secretly an edition in small octavo, one copy of which he circuitously sent to Swift by the agency of Samuel Gerrard,[2] who, shortly before he was leaving for Ireland, received from an anonymous sender at his lodgings in Bath a packet for Swift with an unsigned letter inside. Pope was not in Bath at the time. This was in May or June of 1740, just after Pope had (iv. 241) covered his tracks by writing to Gerrard that he had nothing to send to Swift. Rather promptly Swift must have set to work making some small revisions in the volume and one major insertion, his letter of 10 January 1721. Swift's cousin Mrs. Whiteway protested against the publication, but she cannot have concealed the volume (as she said she did) for long, since by 29 July Faulkner with Swift's permission had begun to reprint the letters and sent off to Pope the first two sheets as printed by him.[3] Pope pretended extreme amazement and chagrin, and protested

[1] Swift's slight hesitation in returning Pope's letters may possibly (but not probably) be due to a project he had for printing his own correspondence. Faulkner in his edition of Swift's *Works*, Dublin, 1772, xiv, pp. v–vi, printed a statement to the effect that Swift had suggested printing his letters. The suggestion probably concerned letters other than those from Pope.

[2] See the letter of Lord Orrery, 6 Oct. 1740 (iv. 276).

[3] See Pope to Lord Orrery, 30 Dec. 1740 (iv. 317).

strongly against publication, affecting to wonder that it should be undertaken by desire of Swift. His pretences almost succeeded in stopping the edition; but, tactfully, he did not go so far as that. His willingness to cast false blame upon Mrs. Whiteway and her son-in-law Deane Swift is the most discreditable part of the whole evasion; but the blame got no public attention. Pope saw to it that his London edition of the correspondence, called *The Works of Mr. Alexander Pope in Prose*, vol. ii, appeared just before the Dublin editions, thus protecting his copyright—from all except Curll.

The complicated story of this intrigue is here abbreviated: much more detail will be found in the letters that passed between Pope and, chiefly, Lord Orrery and Mrs. Whiteway. The whole obscure proceeding is considerably clarified by bibliographical and textual evidence found in the footnotes to this edition, in Professor Griffith's *Bibliography*, and in articles published by Professors Mack and Dearing.[1] The identification by Professor Mack of a copy of the clandestine edition (1740), from which the first published editions were printed, and Mack's account of the later reissue of much of the clandestine text as *The Works of Alexander Pope, Esq.*, vol. vii . . . London: Printed for T. Cooper, M.DCC.XLI, have done much to clear up the story. It is necessary to insist that in the summer of 1740 Swift, while not in good health, was perfectly able to revise and authorize the texts of his letters. Senility became clear only two years later. The textual differences, cited here in footnotes to show differences between the London and Dublin texts of 1741, prove that Swift took a hand in some of the revisions.

A LIST OF EDITIONS OF POPE'S LETTERS 1726–1742

To make a completely scientific bibliography of editions of Pope's letters published during his lifetime is next to impossible. Within the same edition or 'issue' there are frequently small typographical variations, due either to the hand processes of book-making and the resulting press-man's errors (and his casual corrections) or to Pope's uncontrollable appetite for small changes in the arrangement or in the texts of letters. To tell the whole story one must see many copies of each edition. Consequently all that is here attempted is to give data that will identify a given edition or issue, coupled, where possible, with a reference to the most satisfactory attempt that we now have towards detailed descriptions of editions, R. H. Griffith's *Alexander Pope: a Bibliography* (2 v., 1922, 1927). Acknowledgements again are

[1] Maynard Mack, 'The First Printing of the Letters of Swift and Pope', in *The Library*, xix (1939), 465–85. See also V. A. Dearing, 'New Light on the First Printing of the Letters of Pope and Swift', in *The Library*, xxiii (1943), 74–86.

due to Professor V. A. Dearing's unpublished thesis. Not all the editions in the following list have been found useful in explaining texts in this edition, but practically all have been collated, and important textual variants are given in footnotes. The volumes collated, and here described, are chiefly those found in the Harvard College Library or in the libraries of the University of Illinois and the University of Chicago.

In citing these editions in footnotes the reference given is to the date only or to the date plus additional symbols as indicated in the following list. A reference such as '1737–42' means that all editions within those years and in intermediate years agree in a reading.

1726 Miscellanea. In Two Volumes. Never before Published. Viz. I. Familiar Letters written to Henry Cromwell Esq; by Mr. Pope. . . . Vol. I. London: Printed in the Year, 1727.

12mo in sixes (G 177). The volume, published by Curll in July 1726, is post-dated. Pope's letters occupy pp. 1–72.

1729 The Posthumous Works of William Wycherley, Esq; In Prose and Verse, Vol. II. Consisting of Letters and Poems Publish'd from Original Manuscripts. London: Printed for J. Robetrs [*sic*] . . . 1729.

8vo in fours. The only copy known to the editor is that in the Bodleian Library. See V. A. Dearing's account of the volume in *PMLA*, lxviii (1953), 223–36. Pope's correspondence with Wycherley occupies pp. 1–51.

1735a1 [Letters of Mr. Pope and Several Eminent Persons.]

8vo in fours (G 374). The first edition of these letters appeared in at least four variant issues, here called a1, a2, a3, and a4, all of which contain considerable parts printed from the same setting of type. 1735a1 lacks a title-page and the prefatory 'To the Reader'. It consists of two volumes bound as one. Vol. i has the letters to and from Wycherley (on sheets B and C–H, reissued from the 1729 printing), Walsh, H. C. [Henry Cromwell], and Several Ladies. Vol. ii has the letters to and from Trumbull, Steele, Addison, Jervas, Digby, Edw. Blount, Gay, *et al.*

1735a2 Letters of Mr. Pope, and Several Eminent Persons. In the Years 1705, &c. to 1717. London: Printed for J. Roberts in Warwick-lane.

8vo in fours (G 375). Here in vol. ii are lacking the sheets P–T and at the very end X and Y. A title-page and 'To the Reader' are added. An easy way to identify the edition is the date 1717 in the title, not found in other editions.

1735a3 Letters of Mr. Pope, and Several Eminent Persons, From the Year 1705, to 1711. Vol. I. London: Printed and sold by the Booksellers of London and Westminster. M.D.CC.XXXV.

8vo in fours, 2 v. as one (G 378). The title-page and 'To the Reader' alone are from a new setting of type. A new (second) paragraph is added in 'To the Reader'. The sheets lacking in 1735a2 are here present.

1735a4 Letters of Mr. Pope, and Several Eminent Persons . . .

8vo in fours, 2 v. as one (G 380). This issue is identical with a3 except for sheet B of vol. i (the beginning of the Wycherley letters), for which the type has been reset.

1735b Mr. Pope's Literary Correspondence for Thirty Years; from 1704 to 1735. Being, A Collection of Letters, Which passed between him and Several Eminent Persons. Volume the First. London: Printed for E. Curll, in Rose-street, Covent Garden. M.DCC.XXXV.

8vo, 2 v. as one (G 376). An entirely new setting of type hastily done by several printers working concurrently on different portions of the volume. It was published on 23 May, and a second edition was advertised in *The Daily Post-Boy*, 31 May. The edition is the first of Curll's series of volumes of similar title. It corrects all the errata specified on the leaf found in 1735a2. In 1735a2–4 these corrections were not made. It has little or no textual importance, but its commentary is spicy and sometimes illuminating.

1735c Letters of Mr. Pope, and Several Eminent Persons, From the Year 1705, to 1711. . . . London: Printed and sold by the Booksellers . . .

8vo, 2 v. (G 381). This edition is from a new setting of type except in vol. i for sheet B (reset for 1735a4) and in vol. ii for sheets P–T, X, and Y, all of which were supplied by the sheets withheld from 1735a2. In vol. ii the letter of 19 January 1716 from Trumbull is on P* (one leaf). The asterisk serves to identify the edition, which is the last to use any of the sheets printed for 1735a1.

1735d Letters of Mr. Pope, and Several Eminent Persons . . .

8vo, 2 v. (G 383). This edition consists largely of sheets of 1735c reissued. The following parts of vol. ii, however, are printed from the new-set type: signatures L–Q reprint signatures P* and P–T of 1735c, and signatures X–Y have been reset.

1735e Letters of Mr. Pope, and Several Eminent Persons, From the Year 1705 to 1735. Vol. I. London. Printed for T. Cooper. and sold by the Booksellers of London and Westminster. MDCCXXXV.

12mo, 2 v. as one (G 384). Hastily printed, presumably to compete with the duodecimo forthcoming from Curll's press, the type was set from two different founts (in two shops?). The second fount begins with signature K (not K*).

1735f Mr. Pope's Literary Correspondence for Thirty Years . . . Volume the First. The Third Edition. . . . London: Printed for E. Curll . . .

12mo, 2 v. as one (G 385). In Curll's counting the earlier editions are 1735a1, a2, and 1735b.

1735g Mr. Pope's Literary Correspondence. Volume the Second. With Letters To, and From, [10 names given]. London: Printed for E. Curll. . . . M.DCC.XXXV.

8vo (G 386). The volume contains nothing new by Pope, but it has two letters to him from Atterbury, which Pope later disowned. There are interesting prefatory documents, and the volume includes a reprint of 'A True Narrative of the Method by which the Private Letters of Mr. Pope have been Procur'd and Publish'd by Edmund Curll'.

1735h1 Letters of Mr. Pope, and Several Eminent Persons, From the Year 1705, to 1735. Vol. I. London: Printed for T. Cooper, at the Globe in Pater-noster-Row. 1735.

12mo, 2 v. in one (G 396). A negligible reprint.

1735h2 Letters of Mr Pope . . .

12mo (G 397). Identical with 1735h1 except for the substitution of a new frontispiece and the replacement of O12 by an unsigned gathering of four leaves to allow the addition of two Atterbury letters taken from 1735g.

1735i Letters of Mr. Pope, and Several Eminent Persons. From the Year 1705. to 1735. N.B. This Edition contains more Letters, and more correctly Printed than any other extant. London: Printed; and sold by the Booksellers. . . . M.DCC.XXXV.

12mo (G 400). This seems a poor reprint of 1735h2; it contains nothing new, and is less correctly printed than most other editions. It is very likely a piracy.

1735j Mr. Pope's Literary Correspondence. Volume the Third. With Letters To, and, From [8 names given]. London: Printed for E. Curll . . . M.DCC.XXXV.

8vo (G 402). A miscellaneous volume. So far as letters go, it contains four by Voiture, printed as from Pope to Martha Blount—though Curll well knew that they came from the translation of Voiture's letters that he himself was just then publishing. There is no reason to think, as Carruthers and Elwin did, that the four letters by Voiture (in Bodley MS. Rawlinson 90) are in Pope's handwriting. There is also a letter from Pope to the Duchess of Buckingham, with the impossible date of 27 January 1720 (in this present edition placed in 1722).

1735k Mr. Pope's Literary Correspondence. Volume the Second. . . . The Second Edition. London: Printed for E. Curll . . .

12mo (G 403). This contains no new letters, but adds details concerning Curll's publication of Pope's letters.

1735m Mr. Pope's Literary Correspondence. Volume the Third . . . The Second Edition. London: Printed for E. Curll . . . M.DCC.XXXV.

12mo (G 404).

1735n Letters of Mr. Pope, and Several Eminent Persons. From the Year 1705, to 1735. N.B. This Edition contains more Letters, and more correctly printed, than any other extant. Printed for J. Smith; and sold by the Booksellers of London and Westminster. M.DCC. XXXV.

12mo in sixes (G 408). Like 1735i, which it follows closely, it is perhaps a piracy.

1735Da1 Letters of Mr. Pope, and Several Eminent Persons, From the Year 1705, to 1711. Vol. I. Dubdin [*sic*]: Re-printed by

George Faulkner, and Sold at his Shop in Essex-Street, by R. Gunne in Caple-Street, by J. Smith and W. Bruce on the Blind Key, 1735.

12mo, 2 v. (G 398). The misprint of 'Dubdin' occurs in the Harvard copy.

Vol. ii has a differing titlepage, as follows: Letters of Mr. Pope, and Several Eminent Persons. From the Year 1711, &c. Vol. II. Dublin: Printed for M. Rhames, For R. Gunne . . . J. Smith and W. Bruce on the Blind-Key, and G. Faulkner, in Essex-street. M DCC.XXXV

1735Da2 Letters of Mr. Pope, and Several Eminent Persons, From the Year 1705, to 1711. Vol. I. Dublin. Re-printed by G. Faulkner. Sold by him in Essex-street, by R. Gunne in Caple-street, and by J. Smith and W. Bruce on the Blind Key. M DCC,XXXV,

12mo, 2 v. (G 399). No Dublin edition except 1741Da (see below) has any textual authority. Da2 differs from Da1 in having a cancel as title-page.

1736a Mr. Pope's Literary Correspondence. Volume the Fourth. With Letters, &c. To, and From, [7 names given]. To which are added, Muscovian Letters. London: Printed for E. Curll . . . M.DCC.XXXVI.

8vo (G 415). In spite of the title, the volume contains not a single letter to or from Pope.

1736b Mr. Pope's Literary Correspondence. Volume the Fourth . . . The Second Edition. . . . M.DCC.XXXVI.

12mo (G 416). Like 1736a it contains no Pope letters.

1736c New Letters of Mr Alexander Pope, and Several of his Friends. [3 lines of Latin] London: Printed Anno Reformationis, 1737.

8vo (G 429). An advertisement by Curll in *The London Evening Post*, 11 November 1736, includes this item, and enumerates with it the contents of a volume corresponding entirely with Curll's fifth volume of Pope's *Literary Correspondence*, later advertised as Volume the Fifth. See 1737c. The 'new letters' are those from Pope and Bolingbroke to Swift (August 1723), really a joint letter, but printed by Curll as two. The item, a segment of Curll's 'Volume the Fifth', seems to have been issued separately as a pamphlet.

1736Da Letters from Alexander Pope, Esq; and the Right Hon. the Lord Bolingbroke, to the Reverend Dr. Swift, D.S.P.D. . . . London: Printed. Dublin: Reprinted by and for George Faulkner. . . . M.DCC.XXXVII.

Small 8vo (G 453). A reprint of a part of 1736c, postdated.

1737a The Works of Alexander Pope, Esq; Vol. V [also VI]. Consisting of letters, Wherein to those of the Author's own Edition, are added all that are genuine from the former

Impressions, with some never before printed. London: Printed for J. Roberts in Warwick-lane. MDCCXXXVII.

Vol. vi has the following title:

The Works of Alexander Pope, Esq; Vol. VI. Containing the Remainder of His Letters. London: Printed for J. Roberts in Warwick lane. MDCCXXXVII.

Small 8vo (G 461). On the importance of this edition see *supra*, pp. xiv–xv. The title indicates that it was published after the 'author's own edition' (1737b); but it was largely prepared and printed earlier.

1737b1 Letters of Mr. Alexander Pope, and Several of his Friends. London: Printed by J. Wright for J. Knapton . . . L. Gilliver . . . J. Brindley . . . and R. Dodsley . . . MDCCXXXVII.

4to (G 454). This with other forms of 1737b constitutes the 'official' edition acknowledged by Pope as his. The large and small folios were separate impressions, but textually they do not significantly differ from the quarto. Corrections (by the pressman?) make some negligible variants. The three impressions are from the same setting of type.

1737b2 Letters of Mr. Alexander Pope. . . . MDCCXXXVII.

Folio (G 456, 457). The title and texts throughout are from the same setting of type as 1737b1 (q.v.).

1737c Mr. Pope's Literary Correspondence. Volume the Fifth . . . London: Printed for E. Curll . . . M.DCC.XXXVII.

8vo (G 462). This is in part a second edition. The first (1736c) antedated 1737b1, pp. 322–32.

1737d [Letters of Mr. Alexander Pope . . . London: Printed for the Company. 1737.]

(G 470). This is Griffith's conjectural title for a piracy, no copy of which is known to survive.

1737e The Works of Alexander Pope, Esq; Vol. V [and VI]. . . . The Second Edition, Corrected. London: Printed for T. Cooper . . . MDCCXXXVII.

Small 8vo (G 472). A revised conflation of the texts of 1737a and 1737b, on which later editions (but not this present edition) have been based. In the present edition the texts of 1737a and b rather than this revision are preferred.

1739a The Works of Alexander Pope, Esq; Vol V [and VI]. . . . London: Printed for T. Cooper in Pater-noster-Row. MDCCXXXIX.

Small 8vo (G 511). A reprint of 1737e. In the inserted half-sheet L (before L1–8) two Atterbury letters are added. The lack of a period after 'Vol.' in the title-page of Volume V may serve to identify the edition as compared with 1739b.

1739b The Works of Alexander Pope, Esq; Vol. V. [and VI]. London: Printed for T. Cooper. . . . MDCCXXXIX.

Small 8vo (G 512). The title-page closely resembles that of 1739a, but the type is reset throughout.

1740 [Letters of Pope and Swift.]

Small 8vo. See 1742La. In the present edition '1740' indicates the clandestine volume sent by Pope to Swift in May or June of 1740. It had no title-page. Modified copies of this printing as issued later are described by Dr. H. Teerink in his *Bibliography of . . . Swift* (1937) as Book 60, by Professor Maynard Mack, and by Professor V. A. Dearing. See *supra*, p. xviii. The copies at Yale and Harvard as well as that described by Teerink have cancels and an insert in sheet B, which were doubtless not present in the original volume sent to Swift in 1740.

1741La1 The Works of Mr. Alexander Pope, in Prose. Vol. II. London: Printed for J. and P. Knapton, C. Bathurst, and R. Dodsley, M.DCC.XLI.

4to (G 531). This is the first London publication of the Swift–Pope letters. The quarto impression was made before those of the folios, but publication of all three formats was simultaneous.

1741La2 The Works of . . . Pope, in Prose. Vol. II.

Folio (G 529, 530). The title-page and text are from the same setting of type used in 1741La1. In shifting to the larger (folio) formes accidents happened that produced variant issues of the texts, but there are none that carry editorial authority.

1741Lb Dean Swift's Literary Correspondence, for Twenty-four Years; from 1714 to 1738. . . . London: Printed for E. Curll. . . . M.DCC.XLI.

8vo (G 534). Curll announced this as a reprint of the Dublin edition, but actually he reprinted the London quarto (1741La1).

1741Da Letters to and from Dr. J. Swift, D.S.P.D. from the Year 1714, to 1738. To which are added, Several Notes and Translations not in the London Edition. Dublin: Printed by and for George Faulkner, MDCCXLI.[1]

8vo. This is the first Dublin edition of the Swift–Pope letters. It was largely prepared before publication of 1741La1, but was published later. It reprints the clandestine volume, as revised by Swift himself.

1741Db [Letters to and from the Rev. Dr. Swift, D.S.P.D. . . . Dublin: For Ed. Exshaw.]

(G 532.) Possibly a variant issue of 1741Da, a variant of which Dilke had a copy. No copy is now known to exist. See C. W. Dilke, *Papers of a Critic* (1875), i. 328.

1741Dc Letters to and from Dr. J. Swift, D.S.P.D. from the Year 1714, to 1738. Dublin: Printed by and for George Faulkner, MDCCXLI.

12mo (G 533).

[1] Teerink includes this edition in his *Bibliography*, pp. 34–35, but does not give a signature collation, which runs as follows:

π^8, B–S^8, T^4, U^8, X^2, $2U^8$, $2X^8$, $2C^2$.

The firstleaf contains a Faulkner book-list; the title is on $\pi 2$. The second series of signatures (2U, 2X, 2C) includes Swift's pamphlet 'Some Free Thoughts upon the Present State of Affairs', which has its own title-page.

1742La The Works of Alexander Pope, Esq; Vol. VII. Containing the Third and Last Part of Letters, Between him and Dr. Swift. London: Printed for T. Cooper, M.DCC.XLII.

Small 8vo (G 560). This is a highly interesting edition since in it signatures C–L are a reissue of the sheets found in the clandestine volume sent to Swift in 1740, except for H6 and I3–6, which are cancels. See *supra*, p. xviii.

1742Lb The Works of Alexander Pope, Esq; Vol. IV. Part I. Containing an Authentic Edition of his Letters. [Two lines from Catullus] London: Printed for T. Cooper in Pater-noster-Row. M DCC XLII.

Small 8vo (G 568). There is no known evidence that suggests that Pope himself read proof or made revisions in these Cooper octavos (1742Lb, c, d).

1742Lc The Works of Alexander Pope, Esq; Vol. IV. Part II. Containing the Second Part of his Letters. London: Printed for T. Cooper. . . . M DCC XLII.

Small 8vo (G 569).

1742Ld1 The Works of Alexander Pope, Esq; Vol. IV. Part III. Containing the Third Part of Letters. London: Printed for R. Dodsley, and Sold by T. Cooper, M DCC XLII.

Small 8vo (G 570).

1742Ld2 The Works of Alexander Pope, Esq: Vol. IV. Part III. . . .

Small 8vo (G 571). It differs from Ld1 only in having a cancel for the title-page.

1742Le The Works of Alexander Pope, Esq; Vol. IV. Part III. Containing the Third Part of Letters. London: Printed for R. Dodsley, and Sold by T. Cooper, M.DCC.XLII.

Small 8vo (G 572). Almost a line-for-line reprint of 1742Lc, but the type is reset.

1742Da The Works of Mr. Alexander Pope in Prose . . . Dublin: Printed opposite Essex Bridge. 1742.

12mo. This is a reprint of 1741La. Its text, which is not that of 1741Da, has no importance.

THE PRESENT EDITION

Although this present edition increases by about one-third the number of letters printed by Elwin and Courthope, it may frankly be confessed that in certain cases the additions are unimportant. Possibly the real advantage of the edition lies less in the increased number of letters than in the arrangement of the letters in a single chronological order. Placed thus, even small letters fill out the picture, and we see Pope moving among his friends and his publishers more vividly than has been possible before. The larger additions include fifty-eight letters to the

Earl and Countess of Burlington as well as numerous additions to the correspondences with William Fortescue, Hugh Bethel, Ralph Allen, and William Warburton. In many correspondences a few additions are made, which, as has been said, fill out the picture notably. In the Victorian period, or earlier, editors would have hesitated to print purely commercial letters dealing with sizes, costs, and methods of production of Pope's various editions. Several letters now included throw light on the exasperating importance of suits to secure or recover copyrights. Pope's experience more than once made rulings in law that still have significance. His difficulties, formerly called 'chicanery', may now upon occasion be blamed on the abnormal confusion in the normally troubled relations of poet and publisher, troubles due to the recent (1709) passing of the first English Copyright Act.

Only a little more than 10 per cent. of the letters included in this edition were printed by Pope, and of the letters printed by him about a third still existed either in his autograph or in contemporary and trustworthy transcripts. As a result the footnotes here make it possible to form conclusions, as indicated already, concerning his manipulations. Most of his changes were made to improve the style, and some such changes are included among the textual variants cited here, but in general only variants that alter the sense are noted. A fully 'critical' edition of Pope's texts has been neglected as not sufficiently rewarding.

TEXTS

Because of the suspicion that has attached to Pope's 'editings' of his letters the aim here has been to reproduce, with doubtless pedantic care, exactly what he wrote whenever possible. This involves the preservation of patent absurdities in spelling, capitalization, and punctuation. The reader should beware of concluding hastily that 'errors' in these matters are accidental in the process of printing. He will find sentences ending with a comma and beginning with a minuscule initial; he will find letters like Wycherley's crammed with commas and find the 2nd Earl of Oxford at times dispensing with all punctuation; he will find proper names spelt in two or more ways on the same page. Spellings not now current of proper names (Peterborow, Argyle) are preserved. Pope's bad habit of leaving a parenthesis unclosed at the end has for clarity frequently been silently corrected (but see, for example, i. 519, ii. 262); his curious use of a question-mark to indicate vague wonder is preserved: it normally shows a tone slightly different from exclamation (iv. 381). Both Pope and his correspondents habitually use the grave accent where better usage demands the acute: this has at times been corrected. Pope's tags of Greek, Latin, or French are frequently set down incorrectly, and frequently 'adapted': he obviously did not verify his quotations. The editor has taken the liberty of lowering all raised letters (M^{rs}, L^{d}ship, &c.), and words beginning with the letter 'y' for 'th' and abbreviated (y^{e}, y^{t}, y^{y}, &c.) have been normalized and expanded. So also have been such abbreviations as L^{d}, S^{r}, wth, w^{ch}, c^{d}, w^{d}, y^{r}, and y^{rs}. In the original letters the salutation almost invariably used by Pope is 'Dear Sir', and, in printing, this form is omitted. Other types of salutation, showing more individual attitudes, are printed. Bracketed words [ ] are such as do not now appear in the source text, but either did before the holograph was damaged or else existed in Pope's intention, though carelessly omitted in his writing. Words in half-brackets ⌜⌝ are thus set off for textual comment. Most frequently the symbols enclose words omitted by Pope in his own printings, though they existed in the original letters.

The letters to John Caryll, sr., offer special problems, and are more fully modernized than other correspondences. These letters were discovered by Dilke in the nineteenth century, preserved in transcripts made apparently in part by Caryll's daughter who was educated in French convents. The transcripts were frequently careless in execution, and there seems to be no reason for preserving abnormalities that certainly were not Pope's. Transcripts of other letters made for Lord Oxford, and now preserved at Longleat, are far more careful, and hence are here treated with more respect.

THE DATING OF LETTERS

For an editor Pope's most exasperating habit is that of incomplete dating of his letters. In his day a business letter should be carefully dated; but a gentleman in a private, friendly correspondence frequently gave an incomplete date. Pope normally omitted the year,[1] and at times entered only the day of the week. In such cases postmarks, if any, are prized. The attempt to arrange Pope's letters chronologically has involved no end of hypothetical argument. Frequently the result satisfies the editor, who hopes others may usually agree with him. Footnotes will explain, perhaps tediously, the processes by which a date has been assigned; but if a date is diffidently assigned, it must be taken *with diffidence*. Even before publication, but too late for rectification, errors have become apparent (see v. 1–2). There are many letters that are impossible to date with any assurance, but it has seemed best to give such letters completely hypothetical placing rather than to enlarge the limbo of undatables here placed near the middle of Pope's career (iii. 515–19). Questionable placing of a letter rather than including it in limbo may promote argument and the eventual fixing of a date.[2]

[1] Practically always when Pope gives the year date for a letter written between 1 January and 24 March, the year is 'Old Style'; that is, to him the date 10 February 1714 means 1714/15. For him the year began with 25 March.

[2] Letters difficult to place within a moderately certain year are normally placed at the beginning of the year. This placing need not imply that the letters were written in January.

HEADINGS OF LETTERS

At the left margin at the beginning of each letter are given the names of the correspondents involved; on the same line at the right margin is given *the editor's* date for the letter, taken from the end of the letter, or from the superscription, or from a postmark, or from the editor's cogitations. At times this editorial date contradicts the holograph date or the date of an earlier editor—in which case footnotes offer explanations. Under the names of the correspondents at the left appears an abbreviated statement of the provenance of the letter. The texts are drawn either from manuscripts or from printed books or periodicals. By manuscripts one means Pope's original autograph letters or transcripts made by his contemporaries. If a transcript is the source, that fact is stated. If the statement of provenance begins with a date (e.g. 1735, 1741, 1941, &c.), that arrangement indicates a printed source, the author or editor of the book being named, unless the editor is Pope himself. In the case of letters reprinted from the editions of Pope's *Works* in the nineteenth century (Bowles, Roscoe, Elwin–Courthope) or letters that come from printed periodicals, the date, if given, occurs after the title of the work, not before. Prefixed at times to the names of correspondents in the headings will appear one of the following symbols: an asterisk (*) for a letter not hitherto included in an edition of Pope's collected letters; a dagger (†) for a letter that rests only upon the authority of Pope's editions; a double dagger (‡) for a letter suspected as a conflation or a fabrication by Pope; and two vertically parallel lines (||) for a letter published by Pope but now available in a more authentic source than his editions.

Since many of these provenances are given in an abbreviated form, it is advisable to print here a list of provenances, which may also constitute grateful acknowledgements to the institutions and the owners who have consented to aid this edition.

PROVENANCES

1. *Sources of Autograph Letters*

INSTITUTIONS have furnished manuscripts of letters as follows: The Bath Municipal Reference Library (2), the Bibliothèque Nationale (1), The Bodleian Library (29), The Boston (Mass.) Public Library (1), The British Museum (553), The Buffalo Public Library (1), The Amon G. Carter Foundation (1), The University of Chicago (1), Christ Church (Oxford) (1), The William Andrews Clark Library (3), The Fitzwilliam Museum (1), The Folger Shakespeare Library (1), Hartlebury Castle (1), Harvard University (62), Haverford College (1), The Huntington Library (17), McGill University (1),

Maine Historical Society (1), Massachusetts Historical Society (1), The National Library of Scotland (3), The New England Historical and Genealogical Society (4 transcripts), The New York Public Library (7), The Historical Society of Pennsylvania (6), The Pierpont Morgan Library (93), Princeton University (1), The Public Record Office (London) (1 transcript), The Royal College of Surgeons of England (13), The John Rylands Library (1), The University of Texas (1), Trinity College (Cambridge) (1), Trinity College (Dublin) (4), Ushaw College (8), The Victoria and Albert Museum (5), The Wellcome Historical Medical Library (1), Wellesley College (2), The Wisbech Museum (1), Yale University (16).

FAMILY ARCHIVES have furnished letters as follows: Alnwick (1), Althorp (2), Blenheim (19), Blickling Hall (2), Chatsworth (68), Cirencester Park (12), Craster Tower (1), Hagley (9), Longleat (247), Mapledurham (57), Nuneham Courtenay (16), Panshanger (1), Rousham (15), Sandon Hall (1), Welbeck–Portland (on deposit in the British Museum) (5).

PRIVATE OWNERS AND DEALERS have furnished letters as follows: Roger W. Barrett (1), the late J. M. Berdan (1), The Bordoni Collection (1), Lady Charnwood (1), Dawson's Bookshop (1), Lieut.-Col. F. D. E. Fremantle (1), Professor R. H. Griffith (1), Professor F. W. Hilles (2), F. J. Hogan (1), The Marseille Holloway Collection (1), Arthur A. Houghton, Jr. (60), The Hyde Collection (7), Maggs Bros. (3), A. Merivale (1), the late E. H. W. Meyerstein (1), Dr. Eric G. Millar (1), Sir John Murray (17), James M. Osborn (3), Parke-Bernet Galleries (1), Dr. Dallas Pratt (1), Lord Rothschild (2), Earl Stanhope (1), C. A. Stonehill (1), Robert H. Taylor (3), Professor C. B. Tinker (6), H. B. Vander Poel (1), Gabriel Wells (1).

2. *Printed Sources of Texts*[1]

1720 Aaron Hill, Preface to *Creation* (1); 1723 The Duke of Buckingham's *Works* (1); 1726 Curll's *Miscellanea* (1: the rhyming epistle to Cromwell); 1729 *The Dunciad* (1); 1729 John Dennis, *Remarks on . . . The Dunciad* (2); 1729 *The Posthumous Works of Wycherley*, vol. ii [edited by Pope] (19); 1732 *Of False Fame* (1: the prefatory epistle); 1735a *Letters of Mr. Pope* (121); 1735g *Mr. Pope's Literary Correspondence*, vol. ii (1); 1735j *Mr. Pope's Literary Correspondence*, vol. iii (1); 1735 *Narrative of the Method by which Mr. Pope's Letters have been Published* (10); 1735 *A General Dictionary* [in the life of Atterbury] (1); 1736c (1); 1737a Roberts octavos (46); 1737b (18); 1739a (2); 1740 [the clandestine volume]

[1] In this list it will be understood that the figures in parentheses after the titles of books do not represent the total number of Pope letters printed in the respective books, but only the number of letters reprinted in this edition (for want of a better source) from these books.

(55); 1741 Da (1); 1741 La (7); 1743 *The Dunciad* (1); 1745 William Ayre, *Life of Pope* (2); 1745 Dodsley's *Miscellanies by Dr. Swift*, vol. x (3); 1746 Swift's *Works* [Faulkner ed.], end of vol. viii (1); 1751 Aaron Hill, *A Collection of Letters* (36); 1752 Orrery's *Remarks* (3); 1753 Aaron Hill's *Works* (21); 1760 Aaron Hill, *Dramatic Works* (2); 1762 Goldsmith, *Life of Beau Nash* (1); 1763 *Letters of Lady Mary Wortley Montagu* (8); 1765 Deane Swift [ed.], *Works of Jonathan Swift*, vol. xvi (3); 1767 *Letters of Lady Mary Wortley Montagu*, vol. iv (2); 1768 Deane Swift [ed.], *Works of Jonathan Swift* (5); 1769 Judith Cowper, *Letters to a Lady* (1); 1769 Ruffhead, *Life of Pope* (4); 1770 Goldsmith, *Life of Parnell* (2); 1772 Duncombe [ed.], *Letters of Several Eminent Persons Deceased* (6); 1776 *Additions to the Works of Pope* (2); 1783 Nichols [ed.], Atterbury's *Correspondence* (1); 1788 Hurd [ed.], Warburton's *Works* (1); 1791 Boswell, *Life of Johnson* (1); 1797 Holliday, *Life of Mansfield* (1); 1797 Polwhele, *History of Devonshire*, vol. i (31); 1797 Warton [ed.], Pope's *Works* (3); 1803 Nichols [ed.], Swift's *Works*, vol. xviii (1); 1804 *Brookiana* [Henry Brooke] (3); 1806 Bowles [ed.], Pope's *Works* (22); 1817 Warner, *Original Letters* (8); 1820 Spence, *Anecdotes* (2); 1824 Roscoe [ed.], Pope's *Works* (6); 1824 *Letters to and from the Countess of Suffolk* (1); 1831 Rose [ed.], *Marchmont Papers* (4); 1833 Thomas Thorpe, *Catalogue* (1); 1857 Carruthers, *Life of Pope* (3); 1861 Mrs. Delany, *Autobiography* (1); 1869–1913 Sotheby Sale Catalogues (12); 1870–89 Elwin and Courthope [eds.], Pope's *Works* (186); 1870 John Weller, *Catalogue* (1); 1880 Lord Clermont, *History of the Fortescue Family* (1); 1885 Hist. MSS. Comm., Report x (2); 1886 *The Autographic Mirror* (1); 1913 Ball [ed.], Swift's *Correspondence* (1); 1923 W. H. Arnold, *Ventures in Book Collecting* (1); 1925 Francis Edwards, *Catalogue* (1); 1931 T. J. Wise, *A Pope Library* (1); 1935 D. Nichol Smith [ed.], *Letters of Swift to Ford* (1); 1941 R. Blanchard [ed.], Steele's *Correspondence* (1).

Of the letters necessarily taken from the Elwin–Courthope edition 121 come from the Broome papers, available for Elwin's work but since lost—temporarily, it is to be hoped. Among others 20 should come from a volume of the 5th Earl of Orrery's papers, crucial in the history of the publication of the Swift letters, which is also now lost. The other principal groups of letters known only in the Elwin–Courthope edition are 10 to Lord Bathurst and 13 to Jonathan Richardson.

Periodical Publications have furnished printed texts as follows: *The Athenaeum*, 17 May 1884 (3); *The Daily Post-Boy*, 22 December 1731 (1); *The European Magazine* 1791, 1792 (2); *Fog's Weekly Journal*, 26 July 1735 (1); *The Gentleman's Magazine*, for 1787 (1); for 1831 (3 to T. Dancastle); for 1835 (1); for 1836 (5 to the

Tonsons); and for 1855 (11, of which 9 are to Charles Bathurst)—a total of 21; *The Quarterly Review* for 1875 (1); *The St. James's Chronicle*, 13 and 27 July 1776 (2); *The St. James's Evening Post*, 12 July 1735 (1): *The Scots Magazine* for 1784 (1); *The Universal Magazine* for 1808 (2).

Out of over 2,100 letters 735 are taken from printed sources. Of this group something like 280 come from Pope's own printings. It must be remembered, again, that in the listings here given the numbers in parentheses do not indicate the number of letters found in a given place but only the number reproduced in this edition from the indicated source. Naturally, where possible, the text of autograph letters or of early transcripts has been preferred to a printed text.

ABBREVIATIONS OF AUTHORITIES CITED

The works here listed are at times cited in footnotes simply by the last name of the author (with at times a brief title) or by an abbreviated title.[1]

AULT, NORMAN. *New Light on Pope.* 1949.
BALL, F. E. (ed.). *The Correspondence of Jonathan Swift.* 6 v., 1910–14.
Biographie universelle ancienne et moderne. 85 v., 1811–62.
BLANCHARD, RAE. *The Correspondence of Richard Steele.* 1941.
BOWLES, W. L. *The Works of Pope.* 10 v., 1806.
Burke's Peerage: SIR B. BURKE, *Burke's Genealogical and Heraldic History of the Peerage*, &c. 1939.
Burke's Commoners: JOHN BURKE, *Burke's Genealogical and Heraldic History of Commoners.* 2 v., 1835.
BUTT, JOHN (ed.). *Pope's Imitations of Horace* (vol. iv in the Twickenham ed. of Pope's *Poems*). 1939.
CARRUTHERS, ROBERT. *The Life of Alexander Pope.* 1857 (rewritten and improved over the ed. of 1853).
COBBETT, R. S. *Memorials of Twickenham.* 1872.
COBBETT, WILLIAM. *Parliamentary History of England.* 36 v., 1806–20.
DNB: *Dictionary of National Biography.* 22 v., 1901–9 (reissue).
DALLAWAY, J. (ed.). *The Works of Lady Mary Wortley Montagu.* 5 v., 1803.
DILKE, CHARLES WENTWORTH. *The Papers of a Critic.* 2 v., 1875.
DUNCOMBE, JOHN (ed.). *Letters of Several Eminent Persons Deceased* [esp. John Hughes]. 2 v., 1772; 2nd ed. 3 v., 1773.
EC. See Elwin.
ELWIN, WHITWELL, and W. J. COURTHOPE (eds.). *The Works of Alexander Pope.* 10 v., 1871–89. (Cited either as *EC* or as *Elwin.*)
A General Dictionary Historical and Critical (based on the *Dictionnaire* of Pierre Bayle) by J. P. Bernard, T. Birch, J. Lockman, *et al.* 10 v., 1734–41.
Gent. Mag.: *The Gentleman's Magazine*, 1731–.

[1] For explanation of the abbreviations used in the headings of letters to indicate provenance, the preceding list of provenances is to be consulted.

GEC Peerage: *The Complete Peerage*, by G. E. C. *et al.* 1910–.
GRIFFITH, R. H. *Alexander Pope: a Bibliography*. 2 v. (Austin, Texas), 1922, 1927.
Hearne's *Collections*: THOMAS HEARNE, *Remarks and Collections*. 11 v., 1885–1921.
Harcourt Papers, ed. Edward W. Harcourt. 14 v., [1880–1905].
HAWKESWORTH, JOHN (ed.). *The Works of Jonathan Swift*. (8vo), 25 v., 1764–79.
Hist. MSS. Comm. (Various reports of the Historical Manuscripts Commission are cited; e.g. Reports v, ix, and x; Reports on the *Bath MSS.*, the *Montagu House MSS.*, and especially the *Portland Papers*.)
Hist. Reg.: *The Historical Register*, 1714–38.
ILCHESTER, THE SIXTH EARL OF. *Lord Hervey and his Friends*. 1950.
IRVING, W. H. *John Gay*. Durham, N.C., 1940.
JEGP: *The Journal of English and Germanic Philology*, 1903–.
LEADHAM, I. S. *The Political History of England 1702–1760*, 1921.
LEP: *The London Evening Post*, 1727–.
Marchmont Papers: *A Selection from the Papers of the Earls of Marchmont*, ed. Sir G. H. Rose. 3 v., 1831.
NED: *A New English Dictionary on Historical Principles* (ed. J. A. H. Murray *et al.*), 1888–1933.
NICHOLS, JOHN (ed.). *The Epistolary Correspondence of Francis Atterbury*. 5 v., 1783–90.
—— and JOHN BOWYER NICHOLS. *Illustrations of the Literary History of the Eighteenth Century*. 8 v., 1817–58.
—— *Literary Anecdotes of the Eighteenth Century*. 9 v., 1812–16.
Orrery's *Remarks*: JOHN (BOYLE), FIFTH EARL OF ORRERY. *Remarks on the Life and Writings of Swift*. 1752.
PMLA: *Publications of the Modern Language Association of America*. 1884–.
PQ: *Philological Quarterly*, 1922–.
Political State of Great Britain, by A. Boyer, 60 v., 1710–40.
POPE, ALEXANDER. (Editions of the letters are cited by date of the edition. See *supra*, pp. xix–xxv. Later editions of his works or letters are cited by the editor's name.)
Richardsoniana, by Jonathan Richardson. 1776.
ROSCOE, WILLIAM (ed.). *The Works of Pope*. 10 v., 1824.
RUFFHEAD, OWEN. *The Life of Alexander Pope*. 1769. (Only the 8vo edition is here cited.)
SHERBURN, GEORGE. *The Early Career of Alexander Pope*. 1934.
SMITH, DAVID NICHOL (ed.). *Letters from Jonathan Swift to Charles Ford*. 1935.
SPENCE, JOSEPH. *Anecdotes*, ed. by S. W. Singer, 1820.
Suffolk Correspondence: *Letters to and from Henrietta, Countess of Suffolk*. 2 v., 1824.
Supplement of 1825: *Supplemental Volume to the Works of Pope*. 1825.
SUTHERLAND, JAMES R. (ed.). *The Dunciad* (vol. v of the Twickenham ed. of Pope's *Poems*). 1943.
SWIFT, DEANE (ed.). *The Works of Jonathan Swift*. 19 v. 1768.

TEERINK, DR. H. *A Bibliography of the Writings in Prose and Verse of Jonathan Swift, D.D.* The Hague, 1937.

THOMAS, W. MOY. *The Letters and Works of Lady Mary Wortley Montagu* (as ed. by Lord Wharncliffe), with a Memoir by Thomas. 1861.

TILLOTSON, GEOFFREY (ed.). *The Rape of the Lock* (vol. ii of the Twickenham ed. of Pope's *Poems*). 1940.

TLS: *The* [London] *Times Literary Supplement*, 1901–.

WARBURTON, WILLIAM (ed.). *The Works of Pope*. 9 v., 1751. (The edition appeared in both large and small octavo formats, with different settings of type and different footnotes. Here only the large octavo is used.)

WARTON, JOSEPH. *Essay on the Genius and Writings of Pope*. 2 v., 1756, 1782: ed. of 1802 is here cited.

—— *The Works of Pope*. 9 v., 1797.

Wentworth Papers: Selected from the Private and Family Correspondence of Thomas Wentworth, Earl of Strafford. 1883.

WHARNCLIFFE, JAMES, LORD (ed.). *The Letters and Works of Lady Mary Wortley Montagu*. 3 v., 1837; 3rd. ed. 1861.

WILLIAMS, SIR HAROLD. *Swift's Poems*. 3 v. 1937.

WILLIAMS, ROBERT FOLKSTONE. *Memoirs and Correspondence of Francis Atterbury*. 1869.

POPE'S OWN PREFACES TO HIS LETTERS, 1729–42

The Posthumous Works of William Wycherley, Esq., Vol. II (1729)

TO THE READER

Having heard that there were, in the *Harley Library*, some Papers of the late Mr. *Wycherley*, beside what are published in the *First Part* of his *Posthumous Works*; and particularly several *Letters*, which we doubted not would be highly acceptable to the Curious: We made it our Business to apply to the Possessor of them, the Right Honourable the *Earl* of *Oxford.* His Lordship has been pleas'd, in the most Generous Manner, to comply with our Request, and to sacrifice a Private Curiosity to the Gratification of the Publick. Tho' we doubt not, one Cause to which we are to attribute this Favour, is the known Benevolence of that Noble Lord to Learned Men, which extends not only to their *Persons*, but to their *Memories.*

It is always some Question, Whether *Posthumous Works* are Genuine? These Poems in particular will be suspected, from the manifest *Disparity* between them, and the *Folio* printed by Mr. *Wycherley* himself in his Life-time; nay, between some and others of these very Verses. We therefore judg'd the ensuing *Letters* of the more Consequence, as they happen to be a Proof (and indeed the *only one*, to all such who have not been favour'd with a Sight of the *Manuscripts*) that some of the said Poems are Genuine, and let us into the History of their Correction, 'till now a Secret.

They will further enable the Reader to distinguish, which of the Pieces were touch'd upon, with the Author's own Consent and Concurrence, by his Friend; and which may have been finger'd after his Death, by others, without any Warrant but their own Arrogance, or Motive but their own Lucre. The Fact is, that tho' none of them had the last Hand, many were once in a better Condition than they now appear; as may be seen by the *Epistle to Mr. Dryden* and a few others, by great Chance preserv'd in the State Mr. *Pope* left them.

It will be ask'd, Why for so long a Time, as from the Beginning of this Design (which appears by the Letters to have been in 1705,) 'till the Death of Mr. *Wycherley* which happen'd in 1715, no farther Progress was made in correcting either these, or the vast Number of other Verses he left behind? We here see the Reasons were many: The known Inability of Mr. *Wycherley* in *Versification*, added to the Decay of his *Memory*; the *Impossibility* which his Friend at last found of rendring them perfect *Pieces of Poetry*, even tho' he should have entirely new-written them; the Conviction by several Instances, that the more he should bring them to approach to it, the less he should obtain the *End propos'd* of having them pass for Mr. *Wycherley's*; and lastly, his sincere Opinion that they would make a worse Figure as Verses unequal and undigested, without Ornament Method or Musick, than as single *Maxims* or *Apothegmes* of good Sense in Prose. Never was more friendly Advice, or a truer Judgment given. It was also a Task which the Author (notwithstanding his unhappy Defects of *Ear* and *Memory*) might *himself* perform, and upon which it appears he had actually begun, by the *three hundred and odd Maxims* found among his Papers, which only of that whole Book (as we are inform'd) were sent to the Press in Mr. *Wycherley's* own Hand.

It is no unpleasing Reflection to us, that (after more than twenty Years, in which this Transaction has been a Secret) we can thus far consult the Fame of Two Eminent Writers, remarkable for so long a Friendship at so great an Inequality of Years, for it appears to have commenc'd when the one was above *Seventy*, the other not *Seventeen*: And that in this we publish an *Example*, (very rarely to be found among any Authors, and never but among the Best,) of so much Temper, Sense of his own Deficiencies, and Deference to the Judgment of a Friend, in the One; and of so much Sincerity, Candor and Zeal for the Reputation of a Friend, in the Other.

There cannot certainly be a greater Injury to a dead or living Author, than to publish such Works, the unfinish'd Parts of which will be ascrib'd to the one, the more finish'd to the other, and yet answerable to the Intent or Character of neither. It was therefore thought, that to represent the True State of this Case, would be doing the best Justice to the Memory of Mr. *Wycherley*.

A few Passages and Parts of the Letters are omitted, for Reasons which will be obvious to any who compare them.

To which End, the *Originals*, in the Author's own Hand-writing, (together with some other material Papers) may, upon Application, be view'd in the HARLEY-LIBRARY, by any Gentleman, or other Person, of such a Character as to be admitted.

LETTERS OF MR. POPE, AND SEVERAL EMINENT PERSONS (1735)

To the Reader[1]

We presume we want no Apology to the Reader for this Publication, but some may be thought needful to Mr. *Pope*: However he cannot

[1] This preface, like the title-page, was lacking in the imperfect 'morning' edition of 12 May, but it appears in the more complete books offered for sale in the afternoon (1735a2) of that day.

think our Offence so great as Theirs, who first separately published what we have here but collected in a better Form and Order. As for the Letters we have procur'd to be added, they serve but to compleat, explain, and sometimes set in a true light those others, which it was not in the Writer's or Our power to recall.[1]

This Collection hath been owing to several Cabinets; some drawn from thence by Accidents, and others (even of those to Ladies) voluntarily given. It is to one of that Sex we are beholden for the whole Correspondence with *H.C.* Esq; which Letters being lent her by that Gentleman, she took the liberty to print; as appears by the following, which we shall give at length, both as it is something Curious, and as it may serve for an Apology for our selves.

[*Here were inserted Pope's letter to Henry Cromwell, Esq; 27 June 1727; Cromwell's reply of 6 July, and the further reply of Cromwell, 1 August. The letters are here printed in their proper chronological positions.*]

Now, should our Apology for this Publication be as ill receiv'd, as the Lady's seems to have been by the Gentlemen concerned; we shall at least have *Her Comfort* of being Thank'd by the rest of the world. Nor has Mr. *P.* himself any great cause to think it much Offence to his Modesty, or Reflexion on his Judgment; when we take care to inform the publick, that there are few Letters of his in this Collection which were not written under Twenty years of age: On the other hand, we doubt not the Reader will be much more surpriz'd to find, at that early period, so much Variety of Style, Affecting Sentiment, and Justness of Criticism, in pieces which must have been writ in haste, very few perhaps ever re-view'd, and none intended for the Eye of the Publick.

PREFACE TO THE QUARTO EDITION OF POPE'S *LETTERS* (1737b)[2]

If what is here offer'd the Reader should happen in any degree to please him, the thanks are not due to the Author, but partly to his Friends, and partly to his Enemies: It was wholly owing to the Affection of the

[1] After this paragraph there appeared in 1735a3 the following paragraph: 'The Letters to Mr. *Wycherley* were procured some Years since, on account of a surreptitious Edition of his Posthumous Works: As those Letters shewed the true state of that Case, the Publication of them was doing the best Justice to the Memory of Mr. *Wycherley*.' The preface then begins the next paragraph 'The rest of this Collection hath been owing . . .'.

[2] This Preface appeared in 1737a and b in differing forms, and some will think it a mistake to print from the official quarto (b) rather than from the Roberts octavo (a). The differences in text are many but are almost always merely rhetorical. The text printed represents Pope's considered revision of the Preface—probably! The matter is confused by a passage in 'The Booksellers to the Reader' prefixed to 1737a, where the 'Booksellers' say, 'We have prefix'd the *Author's Preface*; and to make it known to be such, have put it into the *First Person* (as it stood originally in his Specimen) instead of the *Third* (as he since alter'd it) lest future times shou'd be led to mistake it for some other Editor's.' Quite possibly, of course, Pope here speaks for the 'Booksellers'.

former, that so many Letters of which he never kept copies were preserv'd, and to the Malice of the latter that they were produc'd in this manner.

He had been very disagreeably us'd, in the publication of some Letters written in his youth, which fell into the hands of a Woman who printed them without his, or his correspondent's consent, in 1727. This treatment, and the apprehension of more of the same kind, put him upon recalling as many as he could from those who he imagin'd had kept any. He was sorry to find the number so great, but immediately lessen'd it by burning three parts in four of them: The rest he spar'd, not in any preference of their Stile or writing, but merely as they preserv'd the memory of some Friendships which will ever be dear to him, or set in a true light some Matters of fact, from which the Scriblers of the times had taken occasion to asperse either his Friends or himself. He therefore lay'd by the originals, together with those of his Correspondents, and caus'd a Copy to be taken to deposite in the Library of a noble Friend; that in case either of the revival of slanders, or the publication of surreptitious letters, during his life or after, a proper use might be made of them.

The next year, the Posthumous works of Mr. *Wycherley* were printed, in a way disreputable enough to his memory: It was thought a justice due to him, to shew the world his better judgment; and that it was his last resolution to have suppress'd those Poems. As some of the letters which had pass'd between him and our Author clear'd that point, they were publish'd in 1729, with a few marginal[1] notes added by a friend.

If in these letters, and in those which were printed without his consent, there appear too much of a juvenile ambition of Wit, or affectation of Gayety, he may reasonably hope it will be consider'd *to whom*, and at *what age*, he was guilty of it, as well as how soon it was over. The rest, every judge of writing will see, were by no means Efforts of the Genius but Emanations of the Heart: and this alone may induce any candid reader to believe their publication an act of necessity, rather than of vanity.

It is notorious, how many volumes have been publish'd under the title of his Correspondence, with promises still of more, and open and repeated offers of encouragement to all persons who should send any letters of his for the press. It is as notorious what methods were taken to procure them, even from the Publisher's own accounts in his prefaces, viz. by transacting with people in necessities,[2] or of abandon'd

[1] Printed, rather, as footnotes.

[2] See the Preface to Vol. I. of a Book called Mr. Pope's Literary Correspondence [i.e. 1735b].—Pope, 1737b. [Alluding to the neediness of Mrs. Thomas, who sold the Cromwell letters to Curll.]

characters,[1] or such as dealt without names in the dark.[2] Upon a quarrel with one of these last, he betray'd himself so far as to appeal to the publick in Narratives and Advertisements: like that Irish Highway-man a few years before, who preferr'd a Bill against his Companion, for not sharing equally in the mony, rings and watches, they had traded for in Partnership upon *Hounslow-heath.*

Several have been printed in his name which he never writ, and address'd to persons to whom they never were written;[3] counterfeited as from Bishop *Atterbury* to him, which neither that Bishop nor he ever saw;[4] and advertiz'd even after that period when it was made Felony to correspond with him.

I know not how it has been this Author's fate, whom both his *Situation* and his *Temper* have all his life excluded from rivalling any man, in any pretension, (except that of pleasing by Poetry) to have been as much aspers'd and written at, as any First Minister of his time: Pamphlets and Newspapers have been full of him, nor was it *there only* that a private man, who never troubled either the world or common conversation with his opinions of Religion or Government has been represented as a dangerous member of Society, a bigotted Papist, and an enemy to the Establishment. The unwarrantable publication of his Letters hath at least done him this service, to show he has constantly enjoy'd the friendship of worthy men; and that if a Catalogue were to be taken of his friends and his enemies, he needs not to blush at either. Many of them having been written on the most trying occurrences, and all in the openness of friendship, are a proof what were his real Sentiments, as they flow'd warm from the heart, and fresh from the

[1] Postscript to the Preface to Vol. 4 [i.e. 1736a].—Pope, 1737b. As a document in abuse this Postscript is here added:

'Pray, with my *Respects* to Mr. POPE, tell him I am sorry that *Ill Health, Ill Humour, Ill Weather, and the Want of a Coach,* should all conspire to prevent his paying that Visit to LUCRETIA*, which she lately expected from Him; and tho' she will not by any Means admit of the Term *Affectionate*, he may subscribe Himself her *humble Servant.* The Lady is eloped from her last Lodging, but *He* may hear of his *Deary* at the *Old Place.* She hopes the Picture will please, now the Painter has re-touched it.

'Tis strange! that still our Bard the Truth will shun,
For *Wrong* is *Wrong*, where-ever it be done.

Adv. from *Hor.*'

Curll in a footnote identifies Lucretia* as follows: 'A noted Cast-off-Punk, of his pious *Saint-John.* Mrs. *Griffith*, alias *Butler*, alias *Lucretia Lindo*, who has several Letters of Mr. *Pope*'s not worth Printing.'

[2] Narrative and Anecdotes before Vol. 2 [i.e. 1735g].—Pope, 1737b.

[3] In Vol. 3. Letters from Mr. Pope to Mrs. Blount, &c.—Pope, 1737b. [The reference is to the four letters by Voiture, printed by Curll in 1735j as from Pope to Miss Blount.]

[4] Vol. 2 of the same 8° pag. 20 [i.e. 1735g] and at the end of the Edition of his Letters in 12° by the Booksellers of London and Westminster; and of the last Edition in 12° printed by T. Cooper, 1725.—Pope, 1737b.

The date 1725 is an evident misprint for 1735 [1735i]. Pope refers to the two letters printed as from Atterbury or to him in 1735g, i, and h2. Page 20 (third series) of 1735g contains a letter to Atterbury, pretty certainly not by Pope, though it expresses ideas later found in the *Essay on Man.*

occasion; without the least thought that ever the world should be witness to them. Had he sate down with a design to draw his own Picture, he could not have done it so truly; for whoever sits for it (whether to himself or another) will inevitably find the features more compos'd, than his appear in these letters. But if an Author's hand, like a Painter's, be more distinguishable in a slight sketch than in a finish'd picture, this very carelessness will make them the better known from such Counterfeits, as have been, and may be imputed to him, either thro' a mercenary, or a malicious design.

We hope it is needless to say, he is not accountable for several passages in the surreptitious editions of those letters, which are such as no man of common sense would have publish'd himself. The errors of the press were almost innumerable, and could not but be extremely multiply'd in so many repeated editions; by the Avarice and Negligence of pyratical Printers, to not one of whom he ever gave the least Title, or any other encouragement than that of not prosecuting them.

For the *Chasms* in the correspondence, we had not the means to supply them, the Author having destroy'd too many letters to preserve any Series. Nor would he go about to amend them, except by the omission of some passages, improper, or at least impertinent, to be divulg'd to the publick: or of such entire letters, as were either not his, or not approv'd of by him.[1]

He has been very sparing of those of his Friends, and thought it a respect shewn to their memory, to suppress in particular such as were most in his favour. As it is not to *Vanity* but to *Friendship* that he intends this Monument, he would save his enemies the mortification of showing any farther how well their Betters have thought of him; and at the same time secure from their censure his living Friends, who (he promises them) shall never be put to blush, this way at least, for their partiality to him.

But however this Collection may be receiv'd, we cannot but lament[2] the *Cause* and the *Necessity* of such a publication, and heartily wish no honest man may be reduc'd to the same. To state the case fairly in the present situation. A Bookseller advertises his intention to publish your Letters: He openly promises encouragement, or even pecuniary rewards to those who will help him to any; and ingages to insert whatever they shall send: Any scandal is sure of a reception, and any enemy who sends it skreen'd from a discovery. Any domestick or servant, who can snatch a letter from your pocket or cabinet, is encouraged to that vile practise. If the quantity falls short of a volume, any thing else

[1] In the Roberts octavo (1737a) this sentence read: 'nor would I go about to alter or amend any thing except by the omission of here and there a passage wholly impertinent to the publick, or of a thought or two which I disapprov'd on a review.'

[2] In 1737a this sentence reads: 'But however this collection may be receiv'd, or whatever credit may be deriv'd to me from that part of it which is not my own, I cannot but lament . . .'

shall be join'd with it (more especially scandal) which the collector can think for his interest, all recommended under your Name: You have not only Theft to fear, but Forgery. Any Bookseller, tho' conscious in what manner they were obtain'd, not caring what may be the consequences to your Fame or Quiet, will sell and disperse them in town and country. The better your Reputation is, the more your Name will cause them to be demanded, and consequently the more you will be injur'd. The injury is of such a nature, as the Law (which does not punish for *Intentions*) cannot prevent; and when done, may punish, but not redress. You are therefore reduc'd, either to enter into a personal treaty with such a man, (which tho' the readiest, is the meanest of all methods) or to take such other measures to suppress them, as are contrary to your Inclination, or to publish them, as are contrary to your Modesty. Otherwise your Fame and your Property suffer alike; you are at once expos'd and plunder'd. As an *Author*, you are depriv'd of that Power which above all others constitutes a good one, the power of rejecting, and the right of judging for your self, what pieces it may be most useful, entertaining, or reputable to publish, at the time and in the manner you think best. As a *Man*, you are depriv'd of the right even over your own Sentiments, of the privilege of every humane creature to divulge or conceal them; of the advantage of your second thoughts; and of all the benefit of your Prudence, your Candour, or your Modesty. As a *Member of Society*, you are yet more injur'd; your private conduct, your domestick concerns, your family secrets, your passions, your tendernesses, your weaknesses, are expos'd to the Misconstruction or Resentment of some, to the Censure or Impertinence of the whole world. The printing private letters in such a manner, is the worst sort of *betraying Conversation*, as it has evidently the most extensive, and the most lasting ill consequences. It is the highest offence against *Society*, as it renders the most dear and intimate intercourse of friend with friend, and the most necessary commerce of man with man, unsafe, and to be dreaded. To open Letters is esteem'd the greatest breach of honour; even to look into them already open'd or accidentally dropt, is held ungenerous, if not an immoral act. What then can be thought of the procuring them merely by Fraud, and printing them merely for Lucre? We cannot but conclude every honest man will wish, that if the Laws have as yet provided no adequate remedy, one at least may be found, to prevent so great and growing an evil.

The Works of Mr. Alexander Pope, In Prose. Vol. II. 1741

The Booksellers to the Reader

There having been formerly publish'd, in Folio and Quarto, one Volume of the Works in *Prose* of Mr. *Pope*, being an Authentic

Edition of his *Letters* with those of his *Friends*; we thought it would be agreeable to the Purchasers of that Edition to have likewise the *Letters* between him and Dr. *Swift*: These we have copied from an Impression sent from *Dublin*, and said to be printed by the Dean's Direction.

As it was begun without our Author's Knowledge, and not only continued without his Consent, but after his absolute Refusal, he would not be prevail'd upon to revise those Letters; but gave us a few more of the Dean's, a little to clear up the History of their Publication; which the Reader may see in one View, if he only observes the Passages marked with Comma's in Letters 75, 77, 81, 84, 86, 87, 88, of this Book.[1]

We have also obtain'd the *Memoirs* of SCRIBLERUS, being the beginning of a considerable Work undertaken so long ago as in 1713 by several great Hands. As much of it as is here publish'd, and all the *Tracts* in the same Name, were written by our Author and Dr. *Arbuthnot*, except the *Essay on the Origine of Sciences*, in which Dr. *Parnelle* had some hand, as Mr. *Gay* in the *Memoirs of a Parish-Clerk*. The rest were Mr. *Pope's*. And the Reader may be assured he has now a complete Edition, not only of all this Author has written singly, but of whatsoever he wrote in Conjunction with any of his *Friends*.[2]

[1] The quotation marks spoken of were accidentally omitted in Letter LXXXIV (30 Dec. 1736) in 1741Lab. They appear in the London octavos of 1742. The numbers here given apply only to the quartos and folios of 1741 (1741Lab), but the letters are easily identified since the 'series' begins with the letter of 3 Sept. 1735 and ends with that dated 8 (or 24) Aug. 1738. See here iii. 492, 505; iv. 11–12, 50, 72, 76, 115–16.

[2] This last paragraph is omitted in the London octavos of 1742.

1704–9

Pope's earliest correspondence, as preserved to us, involves almost exclusively three men: Wycherley, Walsh, and Henry Cromwell. The letters to the last named are practically all surely authentic. Those to Walsh we have only from Pope's printings; and the authenticity of those to and from Wycherley has been impugned by Elwin and Courthope very suspiciously, but without too much evidence. The letters *from* Wycherley can in general be trusted. The picture this correspondence gives of the friendship between Pope and Wycherley has been much distorted by these Victorian editors: except for a temporary coolness in 1710 the friendship lasted until Wycherley's death.

The letters of these years have two subject-matters: wit and literary criticism. Appropriately here at the very beginning Pope appears for what he always was, the man of letters. He appears also as a type which, seen in others, he abhorred: he appears as a literary pedant. The wit of these letters, seen in the excessive compliment essential to letters written in the tradition of Voiture and seen also in the indecorous language and jests natural to the Restoration tradition (of which the three elderly correspondents were a part), was regretted by Pope after the change in the literary weather—caused, in part, by *The Spectator*. Pope always pointed to the youthful age at which the letters were written as an excuse for their follies. It is most regrettable that we have so few letters from his correspondence with Sir William Trumbull and other men who were sincerely fond of the young Pope and dazzled by his abilities.

†POPE *to* WYCHERLEY[1] — 26 *December* 1704

1735

Decemb. 26, 1704.

It was certainly a great Satisfaction to me to see and converse with a Man, whom in his Writings I had so long known with Pleasure: But

[1] We have 36 letters that passed between Pope and Wycherley. Of these 11 are by Pope and 25 by Wycherley. Pope printed 26 letters in his *Posthumous Works* of Wycherley, vol. ii (1729), and in 1735 he omitted two and added two others, of which this first letter is one.

Among the Harleian transcripts are preserved 12 of these letters, only 2 of which (22 Mar. 1705/6 and 11 Nov. 1707) were used in part by Pope. The complete texts of the 12 Harleian letters were first printed by Elwin (v. 387–407). The transcripts are here used as texts. The correspondence was from the start imperfectly preserved; for Wycherley mentions by date 7 letters from Pope that have not come down to us. There is no reason to think, with Elwin, that the two friends were permanently estranged in 1710: the last sentence of Wycherley's last letter (27 Apr. 1710) is most friendly. In the opinion of the present editor the unscrupulous editing of Pope does not notably alter the truth concerning his friendship with the great dramatist, who was also an inferior poet.

In all his editions Pope annotated the date of this first letter, 'The Author's Age then Sixteen.' Very likely the letter was polished for publication in 1735. In 1737 Pope added to the superscription, 'Binfield in Windsor Forest.'

it was a high addition to it, to hear you, at our very first meeting, doing justice to your dead friend Mr. *Dryden.* I was not so happy as to know him; *Virgilium tantum vidi*[1]—Had I been born early enough, I must have known and lov'd him: For I have been assur'd, not only by your self, but by Mr. *Congreve* and Sir *William Trumbul*, that his personal Qualities were as amiable as his Poetical, notwithstanding the many libelous Misrepresentations of them (against which the former of these Gentlemen has told me he will one day vindicate him).[2] I suppose those Injuries were begun by the Violence of Party, but 'tis no doubt they were continu'd by Envy at his success and fame: And those Scribblers who attack'd him in his latter times, were only like Gnats in a Summer's evening, which are never very troublesome but in the finest and most glorious Season; (for his fire, like the Sun's, shin'd clearest towards its setting.)

You must not therefore imagine, that when you told me ⌜of⌝ my own performances ⌜that they⌝[3] were above those Criticks, I was so vain as to believe it; and yet I may not be so humble as to think my self quite below their notice. For Critics, as they are Birds of Prey, have ever a natural inclination to Carrion: And though such poor Writers as I, are but Beggars, however no Beggar is so poor but he can keep a Cur, and no Author is so beggarly but he can keep a Critic. So I'm far from thinking the Attacks of such people either any honour or dishonour, even to me,[4] much less to Mr. *Dryden.* I think with you, that whatever lesser Wits have risen since his Death, are but like Stars appearing when the Sun is set, that twinkle only in his absence, and with the Rays they have borrowed from him. Our Wit (as you call it) is but Reflexion or Imitation, therefore scarce to be call'd ours. True Wit I believe, may be defin'd a Justness of Thought, and a Facility of Expression; or (in the Midwives phrase) a perfect Conception, with an easy Delivery. However this is far from a compleat definition; pray help me to a better, as I doubt not you can. | I am, &c.

[1] When a very young Boy, he prevailed with a friend to carry him to a Coffee-house which Dryden frequented; where he had the satisfaction he speaks of.—Warburton, 1751. See also Spence, p. 332.

[2] He since did so, in his Dedication to the Duke of *Newcastle*, prefix'd to *Tonson's Duodecimo* Edition of *Dryden's* Plays. 1717.—Pope, 1735–42.

[3] Pope improved this sentence first in 1737 by the omissions here in half-brackets. Such concision is the most typical change made by Pope in his various editions.

[4] The passage seems strange coming from a sixteen-year-old poet who has published nothing. It is not, however, impossible; Wycherley has told him that his verses were (or would be) above criticism, but the young poet trembles at the possibly unfavourable reception the Rymers and Dennises of the day might give.

†WYCHERLEY *to* POPE[1] 25 *January* 1704/5

1729

Jan. 25, 1704–5.

I have been so busy of late in correcting and transcribing some of my Madrigals, for a great Man or two who desir'd to see them, that I have (with your Pardon) omitted to return you an Answer to your most ingenious Letter: So Scribblers to the Publick, like Bankers to the Publick, are profuse in their voluntary Loans to it, whilst they forget to pay their more private and particular, as more just Debts, to their best and nearest Friends. However, I hope, you who have as much good Nature as good Sense, (since they generally are Companions) will have Patience with a Debtor, who ⌜you think⌝[2] has an Inclination to pay you his Obligations, if he had wherewithal ready about him; and in the mean time should consider, when you have oblig'd me beyond my present Power of returning the Favour, that a Debtor may be an honest Man, if he but intends to be just when he is able, tho' late. But I should be less just to you, the more I thought I could make a Return to so much Profuseness of Wit and Humanity together; which tho' they seldom accompany each other, in other Men, are in you so equally met, I know not in which you most abound. But so much for my Opinion of you, which is, that your Wit and Ingenuity is equal'd by nothing but your Judgment, or Modesty; which (though it be to please my self) I must no more offend, than I can do either right.

Therefore I will say no more now of them, than that your good Wit ne'er forfeited your good Judgment, but in your Partiality to me and mine; so that if it were possible for a harden'd Scribbler to be vainer than he is, what you write of me would make me more conceited, than what I scribble my self; yet I must confess I ought to be more humbled by your Praise than exalted; which commends my little Sense with so much more of yours, that I am disparag'd and dishearten'd by your commendations; who give me an Example of your Wit in the first Part of your Letter, and a Definition of it in the last: to make writing well (that is like you) more difficult to me than ever it was before. Thus the more great and just your Example and Definition of Wit are, the less I am capable to follow them. Then the best way of shewing my Judgment, after having seen how you write, is to leave off writing; and the best way to shew my Friendship to you, is to put an end to your Trouble, and to conclude | Your, &c.

[1] Omitted in the quarto and folio of 1737. The letter was first printed in 1729, but in the editions of 1735 resetting of the type for this letter was made necessary by the insertion of the letter of 26 Dec. 1704.

[2] you think] *omitted in 1737–42.*

†POPE *to* ——[1] 1 *March* 1704/5

1735

Madam,—I send you the book of Rudiments of *Drawing*, which you were pleas'd to command, and think my self oblig'd to inform you at the same time of one of the many excellencies you possess without knowing of 'em. You are but too good a Painter already; and no Picture of *Raphael's* was ever so beautiful, as that which you have form'd in a certain heart of my acquaintance. Indeed it was but just that the finest lines in nature shou'd be drawn upon the most durable ground, and none cou'd ever be met with that wou'd so readily receive, or so faithfully retain them, as this Heart. I may boldly say of it that you will not find its fellow in all the *Parts* of the *Body* in this book. But I must complain to you of my hand, which is an arrant traitor to my heart; for having been copying your picture from thence and from *Kneller* these three days, it has done all possible injury to the finest Face that ever was made, and to the liveliest Image that ever was drawn. I have imagination enough in your absence, to trace some resemblance of you; but I have been so long us'd to lose my judgment at the sight of you, that 'tis past my power to correct it by the life. Your Picture seems least like when plac'd before your eyes, and contrary to all other pictures receives a manifest disadvantage by being set in the fairest Light in the world. The Painters are a very vain generation, and have a long time pretended to rival Nature; but to own the truth to you, she made such a finish'd piece about three and twenty years ago, (I beg your pardon Madam, I protest I meant but two and twenty) that 'tis in vain for them any longer to contend with her. I know You indeed made one something like it, betwixt five and six years past: 'Twas a little girl, done with abundance of spirit and life: and wants nothing but time to be an admirable piece: But not to flatter your work, I don't think 'twill ever come up to what your Father made. However I wou'd not discourage you; 'tis certain you have a strange happiness, in making fine things of a sudden and at a stroke, with incredible ease and pleasure. | Madam, I am, &c.

[1] Omitted from the quarto and folio of 1737. The date is added in the octavos of 1737–42, but need not be taken too seriously. It is possible that Pope was copying portraits as early as 1705. The letter is in his (?) early witty style. Curll (*Pope's Literary Correspondence*, iii [1735], xvi) commented, 'I find you have very politely pillaged his [Voiture's] Letters: Your *First*, To a Lady, with a *Book* of *Drawings*, is evidently taken from *One* he wrote to *Madame Rambouillet*, in the name of *Callot* the Engraver.' The resemblance, while real, does not extend to plagiarism.

It seems impossible to speculate surely as to the identity of the lady concerned.

†POPE *to* WYCHERLEY 25 *March* 1705

1729

March 25, 1705.

When I write to you, I foresee a long Letter, and ought to beg your Patience beforehand; for if it proves the longest, it will be of course the worst I have troubled you with. Yet to express my Gratitude at large for your obliging Letter, is not more my Duty than my Interest; as some People will abundantly thank you for one Piece of Kindness, to put you in mind of bestowing another. The more favourable you are to me, the more distinctly I see my Faults; Spots and Blemishes you know, are never so plainly discover'd as in the brightest Sunshine. Thus I am mortified by those Commendations which were design'd to encourage me: for Praise to a young Wit, is like Rain to a tender Flower; if it be moderately bestow'd, it chears and revives, but if too lavishly, overcharges and depresses him.[1] Most Men in years, as they are generally discouragers of Youth, are like old Trees, that being past Bearing themselves, will suffer no young Plants to flourish beneath them: But as if it were not enough to have out-done all your Coævals in Wit, you will excel them in good Nature too. As for my green Essays,[2] if you find any pleasure in 'em, it must be such as a Man naturally takes in observing the first Shoots and Buddings of a Tree which he has rais'd himself: and 'tis impossible they should be esteem'd any otherwise, than as we value Fruits for being early, which nevertheless are the most insipid, and the worst of the Year. In a word, I must blame you for treating me with so much Compliment, which is at best but the Smoak of Friendship.[3] I neither write, nor converse with you, to gain your Praise but your Affection. Be so much my Friend as to appear my Enemy, and tell me my Faults, if not as a young Man, at least as an unexperienc'd Writer. | I am, &c.

†WYCHERLEY *to* POPE[4] 29 *March* 1705

1729

March 29, 1705.

Your Letter of the Twenty-fifth of *March* I have receiv'd, which was more welcome to me than any thing cou'd be out of the Country, tho' it were one's Rent due that Day: and I can find no fault with it, but that it charges me with Want of Sincerity, or Justice, for giving you your Due; who shou'd not let your Modesty be so unjust to your Merit, as to reject what is due to it, and call that Compliment which is

[1] Very similar imagery and thought are found in a letter to Caryll, 31 July 1710.
[2] His *Pastorals*, written at 16 Years of Age.—Pope, 1729–42.
[3] Again the imagery resembles that used to Caryll in the letter of 31 July 1710.
[4] Omitted in the quarto and folio of 1737.

so short of your desert, that it is rather degrading than exalting you. But if Compliment be the Smoak only of Friendship (as you say) however you must allow there is no Smoak but there is some Fire; and as the Sacrifice of Incense offer'd to the Gods wou'd not have been half so sweet to others, if it had not been for its Smoak; so Friendship like Love, cannot be without some Incense, to perfume the Name it wou'd praise and immortalize. But since you say you do not write to me to gain my *Praise*, but my *Affection*, pray how is it possible to have the one without the other? We must admire before we love. You affirm, you would have me so much your Friend as to appear your Enemy, and find out your Faults rather than your Perfections: But (my Friend) that would be so hard to do, that I who love no Difficulties, can't be persuaded to it. Besides, the Vanity of a Scribbler is such, that he will never part with his own Judgment to gratify another's; especially when he must take Pains to do it: And tho' I am proud to be of your Opinion, when you talk of any Thing, or Man but your self, I cannot suffer you to murther your fame, with your own hand, without opposing you; especially when you say your last Letter is the worst (since the longest) you have favoured me with; which I therefore think the best, as the longest Life (if a good one) is the best, as it yields the more Variety and is more Exemplary; as a chearful Summer's Day, tho' longer than a dull one in the Winter, is less tedious and more entertaining: Therefore let but your Friendship be like your Letter, as lasting as it is agreeable, and it can never be tedious, but more acceptable and obliging to | Your &c.

†WYCHERLEY *to* POPE[1] 7 *April* 1705

1729

April 7, 1705.

I have receiv'd yours of the Fifth, wherein your Modesty refuses the just Praise I give you, by which you lay claim to more, as a Bishop gains his Bishoprick by saying he will not Episcopate: But I must confess, whilst I displease you by commending you, I please my self; just as Incense is sweeter to the Offerer than the Deity to whom 'tis offered, by his being so much above it: For indeed, every Man partakes of the Praise he gives, when it is so justly given.

As to my enquiry after your Intrigues with the *Muses*, you may allow me to make it, since no old Man can give so young, so great, and able a Favourite of theirs, Jealousy. I am, in my Enquiry, like old Sir *Bernard Gascoign*,[2] who us'd to say, That when he was grown too

[1] Omitted in the quarto and folio of 1737. Pope's letter 'of the Fifth' is unknown.

[2] A gentleman of Italian birth (1614–87), who served in the armies of Charles I, and was rewarded by Charles II, in whose court he was highly favoured.—*DNB*.

old to have his Visits admitted alone by the Ladies, he always took along with him a young Man, to ensure his Welcome to them; who, had he come alone had been rejected, only because his Visits were not scandalous to them. So I am (like an old Rook, who is ruin'd by Gaming) forc'd to live on the good Fortune of the pushing young Men, whose Fancies are so vigorous, that they ensure their Success in their Adventures with the Muses, by their Strength of Imagination.

Your Papers are safe in my Custody[1] (you may be sure) from any one's Theft but my own; for 'tis as dangerous to trust a Scribbler with your Wit, as a Gamester with the Custody of your Money.—If you happen to come to Town, you will make it more difficult for me to leave it, who am, dear Mr. *Pope*, | Your, &c.

†WALSH *to* WYCHERLEY[2] 20 *April* 1705

1735

Apr. 20. 1705.

I return you the Papers[3] you favour'd me with, and had sent them to you yesterday morning, but that I thought to have brought them to you last night my self. I have read them over several times with great satisfaction. The Preface[4] is very judicious and very learned; and the Verses very tender and easy. The Author seems to have a particular Genius for that kind of Poetry, and a Judgment that much exceeds the years you told me he was of. He has taken very freely from the Ancients, but what he has mixt of his own with theirs, is no way[5] inferior to what he has taken from them. 'Tis no flattery at all to say, that *Virgil* had written nothing so good at his Age.[6] I shall take it as a favour if you will bring me acquainted with him; and if he will give himself the trouble any morning to call at my House, I shall be very glad to read the Verses over with him, and give him my opinion of the particulars more largely than I can well do in this Letter. I am, | Sir, | Your most faithful | and most humble Servant, | W. Walsh.

[1] It is interesting to see Pope thus early fearing that his papers might be stolen.

[2] Preceding the group of six Walsh letters, of which this was the first in Pope's editions, was a footnote to the first mention of Walsh's name: 'Of *Abberley* in *Worcestershire*, Gentleman of the Horse in Queen *Anne's* reign, Author of several beautiful pieces in Prose and Verse, and in the Opinion of Mr. *Dryden*, (in his Postscript to *Virgil*), the Best Critic of our Nation in his time.' The note is found in all Pope's editions that print the letter. The letter is omitted in the quarto and folio of 1737.

[3] Mr. *Pope's* Pastorals.—Pope, 1735–42.

[4] The Preface was not published with the Pastorals in 1709, but was first printed in Pope's *Works* in 1717.

[5] no way] not 1737–42.

[6] Sixteen.—Pope, 1735–42.

†POPE *to* WYCHERLEY *30 April 1705*

1729

April 30, 1705.

I cannot contend with you. You must give me leave at once to wave all your Compliments, and to collect only this in general from 'em, that your Design is to encourage me. But I separate from all the rest that Paragraph or two, in which you make me so warm an Offer of your Friendship. Were I possess'd of That, it would put an End to all those Speeches with which you now make me blush; and change them to wholsome Advices, and free Sentiments, which might make me wiser and happier. I know 'tis the general Opinion, that Friendship is best contracted betwixt Persons of equal Age: but I have so much Interest to be of another Mind, that you must pardon me if I cannot forbear telling you a few Notions of mine, in opposition to that Opinion.

In the first place 'tis observable, that the Love we bear to our Friends is generally caused by our finding the same Dispositions in them, which we feel in our selves. This is but Self-love at the Bottom: Whereas the Affection betwixt People of different Ages cannot well be such, the Inclinations of such being commonly various. The Friendship of two young Men is often occasioned by Love of Pleasure or Voluptuousness, each being desirous, for his own sake, of one to assist or incourage him in the Courses he pursues; as that of two old Men is frequently on the score of some Profit, Lucre, or Design upon others: Now, as a young Man who is less acquainted with the Ways of the World, has in all probability less of Interest; and an old Man who may be weary of himself, less of Self-love; so the Friendship between them is the more likely to be true, and unmix'd with too much Self-regard. One may add to this, that such a Friendship is of greater Use and Advantage to both; for the old Man will grow more gay and agreeable to please the young one; and the young Man more discreet and prudent by the help of the old one; so it may prove a Cure of those epidemical Diseases of Age and Youth, Sourness and Madness. I hope you will not need many Arguments to convince you of the Possibility of this; One alone abundantly satisfies me,[1] and convinces to the very Heart; which is, that I am, &c.

[1] Mr. *Wycherley* was at this time about Seventy Years old, Mr. *Pope* under seventeen.—Pope, 1729–42. Professor Howard Vincent in a letter to *TLS* (3 March 1932) places Wycherley's birth on 28 May 1641.

‡POPE *to* WYCHERLEY[1] 23 *June* 1705

1735

June 23, 1705.

I shou'd believe my self happy in your good Opinion, but that you treat me so much in a Style of Compliment. It has been observ'd of Women, that they are more subject in their youth to be touch'd with Vanity than Men, on account of their being generally treated this way; but the weakest Women are not more so than that weak class of Men, who are thought to pique themselves upon their Wit. The World is never wanting, when a Coxcomb is accomplishing himself, to help to give him the finishing Stroke.

Every Man is apt to think his Neighbour overstock'd with Vanity, yet I cannot but fancy, there are certain Times, when most people are in a disposition of being inform'd; and 'tis incredible what a vast Good a little Truth might do, spoken in such seasons. A very small Alms will do a great kindness, to people in extream necessity.

I could name an acquaintance of yours, who wou'd at this time think himself more obliged to you for the Information of his Faults, than the Confirmation of his Follies. If you would make those the subject of a Letter, it might be as long as I could wish your Letters always were.

I do not wonder you have hitherto found some difficulty (as you are pleas'd to say) in writing to me, since you have always chosen the Task of commending me: Take but the other way, and I dare ingage you will find none at all.

As for my Verses which you praise so much, I may truly say they had never been the cause of any Vanity in me, except what they gave me when they first occasion'd my acquaintance with you. But I have several times since been in danger of this Vice, as often I mean as I receiv'd any Letters from you.

'Tis certain, the greatest magnifying Glasses in the World are a Man's own Eyes, when they look upon his own Person; yet even in those, I cannot fancy my self so extremely like *Alexander the Great*, as you wou'd persuade me: If I must be like him, 'tis you will make me so, by complimenting me into a better opinion of my self than I deserve: They made him think he was the *Son of Jupiter*, and you assure me I am a Man of Parts. But is this all you can say to my honour? You said ten times as much before, when you call'd me your

[1] This letter is fabricated from two letters to Caryll—those of 31 July 1710 and 25 Jan. 1710/11. The letter was not published in the 1729 volume, but was inserted in 1735 on a specially printed quarter sheet, *C.

Only a detailed comparison of this letter with the two from which it is largely drawn will show the skill Pope had in such adaptations.

Friend. After having made me believe I possess'd a share in your affection, to treat me with Compliments and sweet Sayings, is like the proceeding with poor *Sancho Pança*: They had persuaded him that he enjoy'd a great Dominion, and then gave him nothing to subsist upon but *Wafers* and *Marmalade*. In our Days, the greatest obligation you can lay upon a Wit, is to make a Fool of him. For as when Madmen are found incurable, wise Men give them their Way, and please them as well as they can; so when those incorrigible things, Poets, are once irrecoverably Be-Mus'd, the best way both to quiet them, and secure your selves from the effects of their Frenzy, is to feed their Vanity; (which indeed for the most part is all that is fed in a Poet.)

You may believe me, I could be heartily glad that all you say were as true, apply'd to me, as it wou'd be to your self, for several weighty Reasons; but for none so much, as that I might be to you what you deserve; whereas I can now be no more, than is consistent with the small tho' utmost Capacity of, | Dear Sir, | Your ever affectionate Servant.

†SIR WILLIAM TRUMBULL[1] *to* POPE 19 *October* 1705

1737

Oct. 19, 1705.

Sir,—I return you the Book[2] you were pleas'd to send me, and with it your obliging letter, which deserves my particular acknowledgment; for next to the pleasure of enjoying the company of so good a friend, the welcomest thing to me is to hear from him. I expected to find, what I have met with, an admirable genius in those Poems, not only because they were Milton's, or were approved by Sir Hen. Wootton, but because you had commended them; and give me leave to tell you, that I know no body so like to equal him, even at the age he wrote most of them, as your self. Only do not afford more cause of complaints against you, that you suffer nothing of yours to come abroad; which in this age, wherein wit and true sense is more scarce than money, is a piece of such cruelty as your best friends can hardly pardon. I hope you will repent and amend; I could offer many reasons to this purpose, and such as you cannot answer with any sincerity; but that I dare not enlarge, for fear of engaging in a stile of Compliment, which has been so abused by fools and knaves, that it is become almost scandalous. I

[1] Secretary of State to King William the Third.—Pope, 1737–42. During the Binfield period Sir William was perhaps the most important influence on the young poet. Pope told Spence (*Anecdotes*, p. 194) that Sir William 'loved very much to read and talk of the classics in his retirement. We used to take a ride out together, three or four days in the week, and at last, almost every day'. Sir William, a former Fellow of All Souls, may be thought of as Pope's tutor in the classics.

[2] *L'Allegro*, *Il Penseroso*, *Lycidas*, and the Masque of *Comus*.—Pope, 1737–42.

conclude therefore with an assurance which shall never vary, of my being ever, &c.

†POPE *to* WYCHERLEY 26 *October* 1705

1729

Oct. 26, 1705.

I have now chang'd the Scene from the Town to the Country; from *Will's* Coffee-House to *Windsor* Forest. I find no other difference than this, betwixt the common Town-Wits, and the downright Country Fools; that the first are pertly in the Wrong, with a little more Flourish and Gaiety, and the last neither in the Right nor the Wrong, but confirmed in a stupid, settled Medium betwixt both. However, methinks these are most in the Right, who quietly and easily resign themselves over to the gentle Reign of Dulness, which the Wits must do at last, tho' after a great deal of Noise, Pother, and Resistance. Ours are a sort of modest, inoffensive People, who neither have Sense, nor pretend to any, but enjoy a jovial Sort of Dulness. They are commonly known in the World by the Name of honest, civil Gentlemen. They live much as they ride, at random; a kind of hunting Life, pursuing with earnestness and hazard, something not worth the catching; never in the way, nor out of it. I can't but prefer Solitude to the Company of all these; for tho' a Man's self may possibly be the worst Fellow to converse with in the World, yet one would think the Company of a Person whom we have the greatest regard to, and affection for, could not be very unpleasant: As a Man in love with a Mistress, desires no Conversation but hers, so a Man in love with himself, (as most Men are) may be best pleased with his own. Besides, if the truest and most useful Knowledge, be the knowledge of our selves, Solitude conducing most to make us look into our selves, should be the most instructive State of Life. We see nothing more commonly, than Men, who for the sake of the circumstantial Part, and meer outside of Life, have been half their Days rambling out of their Nature, and ought to be sent into Solitude to study themselves over again. People are usually spoil'd instead of being taught, at their coming into the World; whereas by being more conversant with Obscurity, without any Pains, they would naturally follow what they were meant for. In a word, if a Man be a Coxcomb, Solitude is his best School; and if he be a Fool, it is his best Sanctuary.

These are good Reasons for my own Stay here, but I wish I could give you any for your coming hither, except that I earnestly invite you. And yet I can't help saying, I have suffer'd a great deal of discontent that you do not, tho' I so little merit that you should.

I must complain of the shortness of your last: Those who have most

Wit, like those who have most Money, are generally most sparing of either.

†WYCHERLEY *to* POPE[1] 5 *November* 1705

1729

Nov. 5, 1705.

Yours of the 26th of *October* I have receiv'd, as I have always done yours, with no little Satisfaction, and am proud to discover by it, that you find fault with the shortness of mine, which I think the best Excuse for it: And tho' they (as you say) who have most Wit or Money, are most sparing of either; there are some who appear Poor to be thought Rich, and are Poor, which is my Case: I cannot but rejoyce, that you have undergone so much discontent for want of my company; but if you have a Mind to punish me for my fault, (which I could not help) defer your coming to Town, and you will do it effectually. But I know your Charity always exceeds your Revenge, so that I will not dispair of seeing you, who, in return to your inviting me to your Forest, invite you to my Forest, the Town; where the Beasts that inhabit, tame or wild, of long Ears or Horns, pursue one another either out of Love or Hatred. You may have the Pleasure to see one Pack of Bloodhounds pursue another Herd of Brutes, to bring each other to their Fall, which is their whole Sport: Or, if you affect a less bloody Chace, you may see a Pack of Spaniels, called *Lovers*, in hot pursuit of a two-legg'd *Vixen*, who only flies the whole low'd Pack to be singled out by one Dog, who runs mute to catch her up the sooner from the rest, as they are making a Noise, to the Loss of their Game. In fine, this is the Time for all sorts of Sport in the Town, when those of the Country cease; therefore leave your Forest of Beasts, for ours of Brutes, call'd Men, who now in full Cry, (pack'd by the Court or Country) run down in the House of Commons, a deserted horned Beast of the Court,[2] to the satisfaction of their Spectators: Besides, (more for your Diversion) you may see not only the two great Play-houses of the Nation, those of the Lords and Commons, in Dispute with one another; but the two other Play-houses in high Contest,[3] because the Members of one House are remov'd up to t'other, (as it is often done by the Court for Reasons of State.) Insomuch that the lower Houses, I mean the Play-houses, are going to act Tragedies on one another without Doors, and the Sovereign is put to it (as it

[1] Omitted from the quarto and folio of 1737.

[2] Bowles identified this 'beast' as Sir Nathan Wright, who had long been under violent attack and had been removed from the post of lord keeper in October.

[3] The Drury Lane company was now acting in the new theatre in the Haymarket, first opened in Apr. 1705. Presently it was found to be fitted for opera rather than for spoken drama. See A. Nicoll, *Early Eighteenth Century Drama* (1925), pp. 46–47.

often happens in the other two Houses) to silence one or both, to keep Peace between them: Now I have told you all the News of the Town. I am, &c.

†WYCHERLEY *to* POPE 5 *February* 1705/6

1729

Feb. 5, 1705/6.

I have receiv'd your kind Letter, with my Paper[1] to Mr. *Dryden* corrected. I own you have made more of it by making it less, as the *Dutch* are said to burn half the Spices they bring home to inhance the Price of the remainder, so to be greater Gainers by their Loss, (which is indeed my Case now.) Well; you have prun'd my fading Lawrels of some superfluous, sapless, and dead Branches, to make the remainder live the longer; thus like your Master *Apollo*, you are at once a Poet and a Physician.

Now, Sir, as to my impudent invitation of you to the Town, your good Nature was the first Cause of my confident request; but excuse me, I must (I see) say no more upon this Subject, since I find you a little too nice to be dealt freely with; tho' you have given me some Encouragement to hope, our Friendship (tho' young) might be without Shyness, or criminal Modesty; for a Friend like a Mistress, tho' he is not to be mercenary to be true, yet ought not to refuse a Friend's kindness because it is small or trivial: I have told you (I think) that a *Spanish* Lady said to her poor, poetical Gallant, that a Queen if she lay with a Groom, would expect a Mark of his kindness from him, tho' it were but his Curry-comb. But you and I will dispute this Matter when I am so happy as to see you here; and perhaps 'tis the only Dispute in which I might hope to have the better of you.

Now, Sir, to make you another Excuse for my boldness in inviting you to Town, I design'd to leave with you some more of my Papers, (since these return so much better out of your Hands than they went from mine) for I intended (as I told you formerly) to spend a Month, or six Weeks this Summer, near you in the Country, for you may be assured there is nothing I desire so much, as an Improvement of your Friendship,—

[1] The same which was printed in the Year 1717, in a *Miscellany* of *Bern. Lintot's*, and in the present Edition of the Posthumous Works of Mr. *Wycherley*.—Pope, 1729.

This note appears not only in the editions of 1735 that simply reissued the unsold sheets of 1729 but also in the later octavos of 1735. In all later editions (1737–42) the words *present Edition* were appropriately dropped. See Norman Ault's edition of Lintot's *Poems on Several Occasions* (1717) called *Mr. Pope's Own Miscellany* (1935), where the first poem is 'An Epistle to Mr. Dryden from Mr. Wycherley. Occasion'd by his proposal to write a Comedy together'.

This letter dates the beginning of Pope's labours as reviser of Wycherley's poems.

||WYCHERLEY *to* POPE[1] 22 *March* 1705/6

Longleat Portland Papers, xiii (Harleian transcripts)

March 22d. 1705/6

My great Little Friend,—I have Receiv'd yours of the 17th Instant Yesterday, being the 21 and your Letter was the best, and most Wellcome thing I have Receiv'd since I came down, tho' I have receiv'd some Monny; But I must confess, you try my patience (as you say) in the begining of your Letter; not by the many Lines in it, but the too many Compliments you make me for nothing; in which you prove yourselfe (tho' a sincere Friend) a man of too much fiction for I have not seen so much Poetry in Prose a great while, since your Letter is filled with so many fine words, and Acknowledgments of your Obligations to me (the only aseverations of yours I dare contradict) for I must tell you your Letter is like an Authors Epistle before his Book, written more to shew his wit to the World than his Sincerety, or gratitude to his Friend, whom he Libells with Praise, so that you have provokd my Modesty ev'n whilst you have Soothd my Vanity for I know not whether I am more Complimented than abused; since too much praise turns Irony, as too great thanks for smal favors turns ingratitude, or too much Cerimony in Religion, Hipocricy, but if you woud have commanded my Judgment You should only have sayd you thought me your true Friend and if you woud have layd some Wit to my Charge, you must have told me, I showd (att least) some when I intended to Submitt all I writ, to the infallibility of your Wit, Judgment, and Sensure who are my Pope.

⌜Now if your Friendship to me shoud make you inquisitive, how I bore my long Journy, att this time of the Year, you must know, it went harder with me in the Coach, than out of it, for there were four Woemen in the Coach, to my Man, and myself, one was handsome and sick so was useless, tother three were well and Ugly enough to make any man Sick, of their Company the first who was Sick if well deserv'd better Jumbling, than that of the Coach nay she might have deservd Jumbling in a Coach in Covent Garden, when it moves whilst the Wheels stand still; the second was too old for Jumbling the third too Young, the fourth was so Ugly 'twas no matter, whether she was old, or young; In short they were all such Damnd batterd Jades, that I shou'd have benn more afrayd of a fall with them, in the Coach, than of a fall that might have thrown me out of the Coach from them so that⌝[2] I have had no sort of Pleasure since I came from you and hardly expect any till I return back to you; which I feare will not be so soon

[1] First printed entire by Elwin (1889), v. 387. Pope in 1729 had printed an adaptation of the last paragraph as if a complete letter, but he did not reprint it after 1735.

[2] Elwin (vi [1871], 27) printed only the last paragraph of the letter.

as I hopd, or Immagind; for I have some thoughts of going from hence to the Bath, being advisd to it by Dr. Radcliff when I was at London as likewise by my Doctor here (if I woud be thouroughly well,) but you may be assurd, I will make hast to you; to be better in the meantime,[1] Pray present my humble Service to your Mother and Father, as likewise to that factious[2] young Gentleman Mr. Englefield and tell him, if I come into Berkshire, I will make him hollow as lowd, in the Tavern at Reading as he did at the Coffee House in London till he dances with his own Dayry Mayds.

Pray let me hear from you the only Satisfaction I can have in this place.

⌜Now after all⌝,[3] I must lay a pennance upon you which is to desire you to look over that Damnd Miscellany of Madrigals of mine[4] to pick out (if possible) some that may be so alterd that they may yet apeare in print again I hope with better Success than they hether to have done. I will give you my Reason for this request of mine when I see you which I am resolvd shall be when I have done here, and at the Bath where I designe to goe and afterwards to spend two Months (God Willing) with You att Binfeild, or near it. ⌜or at Epsham,[5] or else where, in the mean time once more farwell My Deare Little Infallible.⌝

†POPE *to* WYCHERLEY 10 *April* 1706

1729

April 10, 1705/6.[6]

By yours[7] of the last Month, you desire me to select, if possible, some Things from the first Volume of your Miscellanies,[8] which may be alter'd so as to appear again. I doubted your meaning in this; whether it was to pick out the best of those Verses, (as that on the *Idleness of Business*; on *Ignorance*; on *Laziness*, &c.) to make the Method and Numbers exact, and avoid Repetitions? For tho' (upon reading 'em on this occasion) I believe they might receive such an Alteration with

[1] This is the punctuation of the Harleian transcript, but Elwin restores what was probably written by Wycherley by beginning a sentence with 'In the meantime'.

[2] Probably the scribe's error for *facetious*. In his 'Memorial List of Departed Relations and Friends' (EC i, p. ix) Pope enters: 'Anno 1712, mens. Januario, decessit vir facetissimus, juventutis meae deliciae, Antonius Englefield, aet. 75.' Englefield was a friendly Catholic neighbour of the Popes at Binfield, who encouraged the youthful Pope in poetry. He was the grandfather of Martha and Teresa Blount.

[3] Pope in his printings of this paragraph omitted the phrases in half-brackets.

[4] The reference is to his folio volume of *Miscellany Poems* (1704).

[5] Epsom, at least later, was the residence of Henry Cromwell.

[6] The date as given in 1729 was corrected to 1706 in the Errata of the reissued edition of 1735c.

[7] By yours] By one of yours, *1737–42*.

[8] Printed in Folio, in the Year 1704.—Pope, 1729–42.

Advantage; yet they would not be chang'd so much, but any one would know 'em for the same at first sight. Or if you mean to improve the worst Pieces, which are such as to render them very good, would require a great addition, and almost the entire new writing of them? Or, lastly, if you mean the middle sort, as the Songs and Love-Verses? For these will need only to be shortned, to omit repetition; the Words remaining very little different from what they were before. Pray let me know your mind in this, for I am utterly at a loss. Yet I have try'd what I could do to some of the *Songs*,[1] and the *Poems* on *Laziness* and *Ignorance*, but can't (e'en in my own partial Judgment) think my alterations much to the purpose. So that I must needs desire you would apply your Care wholly at present, to those which are yet unpublished, of which there are more than enough to make a considerable Volume, of full as good ones, nay, I verily believe, of better than any in Vol. I. which I could wish you would defer, at least 'till you have finish'd these that are yet unprinted.

I send you a Sample of some few of these; namely, the Verses to Mr. *Waller* in *his old Age*; your new ones on the *Duke of Marlborough*, and two others. I have done all that I thought could be of advantage to them: Some I have contracted, as we do Sun-beams, to improve their Energy and Force; some I have taken quite away, as we take Branches from a Tree, to add to the Fruit; others I have entirely new express'd, and turned more into Poetry. *Donne* (like one of his Successors)[2] had infinitely more Wit than he wanted Versification: for the great dealers in Wit, like those in Trade, take least Pains to set off their Goods; while the Haberdashers of small Wit, spare for no Decorations or Ornaments. You have commission'd me to paint your Shop, and I have done my best to brush you up like your Neighbours.[3] But I can no more pretend to the Merit of the Production, than a Midwife to the Virtues and good Qualities of the Child she helps into the Light.

The few Things I have entirely added, you will excuse; you may take them lawfully for your own, because they are no more than Sparks lighted up by your Fire; and you may omit them at last, if you think them but Squibs in your Triumphs. | I am, &c.

[1] *Vid.* Letter of Nov. 20, 1707. *a.*—Pope, 1729–35. (The *a* refers to note *a* appended to the letter of 1707.)

[2] Wycherley himself.—Elwin.

[3] Several of Mr. Pope's lines, very easy to be distinguished, may be found in the Posthumous Editions of Wycherley's Poems: particularly in those *on Solitude*, *on the Public*, and *on the Mixed Life.*—Warburton, 1751.

JACOB TONSON *to* POPE 20 *April* 1706

Homer MSS. Add. 4807

Sir,—I have lately seen a pastoral of yours in mr. Walsh's & mr Congreves hands,[1] which is extreamly ffine & is generally approv'd off by the best Judges in poetry. I Remember I have formerly seen you at my shop & am sorry I did not Improve my Accquaintance with you. If you design your Poem for the Press no person shall be more Carefull in the printing of it, nor no one can give a greater Incouragement to it; than Sir Your Most Obedient | Humble Servant | Jacob Tonson.

[Gr]ays Inn Gate | April the 20th | 1706

Pray give me a line. per Post.

Address: To Mr. Pope att | Binfield near | Ockingham in | Berkshire | These.
Postmark: AP/20

SIR WILLIAM TRUMBULL *to* POPE 15 *June* 1706

Homer MSS. Add. 4807

15. June. 1706.

Sir,—It is alwayes to my advantage to Correspond with you; For I either have the use of some of your Bookes, or (which I value much more) your Conversation: I am sure it will be my fault, if I do not improve by both. I wish allso I could learn some more skill in Gard'ning from your Father (To whome, with your good Mother all our services are presented, with thankes for the Hartichokes) who has set us a pattern, that I am afraid we shall Copie but in Miniature; For so our Hartichokes are in respect of his.[2] In all things I am ready to yeild, Except in the assurances That no body can be more than I am | Sir | Your most humble & | obedient Servant | Will Trumbull

Poor Jennie is still afflicted with her Ague.

Address: For Mr Alexander Pope.

[1] The MS. of Pope's Pastorals, now in the collection of Arthur A. Houghton, Jr., has the following entry by Pope on the blank page preceding the MS. of 'An Essay on Pastoral': 'Mem: This Copy is that which past thro' the hands of Mr Walsh, Mr Congreve, Mr Mainwaring, Dr. Garth, Mr Granville, Mr Southern, Sir H. Sheers, Sir W. Trumbull, Lord Halifax, Lord Wharton, Marq. of Dorchester D. of Bucks. &c. Only the 3rd Eclog was written since some of these saw the other 3. which were written as they here stand with the Essay, anno 1704.—Ætat. meae, 16. / The Alterations from this Copy were upon the Objections of some of these, or my own.'

[2] The poet's father prided himself on his gardening—as did the son later.

†WALSH *to* POPE 24 *June* 1706

1735

June 24, 1706.

I receiv'd the favour of your Letter, and shall be very glad of the continuance of a correspondence by which I am like to be so great a gainer. I hope when I have the happiness of seeing you again in *London*, not only to read over the Verses I have now of yours, but more that you have written since; for I make no doubt but any one who writes so well, must write more. Not that I think the most voluminous Poets always the best, I believe the contrary is rather true. I mention'd somewhat to you in *London* of a *Pastoral Comedy*, which I should be glad to hear you had thought upon since. I find *Menage* in his observations upon *Tasso*'s *Aminta*,[1] reckons up fourscore Pastoral Plays in *Italian*: And in looking over my old *Italian* Books, I find a great many Pastorals and Piscatory Plays, which I suppose *Menage* reckons together. I find also by *Menage*, that *Tasso* is not the first that writ in that kind, he mentioning another before him, which he himself had never seen, nor indeed have I. But as the *Aminta*, *Pastor Fido*, and *Filli di Sciro* of *Bonarelli* are the three best, so I think there is no dispute but *Aminta* is the best of the three: Not but that the Discourses in *Pastor Fido* are more entertaining and copious in several peoples opinion, tho' not so proper for Pastoral; and the Fable of *Bonarelli* more surprizing. I do not remember many in other Languages, that have written in this kind with success. *Racan*'s *Bergeries* are much inferior to his Lyrick Poems; and the *Spaniards* are all too full of Conceits. *Rapin* will have the design of Pastoral Plays to be taken from the *Cyclops* of *Euripides*. I am sure there is nothing of this kind in *English* worth mentioning, and therefore you have that Field open to your self. You see I write to you without any sort of constraint or method, as things come into my head, and therefore pray use the same freedom with me, who am, &c.

†POPE *to* WALSH[2] 2 *July* 1706

1735

July 2, 1706.

I cannot omit the first opportunity of making you my acknowledgments for reviewing those Papers of mine. You have no less right to correct me, than the same hand that rais'd a Tree has to prune it. I am convinc'd as well as you, that one may correct too much; for in

[1] See Ménage's edition of *Aminta* (1655), esp. pp. 93–100.

[2] In the octavos of 1737 and later Pope dated this letter from 'Windsor-Forest'. Other textual revisions are rhetorical and negligible.

Poetry as in Painting, a Man may lay Colours one upon another, till they stiffen and deaden the Piece. Besides to bestow heightning on every part is monstrous: Some parts ought to be lower than the rest; and nothing looks more ridiculous, than a Work, where the Thoughts, however different in their own nature, seem all on a level: 'Tis like a Meadow newly mown, where *Weeds*, *Grass*, and *Flowers* are all laid even, and appear undistinguish'd. I believe too that sometimes our first Thoughts are the best, as the first squeezing of the Grapes makes the finest and richest Wine.

I have not attempted any thing of Pastoral Comedy, because I think the Taste of our Age will not relish a Poem of that sort. People seek for what they call *Wit*, on all subjects, and in all places; not considering that Nature loves Truth so well, that it hardly ever admits of flourishing: *Conceit* is to Nature what *Paint* is to Beauty; it is not only needless, but impairs what it wou'd improve. There is a certain Majesty in Simplicity which is far above all the Quaintness of Wit: insomuch that the Critics have excluded it from the loftiest Poetry, as well as the lowest, and forbid it to the Epic no less than the Pastoral. I shou'd certainly displease all those who are charm'd with *Guarini* and *Bonarelli*, and imitate *Tasso* not only in the Simplicity of his Thoughts, but in that of the *Fable* too. If surprising discoveries shou'd have place in the story of a Pastoral Comedy, I believe it wou'd be more agreeable to Probability to make them the effects of *Chance* than of *Design*; Intrigue not being very consistent with that Innocence, which ought to constitute a Shepherd's Character. There is nothing in all the *Aminta* (as I remember) but happens by meer accident; unless it be the meeting of *Aminta* with *Sylvia* at the *Fountain*, which is the contrivance of *Daphne*, and even that is the most simple in the world: The contrary is observable in *Pastor Fido*, where *Corisca* is so perfect a Mistress of Intrigue, that the Plot cou'd not have been brought to pass without her. I am inclin'd to think the Pastoral Comedy has another disadvantage, as to the *Manners*: Its general design is to make us in love with the Innocence of a rural Life, so that to introduce Shepherds of a vicious Character must in some measure debase it; and hence it may come to pass, that even the virtuous Characters will not shine so much, for want of being oppos'd to their contraries.—These Thoughts are purely my own, and therefore I have reason to doubt them: but I hope your Judgment will set me right.

I wou'd beg your opinion too as to another point: It is how far the liberty of *Borrowing* may extend? I have defended it sometimes by saying, that it seems not so much the Perfection of Sense, to say things that have *never* been said before, as to express those *best* that have been said *oftenest*; and that Writers in the case of borrowing from others, are like Trees which of themselves wou'd produce only one sort of Fruit, but by being grafted upon others, may yield variety. A mutual commerce makes Poetry flourish; but then Poets like Merchants, shou'd repay with something of their own what they take from others; not like Pyrates, make prize of all they meet. I desire you to tell me sincerely, if I have not stretch'd this Licence too far in these Pastorals? I hope to become a Critic by your Precepts, and a Poet by your Example. Since I have seen your Eclogues, I cannot be much pleas'd with my own; however you have not taken away all my Vanity, so long as you give me leave to profess my self | Your, &c.

†WALSH *to* POPE 20 *July* 1706

1735

July 20, 1706.

I had sooner return'd you thanks for the favour of your Letter, but that I was in hopes of giving you an account at the same time of my Journey to *Windsor*; but I am now forc'd to put that quite off, being engag'd to go to my Corporation of *Richmond* in *Yorkshire.* I think you are perfectly in the right in your Notions of Pastoral, but I am of opinion, that the redundancy of Wit you mention, tho' 'tis what pleases the common people, is not what ever pleases the best judges. *Pastor Fido* indeed has had more admirers than *Aminta*; but I will venture to say, there is a great deal of difference between the admirers of one and the other. *Corisca*, which is a Character generally admir'd by the ordinary judges, is intolerable in a Pastoral; and *Bonarelli's* fancy of making his Shepherdess in love with two men equally, is not to be defended, whatever pains he has taken to do it. As for what you ask of the *Liberty* of *Borrowing*; 'tis very evident the best *Latin* Poets have extended this very far; and none so far as *Virgil*, who is the best of them. As for the *Greek* Poets, if we cannot trace them so plainly, 'tis perhaps because we have none before them; 'tis evident that most of them borrow'd from *Homer*, and *Homer* has been accus'd of burning those that wrote before him, that his Thefts might not be discover'd. The best of the modern Poets in all Languages, are those that have the nearest copied the Ancients. Indeed in all the common Subjects of Poetry, the Thoughts are so obvious (at least if they are natural) that whoever writes last, must write things like what have been said before: But they may as well applaud the Ancients for the Arts of eating and drinking, and accuse the Moderns of having stol'n those Inventions from them; it being evident in all such cases, that whoever live first, must first find them out. 'Tis true, indeed, when

——*unus & alter Assuitur pannus*,[1]

[1] Horace, *De Arte Poetica*, ll. 15–16.

when there is one or two bright Thoughts stol'n, and all the rest is quite different from it, a Poem makes a very foolish figure: But when 'tis all melted down together, and the Gold of the Ancients so mixt with that of the Moderns, that none can distinguish the one from the other, I can never find fault with it. I cannot however but own to you, that there are others of a different opinion, and that I have shewn your Verses to some who have made that objection to them. I have so much Company round me while I write this, and such a noise in my ears, that 'tis impossible I should write any thing but Nonsense, so must break off abruptly. I am, Sir, | Your most affectionate | and most humble Servant.

†WALSH *to* POPE 9 *September* 1706

1735

Sept. 9. 1706.

At my return from the North I receiv'd the favour of your Letter,[1] which had lain there till then. Having been absent about six weeks, I read over your Pastorals again, with a great deal of pleasure, and to judge the better read *Virgil*'s Eclogues, and *Spenser*'s Calendar, at the same time; and I assure you I continue the same opinion I had always of them. By the little hints you take upon all occasions to improve them, 'tis probable you will make them yet better against Winter; tho' there is a mean to be kept even in that too, and a Man may correct his Verses till he takes away the true Spirit of them; especially if he submits to the correction of some who pass for great Critics, by mechanical Rules, and never enter into the true Design and Genius of an Author. I have seen some of these that would hardly allow any one good Ode in *Horace*, who cry *Virgil* wants fancy, and that *Homer* is very incorrect. While they talk at this rate, one would think them above the common rate of mortals: but generally they are great admirers of *Ovid* and *Lucan*; and when they write themselves, we find out all the Mystery. They scan their Verses upon their Fingers; run after Conceits and glaring Thoughts; their Poems are all made up of Couplets, of which the first may be last, or the last first, without any sort of prejudice to their Works; in which there is no Design, or Method, or any thing Natural or Just. For you are certainly in the right, that in all Writings whatsoever (not Poetry only) *Nature* is to be follow'd; and we shou'd be jealous of our selves for being fond of *Similies*, *Conceits*, and what they call saying *Fine Things*. When we were in the North, my Lord *Wharton* shew'd me a Letter he had receiv'd from a certain great General[2] in *Spain*; I told him I wou'd by

[1] Pope's letter is not known to exist.

[2] The Earl of P.—Pope, 1735 (but not thereafter). This opinion of Peterborow's wit

all means have that General recall'd, and set to writing here at home, for it was impossible that a Man with so much Wit as he shew'd, cou'd be fit to command an Army, or do any other Business. As for what you say of Expression: 'tis indeed the same thing to Wit, as Dress is to Beauty; I have seen many Women over-drest, and several look better in a careless Night-gown, with their hair about their ears, than Mademoiselle *Spanheim*[1] drest for a Ball. I do not design to be in *London* till towards the Parliament: then I shall certainly be there; and hope by that time you will have finisht your Pastorals as you would have them appear in the world, and particularly the third of *Autumn* which I have not yet seen. Your last Eclogue being upon the same Subject as that of mine on Mrs. *Tempest*'s Death,[2] I shou'd take it very kindly in you to give it a little turn, as if it were to the Memory of the same Lady, if they were not written for some particular Woman whom you wou'd make immortal. You may take occasion to shew the difference between Poets Mistresses, and other Men's. I only hint this, which you may either do, or let alone just as you think fit. I shall be very much pleas'd to see you again in Town, and to hear from you in the mean time. I am with very much esteem, | Your, &c.

†POPE *to* WALSH[3] — 22 *October* 1706

1735

Oct. 22, 1706.

After the Thoughts I have already sent you on the subject of *English* Versification, you desire my opinion as to some farther particulars. There are indeed certain Niceties, which tho' not much observed even by correct Versifiers, I cannot but think deserve to be better regarded.

1. It is not enough that nothing offends the Ear, but a good Poet will adapt the very Sounds, as well as Words, to the things he treats of. So that there is (if one may express it so) a Style of Sound. As in

is echoed in Pope to Peterborow [May 1723] and in Pope to Swift of Aug. 1723. In his quarto and folio *Letters* (1737) Pope printed the following note on the passage: 'Mr. Walsh's Remark will be thought very innocent, when the Reader is inform'd that it was made on the Earl of Peterborow, just before the glorious Campaigns of Barcelona and Valentia.'

[1] Presumably the daughter of the learned Ezechiel Spanheim, Prussian ambassador to England, 1701–10. She married a French refugee, the Marquis de Montendre, in 1710.

[2] Walsh's eclogue 'Delia, a Pastoral Eclogue; upon the death of Mrs. Tempest, who died upon the day of the late Storm', will be found in Dryden's *Poetical Miscellanies the Fifth Part* (1704), pp. 609–16. See the letter to Pope from Tonson, 20 Apr. 1706.

[3] This letter is closely related to that sent to Cromwell dated 25 Nov. 1710. Pope omitted the last part of the Cromwell letter when printing it, and out of the omission is thought to have fabricated this present letter to Walsh. When transferring a letter from one correspondent to another Pope seldom did the amount of rewriting that is done here. Evidently he felt inclined to emphasize the influence of Walsh, and had relatively few Walsh letters to print. In this present version of the letter we find certain details—the explanation of *hiatus* and of *Alexandrine*, as well as the added diffuseness concerning expletives—that seem needless additions to a more concise statement.

describing a gliding Stream, the Numbers shou'd run easy and flowing; in describing a rough Torrent or Deluge, sonorous and swelling, and so of the rest. This is evident every where in *Homer* and *Virgil*, and no where else that I know of to any observable degree. The following Examples will make this plain, which I have taken from *Vida*.[1]

> Molle viam tacito lapsu per levia radit.
> Incedit tardo molimine subsidendo.
> Luctantes ventos, tempestatesque sonoras.
> Immenso cum præcipitans ruit Oceano Nox.
> Telum imbelle sine ictu, Conjecit.
> Tolle moras, cape saxa manu, cape robora Pastor,
> Ferte citi flammas data[2] tela, repellite pestem.

This, I think, is what very few observe in practice, and is undoubtedly of wonderful force in imprinting the Image on the reader: We have one excellent Example of it in our Language, Mr. *Dryden*'s Ode on St. *Cæcilia*'s Day, entitled, *Alexander*'s *Feast*.

2. Every nice Ear, must (I believe) have observ'd, that in any smooth *English* Verse of ten syllables, there is naturally a *Pause* at the fourth, fifth, or sixth syllable. It is upon these the Ear rests, and upon the judicious Change and Management of which depends the Variety of Versification. For example,

At the fifth. *Where-e'er thy Navy* || *spreads her canvass Wings*,
At the fourth. *Homage to thee* || *and Peace to all she brings*.
At the sixth. *Like Tracts of Leverets* || *in Morning Snow*.[3]

Now I fancy, that to preserve an exact Harmony and Variety, the Pauses of the 4th or 6th shou'd not be continu'd above three lines together, without the Interposition of another; else it will be apt to weary the Ear with one continu'd Tone, at least it does mine:[4] That at the 5th runs quicker, and carries not quite so dead a weight, so tires not so much tho' it be continued longer.

3. Another nicety is in relation to *Expletives*, whether Words or Syllables, which are made use of purely to supply a vacancy: *Do* before Verbs plural is absolutely such; and it is not improbable but future Refiners may explode *did* and *does* in the same manner, which are almost always used for the sake of Rhime. The same Cause has occasioned the promiscuous use of *You* and *Thou* to the same Person, which can never sound so graceful as either one or the other.

[1] For the sources of these lines see the note to the letter to Cromwell of 25 Nov. 1710.
[2] *data*] *date* 1735 h and i. (This proper correction was not made in the octavos.)
[3] The three lines come from Waller: see the note on Pope to Cromwell, 25 Nov. 1710.
[4] Pope but rarely fell into this fault.

4. I would also object to the Irruption of *Alexandrine* Verses[1] of twelve syllables, which I think should never be allow'd but when some remarkable Beauty or Propriety in them attones for the Liberty: Mr. *Dryden* has been too free of these, especially in his latter Works. I am of the same opinion as to *Triple Rhimes*.

5. I could equally object to the *Repetition* of the same Rhimes within four or six lines of each other, as tiresome to the Ear thro' their Monotony.

6. *Monosyllable-Lines*, unless very artfully managed, are stiff, or languishing: but may be beautiful to express Melancholy, Slowness, or Labour.[2]

7. To come to the *Hiatus*, or Gap between two words which is caus'd by two Vowels opening on each other (upon which you desire me to be particular) I think the rule in this case is either to use the *Cæsura*, or admit the *Hiatus*, just as the Ear is least shock'd by either: For the *Cæsura* sometimes offends the Ear more than the *Hiatus* itself, and our language is naturally overcharg'd with Consonants: As for example; If in this Verse,

The Old have Int'rest ever in their Eye,

we should say, to avoid the *Hiatus*,

But th' Old have Int'rest——

The *Hiatus* which has the worst effect, is when one word ends with the same Vowel that begins the following; and next to this, those Vowels whose sounds come nearest to each other are most to be avoided. O, A, or U, will bear a more full and graceful Sound than E, I, or Y. I know some people will think these Observations trivial, and therefore I am glad to corroborate them by some great Authorities, which I have met with in *Tully* and *Quintilian*. In the fourth Book of Rhetoric to *Herennius*,[3] are these words: *Fugiemus crebras Vocalium concursiones, quæ vastam atque hiantem reddunt orationem; ut hoc est, Baccæ æneæ amœnissimæ impendebant.* And Quintilian *l.* 9. *cap.* 4. *Vocalium concursus cum accidit, hiat & intersistit, at*[4] *quasi laborat oratio. Pessimi longè quæ easdem inter se literas committunt, sonabunt: Præcipuus tamen erit hiatus earum quæ cavo aut patulo ore efferuntur. E plenior litera est, I angustior.* But he goes on to reprove the excess on the other

[1] He has not admitted one Alexandrine verse, or triple rhyme, into his Essay on Man, nor into his four Ethic Epistles, nor his Eloisa, nor Dunciad; and but rarely, too rarely Fenton thought, into his Iliad, the ear, in so long a work, wanting some variety.—Elwin (from Warton).

[2] It is curious that Pope repeatedly subscribes to this notion concerning monosyllables. More than one critic has pointed out that Pope himself at times uses monosyllables for speed. *Eloisa*, l. 289, and *Essay on Criticism*, l. 372, have been cited as examples.

[3] *Ad Herennium*, IV. xii.

[4] *at*] *et 1737–42* (*at* is probably a typographical error).

hand of being too sollicitious in this matter, and says admirably, *Nescio an negligentia in hoc, aut solicitudo sit pejor.* So likewise *Tully* (*Orator ad Brut.*)[1] *Theopompum reprehendunt, quod eas literas tanto opere fugerit, etsi idem magister ejus Isocrates*: which last Author, as *Turnebus* on *Quintilian* observe,[2] has hardly one *Hiatus* in all his Works. *Quintilian* tells us that *Tully* and *Demosthenes* did not much observe this Nicety, tho' *Tully* himself says in his Orator, *Crebra ista Vocum concursio, quam magna ex parte vitiosam, fugit Demosthenes.*[3] If I am not mistaken, *Malherbe* of all the Moderns has been the most scrupulous in this point; and I think *Menage* in his Observations upon him says, he has not one in his Poems. To conclude, I believe the *Hiatus* should be avoided with more care in Poetry than in Oratory; and I would constantly try to prevent it, unless where the cutting it off is more prejudicial to the Sound than the *Hiatus* itself. I am, &c.[4]

WYCHERLEY *to* POPE — 19 *February* 1706/7

[See 19 February 1708/9.]

POPE *to* CROMWELL[5] — 12 *or* 13 *July* [1707]

1726 (Curll)

Dear Mr. Cromwell,—May it please ye!
Sit still a Moment; pray be easy—
Faith 'tis not five; no Play 's begun;
No Game at *Ombre* lost or won.
Read something of a diff'rent Nature,
Than *Ev'ning Post*, or *Observator*;
And pardon me a little Fooling,
—Just while your Coffee stands a Cooling.

[1] *Orator*, xliv. 151.

[2] observe] observes *1737–42*. (See, for all this learning, the Rotterdam edition of Quintilian (1665), i. 700, where Turnebus is cited.)

[3] Again *Orator*, xliv. 151.

[4] This being the last letter to Walsh that Pope printed, he appended at the foot of the page in 1735 the following note: 'Mr. *Walsh* died at 49 Years old, in the Year 1708. The Year after, Mr. Pope writ the *Essay on Criticism*, in which he gives him this Elogy,

> Such late was *Walsh*, the Muses Judge and Friend,
> Who justly knew to blame or to commend;
> To failings mild, but zealous for desert,
> The clearest Head, and the sincerest Heart.'

The note was modified in 1737 to omit the two couplets. For a later letter from Walsh to Pope see 21 July 1707.

[5] This letter in verse was printed in Curll's *Miscellanea* (1726) and reprinted in his vol. ii of *Mr. Pope's Literary Correspondence* (1735) with notes. The year, which Curll suggested, is somewhat doubtful. Pope did not reprint the verses, for which no MS. is known.

Since your Acquaintance with one *Brocas*,[1]
Who needs will back the Muses Cock-horse,
I know you dread all those who write,
And both with Mouth and Hand recite;
Who slow, and leisurely rehearse,
As loath t'enrich you with their Verse;
Just as a Still, with Simples in it,
Betwixt each Drop stays half a Minute.
(That Simile is not my own,
But lawfully belongs to *Donne*)
(You see how well I can contrive a
Interpolatio Furtiva)
To *Brocas*'s Lays no more you listen
Than to the wicked Works of *Whiston*;
In vain he strains to reach your Ear,
With what it wisely, will not hear:
You bless the Powers who made that Organ
Deaf to the Voice of such a *Gorgon*,
(For so one sure may call that Head,
Which does not Look, but Read Men dead.)

I hope, you think me none of those
Who shew their Parts as *Pentlow* does,
I but lug out to one or two
Such Friends, if such there are, as you,
Such, who read *Heinsius* and *Masson*,
And as you please to pass their Doom,
(Who are to me both *Smith* and *Johnson*)[2]
So seize them Flames, or take them *Tonson*.

But, Sir, from *Brocas*, *Fouler*, me,
In vain you think to 'scape Rhyme-free,
When was it known one Bard did follow
Whig Maxims, and abjure[3] *Apollo*?
Sooner shall Major-General cease
To talk of War, and live in Peace;
Yourself for Goose reject Crow Quill,
And for plain *Spanish* quit *Brasil*;[4]

[1] Cromwell's circle included obscure persons. Brocas and Fowler wrote verses. Pentlow according to Curll, was a gamester and worse. Whiston, then a professor at Cambridge, was evidently already suspected of heterodoxy. Deprived of his professorship in 1710, he gave popular lectures in London coffee-houses.

[2] Smith and Johnson are characters in *The Rehearsal*.

[3] An allusion to the Whig maxim of abjuring the Pretender.

[4] Brasil was an expensive sort of snuff.

Sooner shall *Rowe* lampoon the UNION,[1]
Tydcombe[2] take Oaths on the Communion;
The *Granvilles* write their Name plain *Greenfield*,
Nay, Mr. *Wycherley* see *Binfield*.

I'm told, you think to take a Step-some
Ten Miles from Town, t'a Place call'd *Epsom*,
To treat those Nymphs like yours of *Drury*,
With—I protest, and I'll assure ye;—
But tho' from Flame to Flame you wander,
Beware; your Heart's no *Salamander*!
But burnt so long, may soon turn Tinder,
And so be fir'd by any Cinder—
(Wench, I'd have said did Rhyme not hinder)
Shou'd it so prove, yet who'd admire?
'Tis known, a Cook-maid roasted *Prior*,
Lardella[3] fir'd a famous Author,
And for a Butcher's well-fed Daughter
Great *D—s*[4] roar'd, like Ox at Slaughter.
(Now, if you're weary of my Style,
Take out your Box of right *Brasil*,
First lay this Paper under, then,
Snuff just three Times, and read again.)

I had to see you some Intent,
But for a curst Impediment,
Which spoils full many a good Design,
That is to say, the Want of Coin.
For which, I had resolv'd almost,
To raise *Tiberius Gracchus* Ghost;
To get, by once more murd'ring *Caius*,
As much as did *Septimuleius*;[5]
But who so dear will buy the Lead,
That lies within a Poet's Head,
As that which in the Hero's pate,
Deserv'd of Gold an equal Weight?

[1] Nicholas Rowe as an ardent Whig supported the Union of Scotland and England, recently accomplished.

[2] Major-General John Tidcombe (1642–1713) was hardly the Catholic Elwin thought him. See *DNB*.

[3] Lardella presumably alludes to an actress who played that role in *The Rehearsal*.

[4] Dennis?

[5] Evidently at various times Pope meditated writing a tragedy. Here he seems to be considering, as Croker thought, the story of Caius Gracchus as a possible fable. Of course the story may be dragged in only as ground for the witticism about lead.

Sir, you're so stiff in your Opinion,
I wish you do not turn *Socinian*;
Or prove Reviver of a Schism,
By modern Wits call'd *Quixotism.*
What mov'd you, pray, without compelling,
Like *Trojan* true, to draw for *Hellen*:[1]
Quarrel with *Dryden* for a Strumpet,
(For so she was, as e'er show'd Rump yet
Tho' I confess, she had much Grace,
Especially about the Face.)
Virgil, when [he] call'd *Pasiphae Virgo*
(You say) he'd more good Breeding; *Ergo*—
Well argu'd, Faith! Your Point you urge
As home, as ever did *Panurge*:
And one may say of *Dryden* too,
(As once you said of you know who)
He had some Fancy, and cou'd write,
Was very learn'd, but not polite—
However from my Soul I judge
He ne'er (good Man) bore *Hellen* Grudge,
But lov'd her full as well it may be,
As e'er he did his own dear Lady.
You have no Cause to take Offence, Sir,
Z—ds, you're as sour as *Cato Censor*!
Ten times more like him, I profess,
Than I'm like *Aristophanes.*

To end with News—the best I know,
Is, I've been well a Week, or so.
The Season of green Pease is fled,
And Artichoaks reign in their Stead.
Th'Allies to *Rond*[2] *Toulon* prepare;
G—d save the pretty Lady's there!
One of our Dogs is dead and gone,
And I, unhappy! left alone.

If you have any Consolation
T'administer on this Occasion,

[1] Who (but not what) this Hellen was is unknown. She was not, as Carruthers thought, Mrs. Thomas, whose early poetic pseudonym was Corinna. See Thoms, *Notes & Queries*, 1 S. xii (1855), 277–9. In his letter to Pope of 6 July 1727 Cromwell calls Mrs. Thomas (E. T.) Sapho, and it is highly probable that at times she is intended by that name in other letters.

[2] *Rond*] bomb *Curll, 1735*. (This detail led Curll to date the letter 1707.)

Send it, I pray, by the next Post,
Before my Sorrow be quite lost.

The twelfth or thirteenth Day of July,
But which, I cannot tell you truly.

WALSH *to* POPE 21 *July* 1707

Homer MSS. Add. 4807

Abberley July 21st: 1707

Sir,—Having receiv'd the favour of your letter of the third of this Month, wherein y[ou] give mee hopes of seeing you here before the E[nd] of it;[1] I am in dayly expectation of receiving your Commands to send a Coach, or Horses to meet you at Worcester, and not put you to the Inconvenience of such Horses as you will finde at the Post house. It was nothing but the fear that you shoud not send mee word time enough for mee to send Horses to meet you, that makes mee give you the trouble of this letter. And I expect no other answer to that Point; as for all others

Nil mihi rescribas, attamen ipse veni,[2]

Your most Humble | Servant | W: Walsh[3]

Address: For | Mr Alex: Pope jun: at | Binfield near | Bagshott | by London
Postmark: IY/23

||WYCHERLEY *to* POPE[4] 11 *November* 1707

Longleat Portland Papers, xiii (Harleian transcripts)

London Novr. the 11th: 1707.

Dear Mr. Pope,—I received yours[5] of the 9th yesterday, which has, like the rest of your Letters, at once pleas'd, and instructed me; so that I can assure you, you can no more write too much, to your absent Friends, than speak too much, to the present; which is a truth, that

[1] Spence records Pope as saying (*Anecdotes*, p. 194), 'I was with him [Walsh] at his seat in Worcestershire, for a good part of the summer of 1705, and showed him my Essay on Criticism in 1706.' Pretty certainly these dates are wrong. There is no record of such a visit to Worcestershire in 1705, and that of 1707 seems to be the only such. Sir William Trumbull in a letter to the Rev. Ralph Bridges, 5 Aug. 1707, says: 'Our little poet is gone a dreadful long journey into Worcestershire, to Mr. Walsh.' See Elwin–Courthope, vi. 59 n. and Sherburn, *Early Career*, p. 56, n. 1.

[2] This tag is used by Pope to the Earl of Oxford, 16 Mar. 1731/2, where he ends, as he says, 'like the schoolboys'.

[3] This letter, first printed (?) in *St. James's Chronicle*, 20 July 1775, is the latest letter preserved in the correspondence with Walsh.

[4] Pope in 1729 printed this letter, making omissions here indicated by half-brackets. He omitted the letter from his quarto and folio of 1737. It was printed in Elwin–Courthope, v. 389, from the Longleat transcripts.

[5] A letter now unknown.

all men own, who have either seen your writings, or heard your discourse,—enough, to make others shew their Judgment, in ceaseing to write, or talk espeacially to you, or in your Company; however I speak, or write to you, not to please you, but myself, since by speaking, or writing to you, I provoke your Answers, which, whilst they humble me, give me Vanity; tho' I am lessen'd, by you, even when you commend me; since you commend my little Sense, with so much more of yours, that you put me out of countenance, whilst you wou'd keep me in it. So that you have found a way, (against the Custom of you great Wits,) to show even a great deal of good nature, with a great deal of good Sense. I thank you, for the Book you promis'd me. I find you wou'd not only correct my Lines, but my Life, and save me here, and hereafter from Damnation: ⌜Now⌝ as to the Damn'd Verses, you say, I intrusted you with, I hope you will let them undergo your Purgatory, to save them, from other Peoples damning them, since the Criticks who are generally the first damn'd in this Life, like the damn'd below, never leave to bring those above them, under their damn'd[1] Circumstances; ⌜whose works having suffer'd the Flames themselves, will have those of all others share their Fates, for their presumption, in seeking their Immortality, which they themselves, by pretending too much to it, the sooner miss'd.

I am sorry your Father is averse to your coming to Town at this time, when ev'ry Body of the two Nations, almost, are in it, and there is likely to be so much Comedy, acted, by the two great Play-Houses of the Nation the House of Lords, and that of the Commons, that me-thinks all People should come to Town but for their diversion, but I fear my Company has given you a Surfit of it; wherefore when my Man returns from the Country, I hope, to come to yours, which will be within a fortnight at farthest, in the mean time⌝ I beg you to peruse, my ⌜damn'd⌝ Papers, and select what you think best, or most tollerable, look over them again, for I resolve suddenly to print some of them, who like a harden'd old Gamster, will, (in spight of all former ill usage, by Fortune,) push on an ill hand in expectation of recovering himself, especially since, I have such a Croupier, or second to stand by me, as Mr. Pope ⌜the Infalible; who shall have with me the Pow'r of the tother Infallible, to damn or save, us by our Works; as t'other Infallible of Rome, since I believe in your Infallibility who am, (Dear Mr. Pope) | Your obliged real Poetick penitent | and humble Servant | W. Wycherley.

My service pray to your Good Father, and Mother, and let me beg of you to use my follies with unmerciful kindness. Mr. Cromwel is your humble Servant, as he tells me.⌝

[1] their damn'd] their own *1729–42*.

†POPE *to* WYCHERLEY[1] 20 *November* 1707

1729

Nov. 20, 1707.

Mr. *Englefyld*[2] being upon his Journey to *London*, tells me I must write to you by him, which I do, not more to comply with his desire, than to gratify my own; tho' I did it so lately by the Messenger you sent hither: I take it too as an opportunity of sending you the fair Copy of the *Poem* on *Dulness*,[3] which was not then finish'd, and which I should not care to hazard by the common Post. Mr. *Englefyld* is ignorant of the Contents, and I hope your prudence will let him remain so, for my sake no less than your own: Since if you should reveal any thing of this nature, it would be no wonder Reports should be rais'd, and there are those (I fear) who would be ready to improve them to my disadvantage. I am sorry you told the great Man, whom you met in the *Court of Requests*, that your Papers were in my hands: No Man alive shall ever know any such thing from me; and I give you this warning besides, that tho' your self should say I had any way assisted you, I am notwithstanding resolv'd to deny it.

The method of the Copy I send you is very different from what it was, and much more regular: For the better help of your Memory, I desire you to compare it by the *Figures* in the Margin, answering to the same in this Letter. The Poem is now divided into four Parts, mark'd with the literal Figures I. II. III. IV. The first contains the *praise* of Dulness, and shews how upon several suppositions, it passes for 1. Religion. 2. Philosophy. 3. Example. 4. Wit. And 5. The cause of Wit, and the end of it. The second Part contains the *advantages* of Dulness: 1st, In Business; and 2dly, at Court; where the Similitudes of the Byass of a Bowl, and the Weights of a Clock, are directly tending to illustrate those advantages of Dulness, tho' introduced before in a place where there was no mention made of them; (which was your only objection to my adding them.) The third contains the *happiness* of Dulness in all Stations, and shews in a great many Particulars, that it is so fortunate, as to be esteem'd some good Quality or other in all sorts of People; that it is thought Quiet, Sense, Caution, Policy, Prudence, Majesty, Valour, Circumspection, Honesty, *&c.* The fourth Part I have wholly added, as a Climax which sums up all the *praise*, *advantage*, and *happiness* of Dulness in a few words, and

[1] Omitted in the quarto and folio of 1737.

[2] See Wycherley to Pope, 22 Mar. 1706/7.

[3] The Original of it in Blots, and with Figures of the References from Copy to Copy, in Mr. *Pope*'s Hand, is in the *Harley-Library*, among other such *Broüillons* of Mr. *Wycherley*'s Poems, corrected by him. *Vid. Lett. Ap.* 10, 1705/6. *Note* (a).—Pope, 1729–35. In 1737–42 Pope substituted for 'in the Harley-Library' the words 'yet extant'.

strengthens them all by the opposition of the *disgrace*, *disadvantage*, and *unhappiness* of Wit, with which it concludes.[1]

Tho' the whole be as short again as at first, there is not one Thought omitted, but what is a Repetition of something in your first Volume, or in this very Paper: Some Thoughts are contracted, where they seem'd encompass'd with too many words; and some new express'd, or added, where I thought there wanted heightning, (as you'll see particularly in the Simile of the *Clock-Weights*;[2] and the Versification throughout, is, I believe such, as no Body can be shock'd at. The repeated permissions you give me of dealing freely with you, will (I hope) excuse what I have done; for if I have not spar'd you when I thought Severity would do you a kindness, I have not mangled you where I thought there was no absolute need of Amputation. As to Particulars, I can satisfy you better when we meet; in the mean time pray write to me when you can, you cannot too often.

†WYCHERLEY *to* POPE[3] 22 *November* 1707

1729

Nov. 22, 1707.

You may see by my Stile, I had the happiness and satisfaction to receive yesterday (by the hands of that Wagg, Mr. *Englefyld*) your extream kind and obliging Letter of the 20th of this Month; which like all the rest of yours, did at once mortify me, and make me vain; since it tells me with so much more Wit, Sense and Kindness than

[1] This is totally omitted in the present edition: Some of the Lines in the H[arley] M[SS.] are these.

> Thus Dulness, the safe Opiate of the Mind,
> The last kind refuge weary Wit can find,
> Fit for all stations, and in each content,
> Is satisfy'd, secure, and innocent;
> No pains it takes, and no offence it gives,
> Un-fear'd, unbated, undisturb'd it lives, &c.—Pope, 1729–35.

'The present edition' refers to Theobald's edition of Wycherley's *Posthumous Works*, i (pt. ii), 12–15, since in Pope's vol. ii of the *Posthumous Works* he prints on p. 11 of the section devoted to 'Miscellaneous Poems' the lines here quoted, with six more, and prints them under the heading 'Verses Omitted in the Panegyrick on Dulness. Vol. I, Page 12.' In the first Booksellers octavo of 1735, where the Wycherley letters were first reprinted from the sheets of 1729, Pope printed the whole twelve lines that Theobald had omitted. In the octavos of 1737–42 the note reverted to its original form, quoting only six lines.

[2] It was originally thus express'd:

> As Clocks run fastest when most Lead is on.

We find it so in a Letter of Mr. *Pope* to Mr. *Wycherley*, dated April 3, 1705, and in a paper of Verses of his, *To the Author of a Poem call'd Successio*, which got out in a Miscellany in 1712, three Years before Mr. *Wycherley* died, and two after he had laid aside the whole design of publishing any Poems.—Pope, 1729. The octavos of 1737–42 omit 'We find it so', thus making the whole note one sentence. No letter of 3 Apr. 1705 is now known.

[3] Omitted from the quarto and folio of 1737.

mine can express, that my Letters are always welcome to you. So that even whilst your Kindness invites me to write to you, your Wit and Judgment forbids me; since I may return you a Letter, but never an Answer.

Now, as for my owning your assistance to me, in overlooking my unmusical Numbers, and harsher Sense, and correcting them both, with your Genius, or Judgment; I must tell you I always own it, (in spite of your unpoetick Modesty) who would do with your Friendship as your Charity; conceal your Bounty to magnify the Obligation; and even whilst you lay on your Friend the Favour, acquit him of the Debt: But that shall not serve your turn; I will always own, 'tis my infallible Pope has, or would redeem me from a poetical Damning, the second time; and save my Rhimes from being condemn'd to the Criticks Flames to all Eternity: But (by the Faith you profess) you know your works of Supererrogation, transfer'd upon an humble acknowledging Sinner, may save even Him; having good Works enough of your own besides, to ensure yours, and their Immortality.

And now for the pains you have taken to recommend my *Dulness*, by making it more methodical, I give you a thousand thanks; since true and natural *Dulness* is shown more by its pretence to form and method, as the sprightliness of Wit by its despising both. I thank you a thousand times for your repeated Invitations to come to *Binfield*:——You will find, it will be as hard for you to get quit of my mercenary kindness to you, as it would for me to deserve, or return to yours; however, it shall be the Endeavour of my future Life, as it will be to demonstrate my self, | Your, &c.

†POPE *to* WYCHERLEY 29 *November* 1707

1729

Nov. 29, 1707.

The Compliments you make me, in regard of any inconsiderable Service I could do you, are very unkind, and do but tell me in other words, that my Friend has so mean an opinion of me, as to think I expect acknowledgments for trifles; which upon my faith I shall equally take amiss, whether made to my self, or to any others. For God's sake, (my dear Friend *Wycherley*) think better of me, and believe I desire no sort of Favour so much, as that of serving you, more considerably than I have yet been able to do.

I shall proceed in this manner, with some others of your Pieces; but since you desire I would not deface your Copy for the future, and only mark the Repetitions; I must, as soon as I've mark'd these, transcribe what is left on another Paper; and in that, blot, alter, and add all I can devise, for their Improvement. For you are sensible, the Omission of

Repetitions is but one, and the easiest Part, of yours and my Design; there remaining besides to rectify the *Method*, to *connect* the *Matter*, and to mend the *Expression* and *Versification*. I will go next upon the [1]Poems of *Solitude*, on the *publick*, and on the *mixt Life*; the *Bill of Fare*; the *Praises of Avarice*, and some others.

I must take some Notice of what you say, of "My pains to make your Dulness methodical;" and of your hint, that "The sprightliness of Wit despises method." This is true enough, if by *Wit* you mean no more than *Fancy* or *Conceit*; but in the better notion of *Wit*, consider'd as propriety, surely *Method* is not only necessary for Perspicuity and Harmony of parts, but gives beauty even to the minute and particular thoughts, which receive an additional advantage from those which precede or follow in their due place: According to a Simile Mr. *Dryden* us'd in conversation, of Feathers in the Crowns of the wild *Indians*, which they not only chuse for the beauty of their Colours, but place them in such a manner as to reflect a Lustre on each other. I will not disguise any of my Sentiments from you: To *methodize* in your Case, is full as necessary as to *strike out*; otherwise you had better destroy the whole Frame, and reduce them into *single Thoughts* in *Prose*, like *Rochfoucault*,[2] as I have more than once hinted to you.

WYCHERLEY *to* POPE[3] *6 December* 1707

Longleat Portland Papers, xiii (Harleian transcripts)

Dear Mr. Pope,—I have received yours of the 29th of Novemr which has so much over paid mine in kindness, that, (as Voiture says) I doubt whether the best Effects, of those fine expressions of your Friendship to me, can be more obligeing, than they themselves; And for my humility you talk of, you have lessen'd it, while you magnify it, as by commending my good Nature with so much more of yours, you have made me almost incapable of being grateful to you: for you have said so many kind things of me, you have hardly left me anything of the same kind, to return you; and the best Actions are not Capable, of making you Amends, for so many good words you have given me; by which you justly magnify them, and your self, by saying they are Sincere, so that, you have obliged me to be vain, rather than not think you, a Plain-dealer.

Thus, (ev'n against your own Opinion,) your freedom with me, proves not you a Fool, but me so, especially if I cou'd think half the good, you say of me, my due.

[1] Some *Broüillons* of these, transcrib'd and very much blotted by Mr. *Pope*, are extant in the *Harley Library*.—Pope, 1729–42, octavos.

[2] See Pope to Wycherley, 2 May 1710 and note.

[3] First printed in Elwin–Courthope, v. 390.

As for the Good Book you sent me, I took it as kindly as the Reprimand from the Good Man, (which I think you heard,) and was that I should not stand in my own light, which was spoken with the Zeal, and Simplicity of a Prophet; So that he will much sooner work my Salvation than all the Doctrines or Examples of our new Inspir'd Prophets, Three of which lately, (I mean of the French Prophets)[1] stood on the Pillory by Order, of the Chief Justice, and our English Prophets are threaten'd with the same Usage; if they persist, in their Enthusiastick Doctrines, to the deluding the People; ⌜amongst which there is one Betty Grey, so pretty and hansome a young Wench, (as they say) that she wou'd be able to turn you to her; and communicate to you some of her Sanctify'd Agitations of Body, by the secret Operations of her Spirits, upon Yours, and put you into such blissful Agitations of an Amorous Extacy, that you would not know where you were, in heav'n or Earth.⌝[2] For Agitation is now the word, because they work out their Damnation here, with fear, and trembling, as the Quakers did formerly; and they are seised, with a Spiritual Ague; which turns to such a Feaver, in their Brains, that they are hot-headed to the degree of Fanatical Prophecy; and so great a Faith, that 'tis said, they believe themselves what they say; and pretend to working Miracles also, as indeed (I think) they may, (to one at least,) Since they have made a Physician a believer; (one Doctor Bifield,[3] famous for his Sal Volatile oliosum,) who is now as Spiritually mad as the rest, beyond the cure of his own Helibore, for he preaches, in the Stile of his Bretheren, and to the Coffeehouses; ev'n to the present Scribes and Pharisees; the Lawyers and Parsons, who frequent them. In fine, as the new Prophets talk to the whole Town, they are the present talk of the whole Town, and are pretty numerous already; nay, they say are like to encrease, for the great Lawyers intend to persecute them, and whip them; and you know, Sanguis Martyrum, est semen Ecclesiae.

I expect my Mans return from Shropshire this day, and if he comes, I will soon after be with you, who am not easy in your absence, because I am | (My Dear Friend) | Your real true Friend, and | humble Servant | W: Wycherley.

[1] The enthusiastic simplicity of these French prophets can be seen in various pamphlets of the time. One octavo volume of about 200 pages was filled, as the title indicates, with *Prophetical Warnings of Elias Marion, Heretofore one of the Commanders of the Protestants . . . in the Cevennes . . . Uttered by him in London, under the Operation of the Spirit.* The publishers of this volume, printed in Apr. 1707, were John Daudé, N. Facio, and Cha. Portales. Were they by chance the three that underwent the correction of the pillory? See also Professor James R. Sutherland, 'John Lacy and the Modern Prophets', in *Background for Queen Anne* (1939), pp. 36–74.

[2] The passage in half-brackets was omitted in Elwin–Courthope.

[3] Dr. Thomas Byfield, a notable quack. The work referred to was published in 1695 as *Horae subsecivae: or Some long-vacation hours redeem'd, for the discovery of the true sal volatile oleosum of the ancient philosophers.* He also published later religious works of an enthusiastic sort.

London Decemr the 6th 1707.

Soft Cromwell salutes you, and eek
Poetical, drunken Tom Cheek.[1]

||POPE *to* CROMWELL[2] 19 *January* 1707/8

The Bodleian Library

Jan 19th 1707

Sir,—I had sent You the Enclosd Papers[3] before this Time but that I entended to have brought them my self & afterwards could find no Opportunity of sending them without Suspicion of their Miscarriage [no]t that they are of the Least Value, but for fear somebody might be foolish Enough to Imagine them so, & inquisitive enough to Discover [t]hose faults which I (by your help) wou'd Correct. I therefore beg the favour of You to Let them go no farther than your Chamber & to be very free of your remarks in the Margins, not only in regard to the Accuracy, but to the fidelity of the Translation: which I have not had time to Compare of Late with its Original. And I desire you to be the more severe as it is much more Criminal for me to make another [s]peak Nonsense than to do it in my own proper Person. For Your better help in Comparing, it may be proper to tell You that this is not an Entire Version of the first Book. There is an Omission from the 128th Line of the Latin which begins—*Sævus amor ruptæque Vices* to the 143d *At nondum Crasso*—& agen[4] from the 167th Line[5] *Iam Murmura Serpunt Plebis Agenoreae*—to the 310th[6] *Interea patriis olim Vagus exul ab oris* (between these two ⸢Last places⸣ *Statius* has a ⸢Noble⸣[7] Description of the *Council* of the *Gods*, & a *Speech* of *Jupiter*; which Contain a peculiar beauty & Majesty; & were Left out for no Other reason but because the Consequence of this Machine appears

[1] On Cheek see also Pope to Cromwell, 25 Apr. 1708.

[2] This letter, printed in 1726 by Curll, with no date, is found with the rest of the Pope–Cromwell letters in Bodley (Rawl. Letters 90, f. 44). It seems to be a contemporary transcript and not in Pope's hand. The date as printed here was lined through when an editor transferred Pope's subscribed address into the superscription. In 1735 Pope, reprinting Curll's text, added the date 'Jan. 22, 1708–9'. Elwin accepted Pope's printed date; but since the date derived only from the poet's faulty memory, it has no real validity. Its plausibility comes from the fact that in 1709 Pope and Cromwell were writing about Statius. But Pope worked intermittently on his pieces over long periods, and he might well have sent Cromwell his version of parts of Statius at the beginning of 1707/8 and not resumed work on it for over a year.

[3] This was a Translation of the first Book of *Statius*, done when the Author was but 14 Years old, as appears by an Advertisement before the first Edition of it in a Miscellany published by B. Lintot, 8°, 1711.—Pope, 1735. (The translation appears in pp. 1–56 of *Miscellaneous Poems and Translations*, published in May 1712.)

[4] These he since translated, and they are extant in the printed Version.—Pope, 1735–42.

[5] from the 128th Line . . . 167th Line] from the 168th Line *1735–42*.

[6] 310th] 312th *1735–42*.

[7] Noble] *omitted 1735–42*; so also 'Last places'.

not till the 2d Book) The Translation goes on from thence to the Words—*Hic vero ambobus rabiem fortuna Cruentam*—where there is an odd account of an Unmannerly[1] Batle at fistycuffs between the *two Princes* on a Very slight Occasion, & at a time when one would think the fatigue of their Journy in so Tempestuous a Night might have renderd 'em Very unfit for such a Scuffle. This I had actualy translated but was Very ill satisfied with it ev'n in my own Words to which an Author cannot but be partial enough of Conscience. It was therefore Omitted in this Copy which goes on above 80 Lines[2] farther at the Words—*Hic primum Lustrare Oculis &c* to the End of the Book.

You will find, I doubt not, ⸢upon reading⸣,[3] that *Statius* was none of the Discreetest poets tho he was the best Versifyer Next *Virgil*: In the Very beginning he Unluckily betrays his Ignorance in the rules of Poetry (which *Horace* had already taught the Romans) when he asks his Muse *where to begin his* THEBAID & seems to doubt whether it should not be, *ab Ovo Ledæo*? when He Comes to the scene of his Poem & the *Prize* in Dispute between the *Brothers* he gives us a Very Mean Opinion of it—*Pugna est de paupere Regno.* Very diffr[ent] from the Conduct of his Master Virgil who at the Entrance of his Poem informs his reader of the Greatness of its Subject. *Tantae Molis erat Romanam Condere Gentem*[4]—there are innumerable Litle fault[s] in him among which I Cannot but take notice of one in this Book where speaking of the implacable Hatred of the *Brothers* he says, *the who[le] World woud be too small a Prize to repay so much Impiety*:

> —Quid si peteretur crimine tanto
> Limes Uterque poli, quem Sol emissus Eoo
> Cardine, aut portu Vergens prospectat Ibero?

This was pretty well one woud think already but he goes on

> Quasque procul Terras obliquo Sydere Tangit
> Avius, aut Boreæ gelidas, madidive tepentes
> Igne Noti?—

After all this what could a Poet think of but *Heaven* it self for the *Pri[ze]* but what follows is astonishing

> —Quid si Tyriæ Phrygiæve Sub unum
> Convectentur Opes?

I do not remember to have met with so great a fall in any ancient Author whatsoever—I should not have insisted so much on the fault[s] of this *Poet* if I did not hope you would take the same freedom with and revenge it upon his *Translator*. I shall be Extreamly glad if the

[1] The word is omitted in all Pope's texts. [2] Actually 72 lines.

[3] Omitted in Pope's texts.

[4] *Gentem*—there] *Gentem.* [Bossu *on Epic Poetry.*] There *1735–42*.

reading this *Essay*[1] can be any Amusement to You; the rather because I had the Dissatisfaction to hear You have been Confind to your Chamber by an Illness which I fear was as troublesome a Companion as I have sometimes been to you in the same Place; where if ever you found any pleasure in my Company it must only[2] have been that which almost evryman takes in Observing the faults & follies of another: a pleasure which You see I take Care to give You even in my absence.

If You will Oblige me at your Leisure with the Confirmation of your recovery Under your own hand it will be extream Gratefull to me for next the pleasure of Serving my friends is that I take in hearing from them & in this particular as beyond all others I [am] beyond all acknowledgments Obligd to Our friend Mr W[ycherley] ⌜who as if it were not enough to have excelld all *Men* in Wit is resolvd to Excell them in *Good Nature* & Humanity too.⌝[3] I know I need no Apology to You for speaking of Mr W[ycherley] whose Example as I am proud of following in all things, so in Nothing More than in professing my self Like him | Sir | Your Most Affectionate & Obedient Servant | A: Pope.

At Binfield near Ockingham per Ockingham Bagg

This immeasurable Long Letter is Like a Large Worthless Countrey present which expects in return a Litle one from the town but of much greater Value.[4]

WYCHERLEY *to* POPE[5] — 19 *January* 1707/8

Longleat Portland Papers, xiii (Harleian transcripts)

My Dear Mr Pope,—I have receivd your most extream kind and entertaining Letter, written upon New Years Day, and I must confess was the best New Years Gift, I receivd this Yeare, tho' some of my Tennants brought me that Day some Monny; but your Letter yet was more wellcome to me, like other acceptable Presents as it was more Copious and bountfull which is no wonder, for you were never a Neggard, of your Wit: I must confess, my Journy (as you aprehend) was very Tedious to me, by reason of the season, but it was yet more insupportable, because every day it encreasd the distance betwixt you, and me; But necessity (which make[s] the old Mare to trot) made me, the old Gelding, Jogg down into Shropshire, haveing two Farmes of

[1] *Essay* is omitted in all Pope's texts.

[2] only] surely *1735–42.*

[3] The compliment to Wycherley, here in half-brackets, was omitted by Pope in 1737 and thereafter.

[4] This last sentence was omitted by Curll (1726) and hence does not appear in any of Pope's texts.

[5] Printed in Elwin–Courthope, v. 392–3.

some Concidderable Rents thrown upp into my hands which might have benn unlet, (for ought I know) for this whole Yeare following, had I not come down nor had I stayd above, woud my Tennants, have come down with the Ready; These were the reasons made me defer the most pleasent Journy to me that which woud have brought me to you, but I am in hopes of this advantage by it; that when I get once again to you I shall have the less reason, or cause to leave you, and the longer time of Enjoying Your agreable Conversation, the thoughts of which make me bear our present Seperation the better or the Damnd Conversation I meet with here and the rather because you have kept up my Spirits by your kind Ingenious Letters, which found me in the Country at an honest Gentlemans house, with whom I made an end of the old Yeare, and began the new one, which is the reason your Letter has been so long unanswerd I haveing been theise four Days out of Shrewsbury.

Now Sir tho your Letter has brought me a great deal of Satisfaction Yet my Dear Little Friend, (as wise men say) there is no happiness without alay

Since your Letter tells me you are forcd to keep your Chamber, uppon so melloncolly an Occasion as that of your Sight, being so Obscurd that you are deprivd of the Conversation you delight so much in (in your Solitude) that of Books, the Consideration of which makes me as Mellencolly here for the Misfortune of your eyes as for that of my own being deprivd of the sight of the Sun or of the sight of you; but your Eyes I suppose know when they have read enough, tho you do not; therefore pray look to your Eyes, because the[y] usd to look so kindly on me; and do not loose your sight in reading, to mend your inward decerning at the expence of your outward, since you may spoyl your Eye Sight and make it become weak or dark but you can hardly emprove your reasons insight which can never fail you; wherefore you may better bear the weakness of your owtward sight, since it is recompenc'd by the strength of your immagination and inward penitration, as your Poetic Forefathers were down from Homer to Milton. But pray (my Dear Friend!) take care of your Eyes and do not read so much as you doe (since you have learned enough) and that I may not be the Occasion (whilst I advise the Preservation of your Eyes) to weaken them (more in vain) by making them read a longer, or more tedious Letter I conclude it, in assureing you, I will make all the hast I can to you; and hope within a Month to come nearer my two best and brightest Friends, you and the Sun for I am Sure I cannot longer bear being at this distance from either of you in the mean time pray give my humble Service to your good Father and Mother and take my advice rather to venter loosing your Eyes by gazeing on the fair Shepherdesses of Your Plains, than by poreing on the Fayrest Impressions of your Authors, which may blind your sight but Scarcely can more improve your inward decerning, therefore pray be rather blind for Love, than knowledge, but if you will be quite blind any way, I will be your Dog, to lead you who every other way woud follow you to serve you and myself because I am | My Dear Little Great Friend | Your most assured Friend and | Unalterable Humble Servant. | W. Wycherley.

Shrewsbury Janry 19th 1707/8

My humble Servis (pray) to your good Father and Mother; wishing them, as you, a happy new Yeare and many more; You may be sure I will make hast to you, My Servise likewise pray to that Catholick Whigg, Mr Englefield.

†WYCHERLEY *to* POPE 28 *February* 1707/8

1729

Feb. 28, 1707/8.

I have had yours of the 23d[1] of this Instant, for which I give you many thanks, since I find by it, that even absence (the usual bane of Love, or Friendship) cannot lessen yours no more than mine. As to your hearing of my being ill;[2] I am glad, and sorry for the report: In the first place, glad that it was not true; and in the next sorry that it shou'd give you any disturbance, or concern more than ordinary for me; for which as well as your concern for my future well-being or life, I think my self most eternally oblig'd to you; assuring, your concern for either will make me more careful of both. Yet for your sake I love this Life so well, that I shall the less think of the other; but 'tis in your power to ensure my Happiness in one and the other, both by your Society and good Example, so not only contribute to my felicity here, but hereafter.

Now as to your Excuse for the plainness of your Stile, or Letter, I must needs tell you, that Friendship is much more acceptable to a true Friend than Wit, which is generally false Reasoning; and a Friend's reprimand often shews more Friendship than his compliment: Nay Love, which is more than Friendship, is often seen, by our Friend's correction of our Follies or Crimes. Upon this Test of your Friendship I intend to put you when I return to *London*, and thence to you at *Binfield*, which I hope will be within a Month.

[1] An unknown letter.

[2] Mr. *Pope* had this from Mr. *Cromwell*, after his Enquiry, in these Words. 'I returned to Town last *Saturday*, and inquiring (as you desir'd) about Mr. *Wycherley*, was told, in two several Places, that he had been very ill, and that he was even gone off our Stage: But I cou'd not imagine this report to be true, or that so great a Man could leave the World without its being instructed to lament so considerable a Loss.'—Pope, 1729–35. Omitted in 1737–42.

Next to the News of your good Health, I am pleas'd with the good News of your going to print some of your Poems, and proud to be known by them to the Publick for your Friend;[1] who intend (perhaps the same way) to be reveng'd of you for your kindness; by taking your Name in vain in some of my future Madrigals: yet so as to let the World know, my love or esteem for you are no more Poetick than my Talent in scribbling. But of all the Arts of Fiction, I desire you to believe I want that of feigning Friendship, and that I am sincerely, | Your, &c,

*POPE *to* [RALPH BRIDGES?][2] — 3 *March* 1707/8

The William Andrews Clark Memorial Library

March the 3rd

Sir,—If you will do me the favour to acquaint me, by a line to Will's Coffeehouse, on what day I may wait on you at Fulham, after Thursday next, I will take the Convenience of the Stagecoach as you formerly directed me. I have some private business with you, and therfore desire it may be a Day when you are like to be much at leisure. I am with a true Sincerity and affection, | Sir | Your humble and | obedient Servant, | A: Pope.

||POPE *to* CROMWELL[3] — 18 *March* 1707/8

The Bodleian Library

Sir,—I believe it was with me when I left the Town, [as] it is with a great many honest[4] Men when they leave the World, whose Loss it self they do not so much regrett, [as] that of their Friends whom they leave behind in it. [F]or I do not know one thing for which I can envy London, but for your continuing there. Yet I guess you [w]ill

[1] Pope dedicated his third Pastoral ('Autumn') to Wycherley, and Wycherley's plan to take Pope's name in vain 'in some of my future Madrigals' may perhaps be indicated in his letter to Pope of 18 May 1708. He published his lines 'To Mr. Pope on his Pastorals' in Tonson's miscellany of 1709, where the Pastorals themselves appeared. It is hardly probable that the heading Pope later gave these lines, 'To Mr. Pope at sixteen years old on occasion of his Pastorals', dates the lines accurately, though Wycherley very likely first saw three of the Pastorals in 1705, if not earlier.

[2] It is temptingly easy to name the recipient and the year of this letter, though the original, now pasted in vol. i of Pope's *Works* (1740), gives no aid. One judges that Pope wishes to consult Bridges (chaplain to the Bishop of London at Fulham) concerning the episode of Sarpedon, which he is preparing as his first translation of Homer. Pope was in town at about this time, and he thanks Bridges for aid in the letter of 5 Apr. [1708]. See also Sir William Trumbull to Pope, 9 Apr. 1708, the next to the last paragraph.

[3] Normally Pope's dating (at the end of the letter) should mean 1708/9; but remarks here about his 'Sapho' tie in with remarks made to Cromwell 25 Apr. 1708, thus settling the year. Printed in 1726 by Curll, the letter is omitted from the quarto and folio of 1737, but appears in all other editions.

[4] honest] *omitted 1735–42.*

expect I shou'd recant this Expression, when I [te]ll you, that Sappho (by which Heath'nish Name [you] have Christen'd a very Orthodox Lady)[1] did not [ac]company me into the Country. ⌜However I will confess myself the less concern'd on that account, because I have no very violent Inclination to lose my Heart, especially in [so] wilde and savage a place as this Forest is: In [th]e Town, 'tis ten to one but a young Fellow may [f]ind his Stray'd Heart again, with some Wilde-Street [o]r Drury-Lane Damsell; but here, where I cou'd have [m]et with no Redress from an unmercifull, virtuous [d]ame, I must for ever have lost my little Traveller in a Hole, where I cou'd never rummage to find him again⌝[2]—Well Sir, you have your Lady in the Town [s]till, and I have my Heart in the Country still, which being wholly unemploy'd as yet, has the more Roome in it for my Friends, and does not want a Corner at your Service—⌜To be serious,⌝[3] you have extreamly obliged me by your Frankness and Kindness to me in Town: And if I have abus'd it by too much Freedome on my part I hope you will attribute it to the natural Openness of my Temper, which hardly knows how to show Respect, where I feel Affection. I wou'd love my Friend, as my Mistress without Ceremony; and hope a little Rough Usage some times may not be more displeasing to one, than it is to the other.

If you have any Curiosity to know in what manner I live, or rather lose a Life, ⌜in the Country⌝;[4] Martial will inform you in one line.[5]

Prandeo, poto, cano, ludo, lego, cæno, quiesco.[6]

Every day with me is litterally Another To-morrow; for it is exactly the same with Yesterday:[7] It has the same Business, which is Poetry; and the same Pleasure, which is Idleness. A Man might indeed pass his time much better, but I question if any Man cou'd pass it much easier. [Human Life (as Plutarch just now told me,[8] is like a Game at Tables, where every one may wish for the best Cast; but after all he is to make his best of that which happens, and go on contentedly.][9] If

[1] The orthodox lady seems to be Mrs. Nelson, a poetical neighbour of Pope's. Cromwell probably called all literary ladies 'Sapho'. He at least had his own Sapho, and called Mrs. Nelson Pope's.

[2] This long passage in half-brackets was omitted in the octavos of 1737–42.

[3] Omitted by Pope in his octavos 1737–42.

[4] Omitted in 1735–42.

[5] In his texts of 1735, but not thereafter, Pope added after the word *line* the following parenthetical remark: '(the Translation of which cost a Friend of ours three in *English*, | *One short*, *one long*, | *One soft*, *one strong*, | *One right*, *one wrong*.)' He borrowed this insertion from his letter to Cromwell of 25 Apr. 1708.

[6] Martial, iv. 90. 7.

[7] Another To-morrow . . . . It has] Another yesterday; for it is exactly the same: It has *1735–42*.

[8] Plutarch's *Moralia*, 'Of Tranquillity of Mind', § 467.

[9] The square brackets, evidently added by a late editor, indicate a sentence omitted in all Pope's editions. It appears in Curll's texts (and the original), but Pope used it, adapted, at the end of his letter to Steele, 18 June 1712.

You will visit our Shades this Spring, which I very mu[ch] desire, you may perhaps instruct me to manage my Game more wisely: but at present I am satisfy'd to triffle away my Time any way, rather than let it stick by me; as Shop-keepers are glad to be rid of those Goods at any rate, which wou'd otherwise be always lying upon their hands.

Sir, if you will favor me sometimes with your Letters, it will be a great Satisfaction to me on severall accounts; and on this in particular, That it will show me, (to my Comfort) that ev'n a Wise Man is sometimes very idle; for so You needs must be when you can find time to write to such a Fellow as | Sir, | Your most Faithfull | & obliged Servant; | A: Pope:

March. 18th. 1708.

[1][P.]S. Pray do not put an Anachronism again upon me, for my Game at Tables out of Plutarch.

I gave your Service to Mr Wycherly yesterday; and desire you to give mine to—Let me see?—Mr Tidcombe.

Address: For Henry Cromwell, Esq: at | the Widow Hambleton's Coffee-house, at the | End of Princes Street, near Drury-Lane, | London.

Postmarks: MR/24 WOCK. N.A.

POPE *to* RALPH BRIDGES[2] 5 *April* [1708]

Add. 36270 (transcript)

Sir,—The favour of your Letter with your Remarks, can never be enough acknowledged; and the speed, with which you Dischargd so troublesome a Task, doubles the obligation. I must own you have pleased me very much by the commendation so ill bestowed upon me; but I assure you, much more by the frankness of your Censure; which I ought to take the more kindly of the two, as it is more advantageous to a Scribler to be improved in his Judgment, then to be sooth'd in his vanity. The greater part of those deviations from the Greek, which you have observd, I was led into by Chapman and Hobbes; who are (it seems) as much celebrated for their knowledge of the Original, as they are decryd, for the baldness of their Translations. Chapman pretends to have restord the genuine Sence of his Author, from the mistakes

[1] All Pope's texts (1735–42) omit the postscript and shorten the ending of the letter to read: 'for so you must needs be when you can find Leisure to write to | Your, &c.'

[2] First published in Dr. Johnson's *Life of Pope*, where it was printed from the original, then in the possession of Lord Hardwicke. The year is determined by Sir William Trumbull's mention (Trumbull to Pope, 9 Apr. 1708) of 'my nephew B's observations'. The letter has no concern with the later project of translating the entire *Iliad*, but rather concerns the passages translated and published in Dryden's sixth Miscellany (1709). The Rev. Ralph Bridges was Sir William Trumbull's 'nephew B.' See Pope to Bridges, 3 Mar. 1707/8.

of all the former Explainers, in several Hundred places: And the Cambridge Editors of the large Homer, in Greek and Latin, attributed so much to Hobbes, that they confess they have corrected the old Latin Interpretation very often by his version. for my part I generally took the Authors meaning to be as you have explaind it; yet their Authority, join'd to the knowledge of my own imperfectness in the Language,[1] over-ruled me. However, Sir, you may be confident I think you in the right, because you happen to be of my opinion: (for men (let 'em say what they will) never approve any other's sense, but as it squares with their own). But you have made me much more proud of, and positive in my Judgment, since it is strenghthend by your's. I think your Criticismes, which regard the Expression, very just, and shall make my profit of them: To give you some proof that I am in earnest, I will alter three verses on your bare objection, tho I have Mr Dryden's Example for each of them. And this I hope you will account no small piece of obedience, from one, who values the Authority of one true Poet above that of twenty Critics or Commentatours. But tho' I speak thus of Commentators, I will continue to read carefully all I can procure, to make up, that way, for my own want of a Critical understanding in the original Beauties of Homer. Though the greatest of them are certainly those of the Invention and Design, which are not at all confin'd to the Language: For the distinguishing Excellencies of Homer are, (by the consent of the best Criticks of all nations) first in the Manners, (which include all the speeches, as being no other than the Representations of each Person's Manners by his words:) and then in that Rapture and Fire, which carries you away with him, with that wonderfull Force, that no man who has a true Poetical spirit is Master of himself, while he reads him. Homer makes you interested and concern'd before you are aware, all at once; whereas Virgill does it by soft degrees. This, I believe, is what a Translator of Homer ought principally to imitate: and it is very hard for any Translator to come up to it, because the chief reason why all Translations fall short of their Originals, is, that the very Constraint they are obliged to, renders 'em heavy and dispirited. The great Beauty of Homer's Language, as I take it, consists in that noble simplicity, which runs through all his works; (and yet his diction, contrary to what one would imagine consistent with simplicity, is at the same time very Copious.) I don't know how I have run into this Pedantry in a Letter, but I find I have said too much, as well as spoken too inconsiderately; what farther Thoughts I have upon this subject, I shall be glad to communicate to you (for my own improvement) when we meet; which is a happiness I very earnestly desire, as I do likewise some opportunity of proving how

[1] In the margin opposite this remark about Pope's confessed 'imperfectness' someone has entered the letters 'N. B.', presumably to signalize the admission of ignorance by Pope himself.

much I think myself obliged to your Friendship, and how truly I am, | Sir, | Your most faithfull | humble servant, | A: Pope.

Aprill the 5th

Endorsement: Copy of a Letter from | Mr Pope to Mr | Bridges at the Bp | of London's at Fulham. | Taken from the Original | in his own hand writing.

†SIR WILLIAM TRUMBULL[1] *to* POPE 9 *April* 1708

1735

I have this moment receiv'd the favour of yours of the 8th instant;[2] and will make you a true excuse, (tho' perhaps no very good one) that I defer'd the troubling you with a letter, when I sent back your Papers,[3] in hopes of seeing you at *Binfield* before this time.[4] If I had met with any fault in your performance, I should freely now (as I have done too presumptuously in conversation with you) tell you my opinion; which I have frequently ventur'd to give you, rather in compliance with your desires than that I could think it reasonable. For I am not yet satisfied upon what grounds I can pretend to judge of Poetry, who never have been practic'd in the Art. There may possibly be some happy genius's, who may judge of some of the natural beauties of a Poem, as a man may of the proportions of a building, without having read *Vitruvius*, or knowing any thing of the rules of architecture: But this, tho' it may sometimes be in the right, must be subject to many mistakes, and is certainly but a superficial knowledge; without entring into the art, the methods, and the particular excellencies of the whole composure, in all the parts of it.

Besides my want of skill I have another reason why I ought to suspect my self, by reason of the great affection I have for you, which might give too much biass, to be kind to every thing that comes from you; but after all, I must say (and I do it with an old-fashion'd sincerity) that I entirely approve of your Translation of those Pieces of *Homer*, both as to the versification and the true sense that shines thro' the whole; nay I am confirmed in my former application to you, and give me leave to renew it upon this occasion, that you wou'd proceed in translating that incomparable Poet,[5] to make him speak good *English*, to dress his admirable characters in your proper, significant, and

[1] Since in 1735 this was the first Trumbull letter to be printed, Pope appended a footnote identifying Sir William, which is here transferred to the letter of 19 Oct. 1705.

[2] Pope's letter of the 8th is unknown.

[3] Pope's translation of the episode of Sarpedon from the *Iliad.*

[4] Pope had written from London?

[5] By this letter Pope established publicly the fact that his Homer was translated at the request of friends. In a sense also he contradicted his statement that Addison was the first to encourage him in the project.

expressive conceptions, and to make his works as useful and instructive to this degenerate age, as he was to our friend *Horace*, when he read him at *Præneste*,[1] *Qui, quid sit pulchrum, quid turpe, quid utile, quid non*, &c. I break off with that *quid non?* with which I confess I am charm'd.

Upon the whole matter I intreat you to send this presently to be added to the Miscellanies, and I hope it will come time enough for that purpose.[2]

I have nothing to say of my Nephew *B.*'s observations,[3] for he sent them to me so late, that I had not time to consider them; I dare say he endeavour'd very faithfully (tho' he told me very hastily) to execute your commands.

All I can add is, that if your excess of modesty shou'd hinder you from publishing this *Essay*, I shall only be sorry that I have no more credit with you, to persuade you to oblige the publick, and very particularly, dear Sir, | Your most faithful | humble Servant, | W. Trumbull.

Apr. 9, 1708.

POPE *to* CROMWELL[4] — 25 *April* 1708

The Bodleian Library

Aprill the 25. 1708.

Sir,—

This Letter greets you from the Shades;
(Not those which thin, unbody'd Shadows fill,
That glide along th'Elysian Glades,
Or skim the flow'ry Meads of *Asphodill:*)
But those, in which a Learned Author said,
Strong Drink was drunk, and Gambolls play'd,
And two Substantial Meals a day were made.
The Business of it is t'express,
From me and from my Holiness,
To you and to your Gentleness,
How much I wish you Health and Happiness;
And much good News, and little Spleen as may be;
A hearty Stomach, and Sound Lady;
And ev'ry Day a double Dose of Coffee,
To make you look as sage as any Sophy.

[1] Horace, *Epistles*, I. ii. 2–3.

[2] *Poetical Miscellanies, the Sixth Part*, publication of which was postponed to 2 May 1709, included Pope's 'essay' at translating from the *Iliad*.

[3] See Pope to the Rev. Ralph Bridges, 5 Apr. 1708.

[4] This letter was printed by Curll in 1726 and 1735, but was never included in Pope's editions of his letters. In 1735 Pope excised the phrase here placed in half-brackets and inserted it in his letter to Cromwell of 18 Mar. 1708.

For the rest, I must be content in plain Prose to assure you, that I am very much oblig'd to you for the favor of your Letter, ⌜and in particular, for the Translation of that one Latine Verse, which cost you three in English.

One short, one long,
One Smooth, one Strong,
One right, one wrong.⌝

But if I may be allow'd to object against any thing you write (which I must do, if it were only to be even with you for your Severity to me) it shou'd be that Passage in yours, where you are pleas'd to call the Whores of *Drury*-Lane, the Nymphs of *Drury*. I must owne it was some time before I cou'd frame to my self any plausible Excuse for this Expression: but Affection (which you know Sir, excuses all things) at last furnish'd me with one in your Justification; which I have here sent you, in Verse, that you may have at least some Rhyme to defend you, tho' you shou'd have no Reason.

If Wit or Critick blame the tender Swain,
Who stil'd the gentle Damsels in his Strain
The Nymphs of *Drury*, not of Drury-Lane;
Be this his Answer, and most just Excuse—
"Far be it, Sirs, from my more civill Muse,
Those Loving Ladies rudely to traduce.
Allyes and Lanes are Terms too vile and base,
And give Idea's of a narrow Pass;
But the well-worn Paths of the Nymphs of Drury
Are large & wide; *Tydcomb* and I assure ye."

I made no question but the News of *Sappho's* staying behind me in the Towne wou'd surprize you. But she is since come into the Country, and to surprize you more, I will inform you, that the first Person she nam'd when I waited on her, was one Mr. *Cromwell*. What an Ascendant have you over all the Sex, who cou'd gain the Fair-one's Heart by appearing before her in a long, black, unpowder'd Perriwig; nay without so much as the very Extremities of clean Linnen in neckloth and Cuffs! I guess that your Friend *Vertumnus* among all the Forms he assum'd to win the good Graces of *Pomona*, never took upon him that of a Slovenly Beau. Well Sir I leave you to your Meditations on this occasion, and to Languish unactive (as you call it:)

But I find I have exceeded my Bounds, & begin to travell on the Confines of Impertinence. However to make you amends, I shall desire Mr. *Wycherley* to deliver you this Letter,[1] who will be sure in

[1] Either Wycherley is taking the letter from Binfield to London or else, more probably, this letter is enclosed to him in a letter not preserved.

less than a quarter of an hour's conversation with you, to give you Wit enough to attone for twice as much Dulness as I have troubled you with. Therfore I shall only give my Respects to some of our Acquaintance, & conclude.

To *Baker*[1] first my Service, pray:
To *Tydcomb* eke,
And Mr *Cheek*:
Last to *yourself* my best Respects I pay,
And so remain, for ever and for ay,
Sir, | Your Affectionate, hum | ble Servant: | A. Pope.

Address: To Henry Cromwell | Esq: | This.

‡POPE *to* CROMWELL[2] — 27 *April* 1708
1735

April 27, 1708.

I have nothing to say to you in this Letter; but I was resolv'd to write to tell you so. Why should not I content my self with so many great Examples, of deep Divines, profound Casuists, grave Philosophers; who have written, not Letters only, but whole Tomes and voluminous Treatises about Nothing? Why shou'd a Fellow like me, who all his life does nothing, be asham'd to write nothing? and that to one who has nothing to do but to read it? But perhaps you'll say, the whole World has something to do, something to talk of, something to wish for, something to be imploy'd about: But pray, Sir, cast up the Account, put all these Somethings together, and what is the Sum Total but just Nothing? I have no more to say, but to desire to give you my Service (that is nothing) to your Friends, and to believe that I am nothing more than | Your, &c.

Ex nihilo nil fit.[3] LUCR.

†POPE *to* CROMWELL — 10 *May* 1708
1735

May 10, 1708.

You talk of Fame and Glory, and of the great Men of Antiquity: Pray tell me, what are all your great dead Men, but so many little

[1] Baker and Cheek are difficult to identify. Elwin suggests Thomas Baker, author of *Tunbridge-Walks* (1703) and other comedies. Cheek, Elwin tells us, is mentioned as an early patron of Pope's in a pamphlet called *Characters of the Times* (1728).

[2] In his 1735 editions Pope was desirous of discrediting Curll's earlier (1726) texts. This letter, for which no original exists, would discredit the letter written only two days earlier (of which Curll had the autograph), which Pope never reprinted and from which he took one bit for insertion in his letter of 18 Mar. 1708. One can only surmise the origin of this present letter.

[3] Lucretius (*De Rerum Natura*, i. 155 f.) phrases the aphorism somewhat differently.

living Letters? What a vast Reward is here for all the Ink wasted by Writers, and all the Blood spilt by Princes? There was in old time one *Severus* a *Roman* Emperor. I dare say you never call'd him by any other Name in your Life: and yet in his days he was styl'd *Lucius, Septimius, Severus, Pius, Pertinax, Augustus, Parthicus, Adiabenicus, Arabicus, Maximus,*—and what not? What a prodigious waste of Letters has Time made! what a Number have here dropt off, and left the poor surviving Seven unattended! For my own part, Four are all I have to take care for; and I'll be judg'd by you if any man cou'd live in less compass?[1] ⌜except it were one Monsieur *D.*[2] and one *Romulus* ⁂ But these, contrary to the common Calamity, came in process of time, to be call'd Monsieur *Boileau Despreaux*, and *Romulus Three-points.*—⌝ Well, ⌜Sir,⌝ for the future I'll drown all high Thoughts in the *Lethe* of Cowslip-Wine; as for Fame, Renown, Reputation, take 'em Critics!

> *Tradam protervis in Mare* Criticum
> *Ventis*[3]—

If ever I seek for Immortality here, may I be d—d! for there's not so much danger in a *Poet*'s being damn'd:

> Damnation follows Death in other Men,
> But your damn'd Poet lives and writes agen.

†WYCHERLEY *to* POPE[4] 13 *May* 1708

1729

May 13, 1708.

I have receiv'd yours of the first of *May.* Your Pastoral Muse outshines, in her modest and natural dress, all *Apollo*'s Court-Ladies, in their more artful, labour'd, and costly Finery; therefore I am glad to find by your Letter, you design your Country-beauty of a Muse shall appear at Court and in Publick; to outshine all the farded, lewd, confident, affected, Town-dowdies, who aim at being honour'd only to their Shame: But her artful Innocence (on the contrary) will gain more Honour as she becomes more Publick; and in spite of Custom will bring Modesty again into Fashion, or at least make her Sister-rivals

[1] The words in half-brackets were omitted in Pope's octavo texts of 1737–42.

[2] Until within a few years of his death Boileau did not put his name at full length to his works, but the titlepages merely stated that they were by the Sieur D***.—Elwin. Was Romulus ⁂ a pawnbroker?

[3] Horace (*Carmina*, I. xxvi. 2) shows Pope making a sort of pun:

> tradam protervis in mare Creticum
> portare ventis. . . .

[4] This letter is omitted from the quarto and folio of 1737. The letter from Pope of 1 May, mentioned in the first sentence, is unknown.

of this Age, blush for Spite, if not for Shame. As for my stale, antiquated, poetical Puss, whom you would keep in countenance, by saying she has once been tolerable, and wou'd yet pass Muster by a little licking over; it is true that (like most vain antiquated Jades which have once been passable) she yet affects Youthfulness, in her Age, and wou'd still gain a few Admirers, (who the more she seeks, or labours for their liking, are but more her contemners.) Nevertheless, she is resolv'd henceforth to be so cautious as to appear very little more in the World, except it be as an attendant on your Muse, or as a Foil, not a Rival to her Wit, or Fame: So that let your Country-gentlewoman appear when she will in the World,[1] my old worn-out Jade of a lost Reputation, shall be her attendant into it, to procure her Admirers; as an old Whore who can get no more Friends of her own, bawds for others, to make Sport or Pleasure yet, one way or other, for Mankind. I approve of your making *Tonson*[2] your Muse's Introductor into the World, or Master of the Ceremonies, who has been so long a Pimp, or Gentleman-Usher to the Muses.

I wish you good Fortune; since a Man with store of Wit, as store of Mony, without the help of good Fortune, will never be Popular; but I wish you a great many Admirers, which will be some Credit to my Judgment as well as your Wit, who always thought you had a great deal, and am | Your, &c.

†WYCHERLEY *to* POPE[3] 18 *May and* 28 *July* 1708

1729

I have made a damn'd Compliment in Verse, upon the printing your Pastorals, which you shall see when you see me.—If you suffer my

[1] This, and the following Extract, are a full Confutation of the Lying Spirit of *John Dennis* and others, who impudently asserted that Mr. *Pope* wrote these Verses on himself, (tho' publish'd by Mr. *Wycherley* six Years before his Death.) We find here it was a voluntary Act of his, promis'd before-hand, and written while Mr. *Pope* was absent. The first *Broüillon* of those Verses, and the second Copy with Corrections, are both yet extant in Mr. *Wycherley*'s own hand; from which will appear, that if they received any alteration from Mr. *Pope*, it was in the Omission of some of his own Praises.—Pope, 1729–42.

This fighting footnote concerns some of the most annoying attacks on Pope, and in his later editions he modified it somewhat. In his errata for the first edition of 1735 he inserted after *extant* the words *viz. in the Harley Library.* In the octavos of 1737–42 the note began less belligerently: 'This, and what follows, is a full confutation of *John Dennis* and others, who asserted . . . .' The phrase about the Harley Library was omitted, and after the word *hand* was substituted: 'In another of his letters of May 18, 1708. are these words. "I have made a damn'd Compliment in verse upon the printing your Pastorals, which you shall see when you see me".'

[2] On 4 Mar. 1707/8 Tonson paid Pope 'for the Tale of Chaucer, and the Eclogues' ten guineas. On 13 Jan. 1708/9 he paid the poet three guineas for the 'Episode of Sarpedon'. Pope's autograph memoranda on these matters are preserved in the Pierpont Morgan Library.

[3] This 'letter' represents the 'following Extract' mentioned in the footnote to the letter of 13 May 1708. It was printed, 1729–35, under the heading 'Extract from two Letters of Mr. Wycherley of May 18 and July 28, 1708'. This is an early and frank example of Pope's manipulating of texts: usually when he combines two letters he gives no warning. In 1737 and thereafter the 'extract' was omitted from Pope's editions.

old Dowdy of a Muse to wait upon your sprightly Lass of the Plains, into the Company of the Town, 'twill be but like an old City-bawd's attending a young Country-beauty to Town, to gain her Admirers, when past the Hopes of pleasing the World herself.

||POPE *to* CROMWELL[1] 1 *November* 1708

The Bodleian Library

Novr the 1st: 1708:

Sir,—I have been so well satisfy'd with the Country ever since I saw you, that I have not so much as thought of the Town, or enquird of any one in it besides Mr. Wycherley and yourself. And from him I understood[2] of your Journy this Summer into Leicestershire; from whence I guess you are return'd, by this time, to your old Apartment [i]n the Widow's Corner;[3] to your old Business of comparing Criticks, & reconciling Commentators; and to your old Diversions of a Losing Game at Picquet with the Ladies, and half a Play, or a quarter of a Play, at the Theatre; where you are none of the malicious Audience, but the [ch]ief of Amorous Spectators; and for the Infirmity of one [Sense][4] which cou'd only there serve to disgust you, enjoy the Vigor [of an]other which ravishes you.

⌜You know, when one Sense is supprest,
It but retires into the rest.

According to the Poetical, not the Learned, Dodwell; who has done one thing worthy of Eternal Memory, wrote two Lines in his life that are not Nonsence!)⌝[5] So you have the advantage of being entertain'd with all the Beauty of the Boxes, without being troubled with any of the Dulness of the Stage. You are so good a Critick, that 'tis the greatest happiness of the Modern Poets that you do not hear their Works; and next, that you are not so arrant a Critick, as to damn them (like the rest) without hearing. But now I talk of those Criticks, I have good news to tell you concerning my self, for which I expect you shou'd congratulate with me: It is that beyond all my Expectations, & far above my Demerits, I have been most mercifully repriev'd by the Sovereign Power of Jacob Tonson, from being brought forth to publick Punishm[ent] and respited from Time to Time from the hands of

[1] In his successive editions of this letter Pope made a number of stylistic improvements that seem factually negligible.

[2] *Understood* is what Pope wrote and Curll printed, but in all Pope's printed texts the word is printed *understand*.

[3] The Widow Hambleton, whose coffee-house Cromwell frequented.

[4] His hearing.—Pope, 1735–42.

[5] The passage in half-brackets was omitted by Pope in the folio and quarto editions of 1737. In the Cooper octavo, later (1737 e), the fact was avowed in a footnote: 'Omitted by the Author in his own edition.' The learned Dodwell doubtless was Henry (d. 1711); the identity of the poetical Dodwell is unknown.

those barbarous Executioners of the Muses, whom I was just now speaking of. It often happens that guilty Poets, like other guilty Criminals, when once they are known and proclaim'd, deliver themselves into the hands of Justice only to prevent others from doing it, more to their disadvantage; and not out of any Ambition to spread th[eir] Fame by being executed in the face of the World, w[hich is] a Fame but of short Continuance. That Poet were a happy Man who cou'd but obtain a Grant to preserve His for Ninety nine Years; for those Names very rarely last so many Days, which are planted either in Jacob Tonson's, or the Ordinary of Newgate's, Miscellanies.

I have an hundred things to say to you which shall be deferr'd till I have the happiness of seeing you in the Town, for the Season now draws on that invites ev'ry body thither. Some of them I had communicated to you by Letters before this time, if I had not been uncertain where you pass'd your time the last Season: So much fine Weather, I doubt not, has given you all the Pleasure you cou'd desire from the Country; and your own Thoughts the best Company in it. But nothing cou'd allure Mr Wycherley to our Forests, he continu'd (as you told me long since he wou'd) an obstinate Lover of the Town, in spite of Friendship & Fair Weather. Therfore henceforward, to all those considerable Qualities I know you possest of, I shall reckon that of Prophecy. But I still believe Mr. Wycherley's Intentions were good, & am satisfyd he [pro]mises nothing but with a real design to perform it; How much soever his other excellent qualities are above my Imitation, his Sincerity, I hope, is not; and it is with the utmost that I am, Sir, Your most humble & obedient Servant. | A: Pope:

Sir, I shall take it as a great favor if you will give me a line or two, directed to me at Binfield near Ockingham, by Ockingham Bagg, Berks: & if Mr. Wycherley be in Town, you will oblige me by letting me know it; for I fear he is not well, having not heard a good while from him, & not knowing where to direct a Letter to him in case he be yet in the Country.

Address: For Henry Cromwell, Esqr: at | the Widow Hambleton's Coffee-house, | in Princes Street, near Drury Lane, | LONDON

Postmarks: NO/3 WOCK-N-AM

WYCHERLEY *to* POPE[1] — 13 *November* 1708

Longleat Portland Papers, xiii (Harleian transcripts)

My Dear Mr Pope,—I came to Town upon Saturday night last, the 6th of this Month; and I assure you the best part of my welcome to

[1] Printed in Elwin–Courthope, v. 394. One may note how artlessly Wycherley flows from one relative clause to another. As he (or the Harleian scribe) wrote the letter it was all a single sentence. It is here completely repunctuated, without warrant from the MS.

Town was your ingenious, kind Letter, another of which I was so happy as to receive at Shrewsbury; to which (I confess) I made no answer, since I intended my return for London in some Days after; but I am to beg your Pardon for not answering sooner your last obliging Letter of the 7th of this Month,[1] which I received since I came to Town, by which I find neither Time or distance can allay or alter your Friendship; for which I think myself not a little obliged to you; as likewise I find by a Letter of yours to Mr Cromwell (which he shew'd me) wherein you make so kind a mention of me that it were ungrateful in me to doubt, (tho' I little deserve it,) what you say; no more than your warmth and reallity of Your Friendship, in spight of absence or Distance, which I value myself much upon, and the more, because you seem jealous in your last of mine. For I think no more in Friendship than in Love Can any man be Jealous without either; so that I am proud of your Quarrel and reproach, for not writing to you oftener, or being capable of forgeting you; but to allay the satisfaction I received by your Letter to me, as by that of yours to Mr Cromwell, you tell me you have been troubled this Month with the Headach, for which I am heartily sorry, that that which gives us so much Pleasure, (with so much ease) shou'd give you so much Pain; but if your head has ak'd, it is but just it should, for its jealousy of me and my Friendship, for not answering sooner your Letters. You and Voiture say, the Woods & Rocks reply; and even the Gods (some say) answer'd (by their Oracles) every dull Pray'r or Praise of them, at what e'er distance it did come to them; so that I confess ev'ry Friend shou'd ev'ry way answer all his Friends kindness and Expectations, (if he cou'd). Therefore no Elivation or Rise (tho' upon the Welch Mountains or at Court) cou'd make me above answering my Friends, especially since my Answers to you wou'd procure yours to me again; which I shou'd Value more than my Lord Treasurers, nay the Queens, to my Petitions as a Poet, in forma Pauperis. But so much for answering; And now for questioning a while. In the first place I desire to know when you will come to Town to make Titcombe and Me bear the Prince's departure from this Life[2] the better; for which the whole Town is going to be sad, as far as black cloth and Crape or muslin will shew their sorrow; for I believe the Truest Mourners are the Silkmen, the Lacemen, the Embroiderers, and Players, who (they say) must shut up their Shops for these Six Months; so consequently be the greatest and truest mourners for the Prince's Death. Nay Titcombe himself is now a sader Fellow than ever; so that the only way to relieve the general sadness here is for you to come to Town, in order to which I can heartily assure and Ensure your welcome to me; for the Chamber

[1] An unknown letter.

[2] Prince George of Denmark died 28 Oct. 1708.

next mine is Empty, and Mrs. Bambers[1] Table is now no more full of Guests than Meat, so that, if you can think of coming to Town, you are sure to be welcome to every body here that knows you, but more especially to | (Dear Mr Pope) | Your real friend, and humble Servant | W: Wycherley

London Novr the 13th 1708.

In the mean time, pray give my humble service to your good Father and Mother, and I beg you to make my Compliment to that most Ingenious, humane, most honourable and most Learned Gentleman Sir Wm Trumbold.

I thank you for the Friendship, as well as the Wit, of your Epigram, which I cou'd praise more, were it less to my Own Praise.

POPE *to* CROMWELL 22 *January* 1708/9

[The letter existing in Rawlinson Letters 90 with the date 19 January 1707[8] was printed in 1726 without date, and in 1735 Pope gave it the date entered above. It is here (p. 36) printed under the original date for the first time.]

||WYCHERLEY *to* POPE[2] 19 *February* 1708/9

Longleat Portland Papers, xiii (Harleian transcripts)

Dear Mr Pope,—I have received yours of the 6th[3] as kind as it is ingenious, for which therefor I most heartily thank you: but it would have been much more welcome to me, had it not inform'd me of your want of Health; ⌜which I am sorry for, who have underwent likewise (of late,) a great deal of Sickness, & trouble, from the Collick, since your leaving the Town, Tho' I thank God, at present, I am pretty well recover'd; if I can keep of, the common Foe the Cold; and shall be contented, to want the Philosophy, sickness may teach a Man; to be a good, harden'd Blockhead, with Health, without Thought, or Sense;⌝ But You, who have a Mind so vigorous, may well be contented, with its crazy habitation; since (you know) the old simmillitude says, the keeness of the Mind, soonest wears out the Body; as the sharpest Sword soonest destroys the Scabbard; so that, (as I say,) you must be satisfy'd, with your apprehension of an Uneasy Life, (tho' I

[1] Mrs. Bambers was evidently Wycherley's landlady. Elwin, without warrant from the transcript, printed *Bambro.*

[2] First printed entire in Elwin–Courthope, v. 395–7. In 1729 Pope included in Wycherley's *Posthumous Works*, ii. 20–22, much of the early part of the letter. He changed the year (which the Harleian transcript gives clearly) to 1706/7. In printing Pope made considerable omissions, here indicated by half-brackets. In 1737 and thereafter Pope did not reprint the letter.

[3] 6th]26th *1729–35*. No letter of either date is known.

hope not a short one, notwithstanding that generally, you sound Wits, (tho' weak Bodys,) are Immortal hereafter, by that Genius, which shortens your present Life, to prolong that of the Future. But I yet hope, your great, Vigorous, and active Mind, will not be able to destroy, your little, tender, and crazy Carcase.

Now to say something to what you writ, concerning the present epidemick distemper of the Mind, and Age, call'd Callumny, I know it is no more to be avoided, (at one time, or another of our Lives,) than a Feaver, or an Ague, and as often those Distempers attend, or threaten, the best Constitutions, from the worst Aire, So does, that malignant Aire, of Calumny soonest atack the sound, and elivated in Mind; as storms of Wind, the tallest, and most fruitful Trees, whilst the low and weak, (for bowing and moving to and fro) are by their weakness, secure from the Danger, and violence, of the Tempest, they undergo. But so much for stinking Rumour, which weakest minds are most afraid of, as Irish men, tho the nastiest of Mankind, are most afraid of, and offended at a Fart,[1] ⌜which is nothing to a Man, who has read Seneca, (as you say) since he is a Doctor, for the weakness of the Mind; wherefore you administer to me some of his prescriptions against the Passions, (the minds Infirmitys) kindly; and confirm me, in his opinion, and yours, Quod nihil est iniquius, quam Secreto credere, palam irasci.[2] Wherefore I have (from my long experience of the World,) learnt, to be slow to believe, as to anger, who, rather, than be unjust to my Friend, by sensureing his Faith too soon, wou'd be treacherous, to my self, by believing my Foes want of Faith to me, too late; but so much, for fear, or doubt of Friendship, which may be as much a signe of it, as Jealousy is of Love. Now next to preserving me, in your Opinion, of my real Friendship to you; I take it, not a little kindly, that you do what you can, to preserve me, in Sir Wm Trumbolds good opinion, and to that end, pray continue to assure him, that no man, is more his humble Servant, than he, who is likewise Yours, by the names of the plain-dealer,[3] and | Wm Wycherley.⌝

London Feb: the 19th 1708/9

⌜Sir,—Since my writing this, I received yours of the 15th[4] which is a second part, to your Former, in relation to your concern for my seeming, to take anything ill of you; but you will (I hope) pardon the crime, which my kindness and Friendship for you, is guilty of; for when our Love is indifferent, our resentments are so; and if a Man did not value his Friends kindness, he wou'd not fear the loss of it: you

[1] At this point Pope's printed text of the letter stops. [2] Seneca, *De Ira*, ii. 25.
[3] One of the frequent associations of the dramatist with his favourite creation, *The Plain Dealer*.
[4] A letter not now known to exist.

desire me to let you know, when the Miscellany comes out, wherein you are concern'd, I can only tell you, that the other night Capt. Steel, who writes the Gazzett, (and is consequently, conversent with Tonson,) told me the Miscellany,[1] would not come out this three weeks yet; so you have a pretty long Reprieve; in the mean time my hearty service to your good Father, and Mother, whilst your Allys, and Friends of the Coffee house, Titcomb, the rough, and Cromwell the Gentle, send you theirs; The one swearing (by God) you are a pretty Fellow, and t'other (y gad) that You are a polite Person, &c.⌉

||POPE *to* CROMWELL *7 May* 1709

The Bodleian Library

May the 7th 1709.

Sir,—You had long before this time been troubled with a Letter from me, but that I deferr'd it till I cou'd send you either the Miscellany,[2] or my Continuation of the Version of Statius. The first I imagin'd you might have [h]ad before now, but since the contrary has happen'd, you may draw this Moral from it, That Authors in general are more ready to write nonsence, than Booksellers are to publish it. I had I know not what extraordinary Flux of Rhyme upon me for three days together, in which time all the Verses you see added, have been written; which I tell you that you may more freely be severe upon them. Tis a Mercy I do not assault you with a number of Original Sonnets & Epigrams, which our modern Bards put forth in the Spring time in as great abundance, as Trees do Blossoms, a very few whereof ever come to be Fruit, & please no longer than just in their Birth. So that they make no less haste to bring [the]ir Flow'rs of Wit to the Press, than Gard'ners to bring their other flow'rs to the [m]arket, which if they can't get off their hands in the morning, are sure to [dye] before night. Thus the same reason that furnishes Common Garden[3] with [those] Nosegays you so delight in, supplies the Muse's Mercury's & Brittish A[pol]lo's (not to say Jacob's Miscellanies) with Verses. And 'tis the happiness of this Age, that the Modern Invention of printing Poems for Pence a piece has brought the Nosegays of Parnassus to bear the same price; whereby the publick-spirited Mr Henry Hills of Black-fryars[4] has been the cause of great Ease & singular Comfort to all the Learned, [w]ho never over-abounding in transitory Coine, shoud not be discontented (methinks) ev'n tho' Poems were distributed Gratis

[1] In which are to appear Pope's *Pastorals*, &c.

[2] *Jacob Tonson*'s sixth Volume of Poetical Miscellanies in which Mr. *Pope*'s Pastorals and some Versions of *Homer* and *Chaucer* were first printed.—Pope, 1735–42. (The volume was published 2 May.)

[3] Pope wrote *Common Garden*, but Curll and he printed *Covent Garden*.

[4] Hills was a notorious piratical printer. See *DNB*.

about the Streets, like Bunyan's Sermons & other pious Treatises, usually publish'd in a like volume & Character.

The Time now drawing nigh, when you use, with Sapho, to cross the Water in an Ev'ning to Spring Garden, I hope you will have a fair opportunity of ravishing her:—I mean only (as Oldfox in ye Plain-dealer says) of ravishing her thro' the Ear with your well-penn'd Verses.—⌜I have been told of a very lucky Compliment of an Officer to his Mistress in the same place, which I cannot but set down, (and desire you at present to take in good part instead of a Latine Quotation) that it may sometime or other be improv'd by your Pronunciation, while you walk, Solus cum Sola, in those Amourous Shades:

> When at Spring-garden Sappho deigns t'appear,
> The Flow'rs march in her Van, Musk in her Rear.⌝[1]

I wish you all the Pleasures which the Season and the Nymph can afford; the best Company, and the best Coffee, and the best news you can desire. And what more to wish you than this, I do not know; unless it be a great deal of Patience to read & examine the Verses I send you; and I promise you in return a great deal of Deference to your judgment, & an extraordinary Obedience to your Sentiments for the future, (to which you know I have been sometimes a little refractory.) If you will please to begin where you left off last, & mark the Margins as you have done in the pages immediately before, (which you will find corrected to your Sense since your last perusal) you will extreamly oblige me, and improve my Translation. Besides those places which may deviate from the Sense of the Author, it wou'd be very kind i[n] you to observe any Deficiencies in the Diction or Numbers. The Hiatus in particular I wou'd avoid as much as possible, which you are certainly in the right to be a professd Enemy to; tho I confess I cou'd not think it possible at all times to be avoided by any writer, till I found, by reading the famous French Poet Malherbe lately, that there is but one throughout all his Poems. [I] thought your Observation true enough to be past into a Rule, but not a Rule [wi]thout Exceptions, nor that ever it had been reduc'd to Practise. But this Exa[mple] of one of the correctest & best of their Poets has undeceivd me, & confirms your Opinion very strongly, and much more than Mr Drydens Authority, who tho he made it a Rule, seldom observd it.—

[1] There is slight doubt that 'Sapho' is Mrs. Thomas. Cromwell in his letter to Pope, 6 July 1727, calls E. T. [Elizabeth Thomas] 'Sapho'. He was likely to apply the name to any literary lady. It was possibly to avoid identification with 'Sapho' that Mrs. Thomas, in Curll's *Mr. Pope's Literary Correspondence*, iii (1735), 10 *bis*, printed an early letter (1703) in which she remarks that 'Sapho was the Name Mr. Cromwell chose' for Mrs. Martland of Winchester. Curll printed this passage entire as Pope wrote it, and so it appeared in the texts of 1735. But in the quarto and folio of 1737 Pope decorously omitted the whole paragraph, and in the Roberts octavo of 1737 and thereafter he printed the first sentence of the paragraph but omitted the portion here placed in half-brackets.

Sir I shall be very proud of a Line or two from you sometimes during this Summer, which will be always very welcome & very obliging to | Sir, | Your most humble and most | obedient Servant, | A: Pope:

[1]I desire you will be so kind to me as not to show what I send, to anybody. I am not certain whether Mr Wycherly be yet in London or no; if he be, I desire you to give him my most hearty Service; & to let him know that I writ to him this very day (for I find Our Letters sometimes miscarry of late). If he be not in Town now, you will favor me by letting me know, if he was in good health when last you saw him.

Address: To | Mr Cromwell; | present

WYCHERLEY *to* POPE[2] 17 *May* 1709

Longleat Portland Papers, xiii (Harleian transcripts)

⌜Dear Mr Pope,—I have had your last, which as all the rest of your Letters, is as ingenious, as it is kind, and which I find lately, came by the hands of your Mother, whom, I shou'd certainly have waited upon, had not the Maid of the House, forgotten, (till two days after,) to tell me, who it was left the Letter for me, at my Lodgings. If you have not heard from me lately, so frequently, as I us'd to write, I must needs tell you the reason; I have had a very odd Accident befall me; upon Friday was fortnight, or rather Saturday morning, the last of April, when I went to, and came from the Painters Tavern, with one Mr Balam, who, being something drunker than I, (because he thought himself sober,) wou'd needs lead me down Stairs; which I refused, and therefore, went down very well, but at the Steps, going into the Street, he turn'd short upon me, to help me again from falling, and so procur'd my Fall; for Balam turning back upon the Ass, not the Ass upon Balam; he fell upon me, and threw me backward, with his Elbow, in my Stomach, and the Hilt of his Sword, in my Eye, bruis'd me so sorely, I was forced to keep my Bed, for two Days; with a great pain in my side, which by the help of Surgeons, is but lately gone; so that I have been almost a fortnight in pain; and thats the reason, you have not heard from me; which, (I suppose) made you imagine, I was gone into Shropshire; but I shall not go till this day come Seavennight, being the 24th of this Month; when I must be forced to goe, and make

[1] This postscript was not printed by Curll; hence Pope could not print it.

[2] First printed entire in Elwin–Courthope, v. 397–9. In 1729 Pope printed a part of the text, beginning with the second paragraph and making several further omissions. These are here placed in half-brackets. Pope omitted his text altogether from the quarto and folio of 1737.

Wycherley's uncouth sense of sentence structure is here, as elsewhere in these letters, amusingly apparent.

a stay in the Country, for about a Month, or six weeks, (at farthest,) when I shall return again, (God willing,) to London, and then, keep my word, better, than I yet have done with you, in visiting you, at Binfield, to redeem the credit of my word with you, (if possible,) and enjoy with you, the remainder of the Summer, in your plaines, where, by your company, the male Rusticks, are civilized, as the Female made incivil, to shew their better breeding.

In the mean time,⌝ I must thank you, for a Book, of your Miscelanies, which Tonson sent me, I suppose, by your Order; and all, I can tell you of it is, that nothing has lately been better received by the Publick than your part of it; so that, you have only displeas'd the Criticks, by pleasing them, too well; having not left them a word to say, for themselves, against you, and your ingenious Performances; so that, now your Hand is in, you must persever, till my Prophisys of you, be fulfill'd. In earnest all the best Judges, of good Sense, or Poetry are Admirers of Yours; and like your part of the Book so well, that the rest is lik'd the worse; this is true, (upon my word,) without Compliment; so that the first Success will make you, for all your Life a Poet, in spight of your Wit; for a Poets Success at first, like a Gamsters fortune at first, is like to make him a Lover at last, and so to be undone, by his good fortune, and merit, by being drawn to farther Adventures, of his future credit, by his first success.

But hitherto your Miscellanys, have safely run the Gantlet, through all the Coffee-houses; which are now entertain'd, with a whimsical new Newspaper, from and to the Coffee houses, called the Tatler, which I suppose you have seen, ⌜and is written, by one Steel, who thinks himself sharp upon this Iron Age, since an Age of War; and who likewise, writes the other Gazetts, and this under the Name of Bickerstaff;⌝ So this is the newest thing I can tell you of, except it be of the Peace, which now (most People say,) is drawing to such a Conclusion, as all Europe is, or must be satisfy'd with,[1] So Poverty (you see) which makes Peace in Westminster Hall, makes it likewise in the Camp, or Field, through the World; So peace be to you, and, to me, who am grown peaceful now ⌜with my Dagger, as well as with my Sword, and to keep my honour, will neither venture it now, with man, or Woman,⌝ and will have no contest with any Man, but him, who says he is more your Friend, or humble Servant, than | Your | Wm Wycherley.

London May the 17th 1709.

⌜You shall hear from me out of Shropshire, in the mean time, pray present my humble service, to your good Father, and Mother, and to Sir Wm Trumbold.⌝

1 Negotiations for peace entered upon in 1709 failed.

†POPE *to* WYCHERLEY 20 *May* 1709

1729

May 20, 1709

I am glad you receiv'd the *Miscellany*,[1] if it were only to show you that there are as bad Poets in this Nation as your Servant. This modern Custom of appearing in Miscellanies, is very useful to the Poets, who, like other Thieves, escape by getting into a Crowd, and herd together like *Banditti*, safe only in their Multitude. Methinks *Strada* has given a good Description of these kind of Collections; *Nullus hodiè mortalium aut nascitur, aut moritur, aut prœliatur, aut rusticatur, aut abit peregrè; aut redit, aut nubit; aut est, aut non est, (nam etiam mortuis isti canunt) cui non illi extemplò cudant Epicædia, Genethliaca, Protreptica, Panegyrica, Epithalamia, Vaticinia, Propemptica, Soterica, Parænetica, Nænias, Nugas.*[2] As to the success which you say my part has met with, it is to be attributed to what you were pleas'd to say of me to the World; which you do well to call your *Prophecy*, since whatever is said in my favour, must be a Prediction of things that are not yet; you, like a true Godfather, engage on my part for much more than ever I can perform. My Pastoral Muse, like other Country Girls, is but out of Countenance, by what you Courtiers say to her; yet I hope you would not deceive me too far, as knowing that a young Scribler's vanity needs no Recruits from abroad: for Nature like an indulgent Mother, kindly takes care to supply her sons with as much of their own, as is necessary for their Satisfaction. If my Verses should meet with a few flying Commendations, *Virgil* has taught me that a young Author has not too much reason to be pleas'd with them, when he considers, that the natural consequence of Praise, is Envy and Calumny.

—Si ultra[3] placitum laudarit, Baccare frontem
Cingite, ne Vati noceat mala lingua futuro:

When once a Man has appear'd as a Poet, he may give up his Pretensions to all the rich and thriving Arts: Those who have once made their court to those Mistresses without Portions, the Muses, are never like to set up for Fortunes. But for my part, I shall be satisfy'd if I can lose my Time agreeably this way, without losing my reputation: As for gaining any, I am as indifferent in the Matter as *Falstaffe* was, and may say of *Fame* as he did of *Honour*, *If it comes, it comes unlook'd for; and there's an End on't.* I can be content with a bare saving game, without being thought an Eminent hand, (with which Title *Jacob* has

[1] *Jacob Tonson*'s sixth Vol. of *Miscellany Poems*.—Pope, 1729–42.

[2] Strada, *Prolusiones academicae*, Lib. III, i. In *Eloquentia Bipartita* (Oxford, 1662), p. 358. Typographical errors in the Latin were indicated in the errata leaf of the first edition of 1735. They have been corrected here.

[3] Corrected from *ulna* (1729–35) in the errata leaf of 1735. See *Eclogue* vii. 27–28.

graciously dignify'd his adventurers and voluntiers in Poetry.) *Jacob* creates Poets, as Kings sometimes do Knights, not for their honour, but for money. Certainly he ought to be esteem'd a worker of Miracles, who is grown rich by Poetry.

What Authors lose, their Booksellers have won,
So Pimps grow rich, while Gallants are undone.

I am, your, &c

WYCHERLEY *to* POPE[1] 23 *May* 1709

Longleat Portland Papers, xiii (Harleian transcripts)

Dear Mr Pope,—I writ to you, last week, to let you know my intention, of leaving the Town this; and accordingly, I begin my Journey towards Shropshire to morrow; where, (as I told you,) I intend my stay shall not be above a Month, to rob the Country and then run out of it as fast as I can (as other Thieves doe;) that I may the sooner come to you, and your Country; for you shall find, (as strainge as you may think it,) that I can at last keep my word; tho' I am long about it. I was extreamly concern'd, (as I told you, in my last,) that I miss'd waiting upon your good Mother, when she was in Town; I have now, no news to send you, but of the Peace, of which so many various things are said, that I think it to no purpose to send you the Particulars; which will soon be communicated to you, by the Tatler Mr Steel, in his Gazett: in the mean time, all that I can observe to you is, Fortune, (like all other Jilts,) leaves those in their Age, who were her Favourites in their Youth; which truth I my self, (as unworthy as I am,) have experienc'd sufficiently; as well as Lewis the Grand (now the Petit,) however, far be it from me to lessen (by any impertinent popular Reflextion) so great a Prince, who, like his Devise, the Sun; for having been all the first part of his days in Glory, may Set at last in a Cloud, but let his declention or going down be what it will, he will leave behind him our Lady the Moon and an abundance of Confederate twinklers, (call'd Starrs of the first magnitude,) but to outshine him, by his own borrow'd light, but I must confess, for the Sun to be Eclips'd by a Holland Cheese wou'd have vexed Lewis the Saint, as well as Lewis the Great, but so much for news, and politick, or moral Reflections; and to return to my promise of making my self happy, in your Company at Binfield; be assur'd, that about six weeks hence (at farthest) I will beat up your Quarters there, and disturb your private Enjoyments, both of your Muse and your Mistress, as most of

[1] Too late for use here the original of this letter was acquired by Harvard. Verbally the original and the transcript are identical. Excessive punctuation is here omitted.

the old Impotent Fumblers do, when they can no more have the Enjoyment of either of their own; and then I have promiss'd Mr Englefield to ride behind you, upon your domestick Pegasus, to wait upon him at his Enchanted Castle, tho' he no more believes it than perhaps you may; but look to't. I'll do't I'll do't,[1] as surely (as I have) been hitherto | (Dear Mr Pope) | Your promissing Friend, tho' | Poetical, that is lying humble | Servant | W: Wycherly.

London May the 23rd 1709

In the mean time, my humble service (pray) to your good Father, and Mother, and my good honourable, and ingenious Patron, Sir Wm Trombold.

†WYCHERLEY *to* POPE — 26 *May* 1709

1729

May 26, 1709.

The last I receiv'd from you, was dated the 22d of *May*.[2] I take your charitable hint to me very kindly, wherein you do like a true Friend, and a true Christian, and I shall endeavour to follow your Advice, as well as your Example,——As for your wishing to see your Friend an Hermit with you, I cannot be said to leave the world, since I shall enjoy in your conversation, all that I can desire of it; nay, can learn more from you alone, than from my long experience of the great, or little vulgar in it.

As to the success of your Poems in the late Miscellany, I told you of in my last; (upon my word) I made you no Compliment, for you may be assur'd, that all sorts of Readers like them, except they are Writers too; but for them, (I must needs say) the more they like them, they ought to be the less pleas'd with 'em: So that you do not come off with a bare *Saving Game* (as you call it) but have gain'd so much Credit at first, that you must needs support it to the last: Since you set up with so great a Stock of good Sense, Judgment and Wit, that your Judgment ensures all that your Wit ventures at. The Salt of your Wit has been enough to give a relish to the whole insipid Hotch-Potch it is mingled with; and you will make *Jacob*'s *Ladder*[3] raise you to Immortality, by which others are turn'd off shamefully, to their Damnation (for Poetick Thieves as they are) who think to be sav'd by others good works, how faulty soever their own are: But the Coffee-house Wits, or rather Anti-wits, the Criticks, prove their Judgments by approving

[1] From the 'flash of a prologue' in *The Rehearsal*, I. ii. 178.

[2] The letter of the 22nd is unknown.

[3] The sixth Volume of [Jacob] *Tonson*'s Miscellanies.—Pope, 1729–35. (The note is omitted in 1737–42.)

your Wit; and even the News-Mongers and Poets will own, you have more Invention than they; nay, the Detracters or the Envious, who never speak well of any Body, (not even of those they think well of in their absence) yet will give you (even in your absence) their good Word; and the *Criticks* only hate you, for being forc'd to speak well of you whether they will or no; and all this is true, upon the word of, | Your, &c.

†POPE *to* CROMWELL 10 *June* 1709

1735

June 10, 1709.

I have receiv'd part of the Version of *Starius*, and return you my thanks for your remarks which I think to be just, except where you cry out (like one in *Horace*'s *Art of Poetry*) *Pulchrè, bené, recté!* There I have some fears, you are often, if not always, in the wrong.

One of your objections, namely on that passage,

> The rest, resolving years shall ripen into Fate,

may be well grounded, in relation to its not being the exact sense of the words—[1]*Cætera reliquo ordine ducam.* But the duration of the Action of *Statius*'s poem may as well be excepted against, as many things besides in him: (which I wonder *Bossu*[2] has not observ'd) For instead of confining his narration to *one year*, it is manifestly exceeded in the very first two books: The Narration begins with *Oedipus*'s prayer to the *Fury* to promote discord betwixt his Sons; afterward the Poet expressly describes their entring into the agreement of reigning a year by turns; and *Polynices* takes his flight for *Thebes* on his brother's refusal to resign the throne. All this is in the first book; in next, *Tydeus* is sent Ambassador to *Etheocles*, and demands his resignation in these terms,

> —Astriferum velox jam circulus orbem
> Torsit, & amissæ redierunt montibus umbræ,
> Ex quo frater inops, ignota per oppida tristes
> Exul agit casus—[3]

But *Bossu* himself is mistaken in one particular, relating to the commencement of the Action; saying in Book 2. Cap. 8.[4] that *Statius*

[1] See the first book of Statius, verse 302.—Pope, 1735–42. Since Pope mentions a specific line he may possibly have had a text with the reading here given. Some of his editors have given the reading more common even in Pope's day: *certo reliqua ordine ducam.*

[2] Le Bossu, *Traité du poëme epique* (1675), Livre II, chap. xviii, 'De la Durée de l'Action', does not mention Statius. In Livre II, chap. viii, he had given a considerable account of the *Thebaid* as illustrating 'Des Fautes qui corrompent l'Unité de l'Action'.

[3] *Thebaid*, ii. 400–4.

[4] *Traité du poëme epique* (2nd ed., 1677), pp. 193–4.

opens it with *Europa*'s *Rape*, whereas the Poet at most only deliberates whether he shou'd or not?

—Unde jubetis
Ire, Deæ? Gentisne canam primordia, diræ,
Sidonios raptus?[1] &c.

but then expressly passes all this with a *Longa retro series*—and says

—Limes mihi carminis esto
Œdipodæ confusa domus—[2]

Indeed there are numberless particulars blame-worthy in our Author, which I have try'd to soften in the version:

—Dubiamque jugo fragor impulit Oeten
In latus, & geminis vix fluctibus obstitit Isthmus[3]

is most extravagantly hyperbolical: Nor did I ever read a greater piece of Tautology than

—*Vacua cum* solus *in Aula*
Respiceres jus omne tuum, cunctosque Minores,
Et nusquam par *stare* caput.[4]

In the Journey of *Polynices* is some geographical error,

—In mediis audit duo litora campis[5]

could hardly be; for the *Isthmus* of *Corinth* is full five miles over: And *Caligantes abrupto sole Mycænas*,[6] is not consistent with what he tell us, in Lib. 4. lin. 305: 'that those of *Mycænæ* came not to the war at this time, because they were then in confusion by the divisions of the Brothers, *Atreus* and *Thyestes*:' Now from the raising the *Greek* army against *Thebes*, back to the time of this journey of *Polynices*, is (according to *Statius*'s own account) three years. | Yours, &c.

WYCHERLEY *to* POPE[7] — 14 *June* 1709

Longleat Portland Papers, xiii (Harleian transcripts)

My Dear Mr Pope,—I received yesturday your last Letter, with the wonted Satisfaction yours use to bring me, yet, I must confess, my Satisfaction was not without some allay, since your letter, likewise brings me the ill news of your wonted Indisposition, which is very

[1] *Thebaid*, i. 3–5. [2] Ibid. 16–17. [3] Ibid. 119–20.
[4] Ibid. 166–8. [5] Ibid. 335. [6] Ibid. 325.
[7] First printed in Elwin–Courthope, v. 400–2, where by a typographical error it is dated 4 June. The Harleian transcript clearly has 14. The transcript is sprinkled with absurdly frequent commas, no less than 40 of which are here silently omitted. The purifying omissions of the Elwin–Courthope text are here set off by half-brackets.

hard for you, that that part of you (your Head) which gives others so much pleasure, should cause you so much pain; which, yet (I believe,) might be eased by another pain, that of your heart, as the pain of the Head is not felt when the Foot is seiz'd with that of the Gout; so that, if you would be heartily in Love, and take the Remedy, for both pains, upon one of your Binfield Nymphs, you wou'd be rid of them; ⌜then Cure your headach with the smart of your Nymphs Taile, and be damn'd—⌝ Now Sir to answer your kind quarel to me, for not seeing you at Binfield yet; I assure you, I have been these five weeks (since my Fall by Balam,) troubled with an akeing side, and the Consequences of it, which retarded my Journey into Shropshire; and must have prevented my journey to Binfield; for I was some time under the Surgeon's hands, and it is not long since I have been totally rid of the pain of my side, who thought, (at this Age,) I shou'd never more have had pain there.

I intend (God willing) to go for Shropshire, upon this Day Sev'n-night, where a Month, will be, the longest Time of my Stay, and then you shall see whether I can keep my Word, or no, with You, at Binfield; in the mean time, I beg you to believe, that I never made a promise yet, to any Man, but with an Intention, of performing it; tho' I believe, you think, I never make my Promises to Men, ⌜(but as you Whoremasters yours to Women,)⌝ only with Intention, to break them; yet (you may believe me,) I seldom break those Promises to my Friends, which wou'd deprive my self of my Pleasure, no more than I would have fail'd formerly an Assignation with my She-Friend, whereby I shou'd have been the greatest Looser.

I find by your Letter to Mr Cromwell, you have dispos'd of the Sappho, (you promis'd me,) to him, so that you have a mind to give me Jealously,[1] but it is rather of your Friendship, than of the Love of your Sappho, since he refus'd, to let me see your last Letter to him; who wou'd be a Lover, or a Friend, by his rude civil-cerimony, too much for Woman or Man to bear; so that I dare swear your Ladys (his acquaintance,) whom you desire him to Salute, in your Name, are Irish-women, by their Intimacy with and Friendship for Him, more than their Names, otherways his hard Face wou'd render inefectual, all the soft things, he cou'd say to them, in praise of theirs; who never discommends anything, and is only a Satyr in his Face, not in his Tongue, and like the Devil Tempts the living Eves to sin most, by his creeping advances, clinging embraces, since the more he bows, and creeps to them, the less they see his Face, which like the Devils were enough to frighten them from what his tempting Tongue wou'd perswade them to; thus he is damn'd to perpetual Flames, of Love here, without hopes of his Fools Paradice in Love; yet like the Devil,

[1] For *jealousy*?

is still tempting Women to his Love, to the Augmentation of their Persecution, and his despare, all this I say a little pevishly of him, because he wou'd not let me see your Letter, but so much for Him who looks like a Devil, Loves like a Tormenter, and damns like a Critick, because he is damn'd himself, but so much for him, you, & me; who am in spight of the Devil, and lying, (as a Poet, or Courtier,) | Your real Friend, and humble Servant | W: Wycherley.

London June the 14th 1709.

My humble service pray, as formerly, give to your good Father, and Mother, and good Sir Wm.

Upon the word of a Plain-dealer, I never saw two such good letters, upon such bad Subjects, Mr Cromwel, and myself; and for my Credit, as much as Yours, I have a good mind to use you as Dennis did me,[1] and print your Letters, the only way for me, to print anything, to oblige the World.

†POPE *to* CROMWELL[2] 11 *July* 1709

The Bodleian Library

July the 11. 1709.

The Morning after I parted with you, I found my self (as I had prophesied) all alone, in an uneasy Stage-Coach; a doleful Change from that agreable Company I enjoyd the Night before! without the least hope of Entertainment, but from my last recourse in such cases, a Book. I then began to enter into acquaintance with the Moralists, and had just receivd from them some cold Consolation for the Inconveniences of this life, & the Incertainty of human Affairs: when I perceivd my Vehicle to stop, & heard from the side of it the dreadful News of a Sick Woman preparing to enter it. 'Tis not very easy to guess at my Mortification, but being so well for[ti]fyd with Philosophy, I stood resign'd with a Stoical Constancy to endure ye [wo]rst of Evils, a Sick Woman! I was indeed a little comforted to find by her [V]oice & Dress, that she was young & a Gentlewoman; but no sooner was her Hood remov'd, but I saw one of the finest Faces I ever beheld, & to increase my Surprize, heard her salute me by my Name. I had never more reason to accuse Nature for making me Shortsighted than now, when I cou'd not recollect I had ever seen those fair Eyes which knew me so well; & was utterly at a loss how to

[1] In *Letters upon several Occasions*, 1696. See also Wycherley to Pope, 11 Aug. 1709.

[2] Formerly dated 17 July. From the autograph the date looks slightly more like 17 than like 11, though the two digits are similar. The postmark is clearly IY/13, and that dictates the choice of 11.

Pope omitted this letter entire from his official quarto and folio of 1737. It is always found in his octavos but with some of his less refined expressions deleted or softened.

address myself, till with a great deal of Simplicity & Innocence she let me know (even before I discover'd my Ignorance) that she was the Daughter of one in our Neighborhood, lately marry'd, who having been consulting her Physicians in Towne, was returning into the Country, to try what good Air and a new Husband[1] cou'd do to recover her. My Father, you must know, has sometimes recommended the Study of Physick to me, but *the Dev'l take me* if ever I had any Ambition[2] to be a Doctor till this Instant. I ventur'd to prescribe her some Fruit (which I happen'd to have in the Coach) which being forbidden her by Her damn'd Doctors,[3] she had the more Inclination to. In short, I tempted, and she Eat; nor was I more like the Devil, than she like Eve. Having the good Success of the foresaid Gentleman[4] before my eyes, I put on the Gallantry of the old Serpent, & in spite of my Evil Forme, accosted her with all the Gayety I was master of; which had so good Effect, that in less than an hour she grew pleasant, her Colour return'd, & she was pleas'd to say, my Prescription had wrought an Immediate Cure. In a Word, I had the pleasantest Journey imaginable,[5] so that now, as once of yore, by means of the *forbidden Fruit*, the *Devil* got into *Paradise*—I shou'd not have us'd this last Phrase but that I know your civill Apprehension will not put any ill Construction upon it, & you will firmly believe that we were as modest—even as Sapho & Mr C~~romwell. Your most obligd and affectionate Servant, A. Pope~~

Thus far (methinks) my Letter has something of the Air of a Romance, tho it be true. but I hope you will look on what follows as the greatest of a[ll] Truths, that I think myself extreamly obligd by you in all points, especially for your kind and honourable Information & Advice in a matter of the utmost Concern to me, which I shall ever acknowledge as the highest Proof at once of your Friendship, Justice, & Sincerity. At the same time be assur'd, that Gentleman we spoke of, shall never by any Alteration in me discover my Knowledge of his Mistake; the hearty Forgiving of which is the Only kind of Return I can possibly make him for so many favors: And I may derive this pleasure at least from it, that whereas I must otherwise have needs been [a] little uneasy to know my Incapacity of returning ⌜to⌝[6] his Obligations, I may now, by bearing his Frailty, exercise my Gratitude & Friendship more, than Himself either is, or perhaps ever will be, sensible of.

1 a new husband] a husband *1737 a–42.*
2 but the Dev'l . . . Ambition] but I never had any Ambition *all Pope's texts.*
3 Her damn'd Doctors] Her Doctors *all Pope's texts.*
4 Gentleman] Tempter *1737 a–42.*
5 Pope, in reprinting from Curll, omitted after *imaginable* all the rest of the paragraph. At the end of this paragraph he concluded the letter, then crossed out the conclusion (as here indicated), and resumed with the next paragraph.
6 Omitted in 1735 n and in the texts of 1737–42.

Ille meos, primus qui me sibi junxit, Amores
Abstulit; ille habeat secum, servetque Sepulchro![1]

But in one thing, I must confess, You have yourself obligd me more than any Man ⌜alive, ev'n than Mr W——⌝;[2] which is, that you have show'd me most of my Faults, to which as you are the more an implacable Enemy, by so much the more are you a Kind Friend to Me. I coud be proud, in revenge, to find a few Slips in your Verses, which I read in London, & since in the Country with more application & pleasure: The Thoughts are very just ⌜& noble⌝,[3] & you are sure not to let 'em suffer by the Versification. If you wou'd oblige me with the Trust of any thing of yours, I shou'd be glad to execute any Commissions you wou'd give me concerning 'em. I am here so perfectly at leisure that nothing wou'd be so agreable an Entertainment to me, but if you will not afford me that, do not deny me at least the satisfaction of your Letters as long as we are absent, if you wou'd not have him very unhappy who is very sincerly | ⌜Dear Sir,⌝ | Your ⌜most obligd & affectionate | Servant, | A: Pope.⌝

⌜Pray give my Service to Mr Tydcombe, & intreat him with all possible Tenderness not to defraud me of the Letter he writ, & which so rightfully belongs to me.⌝[4]

⌜P.S.⌝ Having a vacant Space here, I will fill it with a short Ode on Solitude, which I found yesterday by great accident, & which I find by the Date was written when I was not Twelve years old; that you may perceive how long I have continued in my Passion for a rural life, & in the same Employments of it.

Happy the Man, who free from Care,
The Business and the Noise of Towns,
Contented breaths his Native Air,
In his own Grounds:

Whose Herds with Milk, whose Fields with Bread,
Whose Flocks supply him with Attire,
Whose Trees in Summer yield him Shade,
In Winter, Fire.

[1] *Aeneid*, iv. 28–29.

[2] Omitted in all Pope texts. Curll printed it and expanded 'W——' to 'Wycherley'.

[3] Omitted in all Pope texts.

[4] Elwin says wrongly that the postscript concerning Tidcombe has been cut off from the original letter. It is certainly there; but Pope omitted it from Curll's text, and concluded with 'sincerely, / Your, &c.' He then resumed with 'Having a vacant space. . .'. Curll prints the Ode from Pope's autograph as sent to Cromwell. In Pope's printings of the letter a later improved text of the poem is given. Pope had printed the Ode (in the fifth edition of Lintot's *Miscellany Poems*) shortly before Curll printed it in his *Miscellanea*.

Blest, who can unconcern'dly find
His Years slide silently away,
In Health of Body, Peace of Mind,
Quiet by Day,

Repose at Night; Study & Ease,
Together mixt; sweet Recreation;
And Innocence, which most does please,
With Meditation.

Thus, let me live, unseen, unknown,
Thus, unlamented, let me die,
Steal from the World, & not a Stone
Tell where I lye.

Address: To | Henry Cromwell, Esq: | at the Blue Ball in great Wild- | Street, near Drury-Lane | LONDON

Postmarks: IY/13 BAGSHOT

POPE *to* CROMWELL 17 *July* 1709

[Here dated 11 July 1709.]

†WYCHERLEY *to* POPE[1] 11 *August* 1709

1729

Aug. 11, 1709.

My Letters, so much inferior to yours, can only make up their scarcity of Sense by their number of Lines; which is like the *Spaniards* paying a debt of Gold with a load of brass Money. But to be a Plain-dealer, I must tell you, I will revenge the raillery of your Letters upon mine, by printing them, (as *Dennis* did mine) *without your knowledge too*, which wou'd be a revenge upon your Judgment, for the raillery of your Wit: For some dull Rogues (that is the most in the World) might be such Fools as to think what you said of me, was in earnest: It is not the first time, you great Wits have gain'd Reputation by their paradoxical or ironical Praises; your Forefathers have done it, *Erasmus* and others. For all Mankind who know me must confess, he must be no ordinary Genius, or little Friend, who can find out any thing to commend in me seriously; who have given no sign of my Judgment, but my Opinion of yours, nor mark of my Wit, but my leaving off Writing, to the publick, now you are beginning to shew the World what you can do by yours: whose Wit is as spiritual as your Judgment

[1] Omitted from the quarto and folio of 1737.

infallible; in whose Judgment I have an implicit Faith, and shall always subscribe to it to save my Works in this World, from the Flames and Damnation.——Pray present my most humble Service to Sir *W. Trumbull*;[1] for whom and whose Judgment I have so profound a respect, that his Example had almost made me marry, more than my Nephew's ill Carriage to me; having once resolv'd to have reveng'd my self upon him by my Marriage, but now am resolv'd to make my revenge greater upon him by his Marriage.

||POPE *to* CROMWELL 29 *August* 1709

The Bodleian Library

Aug: 29. 1709.[2]

If I were to write to you as often as I think of you, my Letters wou'd be as bad as a Rent charge; but tho' the one be but too little for your Goodnature, the other wou'd be too much for your Quiet, which is one Blessing Goodnature shou'd indispensably receive from Mankind, in return for those many it gives. I have been inform'd of late how much I am indebted to that Quality of yours, in speaking well of me in my absence; the only thing by which you prove yourself no Wit or Critique: Tho' indeed I have always[3] thought, that a Friend will show just as much Indulgence, & no more, to my faults when I am absent, as he does Severity to 'em when I am present. To be very frank with you, Sir, I must owne that where I receivd so much Civility at first, I cou'd hardly have expected so much Sincerity afterward. But now I have only to wish, that the last were but fully equal to the fi[rst,] & that as you have omitted nothing to oblige me, so you wou'd omit nothing to Improve me.

I caus'd an Acquaintance of mine to enquire twice of your Welfare, by whom I have been inform'd that you have left your Speculative Angle in the Widows Coffeehouse, & bidding adieu for some time to all the Rehearsalls, Reviews, Gazettes, ⌜Tatlers⌝,[4] &c, have ⌜Heroically⌝ marchd off into Lincolnshire. Thus I find you vary your Life in the Scene at least, tho' not in the Action; for tho' Life for the most part, like an old Play, be still the same [, yet] now & then a New Scene may make it more entertaining. As for myself, [I] wou'd not have my life a very Regular Play; let it be a good merry Farce, a

[1] Sir William had married a second time in 1706 at the age of 67.—Elwin. On Wycherley's death-bed marriage in 1715 see Professor Howard P. Vincent, who gives the nephew's story concerning the marriage in 'The Death of William Wycherley', *Harvard Studies and Notes*, xv (1933), 219–42.

[2] Either by accident or by intention all Pope's editions date this letter 19 Aug. If there was intention, the purpose was probably to depreciate Curll's text.

[3] always] often *all Pope's texts.*

[4] Curll had included *Tatlers* and *Heroically*, but Pope curiously omits the words in his texts.

G—ds [name] and a figg[1] for the Critical Unities! ⌜Yet (on the other side) I wou'd as soon write like Durfey, as live like Tidcombe; whose beastly, laughable[2] Life is (if you will excuse such a Similitude) not unlike a Fart, at once nasty & diverting.⌝ For the generality of men, a true Modern Life is like a true Modern Play, neither Tragedy, Comedy, nor Farce, nor one, nor all of these. Every Actor is much better known by his having the same Face, than by his keeping the same Character: For we change our minds as often as they can their Parts, & he who was yesterday Cesar, is to day Sir J. Daw.[3] So that one might, with much better reason, ask the same Question of a Modern Life, that Mr. Rich did of a modern Play; Pray do me the favor, Sir, to inform me; Is this your Tragedy or your Comedy?

I have dwelt the longer on this argument, because I persuade myself it might be usefull at this time when we have no other Theatre, to divert ourselves at this Great one.[4] Here is a glorious Standing Comedy of Fools, at which every Man is heartily merry, and thinks himself an unconcern'd Spectatour. Th[is] (to our singular Comfort) neither my Lord Chamberlain, nor the Queen herself, can ever shut up, or silence.[5] While that of Drury (alas!) lyes desolate, in the profoundest peace! and the melancholly Prospect of the Nymphs yet lingring pensive[6] about its beloved Avenues, appears no less moving, than that of the [Tr]ojan Dames lamenting over their ruin'd Ilium! What now can they hope, dispossessd of their ancient Seats, but to serve as Captives to the Insulting Victors of the Hay-Markett?[7] The afflicted Subjects of France do not, in our Po[st]man,[8] so grievously deplore the Obstinacy of their arbitrary monarch; as thes[e] perishing People of Drury the Obdurate Heart of that Pharaoh, Rich,[9] who like him, disdains all Proposalls of Peace & Accommodation! Several Libells have secretly been affix'd to the great Gates of his Imperial Palace in Bridges Street; and a Memorial, representing the Distresses

[1] be a merry . . . and a fig] be a tolerable farce, and a fig *1737 b*. In 1737 e a footnote is added that calls attention to the omission of the profane remark. It reads: 'Tolerable farce, *in the Author's own Edit.* a God's name *omitted there.*' This note, printed in later editions, shows that Pope continued to pretend no responsibility for any editions except the quarto and folio of 1737.

[2] This entire sentence about Tidcombe (who was only T—e in print) was omitted by Pope in 1737 and thereafter.

[3] Sir John Daw is in Jonson's *Silent Woman*.

[4] The theatres, normally closed during the long vacation, would not be open in August; but because of Rich's unjust treatment of his actors the Lord Chamberlain had ordered Drury Lane to be closed from 6 June 1709.

[5] In the quarto and folio of 1737 the letter ended here. A footnote inserted in 1737 e indicates the fact: 'What follows to the end of this Letter is omitted in the Author's own Edit.' The note appears 1737–42.

[6] *pensive* is omitted in Pope's texts.

[7] During the season of 1709–10 the Drury Lane company acted in the new theatre (opened in 1705) designed by Vanbrugh, in the Haymarket. They shared the theatre that season with the operatic company.

[8] *The Post-man* was a Tory newspaper.

[9] Christopher Rich (d. 1714), theatrical manager.

of these Persons, has been accidentally drop'd (as we are credibly inform'd by a Person of Quality) [out] of his [first] Minister, the Chief Box-keeper's Pocket; at a late Conference [betwixt him and his first Minister about the][1] part of the Confederates, & his Theatrical Majesty on his own part. Of this you may expect a Copy as soon as it shall be transmitted to us from a good hand. As for the late Congress, it [is] here reported, that it has not been wholly ineffectuall; but this wants Confirmation; yet we cannot but hope the concurring Pray'rs and Tears of so many Wretched Ladies may induce this haughty Prince to Reason. I am | Sir | Your most obedient & affectionate Servant | A. Pope.

[2]I have not heard these 2 months from Mr Wycherley, tho' I have written to him twice. I am since told he has been ill, which I am very much concern'd for, & fear is the occasion of his silence since his last Letters, which were the kindest in the world. If you happen at your Return to find him in Town, it will be very obliging to let me know of it; In the mean time a Letter from you will make me the best amends for my Solitude.

Address: [To |][3] H: Cromwell, Esq: to be left | [at the] blue Ball in Great Wild-street, | Lincolns-Inn-Fields, | LONDON

Postmark: AV/31

||POPE *to* CROMWELL 19 *October* 1709

The Bodleian Library

Octob: 19. 1709.

Sir,—I may truly say I am more obligd to you this Summer than to any of my acquaintance, ⌜for had it not been for the two kind Letters you sent me, I had been perfectly, *oblitusque meorum*, *obliviscendus & illis.*⌝[4] The only Companions I had were those Muses of whom Tully says, Adolescentiam alunt, senectutem oblectant, secundas res ornant, adversis perfugium, ac solatium præbent, delectant domi, non impediunt foris, pernoctant nobiscum, peregrinantur, rusticantur. which indeed is as much as ever I expected from them; for the Muses, if you take 'em as Companions, like all the rest,[5] are very pleasant & agreable;

[1] The words in square brackets are supplied from Curll's text of 1726. The original letter was evidently damaged before he read it; for the words supplied are too numerous for the illegible space. In 1735 and later Pope reads: 'Conference of the said Person of quality and others, on the part . . .'

[2] This postscript is omitted in all of Pope's texts: Curll had printed it.

[3] The upper left corner of the address is torn away.

[4] Possibly because aware of his fondness for this tag from Horace, *Epistles*, I. xi. 9, Pope omitted the words in half-brackets in 'his own' editions, the quarto and folio of 1737. He left in his other favourite from Cicero, *Pro Archia*, vii. 16.

[5] like all the rest—*omitted in all Pope's texts.*

but whoever shou'd be forc'd to live or depend upon 'em, woud find himself in a very bad Condition. That Quiet, which Cowley calls the Companion of Obscurity,[1] was not wanting to me unless when it was interrupted by those Fears you so justly guess I had for our Friend's Welfare. Tis extreamly kind in you to tell me the News you heard of him, & you have deliverd me from more Anxiety than he imagines me capable of on his score, as I am convinc'd by his long Silence. However the Love of some things rewards itself, as of Virtue & of Mr Wycherley. I am surpriz'd at the danger you tell me he has been in, and must agree with [yo]u, that our Nation woud have lost in him[2] alone more Wit, Probity, & Good-nature[3] than wou'd have remain'd (for ought I know) in all the rest of it. My Concern for his Friendship will excuse me, (since I know You honor him so much, & since you know I love him above all men) if I vent a part of my Uneasiness to you, & tell you, that there has not been wanting One, (who is every way a Scoundrell but that he has the luck to be born a Gentleman,) that has more than once insinuated malicious Untruths of me to Mr W:[4] which I fear may have had some Effect upon him: If so, he will have a greater Punishment for his Credulity than I cou'd wish him, in that Fellows Acquaintance. The Loss of a faithful Creature is something, tho' of never so contemptible an one: and if I were to change my Dog for such a Man as the aforesaid, I shoud think my Dog undervalu'd; (who follows me about as constantly here in the Country, as I was us'd to do Mr W. in the Towne.)

Now I talk of my Dog, that I may not treat of a worse Subject which my Spleen tempts me to, I will give you some account of him; a thing not wholly unpresidented, since Montaigne (to whom I am but a Dog in comparison) has done the very same thing of his Catt. *Dic mihi quid melius desidiosus agam?* You are to know then, that as 'tis Likeness that begets Affection, so my Favorite Dog is a Little one, a lean one,[5] and none of the finest Shap'd. He is not much a Spaniell in his fawning; but has (what might be worth many a Man's while to imitate from him) a dumb surly sort of Kindness, that rather shows itself when he thinks me ill-us'd by others, than when we Walk

[1] At the end of his essay 'Of Obscurity', in his verses from Seneca's *Thyestes*.

[2] him . . . Wit] him as much Wit . . . as *1737–42*.

[3] Wit, Probity, & Goodnature than] Wit and Probity than *1735*. (In 1737–42 *Goodnature* is still omitted and *than* becomes *as*.)

[4] wanting One . . . to Mr. W.] wanting one to insinuate malicious Untruths of me to Mr. Wycherley *so in all Pope printings*. (Curll in 1726 printed the parenthesis.)

In 1726 Curll added (on p. [156]) this note: 'The Person whom Mr. Pope charges with having *insinuated malicious Untruths* . . . I presume, was Charles Gildon Esq.; who also wrote the Life of Mr. Wycherley, wherein are contained many severe Reflections upon Mr. *Pope*, very unbecoming a Gentleman.'

[5] Pope seems always to have had a dog. Bounce, his later and more famous canine companion, was a Great Dane.

quietly & peaceably by ourselves. If it be the chief point of Friendship to comply with [a] Friend's Motions & Inclinations, he possesses this in an eminent degree; he lyes down when I sitt, & walks where I walk, which Is more than many very good Friends can pretend to, Witness Our Walk a year ago in St. James's Park—Histories are more full of Examples of the Fidelity of Dogs than of Friends, but I will not insist upon many of 'em, because It is possible some may be almost as fabulous as those of Pylades & Orestes, &c. I will only say for the honour of Dogs that the Two most ancient and esteemable Books, Sacred and prophane, extant, (viz: the Scripture and Homer) have shown a particular Regard to these Animals. That of Toby is the more remarkable, because there was no manner of reason to take notice of the Dog besides the great humanity of the Author. And Homer's Account of Ulysses's Dog Argus, is the most pathetic imaginable, all the Circumstances consider'd, and an excellent Proof of the Old Bards Goodnature. Ulysses had left him at Ithaca when he embarkd for Troy, & found him on his return after 20 years, (which by the way is not unnatural, as some Criticks have said, since I remember the Dam of my Dog who was 22 years old when she dy'd: May the Omen of Longevity prove fortunate to her Successour!) You shall have it in Verse.

ARGUS.

When wise Ulysses from his native Coast
Long kept by Wars, and long by Tempests tost,
Arrivd at last, poor, old, disguis'd, alone,
To all his Friends & ev'n his Queen unknown,
Chang'd as he was, with Age, & Toils, & Cares,
Furrowd his rev'rend Face, & white his hairs,
In his own Palace forc'd to ask his Bread,
Scornd by those Slaves his former Bounty fed,
Forgot of all his own Domestic Crew;
His faithful Dog his rightful Master knew![1]
Unfed, unhousd, neglected, on the Clay,
Like an old Servant, now cashier'd, he lay,
And tho' ev'n then expiring on the Plain,[2]
Touch'd with Resentment of ungrateful Man,
And longing to behold his Ancient Lord again.
Him when he Saw—he rose, & crawld to meet,
(Twas all he cou'd) and fawn'd, and kist his feet,
Seiz'd with dumb Joy—then falling by his Side,
Own'd his returning Lord, Look'd up, & Dy'd.

[1] The faithful Dog alone his rightful Master knew—*so in all Pope texts of the letter*. (It is one of the few alexandrines Pope thought proper to allow in his poetry.)

[2] This line is omitted in all Pope texts—to avoid the triplet?

Plutarch[1] (who if I have any Taste, is the greatest of Moral Philosophers) relating how the Athenians were obligd to abandon Athens in the time of Themistocles, steps back again, out of the way of his History, to describe the lamentable Cries [&] Howlings of the poor Dogs, when left behind. He makes mention of one that follow'd his Master across the Sea to Salamis, where he dy'd & was honord with a Tomb by the Athenians, who gave the name of the Dogs Tomb to that part of the Iland where he was buried: This Respect to a Dog from the most polite people of the World is very observable. A Modern Instance of Gratitude to a Dog (tho' we have but few such) is that the Chief Order of Denmark (now call'd the Order of the Elephant) was instituted in memory of the fidelity of a Dog nam'd Wild-brat, by one of their Kings who had been deserted by his Subjects, & gave [his Order][2] this Motto, or to this effect, which still remains; Wild-Brat was faithful. Sir William Trumbull has told me a Story which he heard from one that was present when our King Charls I. being with some of his Court, during his Troubles, and a Discourse arising what Sort of Dogs deservd Pre-eminence, & it being on all hands agreed to belong either to a Spaniell or Greyhound, the King gave his opinion on the Part of the Greyhound, because (said he) it has all the Good-nature of the other, without the fawning.[3] A fine piece of Satire upon his Courtiers, with which I will conclude my Discourse of Dogs. Call me a Cynick or what you please, in revenge for all this Impertinence, I will be contented provided You will but believe me, when I say a bold Word for a Christian, that, of all Dogs, you shall find none more faithfull than | Dear Sir, | Your most Affectionate humble | Servant, | A: Pope:

Address: For Mr. Cromwell, att | the blue Ball in great Wild- | street, near Drury-Lane, | LONDON

Postmark: OC/21

||POPE to CROMWELL 30 *November* 1709

The Bodleian Library

Nov. 30. 1709.

Sir,—About the time that Mr. Wycherley came to London, I troubled you with a Letter of mine, in hopes of prevailing with you to continue

[1] Plutarch, *Life of Themistocles*, x. Pope in all his printed texts omits the parenthetical remark.

[2] The two words in brackets are not in the original letter, but Pope inserted them in all his printed texts.

The tale of Wild-brat came to Pope perhaps through the English version of La Combe de Vrigny's *Relation . . . d'un voyage . . .en Danemark*, under the title of *Travels through Denmark . . . by Way of Journal . . . in 1702* (London, 1707), pp. 295–6. In his revival of the older Order of the Elephants, King Frederick II added to an earlier motto the words: TREU. IST. WILDT. BRAT.

[3] Sir Philip Warwick tells this story in his Memoirs.—Warburton, 1751. (See *Memoires of the Reigne of King Charles I* (1701), p. 329.)

the favor of yours. But I now write, to convince you that Silence is not always the surest Guard against Impertinence: I have too great a Sense of those many Civilities receivd from you, to desist from expressing it, till I receive more: For you not only have acquainted me with many of my Errours in Scribling, but with some in my Conduct; & I owe to you the knowledge of Things infinitely more of concern to my self, than any thing of mine can be to others. The Advantage I have obtain'd from both might indanger your being put upon an endless Trouble of criticising on the rest of my Faults, and therfore you have reason to make some delay with those now under your Examination. Tho' I never cou'd expect you shou'd once look upon them but when you were perfectly at leisure; yet so much Assurance your former Kindness had given me, that I was under some Apprehensions for your Health, on the score of your Silence: and I desir'd Mr. Wycherly to inform me on that subject; which he did not, either thro' forgetfulness, or else believing I shou'd be soon in Town. And I had certainly been there before this time, had It been in my power to comply with his most obliging Invitation, and my Desires of seeing Him & you. But since I find I must not hope for that Satisfaction till after Christmas, I entreat you will not, in the meantime, let me be so unhappy as to doubt of your Welfare; which is the sole business of this Letter, that (to make you some amends for the unconscionable Length of my last) shall not add a Word more but that which I hope you will ever believe, that I am | Dear Sir, Your most oblig'd and most | humble Servant, | A: Pope:

Pray continue to assure Mr W. of my real affection for, and Service to him, and let him know I writ to him 2 Posts since.[1] You will likewise oblige me by giving my Service to Mr Betterton when you see him, who (I am afraid) is not well, not having seen his name among the Actors in the publick Advertisements.

Address: To Henry Cromwell, Esq: | at the blue Ball in Great Wild street, | near Drury Lane, | LONDON

Postmark: PENY POST PAYD

||POPE *to* CROMWELL[2] 15 *December* 1709

The Bodleian Library

Decr. 15. 1709.

I receivd the favour of your kind Letter wherein I find you have obligd me before I expected it, in reviewing the Papers I sent you; I

[1] An unknown letter.

[2] Though printed by Curll from the original, Pope never included this letter in any of his editions.

have been askd, I believe twenty times, by Sr William Trumbull for a sight of that Translation, but have deferrd it till I coud supply the Blank Spaces I left in the fair Copy by your Approbation.[1] If therfore You will send it inclos'd to Mr Thorold the Tobacconist in Duke-street, to be sent me by the Coach, as soon as you can conveniently, It will come very opportunely; since I find I can no longer refuse to show it to Sir William, with any decency. I am mightily plea[sd] with your Objection to my attributing Friendship to Dogs, yet think the Want of Equality is no Obstacle to the Friendship of some Country Gentlemen of my acquaintance, with theirs. I am extremly impatient to enjoy your agreable Conversation, and to let you know how much I prefer it to any here, where indeed Dogs & Men are much on a levell, only the first have more Goodnature & more Sagacity. If I were not at this instant very much afflicted with the headake, I woud offer a few more Considerations in behalf of the four-legg'd Part of the Creation. But I will only add one word, that you and I will never disagree about Dogs, or anything else, for I am with very much Esteem, & ever will be | Your most faithful Friend | & humble Servant | A. Pope.

[2]I design to write to Mr Wycherley by this Post, in answer to the most kind and friendly Letter I ever receiv'd. I shall never be unhappy or melancholly in the Country, as long as he and you will oblige me with your Letters.

Address:[3] For Henry Cromwell, Esqr: at | the blue Ball in great | Wildstreet, near drury lane | LONDON

Postmark: DE/16

[1] 'Sapho to Phaon' appeared in Tonson's publication of Ovid's *Epistles* (Mar. 1712), and Pope's translation of 'The First Book of Statius his Thebais' appeared in Lintott's *Miscellaneous Poems and Translations* (May 1712). Either may here be in question.

[2] The postscript is written in the left margin of the letter.

[3] The address is not in Pope's hand.

1710

In his letters of 1710 Pope shows himself as the complete literary man—with some echoes of coffee-house gossip that mark him as the potential young man about town. For Wycherley he is revising some rather dull and repetitious poems, and revising in a way that was to cause a temporary estrangement. With Cromwell he was exchanging critical—and pedantic—comments, chiefly on the verses of rival poets publishing in Tonson's sixth volume of *Miscellanies* (1709). The year sees only one letter addressed to a third correspondent, the first of many letters to be sent to his friend John Caryll.

WYCHERLEY *to* POPE[1] — 14 *February* 1710

Longleat Portland Papers, xiii (Harleian transcripts)

Dear Mr Pope,—I must needs tell you, in the Stile of the wise Recorder of London;[2] who told King James, after the death of King Charles; he came to him, with Sorrow in one hand, and grief in t'other; (tho' he meant Joy,) So your Letter, brings me sorrow in one Sense, and joy, in another; Sorrow for your indisposition, and joy, that it will not hinder You, from coming to Town; In the mean time, I am not a little concern'd, that, that Head, which gives your Friends, so much pleasure, shou'd give you so much pain; but since it gives you no pain in pleasing the World with its Productions, you must be contented with some pain it gives you otherways. Most things which are most delightful & pleasant give the owners of them most pain; ⌜a Maidenhead, you know, (or shou'd know;) gives a Man, or Woman, most pain, as it gives 'em, most Pleasure,⌝ So that, we must take one with t'other; The most pregnant Womb, is often most vex'd; the most productive, & fruitful Soyl, is most Plow'd, and tourn up; so that, there is no advantage, or pleasure without Labour or Pains; No drunkeness, which gives Joy to the Head and Heart over night, but gives sorrow & pain to both the next morning; So that you see, by less'ning ones Sense, as well as emproving it, the Head must suffer some pain; thus if pain, must be the concomitant of Pleasure, you must not wonder, that your Head, which thinks and writes without Pains, (to give us Pleasure,) shou'd give you otherways so much pains; where-

[1] First printed in Elwin–Courthope, v. 402. Omissions made in that text are here placed in half-brackets. Many commas are here omitted.

[2] Sir George Treby ceased to be Recorder in 1683, and Sir Salathiel Lovell had the office beginning in 1692: who produced the wonderfull gaffe recorded here is uncertain.

fore come to Town, and we will make your Head ake for something; therefore bear the Head-ach heroically, (which you suffer by too much Studdy,) and which will be so far from short'ning your Life, that it will give you Immortality; since your Head (Mr Pope,) like the Head of the Church, can save, or damn, any of your Followers, and their ill works, by the Supererogation of your good works, good example, and infallable Judgment, that is, by your Approbation or Sensure; but I am afraid my Damn'd Works, cannot be sav'd otherways than by Fire, without You lend your Ayd, (Mr Pope) to their Salvation, and mine, by correcting their Faults; and giveing them your plenary Indulgence and me; who am an implicit believer in your Power and the Infallibility of your Judgment, consequently, | Your humble Servant | W: Wycherley.

London. Feb: the 14th 1710

My humble service pray, to your good Father, and Mother, I will endeavour to waite upon Sir Wm Trumbold before he goes out of Town.

||WYCHERLEY *to* POPE[1] 1 *April* 1710

Longleat Portland Papers, xiii (Harleian transcripts)

My Dear Mr Pope,—I have had yours, of the 30th of the last Month, which is kinder, than I desire it shou'd be, since it tells me you cou'd be better pleas'd to be sick again in Town in my Company than to be well in the Country without it; and that you are more impatient to be depriv'd of happiness than of health; ⌜very fine Mr Pope, ye gad! (as Bays wou'd say;)⌝ yet my Dear Friend, set Railery or Compliment aside, I can bear your absence, (which procures your Health, and Ease,) better than I can your Company, when You are in pain; for I cannot see you so, without being so too; your love to the Country, I do not doubt; nor do you (I hope,) my love to it, or you; since there, I can enjoy your Company, without seeing you in pain to give me Satisfaction and Pleasure; There I can have you without Rivals or Disturbers; without the Cromwells too Civil or the Titcombs too Rude;[2] without the noise of the Loud, and the Sensure of the Silent, and wou'd rather have you abuse me there, with the Truth, than at this distance with your Compliment; since now, your buisness of a Friend and kindness to a Friend is by finding fault with his faults, and mending them, by your oblidging severity ⌜to them; wherefore⌝

[1] Printed by Pope with some small omissions, here restored in half-brackets. The Longleat text is found in Elwin–Courthope, v. 403–5. Here, as there, it is repunctuated.

[2] without the Cromwells . . . too Rude] without the C—s too civil, or the T—s too rude *1735*; without the too civil or the too rude *octavos 1737–42. Omitted in the quarto and folio of 1737.*

I hope (in spight[1] of your good nature) you will have no cruel charity, for those Papers of mine, You were so willing to be troubled with, which I take most infinitly kindly of you; and shall acknowledge with gratitude, as long as I live; ⌜since⌝ no friend can do more for his Friend than preserving his Reputation, (nay not by preserving his Life,) since by preserving his Life, he can only make him live about threescore or fourscore Years; but by preserving his Reputation, he can make him live as long as the World lasts; so ⌜give him Immortality here and⌝ save him from damning; when he is gone to the Devil; wherefore,[2] pray condemn me in private, as the Thieves do their Accomplices in Newgate, to save them from Condemnation by the publick, ⌜therefore, I hope you will⌝ be most kindly Unmerciful, to my poetical Faults, and do with my Papers, as you Country Gentlemen do with your Trees; slash, cut, and lopp of the Excressness and dead parts of my wither'd Bays, that the little remainder may live the longer; and ⌜burn the bulk of my writings, to⌝ encrease the value of them, by deminishing the number ⌜of them; as the Dutch, burn three parts of their spices (from the Indies) to add to value of the Remainder; so to magnify their price, by lessening their Store⌝.

I have troubled you with my Papers, rather to give you pains than Pleasure notwithstanding your Compliment, which says you take that trouble kindly: such is your generosity to your Friends, that you take it kindly, to be desir'd by them to do them a Kindness; and think it done to you, when they give you an opportunity to do it to Them; wherefore you may be sure to be troubled with my Letters, out of Interest if not kindness; since mine to You will procure yours to me; so that I write to You, more for my own sake than Yours, less to make you think I write well than to learn from You to write better; thus you see Intrest in my kindness; which is like the Friendship of the world, rather to make a Friend than be a Friend; but I am Yours, ⌜not⌝ as ⌜a feigning lying Poet, but⌝ a true plain Dealer, ⌜(especially) when I tell you I am, ⌜(my Dear Mr Pope)⌝ | Your most obliged Friend, and | real humble Servant, | W: Wycherley⌝

⌜London April the 1st 1710.⌝

⌜Pray let me hear from you before I go out of Town which may be, yet ten days, or there abouts.⌝

⌜My humble service to your good Father, and Mother, and to that most Ingenious, and Honourable Gentleman, good Sir Wm Trumbold, in the mean time, I shall be sure to make your Compliment to Cromwell the gentle, and to the rest of the Coffee house Vertuosos, who are Statesmen, and no Politicians; Sensurers, and no Criticks, Poets, and no Wits.⌝

[1] spight] point *all Pope's texts, 1735–42.*
[2] Devil; wherefore, pray] devil. Therefore I pray *1735–42.*

||POPE *to* CROMWELL 10 *April* 1710

The Bodleian Library

Sir,—I had written to you sooner but that I made some Scruple of sending Profane Things to You in Holy week.[1] Besides Our Family wou'd have been Scandalizd to see me write, who take it for granted I write nothing but ungodly[2] Verses⌈; and They say here so many Pray'rs, that I can make but few Poems: For in this point of Praying, I am an Occasional Conformist. So just as I am drunk or Scandalous in Town, according to my Company, I am for the same reason Grave & Godly here.⌉ I assure you I am look'd upon in the Neighborhood for a very Sober & well-disposd Person,[3] no great Hunter indeed, but a great Esteemer of the noble Sport, & only unhappy in my Want of Constitution for that, & Drinking. They all say 'tis pitty I am so sickly, & I think 'tis pitty Thay are so healthy: But I say nothing that may destroy their good opinion of me. I have not quoted one Latin Author since I came down, but have learn'd without book a Song of Mr Tho: Durfey's, who is your only Poet of tolerable Reputation in this Country. He makes all the Merriment in our Entertainments, & but for him, there wou'd be so miserable a Dearth of Catches, that I fear they wou'd (sans ceremonie)[4] put either the Parson or Me upon making some for 'em. Any Man, of any Quality, is heartily welcome to the best Topeing-Table of our Gentry, who can roundly humm out some Fragments or Rhapsodies[5] of his Works: So that in the same Manner as was said of Homer, to his Detractors; What? dares any man speak against Him who has given so many Men to Eat? (meaning the Rhapsodistes who liv'd by repeating his Verses) So may it be said of Mr Durfey, to his Detractors; Dares any one despise Him, who has made so many men Drink? Alas Sir! this is a Glory which neither You nor I must ever pretend to. Neither you, with your Ovid, nor I with my Statius, can amuse a whole Board of Justices and Extraordinary Esquires, or gain one Humm of Approbation, or Laugh of Admiration! These things (they wou'd say) are too Studious, they may do well enough with such as love Reading, but give us your ancient Poet, Mr Durfey! 'Tis mortifying enough, it must be confess'd; but however let us proceed in the way that Nature has directed us—Multi Multa Sciunt, sed nemo omnia, as it is said in the Almanack. Let us communicate our Works for our mutual Comfort; Se[nd] me Elegies,

[1] In 1710 Easter fell on 9 Apr.

[2] Pope omitted this word and the passage in half-brackets from the purified text of his quarto and folio in 1737.

[3] Neighborhood . . . Person] Neighborhood for a very well-disposed Person *all Pope's texts*; for *becomes* as *in the quarto and folio of 1737*.

[4] The parenthetical expression is missing in all Pope's texts.

[5] can . . . Rhapsodies] can roar out some Rhapsodies *all Pope's texts.*

and you shall not want Heroics. At present I only have these Arguments in Prose to the Thebaid,[1] which you claim by Promise, as I do your Translation of—Pars me Sulmo tenet—and the Ring.[2] The rest I hope for as soon as you can conveniently transcribe 'em, and whatsoever Orders you please to give me shall be punctually obey'd.

Dear Sir, I give you my thanks for abundance of Civility & Good-nature shown to me in Town on all occasions, & desire you to believe me always sensible of the Favors of my Friends, which I never forget, any more than I do my Friends themselvs. 'Tis the chief of my Pleasures here, to be assur'd of their welfare, & I envy the Town for nothing else but their continuing in it. You will oblige me by giving my Service to those at the Coffeehouse that have so little to employ their Thoughts as to inquire of me: and pray when you see Mr Balam, do the same, who (you told me) was so obliging as to intend me his Company before I left London. I am in great impatience of the favor of a line from you, which will be at all times extreamly welcome to | Sir | Your very faithfull and | oblig'd Servant, | A: Pope.

Apr: 10th 1710.

Address: For Henry Cromwell, Esqr: to | be given to Mr. Tho: Thorold, at the | King's head in Duke-street, near | Lincolns-Inn-fields. | London

Endorsements: Carr: paid [on the cover of the letter]. Mr Popes Letters [at the end of the letter. In Cromwell's hand?]

†WYCHERLEY *to* POPE[3] 11 *April* 1710

1729

April 11, 1710.

If I can but do part of my Business at *Shrewsbury* in a Fortnights time (which I propose to do) I will be soon after with you, and trouble you with my Company, for the remainder of the Summer: In the mean time I beg you to give your self the pains of altering, or leaving out what you think superfluous in my Papers, that I may endeavour to print such a Number of them as you and I shall think fit, about *Michaelmas* next;[4] in order to which (my dear Friend) I beg you to be so kind to me, as to be severe to them; that the Criticks may be less so; for I had rather be condemn'd by my Friend in private, than expos'd to my Foes in publick, the Criticks, or common Judges, who are made such by having been old Offenders themselves. Pray believe I have as much Faith in your Friendship and Sincerity, as I have

[1] Pope prefixed a prose 'Argument' to his translation, and perhaps at this time had an argument for each fragment translated (see Pope to Cromwell, 19 Jan. 1707/8).

[2] Cromwell seems to have intended translating Ovid's *Amores*, ii. 15 and 16.

[3] Omitted from the quarto and folio of 1737.

[4] Wycherley did not print—possibly by Pope's advice.

Deference to your Judgment; and as the best Mark of a Friend, is telling his Friend his Faults in private, so the next is concealing them from the publick, 'till they are fit to appear; in the mean time I am not a little sensible of the great kindness you do me, in the trouble you take for me, in putting my Rhimes in Tune, since good Sounds set off often ill Sense, as the *Italian* Songs, whose good Airs, with the worst Words, or Meaning, make the best Musick; so by your tuning my *Welch* Harp, my rough Sense may be the less offensive to the nicer Ears of those Criticks, who deal more in Sound than Sense. Pray then take Pity at once both of my Readers and me, in shortning my barren Abundance, and increasing their Patience by it, as well as the Obligations I have to you; and since no Madrigaller can entertain the Head, unless he pleases the Ear; and since the crowded Opera's have left the best Comedies with the least Audiences, 'tis a sign Sound can prevail over Sense; therefore soften my Words, and strengthen my Sense, and

Eris mihi magnus Apollo.[1]

†POPE *to* WYCHERLEY[2] 15 *April* 1710

1737

April 15, 1710.

I receiv'd your most extream kind letter but just now. It found me over those papers you mention, which have been my employment ever since Easter-monday: I hope before Michaelmas to have discharg'd my task; which, upon the word of a friend, is the most pleasing one I cou'd be put upon. Since you are so near going into Shropshire, (whither I shall not care to write of this matter, for fear of the miscarriage of any letters) I must desire your leave to give you a plain and sincere account of what I have found from a more serious application to them. Upon comparison with the former volume, I find much more repeated than I till now imagin'd, as well as in the present volume, which, if (as you told me last) you would have me dash over with a line, will deface the whole copy extremely and to a degree that (I fear) may displease you. I have ev'ry where mark'd in the margins the page and line, both in this and the other part. But if you order me not to cross the lines, or would any way else limit my commission, you will oblige me by doing it in your next letter; for I am at once equally fearful of sparing you, and of offending you by too impudent a correction. Hitherto however I have crost 'em so as to be legible, because you bade me. When I think all the repetitions are struck out in a copy, I sometimes find more upon dipping in the first volume, and the number increases so much, that I believe more shortning will be requisite

[1] Virgil, *Eclogues*, iii. 104.

[2] First printed in the Roberts octavo in 1737, and included in the later octavos.

than you may be willing to bear with, unless you are in good earnest resolv'd to have no thought repeated. Pray forgive this freedom, which as I must be sincere in this case so I cou'd not but take, and let me know if I am to go on at this rate, or if you would prescribe any other method?

I am very glad you continue your resolution of seeing me in my Hermitage this summer; the sooner you return, the sooner I shall be happy, which indeed my want of any company that is entertaining or esteemable, together with frequent infirmities and pains, hinder me from being in your absence. 'Tis (I am sure) a real truth, that my sickness cannot make me quite weary of my self when I have you with me; and I shall want no company but yours, when you are here.

You see how freely and with how little care, I talk rather than write to you: this is one of the many advantages of friendship, that one can say to one's friend the things that stand in need of pardon, and at the same time be sure of it. Indeed I do not know whether or no the letters of friends are the worse, for being fit for none else to read? 'tis an argument of the trust reposed in a friend's good nature, when one writes such things to him as require a good portion of it. I have experienced yours so often and so long, that I can now no more doubt of the greatness of it, than I hope you do of the greatness of my affection, or of the sincerity with which I am, &c.

||WYCHERLEY *to* POPE[1] — 27 *April* 1710

Longleat Portland Papers, xiii (Harleian transcripts)

⌜My Dear Mr Pope,—I answer'd yours of the 15th (which I think was the last, I had from you) about three days after my receiving it; but having not yet receiv'd any Answer to it from You, I doubt your old pain of the head-ach, has prevented it; which gives me, a great deal of concern for You, in so much, that I have had thoughts, of making You a Visit, before my Journey, into Shropshire; which has been delay'd, by delays, and disappointments to me, out of the Country.⌝

You give me an Account in your Letter, of the trouble you have undergone for me, in Compareing my Papers, you took down with you, with the old printed Volume, and with one another, of that Bundle, you have in your Hands; amongst which, (You say,) you find numerous repetitions[2] of the same thoughts, and Subjects, all which, I must confess my want of memory has prevented me from

[1] Pope printed this letter, making omissions here placed in half-brackets, 1729–42. In 1729 the year date was misprinted as 1718. This was corrected in the errata leaf of 1735. The Longleat text (here given) was printed in Elwin–Courthope, v. 405–7.

[2] The truth of this may be seen in the whole printed Volume of his *Miscellanies* in Folio in 1704, in almost every Page.—Pope, 1729 (omitted, 1737–42).

imagining; as well as commiting them;[1] since of all Figures, that of Tautologie, is the last I would use, or least forgive my self for; but seeing, is believing; wherefore I will take some pains, to examine and compare those Papers in your hands, with one another, as well as with the former printed Coppy, or Book, of my damn'd[2] Miscellanys; all which, (as bad a memory, as I have,) with a little more pains, and care, I think I can remedy; wherefore, I wou'd not have You give your self more trouble about them; which may prevent the pleasure you have, and may give the World, in writing upon new Subjects of your Own, whereby you will much better entertain your self, and the World.[3] Now as to your remarks, upon the whole volume of my Papers; all that I desire of You, is to mark in the Margent, (without defaceing the Coppy at all,) either any Repetition, of words, matter, or Sense, or any thoughts, or words, too much repeated, which, if you will be so kind, as to form,[4] you will supply my want of memory, with your good one, and my deficience of Sense, with the infalibility of yours, which if you do, you will most infinitely oblige me, who almost repent the trouble I have given You, since so much. Now, as to what you call freedom with me, (which you desire me, to forgive ⌜You;⌝) you may be assured, I would not forgive you, unless you did use it ⌜with me⌝; for I am so far from thinking your plainness, ⌜a fault, or⌝[5] an offence to me, that I think it a Charity, & an obligation; which I shall always acknowledge, with all sort of gratitude to you, for it, who am therefore | (Dear Mr Pope) | Your most obliged humble Servant | W: Wycherley.

London April the 27th 1710

All the News I have, to send you is, that poor Mr Betterton, is going to make his Exit from the Stage of this World,[6] the Gout, being gotten up into his Head, and (as the Physicians say,) will certainly carry him of suddenly.

⌜My most humble service pray, to Sir Wm Trombold, and your good Father, and Mother, whilst I can assure you from hence, all the world here, are your Servants, and Friends.⌝

⌜I know not, but I may See You very suddenly at Binfield, after all my broken promisses.⌝

[1] as well... them] as well as made me capable of committing them *1729–42*. (The omission in the transcript is probably an error.)

[2] damn'd] *omitted in 1737 b*. In all Pope's printed texts we have *copies* and *books* instead of the singular forms.

[3] and the World] and others *1729–42*.

[4] to form] to do for me *1729–42*. (Pretty certainly what Wycherley wrote!)

[5] This omission occurs first in the Roberts octavo (1737). It is found thereafter in all Pope's octavos.

[6] Thomas Betterton died the day after this letter was written—28 Apr. 1710.

†POPE *to* WYCHERLEY[1] 2 *May* 1710

1729

May 2, 1710

I am sorry you persist to take ill my not accepting your Invitation, and to find (if I mistake not) your Exception not unmixt with some Suspicion. Be certain I shall most carefully observe your Request, not to cross over, or deface the Copy of your Papers for the future, and only to mark in the Margin the Repetitions: But as this can serve no further than to get rid of those Repetitions, and no way rectify the *Method*, nor *connect* the *Matter*, nor improve the *Poetry* in *Expression* or *Numbers*, without further blotting, adding, and altering; so it really is my opinion, and desire, that you should take your Papers out of my hands into your own; and that no Alterations may be made but when both[2] of us are present; when you may be satisfied with every Blot, as well as every ⌜Alteration and⌝[3] Addition, and nothing be put upon the Papers but what you shall give your own sanction and assent to at the same time.

Do not be so unjust, as to imagine from hence that I would decline any part of this Task: On the contrary you know, I have been at the pains of transcribing some Pieces, at once to comply with your desire of not defacing the Copy, and yet to lose no Time in proceeding upon the Correction. I will go on the same way if you please; tho' truly it is (as I have often told you) my sincere Opinion, that the greater Part would make a much better Figure, as *Single Maxims* and *Reflections* in Prose, after the manner of your favourite *Rochefoucaut*, than in Verse.[4] And this, when nothing more is done but marking the Repeti-

[1] This was the latest of the letters in this correspondence with Wycherley to be printed by Pope. In the 1729 edition more than the latter half of it fell on p. 51, the first leaf in sheet H. In reissuing the Wycherley sheets of 1729 in 1735 it seemed wise to reprint the whole of sheet H. Pope took the opportunity to make two small changes in the text and to lengthen the valedictory footnote.

[2] From this point the type was reset for the editions of 1735. The editor owes this discovery to the acumen of Professor V. A. Dearing.

[3] Alteration and] *omitted 1735–42*.

[4] Here in his editions of 1735–42 Pope appended the following footnote in the nature of valedictory:

'Mr. *Wycherley* lived five Years after, to *December* 1715, but little progress was made in this Design, thro' his Old age, and the increase of his Infirmities. However some of the Verses which had been touch'd by Mr. P. with 308 of these Maxims in Prose were found among his Papers, which having the misfortune to fall into the Hands of a Mercenary, were published in 1728, in Octavo, under the Title of *The Posthumous Works of William Wycherley, Esq.*'

When Curll, ten days after Pope's first edition of 1735 was sold in his shop, reprinted the letters in volume i of *Mr. Pope's Literary Correspondence*, he felt disinclined to fight Pope's battles with 'mercenaries', and so modified Pope's note to read: 'But little Progress was made in this Design, by Mr. *Wycherley*, thro' his old Age, and the Increase of his Infirmities. He died 1715, and was buried in the Vault of St. *Paul*'s Church, *Covent Garden*.' Curll reprinted this note in his later editions.

tions in the Margin, will be an easy Task for your self to do,[1] notwithstanding the bad Memory you complain of. I am unfeignedly, dear Sir, | Your, &c.

[2]⌜The End of Mr. *Wycherley's* Letters.⌝

||POPE *to* CROMWELL 17 *May* 1710

The Bodleian Library

Sir,—After I had recoverd from a dangerous Illness which was first contracted in Town, about a Fortnight after my coming hither, I troubled you with a Letter & a Paper inclos'd,[3] which you had been so obliging as to desire a sight of when last I saw you, promising me in return some Translations of yours from Ovid; Since when I have not had a Syllable from your hands; so that 'tis to be feard that tho' I have escap'd Death, I have not Oblivion. I shou'd at least have expected you to have finishd that Elegy upon me, which you told me you was upon the point of beginning when I was sick in London; If you will but do so much for me first, I will give you leave to forget me afterwards; & for my own part, will dye at discretion, & at my leisure. But I fear I must be forc'd, like many learned Authors, to write my own Epitaph, if I wou'd be remember'd at all; Mons. de la Fontaine's wou'd fitt me to a hair,[4] but 'tis a kind of Sacriledge (do you think it is not?) to steal Epitaphs? In my present, living, dead Condition, nothing wou'd be properer than Oblitusque meorum, obliviscendus et illis—but that unluckily I cannot quite forget my Friends, & the Civilities I receivd from one Mr Cromwell & some others. They say indeed tis one Quality of generous Minds to forget the Obligations they have conferr'd, and perhaps too it may be so, to forget those on whom they conferr'd 'em? Then indeed I must be forgotten to all Intents & purposes. I am, it must be own'd, Dead in a Natural Capacity, according to Mr Bickerstaff;[5] Dead in a Poetical Capacity, as a damn'd

[1] to do] to proceed upon *1735–42*.

[2] This line was dropped in 1735. To it in 1729 Pope had appended the following note, not thereafter reprinted: 'He dy'd five Years after, in *December* 1715. Aged about Fourscore.'

[3] Verses on *Silence* in imitation of the Earl of Rochester's poem on Nothing; done at 14 years old.—Pope, 1737–42.

[4] La Fontaine's epitaph for himself, published in 1671, suited Pope's whim of the moment:

> Jean s'en alla comme il étoit venu,
> Mangea le fonds avec le revenu,
> Tint les trésors chose peu nécessaire,
> Quant à son temps, bien le sut dispenser:
> Deux parts en fit, dont il souloit passer
> L'une à dormir et l'autre à ne rien faire.

See *Œuvres de La Fontaine* (ed. H. de Régnier, 1892), ix. 80.

[5] In *The Tatler* Steele prolonged the joke against the astrologer Partridge by assuming the pseudonym Bickerstaff and by announcing in No. 1: 'I shall from time to time print

Author; and dead in a Civill Capacity, as a useless Member of the Commonwealth ⌜buryd in solitude⌝.[1] But reflect dear Sir, what melancholly Effects may ensue, if Dead Men are not Civil to one another? if He who has nothing to do himself will not comfort & support another in his Idleness? if Those who are to dye themselves will not now and then pay the Charity of Visiting a Tomb and a dead Friend, and strowing a few Flow'rs over him? In the Shades where I am, the Inhabitants have a mutual Compassion for each other: Being all alike *Inanes*, & *Umbratiles*,[2] we Saunter to one anothers Habitations & daily assist each other in doing Nothing at all; All this I mention for your Edification & Example, that *Tout plein de vie*[3] as you are, yet You may not sometimes disdain—*desipere in loco*. At least Remember the Dead, you that are among the Living.[4] Tho you are no Papist, and have not so much regard to the dead as to address yourself to them, (which I plainly perceive by your silence) yet I hope you are not one of those Heterodox, who hold the dead to be totally Insensible of the good Offices & kind Wishes of their living friends, & to be themselves in a dull State of Sleep, without one Dream of those they left behind them? If you are, Let this Letter convince you to the contrary, which assures you I am still, 'tho in a State of Separation, | Sir, | Your most faithfull and affectionate | humble Servant, | A. Pope.

May the 17. 1710.

P.S. This Letter of Deaths, puts me in mind of poor Mr Betterton's;[5] over whom I wou'd have this Sentence of Tully for an Epitaph.[6]

Vitæ bené actæ jucundissima est recordatio.

Address: For Henry Cromwell, Esq; | to be left at the Widow Hambleton's | Coffee house in Princes Street, | near Drury Lane, | LONDON.

Postmark: (illegible).

bills of mortality; and I beg the pardon of all such who shall be named therein, if they who are good for nothing shall find themselves in the number of the deceased.' Pope represents himself as 'good for nothing'. He may have had vaguely in mind a new farce by Mrs. Centlivre, *A Bickerstaff's Burying*, first acted at Drury Lane on 27 Mar. 1710.

[1] buryd in solitude] *omitted in all Pope texts.*

[2] & *Umbratiles*] *omitted in octavos 1737–42.*

[3] *Tout plein de vie*] all alive *1737–42.*

[4] This sentence is omitted in all Pope's texts.

[5] This great actor, one of Pope's earliest friends, died 28 Apr. 1710. Almost the only identifiable painting by Pope still existing is a portrait of Betterton, copied by Pope from Kneller. It has long been in the possession of the descendants of Pope's friend the first Earl of Mansfield. The suggested epitaph is an adaptation of *De senectute*, iii. 9.

[6] Epitaph. | Vitæ] Epitaph, which will serve him as well in his Moral as Theatrical capacity. | Vitæ *1737–42.* (The longer reading first appears in the quarto and folio of 1737, not in the Roberts octavo. It is one of a very few cases where later octavos follow the quarto and folio rather than the Roberts octavo of 1737.)

||POPE *to* CROMWELL 24 *June* 1710

The Bodleian Library

June the 24th 1710.

'Tis very natural for a young Friend, and a young Lover, to think the Persons they love have nothing to do but to please them; when perhaps They, for their parts, had twenty other Engagements before. This was my case when I wonder'd I did not hear from you; but I no sooner receivd your short Letter, but I forgot your long Silence; and so many fine things as you said of me cou'd not but have wrought a cure on my own Sickness, if it had not been of the nature of that, which is Deaf to the Voice of the Charmer. 'Twas impossible you cou'd better have tim'd your Compliment on my Philosophy; it was certainly properest to commend me for it just when I most needed it, and when I cou'd least be proud of it; that is, when I was in Pain. Tis not easy to express what an Exaltation it gave to my Spirits, above all the Cordials of my Doctour; and tis no compliment to tell you that your Compliments were Sweeter than the sweetest of his Juleps & Syrups. But if you will not believe so much,

Pour le moins, vôtre Compliment
M'a soulagé dans ce moment;
Et des qu'on me l'est venu faire,
J'ay chassé mon Apoticaire,
Et renvoyé mon Lavement.

Nevertheless I wou'd not have you entirely lay aside the Thoughts of my Epitaph, any more than I do those of the probability of my becoming (e'er long) the Subject of one. For Death has of late been very familiar with some of my Size; I am told my Lord Lumley and Mr Litton[1] are gone before me; and tho I may now without vanity esteem my self the Least Thing like a Man in England, yet I can't but be sorry two Heroes of such a Make shou'd dye inglorious in their Beds; when it had been a Fate more worthy Our Size, had they met with theirs from an Irruption of Crane[s] or other Warlike Animals, that of old were Enemies to our Pygmaean Ancestors! You of a superior Species little regard what befalls us, Homunciolos Sesquipedales; however, you have no reason to be so unconcern'd, since all Physicians agree, there is no greater Sign of a Plague among Men, than a Mortality among Frogs. ⌜I was the other day in company with a Lady, who rally'd my Person so much, as to cause a total Subversion of my

[1] Aristocratic owners of the quarto and folio text (1737) found these names tactfully concealed as 'Lord L**y and Mr L**n'. Other texts print them as here. The Cooper octavo (1737) and later editions add the footnote: 'The names left out in the Author's Edit.' Viscount Lumley died of smallpox in Apr. 1710. He was evidently small of stature; see *Wentworth Papers*, 1883, p. 75 n.

Countenance: some days after, to be reveng'd on her, I presented her amongst other Company the following Rondeau on that occasion, which I desire you to show Sappho.

You know where you did despise
(Tother day) my little Eyes,
Little Legs, and little Thighs,
And some things, of little Size,
You know where.

You, tis true, have fine black eyes,
Taper Legs, and tempting Thighs,
Yet what more than all we prize
Is a Thing of little Size,
You know where.

This sort of writing calld the Rondeau is what I never knew practis'd in our Nation, and I verily believe it was not⌉[1] in use with the Greeks or Romans, neither Macrobius nor Higynus[2] taking the least notice of it. 'Tis to be observd, that the vulgar Spelling & Pronouncing it Round O: is a manifest Corruption, and by no means to be allow'd of by Criticks. Some may mistakingly imagine that it was a sort of Rondeau which the Gallic Soldiers sung in Caesar's Triumph over Gaul—Gallias Caesar Subegit, &c. as it is recorded by Suetonius in Julio:[3] and so derive its Original from the ancient Gauls to the Modern French: but this is erroneous, the Words there not being exactly rang'd according to the Laws of the Rondeau, as layd down by Clement Marot. If you will say that the Song of the Soldiers might be but the rude Beginning of this kind of Poem, & so consequently imperfect, neither Heinsius nor I are[4] of that opinion. And so I conclude, that we know nothing of the matter.[5]

—But Sir, I ask your pardon for all this Bouffonry, which I cou'd not address to any one so well as to you, since I have found by Experience, you most easily forgive my Impertinencies. 'Tis only to show you that I am mindful of you at all times, that I write at all; and as nothing that I can say can be worth your reading, so I may as well throw out what comes uppermost, as study to be dull.[6] When you are very Idle,

[1] Pope's version of Voiture together with the whole passage in half-brackets was omitted in the quarto and folio of 1737, where Pope substituted: 'I am glad you lik'd the foolish Rondeau I sent you upon my own Littleness: It is the first Rondeau, I believe, in our language. This sort of Poem seems not to have been . . .'

[2] Higynus] Hyginus *all printed texts.*

[3] Suetonius, *De Vita Caesarum*, I. xlix.

[4] are] can be *all Pope's texts.*

[5] In the quarto and folio of 1737 the letter ends here with the word *matter*.

[6] Apart from the quarto and folio texts of 1737 Pope's editions end this letter with the word *dull*. Curll printed (1726) all that is here given except the passages in the postscripted materials indicated in half-brackets. These he omitted, but he printed the postscripts about Englefield, placing the second first.

I hope to hear from you, for at such times you may remember there is in the world such a Thing as | Dear Sir Your most faithfull & humble | Servant | [A. Pope.][1]

⌜You will oblige me, when you have done with the Arguments to Statius, in sending 'em to me, with any Remarks you may have made on that Author. And by informing me when Mr Wycherly is in London.⌝

P.S. Mr Englefyld charges me to give you his most humble Service, & hopes the Ladies of Drury are no less favorable to you now than those of Paris were formerly.

⌜My humble Service, pray, to Mr Bedingfield, & to Mr Balam when you see either of them.⌝

Mr Englefyld always enquires of you, & drinks yours & Mr Wycherly's health with true Country Affection.

Address: To Henry Cromwell Esqr | to be left at the Widow Hambl[e-] | ton's Coffeehouse in Princes st[reet] | [ne]ar Drury lane, | LONDON.

Postmark: IV/26

†CROMWELL *to* POPE 15 *July* 1710

1735

July 15, 1710

At last I have prevail'd over a lazy humour to transcribe this Elegy: I have chang'd the situation of some of the *Latin* Verses, and made some Interpolations, but I hope they are not absurd, and foreign to my Author's sense and manner; but they are refer'd to your censure, as a debt; whom I esteem no less a Critic than a Poet: I expect to be treated with the same rigour as I have practis'd to Mr. *Dryden* and you,

Hanc veniam petimusque damusque vicissim.[2]

I desire the favour of your opinion, why *Priam*, in his speech to *Pyrrhus* in the second *Æneid*, says this to him,

At non ille satum quo te mentiris, Achilles.[3]

He wou'd intimate (I fancy by *Pyrrhus*'s answer) only his degeneracy: but then these following lines of the Version (I suppose from *Homer*'s History) seem absurd in the mouth of *Priam*, viz.

He chear'd my sorrows, and for sums of gold,
The bloodless carcase of my Hector sold.

I am, | Your, &c.

[1] The signature has been cut or worn away except for the top of the P. Curll or someone lined through the paragraph about Statius, presumably for omission.

[2] Horace, *De Arte Poetica*, l. 11.

[3] *Aeneid*, ii. 540.

†POPE *to* CROMWELL[1] 20 *July* 1710

1735

July 20, 1710.

I give you thanks for the Version you sent me of *Ovid*'s Elegy. It is very much an image of that author's writing, who has an agreeableness that charms us without correctness, like a mistress whose faults we see, but love her with them all. You have very judiciously alter'd his method in some places, and I can find nothing which I dare insist upon as an error: What I have written in the margins being meerly Guesses at a little improvement, rather than Criticisms. I assure you I do not expect you shou'd subscribe to my private notions but when you shall judge 'em agreeable to reason and good sense. What I have done is not as a Critic, but as a Friend; I know too well how many qualities are requisite to make up the one, and that I want almost all I can reckon up; but I am sure I do not want inclination, nor I hope capacity, to be the other. Nor shall I take it at all amiss, that another dissents from my opinion: 'Tis no more than I have often done from my own; and indeed, the more a man advances in understanding, he becomes the more every day a critic upon himself, and finds something or other still to blame in his former notions and opinions. ⌜I cou'd be glad to know if you have translated the 11th Elegy of *Lib.* 2. *Ad amicam navigantem.* the 8th of Book 3, or the 11th of Book 3, which are above all others my particular favourites, especially the last of these.⌝[2]

As to the passage of which you ask my opinion in the second *Æneid*, it is either so plain as to require no solution; or else (which is very probable) you see farther into it than I can.

Priam wou'd say, that '*Achilles* (whom surely you only feign to be your Father, since your actions are so different from his) did not use me thus inhumanly. He blush'd at his murder of *Hector* when he saw my sorrows for him; and restored his dead body to me to be buried.' To this the answer of *Pyrrhus* seems to be agreeable enough. 'Go then to the shades, and tell *Achilles* how I degenerate from him:' granting the truth of what *Priam* had said of the difference between them. Indeed Mr. *Dryden*'s mentioning here what *Virgil* more judiciously passes in silence, the circumstance of *Achilles*'s selling *for mony* the body of *Hector*, seems not so proper; it in some measure less'ning the character of *Achilles*'s generosity and piety, which is the very point of which *Priam* endeavours in this place to convince his Son, and to

[1] Pope may have printed the letter from Cromwell immediately preceding this so that in this letter he also could comment on Dryden's couplet which Cromwell had quoted. One wonders if Cromwell in his 'rigour' as a critic of Dryden had unsuccessfully tried to get Dryden to omit the lines. Both Cromwell and Pope agree that the mention of 'sums of gold' (which is not in Virgil) is injudiciously inserted.

[2] The sentence is omitted in the quarto and folio of 1737.

reproach him with the want of. But the truth of this circumstance is no way to be question'd, being expressly taken from *Homer*, who represents *Achilles* weeping for *Priam*, yet receiving the gold, *Iliad* 24: For when he gives the body, he uses these words, 'O my friend *Patroclus*! forgive me that I quit the corps of him who kill'd thee; I have great gifts in ransom for it, which I will bestow upon thy funeral.' I am. &c.

||POPE *to* CARYLL[1] 31 *July* 1710

Add. 28618

Binfield July the 31. 1710.

Sir,—After the kind permission you gave me to write to you, I shall make no more apologies, since a long apology for a dull letter is like a long preface to a dull book, which by endeavouring to make the reader amends, tires him no less than all the rest: For indeed 'tis the constant character of all fools that they are never contented with saying or doing one foolish thing; they will always commit another to maintain or defend it. However, the greatest fools are commonly knowing enough in their own interest, and mine in writing to you is plain enough since you promised to answer me. I may be very unworthy of that favour, but I can't be more undeserving of it than of those others you have obliged me with. And I've one reason to hope I've some share in your affection, which is my having a great deal for you; it being, I believe (as you may've heard me say before), with affections as with arrows, which then make the deepest impression in others' breasts, when they are drawn at first nearest our own. From hence I should confidently believe myself happy in your opinion, but for one thing, and that (to deal frankly with you) is your having treated me so often in a style of compliment; which has been too much honoured in being called the smoke of friendship, for it is a sort of smoke often seen where there is no fire. What the Tatler observes of women,[2] that they are more subject to be infected with vanity than men, on account

[1] In 1735 Pope used parts of this letter in making up the one he printed as to Wycherley, 23 June 1705. This letter is the first of about 150 letters that passed between Pope and John Caryll (1667–1736) of West Grinstead and Ladyholt (Harting). Caryll, a devout Catholic, was nephew and heir of John, Earl Caryll (of a Jacobite creation), who served as Secretary of State to the Old Pretender at St. Germain. The Carylls were connected with the Englefields, the Blounts of Mapledurham, the Pigotts, and with Lord Petre of Ingatestone, hero of *The Rape of the Lock*. The Caryll letters are preserved in somewhat careless transcripts, made before the originals were returned to Pope, who printed some of them but used more of them as materials 'cooked' into letters printed as to other men. In printing a few of the many letters to Caryll Pope did not print Caryll's name, but used the heading 'To the Hon. J. C.' In the ensuing years of Pope's career we shall meet many members of the Caryll family. See Max de Trenqualéon, *West-Grinstead et les Carylls*, 2 v., Paris, 1893.

[2] Possibly an allusion to *Tatler*, No. 120 or 123.

of their being more generally treated with civil things and compliments, is not strictly true in respect to that class of men who are looked upon to pique themselves upon their wit, and are no less usually entertained with fine Flamms, (as the old Earl of Leicester[1] used to call 'em) the world is never wanting, when a coxcomb is upon accomplishing himself, to help to give him the finishing stroke. I know no condition so miserable and blind as that of a young fellow who labors under the misfortune of being thought to think himself a wit; he must from that moment expect to hear no more truth than a prince or an emperor; and can never (if he have any sense) have any satisfaction in his own praise, since if given to his face, it can't be distinguished from flattery, and if behind his back, how can he be certain of it? In short, praise to young scriblers is like rain to young plants; if moderate nothing revives and encourages 'em so much, but if too lavish, nothing more overcharges and injures 'em.

Every man is apt to think his neighbour stocked with vanity and, generally speaking, with reason enough; yet I can't but think there are certain times when most men are in a disposition of being informed, and 'tis incredible what a vast good a very little truth might do, at some seasons! A very inconsiderable alms will do a great kindness to men in extreme necessities. And I could name an acquaintance, sir, of yours, who at this time would think himself more obliged to you for the friendly information of his faults, than for the civil confirmation of his follies. If you would make these the subject of your letters, it would prove so fruitful an one, that you could not complain for the future (as you were pleased lately to do) of any difficulty you could find in answering me, which I do not wonder you then might when you took upon you the task of commending me. But if you'll not be [so] charitable as to do this, at least, sir, be not so uncharitable as to do the other. If you will not instruct me, at least please me, which whatever comes from you certainly will, if your letters are but long enough; but if you said nothing more than that yourself, lady, son, daughter, and brother were well, you would in that single period tell me no less than four or five things that must always please me extremely. You see, sir, with what freedom I write or rather talk upon paper to you. They say a letter should be a natural image of the mind of the writer, but if mine were so it would have been full of nothing else but acknowledgments to you, which I durst not suffer it to be, for fear you should think me too grateful, a fault which none but good men are displeased at, tho' none but such are capable of it. And I know that sometimes a modest benefactor, like a modest mistress, ceases to confer favors when he finds they begin to be talked of.

[1] Robert Sydney (1649–1702), 4th Earl of Leicester, was a close friend of Wycherley's—from whom Pope may have learnt of 'flamms'.

But I am so pleased with writing to you, that nothing but seeing the end of my paper could put me in mind that 'tis high time to leave you to your own better thoughts, among which if you can ever entertain one of me, I beg it may be in the manner most to my advantage, that is to say that you will think me | Dear sir | Your most obliged and affect. humble | Servant | A: P:

P.S. | Mr Dancastle[1] joins with me in desiring all the good family to be assured of our most humble service; but he does it with a gesture and countenance so seriously civil, that 'tis impossible for me to express it, unless I could paint his humble service, as well as write it. All this I had told you, sir, long ago but for almost continual headaches these 3 weeks.

†CROMWELL *to* POPE — 3 *August* 1710

1735

Aug. 3, 1710.

Looking among some *French* Rhymes, I was agreeably surpriz'd to find in the *Rondeau* of [2]*Pour le moins*—your *Apoticaire* and *Lavement*, which I took for your own, so much is your Muse of Intelligence with the Wits of all languages. You have refin'd upon *Voiture*, whose *Ou Vous Sçavez* is much inferior to your *You know where*—You do[3] not only pay your club with your author (as our friend says) but the whole reckoning; who can form such pretty lines from so trivial a hint.

For my[4] Elegy; 'tis confess'd, that the Topography of *Sulmo* in the *Latin* makes but an awkward figure in the Version. Your couplet of the *Dog-Star* is very fine, but may be too sublime in this place. I laugh'd heartily at your note upon *Paradise*;[5] for to make *Ovid* talk of the Garden of *Eden*, is certainly most absurd: But *Xenophon* in his *Oeconomicks*, speaking of a garden finely planted and watered (as is here described) calls it *Paradisos*: 'Tis an interpolation indeed, and serves for a gradation to the *Cœlestial Orb*; which expresses in some sort the

[1] John Dancastle, Esq., of the manor of Binfield, and more especially his brother Thomas (d. 1728), were close friends of the Popes.

[2] In *Voiture's* Poems.—Pope, 1735–42.

[3] You have refin'd . . . *where*—You do] Your Rondeau is a refinement upon Voiture. You do *quarto and folio of 1737*.

[4] Ovid's Amorum, *l.* 2. El. 16. Pars me Sulmo, &c.—Pope, 1735–42.

[5] In Lintott's *Miscellaneous Poems and Translations* (1712) Cromwell printed two translations from the *Amores*: 'To his Mistress' (Bk. II, Elegy 16) and 'The Dream' (Bk. III, Elegy 5). He did not accept Pope's stricture on *paradise*, but printed:

> There 's no supporting of your Absence, here,
> Tho' Paradise was open'd all the Year;
> I'd sooner a Cœlestial Orb forgo,
> Than gain it, by so vast a Loss as you . . . (p. 120).

Sidus Castoris in parte Cœli—How *Trees can enjoy*, let the naturalists determine; but the Poets make 'em sensitive, lovers, bachelors, and married. *Virgil* in his *Georgicks Lib.* 2. *Horace Ode* 15. *Lib.* 2. *Platanus cœlebs evincet ulmos. Epod.* 2. *Ergo aut adulta vitium propagine Altas maritat populos.* Your Critique is a very *Dolce-piccante*; for after the many faults you justly find, you smooth your rigour: but an obliging thing is owing (you think) to one who so much esteems and admires you, and who shall ever be | Your, &c.

||POPE *to* CROMWELL[1] 21 *August* 1710

The Bodleian Library

Aug: 21. 1710.

Your Letters are a perfect Charity to a Man ⌜as much bury'd⌝ in Retirement ⌜as ever Hermit was,⌝ utterly forgotten of all his Friends but you; for since Mr Wycherly left London I have not heard a word from him; tho just before, and once since I writ to him, & tho I know myself guilty of no Offence but of doing sincerely, just what he bid me.[2]—Hoc mihi Libertas, hoc Pia Lingua dedit![3] But the greatest injury he does me, is the keeping me in Ignorance of his Welfare, which I am always very sollicitous for, & very uneasy in the Fear of any Indisposition that may befall him.—⌜I just now receivd notice from one whom I desird to enquire of your health, that you shall be in Town this Fortnight, & then design for Lincolnshire; before which I hope to hear from you, not being able to see you as I fully intended to have done this week. I expect a Solution of the Queries⌝[4] I sent you some time ago, where I think you have not Verse enough to be severe upon, in revenge for my last Critic:[5] in one point of which I must persist, that is to say, my Dislike of your Paradise, in which I take no pleasure; I know very well that in Greek tis not only usd by Xenophon, but is a common word for any Garden; but in English it ever bears the Signification, & conveys the Idea of Eden, which alone is (I think) a reason against making Ovid use it, who will be thought to talk too like a Christian in your Version at least, whatever it might have been in Latine or Greek. As for all the rest of my remarks, since

[1] As a footnote in 1737 e–42 pointed out, 'The beginning of this Letter to the words, In what I sent you, &c. is omitted in Mr. *Pope*'s Edition.' The texts printed by Pope in 1735 and in 1737 a follow Curll's text of 1726 except for omissions made by Pope and here placed in half-brackets.

[2] Correcting his Verses. See the Letters in 1706, and the following Years, of Mr. *Wycherley* and Mr. *Pope*.—Pope, 1735–42.

We have no letters that passed between Wycherley and Pope after 2 May 1710, but Cromwell's letters to Pope indicate that later letters were written.

[3] Ovid, *Heroides*, xv. 68.

[4] As indicated in note 1 the later texts of this letter began at this point, 'In what I sent you some time ago, you have not verse enough . . . .'

[5] Critic] Criticism *all printed texts*. But Pope wrote *critic* for the more modern *critique*.

you do not Laugh at 'em as at this, I can be so civil as not to lay any Stress upon 'em (as I think I told you before) & in particular in the point of *Trees Enjoying*, you have, I must own, fully satisfy'd me that the Expression is not only defensible, but beautifull. I shall be very glad to see your Translation of—*Ad Amicam Navigantem*, as soon as you can; for (without a Compliment to you) Every thing you write either in Verse or prose, is most welcome to me; and you may be confident, if my Opinion can be of any sort of consequence to any thing, that I will never be Unsincere, tho I may be often mistaken. To use Sincerity with you is but Paying you in your own Coin, from whom I have experienced so much of it; and I need not tell you how much I really Esteem ⌜and admire⌝ you, when ⌜I assure you⌝ I esteem ⌜and admire⌝ nothing in the World so much as that Quality. I know you sometimes say Civil Things to me in your Epistolary Style, but those I am to make allowance for, as particularly when you talk of *Admiring*;[1] Tis a word you are so us'd to in Conversation of Ladies, that it will creep into your Expressions in spite of you, ev'n to your friends. But as Women when they think themselvs secure of Admiration, commit a thousand Negligences, which show them so much at disadvantage, and off ⌜of⌝ their Guard, as to lose the little real ⌜Esteem or⌝ Love they had before; so when Men imagine others entertain some Esteem for their abilities, they often Expose all their Imperfections, & foolish Workes, to the disparagement of the little Wit they were thought Masters of: I am going to Exemplify this to you, in putting into your hands (being encoragd by so much Indulgence) some Verses of my Youth, or rather Childhood; which (as I was a great admirer of Waller) were intended in Imitation of his Manner;[2] and are perhaps, such Imitations, as those[3] which awkward Country Dames make, after the fine & well-bred Ladies of the Court. If you will take 'em with you into Lincolnshire, they may serve to save you one hour from the Conversation of the Country Gentlemen & their Tenants (who differ but in Dress and Name) which (if it be there as bad as here) is even worse than my Poetry. ⌜I fancy you have not many Sir Woolaston Dixey's in Lincolnshire, than whom I have not met with a better bred, or better natur'd Gentleman, & to whom I beg you will give my most humble Service.⌝[4] I hope your stay there will be no longer than (as Mr. Wycherley calls it) to Rob the Country, & run away to

[1] It is amusing to see Pope omitting the word *admire* twice so that he may reproach Cromwell with using it! The half-brackets in this part of the letter indicate omissions made in all Pope's texts.

[2] One or two of these were since printed among other Imitations done in his Youth.—Pope, 1737 quarto and thereafter.

[3] as those . . . the fine] as those you see in awkward Country Dames of the fine *all Pope's texts.*

[4] Omitted in all Pope's texts. Dr. Johnson, who lived in Sir Wolstan's house at Market Bosworth in 1732, found the baronet a man of 'intolerable harshness'.

London with your Money. In the mean time I beg the favor of a line from you, and am (as I will never cease to be) | Dear Sir | Your most oblig'd faith- | ful Friend, & humble Servant | A: Pope:

||POPE *to* CROMWELL 12 *October* 1710

The Bodleian Library

Octr 12. 1710.

I deferr'd answering your last, upon the advice I receivd that you were leaving the Town for some time, & expected your Return with Impatience, having then a design of seeing my Friends there, among the first of which I have reason to account yourself. But my almost continual Illnesses prevent that, as well as most other Satisfactions of my Life: However I may say one good thing of Sickness, that it is the best Cure in the world for Ambition, & Designs upon the World or Fortune; It makes a Man pretty Indifferent for the future, provided he can but be Easie, by Intervals, for the present. He will be content to compound for his Quiet only, & leave all the Circumstantial Part & Pomp of Life to those, who have a health vigorous enough to injoy all the Mistresses of their Desires. I thank God, there is nothing Out of myself which [I] wou'd be at the Trouble of seeking, except a Friend; a happiness I once hop'd to have possest ⌜in Mr W. but—Quantum Mutatus ab Illo!⌝[1]—I have for some years been employd much like Children that build Houses with Cards, endeav'ring very busily & eagerly to raise a Friendship, which the first Breath of any illnatur'd By-stander cou'd puff away.—But I will trouble you no further with writing, nor myself with thinking, of this subject.

I was mightily pleas'd[2] to perceive by your Quotation from Voiture that you had Track'd my Muses steps backward so far as France. You see it is with weak Heads as with weak Stomachs, they immediately throw out what they receivd last. And what they read, floats upon the Surface of their Minds, like Oil upon Waters, without incorporating. This, I think however can't be said of the Juvenile[3] Love verses I last troubled you with, where all (I am afraid) is so Puerile, & so like the author, that nobody will suspect any thing to be borrow'd. Yet you, (as a Friend, entertaining a better opinion of 'em) it seems, search'd in Waller, but searchd in vain. Your Judgment of 'em ⌜which you give in French,⌝ is (I think) very right,[4]—⌜for it was my own Opinion

[1] In the quarto and folio of 1737 the phrase in half-brackets is omitted. In all other early texts W. is expanded into Wycherley. *Quantum mutatus* was the posy beneath the famous mezzotint of Wycherley placed in his *Poems* (1704).

[2] Bowles and Elwin doubt the sincerity of Pope's pleasure!

[3] the juvenile Love verses] the Love verses *all Pope's texts.*

[4] In the quarto and folio of 1737 the paragraph ends with *right*, and omits the rest through *Sic servat... sui.* Within this section the other half-brackets indicate ingenious condensations made for Pope's octavo texts.

before. If you think 'em not worth the Trouble of Correcting, pray tell me so freely, & it will save me a Labour: if you think the contrary, you wou'd particularly oblige me by your Remarkes ⌜in the Margins⌝ on the several Thoughts, as they occurr, ⌜& sending me them when you have done.⌝—I long to be nibbling at your Verses, & have not forgot who it was that promisd me Ovid's Elegy ad Amicam Navigantem? Had Ovid been as long composing it, as you [have been in] sending it, the Lady might have saild to *Gades*, & receivd it at her Return. I have really a great Itch of Criticism upon me, & want Matter here in the Country; which I desire you to furnish me with, as I do you in the Towne.

[1]Sic Servat Studii Foedera quisque sui.⌝

I am oblig'd to Mr Caryl (whom you tell me you met at Epsom) for Telling you Truth, as a Man is in these days to any one that will tell Truth to one's advantage, & I think no Truth is more to mine than what he told you, & I shou'd be glad to tell all the world; That I have an extream Affection & Esteem for you.

Tecum etenim longos memini consumere Soles,
Et tecum primas epulis decerpere noctes,
Unum Opus et Requiem pariter disponimus ambo,
Atque verecunda laxamus seria mensa.[2]

By these *Epulae*, as I take it, Persius meant the Portugal Snuff and burn'd Claret which he took with his Master Cornutus, and the *Verecunda Mensa* was, without dispute, some Coffeehouse Table of the Ancients.—I will only observe that these four lines are as elegant & musicall as any in Persius, not excepting those 6 or 7 which Mr Dryden quotes as the only such in all that Author.[3]—I cou'd be heartily glad to repeat the Satisfaction describd in them,[4] ⌜but alas!

Fatis agimur, cedite fatis![5]
Which, in our Tongue, as I translate, is,
Fate rules us: then to Fate give way!
—Now, dreadful Critic! tell me pray,
What have you against this to say?

I am, desiring much to hear from you, | Dear Sir | Your ⌜most affectionate | Friend & faithful Servant | A: Pope:⌝

[6]P.S. ⌜I cou'd be glad to know if Mr Wycherly be in London when next you write:⌝ My *Sapho* (as you heathenishly Christen her) is more

[1] Ovid, *Ex Ponto*, II. v. 60. (*Sic* substituted for *Et*.) [2] Persius, v. 41–44.
[3] See Dryden's explanatory notes on the Sixth Satire of Persius, note 4.
[4] In reprinting from Curll Pope ended the letter at this point.
[5] Seneca, *Oedipus*, 980.
[6] Pope omitted the whole postscript. Curll, rather curiously, omitted the first sentence concerning Wycherley.

properly your Sapho, having been above this half year in Towne. My Service pray, to the Other *Sapho*, who tis to be hopd has not yet cast herself headlong from any of the *Leucades* about *London*, altho her Phaon lately fled from her into Lincolnshire.

Tu—Leucadia potes esse salubrior unda,
Et forma & meritis tu—Phoebus eris.[1]

My *Pylades!* what *Juvenal* says, no Jest is;
Scriptus & in tergo nec dum finitus Orestes.[2]

Address: To Henry Cromwell, Esq | at the Widow Hambleton's Coffee- | house in Princes street, near | Drury Lane, | LONDON | present
Postmark: OC/13

||POPE *to* CROMWELL[3] 28 *October* 1710

The Bodleian Library

The 28th of Octr 1710

I am glad to find by your last letter that you write to me with the freedome of a Friend, setting down your thoughts as they occurr, and dealing plainly with me in the matter of my own Triffles, which I assure you I never valud half so much as I do that Sincerity in you which they were the occasion of discovering to me: & which while I am happy in, I may be trusted with that dangerous weapon, Poetry; since I shall do nothing with it, but after asking & following your advice. I value Sincerity the more, as I find by sad Experience, the practise of it is more dangerous; Writers rarely pardoning the Executioners of their Verses, ev'n tho themselves pronounce sentence upon them.—As to Mr Philips's Pastoralls, I take the first to be infinitely the best, & the second the worst; the third is for the greatest part a Translation from Virgils Daphnis, ⌜& I think a good one.⌝ I will not forestall your judgment of the rest, [4]only observe that [in] that of the Nightingale, there are some very fine lines, & these in particular, (speaking of the Musician's Playing on the harp.)

[1] Ovid, Sapho to Phaon, *Heroides*, xv. 187–8.

[2] Juvenal, i. 6. 'Cromwell', so Elwin writes, 'could not perceive the application of this line, which is a playful apology of Pope for the length of his letter. He compares it to what Juvenal says of Codrus's tragedy of Orestes, which from its prolixity was written, contrary to the ancient custom, upon the back of the parchment as well as the front.' Pope's text, one may perhaps also note, from 'into Lincolnshire' is in part written on the cover, or back (*et in tergo*), of the letter.

[3] Pope omitted this letter from his quarto and folio of 1737, but printed it in his octavo editions with revisions and omissions. The omissions, indicated by half-brackets, show a desire to excise praise of Philips.

[4] only observe . . . (speaking] only observe in that of the Nightingale these lines (speaking *all Pope's texts.*

Now lightly skimming oer the strings they pass,
Like winds that gently brush the plying grass,
& melting Airs arise at their command;
And now, laborious, with a weighty hand,
He sinks into the Cords, with Solemn pace,
& gives the swelling Tones a Manly grace.

To which nothing can be objected but that they are too lofty for Pastorall, especially being put into the mouth of a Shepherd as they are here; In the Poets own person they had been (I believe) more proper. These are more after Virgils Manner than that of Theocritus, whom [yet] in the character of Pastoral he rather seems to imitate. In the whole, I agree with the Tatler, that we have no better Eclogs in our Language. This Gentleman, (if I am not much mistaken in his Talent) is capable of writing very nobly, as I guess by a small Copy of his, publishd in one of the first Tatlers, on the Danish Winter; Tis a very Lively Piece of Poetical Painting, and I recommend it particularly to your Perusall.[1]

Dr. Garths Poem[2] I have not yet seen, but believe I shall be of that Criticks opinion you mention at Will's, who swore it was Good: For tho I am very Cautious of Swearing after Critics, yet I think one may do it more safely, when they Commend, than when they blame.

I agree with you in your Censure of the Use of Sea-Terms in Mr Dryden's Virgill; not only because Helenus was no great Prophet in those matters, but because no Terms of Art, or Cant-Words, suit with the Majesty & dignity of Style [which] Epic Poetry requires—*Cui mens Divinior, atque Os Magna Sonit[urum]*[3]—The Tarpawlin-Phrase can please none but such, *Qui Au[rem] habent Batavam*; They must not expect *Auribus Atticis p[ro]bari*, I find by you. (I think I have brought in two Phrases of Martial[4] here, very dextrously.)

Tho you say you did not rightly take my meaning in the Verse I quoted from Juvenall,[5] in my last, yet I will not Explain it; because, tho' it seems you are resolvd to take me for a Critick; I wou'd by no means be thought a Commentator, and for another reason too, because I have quite forgot both the verse and the application.

I hope it will be no offence to give my most hearty Service to Mr Wycherley, tho' I perceive by his last Letter to me, I am not to trouble him with my Letters, since he there told me he was going instantly out of Town, & till his Return was my Servant, &c. I guess by yours he is

[1] For this sentence, faithfully printed by Curll, Pope substituted in his texts: 'There is a small copy of the same Author publish'd in the *Tatler*, No. 12, on the *Danish* Winter: Tis Poetical Painting, and I recommend it to your Perusal.'

[2] Verses to Lord Godolphin on his Dismissal from the Ministry.—Elwin. These appeared in *The Examiner* for 7 Sept. 1710.

[3] Horace, *Sermones*, I. iv. 43–44. Pope wrote and printed '*Soniturum*'.

[4] Martial, vi. 82 and iv. 87.

[5] See the note to the letter of 12 Oct. 1710.

yet with you; and beg you to do, what you may with all Truth and honour, that is assure him, I have ever born all the respect & kindness imaginable[1] to him, & all that is His. I protest by all that is holy, I do not in the least Know to this hour what it is that has Estrang'd him from me; but [all] this I know, that he may for the future be more Safely [& less] chargeably my friend,[2] since no Invitation he can make shall ever more make me so free with him. I cou'd not have thought any man had been so very cautious and suspicious, as not to credit his own Experience of a Friend. Indeed to believe nobody, may be a Maxime of Safety, but not so much of honesty. There is but one way I know of Conversing safely with all men, that is, not by concealing what we say or do, but by saying or doing nothing that deserves to be conceald, & I can truly boast this Comfort, in my affairs with Mr W.[3] I beg you Sir to pardon my speaking well of my self in this One thing, since I doubt not but Mr W. speaks ill enough of me in some others.[4] But I pardon his Jealousy, which is become his Nature, & shall never be his Enemy whatsoever he says of me—I am most sincerely, & will ever be, | Dear Sir | Your most obligd & affectionate | humble Servant & Friend | A: Pope.[5]

Address: To Henry Cromwell, Esq: | at the Widow Hambleton's | Coffee-house, in Princes street, | near Drury lane, | LONDON | present. |

Postmark: OC/30

†CROMWELL *to* POPE — 5 *November* 1710

1735

Nov. 5, 1710.

I find I am oblig'd to the sight of your Love-verses, for your opinion of my sincerity; which had never been call'd in question, if you had not forc'd me, upon so many other occasions to express my esteem.[6]

I have just read and compar'd [7]Mr. *Row*'s Version of the 9th of *Lucan*, with very great pleasure, where I find none of those absurdities so frequent in that of *Virgil*, except in two places, for the sake of lashing the Priests; one where *Cato* says—*Sortilegis egeant dubii*—and one in the simile of the *Hæmorhois*—*fatidici Sabæi*—He is so errant a Whig, that he strains even beyond his Author, in passion for Liberty, and

[1] imaginable . . . know to this hour] imaginable to him. I do not know to this hour *all Pope's texts.*

[2] safely . . . friend] safely my friend *all Pope's texts.*

[3] Both Curll and Pope expand W. to *Wycherley* in their texts.

[4] This sentence is omitted in all Pope's printed texts.

[5] A postscript seems to have been torn away: neither Curll nor Pope printed one.

[6] This first sentence, printed in Pope's octavo editions, was omitted from the quarto and folio of 1737.

[7] Pieces printed in the 6th vol. of *Tonson's* Miscellanies.—Pope, 1735–42.

aversion to Tyranny; and errs only in amplification. *Lucan* in *initio 9ni*, describing the seat of the *Semidei manes*, says,

> Quodque patet terras inter Lunæque meatus,
> Semidei manes habitant—

Mr. *Row* has this Line,

> Then looking down on the Sun's feeble Ray.

Pray your opinion, if there be an *Error-Sphæricus* in this or no? Yours, &c.

†POPE *to* CROMWELL[1] 11 *November* 1710

1735

Nov. 11, 1710.

You mistake me very much in thinking the freedom you kindly us'd with my Love-verses, gave me the first opinion of your sincerity: I assure you it only did what every good-natur'd action of yours has done since, confirm'd me more in that opinion. The Fable of the Nightingale in *Philips*'s Pastoral, is taken from *Famianus Strada*'s *Latin* Poem on the same subject, in his *Prolusiones Academicæ*; only the Tomb he erects at the end, is added from *Virgil*'s conclusion of the *Culex*. I can't forbear giving you a passage out of the *Latin* Poem I mention, by which you will find the *English* Poet is indebted to it.

> Alternat mira arte fides, dum torquet acutas
> Inciditque graves operoso verbere pulsat—
> Jamque manu per fila volat; simul hos, simul illos
> Explorat numeros, chordaque laborat in omni.—
> Mox silet. Illa modis totidem respondit, & artem
> Arte refert; nunc ceu rudis, aut incerta canendi,
> Præbet iter liquidum labenti e pectore voci,
> Nunc cæsim variat, modulisque canora minutis
> Delibrat vocem, tremuloque reciprocat ore.[2]

This Poem was many years since imitated by *Crashaw*,[3] out of whose Verses the following are very remarkable.

> From this to that, from that to this he flies,
> Feels Musick's Pulse in all its Arteries;
> Caught in a net which there *Apollo* spreads,
> His fingers struggle with the vocal threads:

[1] The first two paragraphs were omitted from the quarto and folio of 1737, in which editions the letter begins with 'I have (as I think I formerly told you) . . .'. In 1737 e and thereafter a footnote was added specifying the omission.

[2] Strada, *Prolusiones*, II. vi. In *Eloquentia Bipartita*, Oxford, 1662, pp. 330–1.

[3] In 'Musicks Duell', from which Pope here quotes.

I have (as I think I formerly told you) a very good opinion of Mr. *Row*'s 9th book of *Lucan*: Indeed he amplifies too much, as well as *Brebœuf*, the famous *French* Imitator. If I remember right, he sometimes takes the whole Comment into the Text of the Version, as particularly in lin. 808. *Utque solet pariter totis se effundere signis Corycii pressura croci.*—And in the place you quote, he makes of those two lines in the *Latin*

> Vidit quanta sub nocte jaceret
> Nostra dies, risitque sui ludibria trunci.

no less than eight in *English*.

What you observe sure cannot be an *Error Sphæricus*, strictly speaking, either according to their *Ptolomaick*, or our *Copernican* system; *Tycho Brahe* himself will be on the Translator's side. For Mr. *Row* here says no more, than that he look'd down on the Rays of the Sun, which *Pompey* might do, even tho' the Body of the Sun were above him.

You can't but have remark'd what a journey *Lucan* here makes *Cato* take for the sake of his fine Descriptions. From *Cyrene* he travels by land, for no better reason than this:

> Hæc eadem suadebat Hyems quæ clauserat æquor.

The Winter's effects on the Sea, it seems, were more to be dreaded than all the Serpents, Whirlwinds, Sands, &c. by Land, which immediately after he paints out in his speech to the soldiers: Then he fetches a compass a vast way round about, to the *Nasamones* and *Jupiter Ammon*'s Temple, purely to ridicule the Oracles: And *Labienus* must pardon me, if I do not believe him when he says—*sors obtulit, & fortuna viæ*—either *Labienus* or the Map, is very much mistaken here. Thence he returns back to the *Syrtes* (which he might have taken first in his way to *Utica*) and so to *Leptis Minor*, where our Author leaves him; who seems to have made *Cato* speak his own mind, when he tells his Army—*Ire sat est*—no matter whither. I am, | Your, &c.

†CROMWELL *to* POPE — 20 *November* 1710

1735

Nov. 20, 1710.

The System of *Tycho Brahe* (were it true, as it is *Novel*) cou'd have no room here: *Lucan*, with the rest of the *Latin* Poets, seems to follow *Plato*; whose order of the Spheres is clear in *Cicero*, *De Natura Deorum*, *De somnio Scipionis*, and in *Macrobius*. The Seat of the *Semidei manes* is *Platonick* too, for *Apuleius de Deo Socratis* assigns the same to the *Genii*, *viz*. the Region of the *Air* for their intercourse with Gods and Men; so that I fancy, *Row* mistook the situation, and I can't be reconcil'd to, *Look down on the Sun's Rays.* I am glad you agree with me about the latitude he takes; and wish you had told me, if the *sortilegi*, and *fatidici*, cou'd license his invectives against Priests? but I suppose you think them (with *Helena*) undeserving of your protection. I agree with you in *Lucan*'s Errors, and the cause of 'em, his Poetic descriptions: for the *Romans* then knew the coast of *Africa* from *Cyrene* (to the South-east of which lies *Ammon* toward *Egypt*) to *Leptis* and *Utica*: But pray remember how your *Homer* nodded while *Ulysses* slept, and waking knew not where he was, in the short passage from *Corcyra* to *Ithaca.* I like *Trapp*'s Versions[1] for their justness; his Psalm is excellent, the Prodigies in the first *Georgick* judicious (whence I conclude that 'tis easier to turn *Virgil* justly in blank verse, than rhyme.) The Eclogue of *Gallus*, and Fable of *Phaeton* pretty well; but he is very faulty in his *Numbers*; the fate of *Phaeton* might run thus,

> —The blasted *Phaeton* with blazing Hair,
> Shot gliding thro' the vast Abyss of Air,
> And tumbled headlong, like a falling Star.[2]

I am, | Your, &c.

||POPE *to* CROMWELL 25 *November* 1710

The Bodleian Library

Nov: 25. 1710.[3]

To make use of that Freedom and familiarity of Style, which we have taken up in our Correspondence, & which is more properly Talking upon Paper, than Writing; I will tell you without any Preface, that I never took Tycho Brahe for one of the Ancients, or in the least an Acquaintance of Lucan's; nay tis a mercy that on this occasion I do not give you an account of his life and conversation, ⌜which perhaps I know a little more of than you imagine;⌝[4] as how he livd some years

[1] In Tonson's *Poetical Miscellanies, the Sixth Part* (1709), appeared the pastorals of both Pope and Philips. Philips's pastorals began the volume, and were followed by Rowe's translation of Lucan ix. The following poems by the Rev. Joseph Trapp were included: 'Paraphrase upon Psalm CIV', 'The Love of Gallus . . . from Virgil's Tenth Eclogue', 'The Description of the Prodigies which attended the Death of Julius Caesar, translated into Blank Verse, from the latter End of the First Book of Virgil's Georgicks', and 'The Story of Phaëton from Ovid's Metamorphoses'.

[2] Trapp's version of the triplet was:

> But *Phaëton* with his sing'd and shining Hair
> Shot like a Meteor gliding thro' the Air;
> Which, if it fell not, seem'd a falling Star.

[3] The original has clearly the date here printed, but somehow Curll (1726) printed 24 Nov., and all Pope's editions copy that date. Brackets here indicate words printed by Curll that have since perished in the autograph. The entire letter is omitted in the quarto and folio of 1737. Half-brackets, as usual, indicate bits omitted from the printed texts found in the autograph letter.

[4] which . . . imagine] *omitted in all Pope's texts.*

like an Enchanted Knight in a certain Iland, with a Tale into the bargain of a King of Denmark's Mistress that shall be nameless—But I have compassion on you, and wou'd not for the world you shou'd stay any longer among the Genii & Semidei Manes, you know where; for if once you get so near the Moon, Sapho will want your presence in [the Clouds] & inferior Regions; not to mention the great Loss Drury Lane will su[stain when] Mr Cromwell[1] is in the Milky-Way. These Celestial Thoughts put m[e in mind] of the Priests you mention, who are a sort of Sortilegi in one sense, because [in their] Lottery, there are more Blanks than Prizes; The Adventurers being at best i[n an] Uncertainty, whereas the Setters up are sure of Something. Priests indeed in the[ir] Character, as they represent God, are sacred; & so are Constables, as they [re]present the King; but you will own a great many of 'em are very odd [fellows] & the devil a bitt of Likeness in 'em. Yet I do assure you, I honor the [good] as much as I detest the bad, & I think that in condemning these, we praise [those.] ⌜I am so far from esteeming ev'n the worst unworthy of my Protection, that I have defended their character (in Congreve's & Vanbrook's Plays) even against their own Bretheren. And so much for Priests in general, now for Trapp in particular, whose⌝[2] Translations from Ovid I have not so good an opinion of as you; ⌜not (I will assure you) on account of any sort of prejudice to him as a Priest, but⌝[3] because I think he has nothing of the main Characteristick of his Au[thor,] a graceful Easiness. For let the Sense be never so exactly renderd[, unless] an Author looks like himself in his Air, Habit, and Manner, tis a [Disguise] and not a Translation. But as to the Psalm, I think David is [much more beholding[4] to him than *Ovid*; and as he treated the Roman like a Jew, so he] has made the Jew speak like a Roman.[5]

⌜Your Mention in this & your last Letter of the Defect in Numbers of several of our Poets, puts me upon communicating a few Thoughts; or rather Doubts of mine on that head, some of which tis likely I may have hinted to you formerly in Conversation: but I will here put together all the little Niceties I can recollect in the Compass of my Observation (1.) As to the Hiatus, it is certainly to be avoided as often as possible; but on the other hand, since the reason of it is only for the sake of the Numbers, so if, to avoid it, we incurr another fault against

[1] Cromwell] C— *in all Pope's texts.*

[2] The Roberts octavo (1737 a) and subsequent octavo texts omit this passage. At the end Pope resumed by changing *whose* to *The* and starting a new sentence.

[3] Also omitted in 1737 a and thereafter.

[4] beholding] beholden *1737 a and later octavos.*

[5] Pope in all his editions ends the letter at this point. The parts omitted bear close resemblance to the letter to Walsh of 22 Oct. 1706. Curll charged Pope with 'transplanting a large shoot from one of the letters to Mr. Cromwell, and grafting it upon Mr. Walsh's stock'; and Elwin and others have naturally assumed that the letter to Walsh was fabricated from this one to Cromwell. If so, Pope did an unusual amount of revising and rewriting.

their Smoothness, methinks the very End of that Nicety is destroyd: As when we say (for instance)

⌜But th' Old have Interest ever in their view.

To avoid the Hiatus—in—The Old have Intrest—Does not the Ear in this [place tell us] that the Hiatus is smoother, less constrain'd, & so preferrable to the Caesur[a? (2.) I w]ou'd except against all Expletives in Verse, as Do before Verbs plural, or [ev'n too] frequent use of Did & Does, to change the Termination of the Rhime; all [the]se being against the usual manner of Speech & meer fillers up of unnecessary syllables. (3.) Monosyllable-Lines, unless very artfully manag'd, are stiff languishing, & hard. (4.) The Repeating the Same Rhimes within 4 or 6 lines of each other: which tire the Ear with too much of the like Sound. [(5.)] The too frequent use of Alexandrines, which are never graceful but [when] there is some Majesty added to the Verse by 'em, or when there cannot be [found] a Word in 'em but what is absolutely needfull. (6.) Every Nice Ear [must] (I believe) have observd, that in any smooth English Verse of ten Syllables, there is naturally a Pause either at the fourth, fifth, or sixth Syllable, as, for example, Waller.[1]

—at the fifth. Where-e'er thy Navy | spreads her canvass wings,
—at the fourth. Homage to thee | and peace to all she brings.
—at the sixth. Like Tracks of Leverets | in Morning Snow.

Now I fancy, that to preserve an exact Harmony & Variety, none of these Pauses shou'd be continu'd above three lines together, without the Interposition of [another]; else it will be apt to weary the Ear with one continu'd Tone; at least [it does] mine. (7.) It is not enough that nothing offends the Ear, that the Verse be (as the French call it) Coulante; but a good Poet will adapt the very Sounds, as well as Words, to the Things he treats of. So that there is (if one may express it so) a Style of Sound: As in describing a gliding stream the Numbers shou'd run easy & flowing, in describing a rough Torrent or Deluge, sonorous & swelling. & so of the rest. This is evident ev'ry where in Homer and Virgill, and no where else that I know of to any observable degree. The following Examples will make this very plain, which I have taken from Vida.[2]

x Molle viam tacito lapsu per levia radit.
x Incedit tardo molimine subsidendo.

[1] Lines 1 and 2 come from 'To the King on his Navy, in the Year 1626'; the third line is from 'Of a Tree cut in Paper'. Most of Pope's editions misprint *tracts* of leverets; two in 1735 (Booksellers) have *tracks*. Waller wrote *track*.

[2] In two cases the lines are from the *Aeneid*; the others are from Vida's *Ars Poetica*. In order the sources are: Vida, iii. 374, 376; *Aeneid*, i. 53; Vida, iii. 425; *Aeneid*, ii. 544–5 (combined); Vida, iii. 422 and 423.

x Luctantes ventos, Tempestatesque Sonoras.
x Immenso cum praecipitans ruit Oceano nox.
—Telum imbelle sine ictu Conjecit.
x Tolle moras, cape saxa manu, cape robora pastor,
Ferte citi flammas, date tela, repellite pestem.

[Thi]s, I think, is what very few observe in Practise, and is undoubtedly of wonderful force in imprinting the Image on the Reader: We have One excellent Example of this in our Language, Mr Dryden's Ode on St. Cecily's day, intitled Alexanders feast, or the Power of Musick.

⌜I ask your pardon for this tedious Letter, & expect a long one in answer to these Notions concerning Versification. I expect also the Voyage of Ovids Mistress with more Impatience than Ovid himself coud her Return. The other Journey you speak of, (mine to London) must yet be deferr'd; but tho I desire nothing more than to enjoy the happiness of your Conversation, yet I have [too] much con[science] to let mine cost you any thing but your Patience. I am heartily sorry for poor Mr Wycherleys Illness, and 'tis to his having been long indispos'd that I partly attribute his Chagrin. I wish he may enjoy all the happiness he desires, tho he has been the occasion of my enjoying much less than I did formerly. I look upon your Kindness to me as doubly engaging at this time, and shall never cease to acknowledge it, or to profess myself | Dear Sir | Your most real Fri[end]⌝[1]

Address: For Henry Cromwell [, Esq:] | at the blue Ball in great | Wilde street, near | Drury lane | London

Postmark: NO/27

†CROMWELL *to* POPE 5 *December* 1710

1735

Decemb. 5, 1710.

The same judgment we made on *Row*'s 9th of *Lucan* will serve for his part of the 6th,[2] where I find this memorable line,

Parque novum Fortuna videt concurrere, bellum
Atque virum.

For this he employs six Verses, among which is this,

As if on Knightly terms in Lists they ran.

[1] The original letter is defective at various edges, and the second leaf has been cut or torn so that no signature is left. The letter seems to have been complete when Curll printed it.

[2] This letter concerns verses in Tonson's sixth *Miscellany* (1709). Rowe's 'Part of the Sixth Book of Lucan' is on pp. 438–64. The particular passage that Cromwell does not approve comes on p. 457. Tickell's 'Description of the Phænix' from Claudian fills pp. 419–28. The offending couplet is on p. 428.

Pray can you trace Chivalry up higher than *Pharamond*? will you allow it an Anachronism?—*Tickell* in his Version of the Phænix from *Claudian*,

> When Nature ceases, thou shalt still remain,
> Nor second Chaos bound thy endless reign.

Claudian thus,

> Et clades te nulla rapit, solusque superstes,
> Edomita Tellure manes—

which plainly refers to the Deluge of *Deucalion* and the Conflagration of *Phaeton*; not to the final Dissolution. Your thought of the *Priests Lottery* is very fine; you play the Wit, and not the Critic, upon the errors of your brother.

Your observations are all very just: *Virgil* is eminent for adjusting his diction to his sentiments; and among the moderns, I find your Practice the Prosodia of your Rules. Your[1] Poem shews you to be, what you say of *Voiture*, *with Books well-bred*: The state of the Fair, tho' satirical, is touch'd with that delicacy and gallantry, that not the Court of *Augustus*, nor—But hold, I shall lose what I lately recover'd, your opinion of my Sincerity; yet I must say, 'tis as faultless as the Fair to whom 'tis address'd, be she never so perfect. The M.G.[2] (who it seems had no right notion of you, as you of him) transcrib'd it by lucubration: From some discourse of yours, he thought your inclination led you to (what the men of fashion call Learning) Pedantry; but now he says he has no less, I assure you, than a Veneration for you. Your, &c.

†POPE *to* CROMWELL — 17 *December* 1710

1735

Decemb. 17, 1710.

It seems that my late mention of *Crashaw*, and my quotation from him, has mov'd your curiosity. I therefore send you the whole Author, who has held a place among my other books of this nature for some years; in which time having read him twice or thrice, I find him one of those whose works may just deserve reading. I take this Poet to have writ like a Gentleman, that is, at leisure hours, and more to keep out of idleness, than to establish a reputation: so that nothing regular or just can be expected from him. All that regards Design,

[1] To a Lady, with the Works of *Voiture*.—Pope, 1735–42. Cromwell had seen the poem in manuscript. It appeared in Lintot's *Miscellaneous Poems and Translations* (1712).

[2] Pope's coffee-house crony John Tidcombe (1642–1713) had been promoted in 1708 from the rank of major-general to that of lieutenant-general, but very likely Cromwell was calling him by his longer-known rank.

Form, Fable, (which is the Soul of Poetry) all that concerns exactness, or consent of parts, (which is the Body) will probably be wanting; only pretty conceptions, fine metaphors, glitt'ring expressions, and something of a neat cast of Verse,[1] (which are properly the dress, gems, or loose ornaments of Poetry) may be found in these verses. This is indeed the case of most other Poetical Writers of *Miscellanies*; nor can it well be otherwise, since no man can be a true Poet, who writes for diversion only. These Authors shou'd be consider'd as *Versifiers* and *witty Men*, rather than as *Poets*; and under this head will only fall the Thoughts, the Expression, and the Numbers. These are only the pleasing parts of Poetry, which may be judg'd of at a view, and comprehended all at once. And (to express my self like a Painter) their *Colouring* entertains the sight, but the *Lines* and *Life* of the Picture are not to be inspected too narrowly.

This Author form'd himself upon *Petrarch*, or rather upon *Marino*. His thoughts one may observe, in the main, are pretty; but oftentimes far fetch'd, and too often strain'd and stiffned to make them appear the greater. For men are never so apt to think a thing great, as when it is odd or wonderful; and inconsiderate Authors wou'd rather be admir'd than understood. This ambition of surprising a reader, is the true natural cause of all Fustian, or Bombast in Poetry. To confirm what I have said you need but look into his first Poem of the *Weeper*, where the 2d, 4th, 6th, 14th, 21st stanza's are as sublimely dull, as the 7th, 8th, 9th, 16th, 17th, 20th, and 23d stanza's of the same copy, are soft and pleasing: And if these last want any thing, it is an easier and more unaffected expression. The remaining thoughts in that Poem might have been spared, being either but repetitions, or very trivial and mean. And by this example in the first one may guess at all the rest; to be like this, a mixture of tender gentile thoughts and suitable expressions, of forc'd and inextricable conceits, and of needless fillers-up to the rest. From all which it is plain, this Author writ fast, and set down what came uppermost. A reader may skim off the froth, and use the clear underneath; but if he goes too deep will meet with a mouthful of dregs: either the Top or bottom of him are good for little, but what he did in his *own*, *natural*, *middle-way*, is best.

To speak of his *Numbers* is a little difficult, they are so various and irregular, and mostly Pindarick: 'tis evident his heroic Verse (the best example of which is his *Musick's Duel*) is carelessly made up; but one may imagine from what it now is, that had he taken more care, it had been musical and pleasing enough, not extreamly majestic, but sweet: And the time consider'd of his writing, he was (ev'n as uncorrect as he is) none of the worst Versificators.[2]

[1] Verse, (which] Verse considering the age he liv'd in, (which *1737 quarto and folio only.*

[2] Warton perhaps was the first to point out Pope's indebtednesses to Crashaw. See also

I will just observe, that the best Pieces of this Author are, a Paraphrase on Psal. 23. On *Lessius*, Epitaph on Mr. *Ashton*, Wishes to his suppos'd Mistress, and the *Dies Iræ.* | I am, &c.

†POPE *to* CROMWELL 30 *December* 1710

1735

Decemb. 30, 1710.

I resume my old liberty of throwing out my self upon paper to you, and making what thoughts float uppermost in my head, the subject of a letter. They are at present upon *Laughter*, which (for ought I know) may be the cause you might sometimes think me too remiss a friend, when I was most intirely so: for I am never so inclin'd to mirth as when I am most pleas'd and most easy, which is in the company of a friend like your self.

As the fooling and toying with a mistress is a proof of fondness, not disrespect, so is raillery with a friend. I know there are Prudes in friendship, who expect distance, awe and adoration, but I know you are not of them; and I for my part am no Idol-worshipper, tho' a Papist. If I were to address *Jupiter* himself in a heathen way, I fancy I shou'd be apt to take hold of his knee in a familiar manner, if not of his beard like *Dionysius*; I was just going to say of his buttons, but I think *Jupiter* wore none (however I won't be positive to so nice a Critick as you, but his robe might be *Subnected* with a *Fibula.*) I know some Philosophers define Laughter, *A recommending our selves to our own favour, by comparison with the weakness of another*: but I am sure I very rarely laugh with that view, nor do I believe *Children* have any such consideration in their heads, when they express their pleasure this way: I laugh full as innocently as they, for the most part, and as sillily. There is a difference too betwixt laughing *about* a thing and laughing *at* a thing: One may find the inferior Man (to make a kind of casuistical distinction) provok'd to folly at the sight or observation of some *circumstance of a thing*, when the *thing itself* appears solemn and august to the superior Man, that is, our Judgment and Reason. Let an Ambassador speak the best Sense in the world, and deport himself in the most graceful manner before a Prince, yet if the *Tail* of *his Shirt* happen (as I have known it happen to a very wise man) to hang out behind, more people shall laugh at that than attend to the other; till they recollect themselves, and then they will not have a jot the less respect for the Minister. I must confess the iniquity of my countenance before you; several Muscles of my Face sometimes take an impertinent liberty with my Judgment, but then my Judgment soon rises, and sets

Gentleman's Magazine, lvi (1786), 311–13, and A. Warren, 'The Reputation of Crashaw', *Studies in Philology*, xxxi (1934), esp. 389–95.

all right again about my mouth: And I find I value no man so much, as he[1] in whose sight I have been playing the fool. I cannot be *Sub-Persona* before a man I love; and not to laugh with honesty, when Nature prompts, or Folly (which is more a second Nature than any thing[2] I know) is but a knavish hypocritical way of making a mask of one's own face.—To conclude, those that are my friends I *laugh with*, and those that are not I *laugh at*; so am merry in company, and if ever I am wise, it is all by my self. You take just another course, and to those that are not your friends, are very civil, and to those that are, very endearing and complaisant: Thus when you and I meet, there will be the *Risus et Blanditiæ* united together in conversation, as they commonly are in a verse: But without Laughter on the one side, or Compliment on the other, I assure you I am with real esteem | Yours, &c.

[1] Corrected to *him* in 1737 a. It was thought necessary in 1741 a to indicate errata in 1737 b, and this was done on page 339 of 1741 a.

[2] than any thing I know] than I know *1737 b*. This error was also corrected in the errata mentioned in the preceding note. The correction itself was erratic: instead of *more a second nature* it read *more ascend nature*.

1711

An important time in Pope's opening career, 1711 saw the publication of his *Essay on Criticism* and a notable widening of his circle of acquaintance. The first publisher of his *Essay*, W. Lewis, had perhaps been an early schoolmate: he was certainly an agent commonly employed by Caryll. Possibly through Caryll Pope was made acquainted with Steele, and improved his acquaintance with Martha and Teresa Blount, Martha being Caryll's god-daughter. Caryll became Pope's ally in the case of those unfortunate ladies Mrs. Weston and Mrs. Cope, who now first appear in the correspondence. Through Cromwell Pope was completely reconciled with Wycherley, and, possibly through the medium of Cromwell, became acquainted with one of his closest friends to be, John Gay. At the end of the year came Addison's commendation of the *Essay on Criticism* in *Spectator* No. 253, and presently he, through Steele's kindness, became Pope's friend.

Concerning his *Essay* Pope met violent attack from John Dennis and some rather stupid reservations from rigorous Catholics. Among the more interesting letters are those to Caryll that explain the poet's views on Catholicism. It is a busy year, occupied with projects in translation, in writing songs for Steele and Clayton, and even (but only jocosely ?) in the writing of a tragedy. The correspondence begins now to record visits—to Caryll at Ladyholt in April, to the Englefields in June and November, to Hallgrove, where his sister lived, and more often to London itself.

POPE *to* CARYLL — 25 *January* 1710/11

Add. 28618

Jany. the 25. 1710/11.

Sir,—In a letter that abounds with so much wit as yours, nothing can be more pleasant than to hear you disclaiming all pretensions to it, like Ovid protesting in very good verse that he would never versify. But some people are so given to say witty things, that, like those who are given to swearing, they never know when they do it. And men that have a great deal of ready wit, like those that have a great deal of ready money, bestow it up and down in a careless manner, and never think they have given away much, because they find their heads and their pockets are full again the next morning. So true it is that 'tis with one that has wit always about him, as with one that constantly carries perfumes: he is not sensible himself of that which delights all besides.

To own the Truth, it was not without a design that I sent you the verses you are pleased to mention so kindly: I meant to give you an opportunity of returning good for evil, in favoring me with a sight of some of yours, for if I made any doubt that you write sometimes, I should hardly have troubled you with what I writ, as not much caring to reveal my poetical sins, but as other sinners commonly do theirs, to those who are equally guilty. As for my verses I may truly say they have never been the cause of any great vanity in me, excepting that they gave me in occasioning my first acquaintance and correspondence with you. Since when indeed I've been often in danger of being notably tainted with this vice, but never more than when I read your last letter. 'Tis certain the greatest magnifying glasses in the world are a mans own eyes, when they look upon his own person; yet even in those, I appear not the great Alexander Mr Caryll is so civil to, but that little Alexander the women laugh at. But if I must be like Alexander, 'tis in being complimented into too good an opinion of my self: they made him think he was the son of Jupiter, and you persuade me I am a man of parts. Alas, Sir! is this all you can say in my honour? you said ten times as much before, when you called me your friend. After having made me believe I possess a share in your affection, to treat me with compliments and sweet sayings, is just like the proceeding with Sancho Pança; first they put it into the poor fellow's head that he enjoyed a vast dominion, and then gave him nothing to subsist upon but a few wafers and marmalade. I fear you observed with what greediness I swallowed whipt syllabubs at your house a year ago? But I have something more to tell you out of Don Quixote. There was once a certain person in Seville who had a very dexterous knack at blowing up young puppies. He made use of your own instrument, a quill, which he clapt to their tails, and puffed 'em up as round as a bladder; then he would ask the standers-by, what think you, gentlemen? is it such an easy matter to blow up a puppy dog? Now to judge impartially betwixt the whelp and the poet, it is a much harder matter to puff up the cur than the creature, and therefore tho' your operation be very like this Spaniard's, you ought not to value yourself so much on the performance. But indeed tho' it be an easy thing enough to make a dull scribbler proud, yet to commend such an one well, is extremely hard, and in this (if you will needs be compared to a quack) you are like him that put into his bills—'Let no man be discourag'd, for this doctor is one that delighteth much in matters of difficulty.' Yet, after all, a man is certainly obliged to any one who can make him vain of himself, since at the same time he makes him satisfied with himself; so nowadays the greatest obligation you can lay upon a wit, is to make a Fool of him. For as when madmen are found incurable, wise men give 'em their way, and please 'em as well as they can; so when those more incorrigible things, poets, are once irrecoverably be-mused, the best way both to quiet them, and to secure ourselves from the effects of their frenzy, is to feed their vanity, which indeed for the most part is all that's overfed in a poet.

But you have taken care I should not have this at least to complain of, by the kind present you sent me; without which, had I kept Lent here, I must have submitted to the common fate of my brethren, and have starved: yet I should (I think) have been the first poet that ever starved for the sake of religion. Now as your lady is pleased to say of my present, that St Luke himself never drew such a Madonna;[1] so I may say of yours, that the prince of the apostles himself, tho' he was a fisherman all his life, never eat so good oysters. And as she tells me that I did a thing I never thought of, and excelled a saint, I may tell you that you have done a thing you was not aware of, and reclaimed a sinner; for you'll be the cause that I shall obey a precept of the Church, and fast this Lent, which I have not done many years before. Which (with my hearty thanks) is all I can say on this subject, for I find upon scratching my head three times, that 'tis not so hard to get pearls out of oysters, as wit.

I have been full an hour upon this foolish letter already, which was only intended to bear off your compliments, and does not pretend to return them. I do but parry your thrusts; I can't hope to hit you. Besides I am unwilling to make tautologies after all the world, as I must, if I should speak of Mr. Caryll. Sir, you may believe me, I could be heartily glad all you say were as true applied to me, as it would be if addressed to yourself: and you need not doubt but I wish I were every way as good a man as you, for several weighty reasons; but for none more than that I might have sense enough to honour you as much as you deserve, whereas as it is, I can do it no more than is consistent with the mean, tho' utmost capacity of | Sir | Your most obliged and affectionate | humble servant | A: Pope

Mr Dancastle and myself join in assuring all your good family of our most humble service. Yesterday I made a letter of mine acceptable at Whiteknights by sending your service in it. (You see, Sir, I improve in my Style by your correspondence; I hope you will continue that satisfaction to me.)

||POPE *to* CROMWELL[2] 10 *May* [1711]

The Bodleian Library

I had not omitted to express my acknowledgments to you for so much Goodnature & Friendship as you lately showd me, till this time;[3] but that I am but just return'd to my own Hermitage, from Mr Caryl's, who has done me so many favors, that I am almost inclin'd to think my Friends Infect one another, and that your Conversation with him

[1] This remark shows that Pope was at this time making presents of his own pictures.

[2] In the rhymed dating at the end of the letter the year is not given. Curll placed the letter in 1710, but the first sentence of the letter to Cromwell of 17 May 1710 makes that impossible. In June 1711 John Dennis attacked the recently published *Essay on Criticism* in his *Reflections Critical and Satyrical* on that poem. In the pamphlet he reflects on Pope's admiration for Aulus Gellius in a manner here anticipated: Lintot had shown Pope the *Reflections* in manuscript. See i. 125. The letter is omitted from the quarto and folio of 1737.

[3] till this time] *omitted in all Pope's texts.*

has made him almost as obliging to me as yourself. I can assure you, he has a sincere respect for you, and this I believe he has partly contracted from me, who am too full of You, not to overflow upon those I converse with. But I must now be contented to converse only with the Dead of This World, that is to say the Dull & Obscure, every way Obscure, in their Intellects as well as their Persons: Or else have recourse to the Living Dead, the Old Authors, with whom you are so well acquainted, even from Virgil down to Aulus Gellius, whom I do not think a Critick by any means to be compar'd to Mr Dennis. And I must declare positively to you, that I will persist in this Opinion, till you become a little more civill to Atticus. Who cou'd have imagin'd, that He who had escapd all the Misfortunes of his Time, unhurt even by the Proscriptions of Antony and Augustus, shoud in these days find an Enemy: more severe & barbarous than those Tyrants [,] and that Enemy, the gentlest too, the bestnatu[rd] of Mortalls, Mr Cromwell? whom I must in th[is] compare once more to Augustus; who seem'd not more unlike himself in the Severity of one part, & the Clemency of the other part of his Life, than You? I leave you to reflect on th[is,] and hope, that Time (which mollifies Stones, and of stiff things makes limber) will turn a resolute Critick to a gentle Reader; and instead of this positive, tremendous, new-fashiond Mr Cromwell, Restore unto us our old Acquaintance, the soft, beneficent, and Curteous Mr Cromwell.

I expect much, towards the Civilizing of you in your Critical capacity, from the Innocent Air and Tranquillity of our Forest, when you do me the favor to visit it: In the meantime, it woud do well by way of preparative, if you wou'd duly & constantly ev'ry Morning, read over a Pastorall of Theocritus or Virgill; and let the Lady Isabella[1] put your Macrobius & A. Gellius somewhere out of your way, for a Month or so: (by which time I shall impatiently expect to see you according to your promise.) Who knows, but Travelling and Daily Airing in an open field, may contribute more successfully to the Cooling a Critics Animosity, than it did to the asswaging of Mr Cheek's Anger, of old? In these Fields you will be secure of finding no Enemy, but the most faithfull and affectionate of your Friends, | Your humble Servant | A. Pope.

The tenth of May; that is (in Meeter)
Just fifty days before St. Peter.[2]

Address: To Henry Cromwell, Esq; | at Mr Naylor's at the blue | ball in great Wildstreet, | near Drury lane, | LONDON.

Postmark: MA/11

[1] His housekeeper, to whom he left a legacy.—Croker–Elwin.
[2] i.e. just fifty days before 29 June, the feast of St. Peter and St. Paul.

||POPE *to* CROMWELL 10 *June* 1711

The Bodleian Library

June 10. 1711.

I was extremely concernd to leave you ill when I parted from the Towne, & desird Mr Thorold[1] to give me an account of the State of your health by the next Coach: he omitted to do it, & I have been since at Mr Englefylds till yesterday, when I receivd the ill Newes that you continu'd ill, or much as I left you: I hope this is not true, & shall be very uneasy in my fears for your health till I have a further account from yourself, which I beg you not to defer. I hope the Air of this Forest may perfectly recover you, & wish you wou'd to that end try it sooner than the end of the month; if you desire Mr Thorold, he will at a day's warning take a place for you. My Father joins in this request, & Mr Englefyld is overjoyd with the hopes of seeing you at his house. When I have your Company, I cannot but be well, & hope from the knowledge of this, that you can't be very ill in mine. I beg you to believe no man can take a greater Interest in your Welfare, or be more heartily affected towards you than myself, who am with all the Esteem & Tenderness of a Friend, | Dr Sir | Your faithful humble | Servant; | A: Pope:

POPE *to* CARYLL 15 *June* 1711

1735

[Under this date in all his editions (1735–42) Pope printed a letter 'To the Hon. J. C. Esq;' which was fabricated from parts of letters here printed from the Caryll transcripts as written under dates of 25 June 1711 and 2 August 1711. For the relation of this fabricated letter to the parts of the genuine letters, see the footnotes appended to them. The fabricated letter was the earliest letter to Caryll that Pope printed.]

||POPE *to* CARYLL[2] 18 *June* 1711

Add. 28618

June 18. 1711.

⌈Having received from you two of the most obliging letters imaginable, I returned by the next post a particular answer to each which I believe did not reach you before you left the town, and I would congratulate you upon the loss of them but that that supposition draws upon you the trouble of these lines.⌉ In your last you most charitably inform[3] me of the mistaken zeal of some people who seem to make it no less their

[1] See Pope to Cromwell, 15 Dec. 1709; i. 77.

[2] Most of this letter, with omissions and very slight revisions, was printed by Pope in 1735–42. Passages omitted by him are placed here in half-brackets.

[3] most charitably inform] inform'd *1735–42*.

business to persuade men they are erroneous, than doctors do that we are sick, only that thereby they may magnify their own cure and triumph over an imaginary distemper. The simile of wit and faith[1] (if you please to cast your eye once more upon it) plainly concludes at the second line, where stands a full stop; and what follows, *meanly they seek &c.*, speaks only of wit, which is meant by *that Blessing*, *that Sun*; for how can the sun of faith be said *to sublime the southern wits and to ripen the genius of northern climates.* I fear these gentlemen understand grammar as little as they do criticism, and perhaps out of good nature to the monks are willing to take from them the censure of ignorance and to have it to themselves. Now the word *They* refers (as I'm sure I meant it and as I thought every one must have known) to those criticks there spoken of, who are partial to some particular set of writers, to the prejudice of all others, and the very simile itself—

> Thus wit, like Faith, by each man is applied
> To one small sect, and all are damned beside.[2]

if read twice may convince them that the censure of damning here lies not on our Church[3] unless they will call our Church one small sect. And the cautious words *by each man*, manifestly show it a general reflection on all such (whoever they are) who entertain such narrow and limited notions of the mercy of the Almighty, which the reformed ministers of the presbyterians are as guilty of as any people living.

Yet after all I promise you, Sir, if the alteration of a word or two will gratify any man of sound faith tho' of weak understanding, I will, (tho' it were from no other principle than that of common good nature) comply with it: and if you please but to particularize the spot where their objection lies (for it is in a very narrow compass) that stumbling block, tho' it be but a little pebble, shall be removed out of their way. If the heat of these disputants who I'm afraid, being bred up to wrangle in the schools, cannot get rid of the humour all their lives, should proceed so far as to personal reflections upon me, I do assure you notwithstanding, I will do or say nothing, however provoked (for some people can no more provoke than oblige), that is unbecoming the character of a true Catholic. I will set before me that excellent example of that great man and great saint, Erasmus,[4] who in the midst of calumny proceeded with all the calmness of innocence, the unrevenging spirit of primitive Christianity! However I would advise them to

[1] The simile . . . plainly] The simile objected to in my Essay,

> (Thus wit, like faith, by each man is apply'd
> To one small Sect, and all are damn'd beside.)

plainly *1735–42*. (In the original letter as here printed the couplet had occurred later.)

[2] In Pope's texts (1735–42) the couplet was printed earlier in the letter; see note 1.

[3] our Church unless] our Church at all, unless *1735–42*.

[4] Pope had praised Erasmus, always one of his heroes, in the *Essay on Criticism*, l. 693.

suffer the mention of him to pass unregarded least I should be forced to do that for his reputation which I would never do for my own, I mean to vindicate so great a light of our Church from the malice of past times and the ignorance of the present, in a language which may extend farther than that in which the trifle about criticism is written.

I wish these gentlemen would be contented with finding faults with one only, who will submit to them right or wrong, as far as I only am concerned. I've too great a regard for the quiet of mankind, to disturb it for things of so little consequence as my credit, and my sence. A little humility can do a poet no hurt, and a little charity would do a priest none: and as St Austin finely says *Ubi charitas ibi humilitas, ubi humilitas, ibi pax.*

⌜I can never enough thank you, dear sir, for your extreme goodness and friendship in acquainting me with everything as you have done of late (tho' unasked) that concerns me. Such a friend is indeed a great treasure (as Solomon calls a friend) and such a freedom as you have begun to use (and more I hope will use) is what may render me the happiest man alive if I make the right use of it. I have all my life from the first years of my reasoning had a disposition to a friendship with some person or other, and if you will accept the most sincere offer of a heart so little worth your acceptance as mine, it is wholly at your service and under this tie, if you please, there can be nothing you advise I shall not be obliged to do from this hour.

⌜The continuance of your letters will be the greatest pleasures I can receive in your absence: which I shall look upon the more kind, the more freely and negligently you write; and if you please, in your next let me know what effect your conference with Sir W. G. had in reference to the lady's business[1] (unless you have already done it to her). I shall be glad to inform her, to whom every little prospect of ease is a great relief in these circumstances. I am certain a letter from yourself or lady would be a much greater consolation to her than your humility will suffer either of you to imagine. To relieve the injured (if you will pardon a poetical expression in prose) is no less than to take the work of God himself off his hands, and an easing Providence of its care: 'Tis the noblest act that human nature is capable of, is in a particular manner your talent, and may you receive a reward for it in heaven; for this whole world has not wherewithal to repay it. I am with the utmost

[1] On the lady's business see *The Athenaeum*, 15 July 1854. She was Elizabeth Weston, estranged wife of John Weston, Esq., of Sutton (Surrey); she was the sister of the first Viscount Gage and of Joseph Gage, who, according to Pope's *Epistle to Lord Bathurst*, l. 128, tried to buy the throne of Poland. Sir W. Goring had been the lady's guardian, and Pope hoped he would continue her friend. Pope's partisanship of the lady in her quarrel with her husband was extreme, and caused coolnesses between himself and Mrs. Nelson and the Englefields, as later letters will show. The Racketts also sided with the husband: see Pope to Martha Blount, 13 Sept. 1717.

esteem and gratitude | dear sir | Your ever obliged friend | and humble servant, | A. P.⌝

⌜My most hearty service attends all your family. I've not yet had the honour of a letter from Mr Steel.⌝[1]

||POPE *to* CARYLL[2] 25 *June* 1711

Add. 28618

June the 25. 1711.

⌜Besides the two letters you last favored me with, I am yet more in your debt for one to Mr Englefield, where you have defended me with all the spirit of friendship, and the very essence of good nature; but one or two things you have there said of me that I'm ashamed to thank you for, they are so extravagantly above my merit; and they prove it true, that a friend is as blind as a lover. I beg you to be cautious of saying these things to others, for I can't answer for their prudence; if they were only said to myself I would for your sake conceal 'em from all besides; and they would then be less dangerous to me too, for I should take 'em only for complimental civilities, whereas when addressed to other people, I might be so vain as almost to imagine you were partly in earnest. I know too well the vast difference betwixt those who truly deserve the name of poets and men of wit, and one who is nothing but what he owes to them; and I keep the pictures of Dryden, Milton, Shakespear, &c., in my chamber, round about me, that the constant remembrance of 'em may keep me always humble: I wish I had Mr Caryll's there, that I might have something to make me proud, when I reflected on his friendship. The extreme goodness with which you accept the offer I too impudently made you of mine, can never be enough acknowledged: I am like a poor fellow who makes his rich landlord a scurvy and worthless present, on the hopes of receiving one of infinitely a greater value in return. But on second thoughts I'm more like one of those many poor neighbors of yours to whom you have done charities, who offer you a small acknowledgment after receiving great benefits from you; for you have been beforehand with me in the proofs of friendship you speak of, and my heart is a debt, not a present. Let this suffice to be told you, and be assured, sir, if I did not esteem your friendship so very much, I would have said a great deal more.⌝

[1] For Steele's connexion with Lord Cutts in 1697, when Caryll redeemed the confiscated estates of his Jacobite uncle, see *The Athenaeum*, 8 May 1858. Caryll may have introduced Pope to Steele.

[2] In part this letter was printed in Pope's editions as 'To the Hon. J. C.' under date of 15 June 1711. Half-brackets indicate omissions made by Pope. In the letter of 15 June he inserted a paragraph from that actually sent to Caryll dated 2 Aug. 1711 (q.v.). In various editions Pope made small changes in his text, the more important of which are here noted.

[1]I send you Mr Dennis's Remarks on the *Essay*, which equally abound in just criticisms and fine railleries: the few observations in my hand in the margin are what only a morning's leisure permitted me to make purely for your perusal, for I am of opinion that such a critic as you will find him by the latter part of his book, is no way to be properly answered but by a wooden weapon: and I should perhaps have sent him a present from Windsor Forest of one of the best and toughest oaken plants between Sunning hill and Oakingham, if he had not informed me in his Preface[2] that he is at this time persecuted by fortune. This I protest I knew not the least of before; if I had, his name had been spared in the *Essay* for that only reason. I can't conceive what ground he has for [so] excessive a resentment, nor imagine how those three lines[3] can be call'd a reflection on his person, which only describe him subject a little to colour and stare[4] on some occasions, ⌜which are revolutions that happen sometimes in the best and most regular faces in Christendom.⌝ I have heard of combatants so very furious as to fall down themselves with that very strength, which they designed to lay so heavy on their antagonists. But if Mr Dennis's rage proceeds only from a zeal to discourage young and inexperienced writers from scribbling, he should frighten us with his verse, not prose; for I've often known that when all the precepts in the world would not reclaim a sinner, some very sad example has done the business.[5] Yet to give this man his due, he has objected to one or two lines with reason, and I will alter them in case of another edition: I will make my enemy do me a kindness where he meant an injury, and so serve instead of a friend. What he observes at the bottom of pag. 20th of his reflections,[6] was objected to by yourself, ⌜at Ladyholt,⌝ and had been mended but for the haste of the press: 'Tis right Hibernian, and I confess it what the English call a bull, in the expression, tho' the sense be manifest enough: Mr Dennis's bulls are seldom in the expression, they are almost always in the sense.[7]

You will see by this, that whoever sets up for wit in these days ought to have the constancy of a primitive Christian, and be prepared

[1] Pope's text of 1735 begins at this point. Dennis's attack was called *Reflections Critical and Satyrical, upon a late Rhapsody, call'd An Essay upon Criticism.*

[2] is no way . . . in his Preface] is but one way to be properly answer'd, and that way I wou'd not take after what he informs me in his preface *1735–42*.

[3] But *Appius* reddens at each word you speak,
And stares tremendous with a threatening eye,
Like some fierce Tyrant in old Tapestry.—Pope, 1735–42.

[4] a little . . . on some occasions] a little to Anger on some occasions *1735–42*.

[5] This Thought we find afterwards put into Verse in the Dunciad, Book I.—Pope, 1735 (not later).

[6] Dennis had criticized, and now Pope was ready to revise, l. 503 of his *Essay*.

[7] At this point in his printed texts Pope inserted from his letter to Caryll of 2 Aug. 1711 (q.v.) the long passage beginning 'I shall certainly never make the least reply', and ending with 'yet he had faults to keep him humble'. See i. 132.

to suffer even martyrdom in the cause of it. But sure this is the first time that a wit was attacked for his religion, as you'll find I'm most zealously in this treatise. And you know, sir, what alarms I have had from the opposite side[1] on this very account? Have I not reason to cry out with the poor fellow in Virgil,[2]

> —Quid jam misero mihi denique restat?
> Cui neque apud Danaos usquam locus, et super ipsi
> Dardanidæ insensi[3] pœnas cum sanguine poscunt!

'Tis however my happiness that you, sir, are impartial.

> *Jove* was alike to Trojan[4] and to Phrygian,
> For you well know, that wit 's of no religion.

The manner in which Mr D. takes to pieces several particular lines detached from their natural places, may show how easy it is to any one[5] to give a new sense, or a new nonsense, to what the author intended, or not intended. And indeed his constructions are not more wrested from the genuine meaning than theirs, who objected to the heterodox parts, as they call 'em. Mr Thomas Southcote[6] is not of that number, who with the utmost candor, and freedom ⌜of a friend,⌝ has modestly told me what others thought; and shown himself one (as he expresses it very well) rather of a *number* than a *party*. ⌜I answer'd his obliging letter some time since, and have received from him a second, to which I will reply immediately when I have ended this.⌝ The only difference between us in relation to the monks is, that he thinks most sorts of learning *flourish'd* among 'em, and I am of opinion that only some sort of learning was barely *kept alive* by 'em. He believes the most natural and obvious sense of that line (A second deluge *learning* over-run) will be thought meant of learning in general, and I fancy it will be understood only, as 'tis meant, of polite learning, criticism, poetry, &c., which is the only learning concerned in the subject of the *Essay*.[7] I am highly obliged to Mr Southcote's zeal in my Commendation and

[1] See the ensuing Letters.—Pope 1735–7. (Later notes printed the singular, *Letter*, referring to that of 18 June, which immediately followed the composite dated 15 June.)

[2] Virgil, *Aeneid*, ii. 70–72.

[3] insensi] infensi *1735–42* (an error of Caryll's scribe?).

[4] Trojan] Latian *1735–42*.

[5] to any one] to a caviller *1735–42*.

[6] English Catholics of this time—at least Pope—frequently spoke of priests as Mr. ——. Mr. Thomas Southcote (1670–1748), son of Sir John, was an abbé by 1735 when Pope, who tends to omit names of persons from his letters, substituted for his name the locution, 'Our friend the Abbé'. (See *Catholic Record Society*, viii. 414: *The Diary of the 'Blue Nuns'*. See also Pope to Fortescue, Jan. 1728/9 and note.)

[7] At this point in his printed texts Pope inserted, from no known letter, the following sentence: 'It is true, that the *Monks* did preserve what learning there was, about *Nicholas* the Fifth's time; but those who succeeded fell into the depth of Barbarism, or at least stood at a stay while others rose from thence, insomuch that even *Erasmus* and *Reuchlin* could hardly laugh them out of it.'

goodness for not concealing what he thinks my errour. And his testifying some esteem for the book, just at a time when his brethren raised a clamor against it, is an instance of great generosity and good nature together, which I shall ever acknowledge. ⌜I ventured to give my most humble service to Mr Southcote when I writ to his brother,[1] and intreat the favour of you to assure that most worthy gentleman of my real esteem and hearty respects. [If] I had the honor of being known to my Lord Petre,[2] I should be so impu[dent as to] desire his acceptance of a thing so inconsiderable as my most humble service. I hope my lord will not, from what Mr Dennis is pleased to say, look upon me as a despiser of Men of Quality, who as they have the greatest advantages of all men, so are worse than the rest of mankind if they are not better; and this may be said (without any danger) to my Lord Petre, who is (by the consent of all who have the happiness to know him) one of those young lords that have wit in our days!

⌜I am glad you design to write to the lady[3] about your conference. I am very confident they can't be united, tho' they may be brought together: 'Tis an easy thing (we daily find) to join two bodies, but in matching minds there lies some difficulty. I could wish every disagreeing pair might be sent for a while to Ladyholt or Grinstead (the best matrimony-schools in England) there to study the happiness of a married life (that hard science to which so very few are born with a genius.) Yet I wish the blessed example may not prove of ill consequence to many others; as we often see that one person's good luck in a lottery is the cause that twenty venture, and lose. Now put the case any of those that past the last Christmas with you, should marry in expectation of such husbands as Mr Caryll, and such wives as his lady; Good God! how confoundedly would most of 'em be disappointed. I have not an inch more of paper to spare, but it shall go hard with me, but I'll find room (tho' in never so great straits) to assure you that I am yours, and all your family's most faithfull humble servant | A. P.

⌜I am just now informed that the tyrant is determined instantly to remove his daughter from the Lady. I wish to God it could be put off by Sir W. G.'s mediation, for I'm heartily afraid 'twill prove of very ill consequence to her.⌝

[1] Mr. Southcote (here believed to be the Abbé) was younger brother to Sir Edward, who lived at Albery Place (Surrey), not too far from Caryll. There were other brothers also. According to Spence (pp. 7–8) Pope, with the aid of Walpole, later got Southcote an abbey in Avignon. Mr. James M. Osborn calls the editor's attention to the date of Pope's effort as given by G. D. Henderson in his *Chevalier Ramsay*, p. 90: 'though negotiations were definitely on foot early in 1723, as the Stuart Papers bear witness, Southcote did not in fact obtain his abbey until after the death of the afflicted de Roure [an insane incumbent] in 1728'. See below, ii. 294 and iii. 6.

[2] Robert, 7th Lord Petre, presently to become the protagonist in *The Rape of the Lock*, was probably visiting Caryll, who was his remote cousin.

[3] Mrs. Weston.

POPE *to* CROMWELL[1] 25 *June* 1711

1726 (Curll) and Bodleian Library

June 25th. 1711.

If my Letter pleas'd you, yours overjoy'd me; and I expect impatiently your kind Visit: A little Room and a little Heart are both at your Service, and you may be secure of being easy in 'em at least, tho' not happy. For you shall go just your own Way, and keep your own Hours, which is more than can be done often in Places of greater Entertainment.—As to your Letter of Critical Remarks on *Dryden*'s VIRGIL,[2] I can only say, most of what you observe are true enough, but of no great Consequence (in my Opinion at least.) *Line* 250. *And sanctify the Shame*—seems to me very beautiful; and so does—'*tis doubly to be dead. Line* 946. *And bandy'd Words still beat about his Ears*,—This I have thought gross as well as you; I agree with you that the 993*d Line* (*And clos'd her Lids at last in endless Night*)—is contradictory to the Sense of *Virgil*, for so, as you say, *Iris* might have been spar'd. And in the main, 'tis to be confess'd that the Translator has been freer with the Character of *Dido* than his modest Author wou'd allow. I am just taking Horse to see a Friend five Miles off, that I have no little Visits abroad to interrupt my Happiness at Home when you are here. So that I can but just assure you, how pleas'd I am in the Expectation of it, and how sincerely I shall ever be, | Dear Sir, | Your most oblig'd and | affectionate Servant, | A. Pope.

P.S. Pray bring a very considerable number of Pint bottles with you; this might seem a strange odd request, if you had not told me you wou'd stay but as many days as you brought bottles; therfore you can't bring too many, tho we are here no Drunkards. 'Tis a fine thing to have a Learned quotation for ev'ry occasion, & Horace helps me to one now.

—non ego te meis
Immunem meditor tingere poculis,
Plena dives ut in domo. Ode 12. lib. 4.

And to another Ep: 5. lib. 1:

Hæc ego procurare & idoneus imperor, & non
Invitus, ne turpe toral, ne sordida mappa
Corruget nares—

And once more Sat. 2. lib. 2.

—bene erit, non piscibus urbe petitis
Sed pullo atque hædo; tum pensilis uva secundas

[1] Only the postscript and the address of this letter are preserved among the other Cromwell letters in Bodley. The main text of the letter is here taken from Curll's 1726 printing.

[2] The lines under discussion are from Book IV of Dryden's *Aeneid*.

Et nux ornabit mensas, cum duplice ficu.

Nil mi rescribas, attamen ipse veni.

P.S. Mr *Lintot* has favord me with a Sight of Mr Dennis's Piece of fine Satire before 'twas publishd; I desire you to read it, & give me your opinion, in what Manner such a Critic ought to be Answer'd?
*Remarks on the Essay on Criticism.[1]

Address: To H: Cromwell, Esqr: | at the blue ball in great | Wildstreet, near Drury lane | London. | present:

||POPE *to* CROMWELL[2] 15 *July* 1711

The Bodleian Library

I send this only to let you know how much our whole family desire to hear of your safe arrival in London, and the Continuance of your health: You have, without Compliment, oblig'd us all so much by your friendly acceptance of so poor an Entertainment here, that you cou'd by nothing have oblig'd us more, but by staying longer. But I take so short a visit only as an Earnest of a more kind one hereafter; as we just Call upon a friend sometimes, only to tell him he shall see us again.—All you saw in this Country charge me to assure you of their humble Service, & the Ladies in particular; who look upon us but as plain Country-fellows since they saw you, & heard more civill things in that one Fortnight than they expect from the whole Shire of us, in an age. The Trophy you bore away from one of 'em, in your Snuffbox, will doubtless preserve her Memory, and be a Testimony of your admiration, for ever.

As long as Moco's happy Tree shall grow,
While Berries crackle, or while Mills shall go;
While smoking streams from Silver Spouts shall glide,
Or China's Earth receive the sable Tyde;
While Coffee shall to British Nymphs be dear;
While fragrant Steams the bended Head shall chear;
Or grateful Bitters shall delight the Tast;
So long her Honour, Name, and Praise shall last![3]

Pray give my Service to all my few friends, & to Mr Gay[4] in particular.

[1] This note is written in (by Curll?) on the original. It was printed in the edition of 1726. Dennis's pamphlet was *Reflections* rather than Remarks. *The Daily Courant*, 21 June 1711, had advertised it as 'just publish'd'.
[2] Curll printed this letter in 1726, but Pope did not reprint it in any of his editions.
[3] These lines anticipate to a certain extent *The Rape of the Lock*, iii. 105–10 and 164–70.
[4] The earliest mention of Gay.

Fare well, that is drink strong Coffee. *Ingere tibi calices Amariores.*[1] I am Dear Sir with all Sincerity, | Your most faithful friend & hum | ble Servant; | A: Pope.

July 15. 1711.

||POPE *to* CARYLL[2] 19 *July* 1711

Add. 28618

July 19, 1711

The concern which you more than seem to be affected with for my reputation by the several accounts you have so obligingly given ⌜me⌝ of what reports and censures the holy Vandals have thought fit to make me the unworthy subject of,[3] makes me desirous of telling so good a friend my whole thoughts of this matter, and of setting before you in a true[4] light the true state of it.

I've ever thought the best piece of service one could do to our religion was openly to expose our detestation and scorn of all those artifices and *piæ fraudes* which it stands so little in need of, and which have laid it under so great a scandal among the enemies. Nothing has been so much a scarecrow to them as the too peremptory and seemingly uncharitable assertion of an utter impossibility of salvation to all but ourselves, invincible ignorance excepted, which indeed some people define under so great limitations and with such exclusions, that it seems as if that word were rather invented as a salvo or expedient, not to be thought too bold with the thunderbolts of God (which are hurled about so freely almost on all mankind by the hands of the ecclesiastics) than as a real exceptive to almost universal damnation. For besides the small number of the truly faithful in our Church, we must again subdivide, and the Jansenist is damned by the Jesuit, the Jesuit by the Jansenist, the strict Scotist by the Thomist, &c. There may be errors, I grant, but I can't think 'em of such consequence as to destroy utterly the charity of mankind, the very greatest bond in which we are engaged by God to one another ⌜as Christians⌝.

Therefore I own to you I was glad of any opportunity to express our dislike of so shocking a sentiment as those of the religion I profess are charged with, and hoped a slight insinuation,[5] introduced so easily, of a casual similitude only could never have given offense, but on the contrary must needs have done good in a nation and time, wherein we are the smaller party, and consequently the most misrepresented and

[1] Catullus, xxvii. 2.

[2] First printed by Pope in 1735. His omissions are in half-brackets.

[3] fitt . . . subject of] fit to pass upon me *1735–42*.

[4] true] clear *1735–42*.

[5] The scribe here wrote something like *insuration*, or *insunation*. Elwin reads *intimation*, but the letter is *s* and not *t*.

most wanting vindication from a slander.[1] For the same reason I took occasion to mention the superstition of some ages after the subversion of the Roman Empire, which is too manifest a truth to be denied, and does in no sort reflect upon the present Catholics,[2] who are free from it. Our silence in these points may with some reason make our adversaries think we allow and persist in those bigotries, which in reality all good and sensible men despise, tho' they are persuaded not to speak against them—I can't tell why, since 'tis now no more the interest even of the worst of our priesthood (as it might be then) to have them smothered in silence; for the opposite sects now prevailing, 'tis too late to hinder our Church from being slandered. 'Tis our business now to show it was slandered unjustly, and to vindicate ourselves from being thought abettors of that which they charge us with. This can't be brought about with serious faces: we must laugh with them at what deserves it, and then we need not doubt of being cleared, even in their opinion.

As to the particulars: you can't but have observed that the whole objection against the simile of *wit* and *faith* lay in the word *they*: when that was beyond all contradiction removed, the very grammar seeming[3] to confute them ⌜(for it seems at St. Omer's they do not learn the English grammar)⌝ then the objection lies against the simile itself: and if that simile will not be objected to, sense and common reason being indeed a little stubborn and not apt to give way to every body, next the mention of superstition must become a crime, as if religion and she were sisters, or else as if it were a scandal upon the family of Christ to say a word against the devil's bastards. Afterwards some more mischief is discovered in a place that seemed very little suspicious[4] at first, and that is in the two lines about schismaticks ⌜at the bottom of page 25⌝;[5] for an ordinary man would imagine the author plainly declared against these schismatics for quitting the true faith out of contempt of the understanding of some few of its believers. But these believers are called *Dull*, and because I say that *These schismatics think some believers dull*, therefore these charitable well-disposed interpreters of my meaning say that *I think all believers dull.* I was telling Mrs. Nelson[6] these fine objections, who assured me I had said nothing which a zealous Catholic need to disown: and I've cause to know that that lady's[7] fault (if she has any) is not want of zeal. She put a notion into my head,

[1] and most wanting . . . slander] and most in need of vindication. *1735–42.*
[2] present Catholics] present professors of our faith *1735–42.*
[3] seeming] serving *1735–42.*
[4] very little suspicious] innocent *1735–42.*
[5] Omitted 1737–42. In 1735 Pope printed 'page 24'.
[6] Mrs. Nelson] Mr. —— *1735–42.* Pope seldom prints a lady's name in his editions of the letters. Mrs. Nelson may have been the 'very orthodox lady' whom Cromwell called Pope's Sapho. See Pope to Cromwell, 18 Mar. 1708, and also to Caryll, 8 Nov. 1712 and 8 Jan. 1712/13.
[7] that lady's] that gentleman's *1735–42.*

which I confess I can't but perfectly acquiesce in, and that was, that ⌜'tis observable⌝ when a set of people are piqued at any truth which they think to their own disadvantage, their method of revenge on the truth-speaker is to attack his reputation a by-way, and not to object to the place they are really galled by. What these therefore in their own opinion are really angry at is that a man[1] whom their tribe oppressed and persecuted ⌜(Erasmus by name)⌝ should be vindicated after a whole age of obloquy, by one of their own people who is free and bold enough[2] to utter a generous truth in behalf of the dead, whom no man sure will flatter, and few do justice to.[3] Others you know, were as angry that I mentioned Mr. Walsh with honour, who, as he never refused to any one of merit, of any party, the praise due to him, so honestly deserved it from all others of never so different interests or sentiments. May I ever be guilty of this sort of liberty and latitude of principle, which gives us the hardiness of speaking well of those whom envy oppresses even after death. As I would always speak well of my friends when they are absent, nay, because they are absent, so I would much more of the dead, in that eternal absence, and the rather because I expect no thanks ⌜from them⌝ for it.

Thus, sir, you see I do in my *conscience* persist in what I have written, yet *in my friendship* I will recant and alter whatever you please in case of a Second Edition,—which I yet think the book will never arrive at, for Tonson's printer[4] told me he drew off a thousand copies in his first impression, and I fancy a treatise of this nature, which not one gentleman in three score even of a liberal education can understand, will hardly exceed the vent of that number. You shall find me a true Trojan in my faith and friendship: in both which I will ever persevere unto the end,[5] and you shall be convinced that both in regard to the determinations of the Church and to your determinations[6] I shall prove a submissive disciple, and renounce all dangerous temptations of the private spirit. I need no bribes to keep me steady, and therefore your flesh-pots of Egypt are lost upon me, and I'm very glad all the venison will fall into so good hands as Mr. Englefield's and Mrs. Blount's.[7] You are pleased to ask me if we bought the horse? Your reason for this question is what I can't readily guess without blushing;[8] and therefore desire you, dear sir, to pardon me, and give me leave to make no answer. I could wish you would not oblige too fast. I love to

[1] a Man] Erasmus *1735–42*. [2] free and bold enough] willing *1735–42*.

[3] and few do justice to] to whom few will do justice *1735–42*.

[4] Tonson was not the publisher of the *Essay on Criticism*, but apparently a printer used by him also printed the *Essay*. The second edition of the poem appeared in Nov. 1712.

[5] All texts of the letter printed by Pope ended at this point.

[6] A superfluous *that* found at this point in the transcript is here omitted for clarity's sake.

[7] Mrs. Blount of Mapledurham was the daughter of Anthony Englefield of Whiteknights and was the mother of Pope's friends Teresa and Martha.

[8] Caryll later presented the horse to Pope. See the letter to Caryll, 15 Dec. [1713].

keep pace with a friend if possible; and 'tis a rule, you know, in walking to let the weakest go foremost: Let me first prove my self your friend (which I shall infallibly do on the first occasion that shall offer itself) and then, sir, do what you will: 'Tis likely this may be a long reprieve for you, and at this rate the first friendly office you are to do for me, may be to pray for my soul; for in all probability in all my whole inconsiderable life I may never be able once to give you a testimony to any purpose, of a thing so true as that I am | Dear Sir | Your ever obliged and most faith- | ful humble servant | A. P.

P.S. | I am infinitely obliged for your bringing me acquainted with Mrs. Cope,[1] from whom I heard more wit and sense in two hours, than almost all the sex ever spoke in their whole lives. She is indeed that way a relation of Mr. Caryll: and that's all I shall say of the lady. My most humble services to Mrs. Caryll, Mr. John Caryll, the young lady, your brother, and Mr. Brown.[2]

Sir, I beg you to pardon the length of this letter. I had not time enough (as Mons. Pascal[3] said of one of his) to make it shorter. This, like most impertinent things, requires no answer, but I should be glad of one to my last. Mr. Weston complains grievously of the manifold mischiefs done his fences and fruits by a certain deer he keeps for you —which he desires you to send for, as I here send you what you required at my hands.

A RONDEAU TO PHILLIS[4]

1.

You know where you did despise
'Tother day my little eyes,
Little legs, and little thighs;
And some things else of little size,
You know where.

2.

You 'tis true have fine blue eyes,
Taper legs and tempting thighs;
But what more than all we prize
Is a thing of little size,
You know where.

[1] Mrs. Cope was a first cousin of Mr. Caryll.—Elwin. She will appear later in the correspondence as a beneficiary of Pope's charity. She was unhappily married, and died on the Continent (Paris) in May 1728.

[2] Mr. Brown was, so Elwin tells us, chaplain to Caryll.

[3] In the postscript to the 16th of his Provincial Letters.—Elwin.

[4] The same rondeau was sent to Cromwell (24 June 1710). It was published by Curll in *Miscellanea* (1726). The appended epigram was published in the Pope–Swift *Miscellanies* (1727: 'the last vol.'), p. 178.

THE BALANCE OF EUROPE. AN EPIGRAM

Now Europe's balanced, and no side prevails;
For nothing's left in either of the scales.

POPE *to* CROMWELL[1] 24 *July* 1711

The Bodleian Library

I receivd your most welcom letter, & am asham'd you shou'd seem to give us Thanks, where you ought to assure us of Pardon, for so ill an Entertainment. Your heroic Intention of flying to the relief of a distressed Lady, was glorious, & noble; such as might be expected from your Character, for as *Chaucer* says (I think)

As noblest Metals are most soft to melt,
So Pity soonest runs in gentle minds.[2]

But what you tell me of her Relation's account of the State of her Mind, is not to be wonder'd at. 'Tis the easiest way they have, to make some seeming excuse for a shameful Indolence & Neglect of afflicted Virtue, to represent it as willing to suffer, & endure the Cross. Alas Sir! These good people of large Estates, & little Souls, have no mind to ease her by bearing it off her Shoulders by a generous assistance! Our Savior himself did not refuse to be Eas'd of the weight of part of his Crosse; tho' perhaps *Simon of Cyrene* might alledge to the Jews that 'twas Christs desire to bear it all himself; and he, for his part, might be willing to go quietly on his Journey, without the trouble——

Be pleas'd to assure Mr Ballam of my faithfull Service; I can never enough Esteem a Zeal so ardent in my Concerns, from one I never cou'd any way oblige, or induce to it. 'Tis an effect of the purest, most dis-interest'd Strain of natural Good-humor in the World. ⌜My humble Service too to Mr Gay, of whose Paper I have made mention to Lewis, who (I believe) will apply to you about it: Therfore if it be Copy'd fairly out, I guess he will be glad of it.⌝[3] Pray at your leisure return me those Papers in my hand which you have, & in Mr Wycherly's,[4] and favour me as often as you can with your Letters, which will ever be the most entertaining Things I can receive in your absence—All those fine Persons you mention return you their humble Service—The Fate of the Ber[ry] moves at once my Compassion, & Envy: It deserves an Elegy but who besides Catullus & Voiture can write

[1] This letter is printed only in Curll's editions, never in Pope's.

[2] Pope misquotes, but from Dryden's 'Palamon and Arcite', ii. 331–2—not from Chaucer.

[3] Curll omitted this sentence about Gay. W. Lewis was a bookseller.

[4] It would seem that in spite of a coolness between himself and Wycherley Pope still had some of Wycherley's 'papers'.

agreably upon Trifles? My humble Service to the Lady in the *Clouds*, whe[re] if I am once more[1] so happy as to be admitted, I will not be put off like *Ixion*, but lay hold on the reall Jun[o.] I am, most Seriously, | Dear Sir | Your most oblig'd and most | affectionate Servant and Friend | A: Pope.

July 24. 1711.

STEELE *to* POPE — 26 *July* 1711

Homer MSS. Add. 4807

July 26th 1711

Sir,—I writ to you the other day and hope you have received my letter. This is for the same end to Know whether You are at Leisure to help Mr Clayton,[2] that is, Me to some Words for Musick against Winter.

Your answer to Me at Wills will be a great favour to, Sir, | Your Most Obedient | Humble Servant | Richard Steele

Address: To | Mr Pope at | Bienfield near | Okingham | Berks

POPE *to* CARYLL[3] — 2 *August* 1711

Add. 28618

2d August 1711.

The letter you writ from my Lord Petre's I received, and answered (in words at least for t'was impossible to answer it in value) near a week before I had your last, with another enclosed in it, by the date of which it appeared that it had been about 8 days coming to me; so that, like most satisfactions of this life, it was long retarded, but the more welcome for having been expected. I beg you to believe I answer all you can say in your letters, even before I receive 'em, in my grateful sense of your unbounded humanity and goodness; and I can no more confine this in words than you can refrain those from overflowing in deeds, and proofs; one of which you have lately given me (as I hear from several hands) in your kind vindication of me from those aspersions which Dennis has endeavored to cast upon my character as a man, no less than an author.

[1] Curll omitted 'more'.

[2] Thomas Clayton was a composer and one of the first to introduce a season of Italian opera (1705) to London. Opera proving unremunerative, Clayton was with Steele in 1711 promoting concerts in the Music Room in York Buildings. See Professor John Loftis, 'Richard Steele's Censorium', in *The Huntington Library Quarterly*, xiv (1950), 43–66.

[3] This letter as a whole was first printed by Elwin, but Pope inserted the second paragraph ('I shall never make the least reply . . .') in the letter to Caryll that he printed in 1735–42 under date of 15 June 1711. He made several stylistic revisions in the text, which do not modify the substance essentially.

I shall never make the least reply to him, not only because you advise me, but because I've ever been of opinion that if a book can't answer for its self to the public, 'tis to no sort of purpose for its author to do it. If I am wrong in any sentiment in that *Essay*, I protest sincerely I don't desire all the world should be deceived, (which would be of very ill consequence) that I myself might be thought right (which is of very little consequence). I'd be the first to recant, for the benefit of others, and the glory of my self, for (as I take it) when a man owns himself to *have been* in an errour, he does but tell you in other words, that he is wiser than he was. But I have had an advantage by [the] publishing that book of Dennis's which otherwise I should never have known. It has been the occasion of making me friends and open abettors of several Gentlemen of known sense and wit; and of proving to me, which I've till now doubted of, that my Trifles[1] are taken some notice of to the world in general, else I should never be attacked thus in particular. I have read that t'was a custom among the Romans, while the general rode in triumph, to have slaves[2] in the streets that railed at him and reproached him; to put him in mind that tho' his services were in the main approved & rewarded, yet he had still faults enough to keep him humble.

I have two letters from Mr Steele,[3] the subject of which is to persuade me to write a musicall interlude to be set next winter by Clayton, whose interest he espouses with great zeal. His expression is, Pray oblige Mr Clayton, that is me, so far as, &c. The desire I have to gratify Mr Steele has made me consent to his request; tho' 'tis a task that otherwise I'm not very fond of.

I delivered the enclosed to the lady.[4] She seemed not to approve of Mrs N—'s writing to the Gentleman, since if sense of honour and a true knowledge of the case, which you have already given him, are too weak to move him, 'tis to be thought nothing else ever will. I cannot but join with you in a high concern for a person of so much merit, as I'm daily more and more convinced by her conversation that she is; whose ill fate it has been to be cast as a pearl before swine. And he who put so valuable a present into so ill hands shall (I own to you) never have my good opinion, tho' he had that of all the world besides. God grant he may never be my Friend! and guard all my friends from such a Guardian! The saying this so freely, and inconsiderately, to you may be a proof with what openness I unfold my whole heart in confidence of your friendship, which I shall ever look upon as a great blessing, and study to return to with all that gratitude and sincerity which is a duty from one who is infinitely obliged a thousand ways, and can only

[1] Trifles] writings *1735–42*.

[2] Slaves] common soldiers *1735–42*.

[3] It is not altogether clear what, if anything, Pope wrote for Steele and Clayton.

[4] The Lady is Mrs. Weston and the Gentleman her husband. Mrs. N— is Mrs. Nelson.

testify how much he thinks himself so, one way; which is that poor vulgar way of assuring you he will always continue | Dear Sir | your most faithful affectionate | friend and obliged servant | A.P.

I have heard of the good health of all at Whiteknights tho' 'tis a great while since I could wait upon 'em. Mr Dancastle returns you, with all heartiness, his humble service, and I intreat your whole family to accept of mine.

POPE *to* CARYLL[1] [Post 4 *September* 1711]

Elwin–Courthope, vi. 156–7

EPITAPH ON JOHN LORD CARYLL

A manly form; a bold, yet modest mind;
Sincere, though prudent; constant, yet resigned;
Honour unchanged, a principle profest;
Fixed to one side, but mod'rate to the rest:
An honest courtier, and a patriot too;
Just to his prince, and to his country true:
All these were joined in one, yet failed to save
The wise, the learn'd, the virtuous, and the brave;
Lost, like the common plunder of the grave!
Ye few, whom better genius does inspire,
Exalted souls, informed with purer fire!
Go now, learn all vast science can impart;
Go, fallen nature, take the heights of art!
Rise higher yet: learn ev'n yourselves to know;
Nay, to yourselves alone that knowledge owe.
Then, when you seem above mankind to soar,
Look on this marble, and be vain no more!

I have a little poetical present to make you, which I dare not trust by the post, and could be glad you would please to direct me a way to send it to you; for I am a little apprehensive of putting it into Lewis's [hand]s, who is too much a bookseller to be trusted with rhyme or

[1] Elwin's manner of printing this letter is peculiar. In the absence of other information one must assume that he is printing from Add. 28618, the source of all other Caryll letters of unspecified provenance. But the letter seems not to be there. The collocation of the epitaph and the remark concerning the 'little poetical present' (obviously an unpublished MS., which he is unwilling to send through Lewis the bookseller, who is also Caryll's London agent for parcels, &c.) would seem to indicate that the present is the epitaph, which (in a transcript?) has been attached to the letter that concerns it. Elwin thought the present was *The Rape of the Lock*, but while Pope would not wish to trust that MS. to Lewis, it would not be so appropriately a 'present' as the epitaph. Caryll's uncle, the Jacobite earl, died in France on 4 Sept. 1711. Presumably he was buried there and the epitaph was not used. Pope, as Elwin tells us, 'afterwards took the first six lines for an epitaph to Sir William Trumbull, and remodelled the rest to become a part (ll. 50–54) of the Epistle to Jervas'.

reputation. * * * What application that was which was made to Mr. Steele on my account I cannot imagine, unless it was made from yourself; for, indeed, I know no other friend who would have been so generous for my sake, and I know nothing you would not attempt to oblige those you once profess a kindness to. I desire your whole family to accept my most humble service, and am, with all sincerity, dear sir, your ever obliged friend and servant.

†CROMWELL *to* POPE[1] 26 *October* 1711

1735

October 26, 1711.

Mr. *Wycherley* visited me at the *Bath* in my sickness, and express'd much affection to me: hearing from me how welcome his letters wou'd be, he presently writ to you; in which I inserted my Scrall, and after a second. He went to *Gloucester* in his way to *Salop*, but was disappointed of a boat and so return'd to the *Bath*; then he shew'd me your answer to his letters, in which you speak of my good nature, but I fear you found me very froward at *Reading*; yet you allow for my illness. I cou'd not possibly be in the same house with Mr. *Wycherley*, tho' I sought it earnestly; nor come up to town with him, he being engag'd with others; but whenever we met we talk'd of you. He praises your Poem,[2] and even outvies me in kind expressions of you. As if he had not wrote two letters to you, he was for writing every Post; I put him in mind he had already. Forgive me this wrong, I know not whither my talking so much of your great humanity and tenderness to me, and love to him; or whether the return of his natural disposition to you, was the cause; but certainly you are now highly in his favour: now he will come this Winter to your house, and I must go with him; but first he will invite you speedily to town.—I arrived on *Saturday* last much wearied, yet had wrote sooner, but was told by Mr. *Gay* (who has writ a pretty Poem to *Lintot*,[3] and who gives you his service) that you was gone from home. *Lewis* shew'd me your letter which set me right, and your next letter is impatiently expected by me. Mr. *Wycherley* came to town on *Sunday* last, and kindly surpriz'd me with a visit on *Monday* morning. We din'd and drank together; and I saying, *To our Loves*, he reply'd, *'Tis Mr.* Pope's *health*: He said he would go to Mr. *Thorold*'s and leave a letter for you. Tho' I cannot answer for the event of all this, in respect to him; yet I can assure you, that when you please to come you will be most desirable to me, as always by inclination so now by duty, who shall ever be | Your, &c.

[1] Printed in Pope's octavo editions; he omitted it from his quarto and folio of 1737.

[2] *Essay on Criticism*.—Pope, 1735–42.

[3] Gay's *Epistle* to Lintot appeared in the publisher's *Miscellaneous Poems and Translations* (1712). The poem mentioned Pope with high praise. See Pope to Cromwell, 21 Dec. 1711.

||POPE *to* CROMWELL[1] 12 *November* 1711

The Bodleian Library

⌜Binfield,⌝ Novr 12. 1711.

I receivd the Entertainment of your Letter the Day after I had sent you one of mine; and I am but this morning returnd hither, ⌜from a Weeks Visit at Mr Englefyld's.⌝ The News you tell me of the many difficulties you found in your Return from *Bath* gives me such a kind of pleasure as we usually take in accompanying our Friends in their mixt adventures; for methinks I see you labring thro all your Inconveniences, of the rough Roads, the hard Saddle, the Trotting Horse, and what not? What an agreable Surprize wou'd it have been to me, to have met you by pure accident ⌜at *Bagshot*,⌝ which I was within an ace of doing, ⌜being at *Hallgrove*[2] that very day?⌝ And to have carry'd you off triumphantly ⌜to *Binfield*,⌝ sett you on an easier Pad, & relievd the wandring Knight with a Nights Lodging, & rural Repaste, at our Castle in the Forest? But these are only the pleasing Imaginations ⌜& Amorous Idæa's⌝ of a disapointed Lover, who must suffer in a melancholy absence yet these 2 months. In the meantime I take up with the Muses for want of your better Company; the Muses, *Quae nobiscum pernoctant*, *peregrinantur*, *rusticantur*.[3] Those Aeriall Ladies just discover to me enough of their Beauties to urge my Pursuit, and draw me [on][4] in a wandring Maze of Thought, still in hopes (& only in hopes) of attaining those favors from 'em, which they confer on their more happy admirers elsewhere. We grasp some more beautifull Idea in our Brain, than our Endeavors to express it can set to the view of others; & still do but labour to fall short of our first Imagination. The gay Colouring which Fancy gave to our Design at the first transient glance we had of it, goes off in the Execution; like those various Figures in the gilded Clouds, which while we gaze long upon, to seperate the Parts of each imaginary Image, the whole faints before the Eye, & decays into Confusion.

I am highly pleas'd with the knowledge you give me of Mr W[ycherley]'s[5] present Temper which seems so favorable to me: I shall ever have such a Fund of Affection for him as to be agreable to myself when I am so to him, & cannot but be Gay when he's in good humor, as the Surface of the Earth (if You will pardon a Poetical Similitude) is clearer, or gloomier, just as the Sun is brighter, or more overcast.—

[1] Throughout this letter the half-brackets indicate omissions made in all of Pope's texts—made, typically, so as to excise trivial, specific details of no public relevance, so he would think.

[2] Pope's half-sister, Mrs. Charles Rackett, lived at Hallgrove near Bagshot.

[3] In the quarto and folio of 1737 Pope omitted this favourite passage from Cicero's *Pro Archia*, vii. 16.

[4] [on] appears in all Pope's texts.

[5] Curll expanded *W—'s* to the complete name.

⌜Pray assure Mr Gay of my Service.⌝[1] I shou'd be glad to see the *Verses* to *Lintott*[2] which you mention, for methinks something very odly agreable may be produc'd from that Subject.[3]—For what remains, I am so well, that nothing but the assurance of your[4] being so can make me better; & If you wou'd have me live with any satisfaction, these dark Days in which I cannot see you, it must be by your writing sometimes to | Dear Sir, | Your most affectionate Friend | & most humble Servant | A: Pope:

Address: To Henry Cromwell Esq: | at the Blew Ball in great | Wildstreet near | Drury lane | LONDON

†CROMWELL *to* POPE — 7 *December* 1711

1735

Dec. 7, 1711.

Mr. *Wycherley* has, I believe, sent you two or three letters of invitation; but you, like the Fair, will be long sollicited before you yield, to make the favour the more acceptable to the Lover. He is much yours by his talk; for that unbounded Genius which has rang'd at large like a libertine, now seems confin'd to you: and I shou'd take him for your Mistress too by your simile of the Sun and Earth: 'Tis very fine, but inverted by the application; for the gaiety of your fancy, and the drooping of his by the withdrawing of your lustre, perswades me it wou'd be juster by the reverse. Oh happy Favourite of the Muses! how *per-noctare*, all night long with them? but alas! you do but toy, but skirmish with them, and decline a close Engagement. Leave Elegy and Translation to the inferior Class, on whom the Muses only glance now and then like our Winter-Sun, and then leave 'em in the dark. Think on the Dignity of Tragedy, which is of the greater Poetry, as *Dennis* says,[5] and foil him at his other weapon, as you have done in Criticism. Every one wonders that a Genius like yours will not support the sinking *Drama*; and Mr. *Wilks* (tho' I think his Talent is Comedy) has express'd a furious ambition to swell in your Buskins. We have had a poor Comedy of *Johnson*'s (not *Ben*) which held seven nights, and has got him three hundred pounds,[6] for the town is sharp-set on new Plays. In vain wou'd I fire you by Interest or Ambition,

[1] Curll here for the second time cuts out a friendly remark about Gay. See 24 July 1711 (to Cromwell).

[2] A *Receipt* to Make a *Miscellany*. By Mr. *Gay*.—Curll, 1726.

[3] Pope omitted this sentence from 1737 b.

[4] In opening the letter Cromwell had torn the text at the seal. Curll supplied the words *your* and *live*. Apparently a postscript has been cut away.

[5] See especially Dennis's *Grounds of Criticism in Poetry* (1704), ch. iii, in Dennis's *Critical Works*, ed. E. N. Hooker, i. 338.

[6] Charles Johnson's *Wife's Relief: or the Husband's Cure*, first acted 12 Nov. 1711, proved to be about the most popular of this prolific playwright's pieces.

when your mind is not susceptible of either; tho' your Authority (arising from the General esteem, like that of *Pompey*) must infallibly assure you of success; for which in all your wishes you will be attended with those of | Your, &c.

||POPE *to* CROMWELL[1] 21 *December* 1711

The Bodleian Library

Decr 21. 1711

If I have not writ to you so soon as I ought, let my writing now attone for the delay; as it will infallibly do, when you know what a Sacrifice I make you at this Time, and that every moment my Eyes are employed upon this paper, they are taken off from Two of the finest faces[2] in the Universe: ⌜For I am at this instant placd betwixt Two such Ladies that in good faith 'tis all I'm able to do, to keep my self in my Skin. *He! Monsieur Cromvell! Entendez-vous bien?*⌝[3] But indeed 'tis some Consolation to me to consider, that while I but write this Period, I escape some hundred fatal Darts from those unerring eyes, and about a thousand Deaths, or better. Now You, that delight in dying, wou'd not once have dreamt of an absent Friend in these Circumstances, You that are so nice an Admirer of Beauty, or (as a Critic wou'd say) *so Elegant a Spectator of Forms?* You must have a sober Dish of Coffee, and a Solitary Candle at your side, to write an Epistle Lucubratory to your Friend; where as I can do it as well with two Pair of radiant Lights, that outshine the Golden God of Day, & Silver Goddess of Night, with all the refulgent Eyes of the Firmament. —You fancy now that *Sapho's* Eyes are a Couple of these my Tapers, but 'tis no such matter Sir; these are Eyes that have more Persuasion in one Glance than all *Sapho's* Oratory and Gesture together, let her put her Body into what *moving Postures* she pleases. Indeed, indeed my Friend, you cou'd never have found so improper a Time to tempt me with Interest or Ambition: Let me but have the Reputation of these in my keeping,[4] & as for my own, let the Devil, or let Dennis, take it for ever! How gladly wou'd I give all I am worth, that is to say, my *Pastorals* for *one* of their *Maidenheads*,[5] & my *Essay*[6] for the other? I wou'd lay out all my *Poetry* in *Love*; an *Original* for a *Lady*, &

[1] In 1726 Curll printed a faithful text of this letter; in 1735 in his *Mr. Pope's Literary Correspondence*, vol. i, he reproduced Pope's text of that year. In vol. ii of his series he printed the excisions made by Pope (and himself) in 1735.

[2] Naturally, but not too certainly, one identifies the 'two finest faces' as those of Teresa and Martha Blount.

[3] Omitted in all Pope's texts.

[4] See Pope's epigram at the end of his letter to Martha Blount here placed in the middle of Feb. 1714/15.

[5] their Maidenheads] them *1735–42*

[6] 'on Criticism' was added in the margin of the original (by Curll?).

a *Translation* for a *Waiting Maid*! ⌜And now (since you find what a blessed disposition I am in)

> Tell me, by all the melting joys of Love,
> By the warm Transports & entrancing Languors,
> By the soft Fannings of the wafting sheets,
> By the dear Tremblings of the Bed of Bliss;
> By all these tender Adjurations tell me,
> —Am I not fit to write a Tragedy?

And wou'd not these Lines sound admirably in the Mouth of *Wilks*, especially if he humourd each period with his Leg, & stamp'd with just alacrity at the Cadences? But⌝[1] alas! what have I to do with *Jane Gray*?[2] as long as Miss *Molly*, Miss *Betty*, or Miss *Patty*, are in this World? Sh[all] I write of *Beauties murderd long ago*, when there are those at this [in]stant that *murder me*? I'll e'en compose my own Tragedy, & the Poet sh[all] appear in his own Person to move Compassion. 'Twill be far more effectu[al] than *Bays* his[3] entring with a Rope about his neck,[4] and the World w[ill] own, there never was a more miserable Object brought upon the Stage.[5]

Now you that are a Critic, pray inform me in what manner I may Connect the foregoing Part of this Letter with that which is to foll[ow] according to the Rules? I wou'd willingly return Mr *Gay* my than[ks] for the favor of his *Poem*, & in particular, for his kind mention of me.[6] I hop'd, when I heard a new Comedy had met with success upon the Stag[e,] that it had been his, to which I really wish no less; and (had it been [any] way in my power) shoud have been very glad to have contributed to its [in]troduction into the World. His Verses to *Lintot*[7]

[1] The whole passage in half-brackets was omitted in Pope's texts.

[2] Rowe's tragedy on Jane Grey was acted in 1715. Quite possibly he was meditating the subject thus early, and Cromwell, who seems not to have liked Rowe, may have suggested that Pope would do the subject much better.

[3] Bayes his] Bayes's *Curll, 1726; and thereafter Pope.*

[4] In *The Rehearsal.*

[5] Pope here inserted a line to separate the two parts of the letter.

[6] On a *Miscellany* of *Poems.*—Curll, 1726 (The mention of Pope occurs in lines 80–86 of Gay's *Epistles.*)

[7] These Verses are printed in Dr. Swift's, and our Author's Miscellanies in 3 Vols. 8vo.—Pope, 1735–42.

It is 'the whim' and not Gay's *Epistle* to Lintot that will be found in the 'last' volume of the *Miscellanies* (1727), p. 105. Pope seems here by ambiguous placing of his footnote to try to shift the authorship of the verses (*Some Colinaeus praise, some Bleau*) from himself to Gay. Curll's notes are also confusing. To the words 'His Verses' Curll adds: 'Verses to be prefix'd to Bernard Lintot's New Miscellany', when he should have stuck to the title he gave in his previous note ('On a Miscellany of Poems'). Curll in another note to the end of the sentence ('the opposite page') says of 'the whim': 'This Copy of Verses will be found in our Second Volume' (Curll, 1735). His vol. ii, pp. 136–7, contains 'Verses to be prefix'd to Bernard Lintot's New Miscellany', and these must be what Cromwell was 'troubled with in the opposite page'. In his *Miscellanea* (1726) Curll had printed these verses after the letter, of which they were evidently a part. Reproducing Pope's text of 1735 he omitted the verses from the letter in vol. i, but included them among the 'castrations' restored in vol. ii of *Mr. Pope's Literary Correspondence.*

have put a Whim in[to] my head, which you are like to be troubled with in the opposite p[age]. Take it as you find it, the Production of half an hour, to[ther] Morning. I design very soon to put a Task of a more serious nature up[on] you, in reviewing a Piece of mine that may better deserve Criticisme and by that time you have done with it, I hope to tell you in Person with how much ardour and fidelity I am | Dear Sir | Your ever affectionate | Friend & Obligd Servant | A. Pope

Decr 21. 1711.[1]

POPE *to* STEELE[2] 30 *December* 1711

Harvard University

Binfield, Decr 30. 1711

Sir,—I have past part of this Christmass with some honest Country Gentlemen, who have Wit enough to be Good-Natur'd, but no manner of Relish for criticisme or polite writing, as you may easily conclude when I tell you they never read the Spectator. This was the reason I did not see That of the 20th till yesterday,[3] at my return home; wherein, tho it be the highest Satisfaction to find oneself commended by a Person whom all the world commends, yet I am not more obligd to you for that, than for your Candor and Frankness in acquainting me with the Errour I have been guilty of in speaking too freely of my Brother-Moderns: 'Tis indeed the common Method of all Counterfits in Wit, as well as in Physic, to begin with warning us of others' cheats, in order to make the more way for their owne. But if ever this Essay be thought worth a Second Edition, I shall be very glad to strike out all such Strokes which you shall be so kind as to point out to me: I shall really be proud of being corrected; for I believe 'tis with the Errors of the Mind as with the Weeds of a Field, which if they are consum'd upon the place, enrich & improve it more, than if none had ever grown there. Some of the Faults of that Book I have myself found, & more (I am confident) others have, enough at least to have made me very humble, had not you given this publick Approbation of it, which I can look upon only as the Effect of that Benevolence you

[1] This is the last of the letters sold by Mrs. Thomas to Curll.

[2] This letter, without cover or address, was discovered by Miss Lucy Aiken, who first printed it in her *Life of Joseph Addison* (1843), ii. 73–74. She assumed that it was to Addison since it was found among the papers of the Tickell family with other papers preserved by Addison's executor, Thomas Tickell. But Steele's reply (20 Jan. 1711/12) makes it quite apparent that the letter was addressed to him and passed on to Addison, the author of the *Spectator* paper that concerned Pope's *Essay*. It was printed as to Steele by Elwin.

[3] *The Spectator* (No. 253) for 20 Dec. 1711 highly praised Pope's *Essay on Criticism* but made reservations about unspecified strokes of ill nature. These, of course, concerned John Dennis.

have ever been so ready to show to Any, who but make it their Endeavour to do well. But as a little Rain revives a Flower which too much overcharges & depresses, so moderate Praise encourages a young Writer, but a great deal may injure him: and you have been so lavish in this point,[1] that I almost hope (not to call in question your Judgment in the Piece) that 'twas some particular partial Inclination to the Author which carryd you so far. This wou'd please me much more than I can express, for I shou'd in good earnest be fonder of your Friendship than of the world's Applause. I might hope too to deserve it better, since a man may more easily answer for his own Sincerity, than his own Witt. And if the highest Esteem built on the justest ground in the world, together with Gratitude for an Obligation so unexpectedly conferr'd, can oblige a man to be ever yours, I beg you to believe no one is more so than | Sir | Your most Faithfull & obedient | humble Servant, | A: Pope.

[1] A letter to Caryll (31 July 1710) uses this same figure and very similar phrasing. So also does an earlier letter to Wycherley (25 March 1705). When preparing the Wycherley letters for publication Pope probably had the original of the Caryll letter in his possession, and he may have elaborated the figure in fabricating the letter to Wycherley (as Elwin inclined to believe). The three passages (here and in i. 5 and i. 94) are very close in phrasing. The Wycherley text, however, has the early artificial style that Pope had ceased to affect before 1729. In one or two words the Wycherley text is closer to this letter to Steele (which Pope did not have in 1729) than it is to the Caryll letter. Evidently the figure is a favourite, and the passages may simply be an example of Pope's astonishing memory for phrase.

1712

This year Pope's new pieces came out only in miscellanies or periodicals. *Sapho to Phaon* appeared in March in Tonson's *Ovid's Epistles, Messiah* in a May *Spectator,* and *The Rape of the Lock* (first form) with other pieces appeared, also in May, in Lintot's *Miscellaneous Poems and Translations,* a miscellany assembled at least in part by Pope for Lintot. During the year he worked on *The Temple of Fame* and *Windsor Forest,* and composed *The Dying Christian to his Soul* as a result of his interest in Hadrian's verses. His personal relations with Steele, and Addison, were at their most cordial this year, and the friendship with John Gay became closer. Some of his letters to Caryll continue his controversy over possibly heterodox ideas in the *Essay on Criticism,* but more commonly they concern Mrs. Weston's unhappy lot or other personal matters—at times financial.

STEELE *to* POPE[1] — 20 *January* 1711[12]

Homer MSS. Add. 4807

Jan: 20th 1711

I have received Your very kind letter. That part of it which is grounded upon Your beleif that I have much affection and Freindship for You I receive with great pleasure, that which acknowledges the Honour done to your essay I have no pretence to. The paper was written by one with whome I will make you acquainted which is the best return I can make to you for your favour to Sir | Your Most obliged Humble Servant | Richard Steele

Mr Pope:

Address: To | Mr Pope | To be left at Mr Lewis's | Bookseller in Russell-street | Covent-Garden

EDWARD BEDINGFIELD *to* POPE[2] — 16 *May* 1712

Homer MSS. Add. 4807

Graysin May the 16th [1]712[3]

Sir,—Last Night I had the favour of yours of the eleventh Instant and according to the directions therein I have enclosed the Copys for

[1] In the margin has been written an entry, now practically undecipherable, which may have been 'The Spectator of | Decr 20 is writ | by Mr Addison'.

[2] Mr. Bedingfield was the third son of Sir Harry Bedingfield, and was a relative of Caryll's. Pope may have met him in the coffee-houses, for he sends service by Cromwell (see letter of 24 June 1710).

[3] Dated 26 May by Elwin.

Lord Petre and that for Mrs Belle Fermor[1]—she is out of Towne and therefore all I can do is to leave her pacquet at her lodgeing—the Gout has seised 2 fingers of my right hand which as it putts me on the necessety of concludeing abrutly will oblige you to pardon it in | Sir | Your very Humble Servant | Edw. Bedingfeld

†CARYLL *to* POPE 23 *May* 1712

1735

May 23, 1712.

I am very glad for the sake of the Widow and for the credit of the deceas'd, that *Betterton*'s remains[2] are fallen into such hands as may render 'em reputable to the one and beneficial to the other. Besides the publick acquaintance I long had with that poor man, I also had a slender knowledge of his parts and capacity by private conversation, and ever thought it pity, he was necessitated by the straitness of his fortune, to act (and especially to his latest hours) an imaginary and fictitious part, who was capable of exhibiting a real one, with credit to himself and advantage to his neighbour.

I hope your health permitted you to execute your design of giving us an imitation of *Pollio*,[3] I am satisfy'd 'twill be doubly *Divine* and I shall long to see it. I ever thought church-musick the most ravishing of all harmonious compositions, and must also believe sacred subjects, well handled, the most inspiring of all Poetry.

But where hangs the *Lock* now? (tho' I know that rather than draw any just reflection upon your self, of the least shadow of ill-nature, you would freely have suprest one of the best of Poems.) I hear no more of it—will it come out in *Lintot*'s Miscellany[4] or not? I wrote to Lord *Petre* upon the subject of the Lock, some time since, but have as yet had no answer, nor indeed do I know when he'll be in *London*. I have since I saw you corresponded with Mrs. *W*. I hope she is now with her Aunt,[5] and that her journey thither was something facilitated by my writing to that Lady as pressingly as possible, not to let any thing whatsoever obstruct it. I sent her obliging answer to the party it most concern'd; and when I hear Mrs. *W*. is certainly there, I will write again to my Lady, to urge as much as possible the effecting the only thing that in my opinion can make her Niece easy. I have run out my extent of paper, and am | Your, &c.

[1] *The Rape of the Lock* was on sale the 20th. Advance copies were evidently sent to the parties most concerned. Caryll had not received his on 23 May. See his letter of that date.

[2] A Translation of some Part of Chaucer's Canterbury Tales, the Prologues, &c. printed in a Miscellany with some works of Mr. Pope, in 2 Vol. 12° by B. Lintot.—Pope, 1735–42.

[3] The imitation of Pollio, Pope's *Messiah*, had already appeared in *Spectator*, No. 378 for 14 May 1712.

[4] *The Rape of the Lock*, in its first form, had appeared on 20 May in Lintot's *Miscellaneous Poems and Translations*.

[5] Mrs. Weston's aunt, Catherine Gage, had married Walter, Lord Aston of Forfar.

POPE *to* MARTHA BLOUNT 25 *May* 1712

Mapledurham

May the 25. 1712.

Madam,—At last I do myself the honour to send you the Rape of the Locke; which has been so long coming out, that the Ladies Charms might have been half decay'd, while the Poet was celebrating them, and the Printer publishing them. But yourself and your fair Sister must needs have been surfeited already with this Triffle; and therfore you have no hopes of Entertainment but from the rest of this Booke, wherein (they tell me) are some things that may be dangerous to be lookd upon; however I think You may venture, tho' you shou'd Blush for it, since Blushing becomes you the best of any Lady in England, and then the most dangerous thing to be lookd upon is Yourself—Indeed Madam, not to flatter you, our Virtue will be sooner overthrown by one Glance of yours, than by all the wicked Poets can write in an Age, as has been too dearly experienc'd by the wickedest of 'em all, that is to say, by | Madam | Your most obedient | humble Servant, | A: Pope:

Address: To Mrs Martha Blount, | Present.

||POPE *to* CARYLL[1] 28 *May* 1712

Add. 28618

May 28. 1712.

It is not only the disposition I always have of conversing with you, that makes me so speedily answer your obliging lines, but the apprehension lest your charitable intent of writing to my Lady A[ston] on Mrs W[eston]'s affair[2] should be frustrated by the short stay she makes there, (which from all I can learn will not be above a fortnight) she went thither on the 25th with that mixture of expectation and anxiety with which people usually go into unknown or half discovered countries, utterly ignorant of the dispositions of the inhabitants, and the treatment they are to meet with. ⌜I only wish it may be such as is due to her merit, and then I think it must be as good as ever woman found.⌝ The unfortunate of all people are the most unfit to be left alone; yet we see the world generally takes care they shall be so, by abandoning 'em: whereas if we took a right[3] prospect of human nature,[4] the business and study of the happy and easy, should be to divert and humour, as well as pity and comfort, the distressed. I cannot therefore excuse some near allies of mine for their conduct of late towards this lady,

[1] Parts of this letter were printed by Pope in 1735. His omissions are here indicated by half-brackets.
[2] See above, i. 119 n., 123, 132, 142, &c.
[3] right] considerate *1735–42*.
[4] human nature] the world *1737–42*.

which has given me a great deal of anger as well as sorrow. All I can say to you of them at present is, that they have not been my relations these two months[1]—The consent of opinions in our minds is certainly a nearer tie than can be contracted by all the blood in our bodies; and I am proud of finding I've something congenial with ⌜Mr Caryll in me⌝.[2] Will you permit me, ⌜dear sir, in friendship⌝ to confess to you, that all the favors and kind offices you have shown towards me have not so strongly cemented me yours, as the discovery of that generous and manly compassion you manifested in the case of this unhappy lady? ⌜Nothing (without flattery) ever touched me more than the sentiment you expressed on my first opening that matter in your coach as we past on the road. Forgive my saying thus much, in consideration of my suppressing so much more, which I could vent on this subject.⌝

I am afraid to insinuate to you how much I esteem you. Flatterers have taken up the style which was once peculiar to friends only, and an honest man has now no way left to express himself ⌜by⌝, besides the common one of knaves, so that true friends nowadays differ in their address from flatterers, much as right mastiffs do from spaniels, and show themselves by a dumb, surly, sort of fidelity, rather than by the complaisant and open manner of kindness. ⌜This last, however, is what you use to me, and which I account for the best way, tho' I should suspect it in most others.⌝ Will you never leave commending my poetry? In fair truth, sir, I like it but too well myself already. Expose me no more, I beg you, to the great danger of vanity, (the rock of all men, but most of young men) and be kindly content for the future when you would please me thoroughly, to say only, you like what I write.[3] ⌜The eclogue on the Messiah in imitation of Pollio, I had transcribed a week since with design to send it to you; but finding it printed in the *Spectator* of the fourteenth (which paper I know is constantly sent down to you) I gave it to Mr Englefield. I hope Lewis[4] has conveyed you by this time the *Rape of the Lock*, with what other things of mine are in Lintot's collection; the whole book I will put into your hands when I have the satisfaction to meet you at Reading, which unfeignedly I passionately long for. What hitherto reprieved you from my company was my long illness, which was no sooner over, but Mr Eng[lefield] told me you was upon the point of going in Warwickshire,[5] from whence I hope you will bring home all you express; that

[1] The Racketts sympathized with Mr. Weston in his troubles with his wife.

[2] with Mr. Caryll in me; will] with you. Will *1735–42*.

[3] The text as printed in 1735 ended here.

[4] W. Lewis, a Catholic bookseller and a friend of Pope's and Caryll's.

[5] The wedding of Mr. John Caryll, Jr., and Lady Mary Mackenzie took place apparently on 15 July in Warwickshire. The plan was that Pope should accompany the bridal pair from London to Ladyholt. Lady Mary was the daughter of the 4th Earl of Seaforth, who had been attainted as a Jacobite. He died in Paris in 1701, and his countess, who at times lived at Twickenham, also died in Paris in 1732.

is, all that man desire[s]. I shall partake so much of the young gentleman's joy, that I fear the nice casuists may account it a sort of enjoying my neighbor's wife, in spirit. But seriously, no friend you have can be more nearly concerned in any thing that regards your happiness and family's than I am. I only hope (as I told Mr Bedingfield the other day, who has done me the favor to send some books of the Rape, to my Lord Petre, and Mrs Fermor) that extreme happiness, which usually causes people to forget old acquaintance, will not make young Mr Caryll entirely forget me in the number of his humble servants. If I might presume to offer any advice in this important change of his life, it should be comprehended in this short sentence, Let him fear the Lord, love his lady, and read the Tatler.

To conclude, as no happiness comes without some allay, so it seems the young gentleman must carry me down with his fair lady: and I shall supply the place of the Egyptian skeleton at the entertainments on your return. But I'll be satisfied to make an odd figure in your triumphs, for the pleasure I shall take in attending 'em. The *Imperatrix Triumphans* shall not be without a slave in her chariot, to hold a wreath over the conqueress. I am, dear sir, with the sincerest respect and affection | your most faithfull friend and | humble servant | A:P:⌉

⌈I beg your lady and the whole family may be assured of my most humble service.⌉

†STEELE *to* POPE 1 *June* 1712

1735

June 1, 1712

I am at a solitude, an house between *Hampstead* and *London* wherein Sir *Charles Sedley* died.[1] This circumstance set me a thinking and ruminating upon the employments in which Men of wit exercise themselves. It was said of Sir *Charles*, who breath'd his last in this room,

> Sedley has that prevailing gentle art,
> Which can with a resistless charm impart,
> The loosest wishes to the chastest heart;
> Raise such a conflict, kindle such a fire
> Between declining Virtue and Desire,
> Till the poor vanquish'd Maid dissolves away
> In dreams all night, in sighs and tears all day.[2]

[1] Pictures of the house may be found in Howitt's *Heights of London*, p. 214, and in Park's *Topography and Natural History of Hampstead.* Professor Blanchard (Steele's *Correspondence*, p. 54) reproduces the mezzotint made from Constable's painting.

[2] From the Earl of Rochester's 'Allusion to Horace the Tenth Satire of the First Book'.

This was an happy talent to a man of the Town, but I dare say, without presuming to make uncharitable conjectures on the author's present condition, he would rather have had it said of him that he had pray'd,

—Oh thou my voice inspire,
Who touch'd Isaiah's hallow'd lips with fire![1]

I have turn'd to every verse and chapter, and think you have preserv'd the sublime heavenly spirit throughout the whole, especially at —*Hark a glad voice*—and—*The lamb with wolves shall graze*—There is but one line which I think below the original,

He wipes the tears for ever from our eyes.

You have express'd it with a good and pious, but not with so exalted and poetical a spirit as the prophet. *The Lord God will wipe away tears from off all faces.* If you agree with me in this, alter it by way of paraphrase or otherwise, that when it comes into a volume it may be amended. Your Poem is already better than the *Pollio.* I am | Your, &c.

†POPE *to* STEELE[2] 18 *June* 1712

1735

June 18, 1712.

You have oblig'd me with a very kind letter, by which I find you shift the scene of your life from the town to the country, and enjoy that mix'd state which wise men both delight in, and are qualify'd for. Methinks the Moralists and Philosophers[3] have generally[4] run too much into extremes in commending[5] intirely either solitude, or publick life. In the former, men for the most part[6] grow useless by too much rest, and in the latter are destroy'd by too much precipitation; as waters lying still, putrify and are good for nothing, and running violently on do but the more mischief in their passage to others, and are swallow'd up and lost the sooner themselves. Those indeed who can be useful[7] to all states, should be like gentle streams, that not only glide thro' lonely valleys[8] and forests amidst the flocks and the shep-

[1] From *Messiah*, ll. 5–6.

[2] This letter is probably the first of Pope's to appear in print. Since it appeared in *The Spectator* for 16 June 1712, the date Pope casually gave it in 1735 is obviously impossible. The text here printed is that of 1735, presumably a revision of the *Spectator* text. Since Addison and Steele habitually revised letters sent in before they printed them, it is conceivable that Pope's text is the more authentic—but not probable. Under the circumstances all verbal differences between the two texts are noted.

[3] the Moralists and Philosophers] most of the Philosophers and Moralists *1712.*

[4] generally] *omitted in 1712.*

[5] commending] praising *1712.*

[6] for the most part] generally *1712.*

[7] Those . . . useful] Those who, like you, can make themselves useful *1712.*

[8] valleys] vales *1712.*

herds, but visit populous towns in their course, and are at once of ornament and service to them. But there are[1] another sort of people who seem design'd for solitude, such I mean as[2] have more to hide than to show: As for my own part, I am one of those of whom *Seneca* says, *Tam umbratiles sunt, ut putent in turbido esse quicquid in luce est.*[3] Some men like some[4] pictures, are fitter for a corner than a full light; and I believe such as have a natural bent to solitude (to carry on the former similitude)[5] are like waters which may be forc'd into fountains and exalted into a great height, may make a noble figure and a louder noise,[6] but after all they[7] would run more smoothly, quietly[8] and plentifully, in their own natural course upon the ground.[9] The consideration of this would make me very well contented with the possession only of that Quiet which *Cowley* calls the *Companion of Obscurity.*[10] But whoever has the Muses too for his companions, can never be idle enough to be uneasy. Thus Sir you see I would flatter my self into a good opinion of my own way of living. *Plutarch* just now told me, that 'tis in human life as in a game at tables, where a man[11] may wish for the highest cast, but if his chance be otherwise, he is e'en to play it as well as he can and to make the best of it. I am | Your, &c.

†POPE *to* STEELE[12] — 15 *July* 1712

1735

July 15, 1712.

You formerly observ'd to me, that nothing made a more ridiculous figure in a man's life, than the disparity we often find in him sick and well: Thus one of an unfortunate constitution is perpetually exhibiting a miserable example of the weakness of his mind, and of his body, in their turns. I have had frequent opportunities of late to consider my self in these different views, and I hope have receiv'd some advantage by it, if what Mr. *Waller* says be true, that

> The soul's dark cottage, batter'd and decay'd,
> Lets in new light thro' chinks that time has made.[13]

[1] are] is *1712.* [2] such . . . as] those . . . who *1712.*

[3] Pope varies from Seneca, *Ep.* iii. 6: 'quidam adeo in latebras refugerunt, ut putent in turbido esse, quicquid in luce est.' [4] like some pictures] like Pictures *1712.*

[5] The parenthetical expression is omitted in 1712.

[6] make a noble . . . noise] make a much nobler Figure, and a much louder Noise *1712.*

[7] they] *omitted in 1712.* [8] quietly] equally *1712.*

[9] The foregoing Similitudes our Author had put into Verse some years before and inserted into Mr. *Wycherley*'s Poem on *Mixt Life*. We find him apparently in the Versification of them, as they are since printed in *Wycherley*'s posthumous Works [ed. by Theobald], 8° Page 3d and 4th.—Pope, 1735–42 (omitted in the quarto and folio of 1737).

[10] In one of Pope's favourite passages, Cowley's verses at the end of his essay 'Of Obscurity'.

[11] where a man] one *1712.*

[12] First printed in *The Guardian*, No. 132, for 12 Aug. 1713. Differences in the texts are negligibly slight.

[13] In Pope's day a very popular quotation from Waller's 'Of the last Verses in the Book'.

Then surely sickness, contributing no less than old age to the shaking down this scaffolding of the body, may discover the inward structure more plainly. Sickness is a sort of early old age; it teaches us a diffidence in our earthly state, and inspires us with the thoughts of a future, better than a thousand volumes of philosophers and divines. It gives so warning a concussion to those props of our vanity, our strength and youth, that we think of fortifying our selves within, when there is so little dependance upon our out-works. Youth at the very best is but a betrayer of human life in a gentler and smoother manner than age: 'Tis like a stream that nourishes a plant upon a bank, and causes it to flourish and blossom to the sight, but at the same time is undermining it at the root in secret. My youth has dealt more fairly and openly with me, it has afforded several Prospects of my danger, and given me an advantage not very common to young men, that the attractions of the world have not dazzled me very much; and I begin where most people end, with a full conviction of the emptiness of all sorts of ambition, and the unsatisfactory nature of all human pleasures. When a smart fit of sickness tells me this scurvy tenement of my body will fall in a little time, I am e'en as unconcern'd as was that honest *Hibernian*, who being in bed in the great storm some years ago, and told the house would tumble over his head, made answer, What care I for the house? I am only a lodger. I fancy 'tis the best time to die when one is in the best humour, and so excessively weak as I now am I may say with conscience, that I am not at all uneasy at the thought that many men whom I never had any esteem for, are likely to enjoy this world after me. When I reflect what an inconsiderable little attom every single man is, with respect to the whole creation, methinks 'tis a shame to be concern'd at the removal of such a trivial animal as I am. The morning after my Exit, the sun will rise as bright as ever, the flowers smell as sweet, the plants spring as green, the world will proceed in its old course, people will laugh as heartily, and marry as fast as they were us'd to do. The memory of man, (as it is elegantly express'd in the wisdom of *Solomon*)[1] passeth away as the remembrance of a guest that tarrieth but one day. There are reasons enough, in the fourth chapter of the same book, to make any young man contented with the prospect of death. *For honourable age is not that which standeth in length of time, or is measur'd by number of years. But wisdom is the gray hair to men, and an unspotted life is old age. He was taken away speedily, lest wickedness should alter his understanding, or deceit beguile his soul,* &c. I am | Your, &c.[2]

[1] Verses 8 to 12.

[2] Shortly after this letter was written Pope went to visit Caryll in Sussex, where he spent two months. During the visit Caryll sent venison to Steele, who thanked him in a brief note dated 27 Aug. 1712 (Add. MS. 28618, f. 85*v*). To the note was appended a postscript: 'Mr Addisson gives his Service to Mr Pope.' See *Correspondence of Steele* (ed. R. Blanchard), p. 60.

POPE *to* MRS. MARRIOT 19 *July* [1712?]

Elwin–Courthope, ix. 470

[See 19 July 1713.]

†POPE *to* STEELE[1] *7 November* 1712

1735

Nov. 7. 1712.

I was the other day in company with five or six men of some learning; where chancing to mention the famous verses which the Emperor *Adrian* spoke on his deathbed, they were all agreed that 'twas a piece of Gaiety unworthy of that Prince in those circumstances. I could not but differ from this opinion: Methinks it was by no means a gay, but a very serious soliloquy to his soul at the point of his departure; in which sense I naturally took the verses at my first reading them when I was very young, and before I knew what interpretation the world generally put upon them.

> Animula vagula, blandula,
> Hospes comesque corporis,
> Quæ nunc abibis in loca?
> Pallidula, rigida, nudula,
> Nec (ut Soles) dabis joca!

"Alas, my soul! thou pleasing companion of this body, thou fleeting thing that art now deserting it! whither art thou flying? to what unknown Scene?[2] all trembling, fearful, and pensive. Now what is become of thy former wit and humour? thou shalt jest and be gay no more."

I confess I cannot apprehend where lies the trifling in all this? 'Tis the most natural and obvious reflection imaginable to a dying man: and if we consider the Emperor was a heathen, that doubt concerning the future fate of his soul will seem so far from being the effect of want of thought, that 'twas scarce reasonable he should think otherwise; not to mention that here is a plain confession included of his belief in its immortality. The diminutive epithets of *vagula*, *blandula*, and the rest, appear not to me as expressions of levity, but rather of endearment and concern; such as we find in *Catullus*, and the authors of *Hendeca-syllabi*

[1] Steele promptly printed this letter (without the verses) in *Spectator*, No. 532, for 10 Nov. Pope's text of 1735 added the verses, but otherwise made only one slight change in his text. The verses were first printed in the miscellany of David Lewis in 1730. Pope omitted them from the letter in his quarto and folio of 1737. See also Pope to Caryll, 12 June 1713. In commenting on the letter in *Spectator*, No. 532 Steele says Pope had enclosed 'for my perusal . . . an admirable poem'—doubtless *The Temple of Fame*.

[2] unknown Scene? all trembling] unknown Region? Thou art all trembling *1712*.

after him, where they are us'd to express the utmost love and tenderness for their mistresses.—If you think me right in my notion of the last words of *Adrian*, be pleas'd to insert it in the *Spectator*, if not, to suppress it. I am | Your, &c.

ADRIANI Morientis
AD
ANIMAM,
Translated.

Ah fleeting Spirit! wand'ring Fire,
 That long hast warm'd my tender breast,
Must thou no more this Frame inspire?
 No more a pleasing, chearful Guest?

Whither, ah whither art thou flying!
 To what dark, undiscover'd Shore?
Thou seem'st all trembling, shiv'ring, dying,
 And Wit and Humour are no more!

POPE *to* JOHN CARYLL, JR.[1] — 8 *November* 1712

Elwin–Courthope, vi. 161–4

Nov. 8, 1712.

There is a passage in your last letter which, I may reasonably say, makes it the kindest I ever received; but as people are never more apt to take little exceptions than when they love most, so there are two things in yours which I will blame no farther than in barely mentioning them,—that compliment you pass upon my wit, as if I writ rather to soothe my own vanity than to prove my affection, and the excuse you seem to make for not writing sooner, as if I pretended to so ridiculous a dominion over your time, or expected you to be very punctual where you are not in debt. One might as well be displeased at the sun for not shining out every day we would wish him to do so, though he be always serviceable to us when most he seems retired, as at a friend, who is ever in a kind disposition towards us, for not manifesting it every day by writing. But if the inclination of a friend towards us, and his bare good will and benevolence be ever to be acknowledged, how much more that convincing rhetoric of action and protection, which you so gallantly slur over with the gay term of *wrestling for a friend*. But consider, sir, your person and limbs are not absolutely your

[1] The original of this letter was in 1884 the property of Alfred Morrison, Esq., of Fonthill House, Hindon, Wilts. See *Hist. MSS. Comm.*, Report IX, ii. 471, where it is printed. The address, not given by Elwin, is here taken from the *Hist. MSS. Comm.* Report.

own; there is a lady has her part in them, who would lament much more if but a nerve of yours were sprained, than all the friends I have would ever do though my brains were beat out; for, to tell you the plain truth, this is the opinion I entertain of almost all those who are generally styled such in the world—our nominal, unperforming friends. As for my own part, whom have I been ever able to oblige? whom have I ever served to that degree? by what right or merit can I pretend to expect a signal service from any man? I am seriously far from imagining that because people have twice or thrice been civil to me, they are bound always to serve me; the prior obligation was mine, not theirs. Or, if they like my poetry, that because they *laugh with me*, they will *cry for me*. But I must be content to take my fortune, with all my own sins upon my own head. Sir Plume[1] blusters, I hear; nay, the celebrated lady herself is offended, and, which is stranger, not at herself, but me.[2] Mr. W[eston],[3] they say, is gloomy upon the matter, —the tyrant meditates revenge; nay, the distressed dame herself has been taught to suspect I served her but by halves, and without prudence. Is not this enough to make a man for the future neither presume to blame injustice or pity innocence? as in Mr. Weston's case; to make a writer never be tender of another's character or fame? as in Belinda's; to act with more reserve and write with less?

I have another storm, too, rising from the bigot, the most violent of animals, on the score of not having altered some true lines in the second edition of the Essay on Criticism. Yet, as to the two first quarrels, I can be satisfied in my conscience of having acted with honour; and as to the last, I dare stand to posterity in the character of an unbigoted Roman Catholic and impartial critic. I dare trust future times, and lie down contented under the impotence of my present censurers, which, like other impotence, would naturally vex and tease one more the less it can do. As to my writings, I pray God they may never have other enemies than those they have met with—which are, first, priests; secondly, women, who are the fools of priests; and thirdly, beaus and fops, who are the fools of women.

You see I write in some heat, but I would not do so if I had not a great [idea] of the friendship of him to whom I write. This frankness, the [less] discreet it is, is the more an act of trust in me to you. My [temper] is really a little soured by all this, and yet more by a piece of s[curvy] news Mr. Southcote yesterday sent me, that the rascally

[1] Sir Plume was early identified with Sir George Brown. See G. Tillotson's edition of *The Rape of the Lock* (Twickenham ed., Pope's *Poems*, vol. ii), pp. 83–84, 90, &c.

[2] Miss Fermor was evidently placated by the enlarged version of the poem—and by the fact that readers found Pope's portrayal of her behaviour amusing rather than denigrating.

[3] Probably this sentence should begin a new paragraph, since no connexion of Weston with *The Rape* is known. The cause of his gloom and revengeful thoughts was Pope's intervention in his marital difficulties.

scri[bbler], the Flying Post, has maliciously reflected upon Mr. Caryll, on [account] of his crossing the seas at this time.[1] Whether he is yet returned I know not; but if he be, I beg you to offer him my utmost service, if he can think me capable of any, with the only weapon I have, my pen, in reply to, or raillery upon, that scoundrel, and in whatever method he thinks most proper. I am on fire to snatch the first opportunity I ever had of doing something, or at least endeavouring to do something, for your father and my friend. I hope he is not now to be told with what ardour I love, and with what esteem I honour him, any more than you how sincerely and affectionately I shall ever be, dear sir, your most faithful and obedient and obliged humble servant.

The verses you inquire about were never written upon you anywhere else than in the letter I sent you. It was a mere piece of raillery as you will see, if you have not yet done justice upon them, being only Mrs. N[elson]'s verses on your lady[2] altered in a whimsical way, and applied to yourself. My most humble service attends the whole family. I have given order to Lewis to send two of my Essays to Ladyholt.

Address: To John Caryll esq. Junior, Ladyholt by Midhurst, Sussex.

†STEELE *to* POPE — 12 *November* 1712

1735

Nov. 12, 1712.

I have read over your *Temple of Fame* twice, and cannot find any thing amiss of weight enough to call a fault, but see in it a thousand thousand beauties. Mr. *Addison* shall see it to morrow: After his perusal of it, I will[3] let you know his thoughts. I desire you would let me know whether you are at leisure or not? I have a design which I shall open a month or two hence,[4] with the assistance of the few like your self. If your thoughts are unengaged, I shall explain my self further. I am | Your, &c.

[1] The issue of *The Flying Post* that attacked Caryll has not been found. Caryll had crossed to France to settle the estate of his uncle, John, titular Earl Caryll, for whom Pope had sent an (unused?) epitaph. See the letter to Caryll, sr., here placed as [Post 4 Sept. 1711].

[2] Mrs. Nelson had lately written some lines on Lady Mary Caryll (young Caryll's bride), whom she describes in a letter as 'one of the noblest ornaments of her sex.'—Elwin. (Mrs. Nelson's letter is to be found among the Caryll transcripts: Add. MS. 28618, f. 86.)

[3] *will* is corrected from *well* in the errata leaf of the first octavo of 1735.

[4] Formerly this 'design' was thought to be *The Guardian*, No. 1 of which appeared on 12 Mar. 1712/13. Recently it has been urged by Professor Blanchard (*Steele's Correspondence*, pp. 63–64) and Professor John Loftis ('Richard Steele's Censorium', in *The Huntington Library Quarterly*, xiv [1950], 43–66; see esp. p. 50) that the 'design' is more probably Steele's Censorium. It might be either.

†POPE *to* GAY 13 *November* 1712

1735

Nov. 13, 1712.

Sir,—You writ me a very kind Letter some months ago, and told me you were then upon the point of taking a journey into *Devonshire.*[1] That hindered my answering you, and I have since several times inquir'd of you, without any satisfaction, for so I call the knowledge of your welfare, or of any thing that concerns you. I past two months in *Sussex*, and since my Return have been again very ill.[2] I writ to *Lintot* in hopes of hearing of you, but had no answer to that point. Our Friend Mr. *Cromwell* too has been silent all this year; I believe he has been displeas'd at some or other of my Freedoms; which I very innocently take, and most with those I think most my friends. But this I know nothing of, perhaps he may have open'd to you: And, if I know you right, you are of a Temper to cement Friendships, and not to divide them. I really much love Mr. *Cromwell*, and have a true affection for your self, which if I had any Interest in the world, or Power with those who have, I shou'd not be long without manifesting to you. I desire you will not, either out of Modesty, or a vicious Distrust of another's value for you, (those two Eternal Foes to Merit) imagine that your Letters and Conversation are not always welcome to me. There's no man more intirely fond of good-nature or ingenuity than myself, and I have seen too much of those qualities in Mr. *Gay* to be any thing less than his | most affectionate Friend | and real Servant, | A. Pope.

[3]*Binfield*, | No. 13, | 1712.

†POPE *to* STEELE 16 *November* 1712

1735

Nov. 16, 1712.

You oblige me by the indulgence you have shewn to the Poem I sent you, but will oblige me much more by the kind severity I hope for from you. No errors are so trivial, but they deserve to be mended; but since you say you see nothing that may be call'd a fault, can you but think it so, that I have confin'd the attendance of Guardian spirits[4] to Heaven's favourites only? I could point you to several, but 'tis my business to be informed of those faults I *do not* know, and as for those

[1] Gay was born and brought up at Barnstaple.

[2] Pope had been ill also in the spring; see his letter to Caryll of 28 May.

[3] The double dating, in superscription as well as here at the end, suggests that possibly Pope in this case sent the original letter to the printer.

[4] This is not now to be found in *The Temple of Fame*, of which Poem he speaks here.—Pope, 1735–42.

I do, not to talk of 'em but to correct 'em. You speak of that Poem in a style I neither merit, nor expect; but I assure you, if you freely mark or dash out, I shall look upon your blots to be its greatest beauties. I mean if Mr. *Addison* and Your self shou'd like it in the whole; otherwise the trouble of correction is what I would not take, for I was really so diffident of it as to let it lie by me these[1] two years, just as you now see it. I am afraid of nothing so much as to impose any thing on the world which is unworthy of its acceptance.

As to the last period of your letter, I shall be very ready and glad to contribute to any design that tends to the advantage of mankind, which I am sure all yours do. I wish I had but as much capacity as leisure, for I am perfectly idle: (a sign I have not much capacity.)

If you will entertain the best opinion of me, be pleas'd to think me your friend. Assure Mr. *Addison* of my most faithful service, of every one's esteem he must be assur'd already. I am | Your, &c.

POPE *to* CARYLL[2] — 19 *November* 1712

Add. 28618

Binfield, Nov 19. 1712.

I am more joyed at your return and nearer approach to us than I could be at that of the sun, so much as I wish him this melancholy season, and tho' he brings along with him all the pleasures and blessings of nature. But 'tis his fate too, like yours, to be displeasing to owls and obscene animals, who can't bear his lustre. What put me in mind of these night birds, was that jail-bird the *Flying Post* whom I think you are best revenged upon as the sun[3] in the fable was upon those bats and beastly birds above mentioned, only by *shining on*, by being honest and doing good. I am so far from esteeming it any misfortune to be impotently slandered, that I congratulate you upon having your share in that, which all the great men, and all the good men that ever lived have had their part of, envy and calumny! To be uncensured and to be obscure, is the same thing. You may conclude from what I here say that it was never in my thoughts to offer you my poor pen in any direct reply to such a scoundrel[4] (who like Hudibras needs fear no blows but such as bruise), but only in some little raillery in the most contemptuous manner thrown upon him, not as in your defence expressly, but as in scorn of him *en Gaieté de Cœur*. But indeed your

[1] Hence it appears this Poem was writ before the Author was 22 Years old.—Pope, 1735–42.

[2] Pope deftly remade parts of this letter into a letter that he printed as sent to Addison under date (in the editions of 1735) of 30 July 1713 or (in the editions of 1737–42) of 20 July 1713. See under date of 30 July 1713 (i. 183).

[3] The transcript seems to read *Swan*, but Pope printed *Sun*, which is essential.

[4] The 'scoundrel' who attacked Caryll in *The Flying Post* was made into John Dennis in the fabricated letter to Addison.

opinion that 'tis entirely to be neglected would have been my own, at first, had it been my own case, but I felt some warmth at the first motion which my reason could not suppress here (as it did when I saw Dennis's book against me, which made [me] very heartily merry in two minutes time.) 'Twas well for us that these sparks' quarrel was to our persons. One does not like your looks, nor tother my shape. This can do us no harm; but had these gentlemen disliked our sense or so, we might have had reason to think so very well of our understandings, as to become insufferably proud and conceited, upon their disapprobation.

I must not omit here to do justice to Mr Thomas Southcote, whose zeal in your concern was most worthy a friend, and honourer of you. He writ to me in the most pressing terms about it, tho' with that just contempt of the slanderer that he deserves. I think that in these days one honest man is oblig'd to acquaint another who are his friends? when so many mischievous insects are daily at work to make people of merit suspicious of each other, that they have the satisfaction of seeing them looked upon no better than themselves.

We are all very much obliged to you for the care of our little affair abroad, which I hope you'll have an account of, or else we may have great cause to complain of Mr A—'s[1] or his correspondent's negligence, since he promised my father to write (as he pressed him to do) sometime before your journey.[2] He has received the 5ll. bill,[3] but it seems the interest was agreed at 5ll. 10*s*. per cent. in the bond, which my father lays his commands upon me to mention, as a thing he doubts not you forgot. I plead this excuse for suffering any consideration so dirty as that of money to have place in a letter of friendship, or in any thing betwixt you and me.

I enclose a few lines upon the subject you were pleased to propose, only to prove my ready obedience, for 'tis such a bastard as you'll scarce, I fear, be willing to father, especially since you can make so much handsomer things of your own, whenever you please. Some little circumstances possibly may require alteration, which you will easily mend. You see my letters are scribbled with all the carelessness and inattention imaginable: my style, like my soul, appears in its natural undress before my friend. 'Tis not here I regard the character of a wit. Some people are wits all over, to that degree that they are fools all over. They are wits in the church, wits in the street, wits at a funeral, nay the unmannerly creatures are wits before women! There is nothing more wrong than to appear always in the pontificalibus of one's profession, whatever it be. There's no dragging your dignity about with you every where, as if an alderman should constantly wear his chain in his shop. Mr Roper, because he has the reputation of keeping

[1] Mr. Arthur, the banker of King Street, London.—Elwin. [2] To Paris.

[3] Pope's father lent Caryll 200*l*. upon bond on 1 June 1710, at 5½ per cent.—Elwin. This investment will reappear in later letters. The loan was repaid in 1727 (Pope to Caryll, 28 Mar. [1727]).

the best pack of fox hounds in England, will visit the ladies in a hunting dress.[1] And I have known an author,[2] who for having once written a tragedy has never been out of buskins, since he can no more suffer a vulgar phrase in his own mouth than in a Roman's; and will be as much out of countenance if he fail of the true accent in his conversation, as an actor would, were he out upon the stage. For my part, there are some things I would be thought besides a wit; as a Christian, a friend, a frank companion, and a well natured fellow, and so forth. And in particular I would be thought | Dear Sir | Your most faithful and | obliged friend and servant | A.P.

My most hearty service waits on Mr Caryll (with whose Correspondence I think my self highly favoured) and the whole good family

I have an odd request to you that if you ever thought any of my epistles worth preserving, you will favour me with the whole cargoe, which shall be faithfully returned to you.[3] I never kept any copies of such stuff as I write; but there are several thoughts which I throw out that way in the freedom of my soul, that may be of use to me in a design I am lately engaged in, which will require so constant a flux of thought and invention, that I can never supply it without some assistance and 'tis not impossible but so many notions, written at different times, may save me a good deal of trouble. Pray forgive this, and keep my secret which is of consequence. | Yours A.P.

POPE *to* CARYLL[4] [29 *November* 1712]

Add. 28618

Binfield.

Just after I had dispatched my last to you, I received the favour of another of your letters, which gave me an account of the affair you so obligingly took upon you to inform us of. Mr Arthur having been pressingly desired by my father to cause an attested copy to be delivered to Mr Whitford, it is surprising enough that they did not; our chief satisfaction depending on that, since we have nothing to show for our right but Mr A's note, (without the attestation). My father thinks he cannot give a procuration to another without discharging Mr A, *ipso facto*, 'till he has this security; so is as much at a loss as ever; tho' it was

[1] Edward Roper, Esq., of Eltham (Kent) was connected with Caryll's neighbours the Butlers. He rented Ladyholt for a time, and after the death of Caryll, jr., leased the stables and kennel at Finden. In 1723 at the age of 84 he was killed 'from the hurt he received by a fall from his horse, as he was hunting a fox'.—Elwin.

[2] The author might well be Ambrose Philips.

[3] This is Pope's earliest request for the return of letters. He commonly considered letters as a part of his literary 'product'. Here he evidently plans to use at least hints from them for *Guardian* papers, or for Steele's Censorium. See above, p. 152 n. 4, Steele to Pope, 12 Nov. 1712. There is no evidence that Pope made any present use of the letters.

[4] The letter to Steele immediately following this and derived from this has the date given above. It seems from all the internal evidence to be approximately correct.

impossible (as we are all sensible) for any one to perform more effectually what we desired, than you have so kindly done, or to give us a fuller satisfaction in the point, since they would not comply with our request.

Tho' you have no great opinion of Mr Tickell's verses to the *Spectator*,[1] I believe you'll think his poem upon the peace to have its beauties especially in the versification. There are also several most poetical images and fine pieces of painting in it, particularly the lines in pag. 13. of the child's emotion at sight of the trophies at Blenheim, and the description of the fields after the wars in p. 5, beginning—*content to see the Honours, &c.*, the 4 excellent verses in p. 12. *our owne strict Judges, &c.*, and the artful introduction of the praise of several noblemen by fancying coins will be struck of them in gold of Indies, are strokes of mastery. And lastly, the description of the several parts of the world in regard to our trade: which has interfered with some lines of my own in the poem called Windsor Forrest, tho' written before I saw his; I transcribe both and desire your sincere judgment whether I ought not to strike out mine, either as they seem too like his, or as they are inferior.

Fearless the merchant now pursues his gain,
And roams securely o'er the boundless main.
Now o'er his head the polar bear he spies,
And freezing spangles of the Lapland skies;
Now swells his canvass to the sultry line,
With glitt'ring spoils where Indian grottoes shine.
Where fumes of incence glad the southern seas,
And wafted citron scents the balmy breeze.

The following are mine.

Now shall our fleets the bloody cross display
To the rich regions of the rising day,
Or those green iles, where headlong Titan steeps
His hissing chariot in th'Atlantick deeps,
Temp[t] icy seas, where scarce the waters roll,
Where clearer flames glow round the frozen pole,
Or under southern skies exalt their sails,
Led by new stars, and born by balmy gales.

Pray use me as a friend in impartially giving your opinion in this matter, as you did in the verse of Adrian, which I took very kindly. I only sent it as my private notion to Mr Steele, which yet I doubted of (as you see by the last lines of the letter itself) not in the least dreaming

[1] For Tickell's verses see *Spectator*, No. 532 (10 Nov.) along with Pope's letter to Steele (7 Nov.) initiating the discussion of Hadrian's lines. Tickell's poem *On the Prospect of Peace* had been published before 1 Nov.

that he would publish me as the author of it by name. The supposition you draw from the suspicion that Adrian was addicted to magic, seems to me a little uncharitable, that he might fear no sort of deity, good or bad, since in the third verse he plainly testifies his apprehension of a future state, by being solicitous whither his soul was going? As to what you mention of his using gay and ludicrous expressions, I have owned my opinion that the expressions are not so, but the diminutives are as often in Latin taken for expressions of tenderness and concern. *Anima* is no more than *my soul. Animula* has the force of *my dear soul.* To say *Virgo bella* is not half so endearing as *virguncula bellula.* And had Augustus only called Horace, *lepidum hominem* it had amounted to no more than he thought him a *pleasant fellow*; 'Twas the *homunciolum* that expressed the love and tenderness that great emperour had for him. And perhaps I should my self be much better pleased, if I were told Mr Caryll called me his *little friend* than if he complimented me with the title of a great Genius, or the like. I am dear sir | Your most obedient servant | and affectionate friend | A: P:

I beg you will believe your thoughts are ever most entertaining to me, and will be doubly useful, in case I should be engaged in writing: therefore I desire to have 'em at all times. I had sent with this a letter to Mr John Caryll, but that the headache is very severe upon me; I should not complain thus (quite across a country too) according to Mrs Blewet's maxim,[1] that no one ever values another for being sick: nor if I had profited as I should by Mrs Cath. Caryll's[2] example, who can suffer in such a manner, that those who are nearest her cannot perceive it. Such an example is of greater force than all Tully's discourse *de dolore tolerando* a thousand times over: but I find from too many instances that I am incapable of amending either by example or precept.

‡POPE *to* STEELE[3] 29 *November* 1712

1735

Nov. 29, 1712.

I am sorry you publish'd that notion about *Adrian*'s *Verses* as mine; had I imagin'd you wou'd use my name, I shou'd have express'd my

[1] Mrs. Blewet was Mrs. Cope's sister and, like her, unhappily married. Both ladies were Mr. Caryll's first cousins.

[2] The daughter of Mr. Caryll and very possibly his scribe in transcribing (badly!) some of Pope's letters.

[3] This letter is doubtless fabricated from the letter of the same date to Caryll. At the time of Steele's death (1729) Pope was asking correspondents to return his letters, and of course he may have got some of his letters to Steele back about that time. The present fabrication, however, makes that seem improbable. Evidently Pope must have written Steele in a somewhat similar manner, but this letter in part repeats to Steele what Pope had said about diminutives in his letter to Steele of 7 Nov.

sentiments with more modesty and diffidence. I only sent it to have your opinion, and not to publish my own, which I distrusted. But I think the supposition you draw from the notion of *Adrian*'s being addicted to Magick, is a little uncharitable, ('that he might fear no sort of Deity, good or bad') since in the third verse he plainly testifies his apprehension of a future state, by being sollicitous *whither* his soul was going? As to what you mention of his using gay and ludicrous expressions, I have own'd my opinion to be that the expressions are not so, but that diminutives are as often in the *Latin* tongue used as marks of tenderness and concern.

Anima is no more than my soul, *Animula* has the force of my dear soul. To say *Virgo Bella* is not half so endearing as *Virguncula bellula*, and had *Augustus* only call'd Horace *Lepidum Hominem*, it had amounted to no more than that he thought him a pleasant fellow: 'Twas the *Homunciolum* that exprest the love and tenderness that great Emperor had for him. And perhaps I should my self be much better pleas'd, if I were told you call'd me your little friend, than if you complimented me with the title of a great Genius, or an Eminent hand (as *Jacob* does all his authors.) I am | Your, &c.

†STEELE *to* POPE[1] — 4 *December* 1712

1737

Decemb. 4, 1712.

This is to desire of you that you would please to make an Ode as of a chearful dying spirit, that is to say, the Emperor Adrian's *Animula vagula* put into two or three stanzas for musick. If you comply with this, and send me word so, you will very particularly oblige your, &c.

†POPE *to* STEELE[2] — [*December* 1712]

1737

I do not send you word I will do, but have already done the thing you desire of me. You have it (as Cowley calls it) just warm from the brain.[3] It came to me the first moment I waked this morning: Yet

[1] First printed in the Roberts octavo (1737 a). It is omitted from the quarto and octavo of that year, but appears in the octavos, 1737–42.

The fact that the lines are to be set to music indicates their probable use in Steele's Censorium.

[2] Printed in the octavos, 1737–42. It is not in the quarto and folio of 1737.

[3] Warton in his *Essay on Pope*, i (1756), 87, pointed out that Pope was clearly indebted also to Thomas Flatman, 'an obscure and forgotten rhymer of the age of Charles the second'. Elwin was troubled by the disingenuousness of alleging that this version of 1737 came just 'warm from the brain' in 1712. The poem in the form here given postdates 1730, when in David Lewis's *Miscellaneous Poems by Several Hands* the version sent to Caryll in Pope's letter of 12 June 1713 was printed. The whole matter is thoroughly discussed by Ault, *New Light*, pp. 60–67.

you'll see it was not so absolutely inspiration, but that I had in my head not only the verses of Adrian, but the fine fragment of Sapho. | &c.

The Dying Christian to his Soul

ODE

I.

Vital Spark of heav'nly flame!
Quit, oh quit this mortal frame;
Trembling, hoping, ling'ring, flying,
Oh the pain, the bliss of dying!
Cease, fond Nature, cease thy strife,
And let me languish into life.

II.

Hark! they whisper; Angels say,
Sister Spirit, come away!
What is this absorbs me quite?
Steals my senses, shuts my sight,
Drowns my spirits, draws my breath?
Tell me, my soul, can this be Death?

III.

The world recedes; it disappears!
Heav'n opens on my eyes! my ears
With sounds seraphick ring:
Lend, lend your wings! I mount! I fly!
O Grave! where is thy Victory!
O Death! where is thy Sting?

POPE *to* CARYLL[1] 5 *December* 1712

Add. 28618

Dec. 5. 1712.

You have at length complied with the request I have often made to you; for you have shown me I must confess several of my faults in the light of those letters. Upon a review of them I find many things that would give me shame, if I were not more desirous to be thought honest than prudent; so many things freely thrown out, such lengths of unreserved friendship, thoughts just warm from the brain without any polishing or dress, the very *déshabille*[2] of the understanding. You have proved yourself more tender of another's embryos than the fondest

[1] In his editions of his letters Pope printed the first half of this letter with only slight revisions. His omissions are placed in half-brackets.

[2] The transcript reads *deshabilée*—an indication of Pope's 'skill' in French?

mothers are of their own, for you have preserved every thing that I miscarried of. Since I know this I shall be in one respect more afraid of writing to you than ever at this careless rate, because I see my evil works may again rise in judgment upon me: yet in another respect I shall be less afraid, since this has given me such a proof of the extreme indulgence you afford to my thought.[1] ⌜This, dear sir, let me assure you, that⌝ the revisal of those letters has been a kind of examination of conscience to me; so fairly and faithfully have I set down in 'em from time to time the true and undisguised state of my mind.[2] But I find that these which were intended as sketches of my friendship, give as faint imperfect images of it, as the little Landskips we commonly see in black and white do of a beautiful country: they can represent but a very small part of it and that deprived of the life and lustre of nature. I perceive that the more I endeavoured to render manifest the real affection and value I ever had for you, I did but injure it by representing less and less of it, as glasses which are designed to make an object very clear, generally contract it ⌜into a smaller compass.⌝ Yet as when people have a just idea of a thing fixed upon their own knowledge, the least ⌜sketches or⌝ traces of it serve to refresh the rememberance,[3] and are not displeasing on that score, so I hope ⌜'tis⌝ the knowledge[4] you have of the esteem I have for you, ⌜that⌝ is the reason you do not dislike my letters.

They will not be of any great service to the design I mentioned to you. I believe I had better steal from a richer man and plunder your letters (which I have kept as carefully as I would letters patent since they entitle me to what I more value than titles of honor.) You have some cause to apprehend this usage from me, if what some say be true, that I am a great borrower. However, I have hitherto had the luck that none of my creditors have challenged me for it. And those who say it are such whose writings no man ever borrowed from; so have the least reason to complain. Their works are granted on all hands to be but too much their own. Another has been pleased to declare that my verses are corrected by other men. I verily believe theirs were never corrected by any man: but indeed if mine were not, 'twas not my fault, I have endeavoured my utmost that they should. These things are only whispered therefore I'll not encroach upon my brother Bayes' province and pen whispers.[5] ⌜But some other calumnies I might think

[1] to my thought] to my slightest thoughts *1735–42*. 'This' should be 'Thus'?

[2] Caryll has returned Pope's letters to him, and they prove useless, Pope says, to the design earlier mentioned to Caryll.

[3] It is notable that here as elsewhere Pope has the insight to perceive that the smallest detail may stimulate the imagination to remembrance.

[4] knowledge] foreknowledge *1735–42*.

[5] At this point Pope's printed texts of the letter end, with the addition of 'so hasten to conclude'. The allusion to Bayes concerns the beginning of Act II of *The Rehearsal*.

of more importance, which have been dispersed in a neighboring family[1] I have been always a true friend to. I find they show a coldness, without enquiring first of myself concerning what they have heard of an old acquaintance from a new one. I shall fairly let them fall, and suffer 'em to continue deceived for their credulity. When flattery and lying are joined and carried as far as they will go, I drop my arms of defence, which are of another kind, and of no force against such unlawful weapons. A plain man encounters them at a great disadvantage; as the poor naked Indians did our guns and fire arms. *Virtute meâ, me involvo*, as Horace expresses it:[2] I wrap myself up in the conscience of my integrity, and sleep after it as quietly as I can.

Be pleased to send the inclosed[3] to your son, whom I really love, because he is so much your son. I waive the ceremony of sealing it, for as I'm sure your hearts are open to each other, I doubt not but every thing else may. I was very much put in mind of you both by a passage in the *Spectator* I chanced to read yesterday. 'Tis in the 3d Vol. Number 192, which I desire you to turn to.—By the way I could be glad to know whether you take in the *Spectators* or not. The poem of *Windsor Forest* has undergone many alterations, and received many additions since you saw it, but has not yet been out of my hands to any man, so was not what Mr Steel mentioned[4]—I expect your opinion frankly of the question I asked in my last.

I beg of you to write to me as often as, with ease to yourself, you can so far oblige me, and particularly that you will not fail to acquaint me some little time before you go to London this winter that I may enjoy your conversation for some time there; or if you go not yourself, if Mr J. Caryll does? Till I hear I will defer my journey thither—Dear sir, I entreat you will ever believe this of me (whatever else may not be allowed me) that I am a Christian and a Catholic, a plain friend without design or flattery | Your most obliged faithful and | affectionate servant | A.P.⌉

⌈My most humble Service to Mrs Caryll, Lady Mary, and Mrs Catherine. Mr Dancastle returns you his with (I dare Say) an unfeigned respect.⌉

[1] Possibly the Englefields of Whiteknights, who, unlike Pope, did not support Mrs. Weston's cause, and were annoyed that Pope did.

[2] Horace (*Carmina*, III. xxix. 54–55) wrote *mea virtute*.

[3] The letter to Caryll, jr., which immediately follows this.

[4] Pope's 'admirable poem' mentioned but not named by Steele in *Spectator*, No. 532 was probably *The Temple of Fame*, which did not appear in print until 1715. See Pope to Caryll, 21 Dec. 1712.

POPE *to* JOHN CARYLL, JR.[1] 5 *December* 1712

Harvard University

Binfield Decembr 5. 1712.

While you are pursuing the Sprightly Delights of the Field, springing up with activity at the Dawning Day, rouzing a whole Country with Shouts and Horns, & inspiring Animalls & Rationalls with like Fury and Ardor; while your Blood boils high in ev'ry Vein, your Heart bounds in your breast, & as vigorous a Confluence of Spirits rushes to it at the sight of a Fox as cou'd be stirrd up by that of an Army of Invaders; while the Zeal of the Chace devours the whole man, & moves him no less than the Love of our Country or the Defence of our Altars could do. While—I say, (& I think I say it like a modern Orator, considering the Length of my Period, and the little Sence that is to follow it) while you are thus imployed, I am just in the reverse of all this Spirit & Life, confind to a narrow Closet, lolling on an Arm Chair, nodding away my Days over a Fire, like the picture of January in an old Salisbury Primer. I believe no mortal ever livd in such Indolence & Inactivity of Body, tho my Mind be perpetually rambling (it no more knows whither than poor Adrian's did when he lay adying) Like a witch, whose Carcase lies motionless on the floor, while she keeps her airy Sabbaths, & enjoys a thousand Imaginary Entertainments abroad, in this world, & in others, I seem to sleep in the midst of the Hurry, even as you would swear a Top stands still, when tis in the Whirle of its giddy motion. 'Tis no figure, but a serious truth I tell you when I say that my Days & Nights are so much alike, so equally insensible of any Moving Power but Fancy, that I have sometimes spoke of things in our family as Truths & real accidents, which I only Dreamt of; & again when some things that actually happen'd came into my head, have thought (till I enquird) that I had only dream'd of them. This will shew you how little I feel in this State either of Pleasure or Pain: I am fixt in a Stupid settled Medium between both.

But possibly some of my good Friends, whom we have lately spoke of in our last letters may give me a more Lively Sense of things in a short time, & awaken my Intellects to a perfect Feeling of Myself & Them. Dull fellows that want Witt, (like those very dull fellows that want Lechery) may, by well-applyd Stroaks & Scourges, be fetchd up into a little of either. I therfore have some reason to hope no man that calls himself my Friend (except it be such an obstinate, refractory Person as yourself) will do me the Injury to hinder these well-meaning Gentlemen from Beating up my Understanding. Whipt wits, like whipt Creams, afford a most sweet & delectable Syllabub to the Taste of the Towne, and often please them better with the Dessert, than all

[1] Roscoe, viii (1824), 245, prints a modernized text of this letter.

the meal they had before. So, if Sir Plume shoud take the pains to Dress me,[1] I might possibly make the Last Course better than the first. When a stale cold Fool is well heated, and hashed by a Satyrical Cooke, he may be tost up into a Kickshaw not disagreeable.

What you mention of the Satisfaction I may take in seeing an Enemy punish himself & become ridiculous by attacking me, I must honestly tell you is, and can be, none to me. I can hate no man so much as to feel a pleasure in what can possibly do my Person no good, his Exposing himself. I am no way the wiser for anothers being a fool, and receive no Addition of credit from another's Loss of it.—As to the other Case, which you own would give a man the Spleen, (the being misconstrued by the very people we indeavour to serve) I have ever made it my fixt maxime, never to seek for any thing from a good action but the action itself, and the Conscious pleasure of a sincere Intention. As some proof that this is my real thought, I was not ignorant of such misconstruction even during the Time I pressed the most to serve that Lady. It may perhaps be often a Blessing of God that a man wants the Fortune & Power he wishes for; which if he had, he woud imploy, possibly, in some sort of Services to others which might be fatall to himself.

I beg you to believe I am very sensible of your good will towards me, which you express so much in taking notice of every thing which I seem concern'd about. I cou'd be very glad to be with you and Mr Stafford[2] at Finden, tho I verily believe you would run away from me as fast as your Horses cou'd carry you. Besides two accidental Reasons that make me very desirous of knowing Mr Stafford, (one, that he is much your Friend, & the other that I have particular obligations to his Father) I have a generall one, which is likewise a very strong Inducement; that Universal good Character which I find he has, even among people that scarce commend any man. I make him no compliment when I say, that I have heard the Vain commend him for his Modesty, & the Drunkard for his Temperance. And a man in these days must have excellent qualities indeed, who gains the Esteem of the World, without complying with its Vices and Follies.—I am, with all Truth, most heartily, | Dear Sir, | Your affectionate & obligd Servant, | A Pope.

My humble Service to Mr Richard Caryll,[3] who I hear is with you at Finden.

Address: To | Mr Caryll, junior. | att Finden.

[1] This passage confirms the received opinion that Sir George Brown was so highly displeased at being represented under the character of Sir Plume as to have threatened personal violence to the author.—Roscoe.

[2] Probably John Stafford, younger brother of the 1st Earl Stafford, and father of the 2nd Earl. In his letter to Caryll, sr., 31 Jan. 1733, Pope speaks of having no influence with the 2nd Earl, 'the son, as he is, of my friend Mr. Stafford'. The father of the 2nd Earl died in 1714.

[3] Young Caryll's uncle.

POPE *to* [STEELE?] 6 *December* 1712

[Professor Rae Blanchard in her edition of Steele's *Correspondence*, Oxford, 1941, p. 66, lists, without text, a letter of this date, sold by Tregaskis and listed in his *Catalogue* No. 831 (October 1920) with the following summary: 'asking him to do what he pleases with a paper he has written. Speaks of the Ode left with Steele last winter and refers to Prior and Addison.' Tregaskis apparently got the letter from the Blenheim archives. Professor Blanchard quotes a description of the letter from the Catalogue of the Blenheim MSS. (F I 89) as follows: 'A letter from Pope dated Dec. 6, 1712, referring to his *Temple of Fame*. This letter seems to be addressed to Steele. It refers to Prior and "begs my most humble service to Mr. Addison."'

No further information is available.]

POPE *to* CARYLL 21 *December* 1712

Add. 28618

December 21: 1712.

I think a compliment is the worst natured thing, a man can with honesty be guilty of to a friend, whom there [are] but two civil ways of abusing, raillery and compliment; and of these compliment is the civilest and unfairest. Yet tho' I think I never was in a worse humour, than at the writing my last I do not recollect that I used this play towards you, as you accuse me when you call compliments my popish tricks. It had been more just and less severe upon your friend had you called 'em Catholic tricks, since they must be granted to be in a manner universal. But if I said any thing so openly true in your praise, as to seem in your eyes, what most things said to your praise I know will do, I beg your pardon and promise you faithfully for the future to do you as much injustice in my words, as you do yourself in your thoughts. What Caesar said of his wife, that 'twas not sufficient she should be really chaste, but must not be so much as suspected, one may apply to friendship: it should not only be free from what is really compliment, but from the very shadow of it. I will not therefore tell you how great a misfortune I account it that I cannot wait upon you at Ladyholt, nor how much I am obliged by that invitation. My ill state of health ever since the cold weather began renders vain any such pleasing thoughts as of the enjoyments of your fireside: I cannot express how thoroughly I'm penetrated by the sharpness of it. I feel no thing alive but my heart and head; and my spirits, like those in a thermometer mount and fall thro' my thin delicate contexture just as the temper of air is more benign or inclement. In this sad condition I'm forced to take volatile drops every day: a custom I have so long continued, that my doctor tells me I must not long expect support from them, and adds that unless I use some certain prescriptions, my tenement will not last long above ground. But I shall not prop it (as decayed as it [is]) with his rotten fulciments: if it falls (as the honest Hibernian said of the house), I care not, I'm only a lodger.[1] The severity of the cold has turned my studies to those books, which treat of the descriptions of the Arctic regions, Lapland, Nova Zembla and Spitsberg; deserts of snow, seas of ice and frozen skies might administer some odd kind of shivering satisfaction (or as the vulgar have it cold comfort), in the comparison with my own case. This, I say, some people would imagine who are of opinion that the knowledge of others' sufferings alleviate our own: but I never could conceive this sorry and inhuman consolation, nor am one degree the less chill for all I read on these subjects.

To fill this paper and to avoid all imputation of compliment I shall here put together several beautiful winter pieces of the poets, which have occurred to my memory on this occasion: It may not perhaps be disagreeable to you to compare what lively images nature has presented in different views to some of the greatest Geniuses for description, which the world ever bred. I shall confine myself to one circumstance only—that of snow, which is thus described by Homer, *Iliad* 12, as I find it translated to my hand: for Greek characters might possibly be taken for cyphers should this letter be intercepted by any zealously affected to the government.—

Hom. *Iliad* 12.

Thus on a wintry day the flaky snow
Incessant falls, when Jove the treasure opens
Of snowy tempests, and of hoary frosts:
He scatters o'er the world a fleecy deluge;
A depth of snow conceals the mountain tops,
The verdant meadows and the manur'd fields,
The banks of rivers, and the Ocean's shores
While the wide main receives into its bosom
A snowy inundation from the skies.[2]

Again. *Iliad* 19.

As when the freezing blasts of Boreas blow,
And scatter o'er the fields the driving snow.
From dusky clouds the fleecy winter flies
Whose dazling lustre whitens all the skies.[2]

[1] Pope uses this quip again in writing to Jervas, 29 Nov. 1716—but not of his own 'house'! See also i. 148.

[2] The passage from Book XII of the *Iliad* comes from a version by Broome, included in the complete English *Iliad* published in 1712 by John Ozell, Broome, and Oldisworth. Broome did Books X–XV. The version was in blank verse printed as prose; but since the beginnings of lines were indicated by capital letters, Pope has given the passage verse form. The second passage, from *Iliad* xix, is interesting in that it gives us two couplets used by Pope in his translation (Bk. XIX, ll. 380–3) first published in 1720. (In 1720 Pope changed *freezing* to *piercing*.) It would be interesting to know how much of the *Iliad* Pope had translated at this time.

Virgil *Geo: 3.* [353–9; 367–9].

——————————neque ullæ
Aut herbæ campo apparent, aut arbore frondes;
Sed jacet aggeribus niveis informis, et alto
Terra gelu late, septemque; assurgit in ulnas
Semper hiems, semper spirantes frigora [Cauri.]
Tum sol pallentes haud unquam discutit umbras
Nec cum invectus equis altum petit aethera, nec cum
Præcipitem Ocean[i] rubro lavit æquore currum
Interea toto non setius ære ningit,
Intereunt pecudes, stant *circumfusa* pruinis
Corpora magna boum——

Hor. *Lib. I. Ode* [9]

Vides ut *alta* stet nive *candidum*
Soracte nec jam sustineant *onus*
Sylvae *laborantes*?——

We have a fine description wrought up from thence with amplification by Mr Congreve, as follows:

Big with the offspring of the north,
 The frozen clouds bring forth;
A shower of soft and fleecy rain
Falls to new cloathe the earth again:
 And see, how by degrees
The universal Mantle hides the trees
 In hoary flakes that downward fly
As if it were the autumn of the sky,
 Whose fall of leaf would theirs supply.
Trembling the trees sustain the weight and bow
 Like aged limbs that feebly go
Beneath a venerable head of snow.[1]

Milton: *Par: Lost* [ii. 488–91]

——————————So the clouds
Ascending while the north wind sleeps, o'erspread
Heavens chearful face; the Lowring Element
Scowls o'er the darkend landskip, snow or show'r.

Mr Philips has two lines which seem to me what the French call very *picturesque*, that I cannot omit to you—

[1] Congreve later revised this version of Horace notably.

All hid in snow, in bright confusion lie,
And with one dazling waste fatigue the eye.[1]

These are the scenes the season presents to me, and what can be more ridiculous than that in the midst of this bleak prospect that sets my very imagination a shivering, I am endeavouring to raise up round about me a painted scene of woods and forests in verdure and beauty, trees springing, fields flowering, Nature laughing.[2] I am wandering thro' Bowers and Grottos in conceit, and while my trembling body is cowering o'er a fire, my mind is expatiating in an open sunshine.

—Videor pios errare per lucos, amœnæ
Quos et aquæ subeunt et auræ.[3]

As to the questions you ask me[:] that the *Temple of Fame* was the poem mentioned in the *Spectators* I thought I told you in my last, *Windsor Forest* will come out first, but I do not yet know when. I had not mention[ed] to you or any other, what I apprehended of the misconstruction of some of my neighbours, but that I could not tell but that something of that nature might be whispered to you, as it has been to them. More men's reputations, I believe, are whispered away, than any other ways destroyed: but I depend upon the justice and honesty of your nature, that you would give me a hearing before you passed the verdict. What I'm certain of is that several false tales have been suggested, and, I fear, many believed by them, since they never opened themselves to me upon the subject: but I shall make a farther trial, till when 'twould not be just to give a farther account. I have sent the letters as leaves[4] sealed up.—Believe, dear sir, I am so sincerely a friend to your whole family that 'tis equally past my power of concealing it or expressing it. I hope this ill weather will put off your journey to London till after Christmas. When I know you are going, I'll be so good conditioned to myself as to meet you there, being ever yours | A.P.

†POPE *to* GAY — 24 *December* 1712

1735

Dec. 24, 1712.

It has been my good fortune within this Month past, to hear more things that have pleas'd me than (I think) almost in all my time beside. But nothing upon my word has been so Home-felt a satisfaction as the

[1] Ambrose Philips's 'Epistle to the Earl of Dorset from Copenhagen' was first printed in *The Tatler*, No. 12 (7 May 1709). Pope's use of the word 'picturesque' is early and hence interesting.

[2] Possibly, as Elwin surmised, this passage means that Pope is revising *Windsor Forest*.

[3] Horace, *Carmina*, III. iv. 6–8.

[4] as leaves] to Lewis *Elwin* (a quite possible reading).

News you tell me of your self: and you are not in the least mistaken, when you congratulate me upon your own good Success,[1] for I have more People to be happy out of, than any ill-natur'd man can boast. I may with honesty affirm to you, that notwithstanding the many Inconveniencies and Disadvantages they commonly talk of in the *Res angusti domi*, I have never found any other, than the inability of giving people of Merit the only certain proof of our value for them, in doing 'em some real service. For after all, if we could but Think a little, Self-love might make us Philosophers, and convince us, *Quantuli indiget Natura!* Ourselves are easily provided for; 'tis nothing but the Circumstantials, and the Apparatus or Equipage of humane life that costs so much the furnishing. Only what a luxurious Man wants for horses and foot-men a good-natur'd Man wants for his friends, or the indigent.

I shall see you this Winter with much greater pleasure than I could the last; and I hope as much of your Time as your Attendance on the Dutchess[2] will allow you to spare to any friend, will not be thought lost upon one who is as much so as any man. I must also put you in mind, tho' you are now Secretary to this Lady, that you are likewise Secretary to Nine other Ladies, and are to write sometimes for them too. He who is forc'd to live wholly upon those Ladies favours, is indeed in as precarious a condition as any He who does what *Chaucer* says for *Sustenance*;[3] but they are very agreeable Companions, like other Ladies, when a Man only passes a Night or so with[4] them at his leisure, and away. I am, | Your, &c.

[1] Gay had been made domestic steward to the Duchess of Monmouth.—Irving, *John Gay*, p. 68.

[2] The Duchess of Monmouth, widow of the beheaded son of King Charles II.

[3] Professor B. J. Whiting suggests the reference is to the last couplet of the unfinished Cook's Tale (*Canterbury Tales*, i (A), 4421–2).

[4] passes a night . . . with] passes a few hours with *1737 b*.

1713

In many ways this was a more exciting year than a casual reading of the letters would indicate. The Peace of Utrecht was signed 31 March (O.S.), and *Windsor Forest* anticipated the happy event by about three weeks. Party politics ran high throughout the year. Steele was so violent a Whig that Jacobite and Tory friends reproached Pope for his part in *The Guardian*. On the surface very friendly relations continued with both Addison and Steele; but in the letters 'Whig' seems increasingly an uncomplimentary term. The influence of Swift and other Tories increased, but the poet was 'clapped into a Whig' by the hearers of his Prologue to *Cato* in April. By the end of the year, however, a covert dissatisfaction was separating Addison and Pope. In July Pope pretended to defend Addison against Dennis's attack on *Cato* by publishing his *Narrative of Dr. Robert Norris*—perhaps his best piece of burlesque writing, if not his tenderest! One wonders if Addison made his displeasure at the *Narrative* as clear to Pope as he did to Dennis. Much of the year Pope spent in town, at Jervas's house in Cleveland Court, long to be his preferred London address. Here he studied painting, a favourite art with him. Encouraged by admiring literary friends, he was persuaded in October to issue Proposals for a translation of the *Iliad*—doubtless the most important act of his year.

POPE *to* CARYLL — 8 *January* 1712/13

Add. 28618

Binfield. Jan. 8. 1712/13.

I am extremely concerned I had no hint of your journey to London a little beforehand, for I should have put hard to have met you, tho' I have been indeed much indisposed of late, rather weak and faint than sick. In this condition nothing raises me so much life as the presence of a friend; and if you yet stay in Town after Munday and give me by the post next Saturday but the hopes of having one glimpse of you from your hurry of business, I will come infallibly. Or if you have any prospect of visiting the Town again in a month or thereabouts I'll defer it till then, and wait upon you in the meantime at Whiteknights.—I have many things to say to you, many hearty wishes to give you, and yet a great many more which I can never be able to say. This is no compliment upon the faith of an honest man who has been much traduced of late, and may 'tis possible, be yet more so. What I complained of to you I find was only a little letchery of the tongue in a lady, which must be allowed her sex, nor would be any concern to me if every married man were but as wise as Mr Caryll. 'Tis a common practice now for ladies to contract friendships as the great folks in ancient times entered into leagues. They sacrificed a poor animal betwixt 'em, and commenced inviolable allies, *ipso facto*; so now they pull some harmless little creature into pieces, and worry his character together very comfortably; Mrs Nelson and Mrs Englefield[1] have served me just thus, the former of whom has done me all the ill offices that lay in her way, particularly with Mrs W[eston] and at White-knights. I have undeniable reasons to know this, which you may hereafter hear: nor should I trouble you with things so wholly my concern but under the sacred seal of friendship, and to give some warning lest you might too readily credit any thing reported from the bare word of a person of whose veracity and probity I wish I could speak as well as I can of her poetry and sense. For the rest, I know many good conditioned people are subject to be deceived by tale-bearers, and I can't be angry at them tho' they injure me. The same gentleness and open temper which makes them civil to me, make 'em credulous to any other. And [it] would be to no purpose to expostulate with such; 'tis a fault of their very nature, which they would relapse into the next week. Every man has a right to give up as much as he pleases of his own character, and I will sacrifice as much of mine as they have injured, to my ease, rather than take inglorious pains of a chattering eclaircissement with women (or men) of weak credulity. Ovid indeed tell[s] us[2] of a contention there was once betwixt the Muses and certain magpies, but I don't much care to moralize the fable in my own example. You'll find by this hint that I have some share in a scribbler's vanity, or at least some respect for myself; which if it be ever pardonable to show, it is certainly when others regard us less than we deserve from them. However, I am perfectly contented, as long as you and a few such as you, entertain no ill opinion of me; who I am confident are above such weak credulity of every tale or whisper against a man who can have no [other] interest in your friendship than the friendship itself. And believe me, dear sir, no one living more truly values yours, or shall in all things he is able more gratefully return to it, than | Your ever obliged friend and | most humble servant | A: P:

After what I have told you, I need not enjoin your silence as to this affair, for I design no more than to be a civil acquaintance at Wh[ite-knight]s.

[1] Mrs. Henry Englefield. Her husband was the uncle of Teresa and Martha Blount. He died in 1720, and in 1732 his widow married Webb, Pope's former schoolmate. So far Elwin. It may be noted that Thomas Hearne, normally a first-class informant, in his *Collections*, names Charles Englefield as dying suddenly in 1720.

That Mrs. Nelson made trouble for more people than Pope is pointed out by Elwin (vi. 180 n.).

[2] *Metamorphoses*, v. 294 ff.

†POPE *to* LORD LANSDOWNE[1] — 10 *January* 1712/13

1737

Binfield, Jan. 10, 1712.

I thank you for having given my poem of Windsor Forest its greatest ornament, that of bearing your name in the front of it. 'Tis one thing when a person of true merit permits us to have the honour of drawing him as like as we can; and another, when we make a fine thing at random, and persuade the next vain creature we can find that 'tis his own likeness; which is the case every day of my fellow scribblers. Yet my Lord, this honour has given me no more pride than your honours have given you;[2] but it affords me a great deal of pleasure, which is much better than a great deal of pride; and it indeed would give me some pain if I was not sure of one advantage; that whereas others are offended if they have not more than justice done 'em, you would be displeas'd if you had so much: therefore I may safely do you as much injury in my words, as you do your self in your own thoughts. I am so vain as to think I have shewn you a favour, in sparing your modesty, and you cannot but make me some return for prejudicing the truth to gratify you: This I beg may be the free correction of these verses, which will have few beauties, but what may be made by your blots. I am in the circumstance of an ordinary painter drawing Sir Godfrey Kneller, who by a few touches of his own could make the piece very valuable. I might then hope, that many years hence the world might read, in conjunction with your name, that of, | Your Lordship's, &c.

POPE *to* CARYLL — [*February* 1712/13?]

Add. 28618

London

I have just now stolen myself from a tumult of acquaintance at Will's, into my chamber, to enjoy the pleasing melancholy of an hour's reflection alone. There is an agreeable gloominess which instead of troubling, does but refresh and ease the mind, and has an effect upon it not unlike the relief a sudden cloud sometimes gives the eye, when it has been aching and too much distended with the glaring of a summer's day. In one of these moments I have past over the pleasures I last tasted in your Company. I remember Horace in one of his Odes,[3] to express the friendship Septimius bore him, addresses him as one who would travel the world over in his company, and makes this the chief

[1] First printed in the Roberts octavo of 1737.

[2] Pope is honoured by his lordship's permission to dedicate *Windsor Forest* to him. Lord Lansdowne's honours (elevation to the peerage) had come at the beginning of 1712, when the twelve Tory peers were created. Pope mentioned Lansdowne as 'Granville the polite' in the *Epistle to Dr. Arbuthnot*, l. 135

[3] Horace, *Carmina*, II. vi.

part of the character by which he recommends him to posterity. Tibullus, who (if we may give credit to his own account of himself) loved Messala as well as I do Mr Caryll, fell sick in his journey with his friend, and desired to be remembered only by this circumstance, when the prospect of death was before him.

Hic jacet immiti consumptus morte Tibullus,
Messalam terra, dum sequiturque, mari.[1]

An epitaph which would very well have agreed with me, had it been my fate to have perished in the flames in your company betwixt old and new Windsor.

I have had lately the entertainment of reading Mr Addison's tragedy of *Cato*.[2] The scene is in Utica, and the time, the last night of his life. It drew tears from me in several parts of the fourth and fifth acts, where the beauty of virtue appears so charming that I believe (if it comes upon the theatre) we shall enjoy that which Plato thought the greatest pleasure an exalted soul could be capable of, a view of virtue itself great[3] in person, colour, and action. The emotion which the mind will feel from this character and the sentiments of humanity which the distress of such a person as Cato will stir up in us, must necessarily fill an audience with so glorious a disposition, and so warm[4] a love of virtue, that I question if any play has ever conduced so immediately to morals as this.

I have just sent the poem of *Windsor Forest* to the press,[5] which I will take care to order some copies of to Ladyholt. I was at the same time both glad and ashamed to find (when we were at Old Windsor) that you had more lines than one of that poem by heart. But I must own your partiality to me makes me love myself the better.

I will endeavour, if I can bring it about with any conveniency, to pay a visit to the lady at Hammersmith, who (I know) would receive me much better and think me more her friend and servant, if I came to her in a coach of my own. But I have a real value for her, and shall therefore venture, tho' in a stage coach. As for Sapho,[6] I must confess I shall never be able to esteem her, (tho' I may give all that's due to her poetry), and therefore question whether I shall ever dissemble so far as to visit her, but am sure I never shall be so unjust to myself as

[1] Tibullus, I. iii. 55–56. Caryll's scribe wrote *mare* for *mari*.

[2] Since *Cato* was first acted (with a Prologue by Pope) on 14 Apr. 1713, it seems strange that Pope still doubts if it may come upon the theatre. In spite of his pleasure in reading the play Pope evidently had doubts of its theatrical quality. He later said as much to Spence. (*Anecdotes*, p. 196.)

[3] great] drest *Elwin*. The transcriber wrote, clearly, *dreat*.

[4] so warm] sovereign *Elwin* (wrongly!).

[5] For *Windsor Forest* Lintot paid Pope £32. 5*s*. on 23 February 1713.—Griffith, p. 21. The printing of the poem (published 7 Mar.) dates the letter.

[6] Sapho is Mrs. Nelson.—Elwin.

to dispute with her, tho' she invite me to a learned debate in terms ne'er so pathetic.

Pardon my desultory manner of scribbling, for 'tis with difficulty I snatch half an hour to write in. I have ten different employments at once that distract me every hour: five or 6 authors have seized upon me, whose pieces of quite different natures I am obliged to consider, or falsify the trust they repose in me—and my own Poem to correct too—besides an affair with Mr Steele,[1] that takes up much consultation daily, and add to all this a law business, which my father uses me in. Guess if I have time upon my hands, and if the labours of the head outweigh those of the body, you'll own no one can well be more busy than I. Yet I must not forget to pay my most humble thanks for Lady Mary's obliging thought on my account as a lover of painting (the pursuit of which is another of my employs). I beg her ladyship to accept my humble service, as well as your whole good family, which I shall ever pray for (after the best manner I am able to pray for any thing) and I beg you, dear sir, to believe none love you more unaffectedly and entirely than, | Your most faithful obedient humble servant | A: P:

I shall continue here[2] 'till Easter, a line from you as often as you can will please me above all things.

POPE *to* CARYLL[3] — 30 *April* 1713

Add. 28618

London. April 30. 1713.

⌜I think it very happy for me, that the circumstances of our friendship are so much changed since I first knew you, as it now requires an excuse when I do not write to you, no less than it once required one when I did. I can assure you, dear sir, nothing less than the pardon you freely promised me when last I saw you, in case of such omission on my part, could have made me satisfied so long without accosting you by way [of] letter.⌝ I've been almost every day employed in following your advice[4] in learning to paint, in which I am most particularly obliged to Mr Gervase,[5] who gives me daily instructions and examples. As to poeticall affairs I am content at present to be a bare looker on, and from a practic[io]ner turn an admirer, which is (as the world goes) not very usual. Cato was not so much the wonder of Rome ⌜itself,⌝ in his days, as he is of Britain in ours; and tho' all the foolish industry

[1] Presumably Pope's co-operation in *The Guardian*, or in the Censorium.

[2] At Jervas's house in Cleveland Court?

[3] In 1735 parts of this letter were printed as a letter to Sir William Trumbull. Pope's omissions made in 1735 are here placed in half-brackets, and his textual revisions are indicated in notes. Reprinting the text avowedly sent to Sir William is consequently superfluous.

[4] advice . . . in which] advice and amusing my self in Painting, in which *1735–42*.

[5] *Gervase* was a common spelling for *Jervas*.

possible has been used to make it a party play, yet what the author once said of another[1] may be the most properly in the world applied to him on this occasion.

> Envy it self is dumb, in wonder lost,
> And factions strive, who shall applaud him[2] most.

The numerous and violent claps of the Whig party on the one side the theatre, were echoed back by the Tories on the other, while the author sweated behind the scenes with concern to find their applause proceeded more [from] the hand than the head. This was the case too of the prologue-writer,[3] who was clapped into a stanch Whig sore against his will, at almost every two lines. I believe you have heard that after all the applauses of the opposite faction, my Lord Bullingbrooke sent for Booth who played Cato, into the box, between one of the acts and presented him with 50 guineas; in acknowledgment (as he expressed it) for ⌜his⌝ defending the cause of liberty so well against a *perpetuall dictator*:[4] the Whigs are unwilling to be distanced this way, ⌜as 'tis said,⌝ and therefore design a present to the said Cato very speedily; in the meantime they are getting ready as good a sentence as the former on their side. So betwixt them, 'tis probable that Cato (as Dr Garth expressed it) may have something to live upon, after he dies.

⌜This play was published but this Monday[5] and Mr Lewis tells me it is not possible to convey it to you before Friday next. The town is so fond of it, that the orange wenches and fruit women in the Park offer the books at the side of the coaches, and the Prologue and Epilogue are cried about the streets by the common hawkers.

⌜But of all the world none have been in so peculiar a manner enamoured with *Cato*, as a young gentleman of Oxford, who makes it the sole guide of all his actions, and subject of all his discourse; he dates everything from the first or third night, &c., of *Cato*: he goes out of town every day it is not played, and fell in love with Mrs Oldfield for no other reason than because she acted Cato's daughter! [6]This has

[1] 'What the author once said of another' is quoted, with changes, in Steele's 'Verses to the Author of the Tragedy of Cato'. The two lines come from Addison's *Campaign*, ll. 45–46. Steele's verses were not published in the first edition of *Cato*, and so presumably postdate Pope's application of the lines to Addison. Of course Steele's lines may have been *written* before Pope wrote this letter.

[2] him] his *Caryll's scribe's error.*

[3] Pope himself. One may compare Pope's account of the first performance of *Cato* with that of the philosopher Berkeley in his letter to Percival. See B. Rand, *Berkeley and Percival*, pp. 113–14. See also Gay's letter to Maurice Johnson (23 Apr. 1713) printed in Nichols's *Bibliotheca Topographica Britannica* (1790), III. xxii, and now preserved in the Gay Collection at Harvard.—Irving, *John Gay*, p. 81.

[4] Marlborough is thus aimed at because of his desire to be appointed Captain-General or life.

[5] Published 27 Apr.

[6] Elwin omitted this sentence and the verses following.

occasioned the following epigram, which was dispersed about the coffee houses in Holy Week, and is much approved of by our wits.

> You ask why Damon does the College seek?
> 'Tis because *Cato*'s not rehears'd this week;
> How long at Oxford then will Damon stay?
> Damon returns not till they *Cato* play:
> Oldfield wants Damon—when will he be at her?
> Oh, not till Oldfield shall be Cato's daughter:
> Why then, if I can guess what may ensue,
> When Cato's clapped, Damon will be so too.

⌜But I find my self just at the end of my paper; and have only room to assure you that I should write with more ceremony and care, if I loved and esteemed you less: and to entreat the continuance of your obliging letters and wonted favours to | Dear Sir | Your ever obligd affectionate humble | Servant | A. P.

⌜I shall go to Binfield next week, from whence I intend to accost Mr John Caryll by way of epistle, in the mean time be pleased to assure him, and the whole family how truly I am their servant.⌝

‡POPE *to* SIR WILLIAM TRUMBULL — 30 *April* 1713

[In 1735 Pope printed portions of his letter of this date addressed to Caryll as if sent to Sir William. See the preceding letter.]

POPE *to* CARYLL[1] — 12 *June* 1713

Add. 28618

London June 12. 1713.

I have been prevented in the design of writing to you by several who have told me you would certainly be here in a few days. But I find this happiness, like most others, still farther off, the nearer we fancy we approach 'em. I therefore resolved no longer to delay the pleasure I always take in assuring you how faithfully I am yours.

As I hope, and would flatter myself that you know me, and my thoughts so entirely as never to be mistaken in either, so 'tis a pleasure to me that you guessed so right in regard to the author of that *Guardian* you mentioned. But am sorry to find it has taken air that I have some

[1] In all his editions (1735–42) Pope printed as to Addison a letter made up from three letters to Caryll, one of which was this of 12 June. The others were those of 23 June and 17 Oct.—all three of 1713. Pope printed his composite without date, but placed it just after his letter from Addison, 2 Nov. 1713, where, as a curiosity, it is preserved in the present edition. From this letter of 12 June Pope borrowed most of the second and fourth paragraphs. His omissions within the borrowed passages are signalized by half-brackets.

hand in those papers, because I write so very few as neither to deserve the credit of such a report with some people, nor the disrepute of it with others. An honest Jacobite ⌜that we met on the 10. of June,⌝ spoke to me, the sense, or nonsense of the weak part of his party, very fairly ⌜and innocently:⌝ that the good people took it very ill of me that I write with *Steele*, tho' upon ever so indifferent subjects.——This I know you will laugh at as well as myself, yet I doubt not but many little calumniators and persons of sowered dispositions will take occasion hence to bespatter me. I confess I scorn narrow souls, of all parties, and if I renounce my reason in religious matters, I'll never do it in any other ⌜affair. But enough of this trifle⌝.

One word, however, of a private trifle; Honest Mr Eng—d[1] has not shown the least common civility to my father and mother; by sending, or enquiring of them from our nearest neighbours, his visitants or any otherwise, these five months. I take the hint, as I ought, in respect to those who gave me being; and he shall be as much a stranger to me, as he desires. I ought to prepare myself by such small trials, for those numerous friendships of this sort which in all probability I shall meet with in the course of my life.

⌜I shall stay in town yet this fortnight, or thereabouts, in which time if you come, you'll find me in the close pursuit of the advice you gave me three months since; painting at Mr Gervase's in Cleveland Court by St. James's.⌝ I generally employ the mornings this way, and the evenings in the conversation of such as I think can most improve my mind, of whatever party or denomination they are. ⌜But as⌝ I ever must set the highest value upon men of truly great, that is honest principles, of equal capacities; ⌜so 'tis no compliment to assure you I shall persist in my old way of preferring your company to all other whensoever you will give me the opportunity of enjoying it:⌝ The best way I know of overcoming calumny and misconstruction is by a vigorous perseverance in every thing we know to be right, and a total neglect of all that ensue from it. 'Tis partly from this maxim that I depend ⌜on all times⌝ upon your friendship, because I believe it will do justice to my *intentions* in every thing; and give me leave to tell you that as the world goes this is no small assurance I repose in you.[2] I've long since been exalted in my real esteem of you, above all compliment, or ostentatious professions, and I beg you to believe me with the same openness that I style my self | Dear sir | Your most faithful and ever affectionate | humble servant | A: P:

My most hearty service to Mr John Caryll in particular.

[1] Henry Englefield, Esq., uncle of Teresa and Martha Blount, and neighbour of the Popes.

[2] Pope's composite printed as to Addison ended at this point.

Adriani Morientis ad Animam.[1]

Poor, little, pretty fluttering Thing!
Must we no longer live together?
And dost thou prune thy doubtful wing,
To take thy flight thou know'st not whither?

Thy hum'rous vein, thy pleasing folly,
Lies all neglected, all forgot,
And pensive, wav'ring, melancholy,
Thou dread'st and hope'st thou know'st not what!

The Same by another Hand.

Ah fleeting Spirit! wandring Fire,
That long hast warm'd my tender breast,
Must thou no more this frame inspire?
No more a pleasing, chearful guest?

Whither, ah whither art thou flying!
To what dark, undiscover'd shore?
Thou seem'st all trembling, shiv'ring, dying,
And wit and humour are no more.

Christiani Morientis ad Animam.

1.

Vital Spark of Heavenly Flame!
Dost thou quit this mortal frame?
Trembling, hoping, ling'ring, flying;
Oh the pain, the bliss of dying;
Cease, fond Nature, cease thy strife,
Let me languish into Life.

2.

My swimming eyes are sick of light,
The less'ning world forsakes my sight,
A damp creeps cold o'er ev'ry part,
Nor moves my pulse, nor heaves my heart.
The hov'ring soul is on the wing;
Where, mighty Death! oh where's thy sting?

[1] The first version of Hadrian is by Prior; the second is by Pope, and the third (written at Steele's request as an 'Ode of a chearful dying spirit') is also by Pope, in spite of the last sentence following the poems. Pope had sent his version of *Christiani Morientis* to Steele, in a letter of shortly after 4 Dec. 1712, but he printed that letter (doubtfully genuine, of course) with a later revised text of the verses. See Pope to Steele, Dec. 1712, and also N. Ault, *New Light*, pp. 60–67.

3.

I hear around soft musick play,
And angels beckon me away!
Calm as forgiven hermits rest,
I'll sleep, or infants at the breast;
Till the trumpet rends the ground;
Then wake with pleasure at the sound.

I desire your opinion of these verses, and which are best written. They are of three different hands.[1]

POPE *to* CARYLL — 23 *June* 1713

Add. 28618

June 23. 1713.

Tho' I was always assured that men of true sense can never be punctilious, yet I cannot deny but I found a pleasure in hearing you had twice written to me, tho' the letter you mention sent by Mr Englefield's servant never came to Binfield, nor to my hands. [2]Your last is the more obliging as it hints at some little niceties in my conduct, which your candor and affection prompt you to recommend to me, and which (so trivial as things of this nature seem) are yet of no slight consequence to people whom every body talks of, and every body as he pleases. 'Tis a sort of tax that attends an estate in Parnassus which is often rated much higher than agrees with the proportion of the small possession an author holds. For indeed an author who is once come upon the town ⌜like a whore that's come upon the town⌝ is enjoyed without being thanked for the pleasure, and sometimes ill treated, even by those very persons who first debauched him. Yet to tell you the bottom of my heart, I am no ways displeased that I have offended the *violent* of all parties already; and at the same time I assure you conscientiously, I feel not the least malevolence or ⌜embittered⌝ resentment against any of those who misrepresented me, or are dissatisfied with me. This frame of mind is so easy, that I am perfectly content with my condition. You must not think it any defect in friendship that I talk so much of myself to you, when according to the way of the world I ought to be tendering respects to you. For what makes me do this, is the persuasion I have that you interest yourself

[1] The statement is untrue. Ault is doubtless right in assuming that Pope's rather innocent lie was designed to secure from Caryll a comment completely unbiased by friendship.

[2] The passage beginning here and ending with 'I am perfectly content with my condition' formed the first paragraph of Pope's composite letter to Addison printed (1735–42) with no date but placed, as here, just after Addison to Pope, 2 Nov. 1713. Pope's two omissions are here placed in half-brackets. The other letters pillaged to form this composite were letters to Caryll dated 12 June and 17 Oct. 1713.

not a little in my concerns, which is, in one word, the strongest assurance that can be given, of my sense of your affection. Let us pretend what we will, no mortal loves any man so well, as that man who, he thinks, loves him most. As therefore I have not the vanity to believe any one here is so truly my friend as yourself, so (without flamm or compliment) no company here can detain me agreeably from the enjoyment of yours in the country. This is so natural a reason that I hope you will credit it.

To confirm you yet farther how nearly my friendship and interest are allied, I have a kindness to beg of you. That you would please to engage either your son or some other correspondent you can depend upon at Paris, to take the trouble of looking himself into the books of the Hôtel de Ville, to be satisfied if our name be there inserted, for 3030 livres at ten per cent life rent, on Sir Rich: Cantillion's life,[1] to begin midsummer 1705. And again, in my father's name for my life, for 5220 livres at 10 per cent also, to begin July 1707.

I should not trouble you with this enquiry, but for my father's ease, who by any solicitations we yet could urge cannot obtain an attested copy of the contract from Cantillion, or Mr Arthur, who lays the neglect on his correspondent.

I wholly agree with you in your opinion of the *Guardian* in general; only I must do Mr Steel the justice to assure you, those he writes himself are equal to any he has wrote. The grand difference is caused by the want of Mr Addison's assistance, who writes as seldom as I do, one a month or so. (By the way, that on Tom Durfey was his, as the receipt for an Epic Poem was your servant's.[2])

Your judgment on the three copies of verse I sent you, is what you need not doubt I think good, because the last of them was my own.

Dear sir, excuse my neglect of method and style; these are what a friend and honest man may neglect; and I assure you faithfully that the true reason I neglect my expression when I write to you, is because I am beyond all expression, entirely | Your affectionate obliged | Friend and faithful servant | A: P:

POPE *to* MRS. MARRIOT[3] 19 *July* [1713?]

Harvard University

London, July the 19th.

Madam,—The same cause that commonly occasions all sorts of negligence in our Sex to yours, has hinder'd thus long my answering your

[1] One wonders if Sir Richard is the celebrated economist who was murdered in 1734. See *DNB*.

[2] *Guardian*, No. 67 (on Tom Durfey) was apparently Addison's first contribution to the periodical. Pope's recipe to make an epic poem (No. 78) appeared on 10 June 1713.

[3] Elwin, printing from a transcript made by Croker from the original, dated this letter 1712. As between 1712 and 1713 there is not much to choose; but in 1712 Pope must have

most obliging Letter; I mean A Rambling way of Life which I have run into these two months & upwards. It is some kind of commendation to bear our duty long in mind, and I assure you I have every day Thought of writing to you. But, Madam, you ought to consider, that to reply to a very witty Epistle, such as yours, requires of necessity a good deal of Time. If I were so wise as to proceed cautiously, I should summon a Council of all the Witts at Button's Coffee house before I attempted it. In plain terms, Madam, I am but a lone man, & no way a match for you. Therefore, for God's sake, and for my comfort, write a dull Letter next; which, considering it comes from your hands, will be the greatest Rarity in the world.

After all I have said, let me whisper you in your Ear, and tell you a little Truth. Faith, Madam, I have never seen nor read your Letter. It came to Binfield when I was in Town, & my Politick Father detained it there to be a motive of drawing me into the Country. I have manfully resisted the Temptation these three weeks, but find I must see your Letter or dye. I believe 'tis with Impatience for this that I have neither Eat nor Slept of late: for upon my word I have scarce layn four hours asleep nor received the nourishment natural to me all this time. I have during those short slumbers dreamt of so many fine things in your Letter that I almost fear 'twill hardly answer my Idæa of it when I read it. Methought t'other night Mrs. Betty Marryot (like a Wagg as she is) snatched it out of my hand & offered me a Kiss to part with it, which I refused, though, in my conscience, she looked more amiable in that Dream than I had ever thought her awake; she was then handsomer than Herself, and before she was only handsomer than all others.

Dreams, they say, are often Propheticall, and I can't but fancy they have told me truth in what they represent to be the contents of your Letter. You railly me cruelly upon my Solitary Life in the Country; while I am distracting my self all about the Towne, you set before my Eyes the entertainments of Balls and Masquerades, Parties of Pleasure in Spring Gardens, Plays and Music meetings, Raffling Shops, and all those things which your fair daughter hates in her heart, & is so very glad to avoid in the shades of Suffolk. But since you insult me to such a degree (as I am sure you do in that cursed Letter), I'll return you such Thanks as it deserves, that is, I'll curse you and your daughter heartily.

In the first place, then, may Providence consent to my wishes, and

been preparing to go to Sussex with Caryll, Jr., and his bride; and there is no mention of such a projected journey—which in July 1712 would have been imminent. According to Gay (see a Morgan Library letter from Gay to Fortescue, 5 Oct. 1713) Pope spent 'all summer' in town in 1713. The original letter, part of the collections of Frederick Locker-Lampson, has recently been deposited in the Harvard College Library.

The Marriots lived in Sturston, the parish in which Broome was presently the clergyman.

cause you both to forsake your House and home; may your Possessions be alienated and put into the hands of Strangers; may your Fields bear Harvests for other people, & those who are now your Tenants be the Dependants of New Possessours. May you quit the Country, the Seat of Innocence and pure Delights, & live in the very Sink of all wickedness, this Towne, in the midst of Vices and Follies. Nay, may you be deprived of the best Companion & comfort you have, your fair Daughter above mentioned; may she forsake you for a Man, and love that man as well or better than yourself all her days. And to cutt you off for ever from any prospect of a return of her whole affection to you, may that man love her so well as to engage her eternally to himself.

After all these heavy curses, for the Accomplishment of which I sincerely pray to Heaven, I have yet so good an Opinion of your Christianity as to believe you will be so charitable as to forgive me—nay, as to think me | Dear Madam, | your most faithful & | obedient humble servant.

I beg the continuance of the favour of your correspondence. If you can't write yourself at any time, let Mrs. Betty do it in your stead; & I'll be so good humour'd as to answer her, let her say whatever she pleases.

POPE *to* TERESA *and* MARTHA BLOUNT[1] [*July* 1713?]

Mapledurham

FRAGMENT

. . . voyd of all Witt; but I assure you as long as I have any Memory, I shall never forget that Piece of Humanity in you. I must owne I should never have look'd for Sincerity in your Sexe, & nothing was so surprising as to find it, not only in your Sexe, but in two of the Youngest and Fairest of it. If it be possible for you to pardon this last folly of mine, 'twill be a greater Strain of Goodness than I expect ever from Yourselves: But whether you can pardon it or not, I think myself obliged to give you this Testimony under my hand, that I must ever have that Value for your Characters, as to express it for the future on all Occasions, & in all the Ways I am capable of.

[1] From this fragment Carruthers (pp. 68, 69) printed the first two incomplete paragraphs, beginning 'But I assure you'. Elwin reprinted from Carruthers the first paragraph only. The last paragraph seems not yet to have been printed. Since the ladies are apparently still resident at Mapledurham, the letter should antedate 1716. Since the gentleman enjoying the friendship of both ladies was at that time H. Moore, Esq., of Fawley Court, and since this gentleman was writing to them frequently in 1713, that seems a possible year. Pope even thus early has been the subject of calumny, and here thanks the ladies for humanity and sincerity (in his defence?). Moore (now known *not* to be James Moore Smythe: see *Modern Language Notes*, xl (1925), 88–91) had on 30 July 1713 written to the ladies, 'I was some hours with Mr. Pope yesterday, who has, to use his own words, a mighty respect for the two Miss Blounts' (Carruthers, p. 71). It is a large editorial assumption that Pope somewhat before this time wrote the letter here given as now preserved.

That Gentleman who is so happy to have you both his Friends, is above all other Friendship; but if he pleases to accept of mine, he may (in spight of all Calumny) be assur'd of it. The same Method that is used to make him doubt of my Honesty, has been practisd formerly to cause my Distrust of his, & by the same Persons. And he may be confident that nothing but the Value I have for him [*words lacking*]

You see Ladies, I can write Seriously when [I am truly] myself, tho' I only Railly when I am displeasd [with others. The] most that any one shall get from me who would c[ause misunder-]standings, is Contempt & Laughter; Those who [Detest that evil] way can have nothing less than an Entire Este[em such as will] [make] me always | Ladies, | Your most obliged [obedient] | humble Servant, | A. Po[pe].

Address: To the Young Ladies, | att | Mapledurham.

‡POPE *to* ADDISON[1] 30 *July* 1713

1735

July 30, 1713.

I am more joy'd at your return than I should be at that of the Sun, so much as I wish for him this melancholy wet season; but 'tis his fate too, like yours, to be displeasing to Owls and obscene animals, who cannot bear his lustre. What put me in mind of these night-birds was *John Dennis*, whom I think you are best reveng'd upon, as the Sun was in the fable upon those batts and beastly birds above-mention'd, only by *Shining on*. I am so far from esteeming it any misfortune, that I congratulate you upon having your share in that, which all the great men and all the good men that ever liv'd have had their part of, Envy and Calumny. To be uncensur'd and to be obscure, is the same thing. You may conclude from what I here say, that 'twas never in my thoughts to have offer'd you my pen in any direct reply to such a Critic, but only in some little raillery; not in defence of you, but in contempt of him.[2] But indeed your opinion that 'tis intirely to be neglected, would have been my own had it been my own case: but I felt more warmth here than I did when first I saw his book against myself, (tho' indeed in two minutes it made me heartily merry). He has written against every thing the world has approv'd these many

[1] This letter was fabricated from parts of that addressed to Caryll, 19 Nov. 1712 (q.v.). The changes of names, &c., are so ingeniously done that the letter, pure fabrication though it is, deserves reprinting as perhaps Pope's masterpiece in this kind. The 'melancholy wet season', to be sure, fits November better than July, but the whole is most deftly 'translated'. In editions of 1737–42 the date is given as 20 July, but since Pope's *Narrative of Dr. Robert Norris* was published, according to *The Post Boy*, on 28 July, the 30th is more probable as date. Even the 30th is improbably prompt for a reply to a reaction from Addison. Since the whole is a fabrication, the date matters only in so far as the letter represents *what may have happened*, even if Pope had no copy of any letter he may have written on the subject.

[2] This relates to the Paper occasion'd by Dennis's *Remarks* upon *Cato*, call'd *Dr. Norris's Narrative of the Frenzy of John Den—*. Pope, 1735–42.

years: I apprehend but one danger from *Dennis*'s disliking our sense; that it may make us think so very well of it, as to become proud and conceited, upon his disapprobation.

I must not here omit to do justice to Mr. —,[1] whose zeal in your concern is worthy a friend, and honourer of you. He writ to me in the most pressing terms about it, tho' with that just contempt of the Critic that he deserves. I think in these days one honest man is oblig'd to acquaint another who are his friends; when so many mischievous insects are daily at work to make people of merit suspicious of each other; that they may have the satisfaction of seeing them look'd upon no better than themselves. I am | Your, &c.

STEELE *to* LINTOT[2] — 4 *August* 1713

1729

August 4, 1713.

Mr. *Lintot*,—Mr. *Addison* desir'd me to tell you, that he wholly disapproves the Manner of Treating Mr. *Dennis* in a little Pamphlet, by way of Dr. *Norris*'s Account.[3] When he thinks fit to take Notice of Mr. *Dennis*'s Objections to his Writings, he will do it in a Way Mr. Dennis shall have no just Reason to complain of. But when the Papers above-mentioned, were offer'd to be communicated to him, he said he could not, either in Honour or Conscience, be privy to such a Treatment, and was sorry to hear of it. I am, | Sir, | Your very Humble Servant, | Richard Steele.

NICHOLAS ROWE *to* POPE[4] — [1713]

Homer MSS. Add. 4807

If you will favour me with your Prologue by this bearer I will Return it to morrow & allways Reckon it among the Obligations you have been so kind as to lay upon | Your most faithfull | humble Servant | N Rowe.

[1] Mr. Gay *1737–42.*

[2] The text is taken from Dennis's *Remarks upon Mr. Pope's Dunciad* (1729), p. 42.

[3] Dennis had been more than once the object of satire in *The Tatler* and *Spectator*, so he thought; and, sensitive because of these or because his misguided critical integrity led him on, he had published (11 July) adverse *Remarks upon the Tragedy of Cato*. Pope, ostensibly to defend Addison but evidently to ridicule Dennis, published (28 July) through Bernard Lintot his *Narrative of Dr. Robert Norris concerning the Strange and Deplorable Frenzy of Mr. John Dennis.* Steele's letter to Lintot expressing Addison's disapproval of Pope's 'defence' was evidently passed on to Dennis, who in 1729 printed it.

[4] For Rowe's tragedy of *Jane Shore* (first acted in Feb. 1714) Pope wrote the epilogue. No prologue by him for any Rowe play is known; hence one suspects Rowe miswrote *prologue* for *epilogue*. It is perhaps possible that Rowe is consenting to read Pope's Prologue for Addison's *Cato*, in which case the letter should come some months earlier. Ault would make the Prologue that published in *Jane Shore* (1715) as 'Sent by an Unknown Hand'. This seems to the editor improbable—especially as Ault agrees that this part of the *Iliad* (Book VI) is translated on the backs of letters (this of Rowe being one) practically all of which date from 1713. See Ault, *New Light*, pp. 138–44.

POPE *to* CARYLL[1] 14 *August* 1713

Add. 28618

August 14. 1713.

I have been lying in wait for my own imagination this week and more, and watching what thoughts of mine came up in the whirl of fancy that were worth communicating to you in a letter. But I am at length convinced that my rambling head can produce nothing of that sort; so I must e'en be contented with telling you the old story, that I love you heartily. I have often found by experience that nature and truth, tho' never so low or vulgar, is yet pleasing when openly and without artifice[2] represented; ⌜insomuch that⌝ it would be diverting to me to read the very letters of an infant, could it write its innocent inconsistencies and tautologies, just as it thought 'em. This makes me hope a letter from me will not be unwelcome to you, when I am conscious I write with more unreservedness than ever man wrote, or perhaps talked to another. I trust your good nature with the whole range of my follies, and really love you so well that I would rather you should *pardon* me than *esteem* me, since one is an act of goodness or benevolence, the other a kind of constrained deference.

You can't wonder my thoughts are scarce consistent, when I tell you how they are distracted! Every hour of my life, my mind is strangely divided. This minute, perhaps, I am above the stars, with a thousand systems round about me, looking forward into the vast abyss of eternity,[3] and losing my whole comprehension in the boundless spaces of the extended Creation, in dialogues with W⌜histon⌝[4] and the astronomers; the next moment I am below all trifles, even grovelling with T⌜idcombe⌝ in the very center of nonsense: now am I recreating my mind[5] with the brisk sallies and quick turns of wit, which Mr Steele in his liveliest and freest humours darts about him; and now levelling my application to the insignificant observations and quirks of grammar of Mr C⌜romwell⌝ and D⌜ennis⌝.

Good God! what an Incongruous Animal is Man? how unsettled in

[1] Pope printed (1735–42) practically this entire letter under date of 14 Dec. 1713 as if to Addison. Small textual variants are noted below, and Pope's omissions are placed in half-brackets.

[2] is . . . without artifice] are . . . artlessly *1735–42.*

[3] the vast abyss of eternity, and] a vast abyss, and *1735–42.*

[4] In his *Memoirs* Whiston speaks highly of Addison as his 'particular friend; and who with his friend Sir *Richard Steel*, brought me, upon my banishment from *Cambridge* [October 1710], to have many astronomical lectures at Mr. Button's coffee-house, near *Covent Garden*, to the agreeable entertainment of a good number of curious persons, and the procuring me and my family some comfortable support under my banishment'. In his first (rhymed) letter to Cromwell Pope had called Whiston 'wicked'. Although Whiston's Arianism was notorious only after 1710, his *New Theory of the Earth* (1696) and his *Eight Sermons* (the Boyle lectures for 1707) evidently shocked some. Pope is here not hostile to Whiston, from whom he evidently got 'agreeable entertainment'—and perhaps scientific instruction.

[5] am recreating my mind] am recreated *1735–42.*

his best part, his soul; and how changing and variable in his frame of body? The constancy of the one, shook by every notion, the temperament of the other, affected by every blast of wind. ⌜What an April weather in the mind! In a word⌝, what is Man altogether, but one mighty inconsistency.

Sickness and pain is the lot of one half of us, doubt and fear the portion of the other! What a bustle we make about passing our time, when all our space is but a point? What aims and ambitions are crowded into this little instant of our life, which (as Shakespear finely words it) is *rounded with a sleep*? Our whole extent of being no more in the eyes of him who gave it, than a scarce perceptible atom[1] of duration. Those animals whose circle of living ⌜and date of perception⌝ is limited to three or four hours, as the naturalists assure us, are yet as long-lived and possess as wide a scene of action as man, if we consider him with an eye[2] to eternity. Who knows what plots, what achievements a mite may perform, in his kingdom of a grain of dust, within his life of some minutes? And of how much less consideration than even this, is the life of man in the sight of that God, who is from ever, and for ever!

Who that thinks in this train, but must see the world and its contemptible grandeurs lessen before him at every thought? 'Tis enough to make one remain stupified in a poise of inaction, void of all desires, of all designs, of all friendships. But we must return (thro' our very condition of being) to our narrow selves, and those things that affect ourselves. Our passions, our interests, flow in upon us, and unphilosophize us into mere mortals. For my part I never return so much into my self, as when I think of you, whose friendship is one of the best comforts I have for the insignificancy of my self. I am ⌜with the utmost sincerity without the senseless ostentation of compliments | Dear sir⌝ | Your ⌜most faithful and obliged | Friend and servant | A.P.⌝

⌜I am again at Mr Jervas's where I hope for the pleasure of a line from you. My faithful service and sincere good wishes always attend your whole family.⌝

NICHOLAS ROWE *to* POPE — 20 *August* 1713

Homer MSS. Add. 4807

Thursday. Aug. 20th 1713

I Don't know that I have a Long time Receiv'd a Billet with greater pleasure than yours. Depend upon it nothing Could have been more agreable but your self. To do something, then, that is perfectly kind

[1] atom] moment *1735–42*.
[2] with . . . eternity] with a view to all Space, and all Eternity *1737–42*.

Come & Eat a Bit of mutton with me to morrow at Stockwell. Bring whom you will along with you, tho' I Can give you nothing but the aforesaid mutton & a Cup of Ale. It is but a little mile from Fox:hall. & you Don't know how much you will oblige your most | affectionate & faithfull | humble servant | N. Rowe.

Address: To Mr. Pope att Mr | Jervas's in Cleaveland:Court | by St James's house or | att Button's Coffee house | in Coventgarden.

†POPE *to* GAY — 23 *August* 1713

1735

Aug. 23, 1713.

Just as I receiv'd yours, I was set down to write to you with some shame that I had so long defer'd it. But I can hardly repent my neglect, when it gives me the knowledge how little you insist upon Ceremony, and how much a greater share in your memory I have than I deserve. I have been near a week in *London*, where I am like to remain, till I become by Mr. *J—s*'s[1] help, *Elegans Formarum Spectator*.[2] I begin to discover Beauties that were till now imperceptible to me. Every Corner of an Eye, or Turn of a Nose or Ear, the smallest degree of Light or Shade on a Cheek, or in a dimple, have charms to distract me. I no longer look upon Lord *Plausible* as ridiculous, for admiring a Lady's fine Tip of an Ear and pretty Elbow (as the *Plain-dealer* has it) but am in some danger even from the Ugly and Disagreeable, since they may have their retired beauties, in one Trait or other about 'em. You may guess in how uneasy a state I am, when every day the performances of others appear more beautiful and excellent, and my own more despicable. I have thrown away three Dr. *Swift*'s, each of which was once my Vanity, two Lady *Bridgwaters*, a Dutchess of *Montague*, besides half a dozen Earls, and one Knight of the Garter. I have crucify'd *Christ* over-again in effigie, and made a *Madona* as old as her mother St. *Anne*. Nay, what is yet more miraculous, I have rival'd St. *Luke* himself in Painting, and as 'tis said an Angel came and finish'd

[1] *J—s*'s] *Jervas*'s *1735–42*.

[2] Pope was evidently copying portraits painted by Jervas, whose favourite subject was the Countess of Bridgewater. The Countess was sister of the Duchess of Montagu and daughter of the Duke of Marlborough. 'Churchill's race' is commended in Pope's Epistle to Jervas. It is regrettable that so little from Pope's brush has come down to us. Lord Mansfield has Pope's copy of Kneller's Betterton; and at Bryn Mawr College one may see (on loan from Mrs. A. E. Newton) a painting by Pope with a curious history. It was first described in Carruthers's *Life* (1857), pp. 462–3, as a drawing or painting (he had not seen it personally) of the prodigal son. At some later date the picture began to be publicized as a self-portrait by Pope. It is basically the painting by Pope from which in 1744 a frontispiece was engraved for the *Essay on Man*, but the figure of a ragged rake (or of Pope himself?) has been superposed on the original background. Pope was perhaps painting as early as 1705 and as late as 1728–30 (Spence, p. 23); but 1713 is the year of his intensive study of painting. In the inventory of his goods taken at his death is an item of seventeen drawings by him found in the garret. (See *Notes & Queries*, 6 S., v [1882], 363–5.)

his Piece, so you would swear a Devil put the last hand to mine, 'tis so begrim'd and smutted. However I comfort my self with a christian Reflection, that, I have not broken the Commandment, for my Pictures are not the likeness of any thing in heaven above, or in earth below, or in the waters under the earth. Neither will any body adore or worship them, except the *Indians* should have a sight of 'em, who they tell us, worship certain Pagods or[1] Idols purely for their Ugliness.

I am very much recreated and refreshed with the News of the Advancement of the *Fan*,[2] which I doubt not will delight the Eye and Sense of the Fair, as long as that agreeable Machine shall play in the Hands of Posterity. I am glad your *Fan* is mounted so soon, but I wou'd have you varnish and glaze it at your leisure, and polish the Sticks as much as you can. You may then cause it to be born in the Lands[3] of both Sexes, no less in *Britain*, than it is in *China*; where it is ordinary for a *Mandarine* to fan himself cool after a Debate, and a Statesman to hide his face with it when he tells a grave Lye, | I am, &c.

POPE *to* CARYLL — 31 *August* 1713

Add. 28618

London 31. Aug. 1713.

They say virtue rewards itself, yet every one is well enough pleased to receive some temporal blessings from it. So tho' the pleasure of writing to you always pays itself, yet I cannot but wish still to have the favour of a line from you. Some testimony now and then, that one is in the good graces of a friend, encourages no less our ardour for him, than those testimonies that we are [well] with Heaven enhance our zeal and devotion to it. I hope a letter of mine, not quite a fortnight since, reached your hands; tho' I am uncertain whether you were then at Grinsted or at Ladyholt. I must tell you fairly, sir, I'm much more concerned and impatient to be informed of every motion you make, and every employment you are engaged in, than of the advances of any foreign armies or any domestic negotiations whatever. A letter of yours has infinitely more charms to me, than the newest mail to the most ardent semipolitician. Bickerstaff's upholsterer[4] was never in half that solicitude on a post-night to know how the world went, as I am how affairs pass in one single family of yours, where there is not a member or individual that does not challenge a particular regard for me. The welfare of 'em all is to me of much more importance, than to the

[1] Pagods or] *omitted 1737–42.*

[2] Gay's poem *The Fan* was published 8 Dec. 1713.

[3] Corrected in 1737 to 'born in the hands'.

[4] Bickerstaff's Upholsterer, created by Addison in *Tatler* No. 155, was an exhibit from the first journalistic generation. He became a popular comic type.

Government that of all or any Branch of the most illustrious House of Hanover.

I can give you little account of the State of the literati in this place. Mr Steele, you know, has carried his election, tho' 'tis said a petition will be lodged against him, and he is of that opinion himself. Some people say, that passage in Scripture may be applied to him, upon the resignation of his places:[1] *I have left all and have followed you.* But whether or no *his Reward will therefore be great* is hard to determine. I made him my compliments in wishing he might become a pensioner.

Now sir, as 'tis usual in newspapers after the account of all material transactions, to descend to more trivial particulars (as for instance after the miseries of the Catalonians,[2] to tell who and who are married) so I beg leave here to give you some notices of my self, who am so entirely immersed in the designing art, (the only sort of designing I shall ever be capable of) that I have not heard a rhyme of my own gingle this long time. My eyes have so far got the better of my ears, that I have at present no notion of any harmony besides that of colors. But I have been hitherto as unsuccessful in uniting them, as the grand ministers have in uniting the kingdoms of England and Scotland: tho' I can indeed, like them, make a shift just to stick carnations and dirt together. They tell us, when St Luke painted, an angel came and finished the work; and it will be thought hereafter, that when I painted, the devil put the last hand to my pieces, they are so begrimed and smutted. 'Tis, however, some mercy that I see my faults; for I have been so out of conceit with my former performances, that I have thrown away three Dr Swifts, two Dutchesses of Montague, one Virgin Mary, the Queen of England, besides half a score earls and a Knight of the Garter. I will make essays upon such vulgar as these, before I grow so impudent as to attempt to draw Mr Caryll: tho' I find my hand most successful in drawing of friends and those I most esteem; insomuch that my master-pieces have been one of Dr Swift, and one Mr Betterton. When I talk of friends I can't but think of Mr Tooker[3] who is with you, and whom I beg to be assured of my most hearty service. Be pleased to intreat Mr John Caryll to accept it and to believe me ever his and his father's | most obliged and most affectionate friend | and servant | A: P:

Scriptus et in tergo, nec dum finitus Orestes.[4]

[1] Steele resigned places incompatible with a seat in Parliament, and if he was to be expelled (as shortly he was) his reward was loss and nothing more.

[2] These unfortunate people had cast their lot with the allies against Spain just before the unexpected end of the war, but neither by the Treaty of Utrecht nor by other means did their former friends protect them from the ferocity of Spanish revenge. The 'betrayal' of the Catalans was long a ground of reproach to the Tory Ministry.

[3] Mr. Tooker was probably a neighbour of Caryll's. See Pope to Caryll, 23 Oct. 1733 and note. See also v. 3–4.

[4] See the end of the letter to Cromwell, 12 Oct. 1710.

||POPE *to* CARYLL[1] 20 *September* [1713]

Add. 28618

Cleveland Court. Sept. 20.

I am just returned from the country, whither Mr Rowe did me the favour to accompany me and to pass a week at Binfield.[2] I need not tell you how much a man of his turn could not but entertain me, but I must acquaint you there is a vivacity and gayety of disposition almost peculiar to that gentleman,[3] which renders[4] it impossible to part from him without that uneasiness ⌜and chagrin⌝ which generally succeeds all great[5] pleasures. I have been just taking a solitary walk by moonshine ⌜in St James's park,⌝ full of the reflections of the transitory nature of all human delights, and giving my thoughts a loose into the contemplation of those ⌜sensations of⌝ satisfaction which probably we may taste in the ⌜more exalted⌝ company of separate spirits, when we range[6] the ⌜starry⌝ walks above, and gaze[7] on this world at a vast distance, as now we do on those.[8] The pleasures we are to enjoy in that conversation must undoubtedly be of a much nobler kind, and not unlikely may proceed from the discoveries each soul shall communicate to another of God and of nature: for the happiness of minds can surely be nothing but knowledge. The highest gratification we receive here below,[9] is mirth, which at the best, is but a fluttering unquiet motion that beats about the breast for a few moments, and after leaves it void and empty. ⌜So little is there in the thing we so much talk of, and so much magnify.⌝ Keeping good company, even the best, is but a less shameful art of losing time.

What we call science here,[10] and study, is little better: the greater number of arts to which we apply ourselves, are mere groping in the dark, and even the search of our most impatient[11] concerns in a future being, is but a needless, anxious, and uncertain haste to be knowing sooner than we can, what without all this solicitude we should[12] know a little after.[13] We are but curious impertinent[s] in the case of futurity.

[1] Much of this letter was printed (1735–42) as addressed to Edward Blount under the improbable date of 10 Feb. 1715/16. Various revisions and omissions (all made for improvement of the style) are noted below. The omissions are placed in half-brackets. The Caryll transcript gives no year, but Elwin suggested 1713 on the slight grounds of Pope's being with Jervas and busy at painting. Pope's *Guardian* essay for 29 Sept. 1713 suggests that Rowe may have been the friend there mentioned as having been recently in the country with Pope.

[2] did me . . . Binfield] accompanied me and pass'd a Week in the Forest *1735–42*.

[3] that Gentleman] him *1735–42*.

[4] renders] make *1735–42*.

[5] great pleasures] our pleasures *1735–42*.

[6] range] shall range *1735–42*.

[7] gaze] perhaps gaze *1735–42*.

[8] at a vast . . . those] at as vast a distance as we now do on those Worlds *1735–42*.

[9] here below] here from Company *1735–42*.

[10] call science here] here call Science *1735–42*.

[11] impatient] important *1735–42*. (The transcript is clear.)

[12] should] shall *1735–42*.

[13] after] later *1735–42*.

'Tis not our business to be guessing what the state of souls is, but to be doing what [may] make[1] our own happy.[2] We cannot be knowing, but we can be virtuous. If this be my notion of a great part of the gravest of sciences, divinity, you may easily imagine how little stress I lay upon any of the lighter arts.[3] I really make no other use of poetry[4] now, than horses ⌜do⌝ of the bells that gingle about their ears (tho' now and then they toss their heads as if they were proud of 'em), only to travel[5] on a little more merrily.[6] I have nothing new in hand, that I may answer your question; nor if I had, would the theatre be in my thoughts; for I am perfectly of your opinion as to writing that way, tho' I could be glad to hear what particular reasons you may have to strengthen me in that opinion. I heartily desire some opportunity of our conferring together, and am very sorry not to be able to embrace that which you so kindly offer me, of waiting upon you and your good family at Ladyholt, all whom I entreat to be assured of my most faithful humble service. I shall yet continue here till the winter, in hopes of seeing you when your business is so favorable to my desire as to bring you to town, and in the meantime of hearing from you, a pleasure which is ever the greatest in the world to | Dear Sir | your most faithful and most obliged | friend and servant. | A: P:

My master[7] returns you with all respects his most humble service.

*JACOB TONSON, JR., *to* POPE[8] — 5 *October* 1713

Egerton 1951

Mr Tonsons Agreement to Mr Pope:

I acknowledge my self bound by this agreement to Mr Pope, that notwithstanding any consideration given him for any poems of his printed by me, the said Mr Pope shall have full liberty, whenever he thinks fit, to cause the said poems to be reprinted by any other book-seller in what volume he pleases, and that neither himself nor that bookseller shall suffer any hindrance or molestation from me, that

[1] what make] what may make *1735–42*. [2] own happy] own State happy *1735–42*.

[3] part of the gravest . . . arts] part of that high Science, Divinity; you will be so civil as to imagine I lay no mighty Stress upon the rest *1735–42*.

[4] I really . . . than horses] Even of my darling Poetry I really make no other use, than Horses *1735–42*.

[5] travel] jogg *1735–42*.

[6] At this point Pope abandons Caryll as copy for Blount and derives the rest of his letter to Blount (10 Feb. 1715/16) from an unknown source—possibly even from a letter to Blount of the date printed in 1735.

[7] Jervas.

[8] The postmark and date on the verso of this agreement require explanation. The agreement itself is plausibly dated; but in 1713 Pope did not live at Twickenham, and October is not August. In the Berg Collection (New York Public Library) there is preserved a receipt for fifteen guineas dated 5 Oct. 1713 in payment for 'The Wife of Bath's Prologue' and a part of *Odyssey* XIII, which Tonson bought for his *Poetical Miscellanies* (published by Steele) of 1714. Hence one assumes that Pope saw Tonson on 5 Oct. The agreement as preserved may be a copy sent to Pope in or after 1719 when he did live at Twickenham.

bookseller allowing me books in proportion to the number of sheets the said poems amount to in such volume and in proportion to the impression.

And I likewise engage my self to Mr Pope that in case he shall desire me to reprint all his poems in a collection, I will therein cause to be reprinted all such pieces of his as have been before printed by any other bookseller in what Volume and manner he shall appoint.

Witness my hand this 5th of October | 1713.

Jacob Tonson junior.

Address: To | Alexander Pope Esqr at | Twick'nham | in | Middx. | present.
Postmark: 11/AV

†POPE *to* ANTHONY HAMILTON[1] 10 *October* 1713[2]

1735

If I could as well express, or (if you will allow me to say it) translate the sentiments of my heart, as you have done those of my head, in your excellent version of my Essay; I should not only appear the best writer in the world, but what I much more desire to be thought, the most your servant of any man living. 'Tis an advantage very rarely known, to receive at once a great honour and a great improvement. This Sir, you have afforded me, having at the same time made others take my sense, and taught me to understand my own; if I may call that my own which is indeed more properly yours: Your verses are no more a translation of mine, than *Virgil*'s are of *Homer*, but are like his, the justest Imitation and the noblest Commentary.

In putting me into a *French* dress, you have not only adorned my outside, but mended my shape; and if I am now a good figure, I must consider you have naturaliz'd me into a country which is famous for making every man a fine gentleman. It is by your means, that (contrary to most young travellers) I am come back much better than I went out.

I cannot but wish we had a bill of commerce for Translation established the next parliament, we could not fail of being gainers by that, nor of making our selves amends for all[3] we have lost by the war. Nay tho' we should insist upon the *demolishing* of *Boileau*'s works;[4] the *French*, as long as they have writers of your form, might have as good an Equivalent.

[1] Printed (1735–42) under the heading 'To General Anthony Hamilton upon his having translated into French Verse the *Essay on Criticism*'. In the editions of 1735 Hamilton's name was omitted. To the name in 1737–42 was appended the footnote: 'Author of the Memoirs of the *Count de Grammont*, *Contas*, and other pieces of note in *French*.' The letter was omitted from the quarto and folio of 1737.

[2] The date first appears in the octavos of 1737.

[3] all] any thing *1737–42*.

[4] Alluding to the English insistence that the 'works' at Dunkirk be demolished.

Upon the whole, I am really as proud, as our Ministers can[1] be, of the terms I have gain'd from abroad; and I design like them, to publish speedily to the world the benefits accruing from them; for I cannot resist the temptation of printing your admirable translation here;[2] to which if you will be so obliging to give me leave to prefix your name, it will be the only addition you can make to the honour already done me. I am, | Your, &c.

||POPE *to* CARYLL[3] 17 *October* 1713

Add. 28618

London. Oct. 17. 1713.

You tell me that when you lay ill in town, my company could mitigate your anguish; and if I would answer in the same style, I should say 'tis a peculiar felicity to you now, in your illness, that you have but one persecution to endure, since you are not troubled with me. It is the unfortunate consequence of a compliment, that a man, for hearing a great deal more than his due said of him by another, must afterwards say a great deal less than his due of himself. But, sir, to set this whole matter right, I must tell you honestly, that if it be a satisfaction to me to be with you when you are ill, it is a happiness when you are well; and I do believe, since you could bear me at that time, you can do it at any other.

In all sincerity, I am as much concerned at any pain you suffer as the nearest friend you have; so that your late long silence, tho' I began to complain of it in my heart, was of advantage to me, in letting me know so late of your indisposition: and I thank your friendship which suffered me to be easy while you were ill.

As to your queries: [4]I can't imagine whence it comes to pass that the few *Guardians* I have written are so generally known for mine: that in particular which you mention I never discovered to any man but the publisher till very lately: yet almost every body I met with told me of it.

The true reason that Mr S[teele] laid down the paper, was a quarrel between him and Jac[ob] Tonson. He stood engaged to his bookseller, in articles of penalty, for all the *Guardians*; and by desisting 2 days, and altering the title of the paper to that of the *Englishman*, was quit of his obligation. These papers being printed by Buckley.

[1] can] ought to *1737–42*.

[2] This was never done, for the two printed *French* Versions are neither of this hand. The one was the work of Monsieur *Roboton*, private Secretary to King *George* the first, printed in 4° at *Amsterdam* and at *London* 1717. The other by the Abbé *Resnel*, in 8° with a large Preface and Notes, at *Paris*, 1730.—Pope, 1735–42.

[3] From the third and fourth paragraphs of this letter Pope culled matter for the undated letter to Addison (placed late in 1713). In making the transfer to Addison Pope made only one verbal change, an omission here placed in half-brackets.

[4] With 'I can't' begins the material used in the undated letter to Addison. See below, p. 198.

As to his taking a more politic turn, I cannot any way enter into that secret, nor have I been let into it, any more than into the rest of his politics, tho' 'tis said he will take into these papers also several subjects of the politer kind, as before. But I assure you, as to myself, I have quite done with 'em, for the future. The little I have done, and the great respect I bear Mr Steele as a man of wit, has rendered me a suspected Whig to some of the ⌜over zealous and⌝ violent. But (as old Dryden said before me), 'Tis not the violent I design to please.[1] And in very truth, sir, I believe they will all find me, at long run, a mere papist. As to the whim upon Dennis,[2] Cromwell thought me the author of it, which I assured him I was not, and we are, I hope very far from being enemies. We visit, criticize, and drink coffee as before. I am satisfied of his merit in all respects, and am truly his friend.

I will enquire for the German of whom I had the seals, tho' I have forgot the house I was at, and send you the seals you desire. Let me know if you would have 'em set, or that care left to your own fancy.

I shall be rejoiced beyond expression when I see you here, It is no flamm, but the most home-felt truth in the world, that I entirely love you for a thousand qualities, which in this age are very rarely, if any where else, to be found, or if any where else, not to be found at least by me.

What poetical news I have to tell you shall be deferred till our meeting. I shall be still at Mr Jervas's, (who gives you his most humble service) except for a fortnight at Binfield (which some poetical affairs of mine require[3]). I therefore beg to know a week (or two rather) before you come up, that I may manage accordingly.

I had some hopes given me of seeing Mr John Caryll speedily in town. I beg you to assure him I am truly his, and to believe me entirely | Your most faithful affectionate obliged | Servant. | A: P:

I have herewith sent you all the *Guardians* I had any hand in.

†LORD LANSDOWNE *to* POPE — 21 *October* 1713

1737

Oct. 21, 1713.

I am pleas'd beyond measure with your design of translating Homer: The tryals which you have already made and published on some parts

[1] The matter borrowed for the letter to Addison stops here. Dryden's remark occurs in his preface to *Absalom and Achitophel.*

[2] This probably refers to *The Narrative of Dr. Robert Norris concerning . . . John Dennis.* If so, Pope lied to Cromwell as to the authorship.

[3] The fortnight was probably to be devoted to some part of the work of enlarging *The Rape of the Lock.* The enlarged poem was published 4 Mar. 1714. Lord Lansdowne's letter, immediately following this, allows the further possibility that the young poet wished to discuss the translation of the *Iliad* with his parents.

of that author have shewn that you are equal to so great a task: and you may therefore depend upon the utmost services I can do you in promoting this work, or any thing that may be for your service.

I hope Mr. Stafford[1] for whom you was pleas'd to concern your self, has had the good effects of the Queen's Grace to him. I had notice the night before I began my journey, that Her Majesty had not only directed his pardon, but order'd a Writ for reversing his Out-lawry. | Your, &c.

†POPE *to* GAY[2] 23 *October* [1713]

1735

Oct. 23.

I have been perpetually troubled with sickness of late, which has made me so melancholy that the Immortality of the Soul has been my constant Speculation, as the Mortality of my Body my constant Plague. In good earnest, *Seneca* is nothing to a fit of illness.

Dr. *Parnelle* will honour *Tonson*'s Miscellany with some very beautiful Copies, at my request.[3] He enters heartily into our design, I only fear his stay in town may chance to be but short. Dr. *Swift* much approves what I proposed even to the very title, which I design shall be, *The Works of the Unlearned*,[4] published monthly, in which whatever Book appears that deserves praise, shall be depreciated Ironically, and in the same manner that modern Critics take to undervalue Works of Value, and to commend the high Productions of *Grubstreet*.

I shall go into the country about a month hence, and shall then desire to take along with me your Poem of the *Fan*,[5] to consider it at full leisure. I am deeply ingaged in Poetry, the particulars whereof shall be deferr'd till we meet.

I am very desirous of seeing Mr. *Fortescue*[6] when he comes to Town before his journey; if you can any way acquaint him of my desire, I believe his good nature will contrive a way for our meeting. I am ever, with all sincerity, dear Sir, | Your, &c.

[1] Probably the Hon. John Stafford, brother of the 1st and father of the 2nd Earl Stafford. They were a Jacobite family.

[2] This letter was not reprinted by Pope after 1735. The year offers difficulties, but 1713 seems most probable. The present editor has elsewhere argued for 1712, but ineffectually.

[3] Parnell had four poems in Tonson's *Poetical Miscellanies . . . Publish'd by Mr. Steele* late in 1713, and dated 1714.

[4] A design of this same name had been presented in *Spectator* No. 457 (14 Aug. 1712), possibly by Pope himself. The project is evidently one of those evolved by the Scriblerus Club. It has no sure connexion with the later *Grub-street Journal* (1730–7).

[5] Since *The Fan* was advertised as published on 8 Dec., it is unlikely that Pope could consider it 'at full leisure' after 23 Nov., when it would be in the printer's hands.

[6] This is the first mention of Gay's friend William Fortescue, who was to become one of Pope's closest friends.

‡ADDISON *to* POPE[1] 26 *October* 1713

1735

October 26, 1713.

I was extreamly glad to receive a letter from you, but more so upon reading the contents of it. The Work[2] you mention will I dare say very sufficiently recommend itself when your name appears with the Proposals: And if you think I can any way contribute to the forwarding of them, you cannot lay a greater obligation upon me than by employing me in such an office. As I have an ambition of having it known that you are my Friend, I shall be very proud of showing it by this, or any other instance. I question not but your Translation will enrich our Tongue and do Honour to our Country: for I conclude of it already from those performances with which you have oblig'd the publick. I would only have you consider how it may most turn to your advantage. Excuse my impertinence in this particular, which proceeds from my zeal for your ease and happiness. The work wou'd cost you a great deal of time, and unless you undertake it will I am afraid never be executed by any other, at least I know none of this age that is equal to it besides your self.

I am at present wholly immersed in country business, and begin to take delight in it. I wish I might hope to see you here sometime and will not despair of it, when you engage in a work that will require solitude and retirement. I am | Your, &c.

†ADDISON *to* POPE 2 *November* 1713

1735

Nov. 2, 1713.

I have receiv'd your letter and am glad to find that you have laid so good a scheme for your great undertaking. I question not but the Prose[3] will require as much care as the Poetry, but the variety will give your self some relief, and more pleasure to your readers.

You gave me leave once to take the liberty of a friend, in advising you not to content your self with one half of the Nation[4] for your

[1] Suspected as a fabrication, this letter, in view of Tickell's translation of *Iliad* I, forms a clear indictment of Addison's sincerity. In the Preface to his *Iliad* (June 1715) Pope remarked that 'Mr. *Addison* was the first whose Advice determin'd me to undertake this Task, who was pleas'd to write to me upon that Occasion in such terms as I cannot repeat without Vanity'. Evidently, then, an encouraging letter came from Addison, and this may well be it. Twenty years later, when the fabrication might be imagined to be made, Pope would hardly recollect the fact of Addison's being 'immersed in country business'—as he actually was at this time. Even in 1735, when he printed the letter, Pope did not know that Tickell on 31 May 1714 signed an agreement (kept very secret?) to translate the entire *Iliad* for Tonson.

[2] The Translation of the *Iliad*.—Pope, 1735–42.

[3] The notes to his translation of Homer.—Warburton, 1751.

[4] That is, of one party. Addison here continues his attitude of superiority to Whig–Tory bitterness, which he had established in *The Spectator*. The attitude motivates the name of 'Atticus' in the *Epistle to Dr. Arbuthnot*.

Admirers when you might command them all: If I might take the freedom to repeat it, I would on this occasion. I think you are very happy that you are out of the Fray, and I hope all your undertakings will turn to the better account for it.

You see how I presume on your friendship in taking all this freedom with you, but I already fancy that we have lived many years together, in an unreserved conversation, and that we may do[1] many more, is the sincere wish of | Your, &c.

‡POPE *to* ADDISON[2] [*December* 1713?]

1735

Your last is the more obliging, as it hints at some little niceties in my conduct, which your candor and affection prompt you to recommend to me, and which (so trivial as things of this nature seem) are yet of no slight consequence, to people whom every body talks of, and every body as he pleases. 'Tis a sort of Tax that attends an estate in *Parnassus*, which is often rated much higher than in proportion to the small possession an author holds. For indeed an author who is once come upon the town, is enjoy'd without being thank'd for the pleasure, and sometimes ill-treated by those very persons that first debauch'd him. Yet to tell you the bottom of my heart, I am no way displeas'd that I have offended the violent of all Parties already; and at the same time I assure you conscientiously, I feel not the least malevolence or resentment against any of those who misrepresent me, or are dissatisfied with me. This frame of mind is so easy, that I am perfectly content with my condition.

As I hope and would flatter my self, that you know me and my thoughts so entirely as never to be mistaken in either, so 'tis a pleasure to me that you guess'd so right in regard to the Author of that *Guardian* you mention'd. But I am sorry to find it has taken air that I have some hand in those Papers, because I write so very few as neither to deserve the credit of such a report with some people, nor the disrepute of it with others. An honest *Jacobite* spoke to me the sense or nonsense of the weak part of his Party very fairly, that the good people took it ill of me, that I writ with *Steele*, tho' upon never so indifferent subjects ——This I know you will laugh at as well as I do: yet I doubt not but many little calumniators and persons of sower dispositions will take

[1] do many] do so many *1737–42*.

[2] This letter is fabricated almost verbatim from passages in three letters of 1713 to Caryll. The first paragraph comes from a letter of 23 June; the second and last come from that of 12 June; the third, fourth, and fifth from that of 17 Oct. It is printed here merely as a curiosity, since the fabrication is lacking in subtlety. Why should Pope tell Addison things about *The Guardian* that he should have known as well as Pope?

In his editions Pope placed this fabrication after a letter of 2 Nov. and before one of 14 Dec. That was careless of him, since he writes as if *The Guardian* were still continuing, and it ceased to appear after 1 Oct.

occasion hence to bespatter me. I confess I scorn narrow souls, of all parties, and if I renounce my reason in religious matters, I'll hardly do it in any other.

I can't imagine whence it comes to pass that the few *Guardians* I have written are so generally known for mine: that in particular which you mention I never discover'd to any man but the publisher, till very lately: yet almost every body I met told me of it.

The true reason that Mr. *Steele* laid down the Paper, was a quarrel between him and *Jacob Tonson.* He stood engag'd to his bookseller, in articles of penalty, for all the *Guardians*: and by desisting two days and altering the title of the paper to that of the *Englishman*, was quit of his obligation: these papers being printed by *Buckley.*[1]

As to his taking a more Politick turn, I cannot any way enter into that secret, nor have I been let into it, any more than into the rest of his politicks. Tho' 'tis said, he will take into these papers also several subjects of the politer kind, as before: But I assure you as to my self, I have quite done with 'em, for the future. The little I have done, and the great respect I bear Mr. *Steele* as a Man of Wit, has render'd me a suspected Whig to some of the violent, but (as old *Dryden* said before me) 'Tis not the Violent I design to please.

I generally employ the mornings in painting with Mr. *Jervas*;[2] and the evenings in the conversation of such, as I think can most improve my mind, of whatever Party or Denomination[3] they are. I ever must set the highest value upon men of truly great, that is honest Principles, with equal capacities. The best way I know of overcoming Calumny and Misconstruction, is by a vigorous perseverance in every thing we know to be right, and a total neglect of all that can ensue from it. 'Tis partly from this maxim that I depend upon your friendship, because I believe it will do justice to my intention in every thing; and give me leave to tell you, that (as the world goes) this is no small assurance I repose in you. I am | Your, &c.

POPE *to* SWIFT[4] 8 *December* 1713

Harvard University (Orrery transcript)

Binfield. Decr 8th. 1713.

Not to trouble you at present with the Recital of all my Obligations to you, I shall only mention two Things, which I take particularly

[1] In 1737–42 Pope omitted this whole paragraph. Possibly such an omission might have two purposes—either to keep himself from obviously giving Addison superfluous information, or, by omitting such information, to create the impression that he had never written such a paragraph and was finally printing a true text.

[2] See Mr. *Pope's* Epistle to him in Verse, writ about this time.—Pope, 1735–42 (but omitted in 1737 b).

[3] whatever Party or Denomination] whatever denomination *1737–42.*

[4] This letter was first printed in Lord Orrery's *Remarks* (1752). It is here reprinted from

well of you; your Desire that I should write to you;—and your Proposal of giving me twenty Guineas to change my Religion, which last you must give me Leave to make the Subject of this Letter.

Sure no Clergyman ever offered so much, out of his own Purse, for the Sake of any Religion. 'Tis almost as many Pieces of Gold, as an Apostle could get of Silver from the Priests of old, on a much more valuable Consideration.

I believe it will be better worth my while to propose a Change of my Faith by Subscription, than a Translation of Homer. And to convince you how well disposed I am to the Reformation, I shall be content, if you can prevail with my Lord Treasurer, and the Ministry, to rise to the same Sum, each of them, on this pious Account, as my Lord Halifax has done on the prophane one.[1] I am afraid there is no being at once a Poet, and a good Christian; and I am very much straitned between Two, while the Whigs seem willing to contribute as much to continue me the one, as you would to make me the other. But if you can move every Man in the Government, that has above ten Thousand Pounds a Year, to subscribe as much as your self, I shall become a Convert, as most Men do, when the Lords turn[2] it to my Interest. I know they have the Truth of Religion so much at Heart, that they would certainly give more to have one good Subject translated from Popery to the Church of England, than twenty heathenish Authors out of any unknown Tongue into ours. I therefore commission you, Mr Dean, with full Authority to transact this Affair in my Name, and to propose as follows.

First,—That as to the Head of our Church, the Pope, I may engage to renounce his Power, whensoever I shall receive any particular Indulgences from the Head of your Church, the Queen.

As to Communion in one Kind, I shall also promise to change it for Communion in both, as soon as the Ministry will allow me ⌜wherewithal to eat, and to drink.⌝[3]

For Invocations to Saints, mine shall be turned to Dedications to Sinners, when I shall find the Great Ones of this World as willing to do me any Good, as I believe those of the other are.

You see, I shall not be obstinate in the main Points. But there is one Article I must reserve, and which you seemed not unwilling to allow me, Prayer for the Dead. There are People, to whose Souls I wish as well as to my own, and I must crave Leave humbly to lay before them,

an early transcript made by Lord Orrery, now preserved in the Harvard College Library, which offers a slightly better text. The transcript bears the heading: 'Mr Pope to Dr Swift, in Answer to a Letter from the Dr persuading Mr Pope to Change his Religion.'

[1] Lord Halifax subscribed for ten sets of the translation of the *Iliad*, at six guineas a set.—Elwin.

[2] Lords turn] Lord turns Orrery, *Remarks*

[3] Omitted by Orrery and by succeeding editors of Pope.

that tho' the Subscriptions above mentioned will suffice for my self, there are necessary Perquisits, and Additions, which I must demand on the Score of this charitable Article. It is also to be considered, that the greater Part of those, whose Souls I am most concerned for, were unfortunately Heretics, Schismatics, Poets, Painters, or Persons of such Lives, and Manners, as few, or no Churches are willing to save. The Expence will be therefore the greater to make an effectual Provision for the said Souls.

Old Dryden, tho' a Roman Catholick, was a Poet; and 'tis revealed in the Visions of some ancient Saints, that no Poet was ever saved under some Hundreds of Masses. I cannot set his Delivery from Purgatory at less than Fifty Pounds sterling.

Walsh was not only a Socinian, but (what you'll own is harder to be saved) a Whig. He cannot modestly be rated at less than a Hundred.

L'Estrange being a Tory, we compute him but at Twenty Pounds, which I hope no Friend of the Party can deny to give, to keep him from damning in the next Life, considering they never gave him Sixpence to keep him from starving in this.

All this together amounts to 170 Pounds.

In the next Place, I must desire you to represent, that there are several of my Friends yet living, whom I design, God willing, to outlive, in consideration of Legacies, out of which it is a Doctrine in the Reformed Church that not a Farthing shall be allowed, to save their Souls, who gave them.

There is One, who will dye within these few Months, with one[1] Mr Jervas, who hath grievously offended in making the Likeness of almost all Things in Heaven above, and Earth below. And one Mr Gay, an unhappy Youth, that writes Pastorals during the Time of Divine Service, whose Case is the more deplorable, as he hath miserably lavished away all that Silver he should have reserved for his Soul's Health, in Buttons and Loops for his Coat.[2]

I cannot pretend to have these People honestly saved under some Hundred Pounds, whether you consider the Difficulty of such a Work, or the extreme Love and Tenderness I bear them, which will infallibly make me push this Charity as far as I am able. There is but One more, whose Salvation I insist upon, and then I have done: But indeed it may prove of so much greater Charge than all the rest, that I will only lay

[1] After both occurrences of the word *One* in this sentence Orrery's *Remarks* insert asterisks as if a name were suppressed. Possibly after the first *One* a name was omitted.

[2] John Gay's six pastorals, *The Shepherd's Week*, were evidently composed by this time, whether during divine service or not. They were published in Apr. 1714 with a poetic 'Prologue to the Right Honourable the Lord Viscount Bolingbroke', which did not advance Gay's fortunes with the Whigs. It did contain the lines Pope here alludes to:

> I sold my sheep and lambkins too,
> For silver loops and garment blue,

the Case before you, and the Ministry, and leave to their Prudence and Generosity what Summ they shall think fit to bestow upon it.

The Person I mean is Dr Swift, a dignified Clergyman, but One who, by his own Confession, has composed more Libels than Sermons. If it be true, what I have heard often affirmed by innocent People, that too much Wit is dangerous to Salvation, this unfortunate Gentleman must certainly be damned to all Eternity. But I hope his long Experience in the World, and frequent Conversation with Great Men, will cause him (as it has some others) to have less and less Wit every Day. Be it as it will, I should not think my own Soul deserved to be saved, if I did not endeavour to save his, for I have all the Obligations in Nature to him. He has brought me into better Company than I cared for, made me merrier, when I was sick, than I had a Mind to be, put me upon making Poems on Purpose that he might alter them, &c. I once thought I could never have discharged my Debt to his Kindness, but have lately been informed, to my unspeakable Comfort, that I have more than paid it all. For Monsieur de Montayne[1] has assured me, that the Person, who receives a Benefit, obliges the Giver; for since the chief Endeavour of one Friend is to do Good to the other, He, who administers both the Matter, and Occasion, is the Man that is Liberal. At this Rate it is impossible Dr Swift should be ever out of my Debt, as matters stand already; and for the future he may expect daily more Obligations from | His most Faithful, Affectionate, | Humble Servant | A. Pope.

I have finished the Rape of the Lock,[2] but believe I may stay here till Christmas without Hindrance of Busyness.

‡POPE *to* ADDISON[3] 14 *December* 1713

1735

Dec. 14, 1713.

I have been lying in wait for my own imagination, this week and more, and watching what thoughts came up in the whirl of the fancy, that were worth communicating to you in a letter. But I am at length convinc'd that my rambling head can produce nothing of that sort; so I must e'en be contented with telling you the old story, that I love you heartily. I have often found by experience, that nature and truth, tho' never so low or vulgar, are yet pleasing when openly and artlessly

[1] Montaigne, *Essais*, I. xxviii, *De l'amitié*: 'Si, en l'amitié dequoy je parle, l'un pouvoit donner à l'autre, ce seroit celuy qui recevroit le bien-fait, qui obligeroit son compagnon.' (Ed. Armaingaud, Paris, 1924, ii. 205.)

[2] The enlarged version.

[3] This letter, with slight revisions, is that actually sent to Caryll dated 14 Aug. 1713 (q.v.). The postscript of the Caryll letter is here omitted entirely; otherwise the adaptations and later revisions are purely stylistic.

represented; it would be diverting to me, to read the very letters of an infant, could it write its innocent inconsistencies and tautologies just as it thought 'em. This makes me hope a letter from me will not be unwelcome to you, when I am conscious I write with more unreservedness than ever man wrote, or perhaps talk'd to another. I trust your good nature with the whole range of my follies, and really love you so well, that I would rather you should pardon me than esteem me, since one is an act of goodness and benevolence, the other a kind of constrain'd deference.

You can't wonder my thoughts are scarce consistent, when I tell you how they are distracted. Ev'ry hour of my life, my mind is strangely divided; this minute perhaps I am above the stars, with a thousand systems round about me, looking forward into a vast Abyss, and losing my whole comprehension in the boundless space of creation, in dialogues with *W*——[1] and the Astronomers; the next moment I am below all trifles, groveling with *T*——[2] in the very center of nonsense. Now I am recreated with the brisk sallies and quick turns of wit, which Mr. *Steele* in his liveliest and freest humours darts about him; and now levelling my application to the insignificant observations and quirks of *Grammar* of Mr. — and *D*—[3]

Good God! What an incongruous animal is Man? how unsettled in his best part, his Soul; and how changing and variable in his frame of Body? The constancy of the one shook by every Notion, the temperament of the other affected by every blast of wind! What is Man altogether, but one mighty Inconsistency! Sickness and Pain is the lot of one half of us; Doubt and Fear the portion of the other! What a bustle we make about passing our time, when all our space is but a point? What aims and ambitions are crowded into this little instant of our life, which (as *Shakespear* finely words it) is *Rounded with a Sleep*? Our whole extent of Being no more, in the eyes of him who gave it, than a scarce perceptible moment of duration. Those animals whose circle of living is limited to three or four hours, as the Naturalists assure us, are yet as long-lived and possess as wide a scene of action as man, if we consider him with an eye to all Space, and all Eternity. Who knows what plots, what atchievements a mite may perform in his kingdom of a grain of dust, within his life of some minutes? and of how much less consideration than even this, is the life of man in the sight of that God, who is from Ever, and for Ever!

Who that thinks in this train, but must see the world and its contemptible grandeurs lessen before him at every thought? 'Tis enough

[1] *Whiston* *1737–42*.

[2] *Tidcombe* is the reading of the Caryll letter. The name is not given in Pope's texts.

[3] Mr. — and *D*—] *C** and *D** *1737–42*. (Elwin inserted *Cromwell* and *Dennis* from the letter to Caryll.)

to make one remain stupify'd, in a poize of inaction, void of all desires, of all designs, of all friendships.

But we must return (thro' our very condition of being) to our narrow selves, and those things that affect our selves: our passions, our interests, flow in upon us, and unphilosophize us into meer mortals. For my part I never return so much into my self, as when I think of you, whose friendship is one of the best comforts I have for the insignificancy of my self. I am | Your, &c.

POPE *to* CARYLL 15 *December* [1713].

Add. 28618

Binfield December 15.

I had sooner accosted you by way of letter, but that Mrs Blount told me at Mapledurham, you had again returned the last week, to the town, which I had not left as I did, but upon the supposal I should not have seen you there again so soon; but hearing nothing farther I believe it was a groundless report. I came into these parts by the way of Reading, to have the opportunity of seeing my old acquaintance at the place above mentioned, and at Whiteknights. I have since experienced the effect of your favours to me in making frequent use of the palfrey you equipped me with. I believe the most effectual means in the world to make a friend often mindful of one is to sort one's present to his occasions. To present a book (as I have done sometimes) to a man who never reads, or a gun to one who never shoots, is a great errour in the discerning faculty. Your present was of that nature that I cannot so much as stir, but I must think of you. The last day you was in London, I heard you were so kind as to stay at Common Garden Coffeehouse a considerable time expecting me. The truth was this: I was invited that day to dinner with my Lady Winchelsea,[1] and after dinner to hear a play read, at both which I sat in great disorder with sickness at my head and stomach. As soon as I got home which was about the hour I should have met you, I was obliged to goe directly to bed.

I have been employed, since my being here in the country, in finishing the additions to the *Rape of the Lock*, a part of which I remember I showed you. I have some thoughts of dedicating that poem to Mrs Fermor by name, as a piece of justice in return to the wrong interpretations she has suffered under on the score of that piece.[2]

[1] Anne, wife of Heneage Finch, 5th Earl of Winchelsea, wrote poems and at least two plays. Professor Myra Reynolds conjectured that the play read was Lady Winchelsea's *Love and Innocence* (unpublished). See *Poems of Anne Countess of Winchelsea* (ed. Reynolds, Chicago, 1903), p. lvi. But since there is no evidence that the countess was ever desirous of having her plays acted, there is little reason for thinking it was one of *her* plays read—or that the play was the cause of Pope's physical distress.

[2] In 1714 Pope did dedicate *The Rape of the Lock* to Miss Fermor. If at first the poem had not pleased her, it evidently gave her later pleasure.

I say nothing to you of the affair of my subscriptions for Homer, since I am sure in my dependence on the utmost of your interest.[1] I would recommend the promoting it with what speed is convenient, since I know the danger there is of letting an affair of this nature cool too much. As to the task it self I am about to undertake, I confess I begin to tremble at it; it is really so great an one, that a disappointment in the subscription will not occasion me any great mortification, considering how much of life I am to sacrifice if it succeeds.

You will excuse the careless freedom with which I write. I know too well the charity of your disposition to doubt of all the indulgence in the world from it. It is certainly the truest maxim in nature that no people are to be so little feared, or so easy to be satisfied with the common course of our actions and addresses, as those of the highest pitch of understanding. The knowledge of this renders me very easy and quiet in the inter[course] I have with some persons, whom I should approach with fear and trembling but for this consolation. I should not else talk at random, or sleep, in the company of Mr Addison[2] and Dr Swift, nor write so fast as my ink can flow to Mr Caryll.

I have just room to entreat you to assure your good family, and Mr John Caryll in a most particular manner, of my most sincere service. I should esteem it a great piece of good nature in him (if the diversions of the field will allow him time) to favour me sometimes with a line or two. The only reason I have not troubled him of late is that I knew his obliging temper would force him to write, even tho' perhaps it was a trouble to him. I am, dear sir, with more truth a thousand times than ceremony, | Your most faithful and | Affectionate servant | A. P.

[1] The subscription had been under way since October, and Caryll was evidently active for Pope. Pope seems not to have begun intensive work on the translation until the success of the subscription was assured.

[2] It is notable that this mention of Addison seems unreservedly friendly.

1714

The winter of 1713–14, most of which Pope spent in Town, was marked by bitter political animosities, which tended to separate Pope from Addison and Steele (who in March was expelled from the House), and made him, with Gay and Parnell, appear as disciples of Swift and Arbuthnot, who were then Tories. These five were playing with their project of writing satirical *Memoirs of Martinus Scriblerus*, until Swift in disgust at the turn of politics ran away to Letcombe, where Gay and Pope visited him in July. The death of Queen Anne (1 August) put an end to more than the Scriblerus Club. In April Pope had gone to Binfield, and there throughout the summer his time was, as he said, 'wholly employed upon Homer'. Apart from translating and from frequent signing of receipts for subscriptions to the *Iliad*, his chief literary occupations were seeing the enlarged *Rape* through the press and the composition of an Epilogue for his friend Rowe's *Jane Shore*. After long and tedious work on Homer, Pope and Parnell (who had been helping) took a holiday at Bath in September and early October. They returned for the Coronation of George I (20 October), and Parnell soon left for Ireland, to which country Swift had in August or September proceeded. In December Pope visited Caryll at Ladyholt—and prepared to publish the first volume of his *Iliad*.

†POPE *to* MRS. BETTY MARRIOT[1] [1714?]

1735

It is too much a rule in this town, that when a Lady has once done a man a favour, he is to be rude to her ever after. It becomes our Sex to take upon us twice as much as yours allows[2] us: By this method I may write to you most impudently, because you once answer'd me modestly; and if you shou'd never do me that honour for the future, I am to think (like a true Coxcomb) that your silence gives consent. Perhaps you wonder why this is address'd to you rather than to Mrs. *M*— with whom I have the right of an old acquaintance, whereas you are a fine Lady, have bright eyes, *&c.* First Madam, I make choice of you rather than of your Mother, because you are younger

[1] Elwin says he prints this letter from a transcript of the original made by Dilke. Since what he prints is exactly the text of the octavo of 1742, one may doubt if Dilke did transcribe the original. It would be unique procedure if Pope printed exactly the original only in an edition which he hardly seems to have revised at all. Pope omitted the letter from the quarto and folio of 1737, but revised the text for the octavos of that year, and kept this revised text thereafter. It is impossible to date the letter. Pope has not seen Mrs. Betty for two winters, and since she may have grown into a giantess, she must still be young. Since the Marriots came (or planned to come) to London in 1715, the letter is placed before that visit, vaguely.

[2] allows] allow *1742 and Elwin.*

than your Mother. Secondly, because I fancy you spell better, as having been at school later. Thirdly, because you have nothing to do but to write if you please, and possibly it may keep you from employing your self worse: it may save some honest neighbouring Gentleman from three or four of your pestilent glances. Cast your eyes upon Paper, Madam, there you may look innocently: Men are seducing, books are dangerous, the amorous one's soften you, and the godly one's give you the spleen: If you look upon trees, they clasp in embraces; birds and beasts make love; the Sun is too warm for your blood, the Moon melts you into yielding and melancholy. Therefore I say once more, cast your eyes upon Paper, and read only such Letters as I write, which convey no darts, no flames, but proceed from Innocence of soul, and simplicity of heart. ⌜However, I can allow you a Bonnet lined with green for your eyes, but take care you don't tarnish it with ogling too fiercely: I am told, that hand you shade your self with this shining weather, is tann'd pretty much, only with being carried over those Eyes—⌝[1] thank God I am an hundred miles off from them[2]—⌜Upon the whole⌝[3] I wou'd sooner trust your hand than your Eyes[4] for doing me mischief; and tho' I doubt not some part of the rancour and iniquity of your heart will drop into your pen, yet since it will not attack me on a sudden and unprepar'd, since I may have time while I break open your letter to cross my self and say a *Paternoster*, I hope Providence will protect me from all you can attempt at this distance. Mr. *B*— tells me[5] you are at this hour as handsome as an Angel, for my part I have forgot your face since two winters,[6] I don't know whether you are tall or short, nor can tell in any respect what sort of creature you are, only that you are a very mischievous one whom I shall ever pray to be defended from. But when Mr. *B*—[7] sends me word you have the small pox, a good many freckles, or are very pale, I will desire him to give thanks for it in your Parish Church, which as soon as he shall inform me he has done I will make you a visit at—without[8] Armour: I will eat any thing you give me without suspicion of poyson, take you by the hand without gloves, nay venture to follow you into an arbour without calling the company. This Madam is the top of my wishes, but how differently are our desires inclined! You sigh out, in the ardour of your heart, Oh Play-houses, Parks, Opera's, Assemblies, *London!* I cry with rapture, Oh Woods, Gardens, Rookeries, Fishponds, Arbours! Mrs. *Betty*[9] *M*—

[1] The passage in half-brackets is omitted in texts of 1737–42.

[2] them] those eyes *1737–42*.

[3] Omitted, 1737–42.

[4] than your Eyes] than them *1737–42*.

[5] Mr. *B*— tells me] I am told *1737–42*.

[6] winters . . . tell] winters. You may be grown into a giantess for all I know. I can't tell *1737–42*.

[7] Mr. *B*—] your Minister *1737–42*. (Broome was the rector of Sturston at this time.)

[8] visit at — without] visit without *1737–42*.

[9] Mrs. *Betty M*—] Mrs. *M*— *1737–42*.

POPE *to* CARYLL *9 January* 1713/14

Add. 28618

London. Jan 9. 1713.

Tho' I believe I am one of the last who has congratulated yourself and Mr Caryll upon the birth of his first born,[1] yet this I dare assure you both—that no man is more rejoiced at that blessing, except the father (unless you will require me to speak more correctly, and say, except the grandfather too). I ought also to felicitate you in particular, that you are so early arrived to the dignity of a patriarch, and that you can bear that venerable name without the stooping in the shoulders and that length of beard, which I have observed to denote one of those sires in all the representations of 'em hitherto. I cannot flatter your son so far as to say any thing fine upon the beauty of the babe, or the near resemblance it has to his own lineaments; not having yet had the pleasure of conversing with the nurse upon that agreeable subject. But I am told here, that few statues of Phidias or Praxiteles themselves made so good a figure the first month of their appearing. ⌜And what very much adds to the perfection and reputation of this piece of work of his, is, that one may affirm of it, as they do of the fine statue in the Place de Victoire, that it was done, all at a *Jette*.⌝[2]

I am thoroughly sensible of your most righteous endeavours to serve me in my new capacity of a Greek translator, and I hope, by the assistance of such solicitours as Mr Caryll, to make Homer's works of more value and benefit to me than ever they were to himself. What I have in particular to desire further is, that you will send me the subscriptions by the first sitting[3] of the parliament at which time it will be necessary for me to know exactly what number we have secure,—there being then to be printed a list of those who already have subscribed or shall to that time: upon the Credit and figure of which persons a great part of the success with the town will inevitably depend.

I now think it pretty certain, that I shall be warmly supported on all sides in this undertaking.

As to the *Rape of the Lock*, I believe I have managed the dedication so nicely that it can neither hurt the lady, nor the author. I writ it very lately, and upon great deliberation; the young lady approves of it; and the best advice in the kingdom, of the men of sense has been made use of in it, even to the Treasurer's.[4] A preface which salved the lady's honour, without affixing her name, was also prepared, but by herself superseded in favour of the dedication. Not but that, after all, fools will talk, and fools will hear 'em.

[1] Born 13 December 1713.—Elwin.

[2] This last sentence was omitted by Elwin.

[3] Parliament sat on 18 February.—Elwin.

[4] The Lord Treasurer was Robert Harley, recently (1711) created Earl of Oxford and Mortimer.

I wish you could inform me by the most convenient opportunity how the matter stands as to the foreign affair. I suppose you had no concern in the *rentes viagères*.[1] This misfortune will go near to ruin me, it being more especially my Concern than my Father's. I shall revenge my self on the mighty monarch, by giving the more spirit to what Homer says of the injustice of kings. I was beginning to think I would go and live upon Mr John Caryll, but have lost all my hopes since he has a child, unless he will maintain me as his huntsman.

Believe me, dear sir, under all circumstances whatever, and in all respects whatever, with the last sincerity and deference | Your most obliged and most faithful | Freind and servant | A: P:

My most humble service attends all the good family even from the grandsire to the grandson. I shall be in London all the winter.

‡POPE *to* ADDISON[2] — 30 *January* 1713/14

1735

Jan. 30, 1713–4.

Your letter found me[3] very busy in my grand undertaking, to which I must wholly give my self up for some time, unless when I snatch an hour to please my self with a distant conversation with you and a few others, by writing.[4] 'Tis no comfortable prospect to be reflecting, that so long a siege as that of *Troy* lies upon my hands, and the campagne above half over, before I have made any progress. Indeed the *Greek* fortification upon a nearer approach does not appear so formidable as it did, and I am almost apt to flatter my self, that *Homer* secretly seems inclined to a correspondence with me, in letting me into a good part of his intentions. There are indeed, a sort of underling auxiliars to the difficulty of a work, call'd Commentators and Critics, who wou'd frighten many people by their number and bulk, and perplex our progress under pretence of fortifying their author. These lie very low in the trenches and ditches they themselves have digg'd, encompass'd with dirt of their own heaping up, but I think there may be found a method

[1] An edict was issued in October 1713, reducing the interest upon the debts contracted by the French Government since the year 1702, to 4 per cent.; and the annuities granted between 1702 and 1710 were reduced a fourth. The elder Pope, in July, 1707, had invested 5220 livres in an annuity on his son's life, at 10 per cent., which is what makes the poet say that it was more his concern than his father's. His notion that the loss would go far to ruin him arose from a report that annuities posterior to 1706 were to be reduced one half, whereas this provision applied only to those which were granted since 1710. As some compensation for so arbitrary a measure the creditors were promised more punctual payment, and a remission of the *dîme* or income-tax.—Elwin.

[2] This letter is really Pope's letter to Caryll dated 1 May 1714 (q.v.), with surprisingly few changes except for improvements in style.

[3] found me very busy] found me at Binfield very busy *Caryll.*

[4] Two sentences concerning a projected visit to Grinstead had to be omitted here as not relevant to Addison.

of coming at the main works by a more speedy and gallant way than by mining under ground, that is, by using the Poetical Engines, Wings, and flying over their heads.

While I am engag'd in the fight, I find you are concern'd how I shall be paid, and are sollicitous that I may not have the ill fate of many discarded Generals, to be first envy'd and malign'd, then perhaps prais'd, and lastly neglected. The former (the constant attendant upon all great and laudable enterprizes) I have already experienc'd. Some have said I am not a Master in the *Greek*, who either are so themselves or are not: If they are not, they can't tell; and if they are, they can't without having catechiz'd me. But if they can read (for I know some Critics can, and others cannot) there are fairly lying before them, some specimens of my translation from this Author in the *Miscellanies*, which they are heartily welcome to. I have met with as much malignity another way, some calling me a Tory, because the heads of that party have been distinguishingly favourable to me; some a Whig because I have been favour'd with yours, Mr. *Congreve*'s, and Mr. *Craggs* his friendship, and of late with my Lord *Halifax*'s Patronage.[1] How much more natural a conclusion might be form'd, by any good-natur'd man, that a person who has been well us'd by all sides, has been offensive to none. This miserable age is so sunk between animosities of Party and those of Religion, that I begin to fear, most men have politicks enough to make (thro' violence) the best Scheme of Government a bad one; and faith[2] enough to hinder their own Salvation. I hope for my own part, never to have more of either than is consistent with common justice and charity, and always as much as becomes a christian and honest man. Tho' I find it an unfortunate thing to be bred a *Papist* here, where one is obnoxious to four parts in five as being so too much, and to the fifth part as being so too little; I shall yet be easy under both their mistakes, and be what I more than seem to be, for I suffer for it. God is my witness that I no more envy you Protestants your places and possessions, than I do our Priests their charity or learning. I am ambitious of nothing but the good opinion of good men, on both sides; for I know that one virtue of a free spirit is more worth, than all the virtues put together of all the narrow-soul'd people in the world. I am | Your, &c.

POPE *to* CARYLL 25 *February* 1713/14

Add. 28618

Feb. 25th 1714.

I had but just a glimpse of Mr Caryll, and an expectation of meeting him another time, of which he disappointed me. I fell ill just after,

[1] For important variance of text in this passage see the letter to Caryll, 1 May 1714.
[2] faith] Belief *1737–42*.

kept my chamber a day or two, and went to wait of him the first morning I could, which was that on which he left London. I had else given him the trouble of taking these 2 books[1] with him, tho' the poem will not be published this week. In this more solemn edition, I was strangely tempted to have set your name at length,[2] as well as I have my own; but I remembered your desire you formerly expressed to the contrary; besides, that it may better become me to appear as the offerer of an ill present, than you as the receiver of it.

Mr Gay's poem[3] was left by him with Lewis as soon as he printed it, but was accidentally mislaid, as Mr Lewis told me, whom I desired forthwith to send it. Mr Gay is much your humble servant.

I agree with you in your opinion of the French translation of the *Essay on Criticism*[4] no less than I do in what you say of the *Crisis.*[5] I believe Mr Steele has hurt himself more, every way, than his worst enemies would have done. I had never read the book till your order reached me; for you are sensible I am the least a politician in the world, tho', by the way, some modern rumors have been thrown about, which would have represented me as more concerned in party affairs than I ever dreamed on; insomuch that I had the honor to be nam'd in the *Leyden*[6] *Gazette* for an enemy to the *Grande Société* at Burton's. But it was laughed at by the chief of my Whig-friends and my Tory-friends. Not being of God, it could not stand.

As to my particular affair at present, which you are so kindly negotiating in the country, the favour I beg is, that you will send me, with what speed you can conveniently, a list of every person who has actually paid you his subscription, or whom you can engage for, on his promise to pay you; for I must print a catalogue of all who have already subscribed in a very short time, and it would be of equal ill consequence either to omit any that have paid, or add any that have not. I wait only for these names to send the catalogue to the press.

I shall now be very much taken up in this work which will keep me a poet (in spite of something I lately thought a resolution to the contrary) for some years longer. I hope in the summer to bring the old blind bard along with me to Ladyholt; where I shall be furnished with much better accommodation to translate his work, than he was when he writ it. In all sincerity, I can't express to you how earnestly I wish for

[1] Two advance copies of *The Rape of the Lock*, which was published on 4 Mar.

[2] The third line of *The Rape* read: 'This Verse to C—l, Muse! is due.' Caryll's name was not given in full in editions supervised by Pope.

[3] *The Fan*, published in Dec. 1713.

[4] See Pope to Anthony Hamilton, 10 Oct. 1713.

[5] Steele's pamphlet, *The Crisis*, which appeared on 19 Jan., was partly responsible for his expulsion from the House of Commons on 18 Mar.

[6] Elwin wrongly printed *London Gazette* for *Leyden*. The *Leyden Gazette* has not been seen. There is no such item in the *London Gazette* for this period. *Burton's* is a miswriting for *Button's* doubtless.

another taste of those agreeable entertainments I have more than once enjoyed with you; and what a pleasure it will be to me to assure every one of your good family in particular how much I am theirs, and | dear sir | your most obliged and affectionate friend | and faithful servant. | A: P:

POPE *to* MRS. *or* MISS MARRIOT 28 *February* [1713/14]

Elwin–Courthope ix. 472

February, the last Day, 1713.

I have of late been so much a man of business[1] that I have almost forgot to write (as I used to do) long letters about nothing. Indeed, I see people every day so very busy about nothing, that I fancy I am no improper historian to write their actions. It would be but filling the paper as they do their lives, no manner[2] with what. [I do not do this] when I write to you who are much too good to have such tricks put upon you. Nor ought I to endeavour to make you pass one quarter of an hour of all your life ill in reading such impertinence, as is but too natural for me to write. What excuse then, can I offer for the poem that attends this letter,[3] where 'tis a chance but you are diverted from some very good action or useful reflection for more hours than one. I know it is no sin to laugh, but I had rather your laughter should be at the vain ones of your own sex than at me, and therefore would rather have you read my poem than my letter. This whimsical piece of work, as I have now brought it up to my first design, is at once the most a satire, and the most inoffensive, of anything of mine. People who would rather it were let alone laugh at it, and seem heartily merry, at the same time that they are uneasy. 'Tis a sort of writing very like tickling. I am so vain as to fancy a pretty complete picture of the life of our modern ladies in this idle town from which you are so happily, so prudently, and so philosophically retired. My friend, Mr. Rowe, in his new play[4] has a description that puts me exceedingly in mind of Sturston:—

> Far from the crowd and the tumultuous city
> There stands a lonely but a healthful dwelling
> Built for convenience, and the use of Life.
> Around it, fallows, meads, and pastures fair,
> A little garden, and a limpid brook,
> By Nature's own contrivance, seem dispos'd;
> No neighbours but a few poor simple clowns,
> Honest and true; with a well-meaning priest.

[1] As a result of the subscription for the translation of the *Iliad*.

[2] *Manner* is a probable misprint. The bracketed emendation is not clearly necessary to the sense.

[3] Evidently an advance copy of *The Rape of the Lock* (1714).

[4] *Jane Shore*, first acted 2 Feb. 1713/14, was an immediate and permanent success. Pope quotes from the melodramatic scene at the end of Act II.

By this well-meaning priest, I mean Mr. Brome, who, Mr. Marriot tells me, is to minister unto you.[1]

†SIR WILLIAM TRUMBULL *to* POPE — 6 *March* 1713/14

1735

March 6, 1713.

I think a hasty scribble shews more what flows from the heart, than a letter after *Balzac*'s manner[2] in studied phrases; therefore I will tell you as fast as I can, that I have receiv'd your favour of the 26th past,[3] with your kind present of *The Rape of the Lock.* You have given me the truest satisfaction imaginable, not only in making good the just opinion I have ever had of your reach of thought, and my Idea of your comprehensive genius; but likewise in that pleasure I take as an *English* Man to see the *French*, even *Boileau* himself in his *Lutrin*, outdone in your Poem: For you descend, *leviore plectro*,[4] to all the nicer touches, that your own observation and wit furnish, on such a subject as requires the finest strokes, and the liveliest imagination. But I must say no more (tho' I could a great deal) on what pleases me so much: and henceforth I hope you will never condemn me of partiality, since I only swim with the stream, and approve what all men of good taste (notwithstanding the jarring of Parties) must and do universally applaud. I now come to what is of vast moment, I mean the preservation of your health, and beg of you earnestly to get out of all Tavern-company, and fly away *tanquam ex incendio.* What a misery it is for you to be destroy'd by the foolish kindness ('tis all one whether real or pretended) of those who are able to bear the Poison of bad Wine, and to engage you in so unequal a combat? As to *Homer*, by all I can learn your business is done; therefore come away and take a little time to breathe in the country. I beg now for my own sake, but much more for yours; methinks Mr. — has said to you more than once,

Heu fuge, nate dea, teque his, ait, eripe flammis![5]

I am | Your, &c.

†POPE *to* SIR WILLIAM TRUMBULL[6] — 12 *March* 1713/14

1735

March 12, 1713.

Though any thing you write is sure to be a pleasure to me, yet I must own your last letter made me uneasy: You really use a style of compli-

[1] Broome had recently become rector of Sturston.

[2] Jean-Louis Guez de Balzac (1594–1654), 'the Christian Socrates', who after 1624, when his first letters were published, exercised great influence in making epistolary style both elaborately noble and excessively formal.

[3] An unknown letter.

[4] Horace, *Carmina*, II. i. 40.

[5] *Aeneid*, ii. 289.

[6] Pope printed this letter as a reply to that of 6 Mar. It makes a most inappropriate reply to that fatherly letter of kind warning.

ment, which I expect as little as I deserve it. I know 'tis a common opinion that a young scribler is as ill pleas'd to hear truth as a young Lady. From the moment one sets up for an author, one must be treated as ceremoniously, that is as unfaithfully,

As a King's Favourite, or as a King.

This proceeding, join'd to that natural vanity which first makes a man an author, is certainly enough to render him a coxcomb for life. But I must grant it is but a just judgment upon Poets, that they whose chief pretence is Wit, shou'd be treated just as they themselves treat Fools, that is, be cajoll'd with praises. And I believe, Poets are the only poor fellows in the world whom any body will flatter.

I would not be thought to say this as if the obliging letter you sent me deserv'd this imputation, only it put me in mind of it; and I fancy one may apply to one's friend what *Cæsar* said of his Wife. *It was not sufficient that he knew her to be chast, himself, but she shou'd not be so much as suspected by others.*

As to the wonderful discoveries, and all the good news you are pleas'd to tell me of my self; I treat it as you who are in the Secret treat common news, groundless reports of things at a distance, which I who look into the true springs of the affair at home, in my own breast, know to have no foundation at all. For *Fame* tho' it be as *Milton* finely calls it, *The last Infirmity of noble Minds*, is scarce so strong a temptation as to warrant our loss of time here: It can never make us lie down contentedly on a death-bed (as some of the ancients are said to have done with that thought). You Sir have your self taught me, that an easy situation at that hour, can proceed from no ambition less noble than that of an eternal felicity, which is unattainable by the strongest endeavours of the Wit, but may be gain'd by the sincere intentions of the Heart only. As in the next world, so in this, the only solid blessings are owing to the goodness of the mind, not the extent of the capacity: Friendship here is an emanation from the same source as Beatitude there: the same benevolence and grateful disposition that qualifies us for the one, if extended farther, makes us partakers of the other. The utmost point of my desires in my present state terminates in the society and good-will of worthy men, which I look upon as no ill earnest and fore-taste of the society and alliance of happy souls hereafter.

The continuance of your favours to me is what not only makes me happy, but causes me to set some value upon my self as part of your care. The instances I daily meet with of these agreeable awakenings of friendship, are of too pleasing a nature not to be acknowledged whenever I think of you. I am | Your, &c.

POPE *to* CARYLL 12 *March* 1713/14

Add. 28618

March. 12. 1714.

Nothing could have mortified me more (amidst all the mortifications I undergo this Lent) than your reproach of my silence, but that[1] I knew it to be undeserved. For upon my word, I answered your kind letter, within a post after Mr Caryll left the town, and accompanied it with two books of *The Rape of the Lock* which Mr Lewis undertook should reach your hands, and sent to one Mr Brown's in order thereto. At the same time he promised to enclose the farce,[2] which had lain in his hands some weeks forgot. He engaged to send *The Rape of the Lock* this post (for I just now come from his shop), which has in four days time sold to the number [of] three thousand, and is already reprinted tho' not in so fair a manner as the first Impression, which I before designed you. But I hope Mr Lewis may recover that packet.

In the letter I entreated the farther favour of you, to send me as soon as you could, a list of the names of those subscribers you had procured, who either had paid the money, or whom you could be sure of, in order to insert them in the printed catalogue now just about to be published.

I was resolved not to omit one post the vindication of myself, in a point so tender to me, as any thing must be which can seem a neglect of you. But I have but three minutes to thank you in, for all your favours, for 'tis now very late. I beg you to believe that not even sickness itself (which has of late been very familiar with me) can make me forget Mr Caryll, at that time when I would gladly forget myself, and could almost be satisfied there were no such thing in the world as | dear sir | Your most faithful and most | affectionate humble servant. | A: P:

I hope in a little time to get into the country, for it begins to be necessary to me: my headaches increasing daily.

POPE *to* CARYLL 19 *March* 1713/14

Add. 28618

19. March. 1714.[3]

After having given you the trouble of reading two of my letters very lately, I can't refrain from sending you a third, in a more particular

[1] Caryll's scribe carefully wrote *what* instead of *that*.

[2] Presumably, as Elwin suggests, this word should be *Fan*, referring to Gay's poem; but the transcriber clearly wrote *Farce*.

[3] Normally Pope dated letters written before 25 Mar. according to Old Style; i.e. normally this date would mean 1715. But as he approached the end of the year (24 Mar.) he sometimes used New Style. So here, unless the year was entered by Caryll. The fact that

manner to thank you for the industry you have used upon my account, as well as for the effects of it on those subscribers you gave me the list of. I think you have been very successful in procuring so many, and too kind in listing so many out of your own family.[1] 'Twill be a satisfactory piece of vanity to me, to have all the world know, and read in this list, how partial the Carylls have been to me. I must own, many of the names in the catalogue I shall exhibit, are of so great figure, that I should not be much mortified even if I failed in my attempt; while posterity would see at least, if I was no good poet, I was the happiest poet that ever appeared upon record, in the good opinion of such a number of such persons.

Yesterday Mr Steele's affair was decided ⌜in his expulsion from the House.⌝[2] I am sorry I can be of no other opinion than yours, as to his whole carriage and writings of late. But certainly he has not only been punished by others, but suffered much even from his own party in the point of character, nor (I believe) received any amends in that of interest, as yet, whatever may be his prospect for the future.

This gentleman, among a thousand others, is a great instance of the fate of all who are carried away by Party-spirit of any side. I wish all violence may succeed as ill, but am really amazed that so much of that vile and pernicious quality should be joined with so much natural good-humour as I think Mr Steele has.

I thought when I sat down to write, to have only thanked you but find I am most at a loss for expressions when I want 'em most. Let me then tell you, I find myself just at the same pitch of affection to you, as I was before you did me this last kindness; that I know you will do me the next I shall ask of you, as readily; that I shall never more pay you a compliment; and that you are never to desire, but always to demand, as your right preferably to any man else, whatsoever you please, of | Dear sir | Your most obliged affectionate | Friend and servant. | A: P:

My most faithful service to the whole family, which I more wish to see than any in England.

I shall be at Binfield in three Weeks.

Pope used paragraphs two and three of this letter for the last two paragraphs of a letter printed by him as to Congreve (19 Mar. 1714/15) suggests that the original was dated 1714, and that in preparing the texts of 1735 Pope wrongly altered the date to 1715, since that would be the normal meaning of his date. The year 1715 should have been to him obviously impossible.

[1] In the list of subscribers to the *Iliad* are Caryll himself, his brother Richard, his son John, and John's wife, Lady Mary.

[2] Steele was, as Pope says, expelled on 18 Mar. 1713/14.

*SCRIBLERUS *to* LORD OXFORD[1] [20 *March* 1713/14]

Longleat Portland Papers, xiii

The Doctor and Dean, Pope, Parnell and Gay
In manner Submissive most humbly do pray,
That Your Lordship would once let Your Cares all alone
And Climb the dark Stairs to Your Friends who have none:
To Your Friends who at least have no Cares but to please You
To a good honest Junta that never will teaze You.

From the Doctor's Chamber past eight;
Mar: 20: $17\frac{13}{14}$

Address: To the Lord High Treasurer

*SCRIBLERUS *to* LORD OXFORD[2] [?*April* 1714]

Longleat Portland Papers, xiii

A Pox of all Senders
For any Pretenders
Who tell us these troublesome Stories,
In their dull hum-drum key
Of Arma Virumque
Hannoniae qui primus ab oris.

A Fig too for H—r[3]
Who prates like his Grandmere
And all his old Friends would rebuke
In spite of the Carle
Give us but our Earle,
And the Devil may take their Duke.[4]

Then come and take part in
The Memoirs of Martin,

[1] This is the earliest of the rhymed notes of invitation sent to Oxford by the Scriblerus Club, meeting in Dr. Arbuthnot's room in St. James's Palace. The note is written in Swift's hand. For similar additional verses not here printed, see *Memoirs of Scriblerus*, ed. Charles Kerby-Miller (1950), Appendix I.

[2] The five men who composed the Scriblerus Club all signed this 'letter' of invitation to attend their meeting, and then some wit overwrote all the names except that of Gay. The overwriting was probably an attempt to superpose a word that described the ruling mood of the name; i.e. Swift becomes *Lustigo*, &c. The words are illegible. The date of the meeting in question is indeterminate: it must come before 21 Apr. when Pope and Parnell went to Binfield, and it must be late enough to fall into the period when Oxford's hold on power was decreasing. It should be a Saturday, and 3 Apr. is a guess. The verses are in Parnell's hand.

[3] Hanmer.

[4] Marlborough.

Lay by your White Staff & gray Habit,
For trust us, friend Mortimer
Should you live years forty more
Haec olim meminisse juvabit.

by order of the Club
A. Pope | J. Gay | J. Swift | J. Arbuthnot | T. Parnell

*LORD OXFORD *to* SCRIBLERUS[1] 10 *April* 1714

Longleat Portland Papers, xiii

Apr: 10: 1714

You merry five who filld with / ful of Blisful nectar
Can Philips sing as Homer chanted Hector
I wil attend to hear your tuneful Lays
And wish your merits meet with one who pays—

*SCRIBLERUS *to* LORD OXFORD[2] [17 *April* 1714?]

Longleat Portland Papers, xiii

My Lord, forsake your Politick Utopians,
To sup, like Jove, with blameless Ethiopians.
Pope.

In other Words, You with the Staff,
Leave John of Bucks,[3] come here and laugh.
Dean

For Frolick Mirth give ore affairs of State,
To night be happy, be to morrow great.
Parnell

Give Clans your money, us your smile
Your Scorn to T—end & Ar—ile.[4]
Doctor

Leave Courts, and hye to simple Swains,
Who feed *no* Flock upon *no* Plains
Gay.

[1] Preserved in Lord Oxford's autograph. The merry five are those who really constituted the Club, and who had addressed his lordship on 20 Mar. (q.v.). The warfare against Philips had been prosecuted by Pope in *Guardian* No. 40 and, more recently, by Gay's pastorals. Gay's *Shepherd's Week* was published 15 Apr. 1714: advance copies might well be circulating on the 10th.

[2] Each of these couplets is beautifully characteristic of its author. Each is in the autograph of the author, whose signature also is autograph. The date, highly hypothetical, is due to the allusion in Gay's couplet to his *Shepherd's Week*. This was then the last Saturday at which all five members were present.

[3] John Sheffield, Duke of Buckingham.

[4] Townshend and Argyle.

POPE *to* JOHN HUGHES[1] 19 *April* [1714]

1772 (Duncombe)

April 19.

Sir,—I make use of the freedom you so obligingly allowed me, of sending you a paper of proposals for 'Homer', and of intreating your assistance in promoting the subscription.

I have added another for Mr. Pate,[2] if he thinks fit to oblige me so far, as you seemed inclined to believe he might.

I have left receipts signed with Mr. Jervas, who will give 'em for any subscriptions you may procure, and be (I am sure) very glad to be better acquainted with you, or entertain you with what paintings or drawings he has. He charges me to give you his most humble service, and I beg you to think no man is, with a truer esteem than I, dear Sir, | Your most obliged | and faithful servant, | A. Pope.

Pray make my most humble service acceptable to Sir Richard Blackmore.[3]

POPE *to* CARYLL 19 *April* 1714

Add. 28618

April 19. 1714.

I began to think it very long since I had the pleasure of a line of yours, when I heard of the accident which disabled your hand. I am perfectly convinced you can never be in the wrong, and that I have always been so, when ever I but began to imagine you could. I sooner believe the Pope may err than that you are capable of erring; so implicitly for the future shall I believe in you, and I hope my faith will make me safe in your friendship. I am sensible I should say something of your hand, upon this occasion, as that 'tis a very unjust and unmerited doom that a hand which gives every one so much pleasure, should feel so much pain, or that That hand should be bound up at this instant, which ever till now was open to all men, or the like. But I am in good earnest of late too much a man of business to mind metaphors and similes. I find subscribing much superior to writing, and there are a sort of little epigrams I more especially delight in, after the manner of rondeaus,

[1] First printed by John Duncombe in his *Letters by Several Eminent Persons Deceased* (1772), i. 85, where it bears the date here given. In a second edition (1773) the letter is dated 13 Apr.

[2] Probably 'Will Pate, the learned woollen-draper,' mentioned as such by Swift in his letter to Stella, Sept. 17 and Oct. 6, 1710.—Duncombe, 1772.

[3] It appears from the above, that Mr. Pope and this poetical knight were then upon terms of friendship, which were first broken by Sir Richard's accusing Mr. Pope of profaneness and immorality (see his 'Essays' [1716], vol. ii, p. 27), on a report from Curl, that he was author of a 'travestie on the first psalm.'—Duncombe, 1772.

which begin and end all in the same words; viz, Received — and A: Pope. These epigrams end smartly, and are each of 'em tagged with two guineas. Of these, as I have learned, you have composed several,[1] ready for me to set my name to, as indeed I never knew you give out in any thing that was either very ingenious or very friendly. I am told you are expected here, and 'tis no small mortification to me to be expected at home, where I am obliged to be in two days. I fully purpose (if you invite me a second time in the proper forms) to see Ladyholt in two or three months, and save the lives of some innocent birds by keeping you a few hours in the day from taking the field. In the meantime I trouble you with a printed proposal of mine, wherein you will find those names inserted which you procured me. As to the money, when you come to town, be pleased to leave it with Mr Jervas, who will give you receipts for each subscriber signed with my hand. I beg the kindness of a word from you, to Binfield, at your first conveniency: be assured, dear sir, nothing is at all times so welcome to | Your most unfeigned friend | and ever affectionate humble servant | A: P:

POPE *to* CARYLL[2] 1 *May* 1714

Add. 28618

May the first 1714.

Your Letter found me ⌜at Binfield,⌝ very busy in my grand undertaking,[3] to which I must wholly give myself up for some time, unless when I snatch an hour to please myself with a distant conversation with you and one or two more by writing ⌜a line or two. I am much afraid I ought not to trust my self at Ladyholt so soon as you mention. The pleasures of that place will take up my head too much to suffer even poetry to enter into competition with them, and Homer himself will have too powerful a rival in Mr Caryll. If I knew your time of returning to Grinsted, I believe I could then be more easy for a Month, after the heat of the work was over, tho' not more happy.⌝ 'Tis no comfortable prospect to be reflecting ⌜(as else I must)⌝ that so long a siege as that of Troy lies upon my hands, and the campaign above half over before I have made any progress. I must confess the Greek fortification does not appear so formidable as it did, upon a nearer approach; and I am almost apt to flatter myself, that Homer secretly seems inclined to correspond with me, in letting me into a

[1] Pope's subscribers, thirty-eight of whom Caryll had secured (so Elwin says), paid two guineas upon subscribing, a guinea additional for each of vols. i, ii, and iii, and half a guinea each for vols. iv and v, when published.

[2] In his editions Pope published this letter, with several revisions, as if to Addison, 30 Jan. 1713/14. Several of his omissions in printing are here placed in half-brackets. For other revisions see the text of the Addison version, i. 208.

[3] The *Iliad.*

good part of his designs. There are, indeed, a sort of underli[n]g auxiliars to the difficulty of the work, called commentators and criticks, who would frighten many people by their number and bulk. These lie entrenched in the ditches, and are secure only in the dirt they have heaped about 'em with great pains in the collecting it. But I think we have found a method of coming at the main works by a more speedy and gallant way than by mining under ground; that is, by using the poetical engines, wings, and flying thither over their heads.

While I am engaged in the fight, I find you are concerned how I shall be paid, and are soliciting[1] with all your might that I may not have the ill fate of many discarded generals, to be first envied and maligned, then perhaps praised, and lastly neglected. The former (the constant attendant upon all great and laudable enterprises) I have already experienced. Some have said I am not a master in the Greek, who either are so themselves or are not. If they are not, they can't tell; and if they are, they can't without having catechised me. But if they can read (for I know some criticks can, and others can't) there are fairly lying before them and all the world, some specimens of my translation from this author in the Miscellanies,[2] which they are heartily welcome to. I have also encountered much malignity on the score of religion,[3] some calling me a Papist and a Tory, the latter because the heads of that party have been distinguishingly favorable to me, ⌜but why the former I can't imagine, but that Mr Caryll and Mr E. Blount have labored to serve me.⌝ Others have styled me a Whig, because I have been honoured with Mr Addison's good word, and Mr Jervas's good deeds, and of late with my Lord Halifax's patronage. How much more natural a conclusion would it be to any good natured man to think a person who has been favoured by all sides has been inoffensive to all. This miserable age is so sunk between animosities of party and those of religion, that I begin to fear most men have politics enough to make the best scheme of government a bad one, thro' their extremity of violence, and faith enough to hinder their salvation. I hope, for my own part, never to have more of either than is consistent with common justice and charity, and always as much as becomes a Christian and honest man, ⌜that is just as much as you.⌝ Tho' I find it an unfortunate thing to be bred a papist, when one is obnoxious to four parts in five as being so too much, and to the fifth part as being so too little, I shall

[1] *Soliciting* in the Addison version is cleverly changed to *solicitous*. Addison, as Pope protested in the 'Testimonies of Authors' in *The Dunciad* of 1729, at first encouraged Pope, but did absolutely no soliciting of subscribers.

[2] In 1709 Pope had published in Tonson's miscellany a translation of the episode of Sarpedon, and in 1714, in Steele's miscellany, had published two other versions from the *Odyssey*.

[3] In the Addison text the rest of this paragraph had to be neatly changed to fit Addison and to avoid stress on religion.

yet be easy under both their mistakes, and be, what I more than seem to be, for I suffer for it. God is my witness, that I no more envy their Protestants their places and possessions than I do our priests their charity or learning. I am ambitious of nothing but the good opinion of all good men of all sides, for I know that one virtue of a free spirit is more worth than all the virtues put together of all the narrow-souled people in the world. ⌜If they promise me all the good offices they ever did, or could do, I would not change for 'em all one kind word of yours.⌝ I am ⌜entirely | dear sir | your obliged, and faithful | Friend and servant | A: P:⌝

⌜What you are so kind as to mention of writing to Mr Stonor,[1] you will oblige me in; as to the rest who know me so well (personally) I beg they may be left to themselves.

I writ to my bookseller to change the Title of the E. of Seafort as you directed.⌝

†THE REV. GEORGE BERKELEY *to* POPE[2] 1 *May* 1714

1735

Leghorne, May 1, 1714.

As I take Ingratitude to be a greater crime than Impertinence, I chuse rather to run the risque of being thought guilty of the latter, than not to return you my thanks for a very agreeable entertainment you just now gave me. I have accidentally met with your *Rape of the Lock* here, having never seen it before.[3] Stile, Painting, Judgment, Spirit, I had already admired in others of your Writings; but in this I am charm'd with the magic of your *Invention*, with all those images, allusions, and inexplicable beauties, which you raise so surprizingly and at the same time so naturally, out of a trifle. And yet I cannot say that I was more pleas'd with the reading of it, than I am with the pretext it gives me to renew in your thoughts the remembrance of one who values no happiness beyond the friendship of men of wit, learning, and good nature.

I remember to have heard you mention some half-form'd design of coming to *Italy*. What might we not expect from a Muse that sings so well in the bleak climate of *England*, if she felt the same warm Sun and breath'd the same Air with *Virgil* and *Horace*?

There are here an incredible number of Poets, that have all the

[1] Mr. Thomas Stonor subscribed to the *Iliad*, probably through Caryll's soliciting. Pope tried to visit him on his journey to Oxford in 1717. See Pope to Martha Blount, i. 729 [post 13 Sept. 1717].

[2] Published in Pope's editions except the quarto and folio of 1737.

[3] Presumably a copy of *The Rape* had been sent to Lord Peterborow, or had been taken with him when he left for Italy in March. Berkeley, of course, is the philosopher.

inclination but want the genius, or perhaps the art, of the Ancients. Some among them who understand *English*, begin to relish our Authors; and I am informed that at Florence they have translated *Milton* into *Italian* Verse. If one who knows so well how to write like the old *Latin* Poets, came among them; it wou'd probably be a means to retrieve them from their cold trivial conceits, to an imitation of their Predecessors.

As Merchants, Antiquaries, Men of Pleasure, *&c.* have all different views in travelling; I know not whether it might not be worth a Poet's while, to travel, in order to store his mind with strong Images of Nature.

Green fields and groves, flow'ry meadows and purling streams, are no where in such perfection as in *England*: but if you wou'd know lightsome days, warm suns, and blue skys, you must come to *Italy*: and to enable a man to describe rocks and precipices, it is absolutely necessary that he pass the *Alps*.

You will easily perceive that it is self-interest makes me so fond of giving advice to one who has no need of it. If you came into these parts I shou'd fly to see you. I am here (by the favour of my good friend the Dean of St. *Patrick's*) in quality of Chaplain to the Earl of *Peterborough*; who about three months since left the greatest part of his family in this town. God knows how long we shall stay here. I am | Your, &c.

†PARNELL AND POPE *to* GAY[1] — 4 *May* 1714

1735

May 4, Binfield 1714.

Dear Gay,—Since by your letter we find you can be content to breath in smoak, to walk in crouds, and divert your self with noise, nay and to make fine Pictures of this way of life, we shou'd give you up as one abandoned to a wrong choice of pleasures. We have however so much compassion on you as to think of inviting you to us, where your taste for books, friendship, and ease, may be indulg'd. But if you do not come, pray leave to tempt us with your description of the Court; for indeed humanity is frail, and we cannot but remember some particular honours which we have enjoy'd in conversation; bate us this one point and we stand you, still untir'd with one another, and fresh to the pleasures of the country. If you wou'd have any news from us, know that we are well at present: This I am sure wou'd have been allow'd by you as news from either of us a fortnight ago. In return to this, send us every thing you imagine diverting, and pray forget not my commissions. Give my respects to the Dean, Dr. *Arbuthnot*, Mr. *Ford*, and

[1] Printed in the editions of 1735 but not thereafter by Pope.

the Provost.[1] Dear *Gay*, adieu. | Your affectionate Friend | and humble Servant. | Tho. Parnell.

Dear Mr. Gay,—Above all other News, send us the best, that of your good Health, if you enjoy it; which Mr. *Harcourt*[2] made us very much fear. If you have any design either to amend your health, or your life, I know no better Expedient than to come hither, where you should not want room, tho' I lay myself in a Trucklebed under the Doctor.[3] You might here converse with the old *Greeks*, be initiated into all their Customs, and learn their Prayers by heart as we have done: The Dr. last *Sunday*, intending to say an *Our Father*, was got half way in *Chryses* Prayer to *Apollo*. The ill effects of Contention and Squabling so lively describ'd in the first Iliad, make Dr. *Parnelle* and myself continue in the most exemplary Union in every thing. We deserve to be worship'd by all the poor, divided, factious, interested Poets of this world.

As we rise in our speculations daily, we are grown so grave, that we have not condescended to laugh at any of the idle things about us this week: I have contracted a severity of aspect from deep meditation on high subjects, equal to the formidable Front of black-brow'd *Jupiter*, and become an awful Nod as well, when I assent to some grave and weighty Proposition of the Doctor, or enforce a Criticism of my own. In a word, *Y—g*[4] himself has not acquired more Tragic Majesty in his aspect by reading his own Verses than I by *Homer*'s.

In this state, I cannot consent to your publication of that ludicrous trifling Burlesque you write about. Dr. *Parnelle* also joins in my opinion, that it will by no means be well to print it.

Pray give (with the utmost fidelity and esteem) my hearty service to the Dean, Dr. *Arbuthnot*, Mr. *Ford*, and to Mr. *Fortescue*. Let them also know at *Button*'s that I am mindful of them. I am, divine Bucoliast! | *Thy loving Countryman.*[5]

*POPE AND PARNELL *to* FORD[6] 19 *May* [1714]

The Pierpont Morgan Library

From the Romantic World.
May 19. By Sunshine.

Now is the Evening Sun, declining from the Hemisphere he had painted with Purple, & intermingled Streaks of Gold; rolling his rapid

[1] Swift's friend Charles Ford was a member of the group at this time. The Provost, according to Dr. Birch and Elwin, was Dr. Benjamin Pratt of Dublin.

[2] The Hon. Simon Harcourt, son of Lord Harcourt, and now getting subscribers for Pope. When young Harcourt died in 1720 Pope wrote an epitaph.

[3] Parnell himself.

[4] Young.

[5] This subscription is borrowed from the end of the Proeme to Gay's *Shepherd's Week*, published in Apr. 1714.

[6] First printed by D. Nichol Smith in his edition of *The Letters of Jonathan Swift to Charles Ford* (1935), pp. 225–6.

Chariot toward the Surface of the Ocean, whose waves begin to Sparkle at his beams; while the silver-footed Thetis, and all her Water Nymphs around, are preparing their Crystal Palaces for his Reception. It seems to us Mortalls, as if his glorious Orbe were prop'd under the Chin by the Tops of the distant Mountains, whose lovely Azure appears sprinkled with the loose Spangles he shakes from his Illustrious Tresses. The lengthening Shadows extend themselves after him, as if they endeavoured to detain him with their long black Arms; or rather (if we consider their Position is directly contrary) they seem the Long Arrows of far-darting Phœbus, which he shoots backward, like a Parthian, as he retreats. The Green Mantle of the Earth is trimm'd with Gold, and the Leaves of the Trees turn'd up with the same. But the God, better pleasd with the Water-Tabby of the Ocean, is resolvd to enrich it with all his Spangles.[1] & now he sinks beneath our Horizon leaving some illustrated tracks of his former beauty behind him, which as they insensibly wear away are suceeded by the silver gleams of his palefacd delegate. From the dark tops of the hills She emerges into Sight to run her inconstant race over the Azure firmament. The Starrs wait around her as a numerous train of Inamorato's who confess the flames of love at the Sight of the celestiall Goddess; the fixed Starrs seem to stand amazd to behold her, while the Planets dance in her presence & wink upon her as a sett of more familiar gallants. But now while I look behold a new & more melancholy scene, a darkning cloud intercepts her streaming glorys, She goes behind it as a matron mounting up into a Mourning Chariot, & now & then peeps through it as a pretty young[2] widdow looking through her crapes. Darkness has now spread its veil over the variety of this terrestriall creation for which rejoyce ye quarrelling Oyster wenches whom it parts & ye fondling Lovers who are to meet in it but what will ye do ye Mooncalves who have stayd late in company in hopes to go home by the light of this second luminary.

By this time it is evident that we have written the day down & the night allmost through which makes it no feignd excuse but a reall reason for us upon the account of want of time to conclude with professing our selves | Your Most Affectionate Friends | & Humble Servants | ɘqoꟼarnell

By Moonshine. May 19.

Address: To Charles Ford Esqr. | at the Secretary's Office | Whitehall | Westminster

Postmark: 21/MA

[1] After this word Parnell took the pen, and the rest is in his hand.

[2] The word is scored over for deletion.

POPE *to* PARNELL[1] [25 *May* or 1 *June* 1714]

Trinity College, Dublin

Binfield near Oakingham
Tuesday

I believe the Hurry you were in hinderd your giving me a word by the last post; so that I am yet to learn whether you got well to town or continue so there? I very much fear both for your Health & your Quiet, and no man living can be more truly concernd in any thing that touches either than my Self. I woud comfort my Self however with hoping that your business may not be unsuccessfull,[2] for your sake; & that at least it may soon be put into other proper Hands; for my own, I beg earnestly of you to Return to us as soon as possible. You know how very much I want you. And that however your Business may depend upon any other my business depends entirely upon you; And yet still I hope you will find your man, even tho' I lose you the mean while; At this time the more I love you, the more I can spare you which alone will, I dare say, be a Reason to you to let me have you back the sooner. The minute I lost you Eustathius with nine hundred pages, and nine thousand Contractions of the Greek Character Arose to my View—Spondanus with all his Auxiliaries in Number a thousand pages (Value three Shillings) & Dacier's three Volumes, Barnes's two, Valterie's three, Cuperus half in Greek, Leo Allatius three parts in Greek, Scaliger, Macrobius, & (worse than 'em all) Aulus Gellius: All these Rushd upon my Soul at once & whelm'd me under a Fitt of the Head Ach, I curs'd them all Religiously, Damn'd my best friends among the rest, & even blasphem'd Homer himself. Dear Sir not only as you are a friend & as you are a Goodnatur'd Man, but as you are a Christian & a Divine come back Speedily & prevent the Encrease of my Sins: For at the Rate I have begun to Rave, I shall not only Damn all the Poets & Commentators who have gone before me, but be damned my Self by all who come after me—To be Serious you have not only left me to the last degree Impatient for your Return, who at all times should have been so (tho never so much as since I knew you in best Health here) but you have wrought Several Miracles upon our Family; you have made old People fond of a Young and gay Person, and Inveterate Papists of a Clergyman of the Church of England—Even Nurse[3] herself is in danger of being in Love in her old Age, and (for all I know) would even marry Dennis[4] for your Sake

[1] First printed by Goldsmith in his Life of Parnell. The Trinity College MS. is not autograph, but is an eighteenth-century copy. Only two Tuesdays are possible for this letter, 25 May or 1 June.

[2] Possibly Parnell's departure for London had something to do with his hope of becoming chaplain to Lord Clarendon on the projected embassy to Hanover.

[3] Pope's nurse, Mary or Mercy Beach, d. 1725, aged 77.

[4] Dennis is hardly the critic; presumably this is the name of Parnell's servant.

because he is your man & loves his master. In short come down forthwith, or give me good Reasons for delaying tho' but for a day or two, by the next post. If I find them Just I will come up to you—tho you know how precious my time is at present my Hours were never worth so much money before But perhaps you are not Sensible of this who give away your own works. You are a Generous Author,[1] I a Hackney Scribler, You are a Grecian & bred at a University, I a poor Englishman of my own Educating; You are a Reverend Person, I a Wagg; in short, you are Dr. Parnelle, with an E at the end of your Name and I | Your most oblidgd & Affectionate | Friend & faithfull Servant | A: Pope

My hearty Service to the Dean, Dr Arbuthnott, Mr Ford, and the true Genuine Shepherd Jno Gay of Devon I expect him down with you.

JERVAS *to* POPE [*Post* 27 *May* 1714][2]

Homer MSS. Add. 4807

Dear Mr Pope,—I intended to have breakfasted with James Eckersall[3] at Drayton but heard by the Way of his being in London, so I jogg'd on to Hammersmith in 5 hours & half without drawing bit. Yesterday I gave a Printed Proposal to Lord Halifax & spoke to the Duke of Devonshire to join my Lord Wharton's Interest & move your affair, that we may set 'em agoing About the Counties—

I have not yet seen the Dear Arch Deacon who is at his old Lodging in St James's plac[e] nor the Dean but have just received a Thing entitled a Prefatory Epistle concerning some Remarks to be publisht on Homer's Iliad, Occasiond by the Proposals of Mr Pope towards a New English Version of the Poems—To the Revd Dr Swift Dean of St Patricks—by Richard Fiddes B.D. Chaplain to the Right Honourable the Earl of Oxford—*Ἀμάρτημ' εὐγενές*—Long.—To Mr Pope from the Author in Manuscript all the Foregoing Elegancies at Proper Distances & Italianiz'd according to form—it came too late for the Coach & is too big for my Priviledge of Frank . . . 8vo 120 pages—Marbled paper.

I find so many Party stroakes in it, That I am afraid it may do your Proposals more harm than good—

[1] Parnell wrote for Pope various things, and possibly Pope is here thinking of the 'Essay on the Life and Times of Homer' included in his translation. It may be a general acknowledgement of the learning that Parnell is so generous with.

[2] The letter is dated, approximately, by the fact that Fiddes's *Prefatory Epistle* was published on 27 May. (adv. in *London Evening Post.*)

[3] Eckersall was a close friend of Jervas, who left him a legacy of a thousand pounds. Pope also was friendly with both Eckersall and Mrs. Eckersall. See letters of Mar. 1720, &c.

My Lord Halifax talkd of a Design to send for you to Bushy Park, I believe with a Coach & Six, or Light Chaise—but did not name the precise Time— . . . I publish your having done the first Book, & begun—I received the Cloak bag safe—I hope you did not pay Carriage—I can't yet guess when I shal be ready for Sir William's[1]—Service &c. | I am Your Servant C.J.

POPE *to* BROOME 30 *May* [1714]

Elwin–Courthope, viii. 30

May 30, [1714].

It is near three months past that I writ to you,[2] with two other letters inclosed in the same packet to Sturston. I have been much afraid for the health of that family[3], as well as for your own, since I received no account of any of them. I hope I uttered no such absurdities in the letters to the ladies as were utterly unpardonable; for all I remember of them is, that I was not quite sober when I writ them. For what remains to trouble you with in this, I beg you will let me know if it fell in your way to make any further advances in the subscription to Homer, at Cambridge or elsewhere? And be so kind to acquaint me what you have received, and from whom? If any were promised, as you sent me word of two, pray receive them as soon as you can conveniently, or any way return them to Lintot with a line to me; for it will be time to make up all my accounts shortly. However it be, pray favour me sometimes with a letter directed to Mr. Jervas's, at Bridgewater House, in Cleveland Court, by St. James's, whither all my letters are directed, wherever I am. I have forty journeys to make this summer, and wish, with all my soul, the first of them were to Sturston. I really love and honour them more than I can express, and wish their happiness more earnestly than my own. For truly, Mr. Broome, I may venture to tell you, now you are a divine, that I despise this world more than I would have it think I do, and have very few ambitions or interests at heart for my own particular. Two fits of the headache make me a philosopher at any time, and I had one yesterday and another this morning.

I wonder I have not heard from you. I hope you have not behaved

[1] Jervas was to paint, or had painted, a 'family piece' of the Trumbulls. As late as 22 Feb. 1714/15 Sir William wrote to Pope his hopes that Jervas would alter parts of the picture. This altering was to be done 'next week', so Pope wrote to Sir William on 15 June 1714, if one can trust a mention in a footnote by Elwin (viii. 4, note 5), who does not print a letter of that date.

[2] Though Pope has written to Broome earlier, this is the first of their long correspondence to be preserved.

[3] Broome had been ordained early in 1713/14 and was now rector of Sturston, where the Marriot ladies lived. Pope's crude letter to Miss Marriot (see 10 Feb. 1714/15) may possibly belong in 1713/14, and be what he is now apologizing for.

yourself so violently in your parish, I mean violently in respect to the young damsels, as to be deprived of your benefice already. I shall be apt to spread this scandal, unless I hear soon from you. I am, very faithfully and affectionately, dear sir, your very humble servant.

*SCRIBLERUS *to* LORD OXFORD [5 *June* 1714?][1]

Longleat Portland Papers, xiii

Tho the Dean has run from us in manner uncivil;
The Doctor, and He* that 's nam'd next to the Devil, [*Pope.
With Gay, who Petition'd You once on a time,
And Parnell, that would, if he had but a Rhyme.
(That Gay the poor Sec: and that arch Chaplain Parnell,[2]
As Spiritual one, as the other is Carnal)
Forgetting their Interest, now humbly sollicit
You'd at present do nothing but give us a Visit.

A. Pope. | T. Parnell | Jo: Arbuthnott | J. Gay.

That all this true is
Witness. E. Lewis.

Endorsement: verses Saturday past | 1714 | Answerd immediatly

*LORD OXFORD *to* SCRIBLERUS 5 *June* 1714

Longleat Portland Papers, xiii

June 5th: 1714

In these Dangerous Times when Popery is Flagrant
And your servant of Oxford would choose to be vagrant
When mercury Dukes set up for Physitians
Or which is the same for state Politicians
He that cares not to Rule wil not fail to obey—
When summond by Arbuthnot, Pope, Parnel & Gay.

Endorsement (in Oxford's hand): Answer to | Dr A: &c | June 5th: 1714.

[1] The date is inferred from the fact that Swift had left town at the end of May, and from the date of Oxford's immediate answer. These verses are in Pope's hand; the signatures are autographs; the lines in 'witness' are in the hand of Erasmus Lewis, and the endorsement is Oxford's.

[2] Gay had an appointment as secretary to Lord Clarendon's mission to Hanover, and left London on 14 June. It had been expected that Parnell might go as chaplain to Clarendon, but at the last moment he failed to get the appointment. Gay's petition to Oxford is contained in the lines sent to Swift, 8 June 1714 (Ball, ii. 144–5).

†POPE *to* CARYLL[1] 8 *June* 1714

1735

June 8, 1714.

The Question you ask in relation to Mr. *Ad*— and *Philips*, I shall answer in a few words. Mr. *Philips* did express himself with much indignation against me one evening at *Button*'s Coffee-house (as I was told) saying, That I was entered into a Cabal with Dean *Swift* and others to write against the *Whig-Interest*, and in particular to undermine his own reputation, and that of his friends *Steel* and *Addison*. But Mr. *Philips* never open'd his lips to my face, on this or any like occasion, tho' I was almost every night in the same room with him, nor ever offer'd me any indecorum.[2] Mr. *Addison* came to me a night or two after *Philips* had talk'd in this idle manner, and assur'd me of his disbelief of what had been said, of the friendship we shou'd always maintain, and desir'd I wou'd say nothing further of it. My Lord *Hallifax* did me the honour to stir in this matter, by speaking to several people to obviate a false aspersion, which might have done me no small prejudice with one Party. However *Philips* did all he could, secretly to continue the report with the *Hanover* Club, and kept in his hands the Subscriptions paid for me to him as Secretary to that Club. The heads of it have since given him to understand, that they take it ill; but (upon the terms I ought to be with a man whom I think a scoundrel) I wou'd not even ask him for this money, but commissioned one of the *Players*, his equals, to receive it. This is the whole matter; but as to the secret grounds of *Philips*'s malignity,[3] they will make a very pleasant History when we meet. Mr. *Congreve* and some others have been much diverted with it, and most of the Gentlemen of the *Hanover* Club have made it the subject of their ridicule on their Secretary. It is to this management of *Philips*, that the world owes Mr. *Gay*'s *Pastorals*.[4] The ingenious Author is extreamly your servant, and would have comply'd with your kind invitation, but that he is just now appointed Secretary to my Lord *Clarendon*, in his Embassy to *Hanover*.[5]

[1] Pope printed this letter in all his editions as 'Mr. Pope to the Honourable . . .'. He never connected it with Caryll, and it is not among the Caryll transcripts; but the letter immediately following in his editions (13 July 1714) has the heading 'To the same', and since that letter is among the Caryll transcripts, both letters are doubtless to Caryll.

[2] This statement constitutes a sort of denial of the story, current (at least later) that Philips brought a rod, which he 'stuck up at the bar of Button's Coffee-house' as a warning to Pope. See the letter of Broome to Fenton, 3 May [1728], and *Pope Alexander's Supremacy and Infallibility Examined* (1729), p. 16.

[3] This 'malignity' was probably largely increased by Pope's attack on Philips's pastorals in *Guardian* No. 40. See Sherburn, *Early Career*, p. 118.

[4] A detailed analysis of the relations of Gay's *Shepherd's Week* to Philips's pastorals, by Professor Hoyt Trowbridge, will be found in *Modern Language Quarterly*, v (1944), 79–88.

[5] On this same day (8 June) Gay wrote to Swift, now at Letcombe, thanking him for help in getting him accepted as secretary to Lord Clarendon. They left for Hanover before the end of June, but the death of Queen Anne (1 Aug.) made this Tory mission futile.

I am sensible of the zeal and friendship with which I am sure you will always defend your friend in his absence, from all those little tales and calumnies, which a Man of any genius or merit is born to. I shall never complain while I am happy in such noble defenders, and in such contemptible opponents. May their envy and ill nature ever increase, to the glory and pleasure of those they wou'd injure; may they represent me what they will, as long as you think me what I am, | Your, &c.

*SCRIBLERUS *to* LORD OXFORD[1] — 12 *June* 1714

Longleat Portland Papers, xiii

June 12 | 1714

To the Right Honourable the | Earl of Oxford.

The Dean to the plain,
& Gay to the Main,[2]
& Pope to the Mountains, retire:
The Dean for his health,
& Gay* for his wealth,
& Pope that the Muse may inspire.

Arbuthnot so tall,
& Parnell so small,
Perceiving their numbers decrease,
Woud have you resume
The chair in our room,
For you never must give up a PLACE.

* Varij Codices from

†POPE *to* SWIFT[3] — 18 *June* 1714

1740

June 18, 1714.

Whatever apologies it might become me to make at any other time for writing to you, I shall use none now, to a man who has own'd himself as splenetick as a Cat in the country. In that circumstance, I know by experience a letter is a very useful, as well as amusing thing: If you are too busied in State-affairs to read it, yet you may find entertainment in folding it into divers figures, either doubling it into a pyra-

[1] The verses are in Parnell's hand, the date in Oxford's. The MS. footnote to Gay's name may be in Gay's hand—added later? The verses seem to indicate the absence from town of all but Arbuthnot and Parnell.

[2] Within the month Gay was leaving for Hanover as secretary to Lord Clarendon.

[3] Printed 1740–2 with practically no changes.

midical, or twisting it into a Serpentine form to light a pipe:[1] or if your disposition should not be so mathematical, in taking it with you to that place where men of studious minds are apt to sit longer than ordinary; where after an abrupt division of the paper, it may not be unpleasant to try to fit and rejoyn the broken lines together. All these amusements I am no stranger to in the country, and doubt not but (by this time) you begin to relish them in your present contemplative situation.

I remember a man, who was thought to have some knowledge in the world, us'd to affirm, that no people in town ever complained they were forgotten by their friends in the country: but my encreasing experience convinces me he was mistaken, for I find a great many here grievously complaining of you, upon this score. I am told further, that you treat the few you correspond with in a very arrogant stile, and tell them you admire at their insolence in disturbing your meditations, or even enquiring of your retreat:[2] but this I will not positively assert, because I never receiv'd any such insulting Epistle from you. My Lord Oxford says you have not written to him once since you went: but this perhaps may be only policy, in him or you; and I, who am half a Whig, must not entirely credit any thing he affirms. At Button's it is reported you are gone to Hanover, and that Gay goes only on an Ambassy to you. Others apprehend some dangerous State-treatise from your retirement; and a Wit who affects to imitate Balsac, says, that the Ministry now are like those Heathens of old, who received their Oracles from the woods. The Gentlemen of the Roman Catholick persuasion are not unwilling to credit me, when I whisper that you are gone to meet some Jesuits commissioned from the Court of Rome, in order to settle the most convenient methods to be taken for the coming of the Pretender. Dr. Arbuthnot is singular in his opinion, and imagines your only design is to attend at full leisure to the life and adventures of Scriblerus.[3] This indeed must be granted of greater importance than all the rest; and I wish I could promise so well of you. The top of my own ambition is to contribute to that great work, and I shall translate Homer by the by. Mr. Gay has acquainted you[4] what progress I have made in it. I can't name Mr. Gay, without all the acknowledgements which I shall ever owe you, on his account. If I writ this in verse, I would tell you, you are like the sun, and while

[1] *to light a pipe* occurs in the clandestine volume (1740) and in Faulkner's octavo (1741 Da). It is omitted from London texts supervised by Pope (i.e. 1741 Labc; 1742 Labc).

[2] Sometime before the Death of Queen *Anne*, when her Ministers were quarrelling, and the Dean could not reconcile them, he retired to a Friend's House in *Berkshire*, and never saw them after. *This note is taken from the Edition printed at* Dublin *by* G. Faulkner.—Pope, 1741 Labc. Since the note first appears in the Faulkner octavo (1741 Da), it seems sure that Swift must have written it: it is not in the clandestine volume.

[3] This, the great project of the Scriblerus Club, was finally published by Pope in 1741.

[4] Gay (8 June 1714) wrote to Swift that Pope had brought the first book of the *Iliad* to town with him.

men imagine you to be retir'd or absent, are[1] hourly exerting your indulgence, and bringing things to maturity for their advantage. Of all the world, you are the man (without flattery) who serve your friends with the least ostentation; it is almost ingratitude to thank you, considering your temper; and this is the period of all my letter which I fear you will think the most impertinent. I am with the truest affection | Yours, &c.

POPE *to* CARYLL — 29 *June* 1714

Add. 28618

Binfield, June 29. 1714

I have formerly told you that I take it for granted, whenever I omit to write to you longer than I ought, you will not fail to attribute it to any thing in nature rather than to a neglect in my friendship. And indeed the pleasure I always find in corresponding with you is too great to be interrupted or delayed by any less cause than close business or sickness. Both these have conspired to prevent my sending a Line till now. Just after I saw your servant in London, I ran into the country with all the peevishness of a disappointed creature, who had really no aim so urgent to carry me to town as a hope of meeting you. I travelled in a open chaise, so exposed to the sun (in my face all the way) that I think I shall covet less to see Italy for the future. It threw me into a kind of fever which I have hardly yet recovered.

I shall attempt to say nothing extraordinary upon the favour you last did me. I look upon money to be one of the least things I am obliged to you for, and I should be heartily ashamed to thank you for forty guineas[2] after I had enjoyed your friendship with silent satisfaction for many years. I begin to look upon myself to have a title to you by long possession, like some of those old servants and tenants who expect your kindness on no other account than because you have long been good to them.

But I can't forbear telling you in the openness of my heart, what an infinite pleasure it was to me to find you snatching the first opportunity you ever had of serving my worldly interests with so distinguishing an alacrity and so warm a pursuit. If other poets had but a few such friends, the whole tribe would grow wealthy in a trice. I protest I am sorry you are not a first minister; for I am satisfied if you were, my fortune were made in as little time as you have been getting subscriptions. And I am sure it would be with less trouble to you, because I know so well how much more difficult, it must be to a man of your temper to ask of others than to give your self.

[1] the sun, and while . . . absent, are] the sun, while . . . absent, you are *1741 Labc.*
[2] The equivalent of twenty subscriptions to the *Iliad.*

May I venture too, without being thought [guilty] of affectation, to say it was not the least of my designs in proposing this subscription, to make some trial of my friends on all sides? I vow to you, I am very happy in the search (contrary to most people who make trials), for I find I have at least six Tory friends, three Whig friends and two Roman Catholic friends: with many others of each who at least will do me no harm.[1] I have discovered two dangerous enemies whom I might have trusted; besides innumerable malevoli, whom I will not honour so far as to suppose they can hurt any body. They say, 'tis in the conduct of life as in that of picquette, one shows most skill in the discarding part of the game. I have besides all this learnt a good deal of particular people's dispositions and humours by this odd way, and could point you several who would make excellent courtiers, if the science of courts required nothing but an artful way of breaking one's word. And all this too without asking one man a question myself, or seeming to aim at any great discoveries. Thus I have been the reverse of a politician, who seems only to aim at knowing the world but really designs purely to get money, whereas I, by seeming to aim at getting money have found a by-way to know the world. Yet after all, the best piece of knowledge I can brag of is, that I know you to be my friend, and myself to be | Dear sir. | Entirely yours. | A: P:

Mr Dancastle made me open the covering of this to assure yourself and the united families of Ladyholt of his faithful service. Mine is always understood.

POPE *to* DR. ARBUTHNOT[2] 11 *July* [1714]

The Royal College of Surgeons of England

Binfield, July 11th

Sir,—I have been so much afflicted with the Headake in the hot weather that I have had perpetual opportunitys of reflecting on those elegant Verses of Dr Scriblerus which you favord us with.[3] This is not a Time for us to make others live, when we can hardly live ourselves; so Scriblerus (contrary to other Maggotts)[4] must lye dead all the Summer, & wait till winter shall revive him. This I hope will be

[1] It is not too easy to identify these men. The Catholics would be Caryll and Edward Blount, but in the next letter to Caryll Pope mentions Southcote as a supporter. The Whigs would certainly include Jervas, the Earl of Halifax, and possibly Congreve. The Tories would include Oxford, Bolingbroke, Swift, and Arbuthnot—possibly also Ford and Erasmus Lewis. The enemies would include Philips and an unknown, possibly Tickell?

[2] This is the earliest letter of the Pope–Arbuthnot correspondence to be preserved, but clearly not the first written. It is endorsed at the top 'No. 44', but the series probably included letters from others than Pope.

[3] Elwin identifies these, with plausibility, as the same the Doctor included in his letter to Swift of 26 June. See Ball, ii. 160.

[4] Elwin cites Dr. Johnson's definition of maggot as 'whimsy, caprice, an odd fancy'.

no disadvantage to him, for Mankind will be Playing the Fool in all Weathers, & affording us materials for That Life, which every mortall contributes his Quota to, and which I hope to see the grand Receptacle of all the oddnesses of the world.

We have paid a Visit to the Dean at 30 miles distance, with whom we stayd some days, & are but just now return'd hither. As I fancy you will be somewhat inquisitive after the manner of his Life, & of our Reception, I will couch the particulars in the way of a News Letter.

From Letcomb near Wantage, July 4th.

This Day the Envoys deputed to Dean S— on the Part of his late Confederates, arrived here, during the Time of divine Service. They were receivd at the Back Door, and having paid the usual Compliments on their part, & receivd the usual Chidings on that of the Dean, were introduced to his Landlady,[1] & entertaind with a Pint of the Lord Bolingbroke's Florence.[2] The Health of that great Minister was drank in this Pint, together with the Lord Treasurer's (whose wine we also wished for). After which were commemorated Dr. Arbuthnot, & Mr Lewis, in a sort of Cyder, plentiful in these parts, & not altogether unknown in the Taverns of London. There was likewise a Side Board of Coffee which the Dean roasted with his own hands in an Engine for the purpose, his Landlady attending, all the while that office was performing. He talked of Politicks over Coffee, with the Air & Stile of an old Statesman, who had known something formerly; but was shamefully ignorant of the Three last weekes. When we mentiond the wellfare of England he laughd at us, & said Muscovy would become a flourishing Empire very shortly. He seems to have wrong notions of the British Court, but gave us a Hint as if he had a Correspondence with the King of Sweden.

As for the methods of passing his time, I must tell you one which constantly employs an hour about noone. He has in his window an Orbicular Glass, which by Contraction of the Solar Beams into a proper Focus, doth burn, singe, or speckle white, or printed Paper, in curious little Holes, or various figures. We chanced to find some Experiments of this nature upon the Votes of the House of Commons. The name of Tho. Hanmer Speaker[3] was much singed, and that of John Barber[4] entirely burn'd out; There was a large Gapp at the Edge

[1] Swift was staying with his old friend the Rev. John Geree (1672–1761), whom he had known at Moor Park. See Nichol Smith, *Letters of Swift to Ford*, p. 15, n. 4.

[2] Elwin quotes the letter from John Barber to Swift, 6 July 1714 (Ball, ii. 172), as indicating that Swift owed his wine to the intercession of Barber. What Barber got for Swift was 'two dozen of red French wine, and one dozen of strong Aaziana white wine'. These seem not to be 'Florence'.

[3] Speaker Hanmer was not much liked by Lord Oxford's friends. Much later Pope was to scorn him as editor of Shakespeare. See *Dunciad*, iv. 105–10.

[4] Why Swift's friend and faithful printer was 'burned out' is not clear.

of the Bill of Schisme,[1] and Several Specks upon the Proclamation for the Pretender.[2] I doubt not but these marks of his are mysticall, & that the Figures he makes this way are a significant Cypher to those who have the Skill to explain 'em—

That I may not conclude this Letter without Some Verses, take the following Epigram which Dr Parnelle & I composed as we rode toward the Dean in the mist of the morning, & is after the Scriblerian Manner. | I am with the truest | Esteem, Sir | Your most oblig'd Servant | A. Pope.

How foolish Men on Expeditions goe!
Unweeting Wantons of their wetting Woe!
For drizling Damps descend adown the Plain
And seem a thicker Dew, or thinner Rain;
Yet Dew or Rain may wett us to the shif[t]
We'll not be slow to visit Dr Swift.

Address: To | Dr Arbuthnott, at his | Lodgings in | St James's.

||POPE *to* CARYLL[3] [13] *July* [1714]

Add. 28618

Binfield, July

You mention the account I gave you a long while ago of the things which Philips said in his foolishness, but I can't tell from anything in your letter, whether you received a long one from me about a fortnight since. It was principally intended to thank you for the last obliging favour you did me, ⌜with regard to the subscriptions,⌝ and perhaps for that reason you pass it in silence. I there launched into some account of my temporal affairs, and intend now to give you some hints of my spiritual. The conclusion of your letter draws this upon you, where you tell me you prayed for me. Your proceeding, sir, is contrary to that of most other friends, who never talk of praying for a man after they have done him a service, but only when they will do him none. ⌜(And I find the person who has done me a kindness must be told of it by others; those who have not will say they have

[1] Within the month Bolingbroke had secured the passage of the Schism Act which forbade Noncoformists to serve as teachers of the youth. Bolingbroke's object was to embarrass Lord Oxford, whose ties with dissenters had been and remained close. It helped to secure the dismissal of Oxford on 27 July, excitement over which may have hastened the death of the Queen on 1 Aug. The Act was repealed in 1719.

[2] On 21 June a Proclamation was issued offering a reward of 5,000*l*. to anyone who should apprehend the Pretender whenever he should land in Great Britain.—Elwin.

[3] With a few small omissions, here placed in half-brackets, Pope printed this letter in the various editions, 1735–42. The text here is from the Caryll transcripts, though the date comes from the editions printed by Pope. Pope's revisions of his own texts are here unimportant. In 1735 he gave the letter the date of 13 July 1714.

themselves: I tell you therefore once more, I am obliged to no Roman Catholic but yourself, Mr Edward Blount and Mr Tho. Southcote.)⌝

Nothing can be more kind than the hint you give me of the vanity of human sciences, which I assure you I am daily more and more convinced of; and indeed I have for some years past looked upon all of 'em no better than amusements. To make them the ultimate end of our pursuit is a miserable and short ambition, which will drop from us at every little disappointment here, and even in case of no disappointment here will infallibly desert us hereafter. The utmost fame they are capable of bestowing is never worth the pains they cost us, and the time they lose us. If you attain the top of your desires that way, all those who envy you will do you harm, and [of] those who admire you, few will do you good. All unsuccessful writers are your declared enemies, and probably some successful ones your secret enemies; for those hate no more to be excelled than these to be rivalled. And ⌜then⌝ at the upshot, after a life of perpetual application, to reflect that you have been doing nothing for yourself, and that the same or less industry might have gained you a friendship that can never deceive or end, a satisfaction which praise cannot bestow, nor vanity feel, and a glory which (tho' in one respect like fame, not to be had 'till after death,) yet shall be felt and enjoyed to eternity. These, dear sir, are unfeignedly my sentiments, whenever I think at all; for half the things that employ our heads deserve not the name of thoughts, they are only stronger dreams or impressions upon the imagination; our schemes of government, our systems of philosophy, our golden words[1] of poetry, are all but so many shadow images and airy prospects, which arise to us but so much the livelier and more frequent as we are more overcast with the darkness, wrapt in the night, and disturbed with the fumes of human vanity.

The same thing that makes old men willing to leave this world, makes me willing to leave poetry. Long habit and weariness of the same track. Homer will work a cure upon me; fifteen thousand verses are equivalent to four-score years, to make me old in rhime. And I should be sorry and ashamed to go on gingling to the last step, like a waggoner's horse in the same road, to leave my bells to the next silly animal that will be proud of them. That man makes a mean figure in eyes of reason who is measuring of syllables and coupling rhimes, when he should be mending his own soul and securing his own immortality. If I had not this opinion, I should be unworthy even of those small limited parts which God has given me, and unworthy the friendship of such a man as you. I am ⌜ever | Dear sir | most affectionately | yours | A: P:⌝

⌜Sir, you will much oblige my father and me, in acquainting us how

[1] Words] worlds *1735–42*.

the affair of the rents in the Hôtel de Ville stand at present, since the alteration; and if there be any different consideration had to foreigners who put in money there, from those of France? Mr Arthur leaves us intirely in the dark in a matter that so much concerns us. Have those whose contracts were altered yet received the new ones? or is any of the rent lately paid? my father's extreme uneasiness must be my apology for this trouble. You guesed right at the cause of Ph[illips']s animosity.⌉

*POPE *to* FORD[1] [19 *July* 1714?]

The Pierpont Morgan Library

I have the plague of the Headake upon me, and write to you in my Anguish. You know it is natural to have recourse to our Friends in our Unhappiness, and I am at present too peevish to converse with any but by Letter. I confess, like a sinful Poet as I am, that I'm justly punishd in the Offending Part: but tho at all times when I write to You my Heart gets the better of my Head, yet it does so now in a particular manner, and you ought to believe all I shall say at this time because I speak with Tears in my Eyes. Tis plain I should not write to you under this circumstance, *Ni Te plus oculis meis amarem*, as Catullus[2] has it. You may expect I should express my Spleen against Poetry, complain about my Subscriptions, curse the Weather & rail at bad Wine: but I will own (as sick as I am) that I think Homer a very good Book, and those subscribers that have payd me very worthy Gentlemen; that England is an excellent Climate, especially in the Latitude of St. James's & Pallmall; and that French Claret is worth 3*s* 6*d* a Bottle, if one had Mr Ford's Company over it. But Dr Parnelle does not deserve the Liquor he has here, by himself, besides the Scandal he gives in a Popish Family by this seperate Communion.

I envy the Town and You excessively at this season. You walk the Streets Invisible, like Heroes, whom the Gods have encompast in a Veil of Clouds. You meet with no Disturbance in your Passage; but have the Noble Gratification of Ambition, to be at large with a great deal of Roome, or to be quite Alone. The great Ones of the Land have abandoned their Palaces to you, and the Queen herself will shortly fly from her Metropolitan City before you. Upon the whole, I cannot but highly applaud your generous Stay in London just at the Time when that grand Objection against the Town-Life, the Vice and Folly of it, is in a fair way to be removed by the Absence of so many thousands of the Wicked.

That we have seen the Dean, Dr Parnelle has informed you; that

[1] Printed by Nichol Smith in *Letters from Swift to Ford*, pp. 226–7. The date is that of the postmark.

[2] xiv. 1.

we long to see you I hope you need not to be informed by one who is so truly & so affectionately | Dear Sir | Your most obliged & most | faithful humble Servant | A. Pope

Pray is Mr Harcourt | in Towne? | The Dr's & my faithful | Service to Mr Lewis.[1]

Address: To | Charles Ford Esqr | at the Secretary's Office | in | Whitehall | London

Postmark: 19/IY

†POPE *to* CARYLL[2] 25 *July* 1714

1735

July 25, 1714.

I have no better excuse to offer you, that I have omitted a task naturally so pleasing to me as conversing upon paper with you; but that my time and eyes have been wholly employ'd upon *Homer*, whom I almost fear I shall find but one way of imitating, which is, in his blindness. I am perpetually afflicted with headach's, that very much affect my sight; and indeed since my coming hither[3] I have scarce past an hour agreeably, except that in which I read your letter. I would seriously have you think, you have no man who more truly knows to place a right value on your friendship, than he who least deserves it on all other accounts than his due sense of it. But let me tell you, you can hardly guess what a task you undertake, when you profess your self my friend; there are some *Tories* who will take you for a *Whig*, some *Whigs* who will take you for a *Tory*, some *Protestants* who will esteem you a rank *Papist*, and some *Papists* who will acount you a *Heretick.*

I find by dear experience, we live in an age, where it is criminal to be moderate; and where no man can be allowed to be just to all men. The notions of right and wrong are so far strain'd, that perhaps to be in the right so very violently, may be of worse consequence than to be easily and quietly in the wrong. I really wish all men so well, that I am satisfied but few can wish me so; but if those few are such as tell me they do, I am content, for they are the best people I know: While you believe me what I profess as to Religion, I can bear any thing the bigotted may say; while Mr. *Congreve* likes my poetry, I can endure *Dennis* and a thousand more like him; while the most honest and

[1] Erasmus Lewis (1670–1754) was a close friend to Jonathan Swift, and a favourite member of Swift's Tory circle. His patron was the first Earl of Oxford, and during the Tory Ministry (1711–14) he was Under-Secretary of State. See *DNB*.

[2] This letter, not found among the Caryll transcripts, is printed in all Pope's editions among the letters 'To the Honourable——'. The variants in Pope's texts are negligible.

[3] *Hither* doubtless means Binfield. It is interesting that Pope seldom mentions Swift in these early letters to Caryll, and one would never guess that Pope and Parnell are just back from visiting Swift at Letcombe.

moral of each party think me no ill man, I can easily support it, tho' the most violent and mad of all parties rose up to throw dirt at me.

I must expect an hundred attacks upon the publication of my *Homer*. Whoever in our times would be a professor of learning above his fellows, ought at the very first to enter the world with the constancy and resolution of a primitive Christian, and be prepared to suffer all sort of publick Persecution. It is certainly to be lamented, that if any man does but endeavour to distinguish himself, or gratify others by his studies, he is immediately treated as a common enemy, instead of being looked upon as a common friend; and assaulted as generally, as if his whole design were to prejudice the State, and ruin the publick. I will venture to say, no man ever rose to any degree of perfection in writing, but through obstinacy and an inveterate resolution against the stream of mankind: So that if the world has receiv'd any benefit from the labours of the Learned, it was in its own despite. For when first they essay their parts, all people in general are prejudiced against new beginners; and when they have got a little above contempt, then some particular persons who were before unfortunate in their own attempts, are sworn foes to them only because they succeed.—Upon the whole, one may say of the best writers, that they pay a severe fine for their fame, which it is always in the power of the most worthless part of mankind to levy upon them when they please. | I am, &c.

†POPE *to* JERVAS[1] 28 *July* 1714

1735

July 28, 1714.

I am just enter'd upon the old way of life again, sleep and musing. It is my employment to revive the old of past ages to the present, as it is yours to transmit the young of the present, to the future. I am copying the great Master in one art, with the same love and diligence with which the Painters hereafter will copy you in another.

Thus I should begin my Epistle to you, if it were a *Dedicatory* one. But as it is a friendly letter, you are to find nothing mention'd in your own praise but what only one in the world is witness to, your particular good-natur'd offices to me. Whatever mankind in general would allow you, that I am not to give you to your face; and if I were to do it in your absence, the world would tell me I am too partial to be permitted to pass any judgment of you.[2]

So you see me cut out from any thing but common acknowledgements, or common discourse. The first you wou'd take ill, tho' I told you but half what I ought; so in short the last only remains.

[1] Published in all Pope's editions.

[2] This sentence is omitted in 1737 and thereafter, and the next sentence then begins (without paragraphing) 'I am cut out . . .'.

And as for the last, what can you expect from a man who has not talk'd these five days? who is withdrawing his thoughts as far as he can, from all the present world, its customs and its manners, to be fully possest and absorpt in the past? When people talk of going to Church, I think of Sacrifices and libations; when I see the parson, I address him as *Chryses* priest of *Apollo*; and instead of the Lord's Prayer, I begin

— God of the silver Bow, &c.

While you in the world are concerned about the *Protestant* Succession, I consider only how *Menelaus* may recover *Helen*, and the *Trojan* war be put to a speedy conclusion. I never inquire if the Queen be well or not,[1] but heartily wish to be at *Hector*'s funeral.[2] The only things I regard in this life, are, whether my friends are well? whether my Translation go well on? whether *Dennis* be writing criticisms? whether any body will answer him, since I don't? and whether *Lintott* be not yet broke? | I am, &c.

WILLIAM ROLLINSON *to* POPE[3] [6 *or* 13 *August* 1714]

Homer MSS. Add. 4807

Fryday morning.

The Venison came last night, a day sooner than I expected it, and the hot weather ha[s] proved so unlucky for carriage that I fear the Haunch will hardly keep sweet [be]yond this day, whereupon I could fret my [self] heartily, and offer you an apology, if [eithe]r were to the purpose, but you must know [I ha]ve found vexation to be a great breeder [of ma]ggots.

If you'l contrive to let me know what day you set forwards I'l be at Oxford the same night. I have long sett my heart upon being merry with you there, & as I am well acquainted with the place I can help you to all the diversions it affords. Dear Sir, | Your very affectionate | Wm Rollinson

Address: To Mr Pope. | These

POPE *to* CARYLL[4] 16 *August* 1714

Add. 28618

Binfield. August 16. 1714.

I think it very long since I had the pleasure and satisfaction of a line

[1] She died 1 Aug.

[2] i.e. at the end of the *Iliad*.

[3] The year is inferred from the placing of the letter in the Homer MSS., and the particular Friday can be nearly deduced from the mention of the trip to Oxford.

William Rollinson was a London merchant, who having made his fortune, retired to live in Oxfordshire. Pope left him £5 in his will, 'to be laid out in a ring or any other memorial'. —Elwin.

[4] Parts of this letter were curiously rearranged and transferred to a letter printed as to Edward Blount under date of 27 Aug. 1714 (q.v.).

of yours. I sent you an epistle three weeks ago,[1] soon after another of mine wherein I entreated the solution of a question from my father concerning a foreign affair of his. I have been told you had some thoughts of a journey this latter season, which I coud be glad to be informed of that I may regulate my motions accordingly; for the chief happiness I hoped for this autumn was to have passed a week or two at Ladyholt. The task I undergo tho'[2] of weight enough in itself, has met with a voluntary increase in my prosecution of it by the enlarging my design of the notes and observations; and the necessity of a certain number of books about me[3] has confined me very much here, tho' I could not but take a trip to London on the death of the Queen,[4] moved by the common curiosity of mankind, who leave their business to be looking upon other men's. I thank God that as for myself, I am below all the accidents of state-changes by my circumstances, and above them by my philosophy. Good will to all, are[5] the points I have most at heart; and I am sure those are not to be broken for the sake of any governors or government. I am willing to hope the best and that I more wish than my own or any particular man's advancement, that this turn may put an end entirely to the divisions of Whig and Tory, that those[6] parties may love each other as well as I love them both, or at least hurt each other as little as I would either; and that our own people may live as quietly as we shall certainly let theirs, that is to say, that want of power itself in us may not be a surer prevention of harm, than want of will in them. I am sure, if all Whigs and all Tories had the spirit of one Roman Catholic that I know, it would be well for all Roman Catholics; and if all Roman Catholics had ever had that spirit, it had been well for all others; and we had never been charged with so wicked a spirit as that of persecution. It is indeed very unjust to judge of us in this nation by what other members of our communion have done abroad. Our Church Triumphant there is very different from our Church Militant here (if I may call that a Church Militant which is every way disarmed). The greatest fear I have under the circumstances of a poor papist is the loss of my poor horse;[7] yet if they take

[1] The allusion is to the letter of 13 July, in which Pope spoke of the foreign affair. Since the date of 13 July came from the editions of 1735, and since Pope probably had to invent the date when printing, he may have affixed an earlier date than he should. If he had dated it 28 July, it would have fitted very well—but he did not.

[2] The scribe wrote *who* for *tho*.

[3] This sentence is transformed in the fabricated letter to Blount, where the necessity of books instead of confining Pope to Binfield has driven him to Oxford.

[4] The political passage on the death of the Queen and the state of parties is used in the letter to Blount, beginning 'I could not but take a trip', and ending with 'as that of Persecution'.

[5] The scribe here is responsible for the bad grammar. Pope's printed text, plausibly authentic here, reads: 'Common charity of man to man, and universal good will to all, are the points . . .'.

[6] For *those* the scribe wrote *they*.

[7] Anti-Catholic laws passed upon the accession of William and Mary were likely to be

it away, I may say with the resignation of Job, tho' not in his very words, *Deus dedit*, *Diabolus abstulit*, I thank God I can walk. If I had a house and they took it away, I could go into lodgings; if I had money and they took it away, I could write for my bread (as much better men than I have been often suffered to do); if my own works would not do, I could turn writing master at last and set copies to children.[1] I remember what Horace said of fortune—

> Si celeres quatit
> Pennas, refigio[2] quæ dedit, et mea
> Virtute me involvo, probamque
> Pauperiem sine dote quæro.

Whatever befalls me, I only desire to keep my own integrity and your love. The rest I leave to Heaven.

I beg the favour of a letter, and am, with the most real and most lasting esteem and affection, | Dear sir | Your obliged, faithful friend | and servant. | A: P:

Dear Sir, Just after writing this, yours came to my hands and was extremely welcome, even tho' it acquainted me of our misfortune,[3] which I am very sorry Mr John Caryll shares with me. Yet under any misfortune, the knowledge that you remember me as a friend will be one of my best consolations.

I am very sorry not to be in London for the only reason you give me to wish myself there, to wait upon Lady Mary,—which I should think the greatest happiness next to waiting upon you. Since you think to be alone, I am inclined to defer my visit to you till towards winter, that I may be able to stay longer (if you will give me leave). It is thought almost necessary to my health to go to the Bath, which I will not however do, unless I am assured of your company afterwards. Believe me more than I can express | Dear sir | Yours

reinvoked now that the death of Queen Anne might bring the succession again in question. One such law forbade Catholics to own a horse that was worth more than £5. Pope mentions his fear for his horse, since it was a gift from Caryll.

[1] Pope had considerable gifts in calligraphy. The manuscript of his Pastorals is beautifully done. For sarcastic comment on his skill with his pen see the second of two letters from Lady Mary Wortley Montagu to Dr. Arbuthnot, here printed (iii. 60) as of Oct. 1729.

[2] *refigio* for *resigno*, a scribal error. See Horace, *Carmina*, III. xxix. 53–56.

[3] The misfortune was the information that the edict which reduced the interest upon the French national debt made no difference between natives and foreigners.—Elwin.

†POPE *to* JERVAS[1] 16 *August* 1714

1735

Aug. 16, 1714.

I thank you for your good offices which are numberless. *Homer* advances so fast, that he begins to look about for the ornaments he is to appear in, like a modish modern author,—

—Picture in the front,
With bays and wicked ryme upon 't.

I have the greatest proof in nature at present of the amusing power of Poetry, for it takes me up so intirely that I scarce see what passes under my nose, and hear nothing that is said about me. To follow Poetry as one ought, one must forget father and mother, and cleave to it alone. My *Rêverie* has been so deep, that I have scarce had an interval to think my self uneasy in the want of your company. I now and then just miss you as I step into bed; this minute indeed I want extremely to see you, the next I shall dream of nothing but the taking of *Troy*, or the recovery of *Briseis*.

I fancy no friendship is so likely to prove lasting as ours, because I am pretty sure there never was a friendship of so easie a nature. We neither of us demand any mighty things from each other; what Vanity we have expects its gratification from other people. It is not I, that am to tell you what an Artist you are, nor is it you that are to tell me what a Poet I am; but 'tis from the world abroad we hope, (piously hope) to hear these things. At home we follow our business, when we have any; and think and talk most of each other when we have none. 'Tis not unlike the happy friendship of a stay'd man and his wife, who are seldom so fond as to hinder the business of the house from going on all day, or so indolent as not to find consolation in each other every evening. Thus well-meaning couples hold in amity to the last, by not expecting too much from human nature; while romantick friendships, like violent loves, begin with disquiets, proceed to jealousies, and conclude in animosities. I have liv'd to see the fierce advancement, the sudden turn, and the abrupt period, of three or four of these enormous friendships, and am perfectly convinc'd of the truth of a Maxim we once agreed in, That nothing hinders the constant agreement of people who live together, but meer vanity; a secret insisting upon what they think their dignity or merit, and an inward expectation of such an Over-measure of deference and regard, as answers to their own extravagant false scale; and which no body can pay, because none but themselves can tell, exactly, to what pitch it amounts? | I am, &c.

[1] Printed in all Pope's editions without notable changes in the text.

†JERVAS *to* POPE[1] 20 *August* 1714

1735

Aug. 20, 1714.

I have a particular to tell you at this time, which pleases me so much, that you must expect a more than ordinary alacrity in every turn. You know I cou'd keep you in suspence for twenty lines, but I will tell you directly that Mr. *Addison* and I have had a conversation, that it would have been worth your while to have been plac'd behind the wainscot, or behind some half-length Picture[2] to have heard. He assured me that he wou'd make use not only of his interest, but of his art to do you some service; he did not mean his Art of Poetry, but his Art at Court; and he is sensible that nothing can have a better air for himself, than moving in your favour, especially since insinuations were spread that he did not care you shou'd prosper too much as a Poet. He protests that it shall not be his fault if there is not the best intelligence in the world, and the most hearty friendship, *&c.* He owns, he was afraid Dr. *Swift* might have carry'd you too far among the enemy during the heat of the animosity, but now all is safe, and you are escap'd even in his opinion. I promis'd in your name, like a good Godfather, not that you should renounce the devil and all his works, but that you would be delighted to find him your friend merely for his own sake; therefore prepare your self for some civilities.[3]

I have done *Homer*'s head,[4] shadow'd and heighten'd carefully; and I inclose the outline of the same size, that you may determine whether you wou'd have it so large, or reduc'd to make room for feuillage or laurel round the oval, or about the square of the Busto? Perhaps there is something more solemn in the Image itself, if I can get it well perform'd.

If I have been instrumental in bringing you and Mr. *Addison* together with all sincerity, I value my self upon it as an acceptable piece of service to such a one as I know you to be. | Your, &c.

†POPE *to* JERVAS 27 *August* 1714

1735

Aug. 27. 1714.

I am just arriv'd from *Oxford*, very well diverted and entertain'd there —all very honest fellows[5]—much concern'd for the Queen's death. No panegyricks ready yet for the King.

[1] Printed without verbal changes in all Pope's editions.

[2] Evidently a remark ventured facetiously concerning Pope's height of 4 feet 6 inches.

[3] Addison's 'civilities' probably consisted of efforts to control the pens of the 'Little Senate' who were already attacking Pope.

[4] The frontispiece for volume i of the *Iliad*.

[5] In the editions of 1737–42 Pope ceased to compliment the Oxonians by omitting this phrase—not omitted in malice, one trusts, but to avoid a certain tone of patronage.

I admire your *Whig-principles* of Resistance exceedingly, in the spirit of the *Barcelonians.* I joyn in your wish for them. Mr. *Addison*'s verses on Liberty, ⌜in his letter from *Italy*⌝,[1] would be a good form of prayer in my opinion, *O Liberty! thou Goddess heavenly bright!* &c.[2]

What you mention'd of the friendly office you endeavour'd to do betwixt Mr. *Addison* and me, deserves acknowledgments on my part. You thoroughly know my regard to his character and my propensity to testify it by all ways in my power. You as thoroughly know the scandalous meanness of that proceeding which was used by *Philips*, to make a man I so highly value, suspect my dispositions toward him. But as, after all, Mr. *Addison* must be the judge in what regards himself, and has seem'd to be no very just one to me; so I must own to you I expect nothing but civility from him, how much soever I wish for his friendship: And as for any offices of real kindness or service which it is in his power to do me, I should be asham'd to receive 'em from any man who had no better opinion of my morals, than to think me a party-man; nor of my temper, than to believe me capable of maligning or envying another's reputation as a Poet. So I leave it to time to convince him as to both, to shew him the shallow depths of those half-witted creatures who mis-inform'd him, and to prove that I am incapable of endeavouring to lessen a person whom I would be proud to imitate, and therefore asham'd to flatter. In a word, Mr. *Addison* is sure of my respect at all times, and of my real friendship whenever he shall think fit to know me for what I am.

For all that pass'd betwixt Dr. *Swift* and me, you know the whole (without reserve) of our correspondence: The engagements I had to him were such as the actual services he had done me, in relation to the subscription for *Homer*, obliged me to. I must have leave to be grateful to him, and to any one who serves me, let him be never so obnoxious to any party: nor did the *Tory-party* ever put me to the hardship of asking this leave, which is the greatest obligation I owe to it; and I expect no greater from the *Whig-party* than the same liberty.——A curse on the word *Party*, which I have been forc'd to use so often in this period! I wish the present Reign may put an end to the distinction, that there may be no other for the future than that of honest and knave, fool and man of sense; these two sorts must always be enemies, but for the rest, may all people do as you and I, believe what they please and be friends. | I am, &c.

[1] Omitted in the quarto and folio of 1737.

[2] Lines 119–40.

‡POPE *to* EDWARD BLOUNT[1] 27 *August* 1714

1735

Aug. 27. 1714.

⌜Whatever studies on the one hand, or amusements on the other, it shall be my fortune to fall into, I shall be equally incapable of forgetting you in any of 'em.⌝ The Task I undertook,[2] tho' of weight enough in itself, has had a voluntary increase, by the inlarging my design of the *Notes*; and the necessity of consulting a number of books has carry'd me to *Oxford*: ⌜But I fear, thro' my Lord *Harcourt*'s and Dr. *Clark*'s[3] means, I shall be more conversant with the pleasures and company of the place, than with the Books and Manuscripts of it.⌝

⌜I find still more reason to complain of the negligence of the Geographers in their Maps of *old Greece*, since I look'd upon two or three more noted names in the publick libraries here. But with all the care I am capable of, I have some cause to fear the Engraver will prejudice me in a few situations. I have been forced to write to him in so high a style, that were my epistle intercepted, it would raise no small admiration in an ordinary man. There is scarce an order in it of less importance, than to remove such and such mountains, alter the course of such and such rivers, place a large city on such a coast, and raze another in another country. I have set bounds to the sea, and said to the land, *thus far shalt thou advance and no further*.[4] In the mean time, I who talk and command at this rate, am in danger of losing my horse,[5] and stand in some fear of a country justice. To disarm me indeed may be but prudential, considering what armies I have at present on foot, and in my service: a hundred thousand *Grecians* are no contemptible body; for all that I can tell, they may be as formidable as four thousand *Priests*; and they seem proper forces to send against those in *Barcelona*.[6] That siege deserves as fine a poem as the *Iliad*, and the machining part of poetry would be the juster in it, as they say the inhabitants expect Angels from heaven to their assistance. May I venture to say, who

[1] This letter is presumably a conflation of at least two letters, one of which is that existing in the Caryll transcripts under date of 16 Aug., and here already printed. The rest of the material may come from a letter actually sent to Blount or from some other source. Passages here placed in half-brackets are not found in the letter to Caryll. Pope seems to be writing from Oxford, a fact not apparent in the Caryll letter. In a letter to Jervas of this same day he announces his return from Oxford.

[2] The Translation of *Homer's Iliad*.—Pope, 1735–42.

[3] Dr. George Clarke (1661–1736), Fellow of All Souls, a notable collector of books, manuscripts, and *objets d'art*. He held various government posts and was Member of Parliament for the University of Oxford, 1717–36, a Tory unacceptable to extreme Jacobites. See Ayre's *Life of Pope* (1745), ii. 22, for an anecdote about religious argument.

[4] This relates to the Map of ancient *Greece*, laid down by our Author in his Observations on the second *Iliad*.—Pope, 1735–42.

[5] The fear of losing his horse is mentioned in the Caryll letter of 16 Aug.

[6] Barcelona had been besieged for more than a year before the date of this letter. Fighting was violent in August, and the city fell on 11 Sept. 1714.

am a *Papist*, and to say to you who are a *Papist*, that nothing is more astonishing to me, than that people so greatly warm'd with a sense of Liberty, should be capable of harbouring such weak Superstition, and that so much bravery and so much folly, can inhabit the same breasts?⌉

[1]I could not but take a trip to *London*, on the death of the *Queen*, mov'd by the common curiosity of mankind, who leave their own business to be looking upon other men's. I thank God that as for my self, I am below all the accidents of State-changes by my circumstances, and above them by my philosophy. Common charity of man to man, and universal good will to all, are the points I have most at heart; and I am sure those are not to [be][2] broken for the sake of any governors, or government. I am willing to hope the best, and what I more wish than my own or any particular man's advancement, is, that this turn may put an end entirely to the division of *Whig* and *Tory*; that the parties may love each other as well as I love them both; or at least hurt each other as little as I would either; and that our own people may live as quietly as we shall certainly let theirs; that is to say, that want of *power* it self in us may not be a surer prevention of harm, than want of *will* in them. I am sure if all *Whigs* and all *Tories* had the spirit of one *Roman-Catholick* that I know, it would be well for all *Roman-Catholicks*; and if all *Roman-Catholicks* had always had that spirit, it had been well for all others, and we had never been charg'd with so wicked a spirit as that of Persecution.

⌈I agree with you in my sentiment of the state of our nation since this change: I find my self just in the same situation of mind you describe as your own, heartily wishing the good, that is the quiet of my country, and hoping a total end of all the unhappy divisions of mankind by party-spirit, which at best is but the madness of many for the gain of a few.⌉[3] I am, &c.

†EDWARD BLOUNT *to* POPE [*September* 1714?]

1737

It is with a great deal of pleasure I see your letter, dear Sir, written in a stile that shows you full of health, and in the midst of diversions: I think those two things necessary to a man who has such undertakings in hand as yours. All lovers of Homer are indebted to you for taking so much pains about the situation of his Hero's kingdoms;[4] it will not

[1] This paragraph comes bodily from the letter to Caryll of 16 Aug.

[2] The word is supplied from the errata printed in the *Letters* in 1735 a2.

[3] In the *Miscellanies*, ii (1727), 338, the first of Pope's 'Thoughts on Various Subjects' became 'Party is the madness of many for the gain of a few'.

[4] The chief English eighteenth-century authority on Homeric geography, Robert Wood, in his *Essay on the Original Genius and Writing of Homer* (1769), as one might expect, found Pope's maps very faulty.

only be of great use with regard to his works, but to all that read any of the Greek Historians; who generally are ill understood thro' the difference of the maps as to the places they treat of, which makes one think one author contradicts another. You are going to set us right; and 'tis an advantage every body will gladly see you engross the glory of.

You can draw rules to be free and easy, from formal pedants; and teach men to be short and pertinent, from tedious commentators. However, I congratulate your happy deliverance from such authors, as you (with all your humanity) cannot wish alive again to converse with. Critics will quarrel with you, if you dare to please without their leave; and Zealots will shrug up their shoulders at a man, that pretends to get to Heaven out of their form, dress, and diet. I would no more make a judgment of an author's genius from a damning critic, than I would of a man's religion from an unsaving zealot.

I could take great delight in affording you the new glory of making a Barceloniad (if I may venture to coin such a word) I fancy you would find a juster parallel than it seems at first sight; for the Trojans too had a great mixture of folly with their bravery: and I am out of countenance for them when I read the wise result of their council, where after a warm debate between Antenor and Paris about restoring Helen, Priam sagely determines that they shall to to supper. And as for the Greeks, what can equal their superstition in sacrificing an innocent lady?

Tantum Religio potuit, &c.[1]

I have a good opinion of my politicks, since they agree with a man who always thinks so justly as you. I wish it were in our power to persuade all the nation into as calm and steady a disposition of mind.

We have receiv'd the late melancholy news, with the usual ceremony of condoling in one breath for the loss of a gracious Queen, and in another rejoycing for an illustrious King. My views carry me no farther, than to wish the peace and welfare of my country; and my morals and politicks teach me to leave all that to be adjusted by our representatives above, and to divine providence. It is much at one to you and me who sit at the helm, provided they will permit us to sail quietly in the great ship. Ambition is a vice that is timely mortify'd in us poor Papists; we ought in recompence to cultivate as many virtues in our selves as we can, that we may be truely great. Among my Ambitions, that of being a sincere friend is one of the chief; yet I will confess that I have a secret pleasure to have some of my descendants know, that their Ancestor was great with Mr. Pope. I am, &c.

[1] Lucretius, i. 101.

*PARNELL *and* POPE *to* FORD[1] 2 *September* 1714

The Pierpont Morgan Library

Binfield Sept: 2 1714.

We whose names will soon be underwritten do thank you for the Letter which you were pleasd to send us from your office, & which we receivd, just at the minute we had promisd our selves. It was unhappy that we did not meet the Dean before he went,[2] & that he did not know he might still stay here. But I desire you woud explain to me still why I may stay, and how long. If I am oblidgd to take the oath in three months or six, if it will do here or in Ireland. I saw something concerning those who had offices and were in England, but I do not know if the words extend to Clergymen and livings; I believe the Provost is sure, lett me know what he does:

And now having finished buisness lett me tell you that the weather grows extream cold which is all the news of the country. I believe in town you are by this time pretty well crowded, State and the hopes of more State employ your thought, and Kings and Coronations in prospect are ever before you. Be pleasd however to descend from those high speculations to answer this letter soon. Then shall you see Gay returning from Hanover, Parnell from Binfield, and Pope following if he does not come along with him. Thus from various parts will we crowd in upon you, to eat your meat, drink your wine, and make nightcaps of your napkins, till warnd by the clock that strikes ten or one more, we retire from you, professing our selves, as we do now Your Affectionate friends and Humble servants | Tho Parnell | A. Pope.

Address: To Charles Ford Esq. at the | blue Perriwig next to the | George Tavern in Pall-Mall, | London.

Postmark: 3/SE

PARNELL *and* POPE *to* DR. ARBUTHNOT

2 *September* 1714

The Royal College of Surgeons of England

Binfield Sept: 2 1714

[Parnell]

Tho we have no buisness to write upon, yet while we have an intire wish to preserve the friendship you were pleasd to show us, we have allways an excuse for troubling you with a letter. It is a pleasure to us to recollect the Satisfaction we enjoyd in your company, when we usd

[1] First printed in *Letters of Swift to Ford* (ed. Nichol Smith, Oxford, 1935), p. 228. The text is in Parnell's hand; both men signed, and Pope addressed the letter.

[2] Swift left Letcombe 'in order to Ireld', as his endorsement of his letter from Ford of 16 Aug. indicates, on 16 Aug. He reached Dublin the 24th. See his letter to Ford (ed. Nichol Smith) of Sept. 1714 (p. 60). Evidently the departure was with little warning to any one—none to Pope or Parnell.

to meet the Dean & Gay with you, and Greatness it self[1] condescended to look in at the Door to us. Then it was that the immortall Scriblerus Smild upon our endeavours, who now hangs his head in an obscure corner, pining for his friends that are Scattering over the face of the earth. Yet art thou still if thou art alive O Scriblerus as deserving of our Lucubrations, tua sectus orbis nomina ducet,[2] still shall half the learned world be called after thy name. Forgive dear Sir this digression by way of Apostrophe to one whom we so much esteem, & be pleasd to lett us know whether indeed he be alive, that at least my wishes in learning may not be like Mr Popes[,] prayrs for the dead. We were lately in Oxford where we mett Mr Harcourt and drunk your health: we thought too to have seen the Dean but were surprizd to hear he was gon for Ireland so suddenly,[3] where I must soon think of following him. But where ever I am I shall still retain a Just Sence of your favours and acknowledge my self allways | Your Most Affectionate Friend and Servant | Tho: Parnell.

If it be proper to give my Duty to my Lord[4] & Mr Pope's—

[Pope]

Tho Dr Parnelle has pre-occupy'd the first Part of this Paper, and so seems to lead the way in this Address to you, yet I must tell you I have several times been inspiring him to joyn with me in a Letter to you, and been prevented by his delays for some posts. And tho' he mentions the name of Scriblerus to avoid my Reproaching him, yet is he conscious to himself how much the Memory of that Learned Phantome which is to be Immortal, is neglected by him at present. But I hope the Revolutions of State will not affect Learning so much as to deprive mankind of the Lucubrations of Martin, to the Encrease of which I will watch all next winter, and grow pale over the midnight Candle. Homer's Image begins already to vanish from before me.[5] The Season of the Campaigne before Troy is near over, and I rejoyce at the prospect of my Amusements in Winter-Quarters with You in London. Our friend Gay will still continue Secretary, to Martin at least,[6] tho I could be more glad he had a better master for his Profit, for his Glory he can have no better. You must not wonder I enlarge upon this head; the remembrance of our agreable Conferences, as well as our Occasional Honours, on your account, will ever dwell upon my thoughts with that Pleasure which I think one honest and

[1] Lord Oxford.

[2] Horace, *Carmina*, III. xxvii. 75–76.

[3] This remark makes it evident that at least part of the visit to Oxford postdated 16 Aug. when Swift left for Ireland.

[4] Presumably Lord Oxford; possibly Bolingbroke.

[5] i.e. Pope has practically completed work on vol. i of his *Iliad*.

[6] Gay had been secretary to the Duchess of Monmouth, and had resigned to become secretary of Lord Clarendon's embassy to Hanover, and was now at liberty, so to speak.

chearful man ought to take in being obliged to another. That we may again enjoy those Satisfactions is heartily my wish, & it is my request to you in the meantime that you will continue to think me, what I sincerely am, | Your most affect: & most faith- | ful humble Servant | A. Pope.

Address: To Dr Arbuthnott, | These

†DR. ARBUTHNOT *to* POPE[1] *7 September* 1714

1737

London, Sept. 7, 1714.

I am extreamly oblig'd to you for taking notice of a poor old distressed courtier, commonly the most despiseable thing in the world. This blow has so rous'd *Scriblerus* that he has recover'd his senses, and thinks and talks like other men. From being frolicksome and gay he is turn'd grave and morose. His lucubrations lye neglected amongst old news-papers, cases, petitions, and abundance of unanswerable letters. I wish to God they had been amongst the papers of a noble Lord sealed up.[2] Then might Scriblerus have pass'd for the Pretender, and it would have been a most excellent and laborious work for the Flying Post[3] or some such author, to have allegoriz'd all his adventures into a plot, and found out mysteries somewhat like the Key to the Lock.[4] Martin's office is now the second door on the left hand in Dover-street,[5] where he will be glad to see Dr. Parnell, Mr. Pope, and his old friends, to whom he can still afford a half pint of claret. It is with some pleasure that he contemplates the world still busy, and all mankind at work for him. I have seen a letter from Dean Swift; he keeps up his noble spirit, and tho' like a man knock'd down, you may behold him still with a stern countenance, and aiming a blow at his adversaries. I will add no more, being in hast, only that I will never forgive you if you don't use my foresaid house in Dover street with the same freedom as you did that in St. James's; for as our friendship was not begun upon the relation of a courtier, so I hope it will not end with it. I will always be proud to be reckon'd amongst the number of your friends and humble servants.

1 Found in all Pope's editions of 1737–42.

2 On 30 Aug. Lord Bolingbroke's office had been sealed up.

3 A leading Whig journal, 1695–1731.

4 Pope's *Key to the Lock*, a burlesque allegorization of his *Rape*, designed to ridicule political writing, was not published until Apr. 1715; but Swift's letter to Pope of 28 June 1715 shows that the *Key* was written before Swift left for Ireland and before the death of Queen Anne.

5 No longer royal physician, the doctor has removed from the palace to a house in Dover Street.

||POPE *to* MARTHA *and* TERESA BLOUNT[1]

[?*September* 1714]

Mapledurham

⌜Fair Ladies—(I would call ye Dear Ladies if I durst)⌝ I returned home as slow, and as contemplative, after I had parted from you, as my Lord ⌜B.⌝ himself retir'd from the Court, and Glory, to his ⌜melancholy⌝ Country Seat, and Wife, a week ago. I found here a dismal, desponding Letter from the Son of another great Courtier who expects the same fate, & who tells me the Great ones of the Earth will take it very kindly of the Mean ones, if they will favor them with a Visit by Daylight. With what joy would they lay down all their Schemes of Glory, did they but know You have the Generosity to drink their Healths once a day? as soon as they are fallen. Thus the Unhappy, by the sole merit of their Misfortunes, become the Care of Heaven and You.—I intended to have put this last into Verse, but in this Age of Ingratitude my best Friends forsake me, I mean my Rhimes—

I desire Mrs P⌜atty⌝ to stay her Stomach with these half hundred Plays, till I can procure her a Romance big enough to satisfie her great Soul with Adventures.[2] May she believe all the Passion & Tenderness exprest in them[3] to be but a faint Image of what I bear her, and may You (who read nothing) take the same truth upon hearing it from me; You will both injure me very much, if you don't think me a truer Friend than ever any Romantic Lover, or any Imitator of their Style, could be.

The Days of Beauty are as the Days of Greatness, and as long as[4] your Eyes make their Sunshine, all the World are your Adorers. I am one of those un-ambitious people who will love you Forty years hence, when your eyes begin to twinkle, in a Retirement,[5] for your own sakes,

[1] Printed by Pope 1735–42 among 'Letters to Several Ladies'. Parts here placed in half-brackets were omitted in Pope's texts, where he gives no indication as to the specific ladies addressed. Here printed from the original at Mapledurham. As to its date, one assumes that Pope is writing after his visit to Mapledurham. Lord Bolingbroke retired to Bucklebury and his (unloved) wife at the end of August when he was removed from office and his papers sealed up. Since Oxford had gone to the country earlier, it was perhaps the son of Lord Harcourt who desired Pope's visits by daylight.

[2] At this point Pope's printed text inserts the following sentence, not found in the original letter: 'As for Novels, I fear she can depend upon none from me but That of *my Life*, which I am still, as I have been, contriving all possible methods to shorten, for the greater ease both of my Historian and the Reader.' (This sentence might sound more natural in 1735 than in 1714.)

[3] them] these Romances *1735–42*.

[4] as long as . . . all the World] so long all the World *1737–42*.

[5] At first Pope wrote 'will love you in a Retirement', and then added 'Forty years . . . twinkle' between the lines. Various phrases about greatness and retirement in this letter suggest phrases used in Pope's Epistle to Robert, Earl of Oxford, published at the end of 1721.

& without the Vanity which every one now will take to be thought | Your Admirer & humble Servant | A. Pope.

My faithful Service to Mrs Blount Mr Blount & Mr Holman.

Address: Au Mademoiselles, | Mademoiselles de Maple- | Durham.

*POPE *to* PARNELL — 13 *September* 1714

Arthur A. Houghton, Jr.

Sept. 13. 1714.

My dear Dr—I went for a Day and a half to Redding,[1] during which Time your Letter came to Binfield, and I had written to you without knowing it. I inclose an Epistle to our friend Mr Berkely whose Illness very much concerns me, I beg you to convey it to him. The Season presses so hard upon us that there is no Day to be lost if you intend for Bath; my Infirmities give me a dreadful prospect of suffering by [the] Weather at my return: I will not detain you 2 days at Oxford.

I thank you very heartily for the Care you testify of the Commissions I gave you to be done at London. But let not the Affair of Sir John Stanley[2] detain you to the prejudice of your health. Leave it to Mr Jervas or recommend it to Mr Harcourt or both. I have receivd your Batrachomuomachia.[3]

Not having heard from you since Wensday, I begin to be in apprehensions for your Welfare. Pray ease me by an account of it, & let me see you speedily.

Be so kind as to assure Dr Arbuthnot, Mr Ford, & Mr Lewis of my most hearty Service. I envy you the Enjoyments of cold chicken and clean Nightcaps in the Pall Mall. I am wrapt up in dull Critical Learning, & have the Headake every Evening. My Father & Mother are impatient for your return; in a coach or two more I shall be spleenatic. Dull I am already, & must be whenever you are absent.

Is Gay come over?[4] Shall we see him here, or when? What can [you s]ay to express how much we both love him? What can I [s]ay to express how much you are loved by | My Dear friend | Your affectionate faithful | Servant | A: Pope.

My most hearty Love | to Mr Jervas.
Could we get Gay with us to Bath?

Address: To the Reverend | Dr Parnelle, at the | Pall Mall Coffehouse in | Pall Mall | London.

[1] Very likely to visit at Mapledurham. [2] One of the subscribers to the *Iliad*.
[3] Published by Pope in May 1717. See Sherburn, *Early Career*, pp. 141, 173, 191.
[4] i.e. returned from Hanover. Gay returned while Pope and Parnell were at Bath. See Pope to Gay, 23 Sept. 1713.

†POPE *to* GAY 23 *September* 1714

1735

Sept. 23, 1714.

Dear Mr. Gay,—Welcome to your native Soil![1] welcome to your Friends! thrice welcome to me! whether return'd in glory, blest with Court-interest, the love and familiarity of the Great, and fill'd with agreeable Hopes; or melancholy with Dejection, contemplative of the changes of Fortune, and doubtful for the future: Whether return'd a triumphant *Whig* or a desponding *Tory*, equally All Hail! equally beloved and welcome to me! If happy, I am to share in your elevation; if unhappy, you have still a warm corner in my heart, and a retreat at *Binfield* in the worst of times at your service. If you are a *Tory*, or thought so by any man, I know it can proceed from nothing but your Gratitude to a few people who endeavour'd to serve you, and whose Politicks were never your Concern. If you are a *Whig*, as I rather hope, and as I think your Principles and mine (as Brother Poets) had ever a Byas to the Side of Liberty, I know you will be an honest man and an inoffensive one. Upon the whole, I know you are incapable of being so much of either Party as to be good for nothing. Therefore once more, whatever you are, or in whatever state you are, all hail!

One or two of your old Friends complain'd they had heard nothing from you since the *Queen*'s death; I told 'em, no man living loved Mr. *Gay* better than I, yet I had not once written to him in all his Voyage. This I thought a convincing proof, how truly one may be a friend to another without telling him so every month. But they had reasons too themselves to alledge in your excuse, as men who really value one another will never want such as make their friends and themselves easy. The late universal Concern in publick affairs, threw us all into a hurry of Spirits; even I who am more a Philosopher than to expect any thing from any Reign, was born away with the current, and full of the expectation of the Successor: During your Journeys I knew not whither to aim a letter after you, that was a sort of shooting flying: add to this the demand *Homer* had upon me, to write fifty Verses a day, besides learned Notes, all which are at a conclusion for this year.[2]

[1] Pope writes from Bath to welcome Gay home from his futile journey to Hanover. The date of the letter must be questionable; for here Pope is at Bath and shows no sign of weariness, and in the letter to Caryll that follows (25 Sept. 1714) he has just arrived on the evening of the 25th and is very weary. Neither date is far wrong so far as the day of the month is concerned. Since Caryll erred in his year, he may also have erred in the day; but it must be remembered that Pope habitually did not date letters in full, and these dates, both of them, may have been added long after the letter was written.

[2] What follows beginning *Rejoice with me* and ending with *kicked his Rosalind* was omitted in the decorous quarto and folio of 1737. The parts in half-brackets were omitted in the octavos 1737–42. In 1737 (octavos) the sentence about the Blouzelindas became and thereafter remained: 'Are not the Rosalinda's of Britain as charming as the Blousalinda's of the Hague?'

Rejoice with me, O my Friend, that my Labour is over; come and make merry with me in much Feasting, ⌜for I to thee and thou to me⌝. We will feed among the Lillies. By the Lillies I mean the Ladies, ⌜with whom I hope you have fed to satiety: Hast thou passed through many Countries, and not tasted the delights thereof? Hast thou not left of thy Issue in divers Lands, that *German Gays* and *Dutch Gays* may arise, to write Pastorals and sing their Songs in strange Countries?⌝ Are not the *Blouzelinda*'s of the *Hague* as charming as the *Rosalinda*'s of *Britain*? or have the two great Pastoral Poets of our Nation renounced Love at the same time? for *Philips*, immortal *Philips*, ⌜*Hanover Philips*,⌝ hath deserted, yea and in a rustick manner kicked his *Rosalind*.——Dr. *Parnelle* and I have been inseperable ever since you went. We are now at the *Bath*, where (if you are not, as I heartily hope, better engaged) your coming would be the greatest pleasure to us in the world. Talk not of Expences: *Homer* shall support his Children. I beg a line from you directed to the Posthouse in *Bath*. Poor *Parnelle* is in an ill state of health.

Pardon me if I add a word of advice in the Poetical way. Write something on the King, or Prince, or Princess. On whatsoever foot you may be with the Court, this can do no harm——I shall never know where to end, and am confounded in the many things I have to say to you, tho' they all amount to this, that I am entirely, as ever, | Your, &c.

POPE *to* CARYLL 25 *September* [1714]

Add. 28618

Bath Sept. 25th 1715 [1]

I deferred my returning an answer to your most kind letter till I came to this place, which I thought would have been before this time, but my companion Dr Parnelle retarded my journey till now. I am this evening arrived extremely weary, and new to all the wonders of the place. I have stared at the Bath, and sneaked along the walks, with that astonished and diffident air which is natural to a modest and ignorant Foreigner. We have scarce any company of figure, no lampoons dispersed, and not a face that promises any. As for my own part, my genius was never turned to that sort of satire, and if I had never so much natural malice, a laborious translation would extinguish all such impetuous emotions. I should be in Dryden's case, of whom it was said:

> He turned the malice of a spiteful satire
> To the safe innocence of a dull translator.

[1] The date of this letter, so far as the year goes, is certainly an error, for the letter describes a first visit to Bath in company with Parnell. Such a visit was made in Sept. 1714. Pope was also in Bath in 1715, but Parnell was not. The day of the month is wrong since Pope pretends to have arrived that evening, and he had written to Gay from Bath on the 23rd.

So that, upon the whole, I walk about here as innocently, and as little dreaded, as that old lion in satire, Mr Wycherley, who now goes tame about this town.[1] I named you to him, and [he] speaks such things of you (to give him his due) as may be heard by your friend with satisfaction. He that dares to despise the great ones of this age, to deny common sense to ministers of state, their small portion of wit to the poets who live by it, and honesty to the maids of fourteen, dares not refuse Mr Caryll his due.

How well the manner of life which all people are obliged to here will agree with my disposition I cannot tell. How far the necessary care of my health may coincide with a duty as indispensable to me at this time, that of finishing my year's task, or how far Homer may be the worse for my being better, are things I am under some doubt about. I hope to give a more reasonable account of myself when I pass a week or two at Ladyholt, where I propose to contrive it so as to meet you rather than at Grinsted, on account of the fear I have of that air in the winter. I see I scarce write common English or grammar at this time, and therefore ought to conclude. I have ten people round me at a tavern-table, and more noise than will agree with my brains, especially when my head aches, as it does after this day's journey. But I would not longer omit to take the occasion of assuring you of the old story, which will be a true one as long as I live that I am unfeignedly | Dear sir | Your most faithful obedient | affectionate servant | A: P:

||POPE *to* TERESA BLOUNT[2] *September* [1714]

Bowles (1806), vii. 182–4

Bath, Sept.

Madam,—I write to you for two reasons: one is because you commanded it, *which will be always a reason to me in any thing*; the other, because I sit at home to take physick, and they tell me I must do nothing that costs me great application *or great pains*, therefore I can neither say my prayers nor write verses. I am ordered to think but slightly of any thing, and I am practising if I can think so of you, which, if I can bring about, I shall be above regarding any thing in nature for the future: I may then think of the world as a hazle nut, the sun as a spangle, and the king's coronation as a puppet-show. When

[1] The mention of Wycherley shows that Pope and he had in some measure at least continued their friendship.

[2] This letter was published, with the paragraphs rearranged and some phrases changed or omitted, by Pope in 1735. Bowles in 1806 printed the original form in a footnote to Pope's version (Bowles, vii. 182–4). He printed from a transcript apparently by Chalmers, which is here reproduced, since the original is not now at Mapledurham.

The date of the letter is fixed by the fact that only in September of 1714 were Pope and Parnell together at Bath.

my physick makes me remember those I love, may it not be said to work kindly? (Hide I beseech you this pun from Miss Patty, who hates them in compliance to the taste of a noble earl, whose *modesty* makes him detest double-meanings.)

Pray tell that Lady, all the good qualities and virtuous inclinations she has, never gave me so much pleasure in her conversation, as that one vice of her obstinacy will give me mortification this month. Ratcliffe[1] commands her to the Bath, and she refuses! Indeed, if I were in Berkshire, I should honour her for this obstinacy, and magnify her no less for disobedience than we do the Barcelonians:[2] I should be charmed with this glorious rebel to Ratcliffe, whom all the great and fair obey as a Tyrant, and from the same servile principle, the fear of death. But people change with the change of places (as we see of late), and virtues become vices when they cease to be for one's interest, with me as with other folks.

Yet let me tell her, she will never look so finely while she is upon earth, as she would in the water. It is not here as in most other instances, but those Ladies that would please extremely must go out of their own element. She does not make half so good a figure on horseback as Christina Queen of Sweden; but were she once seen in the Bath, no man would part with her for the best mermaid in Christendom. Ladies, I have seen you often, I perfectly know how you look in black and white, I have experienced the utmost you can do in *any* colours; but all your movements, all your graceful steps, all your *attitudes* and postures, deserve not half the glory you might here attain, of a moving and easy behaviour in buckram: something betwixt swimming and walking, free enough, yet more modestly-half-naked than you appear any where else. You have conquered enough already by land; show your ambition, and vanquish also by water. We have no pretty admirals on these seas, but must strike sail to your white flags were they once hoisted up. The buckram I mention is a dress particularly useful at this time, when the princess is bringing over the fashion of German ruffs: you ought to use yourselves to some degrees of stiffness before-hand; and when our ladies chins have been tickled a-while with starched muslin and wires, *they may possibly bear the brush of a German beard and whisker.*

Having told you that I am here, I will acquaint you how I got hither: Dr. Parnelle detained me at Binfield some days longer than I proposed when I left Mapledurham,[3] though he came to the country on the day of his appointment. We gave the slip to every body, as you

[1] Dr. John Radcliffe.

[2] On the siege of Barcelona see Pope to Edward Blount, 27 Aug. 1714.

[3] See Pope to Parnell, 13 Sept. 1714, for evidence that Pope had very recently returned from Reading (Mapledurham).

may imagine, when we could pass by your house within two miles of it. The gay Archdeacon had violent yearnings towards you. Thrice he stopped his steed, and thrice he spurred him away; love and inclination pushed him on, but despair withheld: not to add, that the very hairs of his beard stood on end with fear of your eyes; that is to say, he was not shaved. Had he given the parting salute, it had been the most masculine one you ever received. As for me I had the like palpitation of heart towards your sister, for it happened on a day when I defied you and all your works.

You are to understand, Madam, that my *violent* passion for your fair self and your sister has been divided with the most wonderful regularity in the world. Even from my infancy I have been in love with one after the other of you, week by week; and my journey to Bath fell out in the three hundred seventy-sixth week of the reign of my sovereign Lady Martha. At the present writing hereof, it is the three hundred eighty-ninth week of the reign of your most serene majesty, in whose service I was listed some weeks before I beheld her. This information will account for my writing to either of you hereafter, as she shall happen to be Queen Regent at that time.

I could tell you a most delightful story of Dr. Parnelle, but want room to display it in all its shining circumstances. He had heard it was an excellent cure for love, to kiss the Aunt of the person beloved, who is generally of years and experience enough to damp the fiercest flame; he tried this course in his passion for you, and kissed Mrs. Englefyld at Mrs. Dancastle's. This recipe he hath left written, in the style of a divine, as follows: "*Whoso loveth Miss Blount shall kiss her Aunt and be healed. For he kisseth her not as her husband, who kisseth and is enslaved for ever, as one of the foolish ones: but as a passenger who passeth away and forgetteth the kiss of her mouth; even as the wind saluteth a flower in his passage, and knoweth not the odour thereof.*"

When this letter is printed for the wit of it, pray take care that what is underlined be printed in a different character.

Address: To Mrs. Teresa Blount, at Mapledurham, near Redding.

POPE *to* FORD[1] — 2 *October* [1714]

1935 (Nichol Smith)

Bath Octr 2d [1714]

I have been led about from place to place by Dr Parnell, at such a rate, that I have scarcely recovered my self yet of such a series of journeys. If my head were not this moment giddy of the Bath waters, I would

[1] The text is from *The Letters of Swift to Charles Ford*, pp. 229–30. Professor Nichol Smith printed from the original owned by Archdeacon Bright of Lichfield.

tell you I am yet in my senses, and remember with pleasure the kindnesses of Mr Ford. I heartily wish myself with you, in the quiet, indolent station by your Fireside, with a nightcap on: which is a thousand times more to be preferred than this way of catching cold for my health. The dismal prospect of winter affrights me at this distance from London, you, and good company; the sole comforts that can make me live till another summer. When I meet you next, it will be with the same joy that men gett to their native country after a tedious and weary wandring. I cannot think myself in England here, all people are changed in their opinions, manners and looks, since the last view I had of great Britain. How many Degrees are we removed? Is Gay our Countryman, or a High dutch Squire? I have not heard a syllable of his adventures. If he wants consolatory discourses, pray give him what encouragement you can; & desire him to make a visit to Mr Harcourt. If he is afraid of corresponding with Tories, tell him I am a Whig, and he may write to me hither, till the end of next week, by which time I will be at London or in Berkshire. If you have any design for this place pray put a stop to me by a line the next post. Nothing in nature else shall detain me here. We were put in hopes of good company at this Towne, but none appear. I am damnably in the spleen. When shall we see the Dean on this side the water? If you have not heard from Dr Elwood,[1] be so kind to desire the Dean to do that business. I would write to give that Gentleman my thanks as soon as I hear of its being done. Dr Parnelle is intolerably lazie and puts me off from time to time by promising to write jointly with me to all our Friends. I beg you to know me for your most sincere and obedient humble servant | A. Pope.

Address: To Charles Ford Esqr att | the blue Perriwig near | the George Taverne | in Pall Mall | London

Postmark: 4/OC

POPE *to* MARTHA BLOUNT[2] — 6 *October* [1714]

Mapledurham

Bath, Oct. 6th

Madam,—If I may ever be allowed to tell you the Thoughts I so often have of you in your absence, it is at this hour, when I neglect the Company of a great number of Ladies to write this letter: From the

[1] Pope's 'business' with John Elwood, sometime Vice-Provost of Trinity College, Dublin, and university member of Parliament, is obscure. Elwood was a friend of Swift's, and Pope may hope he will try for subscriptions to the *Iliad*.

[2] In all his editions except the quarto and folio of 1737 Pope printed most of the latter part of this letter among his 'Letters to Several Ladies'. The parts printed (indicated below) begin with 'If you ask me how the waters agree with me . . .'. Half-brackets after this point indicate omissions by Pope. Some changes in phrasing are noted; none are important.

Window where I am seated, I command the prospect of twenty or thirty, in one of the finest Promenades in the world, every moment that I take my eye off from this Paper. If Variety of Diversions & new Objects be capable of driving our Friends out of our minds, I have the best excuse imaginable for forgetting you. For I have Slid, I cant tell how, into all the Amusements of this Place: My whole Day is shar'd by the Pump-Assemblies, the Walkes, the Chocolate houses, Raffling Shops, Plays, Medleys, &c. We have no Ladies who have the Face, tho some of 'em may have the Impudence, to expect a Lampoone. The prettiest is one I had the luck to travell with, who has found me out so far as to tell me, that whatever Pretence I make to Gayety, my Heart is not at Bath. Mrs Gage[1] came hither the other day, and did me a double honour, in speaking to me & asking publickly when I saw you last? I endeavor (like all awkward Fellows) to become agreable by Imitation; & observing who are most in favor with the Fair, I sometimes copy the civil Air of Gascoin, sometimes the impudent one of Nash, & sometimes, for Variety, the silly one of a Neighbor of yours who has lost to the Gamesters here that Money of which the Ladies only deserve to rob a man of his age.[2] This mistaken Youth is so ignorant, as to imagine himself as agreable in the Eyes of your Sex to day, as he was yesterday, when he was worth 3 or 4 hundred pounds more, Alas! he knows not, that just as much is lost of a Mistresses Heart, as is emptyd from one's own Pocket! My chief Acquaintances of my own Sex are the aforesaid Mr Gascoin & Mr Nash, of the other, Dame Lindsey & Jenny Man. I am so much a Rake as to be ashamed of being seen with Dr Parnelle. I ask people abroad who that Parson is? We expect better Company this week, and then a certain Lord[3] shall know what Ladies drink his health every day since his disgrace, that You may be in the publick Pamphlets as well as your humble Servant. They say here are Caballs held under pretence of drinking Waters, and this Scandal, like others, refreshes me & elevates my Spirits. I think no man deserves a Monument that could not be wrapd in a Windingsheet of papers writt against him. If Women could digest Scandal as well as I, there are two that might be the happiest Creatures in the Universe.⌝ [4]If you ask how the Waters agree with me, I must tell you, so very well, that I question how you and I should agree, if we were in a roome by ourselves? ⌜But I apprehend you have some notions of the next life that may hinder your happiness in this:⌝

[1] Mrs. Gage is very likely the wife of Thomas Gage, Esq., of Duke Street, Westminster whose possible conversion from Catholicism is satirized in a letter to Teresa Blount from Pope [July 1715].

[2] First Pope wrote, but immediately revised to the present text, the following: 'has lost to the Gamesters here that money which the Ladies only deserve to empty a young man of'

[3] Bowles and Elwin print *Earl*, but the original reads *Lord*. The Lord was almost certainly Robert, Earl of Oxford.

[4] At this point Pope's printed letter begins. Half-brackets indicate his omissions.

Mrs T⌜eresa⌝ has honestly assured me, that but for some whims of that kind which she can't entirely conquer, she would go a Rakeing[1] with me in Man's Cloathes. Even You Madam I fancy (if you would not partake in our adventures) would wait our coming in at the Evening with some Impatience, & be well enough pleasd to hear 'em by the Fireside. That would be better than reading Romances; unless Lady M⌜ary⌝ would be our Historian,[2] for as she is married, she has probably leisure hours in the night to write, or what she will, in. What raises my Desires of this kind of Life, is an acquaintance I am beginning with my Lady Sandwich,[3] who has all the Spirit of the last Age, & all the gay Experience of a pleasurable Life. It were as scandalous an Omission to come to the Bath & not to see my Lady Sandwich, as it had formerly been, to have travelld to Rome without visiting the Queen of Sweden. She is, in a word, the best thing this Country has to boast of, & as she has been all that a Woman of Spirit & delight could be, so she still continues that easie, lively, & independent Creature that a sensible woman always will be.

⌜I have in one week run thro' whatever they call diverting here, & I should be ashamed to pass two just in the same track. I will therfore but take a Trip to Long-leat (which is twelve miles hence) to visit my Lord Lansdowne,[4] and return to London.⌝

I must tell you a Truth which is not however much to my Credit. I never thought so much of yourself & your ⌜fair⌝ Sister as since I have been fourscore miles distant from you. At Binfield[5] I look upon you as good Neighbours, at London as pretty kind of Women, & here as Divinities, Angels, Goddesses, or what you will. In like manner I never knew at what a rate I valued Your Life, till you were upon the point of dying. If Mrs Teresa & You will but fall very sick every Season, I shall certainly dye for you. Seriously I value you both so much that I esteem others much the less for your sakes, You have robbd me of the pleasure of esteeming a thousand fine Qualities in them, by showing me so many in a superior degree in yourselves. There are but two things in the World which can make you indifferent to me which I believe you are not capable of, I mean Ill nature & Malice. I have seen enough of you not to resent any frailty you coud have, & nothing less than a Vice can make me like you less. I expect you should discover, by my common Conduct towards you both, that

[1] go a Rakeing with] go and see the world with *1735–42*. After 1735 even the T of Teresa's name is omitted.

[2] This may be Lady Mary Wortley Montagu or Lady Mary Caryll.

[3] Apparently Lady Sandwich (daughter of the wit and poet, John Wilmot, Earl of Rochester) inherited her father's charm and wit. After 1729, when she became a widow, she lived in Paris (d. 1757).

[4] Lord Lansdowne had married the widow of Thomas Thynne, 1st Viscount Weymouth, of Longleat, in Dec. 1711.

[5] At Binfield] In the Forest *1735–42*. (A typical change to avoid particularity.)

this is true; and that therfore you should pardon a thousand things in me for that one Disposition. Expect nothing from me but Truth and Freedome, & I shall be always thought by you what I always am

⌜Your faithfull obliged humble Servant. A. P.⌝

Address: To | Mrs Martha Blount.

JERVAS *to* POPE[1] [*October* 1714?]

Homer MSS. Add. 4807

Dear Mr Pope.—You remember how frankly I told you of Staying 3 days longer [in] the Country than the Archdeacons Limitation. [Th]e House & we are ready to receive you and Yours—I was Yesterday at Sir John Stanley's Lodgings, but not at home—I saw the Young fellow That is going to try what he can make of Homer's head. I cannot yet Answer for him, but by the end of the next week I shal speak Categorically if he advances as he promises. You will be Time Enough to have it done by Another [if] he loses Operam & oleum. I intend this day to Call at Vertue's[2] [to] see Swift's brought a little more like—And see what is doing to One Pope.

I will give Addison half a dozen Names[3] before you come if you [sta]y till Monday next.

Bring Your Two Exchequer Bills with you, for they must lye [no] longer at 3 per Cent.

Tho' the Cows disappoint us of our Milk Diet, Yet the Oxen [a]fford us Beef as good as ever.

[My] Service to Every body. I expect you on Monday Evening at [the] farthest.

Yours at the old rate | C J—

[Yo]ung Kelsey has got a Place in the Exchequer. [ ]00*l.* per annum.[4]

[1] Elwin placed this letter in 1715, because in that year Jervas paid money to Pope for subscribers to Tickell's Lucan. The sum (£1. 1*s.* 6*d.*), however, would have no relation to a half-dozen subscriptions (see EC viii. 10 n. 6). The engraving of Homer's head for Pope's *Iliad*, mentioned by Jervas in his letter of 20 Aug. 1714, should have been finished before May 1715, Elwin's time for the letter. On 13 Sept. 1714 (a letter that Elwin lacked) Pope writes to Parnell suggesting that Jervas attend to the difficulty with Sir John Stanley, and Jervas here seems to be doing so. In early 1715 Pope was constantly in London: this letter seems addressed to him in Binfield about the time (Oct. 1714) when he and Parnell returned from Bath, and before they went to London for the Coronation. Finally, Archdeacon Parnell was in Ireland in 1715.

[2] George Vertue, the engraver.

[3] Names, so Elwin thought, of subscribers to Lucan; but Jervas and Pope may be hoping (vainly) that Addison will solicit half a dozen subscriptions to the *Iliad.*

[4] The first digit is missing.

†POPE *to* ADDISON[1] 10 *October* 1714

1735

Octob. 10, 1714.

I have been acquainted by one of my friends[2] who omits no opportunities of gratifying me, that you have lately been pleas'd to speak of me in a manner which nothing but the real respect I have for you can deserve. May I hope that some late malevolencies have lost their effect? Indeed it is neither for me, nor my enemies, to pretend to tell you whether I am your friend or not; but if you would judge by probabilities, I beg to know which of your poetical acquaintance has so little Interest in pretending to be so? Methinks no man should question the real friendship of one who desires no real service: I am only to get as much from the *Whigs*, as I got by the *Tories*, that is to say, Civility; being neither so proud as to be insensible of any good office, nor so humble, as not to dare heartily to despise any man who does me an injustice.

I will not value my self upon having ever guarded all the degrees of respect for you; for (to say the truth) all the world speaks well of you, and I should be under a necessity of doing the same, whether I car'd for you or not.

As to what you have said of me, I shall never believe that the Author of *Cato* can speak one thing and think another. As a proof that I account you sincere, I beg a favour of you: It is, that you would look over the two first books of my translation of *Homer*, which are now in the hands of my Lord *Halifax*. I am sensible how much the reputation of any poetical work will depend upon the character you give it: 'tis therefore some evidence of the trust I repose in your good will, when I give you this opportunity of speaking ill of me with justice, and yet expect you will tell me your truest thoughts, at the same time that you tell others your most favourable ones.

I have a farther request, which I must press with earnestness. My Bookseller is reprinting the *Essay on Criticism*, to which you have done too much honour in your *Spectator* of No 253. The period in that paper, where you say, "I have admitted some strokes of ill nature into that Essay", is the only one I could wish omitted of all you have

[1] This sarcastic letter was the last between Pope and Addison to be printed. By October Pope had no hope of 'civilities' from that quarter. One may assume that the letter was so important to Pope that he kept a copy, or one may assume that when preparing his letters for publication (*c.* 1730) he composed this letter, never sent. All the other letters printed as sent to Addison are demonstrably fabricated from letters to Caryll; for this letter there is no 'source'. The mention of *Iliad* I and II as in the hands of Lord Halifax does not perfectly accord with the account set down by Spence twenty years later. See his *Anecdotes*, p. 134.

[2] See two Letters, from Mr. Jervas, and the Answer to it. No. 22, 23.—Pope 1737–42 (first printed in the Cooper octavo *Works*, 1737, 2nd ed., v. 214). Nos. 22 and 23 were the letters from Jervas to Pope, 20 Aug. 1714, and Pope to Jervas, 27 Aug. 1714.

written: but I wou'd not desire it should be so, unless I had the merit of removing your objection: I beg you but to point out those strokes to me, and you may be assured they shall be treated without mercy.

Since we are upon proofs of sincerity (which I am pretty confident will turn to the advantage of us both in each others opinion) give me leave to name another passage in the same *Spectator*, which I wish you would alter. It is where you mention an observation upon *Homer*'s Verses of *Sysiphus*'s Stone, as *never having been made before by any of the Criticks*:[1] I happen'd to find the same in *Dyonisius* of *Halicarnassus*'s Treatise, *περι Συνθεσεος Ονοματον*,[2] who treats very largely upon these Verses. I know you will think fit to soften your expression, when you see the passage; which you must needs have read tho' it be since slipt out of your memory. I am with the utmost esteem, | Your, &c.

||POPE *to* TERESA BLOUNT[3] [*Late October* 1714]

Mapledurham

Madam,—The chief cause I have to repent my leaving the Towne, is the Uncertainty I am in every day of your Sister's State of health. I really expected by every Post to have heard of her Recovery, but on the contrary each Letter has been a new Awakening to my apprehensions, and I have ever since suffer'd Alarms upon Alarms on her account. ⌜A Month ago I should have laughd at any one, who had told me, my Heart would be perpetually beating for a Lady that was thirty miles off from me; and indeed I never imagined my Concern could be half so great for any Young Woman whom I have been no more obliged to, than to so innocent an one as She. But Madam it is with the utmost Seriousness I assure you,⌝ no Relation you have[4] can be more sensibly touched at this, than I; nor any danger of any I have cou'd affect me with more Uneasiness, (tho as I never had a Sister, I can't be quite so good a Judge as You, how far Humanity would carry me.) I have felt some Weaknesses of a tender kind, which I would not be free from; & I am glad to find my value for People so rightly placed, as to perceive them all on this occasion.

[1] These words are since left out in Mr. *Tickel*'s Edition, but were extant all during Mr. *Addison*'s Life.—Pope, 1735–42. 'Left out', that is, from the text of *Spectator* 253 in Tickell's edition of Addison's *Works* (1721). By 1735, when Pope printed all this, he had become in a measure reconciled to Tickell—but not to the memory of Addison!

[2] Pope's Greek for *Περὶ Συνθέσεως 'Ονομάτων*.

[3] This letter seems to be written about the time of the Coronation of King George I (20 Oct. 1714), when Martha Blount had the smallpox. Now that the Coronation is over Pope is leaving town. Presumably because of Martha's health the Blounts left town soon afterwards, and the departure was the occasion of Pope's 'Epistle to a Young Lady [Teresa] on her Leaving Town after the Coronation', first printed in Pope's *Works* (1717).

The letter was printed by Pope in all his editions with the omission of two sentences (excessively tender) in the first paragraph and the whole of the last paragraph. He made hardly a verbal change otherwise. The omissions are in half-brackets. A postscript has been torn away.

[4] no Relation you have] No one *1735–42*.

I cannot be so good a Christian as to be willing (tho no less than God should order it) to resign my own happiness here for hers in another life. I do more than wish for her Safety, for ev'ry wish I make I find immediately changed into a Prayer, and a more fervent one than I had learnt to make till now. May her Life be longer and happier than perhaps herself may desire, that is, as long and as happy as Yourself can desire. May her Beauty be as great as possible; that is, as it always was, or as Yours is: But whatever Ravages a merciless Distemper may commit, I dare promise her boldly what few (if any) of her Makers of Visits & Complements, dare to do; she shall have one man as much her Admirer as ever. As for Your own part Madam, You have him more so than ever, since I have been a Witness to the Generous Tenderness you have shown upon this occasion.

⌜I beg Mrs Blunt & Mr Blunt to believe me very faithfully their Servant, & that your good Mother will accept of a thousand thanks for the Favor of her Maids Letters, & oblige me with the Continuance of them ev'ry post. I intreat her pardon that I did not take my leave of her, for when I parted from you I was under some Confusion, which I believe you might perceive. I thought too that moment, to have snatchd a minute or two more, to have calld agen that night. But when I know I act uprightly, I depend upon Forgiveness from such as [I th]ink you are. I hope you will always be just, [that] is always look upon me as | Madam | Your most obedient faithful | humble Servant⌝

Address: To | Mrs Teresa Blount, next | door to my Lord Salisbury's in | King street, by | St. James's Square

POPE *to* CARYLL[1] 26 *October* [1714]

Add. 28618

October 26. 1715

I have not had the satisfaction of a line from your hands since I writ from Bath. I am now at Binfield, and shall be in London in a week to set Homer forwards in the press. Several little affairs will detain me there a fortnight or three weeks, at the expiration of which I will wait upon you as soon as you will permit me. Tho' if you shall be at Ladyholt betwixt this time and Christmas, I could be glad it might be there I might have that pleasure; both on account of my fears for my health in the air of Grinsted (for I am yet in a very poor state of convalescence) and because I might have the benefit of riding upon dry

[1] The sometimes erratic transcript dates this letter 1715, but Elwin is our authority for the fact that the Caryll family (other than the father) went abroad 13 Oct. 1714 and returned in Aug. 1715. Hence Elwin quite rationally changes the year to 1714.

ground; for I intend to visit you on the palfrey you gave me, which is yet my best vehicle. I hear your whole family is gone abroad, and tho' I shall lose a pleasure in every one of them, yet I can make myself amends in engrossing so much more of you. I have a thousand histories and adventures to tell you, which will be perfectly new, concerning myself and others. The secret story of states and poets intermixed, the policies of government and wit, and how fools are rendered equally serviceable to both. Some things I believe will not displease you, as they tend to making a friend of yours a better Christian, &c. I write this in a hurry, having a learned friend or two at my elbow; jogging me to write other things: and Homer has daily some demands upon me by way of notes and explanations. But let my thoughts be under never so great distractions, they will always be partly employed upon you, and putting me in mind how much I ought to be | Dear sir | Your most faithful affectionate friend | and obedient servant | A. P.

A letter directed to Mr Jervase's in Cleveland Court certainly finds me (wherever I am) in a post or two.

I am extremely concerned for the death of Mr Bedingfield,[1] which I but just now heard of.

POPE *to* BROOME [*November* 1714]

Elwin–Courthope, viii. 32

Sir,—The perpetual hurry my late pretence to business has brought me into, must be my excuse for having omitted to write to you before. I am in a particular manner obliged to your earnestness in doing me a service, and have inserted Sir Robert's name in the list of subscribers.[2] You will add to your favour if you can procure me any of the colleges to subscribe for their libraries, and let me know as soon as any are promised you.

If you have leisure, and can engage, without failing me, to read over in order the commentaries of Eustathius,[3] on the four first Iliads, and to place a mark upon all the notes which are purely critical, omitting the grammatical and geographical and allegorical ones, you will oblige me particularly by informing me. I should be glad you had time to translate them afterwards, and I should think myself under an obligation to pay a lawful tribute for the time you spent in it. Let me know by what means I might convey the books to you securely, if this agree

[1] Caryll's mother was the daughter of Sir Henry Bedingfield, 1st Bt., and the deceased was presumably a relative of Pope's friend.

[2] Sir Robert Cotton was a subscriber.

[3] This is the first mention of the long labours of Broome on Eustathius. Since Broome was now in a comfortable financial state he did all this work without recompense. See his letter to Pope of 29 Oct. 1735 and his letter to Fenton of 15 June [1728].

with your conveniency. Believe me, most affectionately, dear sir, your most obliged and faithful servant.

Be pleased to direct to Mr. Jervas's, at Bridgewater House, near St. James's, whether I am here or in the country.

POPE *to* CARYLL — 19 *November* [1714]

Add. 28618

London November 19.

I am perfectly ashamed of the long omission I've been guilty of, in deferring to write to you. You will allow me to be a very busy fellow, when I tell you I have been perpetually waiting upon the great, and using no less solicitation to gain their opinion upon my Homer than others at this time do to obtain preferments. As soon as I can collect all the objections of the two or three noble judges, and of the five or six best poets, I shall fly to Ladyholt,[1] as a proper place to review and correct the whole for the last time. In which I shall have a peculiar advantage, from a daily conversation and consultation with so good a critick and friend as yourself. I fully purpose to be with you at the beginning of December, and to stay till Christmas, or the time when you shall make your journey to Whiteknights. I think to travel on horseback and could be glad to know if you should do so, or make use of your coach in your journey? As I leave this town on purpose, I beg (if any accident may hinder your being at Ladyholt) that you'll be so kind as to acquaint me soon of it. I hoped to've been with you by this time, but the affair you guess, about publishing the Book, has employed more time in adjusting preliminaries than I expected.

The state of poetry is too low to deserve the least account. Only my friend Mr Gay has writ a little thing, which he sends you with his service.[2]

The thing they have been pleased to call a Receipt to make a Cuckold,[3] is only six lines which were stolen from me, as follows:

> Two or three visits, with two or three bows,
> Two or three civil things, two or three vows,
> Two or three kisses and two or three sighs,
> Two or three *Jesus's!* and *let me die's*,

[1] Pope paid this visit to Caryll, and that they returned together appears from Caryll's account-book: 'Dec. 22. I went this day, with Mr. Pope, to Whiteknights. We lay at Odiham.'—Elwin.

[2] Gay's *Letter to a Lady, Occasion'd by the Arrival of Her Royal Highness the Princess of Wales* (published 20 Nov. 1714) unfortunately took the form of a burlesque of the extreme flattery customary in such epistles, and hence did not further his fortunes at Court. Gay recognized, without regret, his inability to flatter.

[3] These lines appeared in the 2d ed. of Lintot's *Miscellany* (1713–14) and in *Poems and Translations by Several Hands....* Printed for J. Pemberton. This miscellany was collected by John Oldmixon.

Two or three squeezes, and two or three towzes,
With two or three hundred pounds lost at their houses,
Can never fail cuckolding two or three spouses.

I am with all truth and grateful affection | Dear sir | Your faithful friend and servant | A. P.

The book of Count Gabalais[1] is genuine; who translated it I know not. I supose at the instigation of none but the bookseller who paid for it.

POPE *to* MARTHA BLOUNT [*Post* 24 *November* 1714][2]

Mapledurham

Most Divine!—'Tis some proof of my Sincerity towards you that I write when I am prepared by Drinking to speak Truth, and Sure a Letter after twelve at night must abound with that noble Ingredient. That Heart must have abundance of Flames which is at once warm'd by Wine and You; Wine awakens and refreshes the lurking Passions of the Mind, as Varnish does the Colours that are sunk in a Picture, and brings them out in all their natural Glowings. My good Qualities have been so frozen and lockd up in a dull Constitution at all my former Sober hours, that it is very astonishing to me, now I am drunk, to find so much Virtue in me.

In these Overflowings of my heart I pay you my thanks for those two obliging Letters you favord me with of the 18th and 24th Instant. That which begins with Dear Creature, and my charming Mr Pope, was a Delight to me beyond all Expression. You have at last entirely gaind the Conquest over your fair Sister; 'tis true you are not handsome, for you are a Woman and think you are not; but this Good humor and Tenderness for me has a charm that cannot be resisted. That Face must needs be irresistible which was adorned with Smiles even when it could not see the Coronation.[3]

I must owne I have long been shockd at your Sister on several accounts, but above all things at her Pruderie: I am resolved to break with her for ever; and therefore tell her I shall take the first opportunity of sending back all her Letters.

I do suppose you will not show this Epistle out of Vanity, as I doubt not your said Sister does all I writ to her. Indeed to correspond with

[1] *Le Comte de Gabalis* (1670), by the Abbé Montfaucon de Villars, was mentioned as a good book on sylphs in Pope's Dedication (1714) of *The Rape of the Lock.* A new translation of it by John Ozell appeared so shortly after *The Rape* that Pope might naturally be suspected of some sort of co-operation. See Pope's *Poems* (Twickenham ed.), ii. 356, for Professor Tillotson's comments.

[2] The talk of Radcliffe's death (d. 1 Nov. 1714) and the mention of letters of the 18th and 24th instant, date this letter as later than the 24th. Bowles and Elwin somewhat needlessly omitted parts of this letter.

[3] At the time of the Coronation Miss Blount was in London, but was down with smallpox.

Mr Pope may make any one proud who lives under a Dejection of Heart in the Country. Every one values Mr Pope, but every one for a different reason. One for his firm adherence to the Catholic Faith, another for his Neglect of Popish Superstition, one for his grave behavior, another for his Whymsicalness. Mr Tydcomb[1] for his pretty Atheistical Jests, Mr Caryl for his moral and christian Sentences, Mrs Teresa for his Reflections on Mrs Patty, and Mrs Patty for his Reflections on Mrs Teresa.

My Acquaintance runs so much in an Anti-Catholic Channel, that it was but tother day I heard of Mrs Fermor's being Actually, directly, and consummatively, married. I wonder how the guilty Couple and their Accessories at Whiteknights look, stare, or simper, since that grand Secret came out which they so well concealed before. They conceald it as well as a Barber does his Utensils when he goes to trim upon a Sunday and his Towels hang out all the way: Or as well as a Fryer concealed a little Wench, whom he was carrying under his Habit to Mr Colingwood's Convent; Pray Father (sayd one in the Street to him) what's that under your Arm. A Saddle for one of the Brothers to ride with, quoth the Fryer. Then Father (cryd he) take care and shorten the Stirrups—For the Girls Legs hung out—

[2]You know your Doctor is gone the way of all his Patients, & was hard put to it how to dispose of an Estate miserably unwieldy, and splendidly unuseful to him. Sir Sam. Garth says, that for Ratcliffe to leave a Library was as if an Eunuch should found a Seraglio. Dr Shadwell[3] lately told a Lady he wonder'd she could be alive after him; She made answer she wonder'd at it too, both because Dr Ratcliffe was dead, and because Dr Shadwell was alive.

Poor Parnelle is now on the briny Ocean[4] which he increases with his briny Tears for the Loss of You &c. Pray for him, if you please, but not for me. Don't so much as hope I may go to Heaven: tis a place I am not very fond of, I hear no great good of it: All the Descriptions I ever heard of it amount to no more than just this: It is eternal singing, & piping, and sitting in Sunshine. Much good may it do the Saints; and those who intend to be Saints. For my part I am better than a Saint, for I am | Madam | Your most faithfull Admi- | rer, Friend, Servant, | any thing.

I send you Gay's Poem | on the Princess.[5] She is very | fatt. God keep her Husband.

[1] See Pope to Cromwell, 12 July 1707 (p. 27, n. 2).

[2] The paragraph about Dr. John Radcliffe, the fashionable and wealthy practitioner who bequeathed funds for various benefactions including the construction of the Radcliffe Camera at Oxford, was transferred in Pope's editions, except the quarto and folio of 1737, to a letter addressed to Teresa Blount and sometimes dated 13 Sept. 1717.

[3] Dr. Shadwell, later Sir John Shadwell, was physician in ordinary to Queen Anne, George I, and George II.

[4] Returning to Ireland.

[5] Published in Nov. 1714, as *A Letter to a Lady....*

POPE *to* BROOME 29 *November* 1714

Elwin–Courthope, viii. 32

London, Nov. 29, 1714.

I take you at your word, and desire you to read through the commentary of Eustathius on the second book, except the catalogue, which you may save yourself the trouble of. I have read it lately myself,[1] and have a mind to see if we shall not pitch upon the same remarks. It will be a pleasure to me to find our tastes agreeing in what we think the notes most to the purpose.

Be so kind to take this method: translate such notes only as concern the beauties or art of the author—none geographical, historical or grammatical—unless some occur very important to the sense, and none of the poetical history. What are allegorical, if obvious and ingenious, abstract; if far-fetched, omit; but leave out none of the art or contrivance of the poet, or beauties, it being on account of those alone that I put you to this trouble. Be pleased to refer to the pages in your papers. You will find but few of the sort I mention to insist upon, so that the task of writing will not be so great as the trouble of reading, though I suppose you read the Greek with ease. When you have gone through the second book, be pleased to send the pages to Lintot, sealed up and directed to me, by some sure way.

The book will be sent to you by the Bury carrier, so as to be with you on Saturday next. I beg you will be ready to receive it, or send for fear of any accident. It is of considerable value, being the best Roman edition, and of more as belonging to my Lord Halifax.[2] The sooner you could look over this second book the better. I shall not omit any opportunity of returning this kindness you offer me, in such a way as may be most agreeable to you, and best express my gratitude.

You mentioned a gentleman who was ready to subscribe to you; be pleased to receive the subscription, and let me know his name, which was torn out by the seal of your letter, that I may transmit him a receipt. Do the same also in regard to my Lord Cornwallis's, or any others you may find.

The hurry I am in, with different businesses, hinders my answering what you tell me from Mrs. Marriots', or from paying my respects to them by writing. Anything from them is always the most welcome and entertaining to one who is so truly their servant, and so earnestly wishes to see or hear of them. Shall not Mrs. Betty shine this winter

[1] In a letter to Fenton, written in anger at Pope (15 June 1728), Broome expresses doubts if Pope could translate ten lines of Eustathius. Parnell had been helping him at this time. Even Broome at times found it expeditious to derive his comments from Eustathius by way of Mme Dacier!

[2] Lord Halifax (Bufo-like?) was evidently interesting himself in Pope and his translation. For the classic episode narrating Dr. Garth's advice how to trick such a patron see Spence, pp. 135–6.

among the glories of the court and town? Shall foreigners and Germans[1] engross the adorations of all men? Let her come and vindicate English beauty. I am, dear sir, your faithful friend and servant.

||POPE *to* LORD HALIFAX — 3 *December* 1714

Add. 7121

Decembr 3d 1714.

My Lord,—While you are doing Justice to all the World, I beg you will not forget Homer, if you can spare an hour to attend his cause. I leave him with you in that hope, and return home full of acknowledgments for the Favors your Lordship has done me, and for those you are pleasd to intend me.[2] I distrust neither your Will, nor your Memory, when it is to do Good: and if ever I become troublesome or sollicitous, it must not be out of Expectation, but out of Gratitude. Your Lordship may either cause me to live agreeably in the Towne, or contentedly in the Country; which is really all the Difference I sett between an Easy Fortune and a small one. It is indeed a high Strain of Generosity in you, to think of making me easie all my Life, only because I have been so happy as to divert you an hour or two; But if I may have leave to add, because you think me no Enemy to my Country, there will appear a better Reason, for I must be of consequence, as I sincerely am, | My Lord | Your most obliged, most obedi | -ent, & faithful humble Servant, | A. Pope.

Endorsement: Mr Pope

†POPE *to* MRS. ARABELLA FERMOR[3] — [1714–15]

1735

You are by this time satisfy'd how much the tenderness of one man of merit is to be prefer'd to the addresses of a thousand. And by this time, the Gentleman you have made choice of is sensible, how great

[1] In the elegant phrases of Lady Mary Wortley Montagu, the new King George I was 'surrounded by all his German ministers and playfellows, male and female'.

[2] This letter was printed, almost unchanged, in all Pope's editions of his letters, under date of 1 Dec. 1714. It is apparent that in printing Pope preferred to conceal the fact that Lord Halifax's interest was chiefly in Pope's Homer, for instead of the first two sentences as sent Pope printed: 'I am oblig'd to you both for the favours you have done me, and for those you intend me.' The subscription was also abbreviated, and there were two small changes in phrasing in the last sentence. It is possible that the letter was accompanied with an advance copy of Book I of the *Iliad*. It was late to be asking for revisions of the books included in vol. i. The Duke of Chandos received such an advance copy of Book I. See Sherburn, *Early Career*, p. 139, n. 1.

[3] The letter to Martha Blount [post 24 Nov. 1714] tells us that Pope had just heard of Miss Fermor's marriage. Presumably this letter was written shortly thereafter. The grave and formal wit of the letter is significant. Miss Fermor had become Mrs. Francis Perkins.

is the joy of having all those charms and good qualities which have pleas'd so many, now apply'd to please one only. It was but just, that the same Virtues which gave you reputation, should give you happiness; and I can wish you no greater, than that you may receive it in as high a degree your self, as so much good humour must infallibly give it to your husband.

It may be expected perhaps, that one who has the title of Poet, should say something more polite on this occasion: But I am really more a well-wisher to your felicity, than a celebrater of your beauty. Besides, you are now a married woman, and in a way to be a great many better things than a fine Lady; such as an excellent wife, a faithful friend, a tender parent, and at last as the consequence of them all, a saint in heaven. You ought now to hear nothing but that, which was all you ever desired to hear (whatever others may have spoken to you) I mean *Truth*: And it is with the utmost that I assure you, no friend you have can more rejoice in any good that befalls you, is more sincerely delighted with the prospect of your future happiness, or more unfeignedly desires a long continuance of it. I beg you will think it but just, that a man who will certainly be spoken of as your admirer, after he is dead, may have the happiness to be esteem'd while he is living | Your, &c.

1715

The literary event of this year was the triumphant appearance of the first volume of Pope's *Iliad*. Early and scornful attacks upon the projected translation by the 'little Senate' at Button's died before the superiority of Pope's version over that of Tickell, the Buttonian champion. *The Temple of Fame* and *A Key to the Lock* were published early in the year, without drawing great approbation. It was again a time of political turmoil: some of Pope's close friends in the Tory party went either to the Tower (Oxford and Lansdowne) or escaped to France (Bolingbroke and Ormond). Pope and several friends planned a visit to Sir William Wyndham at Orchard Wyndham in August, but within a month of their abandoned project Sir William was arrested at Orchard Wyndham and sent to the Tower. The projected merry journey to the south-west became a quiet ride by Pope and Dr. Arbuthnot to Oxford (and to Bath ?). In expectation of the coming of the Pretender a proclamation in July reinvoked the old law which forbade Catholics to come within ten miles of London. One doubts if our young poet paid any attention to the proclamation. In this year, apparently, the Blount sisters and their mother upon the marriage of their brother left Mapledurham and settled in London. All these changes and the fears attendant upon change made Pope melancholy and philosophical. For two or three years now he had spent so much time in Town that one imagines his parents were more than willing to consider moving nearer to London—which in 1716 they will do.

JOHN DANCASTLE *to* POPE[1] [1715 ?]

Homer MSS. Add. 4807

We are here in continuall apprehentions of being Visite'd and do not think it proper to be from home. At any other time I or my Brother will accompany you. | I am | Dear Sir | Your most | affectionate humble | Servant J. Dan.

Address: To | Mr Pope | These

[1] This letter follows in the Homer MSS. a group of letters that date from the summer of 1715. On this letter Pope began the translation of Book IX of the *Iliad*. On leaves following are two letters to Jervas, which seem to date 1715 or 1716, but immediately after those two when Pope began Book XI (not all leaves contain letters) the poet ran out of 'contemporary' correspondence, and had to use old letters dating from 1711 or earlier. All one can say of the present letter is that it can hardly postdate 1715. The visitation apprehended may be the inspection ordered in 1715 to make sure that Catholics had no firearms, &c., that could be used in the interest of the Pretender.

THE DUKE OF CHANDOS *to* MR. HARCOURT[1]

9 *January* 1714/15

The Huntington Library

To Mr. Harcourt 9 Jan 1714/15

Sir,—I was at your door whilst I was in town to return you my humble thanks for your oblidging present of Mr. Pope's translation of the first book of Homer. A Genius like his can never fail of performing what he undertakes to the satisfaction of true Judges. Nor could he have given a more certain proof of it than in making you sensible, how much he deserves the honour of your approbation.

As I desire to oblidge some friends as early as I can with this great work I intreat you will subscribe for ten sets for me. I think the subscription money is 2 Guin. each, & I enclose a Note for the sum on Mr Zollicoffre who will wait upon you to take it up. I am with the greatest respect &c.

‡POPE *to* CONGREVE[2]

16 *January* 1714/15

1735

Jan. 16, 1714–15.

Methinks when I write to you, I am making a confession, I have got (I can't tell how) such a custom of throwing my self out upon paper without reserve. You were not mistaken in what you judg'd of my temper of mind when I writ last. My faults will not be hid from you, and perhaps it is no dispraise to me that they will not. The cleanness and purity of one's mind is never better prov'd, than in discovering its own faults at first view: as when a Stream shows the dirt at its bottom, it shows also the transparency of the water.

My spleen was not occasion'd however, by any thing an abusive,[3] angry Critick could write of me. I take very kindly your heroick manner of congratulation upon this scandal; for I think nothing more honourable, than to be involved in the same fate with all the great and the good that ever lived; that is, to be envy'd and censur'd by bad writers.

[1] This letter from Chandos to Pope's friend, the son of Viscount Harcourt, is important as answer to the slanders concerning Pope's ingratitude. His dunces alleged that Chandos had given him £500 for his *Iliad*, whereas this letter indicates that the duke was paying the regular price for the translation. Other letters in the Chandos Letterbooks (from vol. xi of which this transcript comes) indicate that His Grace took all the copies he subscribed for.

[2] This letter has seemed—chiefly because of a perhaps too casual footnote by Pope in 1735 (below, note 3)—a fabricated composite. An attack by Dennis would hardly be a 'scandal'; but if Congreve had warned Pope that the Buttonians (Burnet and Duckett) were preparing attacks before they had seen the translation, their work might seem scandalous. The Buttonians were doing precisely that. But Pope said the critic was Dennis.

[3] Dennis, who writ an abusive Pamphlet this Year, intitled, *Remarks on Mr. Pope's Homer*.—Pope 1735. This note was omitted from all Pope's editions after 1735. Dennis's *Remarks* were published in 1717, and could hardly be written before Homer was published.

You do no more than answer my expectations of you, in declaring how well you take my freedom in sometimes neglecting as I do, to reply to your Letters so soon as I ought; those who have a right taste of the substantial part of friendship, can wave the ceremonial. A friend is the only one that will bear the omission; and one may find who is not so, by the very trial of it.

As to any anxiety I have concerning the fate of my *Homer*, the care is over with me. The world must be the judge, and I shall be the first to consent to the justice of its judgment, whatever it be. I am not so arrant an Author, as even to desire, that if I am in the wrong, all mankind should be so.

I am mightily pleas'd with a saying of Monsieur *Tourreil*: "When a Man writes, he ought to animate himself with the thoughts of pleasing all the world: but he is to renounce that desire or hope, the very moment the Book goes out of his hands."[1]

I write this from *Binfield*, whither I came yesterday, having past a few days in my way with my Lord *Bolingbroke*:[2] I go to *London* in three days time, and will not fail to pay a visit to Mr. *M*—,[3] whom I saw not long since at my Lord *Halifax*'s. I hoped from thence he had some hopes of advantage from the present administration: for few people (I think) but I, pay respects to great Men without any prospects. I am in the fairest way in the world of being not worth a groat, being born both a *Papist* and a *Poet*. This puts me in mind of reacknowledging your continued endeavours to enrich me: But I can tell you 'tis to no purpose, for without the *Opes*, *Æquum animum mi*[4] *ipse parabo*. | I am your, &c.

POPE *to* BROOME 29 *January* [1714/15]

Elwin–Courthope, viii. 34

London, Jan. 29.

I gave the first volume of Eustathius to Mr. Marriot[5] a month ago, to be sent down to you by the carrier, and entreated the favour of you

[1] Jacques de Tourreil prefixed to his French translation of Demosthenes a 'Préface historique', of the final sentence of which the quoted passage is a translation. The passage may be found in *Several Orations of Demosthenes . . . English'd from the Greek by Several Hands. To which is prefix'd the Historical Preface of Monsr. Tourreil* (1702), but Pope does not use this English version for his passage.

[2] *The Political State of Great Britain* (ix. 80) records that after a fortnight in town Bolingbroke left for the country on 15 Jan. of this year. The mention is evidence of the early intimacy of Pope and his later 'guide'.

[3] Possibly Mr. (later Sir) Paul Methuen, who in 1716 as Secretary of State forwarded letters from Pope or from Congreve to Lady Mary Wortley Montagu in Constantinople.

[4] animum mi] mi animum *1737–42*.

[5] Probably Jack Marriot of Sturston, to whose sister Elizabeth Pope was presently (10 Feb. 1714/15) to send his letter concerning the visit to a hermaphrodite. Marriot was later curate at Easthampstead, where Fenton lived with the Trumbull family. See Fenton to Broome, 20 Nov. [1725].

to acquaint me of the receipt of it. Since when I have not had a line from you, and have been under some uneasiness in the fears of its having miscarried. I therefore write this word or two in the utmost haste, only for the satisfaction of hearing from you that it came to your hands. Be pleased to direct to me at Mr. Jervas's, in Cleveland Court, by St. James's. The sooner you do it you will the more oblige, dear sir, your most faithful affectionate servant.

I could be glad, if you have done any part, that I had the papers by the first opportunity sent to Lintot, the first volume being now in the press. I must never omit my most unfeigned respects to Mrs. Marriot and Mrs. Elizabeth Marriot, &c.

POPE *to* BROOME — 10 *February* 1714/15

Elwin–Courthope, viii. 35

London, Feb. 10, 1714.

You overjoy me in the news that Mrs. Betty Marriot will be in town. I hope she will give me leave to wait on her toilet sometimes. I beg you to assure Mrs. Marriot of all the hearty wishes of an old friend and the sincere esteem of a true one.

The method you have taken with Eustathius is what I intended. I beg you to continue it through the second book,[1] the catalogue excepted, till you come to town, and to bring it up with you. If you shall not be here soon, go upon the fifth book with what care you can in the same method, for I believe I have done already the same thing to the second that you can do.

Your compliment and the simile about lawyers' fees is not so just as one might expect from a man of your wit. But a similitude is not always a reason, and you must give me leave to please myself in what concerns you in this affair.[2]

I do not hear of anything in Philips's Miscellany[3] that deserves to be ranked with your verses, and I believe you may find a more creditable occasion of putting them in better company hereafter. As to the *Spectator*, that which is now published is not by the former hands,[4] but a paper of no sort of reputation with the town. I tell you this as

[1] The notes or 'Observations' were printed and paginated separately: the verse was already doubtless in print.

[2] This seems to imply an intention on Pope's part to remunerate Broome for his labours. Broome evidently refused compensation. In his letter placed in Nov. 1714 Pope had expressed an intention to pay Broome.

[3] Philips's Miscellany was announced, but not published. He had advertised for contributions in *The London Gazette* of 8 January 1715, and begged 'such gentlemen as were willing to appear' in his collection to send their poems directed to Tonson.—Elwin.

[4] Pope here refers not to the revival of *The Spectator* by Addison and others (not Steele), the last number of which had appeared on 20 Dec. 1714. An added run (Nos. 636–95) had been begun on 3 Jan. 1715 by William Bond and others 'of no sort of reputation'.

a friend, but desire you not to quote my name, since I have often experienced the danger of speaking my mind upon our fellow-writers. One makes a thousand enemies, who are too vain ever to forgive the truth.

I desire to hear from you as you proceed, and send what you have written at proper conveniency. I value you and your writings, and am, dear sir, your faithful and affectionate friend and servant.

If any remarks of your own occur to you as you read, be pleased to set them upon a separate paper. I know they will be too good to be lost.

TO A LADY FROM HER BROTHER[1] [10 *Feb.* 1714/15?]

1735

To a Lady in the Name of her Brother.

⌜If you have not a chaste ear and a pure heart do not peruse this Letter, for as⌝[2] *Jeremy Taylor*[3] says in his *holy living and dying*, the first thing a Virgin ought to endeavour, is to be ignorant of the *distinction of Sexes.*[4]

It is in the confidence I have that you are thus innocent, that I endeavour to gratify your curiosity in a point in which I am sensible none but a Brother could do it with decency.[5]

I shall entertain you with the most reigning Curiosity in the town, I mean a Person who is equally the toast of gentlemen and ladies, and is at present more universally admired than any of either Sex:[6] You know few proficients have a greater genius for Monsters than my self; but I never tasted a[7] monster to that degree I have done this creature: It was not, like other monsters, produced in the Desarts of *Arabia*, nor came from the country of the *Great Mogul*, but is the production of the joint-endeavours of a *Kentish* Parson and his Spouse, who intended

[1] Printed in editions of 1735 but not in Pope's editions of 1737–42. Fragments of the letter in Pope's hand exist at Mapledurham and also among the Marriot papers, from which last Mr. Dilke transcribed it for Elwin and Courthope (see ix. 473–4). Since the text of 1735 varies only slightly from these sources and since it is the only complete text, it is here printed. Footnotes indicate the chief departures from the fragments, which are cited here as *Mapledurham* or *Marriot*. Omissions in 1735 are indicated by half-brackets. The date comes from Dilke's transcript of the Marriot fragments.

[2] Omitted from Mapledurham.

[3] Taylor's *Works* (ed. Heber–Eden, 1861), III. ii. 61.

[4] Sexes.] Sexes and their proper instruments. *Marriot.*

[5] The first Marriot fragment ends here (EC, ix. 473).

[6] I shall entertain . . . Sex] I know you desire to be entertaind every Post with the most reigning Curiosities in Town, and I shall give you an account of a Person who is equally the Toast of Gentlemen and Ladies, and at present has more Admirers than even you yourselves. *Mapledurham.*

[7] a monster] any Monster *Mapledurham.*

in the singleness of heart[1] to have begot a christian but of one sex, and providence has[2] sent them one of two.

There are various opinions concerning this Creature about town, Mr. *Cromwell*[3] observes that the Age is very licentious, and the present Reign very lewd and corrupt, in permitting a Lady *by Authority* (as appears by the printed bills) to expose her personal curiosities[4] for a shilling.

Mr. *P.*[5] looks upon it as a Prodigy portending some great Revolution in the State: to strengthen which opinion he produces the following Prophecy of *Nostradamus*, which he explains politically.

> *When as two Sexes join'd in One,*
> *Shall in the Realm of* Brute *be shown;*
> *Then Factions shall unite, if I know,*
> *To choose*[6] *a Prince* Jure Divino.
> *This Prodigy of common Gender*
> *Is neither Sex but a Pretender,*
> *So the Lord*[7] *shield the Faith's Defender.*

Mrs. *N*—[8] admires what people wonder at so much? and says she is just so her self: The Duchess of *S*—[9] is of the same opinion.

Among these various conjectures, that I might be informed of the truth, I took along with me a Physician and a Divine, the one to inspect the state of its Body, the other to examine that of its Mind: The persons I made choice of were the ingenious Dr. *P*—[10] and the reverend Mr. ——[11] We were no sooner in the room but the Party[12] came to us drest in that habit in which the Ladies affect an Hermaphroditical imitation of Men—your sharp wit,[13] my dear Sister,[14] will immediately conclude that I mean a Riding-habit.[15]

I think it not material to inform you, whether the Doctor, the Divine, or my self look'd[16] first. The Priest you will maliciously fancy[17]

[1] of heart] of their Hearts *Mapledurham.*
[2] providence has] the Lord in his Bounty hath *Mapledurham.*
[3] There . . . Mr. *Cromwell*] Various are the Opinions about Town concerning this Animal. Mr. Cromwell *Mapledurham.*
[4] curiosities] Rarities *Mapledurham.*
[5] *P.*] Poole *Mapledurham.* Benjamin Poole was the father of Mrs. Henry Englefield (the aunt kissed by Parnell; see Pope to Teresa Blount, Sept. 1714).
[6] To choose] To Seke *Mapledurham.* (The holograph has other artificial archaisms, here unspecified.)
[7] So the Lord] And so God *Mapledurham.*
[8] *N*— is presumably Mrs. Nelson. The name is blotted out in the Mapledurham holograph.
[9] *S*—] Sh—y *Mapledurham.* Shrewsbury?
[10] Dr. *P*—] Dr. Purcell *Mapledurham.* John Purcell, M.D. (1674?–1730).
[11] reverend Mr. ——] Sir William Kennedy *Mapledurham.*
[12] the Party came] the Party or Parties came *Mapledurham.*
[13] The second Marriot fragment begins here.
[14] Sister] Sisters *Mapledurham.*
[15] Riding-habit] riding-dress *Marriot.*
[16] look'd] peeped *Marriot, Mapledurham.*
[17] you . . . fancy] (you may be sure) *Mapledurham.*

was in his nature most an Infidel, and doubted most of this Miracle: we therefore propos'd to him to take the surest method of believing, seeing and feeling:[1] He comply'd with both admonitions, and having taken a large pinch of snuff upon it, advis'd us with a nod, that we should by no means regard it as a Female but as a Male, for by so doing we should be guilty of less sinfulness.

The Doctor upon inspection differ'd from this opinion, he wou'd by no means allow it a miracle, or at most a natural one: He said upon the whole it was a woman; that whatever might give a handle to think otherwise, was a trifle, nothing being more common than for a child to be mark'd with that thing which the mother long'd for.

As for this Party's temper of mind, it appears to be a most even disposition, partaking of the good qualities of both sexes: for she is neither so inaccessible as other Ladies, nor is he so impudent as other Gentlemen. Of how obliging and complaisant a turn appears by this, that he tells the Ladies he has the Inclinations of a Gentleman, and that she tells the Gentlemen she has the *Tendre* of a Lady. As a further proof of this affable disposition, he formerly receiv'd visits of the fair sex in their masques,[2] till an impertinent fellow in a female disguise mingled with a party of ladies, and impudently overheard their improving Speculations.

Notwithstanding this, she[3] civilly promised at my request, that my two sisters[4] should be admitted privately whenever you wou'd do her[5] the honour of your consideration.

How agreeable soever this sight has been to me, I assure you it cannot be so pleasing as the sight of you in town, and whatever you may see in the country, I dare affirm[6] no man or woman can shew you the like.

I therefore earnestly desire you to make haste to this place; for tho' indeed like most other brothers, I should be sorry you were married at my expence, yet I would by no means, like them, detain you in the country from your admirers, for you may believe me, no brother in the world ever lov'd a sister as I do you. | I am, *&c.*

[1] to take . . . feeling] to imitate the Method of the Apostle *Mapledurham.* (The Mapledurham fragment ends with the word *Apostle.*) to imitate the method of the Apostle Thomas, to the end he might not be incredulous, but believe. He complied with our *Marriot.* (The second Marriot fragment ends with *our.*)

[2] The third and last Marriot fragment begins at this point.

[3] she] he *Marriot.*

[4] *two sisters* would evidently refer to Teresa and Martha and cause the letter to be supposedly written by Michael Blount.

[5] her] him *Marriot.*

[6] The last fragment of the Marriot text ends with *affirm.*

†POPE *to* MARTHA BLOUNT[1] [*February* 1715?]

1737

Madam,—I am not at all concern'd to think that this letter may be less entertaining than some I have sent: I know you are a friend that will think a kind letter as good as a diverting one. He that gives you his mirth makes a much less present than he that gives you his heart; and true friends wou'd rather see such thoughts as they communicate only to one another, than what they squander about to all the world. They who can set a right value upon any thing, will prize one tender, well-meant word, above all that ever made them laugh in their lives. If I did not think so of you, I shou'd never have taken much pains to endeavour to please you, by writing, or any thing else. Wit, I am sure I want; at least in the degree that I see others have it, who wou'd at all seasons alike be entertaining; but I would willingly have some qualities that may be (at some seasons) of more comfort to my self, and of more service to my friends. I wou'd cut off my own head, if it had nothing better than wit in it; and tear out my own heart, if it had no better dispositions than to love only myself, and laugh at all my neighbours.

I know you'll think it an agreeable thing to hear that I have done a great deal of Homer. If it be tolerable, the world may thank you for it: for if I could have seen you every day, and imagin'd my company cou'd have every day pleas'd you, I shou'd scarce have thought it worth my while to please the world. How many verses cou'd I gladly have left unfinish'd, and turn'd into it, for people to say what they would of, had I been permitted to pass all those hours more pleasingly? Whatever some may think, Fame is a thing I am much less covetous of, than your Friendship; for that I hope will last all my life, the other I cannot answer for. What if they shou'd both grow greater after my death? alas! they wou'd both be of no advantage to me! Therefore think upon it, and love me as well as ever you can, while I live.

⌜Now I talk of fame, I send you my Temple of Fame, which is just come out:[2] but my sentiments about it you will see better by this Epigram.⌝

⌜What's Fame with Men, by custom of the nation,
Is call'd in women only Reputation:
About them both why keep we such a pother?
Part you with one, and I'll renounce the other.⌝

[1] Printed first in the Roberts octavo of 1737. In the quarto and folio editions of that year the last part of the letter, here placed in half-brackets, was omitted. In the later octavos (sold by Cooper) a footnote at the beginning of the last paragraph remarked: 'From hence to the End of this Letter, is left out in the Author's Edit.' It is questionable if Pope authorized the note.

[2] Pope's *Temple of Fame* was published 1 Feb. 1715.

*POPE *to* SIR WILLIAM TRUMBULL 14 *February* 1714/15

Harvard University

Sir,—It is with some Shame I write to you when I reflect how long ago I ought to have done it. Nothing but that which makes men generally forget all offices of Friendship, & Dutyes of sociable Life, Business; could have renderd me guilty of any thing that could seem Forgetfulness of one whom I shall always be most gratefully mindful of. I never was so much employd in my Life, tho I have often been better employd; and particularly at those times when I had nothing to do but to improve my self at [East]hampstead. I must undergo the Drudgery of an [author][1] in correcting Sheets; when had I been (much more wisely) an humble Reader only, I might have corrected my own mind, and been more worthy of what I so justly value, your Friendship.

The enclosed Verses had been ordered you from the Bookseller a week since,[2] but that I resolved to accompany them with my Services: And have been daily in a Hurry till this instant, as my Father (who is the Bearer) can inform you; I beg you to accept of my sincerest wishes for the prosperity of yourself & Family, in a Word for every thing yourself can wish or pray for: I know all your Desires are as just and reasonable as mine is when I desire you to think me ever | Sir | Your most faithfull, obliged | humble servant. | A. Pope.

Mr Jervas is in the most | Zealous manner your most | humble Servant.

Address: To | The Right Honourable Sir William | Trumbull

Endorsement: Mr Pope. 14. Feb. 1714 | with the Temple of Fame

SIR WILLIAM TRUMBULL *to* POPE[3] 22 *February* 1714/15

1737 and Harvard University

Easthampstead, Feb. 22, 1714–15.

I am sensibly oblig'd, dear Sir, by your kind present of the Temple of Fame, into which you are already enter'd, and I dare prophecy for once (tho' I am not much given to it) that you will continue there, with those,

> Who ever new, not subject to decays,
> Spread and grow brighter with the length of days.[4]

[1] Square brackets emend the text where the original is torn. [2] Pope's *Temple of Fame*.

[3] Sir William's complete draft of this letter is preserved, as he wrote it, on the back of Pope's letter to him of 14 Feb. Pope printed the letter first in his octavo (Roberts) of 1737, and since that text is more finished, though differing only slightly from the draft, it is here reprinted. Major departures from the draft are noted.

[4] Adapted from *The Temple of Fame*, ll. 51–52.

There was nothing wanting to compleat your obliging remembrance of me, but your accompanying it with[1] your poem; your long absence being much the severest part of the winter. I am truly sorry that your time, which you can imploy so much better,[2] should be spent in the drudgery of correcting the printers; for as to what you have done your self, there will nothing of that nature be necessary. I wish you could find a few minutes leisure to let me hear from you sometimes, and to acquaint me how your Homer draws on towards a publication, and all things relating thereunto.[3]

I intreat you to return my humble service to Mr. Jervas. I still flatter my self that he will take an opportunity, in a proper season,[4] to see us, and review his picture, and then to alter some things, so as to please himself; which I know will not be, till every thing in it is perfect; no more than I can be, till you believe me to be with that sincerity, and esteem that I am, and will ever continue, your most faithful friend.

||POPE *and* GAY *to* CARYLL[5] — 3 *March* 1714/15

Add. 28618

March. 3rd 1714.

You travel like the sun,[6] who, even while he retreats from us, darts back some rays of comfort. Your epistles in Mr Gay's behalf were sent, attended with a competence of tickets, to my Lord Waldegrave and Mr Plowden: the effect of 'em I do not yet know. You have obliged my friend and me beyond all power, and even decency of expression, and each of us ought to thank you for the other.

The farce[7] has occasioned many different speculations in the town, some looked upon it as a mere jest upon the tragic poets, others as a satire upon the late war. Mr Cromwell hearing none of the words and seeing the action to be tragical, was much astonished to find the audience laugh; and says the Prince and Princess must doubtless be under no

[1] The words *it with* are not in the draft and should not have been inserted by Pope, since what Sir William is evidently trying to say is that he wishes Pope had accompanied his poem to Easthampstead.

[2] can imploy . . . better] can so well imploy *MS.*

[3] At the end of the paragraph Pope made a typical omission. The draft had added: 'A line or 2 sent to me to be left with Mr Rn Morris in G. str. will find me.' (The name *Rn Morris* is guessed at: it is probably wrong!)

[4] in a proper season—the phrase is not in the draft.

[5] In Pope's editions the second paragraph of this letter was printed as the larger part of a letter to Congreve under date of 19 Mar. 1714/15. Departures in the printed text are indicated below.

[6] Caryll had left London on the 21st of February.—Elwin.

[7] Gay's farce *The What d'ye Call It* was a great success, and Caryll had evidently helped promote the profitable benefit night, which (since the farce was first acted on 23 Feb.) should have fallen on 25 Feb.

less amazement[1] on the same account. Several Templars and others of the more vociferous kind of critics, went with a resolution to hiss, and confessed they were forced to laugh so much that they forgot the design they came with. The Court in general has in a very particular manner come into the jest, and the three first nights (notwithstanding two of them were Court nights) were distinguished by very full audiences of the first quality. The common people of the pit and gallery received it at first with great gravity and sedateness, some few with tears; but after the third day they also took the hint, and have ever since been very loud in their clapps. There are still some grave sober men who cannot be of the general opinion, but the laughers are so much the majority, that Mr. Dennis and one or two more seem determined to undeceive the town at their proper cost, by writing some critical dissertations against it: to encourage them in which laudable design, it is resolved a preface shall be prefixt to the farce in the vindication of the nature and dignity of this new way of writing.

I have but just room to assure you of my most hearty service and lasting acknowledgments; for Mr Gay, who has wrought all the above said wonders, challenges a part of the paper. Believe me at all times | Dear sir | Your most affectionate faithful Friend | and Servant | A: P:

He will have made about an 100 ll. of this farce.

London March. 3. 1727.[2]

Sir,—Now my benefit night is over, it should be my first care to return my thanks to those to whom I am mostly obliged; and the civilities that I have always received from you, and upon this occasion too, claim this acknowledgment. The *What'dye call it* met with more success than could be expected from a thing so out of the way of the common taste of the town. It has been played already five nights, and the galleries, who did not know what to make of it, now enter thoroughly into the humour, and it seems to please in general better than at first; the parts in general were not so well played, as I could have wished, and in particular the part of Filbert,[3] to speak in the style of the French Gazette. Penketham did wonders; Mrs Bicknell performed miraculously, and there was much honour gained by Miss Younger tho' she was but a parish child. I hope next week to have the honour to send you this dramatic performance in print, and I shall always think myself very happy when I can have any opportunity to show myself | Your most obliged faithful | humble servant | J. Gay.

[1] The Prince and Princess of Wales, having little English, might understand no more than Cromwell heard.

[2] The date 1727, though clearly written in the Caryll transcript, is obviously wrong.

[3] Johnson played Filbert; Pinkethman was Jonas Dock; Mrs. Bicknell was Kitty, and Miss Younger was 'Peascod's daughter, left on the Parish'. Both ladies were friends of Pope and Gay.

POPE *and* GAY *to* PARNELL 18 *March* [1714/15]

1770 (Goldsmith, *Life of Parnell*)

London, March 18.

I must own I have long owed you a letter, but you must own, you have owed me one a good deal longer. Besides, I have but two people in the whole kingdom of Ireland to take care of; the Dean and you: but you have several who complain of your neglect in England. Mr. Gay complains, Mr. Harcourt complains, Mr. Jarvas complains, Dr. Arbuthnot complains, my Lord complains;[1] I complain. (Take notice of this figure of iteration, when you make your next sermon) some say, you are in deep discontent at the new turn of affairs;[2] others, that you are so much in the Archbishop's good graces, that you will not correspond with any that have seen the last ministry.[3] Some affirm, you have quarrel'd with Pope, (whose friends they observe daily fall from him on account of his satyrical and comical disposition) others, that you are insinuating yourself into the opinion of the ingenious Mr. What-do-ye-call-him. Some think you are preparing your sermons for the press, and others that you will transform them into essays and moral discourses. But the only excuse, that I will allow, is, your attention to the Life of *Zoilus*, the Frogs already seem to croak for their transportation to England, and are sensible how much that Doctor is cursed and hated, who introduced their species into your nation; therefore, as you dread the wrath of St. Patrick, send them hither,[4] and rid your kingdom of those pernicious and loquacious Animals.

I have at length received your poem out of Mr. Addison's hands,[5] which shall be sent as soon as you order it, and in what manner you shall appoint. I shall in the mean time give Mr. Tooke[6] a packet for you, consisting of divers merry pieces. Mr. Gay's new Farce, Mr. Burnet's Letter to Mr. Pope,[7] Mr. Pope's Temple of Fame, Mr. Thomas Burnet's Grumbler on Mr. Gay,[8] and the Bishop of Ailsbury's Elegy,[9] written either by Mr. Cary or some other hand.

[1] My lord might be either Oxford or Bolingbroke; but it is hardly probable that Pope had recently seen either of them.

[2] Having forsaken his Whig friends when the Tories came into power, Parnell was unfortunate now that the new turn had swept the Whigs into office.

[3] Archbishop King was a Whig.

[4] The allusion is to Parnell's translation of *The Battle of the Frogs and the Mice.*

[5] Parnell's poem is unidentified.

[6] The elder Benjamin Tooke (d. 1716) had been a printer in Dublin and was now a bookseller for Swift and others in London.

[7] *Homerides: or, a Letter to Mr. Pope, Occasion'd by his intended Translation of Homer*, by Thomas Burnet (son of the bishop) and George Duckett, appeared about 7 Mar., if one may judge from advertisements in Nos. II and III of *The Grumbler.*

[8] *The Grumbler*, No. IV (17 Mar. 1715) attacks *The What D'ye Call It.* (This copy of *The Grumbler* exists in the Gay Collection at Harvard.)

[9] Gilbert Burnet, Bishop of Salisbury, had died on the day before this letter was written. If, as has been assumed, he is the Bishop of 'Ailsbury', his elegy was prompt!

Mr. Pope is reading a letter, and in the mean time, I make use of the pen to testify my uneasiness in not hearing from you. I find success, even in the most trivial things, raises the indignation of scribblers: for I, for my What-d'-ye-call-it, could neither escape the fury of Mr. Burnet, or the German Doctor;[1] then where will rage end, when Homer is to be translated? Let *Zoilus* hasten to your friend's assistance, and envious criticism shall be no more. I am in hopes that we may order our affairs so as to meet this summer at the Bath; for Mr. Pope and myself have thoughts of taking a trip thither. You shall preach, and we will write lampoons; for it is esteemed as great an honour to leave the Bath, for fear of a broken head, as for a Terrae Filius of Oxford to be expelled.[2] I have no place at court, therefore, that I may not entirely be without one every where, shew that I have a place in your remembrance; | Your most affectionate, | Faithful servant, | A. Pope, and J. Gay.

Homer will be published in three weeks.

‡POPE *to* CONGREVE[3] 19 *March* 1714/15

1735

March 19, 1714–15.

The Farce ⌜of the *What-d'ye-call-it*,⌝ has occasioned many different speculations in the town. Some look'd upon it as meer jest upon the tragic poets, others as a satire upon the late war. Mr. *Cromwell* hearing none of the words, and seeing the action to be tragical, was much astonished to find the audience laugh; and says, the Prince and Princess must doubtless be under no less amazement on the same account. Several templers, and others of the more vociferous kind of criticks, went with a resolution to hiss, and confest they were forced to laugh so much, that they forgot the design they came with. The Court in general has in a very particular manner come into the jest, and the three first Nights, (notwithstanding two of them were court-nights) were distinguish'd by very full audiences of the first quality. The common people of the pit and gallery, receiv'd it at first with great gravity and sedateness, some few with tears; but after the third day

[1] *The High-German Doctor* was a periodical first issued 4 May 1714, and written by Philip Horneck.

[2] Expulsion was a not altogether unexpected fate of these student orators and satirists. Nicholas Amhurst, editor of *The Craftsman*, was expelled in 1719.

[3] The first paragraph of this letter is taken from that found among the Caryll transcripts dated 3 Mar. 1714 [1715] and sent to Caryll. It was used practically without change. The two paragraphs about Steele were borrowed from Pope's letter to Caryll of 19 Mar. 1714: whence Pope's date for his fabrication. Though placing Steele's expulsion in 1715 was a palpable absurdity, Pope kept the date unchanged throughout his editions. He omitted the letter from the quarto and folio of 1737. The authentic letters to Caryll should be consulted for annotations.

they also took the hint, and have ever since been very loud in their claps. There are still some sober men who cannot be of the general opinion, but the laughers are so much the majority, that one or two criticks[1] seem determined to undeceive the town at their proper cost, by writing grave[2] dissertations against it: To encourage them in which laudable design, it is resolv'd a *Preface* shall be prefixt to the *Farce*, in vindication of the nature and dignity of this new way of writing.

Yesterday Mr. *Steele*'s affair was decided:[3] I am sorry I can be of no other opinion than yours, as to his whole carriage and writings of late. But certainly he has not only been punish'd by others, but suffer'd much even from his own party in the point of character, nor (I believe) receiv'd any amends in that of interest, as yet; whatever may be his Prospects for the future.

This Gentleman, among a thousand others, is a great instance of the fate of all who are carried away by party-spirit, of any side. I wish all violence may succeed as ill: but am really amazed that so much of that sower[4] and pernicious quality shou'd be joyned with so much natural good humour as I think Mr. *Steele* is possess'd of. | I am, &c.

POPE *and* GAY *to* CARYLL [*c.* 19 *March* 1714/15][5]

Add. 28618

The calamity of your gout is what all your friends, that is to say, all that know you, must share in. ⌜Mr Gay and myself have often wished ourselves with you, in the nature of comforters, or Merry Andrews (which you should like best), a task we are the fitter for, as we have (since your leaving the town) been employed in that way by a fellow sufferer of yours and a fellow friend of ours, Mr Harcourt; who is now laid up with your distemper.⌝ We desire you, in your turn, to condole with us, who are under a persecution, and much afflicted with a distemper which proves mortal[6] to many poets, a criticisme. We have indeed some relieving intervals of laughter (as you know there are in some diseases), ⌜but the attacks are renewed,⌝ and it is the opinion of divers good guessers that the last fit will not be more violent than advantageous ⌜to us.⌝ For poets assailed by critics are much like men

[1] one or two criticks] Mr. Dennis & one or two more *Caryll MSS.*

[2] grave] critical *Caryll MSS.*

[3] decided: I am sorry] decided in his expulsion from the House. I am sorry *Caryll MSS.* (Steele was expelled from the House of Commons on 19 Mar. 1713/14.)

[4] sower] vile *Caryll MSS.*

[5] The date is approximated by the facts that the letter was written just after the death of Gilbert Burnet, Bishop of Salisbury (d. 17 Mar.) and before Talbot, Bishop of Oxford, was officially announced as Bishop of Salisbury—which occurred on 19 Mar.

The first two paragraphs of the letter were used by Pope (1735–42) in a letter printed as to Congreve 7 Apr. 1715. They form (with alterations and omissions—here indicated in half-brackets) the last half of that letter. The letter did not appear in the quarto and folio of 1737.

[6] mortal] grievous *1735–42*.

bitten by tarantulas: they dance on the faster ⸢the deeper they are stung, till the very violence and sweating makes 'em recover.⸣

Mr Tho: Burnet hath played the precursor to the coming of Homer, in a treatise called *Homerides.*[1] He has[2] since risen very much in his criticismes, and after assaulting Homer, made a daring attack upon the *Whatd'yecall-it.*[3] Yet is there not a proclamation issued ⸢forth⸣ for the burning of Homer and the Pope by the common hangman; nor is the *Whatd'yecall-it* yet silenced by the Lord Chamberlain. They shall survive the conflagration of his father's works, and live after his father is damned; for that the B[ishop] of S[alisbury] already is so, is the opinion of Dr Sacheverell and the Church of Rome.

It remains that I should in a brief and perspicuous manner, acquaint you with the news of this place. The Bishop of Oxford expects the Bishopric of Sarum; Mr Gay expects a present from the Princess:[4] we are invited this day to dinner at my Lord Lansdowne's; we are invited to see the lions at the Tower, gratis;[5] by a lord who expects to have a new lodging given him by the Parliament. Mr Steele declares the farce should not have been acted if he had been in town.[6] The new theatre in Lincolns Inn Fields have thoughts of acting it without his consent. The rest is no news, being only that we are everlastingly | Your most obliged and most | faithful, affectionate Servants.

Sir,[7]—I received your obliging letter, but could wish that honour had not been done me, since it put you to pain in the writing of it. I have given the book as you ordered to Lewis to be sent to you the first opportunity. When any thing of mine is sent to your retirement I cry out

Hei mihi quod Domino non licet ire tuo.

Ovid[8]

[1] See the preceding letter (to Parnell, 18 Mar.).

[2] The Caryll transcript has *was*; here emended to *has*.

[3] For Pope's note on this attack (1735) see his letter to Congreve, 7 Apr. 1715.

[4] A present as acknowledgement of his *Letter to a Lady*, addressed to the Princess on her arrival in England.

[5] It may be that Lord Lansdowne joked about coming to the Tower to see him when he should be lodged there—as he was for over a year beginning 26 Sept. The lord might conceivably be Bolingbroke, who escaped to France on 28 Mar., or Oxford, who went to the Tower on 16 July.

[6] Steele as patentee of Drury Lane could have prevented performance, and might have, since his friend Addison's *Cato* was burlesqued in passages of the farce. But his objection was not strong, evidently, for performances from time to time continued in Drury Lane. It was not acted in Lincoln's Inn Fields.

[7] This added note is by Gay, who is sending by Lewis a copy of his farce. Caryll's gout had made writing for the play painful.

[8] *Tristia*, I. i. 2. Caryll himself very likely inserted Ovid's name at the end of the letter.

GAY *and* POPE *to* CARYLL[1] [*April* 1715]

Add. 28618

London.

Sir,—Mr Pope is going to Mr Jervase's where Mr Addison is sitting for his picture. In the meantime amidst clouds of tobacco at William's[2] Coffee-house I write this letter. ⌜We have agreed to spend this day in visits: he is to introduce me to a lord and two ladies, and on my part, which I think will balance his visits, I am to present him to a dutchess.⌝[3] There is a grand revolution at Will's Coffee-house. Morrice has quitted for a coffee-house in the City, and Titcombe is restored to the great joy of Cromwell, who was at a great loss for a person to converse with upon the Fathers and Church History. The knowledge I gain from him is entirely in painting and poetry; and Mr Pope owes all his skill in astronomy ⌜and particularly in the revolution of eclipses⌝ to him and Mr Whiston, so celebrated of late for his discovery of the longitude in an extraordinary copy of verses[4] ⌜which you heard when you were last in town.⌝ Mr Rowe's *Jane Grey* is to be played in Easter week[5] when Mrs Oldfield is to personate a character directly opposite to female nature; for what woman ever despised Sovereignty? Chaucer has a tale, where a knight saves his head by discovering ⌜that⌝ it was the thing which all women most coveted. ⌜Colonel Frowde[6] puns upon his play, and declares that most of the ladies of Drury Lane will not accept of a crown when 'tis offered them, unless you give them a supper into the bargain; and wonders how people can admire the uncommonness of the character.⌝ Mr Pope's Homer is retarded by the great rains that have fallen of late,[7] which causes the sheets to be long a-drying. This gives Mr Lintott great uneasiness, who is now endeavoring to corrupt the curate of his parish to pray for fair weather, that his work may go on the faster. There's a sixpenny criticism[8] lately

[1] This letter, with additions from that to Caryll [*c.* 19 Mar. 1715], became a letter to Congreve printed in Pope's editions under date of 7 Apr. 1715. Pope's extensive omissions from this present text are indicated in half-brackets. He made two or three verbal changes as noted below.

[2] at William's Coffee house] at a coffee house *1735–42*. (Elwin thinks the reference is to William's near St. James's—which would also be near Cleveland Court where Jervas and Pope lived; but it may be jocose affectation for Will's, which Gay immediately goes on to speak of.)

[3] Gay's former employer, the Duchess of Monmouth?

[4] Called an Ode on the Longitude, in Swift and Pope's Miscellany.—Pope, 1735–42; see Pope to Congreve, 7 Apr. 1715.

[5] Easter fell on 17 Apr., and Rowe's play was acted first on 20 Apr.—before which day this letter was evidently written.

[6] Col. William Frowde and not his brother Philip, the dramatist, as has been thought. W. D. Ellis kindly called the editor's attention to the note in Swift's *Journal to Stella* (ed. Sir Harold Williams), pp. 81–82, on this matter.

[7] Pope had advertised 1 Mar. as the date of publication; the volume appeared 6 June.

[8] This curious Piece was entitled, *A compleat Key to the What-d'ye-call-it*. It was written by one *Griffin* a Player, assisted by *Lewis Theobald*.—Pope, 1735–42; in To Congreve, 7 Apr. 1715.

published upon the tragedy of the *What dye call it*, wherein he with much judgment and learning calls me a blockhead, and Mr Pope a knave. His grand charge is against the *Pilgrim's Progress* being read, which he says is directly levelled at Cato's reading Plato. To back this censure, he goes on to tell you that the *Pilgrim's Progress* being mentioned to be the eight[h] edition makes the reflection evident, the tragedy of *Cato* being just eight times printed.[1] He has also endeavoured to show that every particular passage of the play alludes to some fine part of [the] tragedy, which he says I've injudiciously and profanely abused. Sir Samuel Garth's poem upon my Lord Clare's house[2] I believe will be published in the Easter week. ⌜My Lord Peterborough, I hear, is banished the Court,[3] but I do not know the occasion. Mr Pope and I have thoughts of doing ourselves the honour of making you a visit in Sussex as soon as he hath ended this year's labour with the bookseller, where I promise myself the greatest pleasure and satisfaction. May the gout be favorable to you, that we may walk together in your Park. Mr Pope will make his conditions before he will venture into your company, that you shall not allow him any of your conversation in the morning; he is obliged to pay this self-deniall in complaisance to his subscribers. For my part, who do not deal in heroes or ravished ladies, I may perhaps celebrate a milk-maid, describe the amours of your parson's daughter, or write an elegy upon the death of a hare; but my articles are quite the reverse of his, that you will interrupt me every morning, or ten to one I shall be first troublesome and interrupt you. Let Mr Pope and Mr Homer keep company together. I should think that ancient gentleman a good companion in a garret in London, but not in one of the pleasantest seats in England, where I hope next month to have the happiness of good company.⌝

Thus far Mr Gay—who in his letter has ⌜already⌝ forestalled all the subjects of ⌜raillery and⌝ diversion: unless it should be one, to tell you that I sit up till ⌜one or⌝ two a clock ⌜every night⌝ over burgundy and champagne, and am become so much a modern rake that I shall be ashamed in a short time to be thought to do any sort of business. I must[4] get the gout by drinking, ⌜as above said,⌝ purely for a fashionable pretence to sit still long enough to translate four books of Homer. I hope you'll by that time be up again, and I may succeed to the bed and couch of my predecessor ⌜at Ladyholt.⌝ Pray cause the stuffing to be repaired, and the crutches shortened for me. ⌜I have used my author like a mistress, attacked at first with prodigious violence and warmth

[1] being just eight times printed] having just eight times (as he quaintly expresses it) *visited the press.* *1735–42*; in To Congreve, 7 Apr. 1715.

[2] Garth's *Claremont*, published 2 May, contained a fine compliment to *Windsor Forest.*

[3] Peterborough had been recalled from Italy upon the accession of George I, and when he reached London was ordered not to appear at Court.

[4] I must] I fear I must *1735–42*; see Pope to Congreve, 7 Apr. 1715.

for a month or two, and then left him every day for any sort of idle companion I could light upon. It is with great grudging and melancholy that I now reflect I must at last be obliged to do my drudgery at home, and stick to my old task and daily labor.

That I may tell you some news of another besides myself, know that Richard Steele Esquire is now Sir Richard Steele.[1] What reflections may be made upon this occasion, I leave to you to produce in your next lucubration, which will be received with much pleasure by, | Sir, | your most affectionate faithful | friend and servant | A. P.⌉

‡GAY *and* POPE *to* CONGREVE[2] — 7 *April* 1715

1735

April 7, 1715.

Mr. *Pope* is going to Mr. *Jervas*'s, where Mr. *Addison* is sitting for his picture; in the mean time amidst clouds of tobacco at a coffee-house I write this letter. There is a grand revolution at *Will*'s, *Morrice* has quitted for a coffee-house in the city, and *Titcomb* is restor'd to the great joy of *Cromwell*, who was at a great loss for a person to converse with upon the fathers and church-history; the knowledge I gain from him, is entirely in painting and poetry; and Mr. *Pope* owes all his skill in astronomy to him and Mr. *Whiston*, so celebrated of late for his discovery of the longitude in an extraordinary copy of Verses.[3] Mr. *Rowe*'s *Jane Gray* is to be play'd in *Easter-week*, when Mrs. *Oldfield* is to personate a character directly opposite to female nature; for what woman ever despis'd Sovereignty? You know *Chaucer* has a tale where a knight saves his head, by discovering it was the thing which all women most coveted. Mr. *Pope*'s *Homer* is retarded by the great rains that have fallen of late, which causes the sheets to be long a drying; this gives Mr. *Lintot* great uneasiness, who is now endeavouring to corrupt the Curate of his parish to pray for fair weather, that his work may go on. There is a six-penny *Criticism* lately publish'd upon the Tragedy of the *What-d'ye-call-it*, wherein he with much judgment and learning calls me a blockhead, and Mr. *Pope* a knave. His grand charge is against the *Pilgrims Progress* being read, which he says is directly level'd at *Cato's* reading *Plato*; to back this censure, he goes on to tell you, that the *Pilgrims Progress* being mention'd to be the eighth edition, makes the reflection evident, the Tragedy of *Cato* having just eight times (as he quaintly expresses it) *visited the Press.* He has also endeavoured to show, that every particular passage of the

[1] Steele was knighted according to the records of the Heralds Office on 9 Apr.—Aitken, *Life of Steele* (1889), ii. 57.

[2] This letter is taken from two letters to Caryll here dated [*c.* 19 Mar. 1714/15] and [Apr. 1715]. The first sentence perhaps indicates a last attempt of Jervas to bring Pope and Addison together. Further annotation of the material may be seen in the letters sent to Caryll.

[3] For Pope's note (1735–42) to this passage see his letter to Caryll, i. 288, note 4.

play alludes to some fine part of [the] Tragedy, which he says I have injudiciously and profanely abused.[1] Sir *Samuel Garth*'s Poem upon my Lord *Clare*'s house, I believe will be publish'd in the *Easter-week.*

Thus far Mr. *Gay*—who has in his letter forestall'd all the subjects of diversion; unless it should be one to you to say, that I sit up till two a-clock over *Burgundy* and *Champagne*; and am become so much a rake, that I shall be ashamed in a short time to be thought to do any sort of business. I fear I must get the gout by drinking, purely for a fashionable pretence to sit still long enough to translate four books of *Homer*, I hope you'll by that time be up again, and I may succeed to the bed and couch of my predecessor: Pray cause the stuffing to be repaired, and the crutches shortned for me.[2] The calamity of your gout is what all your friends, that is to say all that know you, must share in; we desire you in your turn to condole with us, who are under a persecution, and much afflicted with a distemper which proves grievous to many poets, a *Criticism.* We have indeed some relieving intervals of laughter, (as you know there are in some Diseases;) and it is the opinion of divers good guessers, that the last fit will not be more violent than advantageous; for poets assail'd by critics, are like men bitten by *Tarantula's*, they dance on so much the faster.

Mr. *Thomas Burnet* hath play'd the precursor to the coming of *Homer*, in a treatise call'd *Homerides.* He has since risen very much in his criticisms, and after assaulting *Homer*, made a daring attack[3] upon the *What-d'ye-call-it.* Yet is there not a proclamation issued for the burning of *Homer* and the *Pope* by the common hangman; nor is the *What-d'ye-call-it* yet silenc'd by the Lord-Chamberlain. ⌜They shall survive the conflagration of his father's works, and live after they and he are damned; (for that the B—p of *S.* already is so, is the opinion of Dr. *Sacheverel* and the Church of *Rome.*) | I am, &c.⌝[4]

POPE *to* PARNELL[5] — *7 April* 1715

Elwin–Courthope, vii. 455

April 7, 1715.

It is presumed the different sorts of ink wherewith you wrote to Mr. Gay and to me might have some effect upon the styles, and you may, by this expedient, if you please, compose a new and elegant essay upon

[1] This curious piece was entitled, *A compleat Key to the What-d'ye-call-it.* It was written by one Griffin, a Player, assisted by Lewis Theobald.—Pope, 1735–42.

[2] From this point the letter is drawn from the earlier letter to Caryll [*c.* 19 Mar. 1715] concerning his gout. For omissions see the original letter sent to Caryll.

[3] In one of his Papers call'd *The Grumbler*; long since dead.—Pope, 1735–42. After 1735 Pope omitted 'long since dead'.

[4] This last sentence was omitted from the printed text in 1737 and thereafter.

[5] Elwin printed this letter from the original, which has now disappeared.

the different styles of prose as well as of poetry.[1] But the natural and obvious reason of that variety we do conceive to have proceeded from hence, that you wrote the one in bad scribbling ink to me at your own house, and the other in good writing ink at the dean's.

I can convey to you the poem I received from Mr. Addison by Mr. Budgell's packets, as I fancy you might the treatise of Zoilus, and the Batrachomuomachia, directed to Mr. Tickell for me.[2] You may now tell Mr. Budgell that he is mentioned in our letters, as he may probably know himself if this should be opened at the office before it reaches your hands. I much long for your promised piece, and beg it may be accompanied with the Pervigilium Veneris.[3] My faithful service to the dean, whom I honour more than an English archbishop. This is all at present, but that I wish you pretensions and potatoes as many as you can digest, ecclesiastical dignities unspeakable, long life, and short sermons. Yours, in all cordial affection for ever.

POPE *to* CARYLL [*June* 1715]

Add. 28618

Binfield

You will have the humanity, I know, to excuse my having deferred writing till now, when you are told that I've writ several hundreds of verses since my coming hither, which was not a fortnight ago. I have scarce allowed myself the discharge of any common civilities to my neighbours here, or the least amusement to myself. The unwearied diligence I observe at this season in the country people about me affords one good lesson: that I ought to make hay whilst the sun shines. No fair day in the fancy is to be neglected, considering what a climate what a right English climate, there is in my head, where few days pass without being clouded, or feverish. It is not the worse for me that Gay did not accompany me hither; for whatever the world may think of my love to the Muses, I never keep 'em company when I can have that of a friend. My Muse is now an old stale wife, and I make bitter dry drudgery of it. This jade of mine, that is so fruitful of abortions, will lie in her month, whatsoever she brings forth, tho' it were but a sooterkin: for so the state and ceremony of the matter requires. As soon as I'm up I'll make 'em a visit at Ladyholt, if Gay will keep his word, and you shall find me as frolicsome again as ever: ⌜like those good wives who are no sooner up, but the old benefactor is troubled

[1] In 1713 Parnell had published his verse *Essay on the Different Styles of Poetry*.

[2] Addison was now secretary to the Lord Lieutenant of Ireland, and Budgell was the under-secretary. Evidently Parnell and Budgell in Ireland were on doubtful terms as were Pope and Tickell in England. Addison was at this time in England.

[3] Parnell's translation of the *Pervigilium* is included in Pope's edition of Parnell's *Poems* (1722).

with them.⌝ I have a little affair of business to add to this letter. You would oblige me if you knew any secure estate, on which I might purchase an anuity[1] for life of about 500 *l.* I believe my unfortunate state of health might, in this one case, [be] of some advantage to me. The kind interest which I know you always take in my fortunes, gives me reason to think such an enquiry will be no trouble to you. I desire to hear if you have any thoughts of coming to Mapledurham yet. If it were about a month hence, we might return with you; for I expect Mr Gay in some weeks, unless matters of more consequence to him prevent. I am, with the truest esteem | Dear sir | Your most obliged and faithful | affectionate servant | A: P:

I hope you have your books from Lintot.[2]

POPE *to* MARTHA BLOUNT 3 *June* [1715]

Mapledurham

Friday the 3d. of Jun.

Madam,—I dare not pretend to instruct a Lady when to take any thing kindly. Their own Hearts are always the best Directors. But if I might, I would tell you that if ever I could have any merit with you, it is in writing to you at a time when I am studying to forget every Creature I ever lov'd or esteemed: When I am concern'd for nothing in the world but the Life of one or two who are to be Impeachd,[3] and the Health of a Lady that has been sick. When I am to be entertain'd only with that Jade whom every body thinks I love, as a Mistress, but whom in reality I hate as a Wife, my Muse. Pitty me, Madam, who am to lye in of a Poetical Child for at least two Months.[4] As soon as I am up again I'll wait upon you: but in the mean time I beg to hear if you are quite recoverd from your Ague, the only thing I desire to hear from anyone in my present State of Oblivion.

Not that I am so vain to expect a Favor from your hands which I never yet receivd; I do not say never merited to receive, for I know both how little, and how much I deserve at your hands, tho it is impossible you should. But if you will send those books of mine which you are weary of, by one of your servants, he may at the same time inform me of your Health. He may add to my Satisfaction by acquainting me of that of Mr Blount, Mrs Blount, & your fair Sister—This Letter may very probably be the only thing that hinders you from a

[1] Pope intended (as later letters show) to say, 'I might purchase for 500*l.* an annuity for life.'

[2] Copies of the *Iliad*, vol. i, published 6 June.

[3] Bolingbroke was impeached on 10 June and Oxford shortly thereafter.

[4] This Poetical Child would seem to be the second volume of the *Iliad*, which Pope must proceed to translate. Volume i had been announced on 31 May for delivery on 6 June, and hence would not be a two-months matter.

total Forgetfulness of me: I would to God I could as easily forget Mapledurham is within Ten miles of me.[1] I am just in the Condition of the poor people in Purgatory, Heaven is in Sight, and the Pain of Loss the greatest I endure. I hope to be happy in a little time and live in that hope.

Yours and Mrs Teresa's most obedient | faithful Servant. | A. Pope.

I desire Mr Blount not to send for his first Vol. of Homer to London: I shall have one for him on a better paper than Ordinary by Thursday next.

Address: For | Mrs Martha Blount, | att | Mapledurham

EDWARD YOUNG[2] *to* POPE — 8 *June* [1715]

Homer MSS. Add. 4807

Just now I receivd the Homers, which with that You design for the publick Library (of which I will take the Care desird) are in Number but Eleven, whereas the List You sent was of Twelve. | I am Dear Sir | Your most Affectionate | Humble Servant E Young

June 8th.

The mistake was Easie, nor would I have You give yourself farther trouble. I will Expect mine at Wasses.[3]

Address: To Mr Pope att | Button's Coffee house.[4]

LINTOT *to* POPE — 10 *June* 1715

Homer MSS. Add. 4807

10. June. 1715.

Sir,—You have Mr Tickles Book to divert one Hour—It is allready condemn'd here and the malice & juggle at Buttons is the conversation of those who have spare moments from Politicks.

[1] i.e. ten miles from Binfield, from which Pope must be writing. His leaving London at the moment *Iliad*, vol. i, was to appear is eloquent concerning his trepidation as to its reception.

[2] The poet Young, a law fellow of All Souls at this time, was evidently Pope's agent in distributing the *Iliad* in Oxford. Ten colleges had subscribed, and Pope had sent a special copy 'for the publick Library' (Bodley's). But see W. D. Macray, *Annals of the Bodleian Library* (2nd ed., 1890), p. 204, where Pope is recorded as presenting copies of the *Iliad* and *Odyssey* in 1725. Pope has failed to include Young's own copy. Young was a friend of Tickell, to whom he conveyed the opinion of Oxford concerning the rival Homers of 1715: 'To be very plain the University almost in general gives the Preference to Popes Translation.' See Sherburn, *Early Career*, pp. 144–5.

[3] 'Wasse' is a guess for an illegible word. Joseph Wasse, rector of Aynhoe, may have been in London at this time. Bentley said, 'According to Whiston, when I am dead, Wasse will be the most learned man in England.' (Nichols, *Lit. Anec.* i. 263.)

[4] The address suggests that Young in Oxford did not realize that Pope in June 1715 was not frequenting Button's. His normal London address was Jervas's house in Cleveland Court.

Sir Jno Germain has his Book.

All your Books were deliverd pursuant to your directions the middle of the Week after you left Us.

The princess is extreamly pleasd with her Book. You shall have your Folios preserv'd.

Mr Broome I have not heard from. Pray detain me not from publishing my Own Book having deliverd the greatest part of the Subscribers allready, upwards of four hundred.

I designd to publish Monday sevennight[1] pray interrupt me not by an Errata.

I doubt not the Sale of Homer if you do not dissapoint me by delaying the Publication. | Yours | Bernard Lintott.

Service to Mr Gay—

Lord Bolinbroke is impeachd this Night The noise the Report makes does me some present damage.

JERVAS *to* POPE *12 June 1715*

Homer MSS. Add. 4807

June the 12th 1715–

Dear Mr P.—I had Your Last in due time.

Shall I send you the £100 in Bills or Cash. and when? Gay had a Copy of the Farewell,[2] with your Injunctions. No other extant.—

Lord Harvey[3] had the Homer & Letter, & bids me thank the Author—

I hear nothing of the Sermon—The Generality will take it for the Deanes and that will hurt neither you nor him.[4] Gay will be with You on Saturday next. He also works hard[5]—Your old Sword went with the Carrier & was tyed to the other Things with a Cord & my folks say very fast. You must make the Carrier responsible, Mine will swear to the Delivery . . . &c. . . .

No Books for you from Lintot.

[1] The first volume of Pope's *Iliad* in quarto was distributed to subscribers beginning on Monday June 6. Tickell's *First Book* was on sale 8 June. In *The St. James's Post* and *The Daily Courant* for 6 June Lintot advertised that his 'fine folio edition' in large and small paper would be published 'next week'. It is not clear at what date Lintot's trade copies were on sale. The earliest advertisement noted occurs in *The London Gazette* for 2 July 1715.

[2] 'A Farewell to London in the Year 1715' was first published in *Additions to Pope's Works* (1776).

[3] Carr, Lord Hervey (d. 1723), unlike his younger brother John, was admired by Pope.

[4] The late Norman Ault argued in his edition of *The Prose Works of Pope* (1936), i, pp. lxxv–xcii, that this passage indicates Pope's authorship of *The Dignity, Use and Abuse of Glass-Bottles. Set forth in a Sermon . . . By the Author of the Tale of a Tub.* This 'sermon' makes casual attacks on Philip Horneck and Thomas Burnet (son of the bishop), who had been attacking Pope, and Ault's argument for Pope's authorship is very ingenious—but not wholly convincing.

[5] On his *Trivia*.—Elwin.

Mrs Raines a Young Lady in the City & one of my Shepherdesses,[1] takes one of the Volumes, has paid her 2 Guineas & is to be a Subscriber in your next list.

I also got 2 Guineas from the Marquess of Dorchester. . . .[2]

Philips[3] sent me a Note for Receipts to be Convey'd to the 11 Members of the Late Hanover Club. Pray Let me have their Names by the first—

I send to Mr. Merril's[4] to day, &c.

Lintot sent me Tickell's Homer for your Government. I cou'd not forbear comparing, And I do not know what the Devil is got into my head, but I fancy I coud make a more Poetical Translation in [a] fortnight. (excepting a very few Lines)[5]

It seemes 'tis publisht merely to Shew as a Specimen of his Ability for the Odysses—Fortescue wou'd have Gay publish a Version of the first Book of the Odysses & tell the World 'tis only to bespeak their Approbation & favor for a Translation of Statius or any other Poet—in short we are merry whether we are Witty or no—My Respects to Dear Sir William[6] & his good Lady & Son and am concerned for any deficiency in his Countenance, but am in no pain for the Paultry Basso rilievo. | Yours. and Yours.

[*Written along the left margin*:] I will remember you to Your friends of my Acquaintance punctually.

POPE *and* JERVAS *to* LINTOT [*? June* 1715]

Add. 12113

To Mr Lintott.

Sir,—Pray deliver the Bearer two Books for the Duke & Dutchess of Rutland one in fine paper, the other in common. and place 'em to my Account—I having made Use of one of Mr Jervas's Books, desire you

[1] That is, one of the ladies painted by Jervas as shepherdesses.

[2] The Marquess of Dorchester was the father of Lady Mary Wortley Montagu. He was created Duke of Kingston later in 1715.

[3] On Philips's slowness in turning in these subscriptions see Pope to Caryll, 8 June 1714. Now apparently Pope is making the eleven wait for their books.

[4] John Merril, Esq., is listed as a subscriber to the *Iliad.*

[5] This is, of course, a prejudiced view of Tickell's rival translation, though in general his translation was not well received. Pope evidently intended to 'govern' the work. His copy of Tickell's volume, now preserved at Hartlebury Castle, has marginalia that show his intention to attack the book. He wisely thought better of the matter, and after Addison's death he and Tickell were somewhat reconciled if not actually friendly. Tickell's address 'To the Reader' certified that the translation of Book I of the *Iliad* was designed to 'bespeak the Favour of the Public to a Translation of Homer's Odysseis'. As a matter of fact Tickell had signed an agreement with Tonson on 31 May 1714 to translate the whole *Iliad.* Pope apparently never learned of this agreement. See Sherburn, *Early Career*, pp. 123–48.

[6] Sir William Trumbull, whose picture Jervas had not yet 'reviewed'. See Trumbull to Pope, 22 Feb. 1714/15.

also to give the bearer another instead of it, from | Your Servant A. Pope.

This you may file for a Receipt of three Bookes.

——— —

Mr Lintott sent Yesterday six Books out of which you design'd one of the best for the Duke of Montagu, which you gave to Sir John Shadwell. Therefore I must have one [in] its room for his Grace. Which makes this a Receipt for four. | Charles Jervas.

POPE *to* BROOME 16 *June* [1715]

Elwin–Courthope, viii. 36

Windsor Forest, June 16.

I am told by Mr. Lintot that you have run through the first volume of Eustathius in the manner I desired. The acknowledgements I am to pay you on that account shall be deferred to a more convenient opportunity. I beg you to send the papers of extracts, &c., sealed up, to me, directed to Lintot, as soon as they are ready, together with the book itself, which belongs to the library of the late Lord Halifax. You will take a particular care in putting it up, and send a letter to Mr. Lintot two posts before, that he may know on what day the book will be in London, and at what inn to meet it, for fear of accidents. I will send the next volume, as soon as I can procure it, afterwards.

There were one or two subscribers to Homer whose names you gave in,—Sir Robert Cotton and my Lord Cornwallis,—neither of which have paid, unless it were to you. I should be glad it were in your hands, and you need not give yourself the trouble to return it. I hope it will not be long before we may contrive to meet. I have ordered Lintot, as soon as he receives the first volume of Eustathius, to send you back by the next return of the same carrier the first volume of my translation, which I desire you to accept.

Mrs. Marriot may believe, with a great deal of truth, that nothing but the utmost hurry in town, and constant attendance to study in the country, could so long have prevented me the pleasure of writing to her. I am really so fatigued with scribbling, that I could almost wish, in the Scripture phrase, that *my hand had forgot its cunning*. Homer will at last do me justice; he was the first author that made me catch the itch of poetry, when I read him in my childhood; and he will now cure me of it entirely. If I outlive this task, which perhaps, sickly as I am, I may, and the memory of it too, I shall be capable of being everything that I now am hindered from being,—I mean I shall be a better man, a better friend, a better correspondent, &c. I am now like a wretched man of business, who regards only himself and his own affairs. But I assure Mrs. Marriot sincerely, I am always hers, and, sir, your most faithful, affectionate, humble servant.

Mrs. Betty Marriot promised I should wait on her in this country, but has disappointed me. Pray tell her, when she returns, that she is in my debt.

LINTOT *to* POPE[1] — 22 *June* 1715

Homer MSS. Add. 4807

June the 22d 1715.

Sir,—The hurry I have been in by the Report from the Comittee of Secrecy[2] to get it publishd has prevented the publication of Homer for the present till the Noise be over, and those whom I expected to be very noisy on Account of your Translation are buried in politicks.[3]

Mr Thornhill[4] sent to me for his Own Book which he paid for to you, as he says,[5] and paid me Eight Guineas for the Subscriptions of Sarah Countess of Winchelsea | Mrs Seymour. | Berkly Seymour Esqr | & | Charles Frotherby Esqr.[6]

Mr Harcourt and Lord Harcourt have had thirteen Books sent to their House, Ten of which were of the finest paper.

I will observe your directions about Mr Broome.

The 2d voll of Homer shall be sent in a day or Two. The project for printing the first Book of Homer with Mr Dryden, and Mr Tickles & Mr Manwarings together is well thought off, I propos'd it to Mr Tonson, but it will not do. I will consider further of it.

The Duke of Ormond is to be impeached for High Treason and E: of Strafford for high Crimes & Misdemeanors.

May Success attend your Studies[7] is the hearty prayer of | Yours to Command | Bernard Lintott.[8]

[1] In the margin of this letter Pope jotted comments here given in footnotes, italicized (though not underlined on the letter).

[2] The Report of the Committee to investigate the Oxford Ministry. Pope's marginal entry is: *send it.*

[3] Pope's marginal entry is *W^t s^d of Tickels* [i.e. what is said of Tickell's translation of *Iliad* I?].

[4] Thomas and Richard Thornhill are among Pope's subscribers. Sir James Thornhill, the painter, is not in the list.

[5] Pope writes in *pd.*

[6] Pope's marginal comment: *These to have Receits, & books w^n sent for.*

[7] Two marginal comments by Pope: *That I proceed* and *Wm Holmes Esq. two receits.* | *To whom deliverd.*

[8] Pope's final entry: *Sheet C. p. 1. for self corr.* [i.e. he wants to correct something on page 1 of sheet C].

†PARNELL *to* POPE[1] 27 *June* 1715

1735

June 27, 1715.

I am writing you a long letter, but all the tediousness I feel in it is, that it makes me during the time think more intently of my being far from you. I fancy if I were with you, I cou'd remove some of the uneasiness which you may have felt from the opposition of the world, and which you should be asham'd to feel, since it is but the testimony which one part of it gives you that your merit is unquestionable: What wou'd you have otherwise, from ignorance, envy, or those tempers which vie with you in your own way? I know this in mankind, that when our ambition is unable to attain its end, it is not only wearied, but exasperated too at the vanity of its labours; then we speak ill of happier studies, and sighing condemn the excellence which we find above our reach.—

My *Zoilus*[2] which you us'd to write about, I finish'd last spring, and left in town,[3] I waited till I came up to send it you, but not arriving here before your book[4] was out, imagin'd it a lost piece of labour. If you will still have it, you need only write me word.

I have here seen the *First Book* of *Homer*,[5] which came out at a time when it cou'd not but appear as a kind of setting up against you. My opinion is, that you may if you please, give *them thanks who writ it*. Neither the numbers nor the spirit have an equal mastery with yours; but what surprizes me more is, that, a scholar being concern'd, there should happen to be some mistakes in the author's sense, such as putting the light of *Pallas*'s eyes into the eyes of *Achilles*; making the taunt of *Achilles* to *Agamemnon*, (that he should have spoils when *Troy* should be taken) to be a cool and serious proposal: the translating what you call *ablution* by the word *Offals*, and so leaving *Water* out of the rite of lustration, *&c.* but you must have taken notice of all this before. I write not to inform you, but to shew I always have you at heart. | I am, &c.

[1] This letter was omitted from the quarto and folio of 1737, but occurs in all other editions by Pope. The date was omitted in his editions after 1735. The Cooper octavo of 1737 printed a note doubtfully authorized by Pope but certainly true: 'This [letter], and the three Extracts following, concerning the Translation of the first *Iliad*, set on foot by Mr. *Addison*, Mr. *Pope* has omitted in his own Edition.'

[2] Printed for B. Lintot 1715, 8o under this Title.—Pope, 1735–42. The phrase *under this Title* is omitted in the Cooper octavo of 1737 and thereafter—wisely, since the 'Life of Zoilus' was printed in 1717 prefixed to Parnell's translation of *Homer's Battle of the Frogs and Mice*, which Pope published in May of that year.

[3] 'Town' here means Dublin.

[4] Vol. i of the *Iliad*.

[5] Tickell's translation of Book I of the *Iliad*.

JERVAS *to* POPE[1] 28 *June* 1715

1776 (*Additions*)

London, June 28th, 1715.

Dear Mr. Pope,— Mrs. Cecil sent to me for some receipts which she is so kind to get distributed. She has given me two or three names, Lady Ranelagh, Lady Cavendish, &c. whom she has not seen lately to solicit for you. Lady Scudamore asks how and what you do, being much concerned we had not a few breakfasts in her closet before you left us.

I have a letter from Mr. Edward Blount, claiming hints of promises to see Blagdon in Devon—[2] all over civil and courteous with an air. I dined yesterday with Mr. Rollinson, who takes it ill that Gay forgot to call him to go to Binfield in his way to Lady Bolenbr—[3]

I saw a glimpse of young Mr. Blount,[4] and he called here, but I was not at home.—I would have ventured to send the Report of the Committee,[5] that you may have time enough to prepare a Preface or Dedication to the memory of your patrons.[6]—The Whigs say, Bolenbroke is the hero of your Preface. Pray make room for Walpole in your next, to keep the balance of power even.

Mr. Samuel Hill, nephew to our neighbour, a subscriber to Mr. Harcourt, but his name forgot in the list. I gave him a receipt.

Most of what you see has been writ a week, in hope of some occurrence worthy your notice. Mr. Fortescue tells me Gay will be in London the first proxim.—Service to every body—Neighbours, &c.

I am yours, &c. | C. J.

That my correspondence may be as little troublesome as possible, you see I take care to procure poetical franks.[7]

[1] Elwin's text does not differ, except in his modernizations, from that given here. He seems to have seen the original letter, which he reports as incomplete through a tear in two places.

[2] The original was, according to Elwin, torn at this point.

[3] The first Lady Bolingbroke (d. 1718) lived at Bucklebury, a few miles west of Binfield.

[4] Young Mr. Blount is Michael, brother of Martha and Teresa.

[5] The report of the Committee of Secrecy to inquire into the conduct of the late Ministry. Walpole was chairman of this committee; hence the mention of him here.

[6] Here again the MS. was incomplete according to Elwin. The 'patrons' of Homer in 1715 were unfortunate. Tickell dedicated to Lord Halifax, who died before the volume was published, and Pope daringly praised Bolingbroke (as well as Halifax) in his Preface, and Bolingbroke was impeached on 10 June.

[7] Possibly by Addison? In the *Iliad* MSS. (Add. 4807) between folios 92*v* and 167*v* occur 19 letters to or from Pope, the backs of which he used for translating. Also found there, not surely tied to any letter, are addresses and franks. Six franks are Addison's, and 4 of the 6 are addressed to Pope in Addison's hand—presumptive evidence that Pope and he were corresponding in 1715, since the surrounding letters date from that year.

†SWIFT *to* POPE 28 *June* 1715

1740

Dublin, June 28, 1715.

My Lord Bishop of Clogher[1] gave me your kind letter full of reproaches for my not writing. I am naturally no very exact correspondent, and when I leave a country without probability of returning, I think as seldom as I can of what I lov'd or esteem'd in it, to avoid the *Desiderium* which of all things makes life most uneasy. But you must give me leave to add one thing, that you talk at your ease, being wholly unconcerned in publick events: for, if your friends the Whigs continue, you may hope for some favour; if the Torys return, you are at least sure of quiet. You know how well I lov'd both Lord Oxford and Bolingbroke, and how dear the Duke of Ormond is to me: do you imagine I can be easy while their enemies are endeavouring to take off their heads?[2] *I nunc, & versus tecum meditare canoros*[3]—Do you imagine I can be easy, when I think of the probable consequences of these proceedings, perhaps upon the very peace of the nation, but certainly of the minds of so many hundred thousand good subjects? Upon the whole, you may truly attribute my silence to the Eclypse, but it was that eclypse which happened on the first of August.[4]

I borrow'd your Homer from the Bishop (mine is not yet landed) and read it out in two evenings. If it pleases others as well as me, you have got your end in profit and reputation: Yet I am angry at some bad Rhymes and Triplets,[5] and pray in your next do not let me have so many unjustifiable Rhymes to *war* and *gods*. I tell you all the faults I know, only in one or two places you are a little obscure; but I expected you to be so in one or two and twenty. I have heard no soul talk of it here, for indeed it is not come over; nor do we very much abound in judges, at least I have not the honour to be acquainted with them. Your Notes are perfectly good, and so are your Preface and Essay.[6] You were pretty bold in mentioning Lord Bolingbroke in that

[1] Dr. St. George Ash, formerly a Fellow of Trinity College, Dublin (to whom the Dean was a Pupil), afterwards Bishop of Clogher, and translated to the See of Derry in 1716–17. Dublin Edit.—1741–2. (Bishop Ashe had just returned from London, and evidently brought Pope's letter to Swift with him.)

[2] Only extremists would have gone so far. The top Whigs were probably glad to have Bolingbroke flee to France in March and Ormond also in June. Lord Oxford remained, and was in the Tower for almost two years. In July 1717 all charges against him were dropped, but he was excepted from the Act of Grace.

[3] Horace, *Epistles*, II. ii. 76.

[4] The date of the death of Queen Anne. There was a total and very dark eclipse of the sun on 22 Apr. 1715, which Pope had probably spoken of in his lost letter, here answered by Swift.

[5] Swift was a far more expert rhymer than Pope. He disliked triplets also. See Swift to Thomas Beach, 12 Apr. 1735 (ed. Ball, v. 162).

[6] The prefatory 'Essay on . . . Homer' was by Parnell. See Pope's remark in the joint letter to Parnell written with Gay, Jervas, and Arbuthnot in 1716. There Pope praises Parnell's prose, which he privately depreciated. See Spence, *Anecdotes*, p. 138.

Preface.[1] I saw the Key to the Lock[2] but yesterday: I think you have changed it a good deal, to adapt it to the present times.

God be thanked I have yet no Parliamentary business,[3] and if they have none with me, I shall never seek their acquaintance. I have not been very fond of them for some years past, not when I thought them tolerably good, and therefore if I can get leave to be absent, I shall be much inclin'd to be on that side, when there is a parliament on this: but truly I must be a little easy in my mind before I can think of Scriblerus.

You are to understand that I live in the corner of a vast unfurnished house; my family consists of a steward, a groom, a helper in the stable, a foot-man, and an old maid, who are all at board-wages, and when I do not dine abroad, or make an entertainment, (which last is very rare) I eat a mutton-pye, and drink half a pint of wine: My amusements are defending my small dominions against the Arch-Bishop,[4] and endeavouring to reduce my rebellious Choir. *Perditur haec inter misero lux.*[5] I desire you will present my humble service to Mr. Addison, Mr. Congreve, and Mr. Rowe, and Gay. I am, and will be always, extreamly yours, &c.

CARYLL *to* POPE 29 *June* [1715]

Homer MSS. Add. 4807

Lady holt. June 29.

The favour of your last follow'd me about the Country 'till att last itt over took me att Parham (Sir Cecill Bishop's) where I had been neer a Weeke, agreably entertaind by the good Sence of the Lady, and wonderfully diverted with the knight's inimitable Manner of thinking and talking. Your Homer came down whilst I was there upon which he ran severall extempore Divisions, And I beleeve had you been privy to them, you would have preferr'd em before some of Rapin's or Madame Dacier's more deliberate Remarks. I am now return'd as you see by the Date of my Letter, and after a Weekes stay here, I hope I shall be att Liberty to goe to Mapledurham, you shall be sure to hear from me soon after I gett thither, in hopes of seeing you there. In the mean while I must needs tell you that I was truly overjoy'd that the

[1] The Preface to the *Iliad.*

[2] *A Key to the Lock* is listed in Lintot's *Monthly Catalogue* (p. 79) as published in Apr. 1715. Evidently from Swift's remark here it was written and seen by him before he left England in 1714. It is mentioned by Arbuthnot in his letter to Pope of 7 Sept. 1714.

[3] This paragraph is obscure. Probably Swift refers to the Irish Parliament and is saying that if he can be free of it he would incline to be in England ('on that side') when the Irish Parliament is in session. But he may be uneasy for fear of penalties because of his pamphlets.

[4] Dr. William King, who opposed what he regarded as Swift's arrogance in asserting decanal prerogatives.

[5] Horace, *Sermones*, II. vi. 59.

Indisposition I left you under att London,[1] went off so well, and to find by your Letter that you are Like to be againe a Man of this World. I hope Mr Gay & I shall putt you to the Proof, if when you and I meet We can agree upon the time. I have try'd in two or three places for such an annuity as you mention, butt they doe not care to deal that Way. All are well abroade & I am in haste butt allwayes | Dear Sir | Your affectionate freind & Servant | J. Caryll

RALPH BRIDGES *to* POPE — 2 *July* 1715

Homer MSS. Add. 4807

Easthampstead July 2. | 1715

The ill weather having long denyed me the pleasure of seeing You, makes me communicate to You a Proposal I lately receiv'd. 'Tis to meet a Gentleman an Acquaintance of Yours at dinner at Sunninghill on Monday next.[2] If You have no Engagement and can spare a few moments from Homer, I will answer that Your Company will be reckond a favor by the Gentleman.

I cannot omit repeating my thanks for the kind present of Your Homer, which at once charms me & surprizes me, that You have bin able to make so renownd an Author appear so well that is so like himself in the English Language. I beg leave to congratulate You upon it & to assure You that I am with all imaginable sincerity & esteem | Sir Your most obedient | humble Servant | R. Bridges.

POPE *to* JERVAS — [*July* 1715]

Homer MSS. Add. 4807

I beg you to let me know if you have any thoughts of the Devonshire Journey this Summer. If you have, I will stay for you, & let Mr Fortescue & Gay travel together. This Resolution must be made with some haste, because they go next Week & I shall want time to prepare.

I thought Mrs Cecil had Receipts before. The Names of Lady Ranelagh & Lady Cavendish were inserted long since in the List.

You may tell Mr Rollinson that Gay was not sure he should go to Lady Bolingbrokes when he came hither; or help him to some Excuse, for his Neglect was scandalous, and has given him much Vexation of Spirit.

I should have been glad to have had the Report of the Committee, & have since writ to Lintot for it. If the Whigs say now B. is the Hero of my preface, the Tories said (you may remember) three years ago,

[1] Caryll had met Pope in London in May.—Elwin.

[2] One guesses that Bridges, visiting Sir William Trumbull, is arranging a dinner-party for Pope, Sir William, and himself, on 4 July (Monday next).

that Cato was the Hero of my Poetry:[1] It looks generous enough to be always on the Side of the Distressed. And my Patrons of the other party may expect great Panegyricks from me, if ever they come to be impeached by the future Justice or Rage of their Opponents. To compliment those who are *dead in Law*, is as much above the Imputation of Flattery, as Tickell says it is, to compliment those who are really *dead*. And perhaps too there is as much *Vanity* in my Praiseing *Bol*— as in his praising Hal— No people in the World are so apt to give themselves Airs as we Authors.

I have just received the Report, but have not yet had time to read any of it. I have gone thro the 5th 6th & 7th books, except a small part at the latter end of the 6th—Pray tell me if you hear any thing said about Mr Tickel's or my translation; if the Town be not too much taken up with Great affairs to take any Notice of either.

I hold the Resolution I told you in my last of seeing you, if you cannot take a trip hither, before I goe. But I would fain flatter myself so far as to fancy we might travel together. Pray give me a Line by Saturdays post.

I am at all times, & in all Reigns, whatever be the fate of the World, or of myself, sincerely & affectionately | (Dear Mr Jervas) Yours. A. P.

All here most truly your Servants.

THE REV. GEORGE BERKELEY *to* POPE[2] — 7 *July* 1715

1735

EXCERPT

July 7, 1715.

—Some days ago, three or four Gentlemen and my self exerting that right which all readers pretend to over Authors, sate in judgment upon the two new Translations of the first *Iliad*. Without partiality to my country-men, I assure you they all gave the preference where it was due; being unanimously of opinion that yours was equally just to the sense with Mr. ——'s, and without comparison more easy, more poetical, and more sublime. But I will say no more on such a thread-bare subject, as your late performance is at this time. | I am, &c.

[1] In the Preface to his *Iliad* Pope had praised Bolingbroke and Halifax both—the one in exile and the other recently deceased. Tickell had dedicated his translation of *Iliad* i to Lord Halifax, who had died before the translation appeared. Three years (rather, *two*) earlier Pope's Prologue to Addison's *Cato* had caused him to be called a Whig. See Pope's 'Epilogue to the Satires', i. 7–8.

[2] This excerpt from a letter was printed in all Pope's editions except the 'authorized' quarto and folio of 1737. 'Mr. ——' of course is Tickell.

†JOHN GAY *to* POPE[1] 8 *July* 1715

1735

EXCERPT

July 8, 1715.

—I have just set down Sir *Samuel Garth* at the Opera. He bid me tell you, that every body is pleas'd with your Translation, but a few at *Button*'s; and that Sir *Richard Steele* told him, that Mr. *Addison* said *Tickel*'s translation was the best that ever was in any language.[2] He treated me with extream civility, and out of kindness gave me a squeeze by the Sore finger.[3]—I am inform'd that at *Button*'s your character is made very free with as to morals, *&c.* and Mr. *A*— says, that your translation and *Tickel*'s are both very well done, but that the latter has more of *Homer*. | I am &c.

DR. ARBUTHNOT *to* POPE[4] 9 *July* 1715

1735

EXCERPT

July 9, 1715.

—I congratulate you upon Mr. *Tickel*'s[5] first Book. It does not indeed want its merit; but I was strangely disappointed in my expectation of a Translation nicely true to the original; whereas in those parts where the greatest exactness seems to be demanded, he has been the least careful, I mean the History of *ancient Ceremonies and Rites*, &c. in which you have with great judgment been exact.

I am, &c.

POPE *to* —— [*Summer of* 1715]

Homer MSS, Add. [illegible]

I have treated you as we commonly do our best Benefactor, make a hasty use of all the advantages he puts us in the capacity of possessing, & thank him afterwards at our idle leisure, if we have the Grace to thank him at all.[6]

[1] This is one of the three 'extracts' concerning the reception of Pope's *Iliad* that he omitted from the quarto and folio of 1737. See his note to Parnell's letter of 27 June 1715. The extracts were from letters from Berkeley, Gay, and Dr. Arbuthnot.

[2] Sir Richard Steele afterwards, in his Preface to an Edition of the *Drummer*, a Comedy by Mr. Addison, shews it to be his opinion, that 'not Mr. Tickel but Mr. Addison himself was the Person that translated this book.'—Pope, 1735–42.

The first four words quoted in this note from Steele (*not Mr. Tickel but*) were omitted from the note after 1735.

[3] Elwin reads, without warrant, *fore-finger.*

[4] The third extract from a letter about his *Iliad* that was omitted by Pope from the quarto and folio editions of 1737. It appears in the other editions of his letters.

[5] *Tickel*'s] T*'s *1737–42*.

[6] This one sentence of a letter occurs on the verso of a leaf in the MS. of Book VIII of the *Iliad*. That almost certainly places it in a vague chronology. Its only interest is its typical manner of apology plus flattery. It was apparently first printed in the *Supplement* of 1825.

†POPE *to* JAMES CRAGGS[1] 15 *July* 1715

1735

July 15, 1715.

I lay hold of the opportunity given me by my Lord Duke of *Shrewsbury*, to assure you of the continuance of that esteem and affection I have long born you, and the memory of so many agreeable conversations as we have pass'd together. I wish it were a compliment to say such conversations as are not to be found on this side of the Water: for the Spirit of Dissention is gone forth among us; nor is it a wonder that *Button*'s is no longer *Button*'s, when *Old England* is no longer *Old England*, that region of hospitality, society, and good humour. Party affects us all, even the wits, tho' they gain as little by politicks as they do by their wit. We talk much of fine sense, refin'd sense, and exalted sense; but for use and happiness give me a little common sense. I say this in regard to some gentlemen, profess'd wits of our acquaintance, who fancy they can make Poetry of consequence at this time of day, in the midst of this raging fit of Politicks. For they tell me, the busy part of the nation are not more divided about *Whig* and *Tory*, than these idle fellows of the Feather about Mr. *Tickel*'s[2] and my Translation. I (like the *Tories*) have the town in general, that is the mob, on my side; but 'tis usual with the smaller Party to make up in industry what they want in number, and that's the case with the little Senate of *Cato*. However if our Principles be well consider'd, I must appear a brave *Whig*, and Mr. *Tickel* a rank *Tory*; I translated *Homer* for the publick in general, he to gratify the inordinate desires of One man only. We have, it seems, a great *Turk* in Poetry,[3] who can never bear a Brother on the throne; and has his Mutes too, a sett of Nodders, Winkers, and Whisperers, whose business is to strangle all other offsprings of wit in their birth. The new Translator of *Homer* is the humblest slave he has, that is to say, his first Minister; let him receive the honours he gives him, but receive them with fear and trembling: let him be proud of the approbation of his absolute Lord; I appeal to the People, as my rightful judges and masters; and if they are not inclin'd to condemn me, I fear no arbitrary high-flying proceedings from the small Court-faction at *Button*'s. But after all I have said of this great Man, there is no rupture between us: We are each of us so civil and obliging, that

[1] This letter, printed in all Pope's editions, was presumably written while Craggs was in France. Elwin thought Pope would hardly write in the tone here used concerning Addison to one of Addison's friends. One has only to read the letters of young Tom Burnet to George Duckett to see that such a tone was not rare in the Addison circle.

[2] *Tickel*'s] T*'s *1737–42*. The name is thus suppressed in its later occurrences in this letter.

[3] This phrase, like others in the letter, obviously anticipates the Atticus portrait (e.g. l. 198) of the *Epistle to Dr. Arbuthnot*. The 'character' of Atticus (Addison) was evidently taking shape at this time. See Sherburn, *Early Career*, pp. 146–7.

neither thinks he is obliged. And I for my part treat with him, as we do with the *Grand Monarch*; who has too many great qualities not to be respected, tho' we know he watches any occasion to oppress us.

When I talk of *Homer*, I must not forget the early Present you made me of *Monsieur de la Motte*'s Book.[1] And I can't conclude this letter without telling you a melancholy piece of news which affects our very Entrails, ——[2] is dead, and Soupes are no more! You see I write in the old familiar way. "This is not to the Minister but to the Friend."[3] —However, it is some mark of uncommon regard to the Minister, that I steal an expression from a Secretary of State. | I am, &c.

||POPE *to* TERESA *and* MARTHA BLOUNT[4] [23 *July* 1715]

Mapledurham

Ladies,—⌜It is a difficult Task you have impos'd upon me, that of writing News; and if you did not think me the humblest Creature in the World, you cou'd never imagine a Poet would dwindle to a Brother of Dyer & Dawkes,[5] from an Associate of Tate and Brady. At this time indeed I might alledge many Excuses for disobeying you in this point; as first, that we have too much News to warrant the writing any; secondly, that it is dangerous; and thirdly & principally that it is troublesome to me.⌝

The Earl of Oxford has behaved so bravely, that, in this Act at least he might seem above Man, if he had not just now voided a Stone to prove him subject to human Infirmities.[6] The utmost Weight of Affliction from Princely[7] Power and Popular Hatred, were almost worth bearing for the Glory of such a dauntless Conduct as he has shown under it.

[1] Houdard de la Motte published a French version of parts of the *Iliad* under the title: *L'Iliade, pöeme, avec un discours sur Homère* (Paris, 1714).

[2] The 1737–42 editions substitute L* for this dash.

[3] The quoted phrase is adapted from part of a letter from Bolingbroke to Matthew Prior (10 Sept. O.S. 1712) that was published in the *Report of the Secret Committee*. See Cobbett, *Parliamentary History*, vii (1811), Appendix, clxix. Bolingbroke writes: 'It is now three a clock in the morning; I have been hard at work all day, and am not yet enough recovered to bear much fatigue; excuse therefore the confusedness of this scroll, which is only from Harry to Matt. and not from the secretary to the minister.'

[4] In 1735 as Letter VIII among his 'Letters to Several Ladies' Pope printed an undated letter, which he reprinted in all his later editions. The first paragraph of this 'Letter VIII' was taken from a letter now at Mapledurham dated 7 Aug. [1716]; the rest of it is from this present letter. He omitted much of the Jacobite news here included, and his omissions are placed in half-brackets. On the date [23 July 1715] see the following page, n. 5.

[5] Originally Pope wrote 'dwindle to a News writer', but he deleted 'a News writer' and added the specific newsmen, John Dyer (d. 1713) and Ichabod Dawkes. Tate and Brady versified the Psalms.

[6] Oxford was committed to the Tower 16 July. In his speech before the Lords on 8 July he remarked, 'I now labour under an Indisposition of Body'.

[7] Princely] ministerial *1737–42*.

⌜The Duke of Ormond is retired[1] & become a Rival of the Courage of that other Noble Lord, whose health is joind with the Duke's at your Table.⌝

⌜You will say you knew thus much, as also that the Pretender is coming (which is more than I, & my Brother Newsmongers know)⌝ You may soon have your Wish to enjoy the Gallant Sights of Armies, Campagnes,[2] Standards waving over your Brother's Cornfields, & the pretty windings of the Thames about *Mapledurham*,[3] staind with the blood of Men. Your Barbarity which I have heard so long exclaim'd against in Town & Country, may have its fill of destruction. I would not add One Circumstance usual in all Descriptions of Calamity, that of the many Rapes committed, or to be committed, upon those unfortunate Women that delight in War. But—God forgive me—in this martial Age—if I could—I would buy a Regiment for your sake—and Mrs Patty's[4]—& some others, whom I have cause to fear no fair Means will prevail upon.

Those Eyes that care not how much Mischief is done, or how great Slaughter committed, so they have but a fine show; those Very-female Eyes will be infinitely delighted with the Camp which is speedily to be form'd in Hyde park. The Tents are carried thither this morning,[5] New Regiments ready rais'd, with new Clothes & Furniture (far exceeding the late Cloth & Linnen designd by his Grace[6] for the Soldiery.) The sight of so many thousand gallant Fellows, with all the Pomp & Glare of Warr yet undeformed with battle, those Scenes which England has for many years only beheld on Stages, may possibly invite your Curiosity to this place.

⌜My Lady Lansdowne held her *Last* Assembly yesterday, where was *not* present the E. of D—d.

⌜I mett my Lord Finch in Red, trimmd with Gold; correspondent to the Gravity of the Nottingham-family. So that he may beg (with Mrs Patty's leave) to be as gay as a *Gold Finch*.

⌜The Princes Secretary M—x,[7] has been so employed in writing

[1] Ormond had been impeached in June, and he withdrew to France on 21 July. All Catholics were ordered on 27 July to withdraw ten miles from London, and in anticipation of this order many had doubtless already gone to the country.

[2] Campagnes] incampments *1735–42*.

[3] Thames about *Mapledurham*, staind] *Thames* about M— stain'd *1735*; Thames stained *1737–42*.

[4] Patty's] P—'s *1735–42*.

[5] It is this statement, taken literally, that dates the letter. Documents show that on 23 July 1715 the camp was formed and 12*s*. paid for carts to carry thither the tents. See Daniel MacKinnon, *Origin and Services of the Coldstream Guards*, i. 344–5, and Sir F. W. Hamilton, *Origin and History of the First or Grenadier Guards*, ii. 66.

[6] The Guards had been rebellious because of unsatisfactory uniforms. To placate them Marlborough had ordered new uniforms and these 'with a liberal donation of beer' 'won them to a sense of duty.'—Elwin. In his quarto and folio editions of 1737 Pope omitted this political parenthesis—a part of his manœuvres to conciliate Sarah, Duchess of Marlborough?

[7] Samuel Molyneux (1689–1728) was an astronomer as well as a courtier. He continued

Dispatches, that his weary hand could hardly shake the Box and Dice 'tother day, at Mr Gage's. The Ladies blamed his Indolence, and he made that Excuse.⌝

[1]Mrs ⌜Nelson⌝ expects the Pretender at her Lodgings, by Saturday sennight. She has bought a Picture of Madam Maintenon to sett her features by, against that time. Three Priests of your Acquaintance are very positive, by her Interest, to be his Father Confessors.

⌜It is reported that the Hon. Thomas Gage[2] Esq. having renouncd the Errors of the Romish Communion is to be created Groom Porter. & that Alex. Pope, Gent. being ready to do the same, will be chosen City-Poet.

⌜The Lord Viscount Dunbar is married to the Daughter of the Lord Clifford: One of the Agents in this Affair was Mr Edward Blount, who (it was thought) might have provided for that noble Vicount much better out of his own Family. The said Mr Blount is this morning gone off for Devonshire, without daring to call at Mapledurham in his way—Some People sigh, & say, Mr Holman stands fair.

⌜Sir Sam. Garth's Journey into Italy is put off; for three Days—That of some others into Devonshire is neither off nor on, like most modern Matches, tho' all the Parties are agreed.

⌜I must stop here till further Advices, which are expected from the Lady Mary Wortley, this afternoon.⌝

By Our latest Accounts from Dukestreet, Westminster, the Conversion of Tho. Gage Esq.[2] is reported in a manner somewhat more particular. That upon the Seizure of his Flanders Mares, he seem'd more than ordinarily disturbd for some hours, sent for his Ghostly father, & resolvd to bear his Loss like a Christian. Till about the hours of seven or eight, the Coaches & Horses of several of the Nobility passing by his Window towards Hyde park, he could no longer endure the disapointment, but instantly went out, took the Oathe of Abjuration, & recover'd his dear Horses which carryd him in triumph to the Ring. The poor distressed Roman Catholicks, now Un-hors'd and Un-charioted, cry out with the Psalmist: Some in Chariots, & some in Horses, but We will invocate[3] the name of the Lord.

There are several other Advices from the Lady M. W. which you shall have in our next. So much for the present, & as for the future, I neither know what will become of myself, or of the nation.

as secretary to the Prince until the Prince became George II. Here, as elsewhere, Pope is inclined to deal in innuendo concerning the Secretary.

[1] This paragraph about Mrs. —— (not even her initial was given in the texts of 1735) was omitted after 1735.

[2] Thomas Gage Esq.] *T. G.* Esq. *1735–42*. Added concealment for Gage was procured in the quarto and folio of 1737 by omitting *from Dukestreet, Westminster*.

[3] *invocate* is neither in the Authorized Version nor in that of Douai.

JERVAS *to* POPE [31 *July* 1715?][1]

Homer MSS. Add. 4807

Dear Mr P.—I intend to see the Doctor & the Duke[2] this Evening having sent several Expresses to fix a Meeting that I may put you out of your pain; perhaps I ought not to let you know that I suspect the Doctor's punctuality as a Practising Physician, besides the Common uncertainty from the present situation of this world[3] in which we have a small Share: The very weather is discouraging & seems in contradiction to a journey of pleasure. The Duke will have the advantage of us prodigiously by his Loving a Bottle, which is alike gratefull in all Seasons, but what Shal we do when we can neither ride nor walk? About 11 at night I may be able to be more positive & defer Sealing til then. I am just going to Vertue to give the last hand to that Enterprize which is our Concern.[4] He has done the King from Kneller, but so wretchedly that I can scarcely imagin how bad the Picture must be from which that Artist has performd so poorly: but it is like & ruefull. 2 Fanns You shal have[5] & you shal pay for 'em in Money if you think that way best. If we set out I will take care of sending your baggage before hand.

I am this Minute come from the Doctor, who seems ready to mount, but the Weather is so extravagant that there must be a day or two of fair for preparation to make the Way tolerable over head & under foot.

The Doctor must lye at Windsor the first Night & take you up next Morning The Duke is gone with Sir William Windham.[6] I shal take Waters for our mutual aid.

Service to all &c Your your your

*POPE *to* TERESA *and* MARTHA BLOUNT[7]

1 *August* [1715]

Mapledurham

Binfield, Augst 1st

Ladies,—It having been the practise of good Catholiques in times of Persecution, to fly to the Protection of the Virgin Mary, and I not

[1] The date is inferred from Jervas's mention in his next letter, 2[August], of having written 'the last post'. It should be approximately correct.

[2] Dr. Arbuthnot and 'Duke' Disney were to be fellow travellers to Devonshire.

[3] The expected Jacobite invasion.

[4] George Vertue was engraving Jervas's portrait of Pope. *The Daily Courant* for 20 Aug. 1715 advertises that Lintot will have it for sale on the 23rd.

[5] The fans were for the Misses Blount. See Pope to Martha Blount [19 Aug. 1715?].

[6] Sir William Windham was in September arrested at his seat in Somerset (Orchard Wyndham) as a Jacobite plotter.

[7] This letter, here first published (?), is an example of the irreverent wit that Pope was capable of—as were others of his day. The year may be doubted, but it seems likely that the poet did visit Mapledurham briefly in Aug. 1715.

being very well acquainted with her, am obliged in the same circumstance to apply to the most heav'nly Virgins I know: Tho I am sensible You are not so easie of Access as that good Lady, who (I have been told) is so indulgent a Mistress to her Servants as to grant the Requests of all that pray to her. Indeed you are perfect Tyrants in comparison; yet not such Tyrants as some people here, who outdoe all your Sex in unreasonable Expectations: For you must know Ladies, they would make me swear things much more impossible, than it is never to love but one or two Women, after one has seen you. Now since I think it hard (as Dr Conquest said) to be plagu'd in this world for having Some Religion, & damn'd in the other for having none; I therfore beg to know if Mapledurham may be my Sanctuary for a day or two? Whether it will be no Inconvenience to Mr Blount, (which the present posture of Affairs[1] renders doubtful to me) and whether the Meeting of Two Toasts and a Poet may not be as great a Riot, as can be made by any five in the Kingdome? If you wonder why I don't write this to Mr Blount, know, that it is much more Catholique to address to the Lady than to the Gentleman. I am most religiously, tho' not Ceremoniously, | Your most obedient | & most faithfull humble Servant | A. Pope.

Address: To | Mrs Teresa Blount, | Mrs Martha Blount. |

JERVAS *to* POPE 2 [*August* 1715][2]

Homer MSS. Add. 4807

Dear Mr P:—Tho' I have not a Syllable to say of more certainty than the Last post Yet I write—I hold my self in a readiness, in spite of a Demand for Pictures.

The Counsellour Bick—[3] has purchasd a Nag for his Equipage & waits our Motions, he was here Yesterday & to Morrow We'nsday Evening we are to tast Devonshire Cyder with Mr Copplestone[4] at his Lodgings.

The Court Opiniâtre is that the P—[5] is coming—They have no Account of Ormond's Arrival in France, tho' they have certain Intelligence that he went off at Shoreham in Sussex Ten days ago. I design to know Arbuthnots Determination to Morrow. Service to every body I am | Yours | Most affectionatly | C. J.

Tuesday 2.

[1] This phrase may refer to the political situation or to the approaching marriage of Mr. Blount, the brother of Teresa and Martha.

[2] 'Tuesday 2' fits the date assigned as do other details of the letter, notably Ormond's flight about 21 July.

[3] Edmund Bickford was a friend or neighbour of Fortescue in Devonshire, as well as an attorney who more than once drew up legal papers for Pope.

[4] Copplestone is also from Devonshire.—Elwin.

[5] The Pretender.

JERVAS *to* POPE 12 *August* 1715

Homer MSS. Add. 4807

Dear M P.—I wou'd not have fail'd by Tuesdays Post[1] but that the Doctor cou'd not be near positive as to the Time, but Yesterday we met on horseback & took two or three Turns near the Camp;[2] partly to see my New horses Goeings & partly to Name something like the Day of setting forth, & the manner thereof, Viz. That on Thursday next (god Willing) Doctor A— D. Disney & C. Jervas, rendevous at Hyde park Corner about Noon & proceed to Mr Hills at Eggam, to lodge there, Ffryday to meet Mr Pope upon the road, to proceed together to Lord Stowell's,[3] there also to Lodge. The next day Saturday to Sir William Windham's & to rest there the Lords day. On Monday forward Again toward Bath or Wilton[4] or as we shal then Agree. The Dr Proposes that himself or his Man ride my Spare horse & that I have all Equipage to be sent to Bath by the Carrier with Your Portmanteau, The Doctor Says he will allow None of us so much as a Nightgown or Slippers for the road, so a Shirt & Cravat in the pocket is all you must think of in his New Scheme, his Servant may be bribed to find room for that. You shal have a shorter & less bridle sent down on Saturday & the other shal be return'd in due Time. The Taylor shal be Chastis'd if 'tis really Negligence in his Art, but if 'tis only Vapors you must beg pardon. The Linnen & Stockings out of yr Portmanteau may go with the bridle. I forgot to tell you that the Third day is to be Oxford University & the Monday following to Sir W. Windham's. . . .

The french King has been indispos'd & Men think he is in an ill Way &c.

Lon[don] [Serv]ice to Every body | Vot Serviteur tres humble C. J.

August 12th 1715.

*CARYLL *to* LINTOT 13 *August* 1715

Add. 12113

Aug. 13. 1715.

Mr Lintott—Sir John Shelley having lost his Receipt for his Subscription Money to Mr Pope's Homer, I desire, that upon Sight of this, You would deliver a Book for him to the Bearer, And this shall be your Discharge to the Author. I am your friend. | J Caryll

To Mr Bernard Lintott | Bookseller in fleetstreet.

[1] Jervas had failed to write on Tuesday the 9th. This much-planned journey to Bath and to Sir William Wyndham's seat, Orchard Wyndham, near Williton, resolved itself into a simpler journey, as later letters show.

[2] In Hyde Park. See Pope to the Misses Blount [23 July 1715].

[3] William, 3rd Lord Stawell, lived at Aldermaston, not far from Newbury. Sir William must have had a house a day's ride west of Oxford—Orchard Wyndham is not here indicated.

[4] For Williton, near Orchard Wyndham.

POPE *to* CARYLL 14 *August* 1715

Add. 28618

Binfield August 14. 1715.

I make some doubt whether these prophane hands, employed as they are in pagan poetry, ought to write to you at present, who have been promoting so godly and even ceremonious a work as that sanctified one of marriage. The genealogies of the Greeks and Trojans have very little to do with propagation of a Catholic posterity: which has doubtless lain very near your heart, in the offices I hear you have been rendering to Sir H: T: and Mr B:[1] and indeed indeed those old people, (tho' by what I can find, little less religious than the moderns) seem to look upon the distinctions of lawful and illegal offspring with less regard than we; as may appear from a passage or two in my present year's task[2] that (at this juncture) I think the fittest to transcribe for your use and edification.

The first is in the fifth book of the *Iliad*, where a lady, the virtuous wife of Antenor the wisest counsellor of Troy, is highly extolled by our author for the tenderness she showed to a natural son of her husband's in educating him in her own family among the lawful issue, as one of her own. That I may not trouble you with Greek, take it in words much inferior to the original.[3]

From Meges' rage the swift Pedæus fled,
Antenor's offspring from a foreign bed,
(Whose gen'rous comfort,[4] Theano the fair,
Nursed the young stranger with a mother's care)

The other passage is in the eighth book, where a young hero having signalized himself in a very uncommon manner by the deaths of several enemies, the general, Agamemnon, runs to him in a rapture, blesses his prowess, and talks to him thus:

O chief, forever dear, (the Monarch cried)
Thus, always thus, thy early worth be tried!
Thy brave example shall retrieve our host;
Thy country's savior, and thy father's boast!

[1] Michael Blount, the brother of Teresa and Martha, is to marry or has just married Mary Agnes, the eldest daughter and co-heiress of Sir Henry Tichborne.—Elwin. There is evidence in 'The Diary of the Blue Nuns' (*Catholic Record Society*, viii. 327) that this marriage took place in 1715.

[2] Caryll's scribe wrote *talk* for *task*.

[3] Pope's *Iliad*, v. 91–94. Pope's printed text changed *rage* to *force* and line 93 finally read:

Whose gen'rous spouse, Theano, heav'nly fair.

[4] Pope may have written *consort*, since in his *Iliad* Pope printed *spouse*; but Caryll's scribe wrote *comfort*. See N. Callan in *RES*, April 1953, pp. 116–17.

Sprung from an alien's bed thy sire to grace,
The vig'rous offspring of a forced embrace!
Proud of his boy, he own'd the gen'rous flame,
And the brave son repays his cares with fame.[1]

This compliment upon a spurious[2] birth is what few people would pay nowadays; nor do I think either Sir Harry or you would say any thing like it to Mr B: upon the birth of his first child. But raillery apart, I know you delight in doing good; and tho' there be some hazard whether a man does any when he helps another to a wife, yet I believe if any man can make marriage a prudent action, it must be by following your advice and example both before and after it, in all that regards that state. If you could get every man as good a wife as you did for your son, all railleries on this subject would be at an end. The very satirists and wits would be the first to apply to you; and even I myself should entreat you to seek out some shepherdess about the hills of Ladyholt for the felicity of your humble servant.

The mention of good wives makes me desirous of knowing if those that belong to that place[3] are yet coming over? if you shall live single or double the next winter? Tho' I cannot say I desire any more company than your own, whenever I entertain hopes of visiting your abode; yet a great many good examples must be of use to me in my unholy circumstances, and therefore it would be a great profit to me to see them with you.

I ought not to have got thus low in my letter, before I apologized for my silence till this time. But I am sure your knowledge of my perpetual remembrance and esteem of you is too just to need any apologies on this head: and when we are once in such a general and constant disposition of friendship, one may be said to write always, as well as to pray always, when one is always inclined to do either. I am just setting out for the Bath in company with Doctor Arbuthnot and Mr Jervas:[4] thence it is not impossible, yet, but I may go into Devonshire. A line of yours directed to Mr Jervas's in London will be sent after me wherever I am and be in all places the most agreeable thing in the world to one so entirely and sincerely yours as | A: P:

[1] Pope's *Iliad*, viii. 339–46. In line 344 *forc'd embrace* became in the printed text *stol'n embrace*.

[2] Caryll's scribe wrote *spunious* for *spurious*.

[3] Caryll's family was in France: Pope speaks here and in the next letter to Caryll of their return.

[4] The journey to Bath seems to have been deferred, though at this time Pope went to Oxford with Arbuthnot but without Jervas. He returned from Bath in October; when he arrived there is doubtful. Edward Blount and Fortescue both lived in Devonshire. It is possible that Pope thought Orchard Wyndham was in that county.

POPE *to* MARTHA BLOUNT [19 *August* 1715?][1]

Mapledurham

Friday.

Madam,—I have long been sensible of Your Foreknowledge of the Will of Heaven, which (as I have often told you) I can attribute to nothing but a Secret Correspondence with Your Fellow-Beauties, the Angels of Light. In very deed my Rambling Associates have deserted me; Jervas has Ladies to paint, & Duke Disney must visit a Bishop in hopes of his Conversion.[2] The Duke is too Sedate for me, notwithstanding he has so much Mercury in him. Only Dr Arbuthnot & I travel soberly and philosophically to Oxford, &c. enquiring into Natural Causes, & being sometimes wise, sometimes in the Spleen. Tis very hard, this World is a Thing which every unfortunate Thinking Creature must necessarily either laugh at, or be angry at: And if we laugh at it, People will say we are Proud, if we are angry at it they'l say we are ill-humor'd. I beg your pardon for my Spleen to which you showd so much Indulgence, and desire yourself & your fair Sister to accept of these Fans as a part of my Penalty. I desird Mr Jervas to chuse two of the best he had, but if these do not chance to hitt your fancy, you'l oblige me by taking your own choice out of twenty when you go to London. What little Discomposure they may receive by the Rumpling, will be recoverd if you keep 'em laid up smooth. (as modest Women do their Petticoats)

I can't tell to whom I am obliged for two Bottels of the white Elder Wine which was given to our Boy unknown to me.[3] But it looks like the good naturd Trick of a kind hearty Motherly Gentlewoman; and therfore I believe I owe it to Mrs Blount, whom I entreat to think me her most faithful Servant—Mr Blount may esteem me so too, if he knows I cannot heartily wish him married[4]—What to wish for Mrs Teresa and You I know not; but that I wish as sincerely as I do for myself, and that I am in love with you both as I am with myself, and

[1] This letter was by Elwin dated [27 July]. Unfortunately in 1715 the 27th fell on a Wednesday, not a Friday. The present very hypothetical date depends on Jervas's letter to Pope, 12 Aug. 1715, which sets the following Friday (the 19th) as the day when Pope should join Jervas, Disney, and Arbuthnot on their long-projected journey. For another mention of the fans for the young ladies see Jervas to Pope [31 July 1715].

[2] Henry Disney (or Desaulnais), commonly called 'Duke', was colonel of an Irish regiment, a member of Swift's Tory Brothers Club, a close friend of General Withers, with whom he lived. Pope wrote an epitaph for the General.

[3] The reference to her indulgence of his splenetic behaviour and to the kind present of the elderberry wine seem to indicate a visit to Mapledurham shortly before the journey with Arbuthnot began. See Pope to the Misses Blount, 1 Aug. 1715, for a suggested visit.

[4] Pope thus indirectly expresses regret for a marriage that will make the mother and sisters of Michael leave their home. The remark would seem to imply that the marriage had not yet taken place, though it did within the year. See Pope to Caryll, 14 Aug. 1715.

find myself most so with all three when I least suspect it. | I am | Madam | Your most obliged & | obedient humble Servant | A. Pope. |

Address: To | Mrs Martha Blount: | Present

POPE *to* JOHN HUGHES[1] — *7 October* 1715

Robert H. Taylor

Binfield, Oct. 7, 1715.

Ever since I had the pleasure to know you, I have believed you one of that uncommon rank of authors, who are undesigning men and sincere friends; and who, when they commend another, have not any view of being praised themselves. I should be therefore ashamed to offer at saying any of those civil things in return to your obliging compliments in regard to my translation of "Homer;" only I have too great a value for you not to be pleased with them; and yet, I assure you, I receive praises from you with less pleasure than I have often paid them to your merit before, and shall (I doubt not) have frequent occasions of doing again, from those useful pieces you are still obliging us with.

If you was pleased with my preface, you have paid me for that pleasure, in the same kind, by your entertaining and judicious essays on Spenser.[2] The present you make me is of the most agreeable nature imaginable, for Spenser has been ever a favourite poet to me: he is like a mistress, whose faults we see, but love her with 'em all.

What has deferred my thanks till now, was a ramble I have been taking about the country, from which I returned home and found your kind letter but yesterday. A testimony of that kind, from a man of your turn, is to be valued at a better rate than the ordinary estimate of letters will amount to. I shall rejoice in all opportunities of cultivating a friendship I so truly esteem, and hope very shortly to tell you, in town, how much I am, Sir, | Your obliged and faithful | humble servant, | A. Pope.

Since you desire to hear of my progress in the translation, I must tell you that I have gone through four more books, which (with the remarks) will make the second volume.

Address: To John Hughes Esq.

[1] The text here reproduced was printed by Duncombe in 1772. It differs from the original, recently acquired by Mr. Taylor, only in capitalization, punctuation, and the occasional use of ampersands. 'Binfield' was inserted by Duncombe in the superscription.

[2] 'An essay on allegorical poetry', 'remarks on the fairy queen', 'on the shepherd's calendar, &c.' prefixed to Mr. Hughes's edition of 'Spenser's works', 1715.—Duncombe, 1772.

POPE *to* TERESA *and* MARTHA BLOUNT[1]

[*Autumn*, 1715?]

Mapledurham

Thursday.

Dear Ladies,—You have here all the Fruit Mr Dancastles Garden affords that I could find in any degree of ripeness: They were on the Trees at eleven this morning, & I hope will be with you before night. Pray return, seald up, by the bearer, every single bit of paper that wraps 'em up: for they are the Only Copies of this part of Homer. If the Fruit is not so good as I wish, let the Gallantry of this Wrapping-paper make up for it. I'm Yours

POPE *to* CARYLL

11 *October* 1715

Add. 28618

Binfield. Oct. 11th 1715

I am newly arrived in the Forest, after my journey from Bath, which was diversified with many agreeable diversions[2] by the way. I could heartily have wished Ladyholt might have been one, but was overruled by my companions,[3] into whose hands I was committed, and I was as little in my power as if they had been the king's messengers. You may justly believe I should never have visited you with more satisfaction, than at a time when I should see you in all the shining circumstances of a *pater familias*, upon the recovery of almost all that is dear to you.[4] Jacob that recovered his son Joseph from the land of Egypt might give one some idea of you. Pray own the truth, did not you begin to *prophesy* when you saw 'em all about you like the old patriarch? Had you no delightful prospects in your mind of the *nati natorum, et qui nascentur ab illis*?[5]—Well, I am but a single careless man; yet the deuce take me, if when I see Ladyholt I don't wish my self [married]. But indeed when I go anywhere else in the world, I am cured of that wish again.

'Tis really some advantage one receives from knowing the world that the more one sees of our fellow creatures, the more willing one grows to part with it and them. Which (to own an humble truth to

[1] This letter might fall in any autumn when Pope was either resident or visitor at Binfield during his 'Homeric' period. But it seems probable that it was written before the Popes removed to Chiswick. It might be 1714 as well as 1715. Thomas Dancastle apparently transcribed the whole of Pope's *Iliad* for the press.

[2] Caryll's scribe carefully wrote *divisions* instead of *diversions* (Elwin's emendation).

[3] Pope's companions may have been Gay and Fortescue, who had been at home in Devonshire during the summer, and possibly Dr. Arbuthnot, if he and Pope had gone on to Bath from Oxford in August.

[4] Caryll's family had returned from France.

[5] *Aeneid*, iii. 98. Also used by Vida, *Poeticorum*, L. iii. See *Opera* (1586), p. 476. See also Pope's debasement of the line in *Dunciad*, iv. 332, and note.

you) is all I ever learned from experience that was to any purpose. If expectation is a jilt, experience is a downright whore, and stares us in the face with such confounded conviction, that it were better to be deceived as at first, unless we can heroically bear to leave this false prostituted thing the world, forever. I hope as a Christian, I can.

Having talked of Christianity, it is proper (as usual) to join it with interest; and so I acquaint you that my father has received yours, and that his son confesses he owed you 20*s.* prodigal as he is, to spend his father's money before it came to his hands![1]

I shall be closely confined to study this fortnight, after which I intend to try my fortune in London and to try my bookseller's fortune too, who tells me with great spirit, he has got much more this year by politics than he can lose by poetry. My next volume will be then put to the press: As it consists entirely of battles, it may perhaps agree with a martial age; but I foresee the translating of Homer will very much prejudice the poets of this time, who may hereby be prevented from stealing descriptions from him. I am really a lover of peace and wish myself out of these battles now, as I formerly wished myself in—just like most people in the case of war.

To say truth I am weary of translating; I am weary of poetry itself; I am weary of prose (thanks to my notes). I begin to hate to write at all, even letters; and possibly in a little time you will see mine consist of three lines, and underneath (what will be the last thing I shall refrain from writing, professing, and being) | Dear Sir | Your most faithful obliged | Friend and humble servant | A: P:

My father desires your acceptance of his most hearty humble service. Your good Lady, Mr Caryll junior his good Lady, Mrs Cath: Caryll, &c., must always believe me theirs or be very much in the wrong, which I fancy they never were.

†POPE *to* MARTHA BLOUNT[2] [1715]

1737

⌜Madam,⌝—The weather is too fine for any one that loves the country to leave it at this season; when every smile of the sun, like the

[1] Caryll, as appears from his accounts, had deducted 1*l.* from the interest due to the elder Pope, and sent a draft for 10*l.* instead of 11*l.*—Elwin.

[2] This letter was first printed in the Roberts octavo of 1737. In the quarto and folio of that year it was dated 1715, but that date does not appear in the octavo editions of 1737–42. Elwin dated the letter 1727 on the ground that the last four sentences (omitted in the quarto and folio of 1737) referred to Gay's declining the appointment as gentleman usher to the Princess Louisa (Oct. 1727). They might equally well refer to Gay's similar situation at the time of another succession, that of George I, and to his fruitless action in publishing his Epistle to the Princess Caroline in Nov. 1714, which might as likely 'charm' Lord Bathurst as Gay's refusal of an absurd appointment. On other grounds Pope's date of 1715 seems preferable. The remarks about being separated from his friends, the Blount ladies, curious at

smile of a coy lady, is as dear as it is uncommon: and I am so much in the taste of rural pleasures, I had rather see the sun than any thing he can shew me, except yourself. I despise every fine thing in town, not excepting your new gown, till I see you dress'd in it (which by the way I don't like the better for the red; the leaves I think are very pretty). I am growing fit, I hope, for a better world, of which the light of the sun is but a shadow: for I doubt not but God's works here, are what come nearest to his works there; and that a true relish of the beauties of nature is the most easy preparation and gentlest transition to an enjoyment of those of heaven; as on the contrary a true town life of hurry, confusion, noise, slander, and dissension, is a sort of apprenticeship to hell and its furies. I'm endeavouring to put my mind into as quiet a situation as I can, to be ready to receive that stroke which I believe is coming upon me, and have fully resign'd my self to yield to it. The separation of my soul and body is what I could think of with less pain; for I am very sure he that made it will take care of it, and in whatever state he pleases it shall be, that state must be right: But I cannot think without tears of being separated from my friends, when their condition is so doubtful, that they may want even such assistance as mine. Sure it is more merciful to take from us after death all memory of what we lov'd or pursu'd here: for else what a torment would it be to a spirit, still to love those creatures it is quite divided from? Unless we suppose, that in a more exalted life, all that we esteemed in this imperfect state will affect us no more, than what we lov'd in our infancy concerns us now.

This is an odd way of writing to a lady, and I'm sensible would throw me under a great deal of ridicule, were you to show this letter among your acquaintance. But perhaps you may not your self be quite a stranger to this way of thinking. I heartily wish your life may be so long and so happy, as never to let you think *quite so far* as I am now led to do; but to think *a little towards it*, is what will make you the happier and the easier at all times.

There are no pleasures or amusements that I don't wish you, and therefore 'tis no small grief to me that I shall for the future be less able to partake with you in them. But let Fortune do her worst, whatever she makes us lose, as long as she never makes us lose our honesty and our independence; I despise from my heart whoever parts with the first, and I pity from my soul whoever quits the latter.

I am griev'd at Mr. G——'s condition in this last respect of dependence. He has Merit, Goodnature, and Integrity, three qualities

first sight, take on meaning if written at the time when they were being exiled from Mapledurham (ten miles from Binfield) to London, which was more distant from Binfield. His praise of rural pleasures and disgust of the town would be a part of this pain felt because of the loss of these 'neighbours'. The autumn, with its unexpectedly fine weather, seems an appropriate time for this letter. But the date must be guess-work.

that I fear are too often lost upon great men; or at least are not all three a match for that one which is oppos'd to them, Flattery.[1] I wish it may not soon or late displace him from the favour he now possesses, and seems to like. ⌜I'm sure his late action deserves eternal favour and esteem: Lord Bathurst was charm'd with it, who came hither to see me before his journey. He ask'd and spoke very particularly of you. To morrow Mr. Fortescue comes to me from London about B—'s suit in *forma pauperis*. The poor man looks starv'd: he tells me you have been charitable to him. Indeed 'tis wanted; the poor creature can scarce stir or speak; and I apprehend he will die, just as he gets something to live upon. Adieu.⌝[2]

†EDWARD BLOUNT *to* POPE[3] 11 *November* 1715

1737

Nov. 11, 1715.

It is an agreement of long date between you and me, that you should do with my letters just as you pleased, and answer them at your leisure, and that is as soon as I shall think you ought. I have so true a taste of the substantial part of your friendship, that I wave all ceremonials; and am sure to make you as many visits as I can, and leave you to return them whenever you please, assuring you they shall at all times be heartily welcome to me.

The many alarms we have from your parts, have no effect upon the genius that reigns in our country,[4] which is happily turn'd to preserve peace and quiet among us. What a dismal scene has there been open'd in the North? what ruin have those unfortunate rash gentlemen drawn upon themselves and their miserable followers, and perchance upon many others too, who upon no account would be their followers? However, it may look ungenerous to reproach people in distress. I don't remember you and I ever used to trouble our selves about politicks, but when any matter happen'd to fall into our discourse, we us'd

[1] The failure of Gay's epistle to the Princess (*A Letter to a Lady*) was probably due to the fact that instead of flattering, as he was expected to do, he spent his lines in ridicule of flatterers. If we accept Pope's date of 1715, the 'favour' then possessed by Gay would be that of the Earl of Burlington.

[2] Omitted in the quarto and folio of 1737. After the sentence ending with *like* was added, *I am, etc.*

[3] In all editions of 1737 and thereafter Pope published this letter under the date given and without textual changes. Unfortunately in his table of contents (1737 a) he described the letter as reflections 'After the affair at Preston'. Since the 'affair' took place on 13 Nov., the letter was suspect. There had, of course, been fighting in the north before Preston, and the letter, when edited fifteen years later, might seem to Pope to deal with the most decisive of the conflicts. It is, however, very likely that Pope inserted the date when editing with his usual carelessness. There is reason to think that the letter reflects Blount's attitude towards the Jacobite rebellion.

[4] He is writing evidently from Blagdon in Devonshire.

to condemn all undertakings that tended towards the disturbing the peace and quiet of our country, as contrary to the notions we had of morality and religion, which oblige us on no pretence whatsoever to violate the laws of charity: how many lives have there been lost in hot blood, and how many more are there like to be taken off in cold? If the broils of the nation affect you, come down to me, and though we are farmers, you know Eumeus made his friends welcome. You shall here worship the Eccho at your ease;[1] indeed we are forc'd to do so, because we can't hear the first report, and therefore are oblig'd to listen to the second; which for security sake, I do not always believe neither.

'Tis a great many years since I fell in love with the character of Pomponius Atticus:[2] I long'd to imitate him a little, and have contriv'd hitherto, to be like him engaged in no party, but to be a faithful friend to some in both: I find my self very well in this way hitherto, and live in a certain peace of mind by it, which I am perswaded brings a man more content than all the perquisites of wild ambition. I with pleasure join with you in wishing, nay I am not ashamed to say, in praying for the welfare temporal and eternal of all mankind. How much more affectionately then shall I do so for you, since I am in a most particular manner and with all sincerity your, &c.

POPE *to* BROOME — 6 *December* [1715]

Elwin–Courthope, viii. 37

Dec. 6.

You will excuse a man who is under so many obligations as myself, to be deficient in his acknowledgements to some, and it is not unnatural to use those persons with most freedom whose candour and friendship we chiefly depend upon. However, if I defer my thanks, I do not forget them; and you must believe me not a little grateful to you for the last packet you sent me. Your own verses, and those of your friend, I shall commit to Mr. Lintot, and take what liberties you allow me with yours. But his Miscellany, he tells me, will scarce be put in hand these two months.[3]

[1] On the eighth enigma or symbol of Pythagoras about the echo see also Pope to Trumbull, 16 Dec. 1715, and from Trumbull, 19 Jan. 1716. Evidently Pope had quoted the enigma to Blount, who here mentions it in reply.

[2] This love of Atticus was probably due to Sir Matthew Hale's *Life and Death of Pomponius Atticus* (1677), which contains the first English version of the life by Nepos, with a sort of courtesy-book comment for all who might wish to remain aloof from faction and still preserve that integrity and beneficence that 'have a great connaturality to human nature'. Pope's later application of the name to Addison was both high compliment and bitter irony: Addison, a potential Atticus, was tied to a private faction, a 'Little Senate'.

[3] In July 1717 Lintot published a volume called *Poems on Several Occasions*, in which Pope had a large hand and to which Broome contributed a number of small pieces. This may be the miscellany of which Pope here speaks. See the edition by Norman Ault called *Pope's Own Miscellany* (1935).

Since my last, I find it necessary to review Eustathius upon the seventh and eighth books. If therefore you had full time to make an abstract of them, it would be particularly obliging: but as it will be wanted for the press in three weeks' time,[1] I fear you may scarce have leisure; however, be pleased to let me know in a post or two.

I shall leave London in a week, designing to pass the Christmas at home in the Forest. From thence I shall be able to write to you more at large than my present hurry will allow me. I heartily wish I could as easily have seen Sturston this winter weather, where the absence of the sun might be imperceptible in the presence of the fair ladies. How many longing wishes shall I send thither, when I am shut up with my old father and mother, or at best only see a country neighbor? Pray represent my affliction to Mrs. Marriot in all the moving terms you can, and let them ever believe me sincerely theirs, as I am your most faithful humble servant.

POPE *to* CARYLL[2] [? *December* 1715]

Add. 28618

I should make you a very long and extraordinary apology for having so long been silent, if I were to tell you in what a wild, distracted, amused, buried[3] state, both my mind and body have been ever since my coming to this town. A good deal of it is so odd, that it would hardly find credit; and more so perplexed that it would move pity in you when you reflect how naturally people of my turn love quiet, and how much my present studies require ease. In a word, the world and I agree as ill, as my soul and body, my appetites and constitution, my books and business. So that I am more splenetic than ever you knew me, concerned for others, out of humour with myself, fearful of some things, wearied with all. As to my crime in regard to you (the only one I

[1] The *Iliad*, vol. ii, was published on 22 Mar. 1716.

[2] The Caryll transcript is undated, and at this point the transcripts are clearly not in good chronological order. Elwin dates the letter 'November or December 1715', but since Pope had written to Caryll on 11 Oct., November would seem early for so elaborate an apology for long silence. Hence December is preferable. If we adopt such a date, we must assume a scribal error (and there are innumerable such in these transcripts) in the sentence where Pope speaks of printing the '1st' volume of his *Iliad.* It is probably an error for *2nd.* Pope's disillusionment with 'the world' and his comment on the 'prodigious ferment of politics' might fit the period after the Jacobite surrender at Preston. Possibly for Dec. 1715 we should have more political details, for on 9 Dec. some scores of the top rebels were jeered through the streets of London, 'each man on horseback, his arms tied with ropes, the horses led by soldiers' (Leadham, pp. 254–5). As a Catholic who probably (like Edward Blount) did not sympathize with the Jacobites Pope might be silent when writing to another Catholic who presumably did secretly favour their cause.

The letter cannot date in late 1714 when the first volume of the *Iliad* was going to press, since then Caryll's family was abroad, and Pope knew of their absence. He here writes of them as now at Ladyholt.

[3] Pope's 'amus'd, buried state' (the clear writing of the scribe) is allowed to stand as meaning 'buried in business' or dead to the world of politics. Elwin silently emended to *hurried.*

shall ever be guilty of), that of not writing, I can only truly tell you 'tis what I have been equally guilty of towards all my best friends of late; and I know your candor and indulgence, so long experienc'd by me, will look with a better eye upon this plain confession of truth, than upon the most artful excuses of respectful compliments.

It is an old thing to tell you how much I love you, and all that's yours; how entirely my own heart makes all your interests mine; and how sensible a stroke to it everything must be, which affects your quiet, or happiness in any kind. Perhaps accident, or distance, or private cares, or public calamities, something in short or other of what human life inflicts upon us, may prevent the usual frequency of our expressions of that friendship, which I'm sure to carry with me to my grave. Our guardian angels, whom we never see, nor hear, are yet constant in their kindness, and perpetual in their good offices to us. And I hope some beings of far inferior species may at least imitate them in this uninterrupted benevolence to each other.—You see I am in a reverie, and will pardon these wild indeterminate ravings of one who must always be thinking of you, whatsoever state or scene of life either of us shall be thrown into. I beg you at all times, to believe me as zealous to continue our friendship, as I was the first moment I began it: and that as it has increased ever since that time, so it shall never suffer any abatement by any intervals of absence or fortune. This town is in so prodigious a ferment of politics that I, who never meddled with any, am utterly incapable of all conversation in it. I long for a retreat, and the necessary attendance upon the press while my first[1] volume is printing, hinders me from that satisfaction.

I heartily wish you are happier at Ladyholt, and that your whole family may enjoy that serenity and lively good humour which I have had the delight of often observing there. I beg them all to accept of my most zealous wishes for their welfare, and most sincere tender of service. I should be glad I could conclude this letter by telling you any news that is agreeable, or tending to the advancement of politeness or arts; but even poetry is become none of my pleasures, nor do I know almost any other I can now boast, but that I believe you think me | Dear Sir | Your most affectionate obedient | Faithful humble servant. | A. P.

†POPE *to* SIR WILLIAM TRUMBULL *16 December* 1715

1735

Decemb. 16, 1715.

It was one of the Enigma's of *Pythagoras, When the Winds rise, worship the Eccho.* A modern Writer[2] explains this to signify, '*When*

[1] In error for *2nd*? or *next*? See the long introductory note above.

[2] The unidentified 'modern writer' had doubtless the more truly Pythagorean interpretation. Stanley in his *History of Philosophy* (1660) translated this eighth Symbol: 'When

popular Tumults begin, retire to Solitudes, or such places where Eccho's are commonly found; Rocks, Woods, &c.' I am rather of opinion it should be interpreted, 'When Rumours increase, and when there is abundance of Noise and Clamour, believe the *second Report*:' This I think agrees more exactly with the *Eccho*, and is the more natural application of the Symbol. However it be, either of these precepts is extreamly proper to be followed at this season; and I cannot but applaud your resolution of continuing in what you call your Cave in the forest, this winter; and preferring the noise of breaking Ice to that of breaking Statesmen, the rage of Storms to that of Parties, and fury and ravage of Floods and Tempests, to the precipitancy of some, and the ruin of others, which I fear will be our daily prospect in *London*.

I sincerely wish my self with you, to contemplate the wonders of God in the firmament, rather than the madness of man on the earth. But I never had so much cause as now to complain of my poetical star, that fixes me at this tumultuous time, to attend the gingling of rymes and the measuring of syllables: To be almost the only trifler in the nation; and as ridiculous as the Poet in *Petronius*,[1] who while all the rest in the ship were either labouring or praying for life, was scratching his head in a little room, to write a fine description of the tempest.

You tell me you like the sound of no arms but those of *Achilles*: for my part I like them as little as the others. I listed my self in the battles of *Homer*, and I am no sooner in war, but like most other folks, I wish my self out again.

I heartily joyn with you in wishing Quiet to our native country: Quiet in the state, which like charity in religion, is too much the perfection and happiness of either, to be broken or violated on any pretence or prospect whatsoever: Fire and sword, and fire and faggot are equally my aversion. I can pray for opposite parties, and for opposite religions, with great sincerity. I think to be a lover of one's Country is a glorious Elogy, but I do not think it so great an one as to be a lover of Mankind.

⌜Mr. *J*— and⌝[2] I sometimes celebrate you under these denominations, and join your health with that of the whole world; a truly Catholick health; which far excels the poor narrow-spirited, ridiculous healths now in fashion, to *this Church*, or *that Church*: Whatever our teachers may say, they must give us leave at least to *wish* generously. These, dear Sir, are my general dispositions, but whenever I pray or wish for particulars, you are one of the first in the thoughts and affections of | Your, &c.

the winds rise, worship the noise.' Pope is trying to apply the enigma to the Jacobite uprising so recently quelled. He had used this same enigma in a lost letter to E. Blount, who replied on 11 Nov. 1715.

[1] *Satyricon*, 115.

[2] Omitted in Pope's texts, 1737–42. (*J*— was probably Jervas.)

POPE *to* JOHN VANDER BEMPDEN[1] [1715?]

Homer MSS. Add. 4807 (draft)

Thursday.

Sir,—Upon what you told me when I was last to wait on you, I deferr'd treating further for the Rentcharge, till you could be more certain what Summ you could conveniently raise in present toward the purchase.

If there were only three or 400 ll wanting, we woud take your Bond, for as to a mortgage on the Rentcharge my father is not qualifyd to take it, for by an Act of Parliament he cannot buy Land, tho he may sell. However if you desire to make the purchace soon, I believe I have a friend who will lend you the 1000 ll on the same Security you offer us. If you have any other Scruple, you'll please to tell it me fairly, but if this purchace be convenient to you we shall think of treating with no other & be ready upon your Answer; since I think what I here propose entirely accommodates all the difficulty you seemd to be at.

I am | Sir, | Your most humble Servant, | A. Pope.

Address: To | John Vander Bempden Esqr | present.

[1] Mr. Hunter supposes, with great probability (Trusts, pp. 37, 38), that this letter relates to the proposed sale of the 'rent-charge' arising out of Ruston, mentioned in the father's will, which one of the Vander Bempden family of Yorkshire were in treaty for.—Elwin–Courthope, x. 231 n.

The letter in draft occurs among the leaves on which *Iliad* xiii was translated. Since this book appeared in vol. iv (1718), all one can say of the draft is that it was evidently written before the death of Pope's father in 1717. The Elwin–Courthope edition dated the letter 1715, but the sale may have been projected in 1716 at the time when the house at Binfield was sold. In 1716 Catholics feared registration of their estates would be followed by added discriminatory taxation.

1716

In the first half of this year the Popes removed to Chiswick, where social engagements made translation more difficult than it had been at Binfield. Pope's friendship —one might almost call it a passion—for Lady Mary Wortley Montagu became more expressive when in the summer she and Mr. Wortley departed for Constantinople, and the famous correspondence between her and Pope began. Pope's second volume of Homer duly appeared in March, but apart from Homer the publication of things by him was furtive and unhappy. Curll for bringing out the *Court Poems*, unauthorized, was given a vomit, and Pope's pamphlets on this espisode began a war with Curll that was to plague the rest of his career. A burlesque of the Tate and Brady version of the First Psalm had to be disowned, hypocritically, and not infrequent attacks on his writing or on his religion gave him uneasy moments. A new correspondence with Francis Atterbury, Bishop of Rochester, led later to political complications when the bishop was exiled for treason in 1723. Because of the invasion of '15 all Catholic estates seemed now in jeopardy.

POPE *to* CARYLL — 10 *January* [1715/16]

Add. 28618

I received some time past your most welcome and friendly letter. It is a true apology I make for not having sooner acknowledged it, that I really intended to have complied with your kind invitation, and made a venturesome trip in the winter to Ladyholt. You see sufficiently the cause that prevents that satisfaction, whenever you look out of your windows, or put your nose out of doors.[1] I very much wish the season had not exerted its severity before I had arrived among you: for I could pardon any of its inclemencies, tho' never so lasting, when they furnish me with a good pretence of staying with you. I sincerely long to enjoy a few more agreeable hours in that conversation I have so often delighted in; with those persons I have so long esteem'd, and in that frankness, ease, and good humour which is hereditary to your family. It is my hearty wish Heaven may continue all those blessings you all deserve, and nothing interrupt the intercourse of so many virtues as you can employ towards each other.

As for myself, who am a single, unconcerned, and independent creature in the world, who have no interests at my heart but those of mankind, a general good will to all men of good will, I shall be content

[1] From late December to February of 1715/16 the winter was extremely cold—perhaps the worst winter of Pope's time. The Thames was frozen over, streets of booths were laid out, and coaches could drive about on the ice.

to wear away a life of no importance in any safe obscurity. The old conceits of fame, and idle pleasures of poetry are seriously over with me, and I think of nothing but entire indolence, resignation, or something between both, which I want a name for. I am really a greater philosopher than I have the vanity to describe to you; and perhaps a better Christian than is consistent with Christian humility to pretend to be.

I have made several offers of visiting Lady Swinburne,[1] but herself and her friends [are] somewhat delicate as to my waiting upon her in the place where she now is. I have given them to understand, however, how desirous I should be of any occasion of testifying for her that benevolence and regard, which both her own merit, misfortune, and, added to those, your friendship for her, challenge from me. The Mapledurham ladies (if they be any longer called so, since their brother makes so much haste to an alienation of his affections another way) are not so unfortunate in particular, but sensible enough (I can assure you) to be very much so in partaking the afflictions of others: Their behaviour is generous and exemplary on this occasion. I question whether, the time considered, their sorrows are not more seasonable than their brother's loves?—To answer your remaining Queries, Mr Plowden's book[2] is in my custody, Gay's poem[3] just on the brink of the press, to which we have had the interest to procure him subscriptions of a guinea a book, to a pretty tolerable number. I believe it may be worth 150 ll to him in the whole.

I beg the whole family of Ladyholt to be assured at all times of my most faithful services: And yourself to believe no man can continue with more ardor than I, Your most affectionate, obliged | Friend, and humble servant | A: P:

London Jan: 10th

†SIR WILLIAM TRUMBULL *to* POPE 19 *January* 1715/16

1735

Jan. 19, 1715/16.

I should be asham'd of my long idleness, in not acknowledging your kind advice about *Eccho*, and your most ingenious explanation of it, relating to Popular tumults; which I own to be very useful: And yet give me leave to tell you, that I keep my self to a shorter receipt of the same *Pythagoras*, which is *Silence*; and this I shall observe, if not

[1] Lady Swinburne, sister of Mrs. Lister Blount and hence aunt of Teresa and Martha, was now in trouble because of the implication of her husband (Sir William) and his brothers in the Jacobite uprisings. Sir William died 17 Apr. 1716.—Elwin.

[2] His copy of the *Iliad*, vol. i?

[3] Gay's *Trivia* was published on 26 Jan. In addition to subscription money Lintot paid him £43 for the copyright. See EC vii. 460 n.

the whole time of his discipline, yet at least till Your return into this country. I am oblig'd further to this method, by the most severe weather I ever felt; when tho' I keep as near by the fire as may be, yet *Gelidus concrevit frigore Sanguis*:[1] and often I apprehend the circulation of the blood begins to be stop'd. I have further, great losses (to a poor farmer) of my poor Oxen—*Intereunt pecudes, stant circumfusa pruinis Corpora magna Boum*,[2] &c.

Pray comfort me if you can, by telling me that your second Volume of *Homer* is not frozen; for it must be express'd very poetically to say now, that the Presses *sweat*.

I cannot forbear to add a piece of artifice I have been guilty of, on occasion of my being oblig'd to congratulate the birth-day of a friend of mine: When finding I had no materials of my own, I very frankly sent him your imitation of *Martial*'s Epigram on *Antonius Primus*.[3] This has been applauded so much that I am in danger of commencing Poet, perhaps Laureat, (pray desire my good friend Mr. *Rowe* to enter a Caveat) provided you will further increase my stock in this bank. In which proceeding I have laid the foundation of my estate, and as *honestly* as many others have begun theirs. But now being a little tender, as young beginners often are, I offer to you (for I have conceal'd the true author) whether you will give me orders to declare who is the Father of this fine child, or not? Whatever you determine, my fingers, pen, and ink are so frozen, that I cannot thank you more at large. You will forgive this and all other faults of, Dear Sir, | Your, &c.

†POPE *to* EDWARD BLOUNT[4] — 21 *January* 1715/16

1735

Jan. 21, 1715/16.

I know of nothing that will be so Interesting to you at present, as some circumstances of the last Act of that eminent Comick Poet, and

[1] *Aeneid*, xii. 905.

[2] *Georgics*, iii. 368 f.

[3] In his editions of 1735 Pope here added a footnote summarizing the life of Sir William (who died in Dec. 1716) and printing his epitaph, which had appeared in Pope's *Works* (1717). Of interest in this note is Pope's statement: 'Our Author celebrated that Retirement [Sir William's] in his Poem on the [Windsor] Forest, and addrest to him his first Pastoral at 16 Years of Age.' The imitation of Martial Pope published in *Poems on Several Occasions* (1717; ed. Norman Ault as *Pope's Own Miscellany*, 1935), p. 39, under the heading 'Sent to Sir Philip Meadows on his Birth-Day, by Sir William Trumbull. In Imitation of Martial, Book 10, *Epig*. 23.' In later (1737–42) editions of his letters Pope substituted for this footnote one that merely printed the first line of Martial's poem together with a revised text of Pope's Imitation.

[4] This interesting letter gives us Pope's account of the death-bed marriage of Wycherley. It is hardly likely that Pope made up the story. The disinherited nephew sued in chancery for his uncle's estate, and told a very different story of Wycherley's last hours. See Professor Howard P. Vincent, 'The Death of William Wycherley', in *Harvard Studies and Notes*, xv (1933), 219–42. Professor Vincent informs the editor that the Lord Chancellor's decision was not favourable to the nephew's story.

our Friend, *Wycherley*. He had often told me, as I doubt not he did all his Acquaintance, that he would Marry as soon as his life was despair'd of. Accordingly a few days before his Death he underwent the Ceremony; and join'd together those two Sacraments which wise Men say should be the last we receive; For if you observe, Matrimony is plac'd after Extreme Unction in our Catechism, as a kind of Hint of the Order of Time in which they are to be taken. The old Man then lay down, satisfy'd in the Conscience of having, by this one Act paid his just Debts, obliged a Woman who (he was told) had Merit, and shewn a heroic resentment of the ill usage of his next Heir. Some hundred pounds which he had with the Lady, discharged those Debts; a Jointure of four hundred a year made her a Recompence; and the Nephew he left to comfort himself as well as he could, with the miserable Remains of a mortgaged Estate. I saw our Friend twice after this was done, less peevish in his Sickness than he used to be in his Health; neither much afraid of dying, nor (which in him had been more likely) much ashamed of Marrying. The Evening before he expired, he called his young Wife to the bedside, and earnestly entreated her not to deny him one request, the last he should make. Upon her Assurances of consenting to it, he told her, *My Dear, it is only this; that you will never marry an old Man again.* I cannot help remarking, that Sickness which often destroys both Wit and Wisdom, yet seldom has power to remove that Talent which we call *Humour*: Mr. *Wycherley* shew'd his, even in this last Compliment; tho' I think his request a little hard; for why should he bar her from doubling her Jointure on the same easy Terms?

So trivial as these Circumstances are, I should not be displeas'd myself to know such Trifles, when they concern or characterise any eminent Person. The wisest and wittiest of Men are seldom wiser or wittier than others in these sober Moments. At least, our Friend ended much in the Character he had lived in: And *Horace*'s Rule for a Play, may as well be apply'd to him as a Playwright.

—Servetur ad imum
Qualis ab inceptu processerit, & sibi constet.[1]

I am, &c.

‡POPE *to* EDWARD BLOUNT[2] 10 *February* 1715/16

1735

Feb. 10, 1715/16.

I am just return'd from the Country, whither Mr. *Rowe* accompanied me, and pass'd a Week in the Forest. I need not tell you how much

[1] Horace, *Ars Poetica*, ll. 126–7. Pope in all editions printed *inceptu*.

[2] This letter is fabricated from that to Caryll, 20 Sept. 1713 (from which the first five paragraphs here are derived) and from two paragraphs—the last two here—from an

a Man of his Turn entertain'd me; but I must acquaint you there is a Vivacity and Gaiety of Disposition almost peculiar to him, which make it impossible to part from him without that uneasiness which generally succeeds all our pleasures. I have been just taking a solitary walk by moonshine, full of reflections on the transitory nature of all human delights; and giving my Thoughts a loose in the contemplation of those Satisfactions which probably we may hereafter taste in the Company of separate Spirits, when we shall range the Walks above, and perhaps gaze on this World at as vast a distance as we now do on those Worlds. The pleasures we are to enjoy in that Conversation must undoubtedly be of a nobler kind, and (not unlikely) may proceed from the Discoveries each shall communicate to another, of God and of Nature; for the Happiness of Minds can surely be nothing but Knowledge.

The highest Gratification we receive here from Company is *Mirth*, which at the best is but a fluttering unquiet Motion, that beats about the breast for a few moments, and after leaves it void and empty.

Keeping good Company, even the best, is but a less shameful Art of losing Time.

What we here call *Science* and *Study*, are little better: The greater number of Arts to which we apply ourselves are mere groping in the Dark; and even the search of our most important Concerns in a future being, is but a needless, anxious, and uncertain haste to be knowing, sooner than we can, what without all this sollicitude we shall know a little later. We are but *Curious Impertinents* in the case of Futurity. 'Tis not our business to be guessing what the State of Souls shall be, but to be doing what may make our own State happy; We cannot be Knowing, but we can be Virtuous.

If this be my Notion of a great part of that high Science, Divinity; you will be so civil as to imagine I lay no mighty Stress upon the rest. Even of my darling Poetry I really make no other use, than Horses of the Bells that gingle about their ears (tho' now and then they toss their Heads as if they were proud of 'em) only to jogg on a little more merrily.

Your Observations on the narrow conceptions of Mankind in that point of Friendship, confirm me in what I was so fortunate as at my first knowledge of you to hope, and since so amply to experience. Let me take so much decent Pride and Dignity upon me, as to tell you, that but for Opinions like these, which I discover'd in your Mind, I had never made the Trial I have done; which has succeeded so much to mine, and I believe not less to your Satisfaction: For if I know you

unknown origin. The February date is obviously improbable for the first group of paragraphs: it may have been taken from the letter (unknown) from which the last two came. Annotations of the first five paragraphs will be found joined to the letter to Caryll.

right, your Pleasure is greater in obliging me, than I can feel on my part, till it falls in my power to oblige you.

Your Remark, that the Variety of opinion in Politics or Religion is often rather a Gratification, than Objection, to people who have Sense enough to consider the beautiful order of Nature in her Variations; makes me think you have not construed *Joannes Secundus* wrong, in the Verse which precedes that which you quote; *Bene nota Fides*,[1] as I take it, does no way signify the *Roman* Catholic Religion, tho' *Secundus* was of it. I think it was a generous thought, and one that flow'd from an exalted mind, that it was not improbable but God might be delighted with the various methods of worshipping him, which divided the whole World. I am pretty sure You and I should no more make good *Inquisitors* to the modern Tyrants in Faith, than we could have been qualify'd for *Lictors* to *Procrustes*, when he converted refractory Members with the Rack. In a word, I can only repeat to you what I think I have formerly said; that I as little fear God will damn a Man who has Charity, as I hope that any Priest can save him without it. | I am, &c.

GAY, JERVAS, ARBUTHNOT, *and* POPE *to* PARNELL[2]

[*February* 1715/16]

Trinity College, Dublin

My Dear Doctor,—I was last Summer in Devonshire [and] am this Winter at Mrs Bonyers;[3] in the Summer I wrote a Poem & in the Winter I have publish'd it, which I have sent to you by Dr Elwood.[4] In the Summer I eat two Dishes of Toad Stools of my own gathering instead of Mushrooms, and in the Winter I have been sick with Wine as I am at this time,

[Two lines here are heavily scored out.][5]

now you know where I have been and what I have done I shall tell you what I intend to do the ensuing Summer. I propose to do the same thing I did last, which was to meet you in any Part of England you would appoint, don't let me have two dissapointments. I have long'd

[1] Johannes Secundus, Epistle xi (*Ad Sibrandum Occonem*), bk. I, l. 29.

[2] This letter was written after the success of Gay's *Trivia* (published 26 Jan.) was assured and before the publication of Pope's *Iliad*, vol. ii, was imminent. Vol. ii was published on 22 Mar. The date of the chop-house dinner at which this letter was produced can thus be only vaguely determined. The writing is strongly redolent of wine.

[3] The name was thus printed by Goldsmith: it might possibly be Bowzer. She was doubtless Gay's landlady.

[4] A senior fellow of Trinity College, Dublin, and at one time the representative of the university in parliament.—Elwin.

[5] Goldsmith (1770) printed this overscored passage as: 'blessed be God for it, as I must bless God for all things. In the summer I spoke truth to damsels; in the winter I told lyes to ladies.'

to hear from you, and to that intent teaz'd you with three or four Letters, but having no Answer, I fear'd both your's & my Letters might have miscarried. I hope my Performance will please the Dean whom I often wish for, and whom I would have often wrote to, but for the same Reasons I neglected writing to you. I hope I need not tell you how I love you, & how glad I shall be to hear from you; which next to seeing you would be the greatest Satisfaction to | Your most Affectionate Friend & | Humble Servant. J G

Dear Mr A. . . .n,[1] Tho' my Proportion of this Epistle shou'd be but a Sketch in Miniature yet I take up half this Page having paid my Club with the good Company both for our Dinner of Chops & for this Paper. The Poets will give you lively Descriptions in their Way, I shal only Acquaint you with that which is directly my own Province. I have just set the last hand to a Couplet, for so I may call two Nymphs in One Piece. They are Pope's Favorites[2] & therefore you will guess must have cost me more pains than any Nymphs can be worth. He has been so unreasonable to expect that I shoud have made them as beautifull upon Canvas as he has done upon paper. If this same Mr P . . . shou'd omit to write for the Dear Frogs & the Pervigilium I must entreat you not to let me languish for 'em as I have done ever since they crost the Seas & us. You remember by what Neglects &c we mist 'em when we lost you & therefor I have not yet forgiven any of those Triflers that let 'em escape & run those hazards. I am going on at the old rate & want you & the Dean prodigiously, and I am in hopes of making you a Visit this Summer & of hearing from you both now you are together. Fortescue I am sure will be concern'd that he is not in Cornhill to set his h[and] to these presents not only as a Witness but as a Serviteur tres humble C. J.[3]

It is so great an honour to a poor Scots man to be Rememberd at this time o'day, especially by an inhabitant of the Glacialis Ierne that I take it very thankfully. & have with my good freinds Rememberd you at our Table in the chop house in exchange Alley Ther wanted nothing to compleat our happiness but Your Company & our Dear Freind the Deans I am sure the whole entertainment would have been to his Relish. Gay has gott so much money[4] by his art of walking the streets, that he is ready to sett up his equipage: he is just going to the bank to negotiate some exchequer Bills. Mr pope delays his Second Volume of his Homer till the Martial Spirit of the Rebells is quite quelld it being judgd that his first part did some harm that way. Our

[1] For 'Dear Mr. Archdeacon'. Parnell was Archdeacon of Clogher.
[2] Jervas's painting of Martha and Teresa Blount is still preserved at Mapledurham.
[3] For 'Charles Jervas'.
[4] On Gay's 'money' see Pope to Caryll, 10 Jan. 1715/16.

love again & again to the Dear Dean. *fuimus Torys*:[1] I can say no more—

When a man is conscious that he does no good himself, the next thing is to cause others to do some: I may claim some merit this way, in hastening this Testimonial from your Friends above-writing. Their Love to you indeed wants no Spur, their Ink wants no Pen, their Pen wants no Hand, their Hand wants no Heart, and so forth (after the manner of Rabelais, which is betwixt some meaning & no meaning.) And yet it may be said, when Present Thought and Opportunity is wanting, their Pens want Ink, their Hands want Pens, their Hearts want Hands, &c. Till Time, Place, and Conveniency concur, to sett them a writing; as at present, a sociable Meeting, a good Dinner, a warm Fire, and an easie Situation do, to the Joint Labour and pleasure of this Epistle.

Wherein, if I should say nothing, I should say much (much being included in my Love) tho my Love be such that if I should say much, I should yet say nothing, it being (as Cowley says) equally impossible either to conceal, or to express it.

If I were to tell you the thing I wish above all things, it is to see you again; the next is to see here your Treatise of Zoilus with the Batrachomuomachia, and the Pervigilium Veneris, both which Poems are Masterpieces in several kinds: and I question not the Prose is as excellent in its sort as the Essay on Homer:[2] Nothing can be more glorious to that great Author, than that the same hand that carvd his best Statue, and deckd it with its old Lawrells, should also hang up the Scare-crow of his miserable Critick, and gibbet up the Carcase of Zoilus to t[he Te]rror of the Witlings of Posterity.

More, much more, upon this & a thousand other subjects will be the matter of my next letter, whe[rein] I must open all the Friend to you. At this time I must be content with telling you I am faithfully | Your most affectionate & humble Servant | A. Pope.

Address:[3] To | The Revd Dr Parnelle, | in | Dublin

*POPE *to* RICHARD GRAHAM[4] — 29 *February* 1715/16

The Huntington Library

Feb. 29th 1715

Sir,—Tho' I have this day so much unforeseen business upon my hands, as to prevent my being able to meet you this Evening, I could

[1] A pun on the motto of the East India Company (which was taken from the *Aeneid*): 'Fuimus Troes.'

[2] Pope came to think less highly of this essay, written for him by Parnell, or else he is insincerely flattering his helper here. See Spence, p. 138.

[3] In Pope's hand, with his individual spelling, *Parnelle*.

[4] This letter concerns the Dedication to the Earl of Burlington speedily to be published

not forbear reading thrice over your Dedication: and with all sincerity assure you, I can see nothing Envy itself could carp at, except the few General Phrases I have crossed out. My Opinion of the noble Person it is inscribed to, is as high as any man's in the world; and I am proud of every the least Opportunity, to give it under my hand, with what extreme regard I honour my Lord Burlington. If, to the rest of his due praises, you think fit (provided he allows it) to add that noble Branch, of His Magnanimity in compassionating even Enemies, which I have interlined: it is all I cou'd wish were added to what you have so well written. I leave it wholly to you; and had not done this, but to obey you. I am very sincerely | Sir | Your Affectionate | & humble Servant. | A. Pope

Address: For | Mr Graham.

Endorsement: 29th Febry 1715. | Mr Pope | about my Dedication | of Fresnoy—

POPE *to* JOHN CARYLL, Jr.[1] [*Early* 1716?]

Add. 32567 (Mitford transcript)

What new Scenes of Life I may enter into are uncertaine, but wherever I may be or however engagd, I hope Mr. Caryll & yourself will ever be so just as to believe my whole heart at your Service: That must still be left to my own disposall and while it is so, must be entirely yours. Be pleasd, Dear Sir, to continue the favour you have always shown to me, & use your interest with your father that he may do the same: the best testimony of which will be the *Satisfaction* you will both some times give me of hearing from you that you have not forgot there [is such] an one in the World as | Sir | Your most faithfull | affectionate, humble Servant | A Pope.

I entreat the whole | good family to accept | my most faithful Service.

Address: To | John Caryll Esqr junior | at Lady Holt in | Sussex. | By Midhurst Bagg.

(10 Mar.) in Graham's edition of Du Fresnoy's *Art of Painting* as translated by Dryden. It is a most flattering Dedication by a man who boasts to the Earl: 'Your Lordship is now in the Fourth Generation of our [the Graham family's] *Patrons* and *Benefactors*.' The volume contained Pope's first printing of the epistle 'To Mr. Jervas, with Fresnoy's *Art of Painting*'. What Pope interlined in the Dedication was very likely the passage relating to the northern rebels. It speaks of 'that exemplary Moderation and Generosity, which mov'd You to intercede for the *Lives* of *those*, against whom You stood prepar'd to hazard *Your own*'.

[1] In 1857 Carruthers printed a text of this letter as coming from the collection of Mr. [Samuel?] Rogers. This Elwin (vi. 135) reprinted. The Mitford transcript, here printed, seems to give a more complete text. Mitford labels the letter imperfect, but whether he means more than that certain words, here supplied in brackets, are missing is uncertain. He may mean that this is only the last paragraph of a letter.

The date is difficult. One assumes that it is written at the time (early 1716) when Catholics were to register their estates and possibly be subject to additional taxation; at the time, that is, when the house at Binfield was sold and before a future place of residence ('new scenes') had been chosen.

||POPE *to* CARYLL[1] 20 *March* 1715/16

Add. 28618

March. the 20th 1715/16

I find that a real concern is not only a hindrance to speaking, but writing too. The more time we give ourselves to think over one's own, or a friend's unhappiness, the more unable we grow to express the grief that proceeds from it. It is as natural to delay a letter, at such a season as this, as to retard a melancholy visit to a person one cannot relieve. And one is ashamed in that circumstance, to pretend [to] entertain people with trifling, insignificant affections of sorrow on one hand, or unseasonable and forced gayeties on the other. 'Tis a kind of prophanation of things sacred to treat so solemn a matter as a generous voluntary suffering, with compliments or heroic gallantries. Such a man as I know you are, has[2] no need of being spirited up into honour, or like a weak Woman praised into an opinion of his[3] own virtue. 'Tis enough to do and suffer what we ought; and men should know that the noble power of suffering bravely is as far above that of enterprising greatly, as an unblemished conscience and inflexible resolution are above an accidental flow of spirits or a sudden tide of blood. If the whole religious business of mankind, be included in resignation to our Maker, and charity to our fellow creatures; there are now some people, who give us the opportunity of affording as bright an example in practising the one, as themselves have given an infamous instance of the violation of the other. Whoever is really brave, has always this comfort when he is oppressed, that he knows himself to be superior to those who injure him. For the greatest power on earth can no sooner do him that injury, but the brave man can make himself greater by forgiving it.

If it were generous to seek for alleviating consolations in a calamity of so much glory, one might say that to be ruined thus in the gross, with a whole people, is but like perishing in the general conflagration, where nothing we can value is left behind us.

Methinks, in our present condition, the more[4] heroic thing we are left capable of doing, is to endeavour to lighten each other's load, and (oppressed as we are) to succour such as are yet more oppressed. If there are too many who cannot be assisted but by what we cannot give, our money, there are yet others who may be relieved by our

[1] In 1735 Pope printed this letter, with practically no changes except the omission of direct mention of Mapledurham, as if sent to Edward Blount of Blagdon. The few verbal changes are indicated below.

[2] Such a man . . . has] Such a Mind as your's has *1735–42*.

[3] his own Virtue] its own Virtue *1735–42*.

[4] more] most *1735–42* (a scribal error?).

counsel, by our countenance, and even by our cheerfulness. The misfortunes of private families, the misunderstandings [of people][1] whom distresses make suspicious, the coldness of relations whom change of religion may disunite,[2] or the necessities of half-ruined estates render unkind to each other,—these at least may be softened some degree, by a general well-managed humanity among ourselves, if all those who have your principles, had also your sense and conduct. But indeed most of them have given lamentable proofs of the contrary; and 'tis to be apprehended that they who want sense are only religious thro' fear,[3] and good-naturd thro' shame: These are narrow-minded creatures that never deal in essentials; their faith never looks beyond ceremonials, nor their [charity] beyond relations. As poor as I am, I would gladly relieve any distressed, conscientious French refugee at this instant: what must my concern then be, when I perceive so many anxieties just now springing in[4] those hearts which I have desired a place in, and such clouds of melancholy rising on those faces I have so long looked upon with affection? I begin already to feel both what some apprehend, and what others are yet too stupid to apprehend. I grieve with the old for so many additional inconveniencies and chagrins more than their small remain of life was to undergo; and with the young for so much of those gayeties and pleasures, the portion of youth, as they will by this means be deprived of. This brings into my mind one or other I love best and among those, the widow and fatherless, late of ⌜Mapledurham.⌝[5] As I am certain no people living had an earlier and truer sense of others' misfortunes, or a more generous resignation as to what might be their own; so I earnestly wish, that whatever part they must bear of these, may be rendered as supportable to 'em, as it is in the power of any friend to make it. ⌜They are beforehand with us in being out of house and home, by their brother's marriage: and I wish they have not some cause already to look upon Mapledurham with such sort of melancholy as we may upon our own seats when we lose them⌝[5]—But I know you have prevented me in this thought, as you always will in any thing that is good or generous. I find by a letter of your lady's (which I have seen) that their ease and tranquillity is some part of your care. Upon my faith I believe there is some fatality in it, that you should always, from time to time, be doing those particular things that make me enamoured of you.

I write this from Windsor Forest, [of] which I am come to take my last look ⌜and leave of⌝.[6] We here bid our ⌜papist⌝-neighbours adieu,

[1] [of people] *added from the printed text of 1735; omitted by scribal error from the MS.*

[2] The pressure upon Catholics to abjure their faith was obviously at this moment terrific. Elwin cites two cases, and there were doubtless many. See Sherburn, *Early Career*, p. 159.

[3] thro' fear] thro' Weakness *1735–42.*

[4] springing in] tearing *1735–42.*

[5] Omitted in editions of 1735–42; replaced by a dash.

[6] The passage serves to date the removal from Binfield, due in part to laws against the

much as those who go to be hanged do their fellow-prisoners, who are condemned to follow 'em a few weeks after. ⌜I was at Whiteknights, where I found the young ladies I just now mentioned spoken of a little more coldly, than I could (at this time especially) have wished.⌝ I parted from honest Mr Dancastle with tenderness; and from old Sir William Trumbull as from a venerable prophet, foretelling with lifted hands the miseries to come ⌜upon posterity⌝, which he was just going to be removed from![1]

Perhaps now I have learnt so far as

—Nos dulcia linquimus arva,

the next may be—Nos patriam fugimus.[2]

Let that, and all else be as Heaven pleases![3] for the rest I shall be ever | Dear Sir, most faithfully and gratefully yours, | and all your family's.

POPE *to* EDWARD BLOUNT 20 *March* 1715/16

1735

[In his editions, 1735–42, Pope printed a letter of this date as to Blount, which is practically identical with that to Caryll of the same date. Assuming that Pope did not send identical letters to both men and that he transferred the Caryll letter to Blount as addressee, the text of 1735 (to Blount) is here omitted. For textual changes see the notes to the Caryll letter.]

†EDWARD BLOUNT *to* POPE 24 *March* 1715/16

1737

March 24, 1715–16.

Your letters give me a gleam of satisfaction, in the midst of a very dark and cloudy situation of thoughts, which it would be more than human to be exempt from at this time, when our homes must either be left, or be made too narrow for us to turn in. Poetically speaking, I should lament the loss Windsor Forest and you sustain of each other, but that methinks one can't say you are parted, because you will live by and in one another, while verse is verse. This consideration hardens me in my opinion rather to congratulate you,[4] since you have the

purchase of land by Catholics or to the fear of double taxation upon Catholic estates. These laws were not rigidly enforced, but at the moment they were threatening. The omissions, seen in half-brackets, in the printed text of this letter indicate Pope's cleverness in revision.

[1] removed from!] remov'd himself *1735–42*. (Sir William was now 77; he died in Dec. 1716.)

[2] Virgil, *Eclogues*, i. 3–4.

[3] After the word *pleases* Pope (1735–42) added a different ending: 'I have provided just enough to keep me a Man of Honour. I believe you and I shall never be asham'd of each other. I know I wish my Country well; and if it undoes me, it shall not make me wish it otherwise.'

[4] The place at Binfield is evidently sold, but the family settles at Chiswick almost a month later than this. See Pope to Caryll, 20 Apr. 1716.

pleasure of the prospect whenever you take it from your shelf, and at the same time the solid cash you sold it for, of which Virgil in his exile knew nothing in those days, and which will make every place easy to you. I for my part am not so happy; my *parva rura* are fasten'd to me, so that I can't exchange them as you have, for more portable means of subsistance; and yet I hope to gather enough to make the *Patriam fugimus* supportable to me: 'tis what I am resolved on, with my *Penates.* If therefore you ask me to whom you shall complain? I will exhort you to leave laziness and the elms of St James's Park, and choose to join the other two proposals in one, safety and friendship, (the least of which is a good motive for most things, as the other is for almost every thing) and go with me where War will not reach us,[1] nor paultry Constables summon us to vestrys.

The future epistle you flatter me with, will find me still here, and I think I may be here a month longer. Whenever I go from hence, one of the few reasons to make me regret my home will be that I shall not have the pleasure of saying to you

Hic tamen hanc mecum poteris requiescere noctem,[2]

which would have render'd this place more agreeable, than ever it else could be to me; for I protest it is with the utmost sincerity that I assure you I am entirely | Dear Sir, | Yours, &c.

POPE *to* MARTHA BLOUNT[3] [*March* 1716?]

Mapledurham

Madam,—I am here studying ten hours a day, but thinking of you in spight of all the learned. The Epistle of Eloise grows warm, and begins to have some Breathings of the Heart in it, which may make posterity think I was in love. I can scarce find in my heart to leave out the conclusion I once intended for it——

I am to pass three or four days in high luxury, with some company at my Lord Burlington's; We are to walk, ride, ramble, dine, drink, & lye together. His gardens are delightfull, his musick ravishing,[4] yet I shall now and then cast a thought on Charles-street.[5]

[1] Blount went abroad in the summer of 1716. He had returned by the spring of 1717, but again withdrew to the continent in July of that year.—Elwin.

[2] Virgil, *Eclogues*, i. 80. (Virgil has *poteras.*)

[3] The date again is mere guess-work. It seems probable that Pope is writing from Binfield in Holy Week (Easter came on 1 Apr. 1716) to Miss Blount, visiting or living in Charles Street. Only this letter connects her with that street.

[4] Since about three weeks after the supposed date of this letter the Popes settled in Chiswick 'under the wing of my Lord Burlington', this visit was preliminary to removal. At this time Burlington's music was in the charge of Handel.

[5] This should be a gallant reference to Miss Blount as in Charles Street. It may, however, be to Lady Mary Wortley Montagu. She is addressed as 'in Charles Street, Westminster',

May you have all possible success both at your Devotions this week, & your Masquerade the next: Whether you repent or Sin, may you do all you wish; and when you think of me, either laugh at me or pray for me, which you please.

POPE *to* CARYLL

20 *April* [1716]

Add. 28618

London April 20.

You will think the better of your friend, and judge more truly of that friendship and regard which must be constant in him, if you consider he never yet neglected to pay you his acknowledgments from time to time, but when business, hurry, and accident prevented. I have had enough of all three of late to make me forget any thing but you: *Imprimis*, my father and mother having disposed of their little estate at Binfield, I was concerned to find out some asylum for their old age; and these cares, of settling, and furnishing a house, have employed me till yesterday, when we fixed at Chiswick under the wing of my Lord Burlington.[1] *Item*, a most ridiculous quarrel with a bookseller, occasioned by his having printed some satirical pieces on the Court[2] under my name. I contrived to save a fellow a beating by giving him a vomit, the history whereof has been transmitted to posterity by a late Grub-street author. I supose Lewis has sent you the Pamphlet which has much entertained the town. *Item*, new designs with some of my friends for a satirical work, which I must've formerly mentioned to you.[3] But were I to tell you all, I should be endless. However, I wrote to you a very long epistle about 3 weeks ago, which I fear you never received, and fear it the more as I spoke my Mind pretty freely upon some

in a letter printed by Dallaway (Lady Mary's *Works*, i [1803], 49), reprinted by Elwin (ix. 410) and dated [1719]. The date assigned is wrong, since in 1719 Lady Mary lived in Covent Garden. The letter, not here reprinted, is preserved in the Pierpont Morgan Library, and since it is an original letter, not a transcript, and since it is unsigned and not in Pope's hand, the present editor cannot regard it as Pope's: hence it is here omitted. In a letter to Lady Mary, 18 Aug. [1716], Pope alleges a melancholy reaction whenever he passes her house: his passing it after her departure suggests that possibly he passed it on his way to another lady (Miss Blount) in the same street. Within the year the Blount ladies were living in Bolton Street, but not certainly in 1716.

[1] Mawson's New Buildings, in which the Popes had now a house, was a short walk from Chiswick House, where Lord Burlington occasionally resided. His Palladian villa, built about 1730–2, had not yet replaced the older house.

[2] At the beginning of his account of the 'vomit' in the pamphlet here unnamed (it was called *A Full and True Account of a Horrid and Barbarous Revenge by Poison on the Body of Edmund Curll*) Pope remarked: 'Every body knows, that the said Mr. Edmund Curll, on Monday, the 26th instant, published a satirical piece, intitled, Court-poems' (Elwin–Courthope, x. 462). Pope himself was the 'Grubstreet Author'.

[3] The projected satirical work is not easily identified. Elwin thought it the *Memoirs* of Scriblerus. The allusion may be to the projected *Works of the Unlearned*. See Sherburn, *Early Career*, pp. 74–75. Less probably the reference might be to *Three Hours after Marriage* (1717) by Gay, Pope, and Arbuthnot.

modern conjunctures. I wish I knew of your receit of it. My not hearing from you made me hope you had thought of seeing the town shortly. As to my being at Ladyholt for a week or two, it is what I earnestly pant after, and Mr Gay has made several appointments with me to that purpose; but hitherto not only what I have mentioned on my part, but this[1] illness has retarded it. We will certainly be disappointed not much longer. In the meantime, I beg to hear from you, and in such amicable long letters as you use to favor me with. You see I aim at nothing in mine but to talk with you, and to tell you without ceremony how sincerely and unfeignedly I am | Dear Sir | Always yours. | A. P.

*POPE *to* THOMAS DANCASTLE[2] 24 *April* [1716]

. . . I have a commission from my Father to trouble you with. . . . It is that you will be so obliging as to speak to Mr. Tanner in his name, to entreat he will order a Comission to be sent to Chiswick, at Mr. Mawson's new Buildings, that my Father and Mother may pass the time there, rather than be at the trouble and fatigue of going to London (which my Mother's infirmities may render dangerous to her health at this time. . . .

You will find I shall talk upon paper to you both, with the same freedom & unthinking friendship that I have so long conversed with you. You shall be convinced I am no more a wit here, than I was at Binfield & have nothing less in my thought than to show my abilities in writing, as I have nothing more in my desires than to prove my Affection for you. I hope in a short time to relieve you from the care of my palfrey, tho I find it not practicable for me to travel upon him. [Etc.] Dear Sir | Your most affectionate & | obliged Servant, | A. Pope

JERVAS *to* POPE[3] [1716?]

Homer MSS. Add. 4807

Lady Mary W——y orderd me by an Express this Wensday Morning, sedente Gayo, et ridente Fortescuvio, to send you a Letter or some

[1] Elwin emends *this* to *his*. There is no further evidence of illness at this time either on Gay's part or on Pope's. Pope is the more likely to plead illness as an excuse.

[2] The first fragment of this unpublished letter is taken from Sotheby's Catalogue for the sale of 28 July 1913 (where it is lot 190). The second fragment comes from Catalogue 187 issued in 1927 by James F. Drake, Inc., of New York. The original letter has not been found. The first part of the letter evidently refers to the obligation of Catholics to register as such upon change of residence. The second part also seems to refer to a recent removal from Binfield, and hence the letter here is dated [1716] in spite of the fact that both catalogues date it [1717]. The palfrey was given to Pope in 1713 by Caryll, and now is presently to be sold.

The second fragment is here provided by the kindness of Professor R. H. Griffith, to whose attention it came.

[3] It is impossible to date this letter, but it was certainly written before Lady Mary departed for Constantinople on 1 Aug. 1716. On the back of it Pope translated a part of Book X

other proper Notice to come to her on Thursday about 5 a Clock which I suppose she meant in the Evening. Gay design'd to have been with you to day & I wou'd have had him deliverd this welcom message, but he durst not venture to answer for your coming upon his asseverations, you having interchangeably so accustom'd yourselves to Lying that you cannot believe One Another, tho' upon never so serious an Occasion. He will be ready to go back with you—Fortescues service & mine to all—We are your humble Servants. | &c.

Wensday 11 a Clock at Noon.

*FORTESCUE *to* GAY[1] [1716]

Homer MSS. Add. 4807

Dear Gay,—[No]t having heard any thing of you to[day] I suppose this may find you at [Chi]swick; pray give my humble service [to] Mrs Pope, Mr Alexander Pope the elder, [and] Mr Alexander Pope the younger [A]nd I'me just going to forget the [chie]f end of my Letter, which is that Mr [ ]t has (as he says) got a very easy [goi]ng little horse, which you may have [for] 5 guineas; he rid him up himself, [and] says he Knows no fault in him; so [if] you don't succeed with my Lord Burlington, [you] may at least with him. my head [ache]s. I am Your most affect. WF.

†POPE *to* SWIFT[2] 20 *June* 1716

1740

June 20, 1716.

I cannot suffer a friend to cross the Irish seas without bearing a testimony from me of the constant esteem and affection I am both obliged and inclined to have for you. It is better he should tell you than I, how often you are in our thoughts and in our cups, and how I learn to sleep

of the *Iliad*. Book X was printed in vol. iii (1717). Probably Pope is now living at Chiswick, since a summons sent to Binfield on Wednesday morning would with difficulty fetch Pope to London by Thursday evening. All this is guess-work. Jervas went to Ireland in the summer of 1716.

[1] On the verso of this letter (forwarded by Gay to Pope?) the poet translated part of Book XI of the *Iliad*. Since the letter mentions Chiswick as residence of the Popes and since Book XI was published in June 1717, the letter dates either 1716 or 1717. It is here regarded as possibly indicating a desire for a substitute for Pope's palfrey, left at Binfield.

[2] The date offers some difficulty, which most likely is to be resolved by assuming that Pope supplied the date when printing in 1741, and that he forgot, what seems clearly the case, namely, that Curll published Pope's scandalous perversion of the first Psalm under the title *A Roman Catholic Version of the First Psalm, for the Use of a Young Lady, By Mr. Pope* ten days after the date assigned to the letter. The burst of advertising of *The First Psalm* in several newspapers on the 30th or later makes the date of this letter improbable; but it is evidently not more than a fortnight off. Charles Ford carried the letter over, and he was in Dublin in July. See Pope to Parnell, 29 July 1716.

less[1] and drink more, whenever you are named among us. I look upon a friend in Ireland as upon a friend in the other world, whom (Popishly-speaking) I believe constantly well-disposed towards me, and ready to do me all the good he can, in that state of separation, tho' I hear nothing from him, and make addresses to him but very rarely. A Protestant divine cannot take it amiss that I treat him in the same manner with my patron-Saint.

I can tell you no news, but what you will not sufficiently wonder at, that I suffer many things as an Author militant: whereof, in your days of probation, you have been a sharer, or you had not yet arrived to that triumphant state you now deservedly enjoy in the Church. As for me, I have not the least hopes of the Cardinalat, tho' I suffer for my Religion in almost every weekly paper. I have begun to take a pique at the Psalms of David (if the wicked may be credited, who have printed a scandalous one in my name.)[2] This report I dare not discourage too much, in a prospect I have at present of a post under the Marquess de Langallerie,[3] wherein if I can but do some signal service against the Pope, I may be considerably advanced by the Turks, the only religious people I dare confide in. If it should happen hereafter that I should write for the holy law of Mohamet, I hope it will make no breach between you and me; every one must live, and I beg you will not be the man to manage the controversy against me. The Church of Rome I judge (from many modern symptoms, as well as ancient prophecies) to be in a declining condition; that of England will in a short time be scarce able to maintain her own family: so Churches sink as generally as Banks in Europe,[4] ⌜and 'tis time to look out for some better security⌝.

I don't know why I tell you all this, but that I always loved to talk to you; but this is not a time for any man to talk to the purpose. Truth is a kind of contraband commodity which I would not venture to export, and therefore the only thing tending that dangerous way which I shall say, is, that I am and always will be with the utmost sincerity, | Yours, &c.

[1] Alluding to his constant custom of sleeping after dinner.—Warburton, 1751.

[2] Pope found it advisable to profess hypocritical ignorance of *The First Psalm* in *The Evening Post* of 2 Aug. See Pope to Teresa Blount, 7 Aug. 1716.

[3] This astonishing person (1656–1717) had passed from the armies of Louis XIV to those of Prince Eugene, of the King of Poland, of the Landgrave of Hesse, and finally to service with the Sultan. In this year he was arrested by order of the Emperor, and he died in prison in 1717. (*Biographie Universelle.*)

[4] In the clandestine edition sent to Ireland for printing and in the first octavo printed there by Faulkner, the text was as given here. In all later editions sponsored by Pope (except his later reissue of the clandestine volume) the last clause about Churches was omitted in favour of the following (added after the word *Europe*): 'and for the same reason; that Religion and Trade, which at first were open and free, have been reduced into the Management of Companies, and the Roguery of Directors'.

||POPE *to* CARYLL[1] 22 *June* 1716

Add. 28618

At Mawson's New Buildings in Chiswick: June the 22nd | 1716.

If a regard both to publick and private affairs may plead a lawful excuse in behalf of a negligent correspondent, I have really a very good title to it. I cannot say whether 'tis a felicity or unhappiness that I am obliged at this time to give up my whole application to Homer; when without that employment my thoughts must turn upon what is less agreeable, the violence, madness and resentment of modern heroes,[2] which are likely to prove (to some people at least) more fatal, than all those qualities in Achilles did to his unfortunate countrymen. ⌜It was a greater loss than in this unlucky season I can well support,—that of your company when you were last on our side of the world; and I know I ought to have expressed my concern at it much sooner; but I dare trust your good temper and friendship with greater omissions than these, and I believe you have humanity and indulgence enough for your friends to apply to 'em what a fine writer says of a less generous passion.

'Tis sure the tend'rest part of love
Each other to forgive.[3]

I seriously long to talk over a thousand things with you, for which I know you will give me the most satisfactory account, and the best and truest advice. In order to which (as well as to obtain a pleasure I shall never lose the relish of, that of the enjoyment of so many agreeable companions as I have found in your family) I fully purpose, the moment my task is over, to amble to your retirement, whether at Grinsted or Ladyholt; tho' I could wish it were at the last of those places. And as I hope this may be done in less than two months, I beg in the meanwhile to be informed of the precise time of your *dèmarches*.⌝

Tho' the change of my scene of life, from Windsor Forest to the water-side at Chiswick, be one of the grand Æra's of my days, and may be called a notable period in so inconsiderable a history, yet you can scarce imagine any hero passing from one stage of life and entering upon another, with so much tranquillity and so easy a transition, and

[1] In 1735–42 Pope printed this letter in his editions as to Edward Blount. In so doing he omitted two-thirds of the first paragraph (placed here in half-brackets) and half of the parenthesis in the last paragraph. The other merely verbal changes—such as substituting 'to the side of the Thames' for 'to the waterside at Chiswick'—are unimportant and very few.

[2] Heroes] War-makers *1735–42*. To 'War-makers' Pope (1735–42) appended the note 'This was written in the year of the affair of *Preston*'. The note became inept when in the Cooper octavo of 1737 and later the letter was misdated—first 1767 and thereafter 1717. Probably Pope was not responsible for these errors.

[3] Pope misquotes slightly from 'The Reconcilement', a song by his friend John Sheffield, Duke of Buckingham.

so laudable a behaviour as myself. I am become so truly a Citizen of the World (according to Plato's expression)[1] that I look with equal indifference on what I have lost, and on what I have gained. The times and amusements past, are not more like a dream to me than those which are present. I lie in a refreshing kind of inaction, and have one comfort at least of obscurity, that the darkness helps me to sleep the better. I now and then reflect upon the enjoyment of my friends whom I fancy I remember much as separate spirits do us, at tender intervals, neither interrupting their own employments, nor altogether careless of ours: but in general constantly wishing us well, and hoping to have us one day in their company.

To grow indifferent to the World is to grow philosophical or religious (whichsoever of those turns we chance to take⌜, or others to give to what we do⌝), and indeed the world is such a thing as one that thinks pretty much must either laugh at, or be angry with. But if we laugh at it, they say we are proud; and if we are angry with it, they say we are ill-natured. So the most politic way is to seem always better pleased than one can be [, to seem] greater admirers, greater lovers, and in short greater fools than we are. So shall we live comfortably with our families, quiet with our neighbours, favoured by our masters, happy with our mistresses. I have filled my paper, and am | Dear sir | Sincerely yours. | A: P:

EDWARD BLOUNT *to* POPE[2] — 23 *June* 1716

Homer MSS. Add. 4807

June 23. 1716.

Yesterday the[3] Bill to oblige Papists to Register their names and Estates pass'd the Lords with many amendments, and this day was sent to the Commons for their Concurrence, which they have put off

[1] The expression may have been assigned to Plato in translations of the episode of his trial in the Aeginean court, where he was acquitted of being an Athenian on the ground that he was a philosopher [citizen of the world?]. See Diogenes Laertius, iii. 19. The expression is somewhat improbably put into the mouth of Socrates by Cicero (*Tusculan Disp.* v. 37, 108) and others. It better fits Diogenes the Cynic. See Diogenes Laertius, vi. 63. The eighteenth century loved the expression and habitually gave it to Plato.

[2] This letter was printed in *The St. James's Chronicle*, 18 July 1775, and has been reprinted since then.

[3] The word *Registry*, at first inserted here, is crossed out. Properly the Bill was called 'An Act for appointing Commissioners to inquire of the estates of certain traitors, and of Popish recusants, and of estates given to superstitious uses, in order to raise money out of them severally for the use of the public'. Royal assent to the Commissioners Bill was given on 26 June. In anticipation of this device to increase taxes on Catholics and possibly because of questionable title to the house and land at Binfield (for Catholics were not allowed to buy land, and the Popes had a sort of concealed ownership of the place at Binfield) the Popes had sold out and moved to Chiswick, there renting a new house. The parents of the poet were doubtless also influenced by a desire to live nearer Town, where their son had now to spend much time.

giving till next Monday. The Commissioners Bill wants nothing but the Royall Assent which there is no doubt will easily be had both to that and the other on Tuesday next. I shall not pretend to make any Remarks, to interrupt your better Thoughts with the very worst of mine. I will not fix any day yet for my coming to see you, but hope first to have that pleasure in Town, which is a solid one to Dear sir | your truly affectionate humble servant | E B:

POPE *to* LADY MARY WORTLEY MONTAGU[1] [*July* 1716]

The Pierpont Morgan Library

Tuesday morning.

Madam,—So natural as I find it is to me, to neglect every body else in your company, I am sensible I ought to do any thing that might please you; and I fancy'd, upon recollection, our writing the Letter you proposed was of that nature. I therfore sate down to my part of it last Night, when I should have gone out of town.[2] Whether or no you will order me, in recompence, to see you again, I leave to you; for indeed I find I begin to behave my self worse to you than to any other Woman, as I value you more. And yet if I thought I shou'd not see you again, I would say some things here, which I could not to your Person. For I would not have you dye deceivd in me, that is, go to Constantinople without knowing, that I am to some degree of Extravagance, as well as with the utmost Reason, | Madam | Your most faithfull & | most obedient humble Servant | A. Pope.

Address: For the Right Honorable | the Lady Mary Wortley.

†POPE [*and* LADY MARY WORTLEY MONTAGU][3] [*to* LADY RICH] [*July* 1716]

1735

The Wits would say, that this must needs be a dull Letter, because it is a marry'd one. I am afraid indeed you will find what Spirit there is

[1] Perhaps July is late for this letter, written not too long before the Wortley Montagus set off for Constantinople. Their departure from London is best dated, as Professor Halsband informs the editor, as coming on Wednesday, 1 Aug. See the *Hist. MSS. Comm.*, *Polwarth MSS.* (1911), i. 49, 52 and *The Evening Post*, 31 July 1716. Moy Thomas mistook the item in *The Weekly Journal; or*, *British Gazetteer*, and chose the Wednesday sennight (25 July).

[2] The letter that Pope stayed in town to write was that printed immediately following this present letter: the joint letter of Pope and Lady Mary to Lady Rich.

[3] This letter was printed by Pope (1735–42) among his 'Letters to Several Ladies' under the heading 'To a Lady, written on the opposite pages of a Letter to her Husband from Lady M.' Roscoe's suggestion, generally accepted, is that we here have the joint letter that Pope speaks of in his letter to Lady Mary printed just before this. Roscoe also suggested that the letter is addressed to Lady Rich, wife of Sir Robert Rich (1685–1768). On Sir Robert see *DNB*. Lady Rich was the daughter of Col. Edward Griffith; she married Sir Robert in 1710, and hence is not the Miss Griffith or Griffin (Pope writes the name

must be on the side of the Wife, and the Husband's part as usual will prove the dullest. What an unequal Pair are put together in this sheet? in which tho' we sin, it is you must do penance. When you look on both sides of this paper, you may fancy that our words (according to a Scripture expression) are as a *Two-edg'd Sword*, whereof Lady *M.* is the shining blade and I only the Handle. But I can't proceed without so far mortifying Sir *Robert* as to tell him, that she writes this purely in obedience to me, and that it is but one of those honours a Husband receives for the sake of his Wife.

It is making court ill to one fine Woman to shew her the regard we have for another, and yet I must own there is not a period of this Epistle but squints toward another over-against it. It will be in vain to dissemble: Your penetrating eyes cannot but discover how all the letters that compose these words lean forward after Lady *M*'s letters, which seem to bend as much from mine, and fly from them as fast as they are able. Ungrateful letters that they are! which give themselves to another man in the very presence of him who will yield to no mortal in knowing how to value them.

You will think I forget my self, and am not writing to you; but let me tell you, 'tis you forget your self in that thought, for you are almost the only Woman to whom one can safely address the praises of another. Besides can you imagine a Man of my importance so stupid, as to say fine things to you before your Husband? Let us see how far Lady *M.* her self dares do any thing like it, with all the wit and address she is mistress of. If Sir *Robert* can be so ignorant (now he is left to himself in the country) to imagine any such matter, let him know from me, that here in town every thing that Lady says, is taken for Satire. For my part, every body knows it is my constant practice to speak Truth, and I never do it more than when I call my self | Your, &c.

‡POPE *to* JERVAS[1] — 9 *July* 1716

1735

July 9, 1716.

Tho', as you rightly remark, I pay my Tax but once in half a Year, yet you shall see by this Letter upon the neck of my last, that I pay a

both ways) mentioned by Pope among the Maids of Honour of the Princess of Wales. It is possibly a sister who was Maid of Honour, and possibly there is a confusion of two families. Lady Mary's part of the letter has apparently not survived. Pope confessedly writes for Lady Mary to read rather than for Lady Rich.

[1] This letter is most obviously 'cooked' since the matter, drawn from different letters (?), fits no one date. Jervas left London for Ireland about 1 Aug. 1716, as Pope to Parnell, 29 July, indicates. The letter might seem to have been written in 1718, but Parnell died at Chester in October of that year, and Eusden became laureate on 24 Dec. 1718. *The Non-Juror* was first performed 6 Dec. 1717. The projected exchange of Eusden and Parnell fits no possible date.

double Tax, as we Non-Jurors ought to do. Your Acquaintance on this side the Sea are under terrible Apprehensions, from your long stay in *Ireland*, that you may grow too Polite for them; for we think (since the great success of so damn'd a Play as the Non-Juror) that Politeness is gone over the Water. But others are of opinion it has been longer among you, and was introduced much about the same time with *Frogs*, and with equal Success. Poor *Poetry*! the little that's left of it here longs to cross the Seas, and leave *Eusden* in full and peaceable Possession of the *British* Laurel: And we begin to wish you had the singing of our Poets, as well as the croaking of our Frogs, to yourselves in *Sæcula Sæculorum*. It would be well in exchange, if *Parnelle*, and two or three more of your Swans, would come hither, especially that Swan, who like a true modern one, does not sing at all, Dr. *Swift*. I am (like the rest of the World) a Sufferer by his Idleness. Indeed I hate that any Man should be idle, while I must translate and comment: And I may the more sincerely wish for good Poetry from others, because I am become a person out of the question; for a Translator is no more a Poet, than a Taylor is a Man.

You are doubtless persuaded of the Validity of that famous Verse,

'Tis Expectation makes a Blessing dear:

but why would you make your Friends fonder of you than they are? There's no manner of need of it—We begin to expect you no more than *Anti-christ*. A Man that hath absented himself so long from his Friends, ought to be put into the Gazette.

Every Body here has great need of you. Many Faces have died for ever for want of your Pencil, and blooming Ladies have wither'd in expecting your return. Even *Frank* and *Betty* (that constant Pair) cannot console themselves for your Absence; I fancy they will be forced to make their own Picture in a pretty Babe, before you come home: 'Twill be a noble Subject for a Family Piece. Come then, and having peopled *Ireland* with a World of beautiful Shadows, come to us, and see with that Eye (which, like the Eye of the World, creates Beauties by looking on them) see, I say, how *England* has altered the Airs of all its heads in your Absence; and with what sneaking City Attitudes our most celebrated Personages appear in the meer mortal Works of our Painters.

Mr. *Fortescue* is much yours; *Gay* commemorates you; and lastly (to climb by just steps and degrees) my Lord *Burlington* desires you may be put in mind of him. His Gardens flourish, his Structures rise, his Pictures arrive, and (what is far nobler and more valuable than all) his own good Qualities daily extend themselves to all about him: Whereof, I the meanest (next to some *Italian* Chymists, Fidlers, Bricklayers, and Opera-makers) am a living Instance.

POPE *to* PARNELL[1] 29 *July* [1716]

Trinity College, Dublin

London, July the 29th

I wish it were not as ungene[rous] as vain, to complain too much of a Man that forgets me, [but] I could expostulate with you a whole day upon your in[hum]an Silence: I call it Inhuman, nor would you think [it le]ss, if you were truly sensible of the uneasiness it gives [me.] Did I know you so ill as to think you proud, I should be [much] less concernd than I am able to be when I know one of [the] best naturd men alive neglects me. And if you know me [so ill] as to think amiss of me with regard to my Friendship [for y]ou, You really do not deserve half the trouble you occa[sion] me.

To tell[2] you that both Mr Gay and myself have written [severa]l Letters in vain, that we are constantly enquiring of [all w]ho have seen Ireland if they saw you, and that (for[gotten] as we are) we are ev'ry day remembring you in our [most] agreable hours; all this is as true as that we are [sincer]ely Lovers of you, and Deplorers of your Absence: and [that] we form no Wish more zealously[3] than that which brings [you ov]er to us, & places you in your old Seat between us.

We have lately had some distant hopes of the Dean's design to revisit England: Will you not accompany him? or is England to lose every thing that has any charm for us? & must we pray for Banishment as a benediction? I have been once a witness of some (I hope all) of your Spleenatic hours; Come and be a Comforter in your turn to me, in mine. I am in such an unsettled State, that I can't tell if I shall ever see you unless it be this year. Whether I do or not, be ever assured you have as large a Share in my thoughts and Good wishes as any man; and as great a Portion of Gratitude in my heart as would enrich a Monarch, could he know where to find it. I shall not dye without testifying something of this nature, and leaving to the world a Memorial of the Friendship that has been so great a Pleasure and Pride to me.

It would be like writing my own Epitaph to acquaint you what I have lost since I saw you, what I have done, what I have thought, where I have lived, & where I now repose in Obscurity. My Friend Jervas, the Bearer of this, will inform you of all particulars concerning me[, & Mr Ford is][4] charged with a thousand Loves, a thousand

[1] The original letter is preserved in an imperfect state. A marginal annotation says: 'Printed in Goldsmith's Life of Parnell. The letter when copied by G was perfect.' The last statement seems probable, and Goldsmith's readings for words on the left margin of page 1 and the right of page 3 are here given in brackets with exceptions noted below.

[2] Goldsmith began this paragraph with the impossible expression 'I need not tell you ...'. The paragraph clearly begins with 'To tell you' and the predicate begins 'all this is true ...'.

[3] zealously] ardently *Goldsmith* (an error).

[4] This sounds as if Ford and Jervas crossed together; but from the letter of Pope to Swift, 20 June (which may be wrongly dated), one would assume that Ford had crossed earlier.

Com[pliments &] Commissions[1] to you, on my part. They [will both tax you] with the neglect of some promises, which [were too agreeable] to us all to be forgot. If you care for [any of us, tell them] so, and write so to me. I can say [no more but that] I love you and am (in spite of the [longest neglect or] Absence)[2] | Dear Sir | Your [most faithful, affec-|tiona[te Friend & Servant] | [A. Pope]

Gay is in Devonshire & from thence goes to Bath. My Father and Mother never fail to commemorate you.

If you ever see Mr Caldwell, assure him [ ] & let him know I have since written to [ ] one letter, with a little parcell I deliverd[3]

Address: To the Revd Dr Parnell, | to be left with Wm Burgh, Esq; | at the Custom house in | Dublin.

POPE *to* TERESA BLOUNT[4]

Mapledurham

To Mrs Teresa Blount

Madam. Since you prefer three hundred pound to two true Lovers, I presume to send you the following Epitaph upon them, which seems to be written by one of your Taste.

> Here lye two poor Lovers, who had the mishap
> Tho very chaste people, to die of a Clap.

I hope Miss Patty will not so much as smile at this: if she does, she may know, she has less pity than I.

I hope you have had (with this) 4 letters from me. Don't I write often enough?

POPE *to* TERESA BLOUNT[5] *7 August* [1716]

Mapledurham

August the 7th

Madam,—I have so much Esteem for you, and so much of the other thing, that were I a handsome fellow I should do you a vast deal of

[1] Loves . . . Commissions] Loves and a thousand Commissions *Goldsmith.* Elwin prints *Complaints* instead of *Compliments.* Goldsmith's text is faulty; all we have of either *complaints* or *compliments* is the first syllable.

[2] neglect or Absence] neglect of happiness *Goldsmith* (an error).

[3] This final postscript was omitted by Goldsmith and other editors. A Caldwell is mentioned in stanza xx of Gay's poem 'Mr. Pope's Welcome from Greece'; but he is unidentified and the postscript conveys little. The address of this letter is not in Pope's hand.

[4] It is perhaps unwise to pretend to place this letter, but since Pope says this is the fourth letter written to Teresa, and since his letter to her of 7 Aug. [1716] is clearly endorsed 'Letter 6', this should precede that letter by an indeterminate interval.

[5] The date on the original is not in Pope's hand. It is presumably in that of the recipient. Pope did not print this letter, but from the second paragraph of it he borrowed all but the first sentence for use at the beginning of the letter here printed as of July 1715. For the

good: but as it is, all I am good for is to write a civil letter, or to make a fine Speech. The truth is, that considering how often & how openly I have declared Love to you, I am astonished (and a little affronted) that you have not forbid my correspondence, & directly said, *See my face no more.* It is not enough, Madam, for your reputation, that you keep your hands pure, from the Stain of Such Ink as might be shed to gratify a male Correspondent; Alas! while your heart consents to encourage him in this lewd liberty of writing, you are not (indeed you are not) what you would so fain have me think you, a Prude! I am vain enough to conclude (like most young fellows) that a fine Lady's Silence is Consent, and so I write on.

But in order to be as Innocent as possible in this Epistle, I'll tell you news. You have askd me News a thousand times at the first word you spoke to me, which some would interpret as if you expected nothing better from my lips: And truly 'tis not a sign Two Lovers are together, when they can be so impertinent as to enquire what the World does? All I mean by this is, that either you or I cannot be in love with the other; I leave you to guess which of the two is that stupid & insensible Creature, so blind to the others Excellencies and Charms.

But to my news—My Lord Burlington's & my Journey to the North is put off till September. Mr Gay has had a fall from his horse, & broken his fine Snuffbox.[1] Your humble Servant has lost his blue Cloak. Mr Ed. Curll has been exercised in a Blanket and whipped at Westminster Schoole by the Boys, whereof the common Prints have given some account.[2] If you have seen a late Advertisement,[3] you will know that I have not told a lye (which we both abhominate) but equivocated pretty genteely: You may be confident twas not done without leave from my Spiritual director. My next News is a triffle, I will wait upon you at Whiteknights in a fortnight or 3 weeks, unless you send me word to the contrary, which I beg you to do if I shall not find you there. Would to God you could go to Grinsted or the Bath; I would attend you to either.

earlier letter Pope combined materials from two still preserved at Mapledurham. This, of course, was his common habit.

[1] Gay's accident is jokingly mentioned in the same terms in *God's Revenge against Punning*, a pamphlet published about this time and possibly written by Pope himself.

[2] *The Original Weekly Journal*, 4 Aug. 1716, gives an account of Curll's punishment. See Sherburn, *Early Career*, pp. 171–2.

[3] Pope's 'genteel equivocation' concerning his burlesque of the First Psalm was by him inserted in *The Postman*, 31 July and in *The Evening Post* for 2 Aug. It is worth reprinting as a specimen of Pope's art:

> 'Whereas there have been publish'd in my Name, certain scandalous Libels, which I hope no Person of Candor would have thought me capable of, I am sorry to find myself obliged to declare that no Genuine Pieces of mine have been printed by any but Mr. Tonson and Mr. Lintot. And in particular, as to that which is entituled, A Version of the first Psalm; I hereby promise a Reward of three Guineas to any one who shall discover the Person or Persons concerned in the Publication of the said Libel, of which I am wholly ignorant. | A. Pope.'

As I am always impertinent in my Questions concerning you, to every body that has seen or heard from you, so I have lately received much gladness, in the belief that you might do so from the late Entertainments of the Lord Cadogan in your neighborhood. I heartily wish many times, You led the same Course of life which I here partly enjoy and partly regrett; for I am not a day without what they call Elegant Company. I have not dined but at great Entertainments these ten days, in pleasant Villas about the Thames: whose Banks are now more populous than London, thro' the neighborhood of Hampton Court.[1] . . . Upon the whole I am melancholy, which (to say truth) is [all one] getts by Pleasures themselves. Yet as I believe melancho[ly hurts] me as little as any one, so I sincerely wish, much r[ather to] be so myself, than that those I value should partake [of it. In] particular, Your Ease & happiness would be a great par[t of my] Study, were I your Guardian angel; as I am, a poor [man], it is one of my most earnest wishes. Believe me | Madam | Your most faithfull humb[le Servant] | A. P[ope]

Pray tell Miss Patty that tho' | she will not write to me, I hear | she writes for me, which I ought to | take as kindly: This was informed | of by Mr Caryll.

POPE *to* THOMAS DANCASTLE *7 August* 1716

The Gentleman's Magazine, ci² (1831), 291–2

Aug. the 7th, 1716.

Several reasons and accidents, too long and too inconsiderable to enumerate, have hinder'd my writing to you for some time. And another, which I take for a better reason than all those, had like to have done it now; which is, that I hope in a very short time to see you at Binfield. A journey into the North, which my Lord Burlington proposed I should take with him this month, being deferr'd till the next. And I have resolved not to lose a whole season (and a season of fruit too) without waiting on your Brother and your self. As to my method of travelling, I will not give him the trouble which I hear by more hands than one, he is ready to take, of sending my Horse hither; since I am equipt otherwise. I only want to know if both of you shall be at home about the 20th of this month; without which precaution I would not begin my Rambles, the first design of which is to have some happy hours in your company.

Notwithstanding this, if you have had leisure to transcribe the Book[2]

[1] At this point the second leaf of the letter is so torn that only fragments of 14 lines remain, fragments that convey little, and are hence omitted. They seem to concern reflections upon the pleasures of fashionable society.

[2] One of the Books of the *Iliad*, doubtless for vol. iii.

I troubled you with, I would rather it were conveyed hither by some safe hand than given me at your house, since I should chuse to leave it with a Critick or two during my journeys.

I have been here in a constant Course of Entertainments and Visits ever since I saw you, which I partly delight in, and partly am tired with; the common case in all pleasures. I have not dined at home these 15 days, and perfectly regrett the quiet, indolence, silence, and sauntring, that made up my whole life in Windsor Forest. I shall therefore infallibly be better company and better pleased than ever you knew me, as soon as I can get under the shade of Priest-Wood, whose trees I have yet some Concern about. I hope, whatever license the freeborn Subjects of your Commons may take, there will yet be Groves enough left in those Forests to keep a Pastoral-writer in countenance. Whatever belongs to the Crown is indeed as much trespas'd upon at this time in the Court as in the Country. While you are lopping his timber, we are lopping his Prerogative.

I desire you to take notice how naturally I talk like a man at St. James's end of the town, and how entirely I have put off the Airs of a Country Gentleman. Thus it is, we always are proud of the last thing we do, and the Condition we put ourselves into, though it be the worst in the world, and immediately treat our Old acquaintance as odd people of an inferior Sphere. I ought upon this principle to rally you upon your harvest time, make pictures of my Friends tossing Wheatsheaves and raising Reeks,[1] imagine I see you in a great Sweat and Hurry; and all that. But this I reserve till I see you; unless I should then on a sudden affect the fine Gentleman, and extoll the Innocence and Exercise of the Rural Life. I know, however I behave myself, and whatever I say or write to you, You'll take in good part upon the knowledge how truly and affectionately I am your good Brother's, and | Dear Sir, Your faithful and humble | Servant, | A. Pope.

Address: To Mr. T. Dancastle, at Binfield near | Oakingham, Berks
Frank: Burlington

||POPE *to* LADY MARY WORTLEY MONTAGU[2]

18 *August* [1716]

The Pierpont Morgan Library

August the 18th

Madam,—I can say little to recommend the Letters I am beginning to write[3] to you, but that they will be the most impartial Representa-

[1] *Obs. for* Ricks.—*OED.*

[2] In all his editions Pope printed this letter without date or identification of the recipient. In 'his own' editions, the folio and quarto of 1737, he described it in his table of contents as 'To a Lady Abroad'. It is here printed from the original. Omissions in the text printed by Pope are in half-brackets. His more interesting verbal changes are indicated below.

[3] I . . . write] I shall write *1735–42*.

tions of a free heart, and the truest Copies you ever saw, tho' of a very mean Original. Not a feature will be soften'd, or any advantageous Light employd to make the Ugly thing a little less hideous, but you shall find it in all respects most Horribly Like. You will do me an injustice if you look upon any thing I shall say from this instant as a Compliment either to you or to myself: whatever I write will be the real Thought of that hour, and I know you'll no more expect it of me to persevere till Death in every Sentiment or notion I now sett down, than you would imagine a man's Face should never change after his picture was once drawn.

The freedome I shall use in this manner of Thinking aloud ⌜(as somebody calls it) or Talking upon paper,⌝ may indeed prove me a fool, but it will prove me one of the best sort of fools, the honest ones. And since what Folly we have will infallibly Buoy up at one time or other, in spite of all our art to keep it down; tis almost foolish to take any pains to conceal it at all, and almost knavish to do it from those that are our friends. If Momus his project had taken of having Windows in our breasts,[1] I should be for carrying it further and making those windows Casements: that while a Man showd his Heart to all the world, he might do something more for his friends, e'en take it out, and trust[2] it to their handling. I think I love you as well as King Herod could Herodias, (tho I never had so much as one Dance with you) and would as freely give you my heart in a Dish, as he did another's head. But since Jupiter will not have it so, I must be content to show my taste in Life as I do my taste in Painting, by loving to have as little Drapery as possible. Not that I think every body naked, altogether so fine a sight as yourself and a few more would be: but because 'tis good to use people to what they must be acquainted with; and there will certainly come some Day of Judgment[3] to uncover every Soul of us. We shall then see how the Prudes of this world owed all their fine Figure only to their being a little straiter-lac'd, and that they were naturally as arrant Squabs as those that went more loose, nay as those that never girded their loyns at all.

But a particular reason to engage you to write your thoughts the more freely to me is, that I am confident no one knows you better. For I find, when others express their Opinion of you, it falls very short of mine, and I am sure at the same time Theirs is such as You would think sufficiently in your favour.

You may easily imagine how desirous I must be of a Correspondence with a person, who had taught me long ago that it was as possible to Esteem at first sight, as to Love: and who has since ruin'd me for

[1] See Lucian, *Hermotimus*, 20.
[2] e'en take it out, and trust] even give it them, and trust *1735–42*.
[3] Judgment to uncover] judgment or other, to uncover *1735–42*.

all the Conversation of one Sex, and almost all the Friendship of the other. I am but too sensible thro' your means that the Company of Men wants a certain Softness to recommend it, and that of Women wants every thing else. How often have I been quietly going to take possession of that Tranquility and indolence I had so long found in the Country, when one Evening of your Conversation has spoild me for a Solitaire too?[1] Books have lost their effect upon me; and I was convinced since I saw you that there is ⌜something more powerful than Philosophy, and since I heard you that there is⌝ one alive wiser than all the Sages. A plague of female Wisdome! it makes a man ten times more uneasy than his own! What is very strange, Virtue herself, when you have the dressing her, is too amiable for one's Repose. What a world of Good might you have done in your time, if you had allowed half the fine Gentlemen who have seen you to have but conversd with you? They would have been strangely caught,[2] while they thought only to fall in love with a fair Face, and You had bewitchd them with Reason and Virtue; two Beauties, that the very Fops pretend to no acquaintance with.

The unhappy Distance at which we correspond, removes a great many of those punctillious Restrictions and Decorums, that oftentimes in nearer Conversation prejudice Truth to save Good breeding. I may now hear of my faults, and you of your good qualities, without a Blush ⌜on either side⌝. We converse upon such unfortunate generous Terms as exclude the regards of Fear, Shame or Design in either of us. And methinks it would be as ungenerous[3] a part, to impose even in a single Thought upon each other, in this State of Seperation, as for Spirits of a different Sphære who have so little Intercourse with us, to employ that little (as some would make us think they do) in putting Tricks and Delusions upon poor mortals.

Let me begin then, Madam, by asking you a question which may enable Me to judge better of my own Conduct than most Instances of my life. In what manner did I behave, the last hour I saw you? what degree of Concern did I discover when I felt a misfortune which I hope you never will feel, That of parting from what one most esteems? For if my Parting lookd but like that of your common Acquaintance, I am the greatest of all the Hypocrites that ever Decency made.

I never since pass by the House,[4] but with the same Sort of Melancholy that we feel upon Seeing the Tomb of a Friend; which only serves to put us in mind of What we have lost. I reflect upon the Circumstances of your Departure,[5] your Behavior in what I may call

[1] for a Solitaire too?] for a *Solitaire!* *1735–42*.

[2] caught] bitt *1735–42, but the folio and quarto of 1737 have the more elegant word* deceiv'd.

[3] ungenerous] paltry *1735–42*.

[4] the House] your house *1735–42*.

[5] Departure, your Behavior] departure which I was there a witness of (your behavior *1735–42*.

Your last Moments, and I indulge a gloomy kind of Satisfaction[1] in thinking you gave some of those last moments to me. I would fain imagine this was not accidental, but proceeded from a Penetration which I know you have in finding out the truth of people's Sentiments, and that you were not unwilling, the last man that would have parted with you, should be the last that did. I really lookd upon you then,[2] as the friends of Curtius might have done upon that Hero in the instant he was devoting himself to Glory, and running to be Lost out of Generosity! I was oblig'd to admire your Resolution in as great a degree as I deplor'd it; and could only wish, that Heaven would reward so much Merit[3] as was to be taken from us, with all the felicity it could enjoy elsewhere.[4] ⌜May that Person for whom you have left all the world be so just as to prefer you to all the world: I believe his good understanding has engagd him to do so hitherto, and I think his Gratitude must for the future. May you continue to think him worthy of whatever you have done, may you ever look upon him with the eyes of a first Lover, nay if possible with all the unreasonable happy Fondness of an unexperienced one, surrounded with all the Enchantments and Idæas of Romance and Poetry. In a word, may you receive from him as many pleasures and gratifications as even I think you can give. I wish this from my Heart, and while I examine what passes there in regard to You, I cannot but glory in my own heart that it is capable of so much Generosity.⌝ I am, ⌜with all unalterable esteem and sincerity | Madam | Your most faithfull obedient | humble Servant, | A. Pope.⌝

||POPE *to* LADY MARY WORTLEY MONTAGU

The Pierpont Morgan Library

20 *August* [1716][5]

[20 Aug.]

Madam,—You will find me more troublesome than ever Brutus did his evil Genius; I shall meet you in more places than one, and often refresh your memory of me before you arrive at Your Philippi. These Shadows of me, my Letters, will be haunting you from time to time, & putting you in mind of the man who has really sufferd by you, and whom you have robbd of the most valuable of his enjoyments, your

[1] Satisfaction] pleasure *1735–42*. [2] you then, as] you just as *1735–42*

[3] Merit] Virtue *1735–42*.

[4] The rest of the letter, except 'I am, &c.' is omitted 1735–42.

[5] The date comes from Pope's postscript.

Pope printed this letter (1735–42) with practically no verbal revisions in the different editions. His departures from the original are here noted. Some of them seem due to misreadings of the copy sent to the printer, a fact that suggests that the letters were printed from a transcript with Lady Mary retaining the original letters. In such case the transcripts would have been made in the early twenties, not by Pope, but for him, when he was still on friendly terms with Lady Mary.

Conversation. The Advantage of learning[1] your Sentiments, by discovering mine, was what I always thought a great one, and even worth the Risque I run of manifesting my own indiscretion. You then rewarded my Trust in you the moment it was given, and was sure to please or inform[2] me the minuit you answered. I must now be contented with more slow Returns; however 'tis some pleasure that your Thoughts upon paper will be more durable,[3] and that I shall no longer have cause to complain of a Loss I have so often regretted, that of any thing you said which I happend to forget. In earnest, Madam, if I were to write to you as often as I think of you, it must be every day of my life. I attend you in Spirit thro' all your Ways, I follow you in Books of Travells ⌜thro' every Stage, I wish for you⌝ and fear for you thro' whole Folio's. You make me shrink at the past dangers of dead Travellers, and when I read of a delightful Place or agreeable Prospect, I hope it yet subsists to give you pleasure. I enquire the Roads, the Amusements, the Company, of every Town and Country you pass through,[4] with as much diligence as if I were to sett out next week to overtake you. In a word, no one can have you more constantly in Mind, not even your Guardian Angel, (if you have one) and I am willing to indulge so much Popery as to imagine,[5] some Being takes care of you, who knows your Value better than you do yourself. I am willing to think Heaven never gave so much Self-neglect and Resolution to a Woman, to occasion her calamity; but have the Piety[6] to believe those Qualities must be intended to conduce to her benefit and her glory.

Your first short letter[7] only serves to show me you are living:[8] It puts me in mind of the first Dove that return'd to Noah, & just made him know it had found no Rest abroad. There is nothing in it that can please[9] me, but when you say[10] you had no Seasickness. I beg your next may give me all the pleasure it can, that is, tell me any that you receive. Nothing that regards the Countries you pass thro' engages so much of my Curiosity or Concern, as what relates purely to yourself.[11] You can make no Discoveries that will be half so valuable to me as those of

[1] learning] hearing *1735–42*.

[2] and . . . inform me] for you pleas'd or inform'd me *1735–42*.

[3] more durable] a more lasting possession to me *1735–42*.

[4] and when . . . pass through] and if I read of a delightful prospect, or agreeable place, I hope it yet subsists to please you. I enquire the roads, the amusements, the company, of every town and country thro' which you pass *1735–42*.

[5] imagine] fancy *1735–42*.

[6] but have the Piety to] but am pious enough to *1735–42*.

[7] Not known. It evidently reported her arrival, with no seasickness in spite of a stormy crossing.

[8] living] alive *1735–42*.

[9] can please] pleases *1735–42*.

[10] say] tell me *1735–42*.

[11] This sentence is shifted into the next one (1735–42), being placed after the word *mind* where four words were omitted, as shown by the half-brackets.

your own mind, ⌜temper, and thoughts: And⌝ Your Welfare, to say truth, is more at my heart than that of christendome.

I am sure I may defend the Truth, tho perhaps, not the Virtue, of this declaration. One is ignorant, or at best doubtful, of the Merits of differing Religions and Governments; but Private Virtues one can be sure of. I can therfore judge[1] what particular Person deserves[2] to be happier than others, but not what Nation deserves to conquer[3] another? You'll say I am not Publick-Spirited, Let it be so; I may have too many Tendernesses, particular Regards, or narrow views; but at the same time I am certain the Man who wants these can never be Publick-Spirited. For how is it possible for Him to love a hundred thousand men, who never loved One?[4]

I communicated your Letter to Mr C⌜ongreve⌝: He thinks of you and talks of you as he ought; I mean as I do, (for one always thinks that to be as it ought.)[5] His health and my own are now so good, that we wish with all our Souls you were a witness of it. We never meet but we lament over you; we pay a Sort[6] of Weekly Rite to your Memory, where we strow Flowers of Rhetorick, and offer such Libations to your name as it were a Prophaness[7] to call Toasting. ⌜I must tell you too, that⌝ the Duke of Buckingham has been more than once Your High Priest, in performing the Office of your praises:[8] and upon the whole I believe, there are as few Men who do not deplore your Departure, as Women that sincerely do.[9] For you who know how many of your Sex want good Sence, know also they must want Generosity.[10] ⌜And I know how much of that virtue is requisite to make the very best not to envy you. But⌝ you have enough of both, to pardon whatsoever you despise.[11] For my part, I hate a great many Women for your sake, and undervalue all the rest. Tis you are to blame, and may God revenge it upon you, with all those Blessings and Earthly Prosperities which the Divines tell us are the cause of our Perdition! for if He makes you happy in this life, I dare trust your own virtue to do it in the other—I am ⌜with the most unfeigned

[1] judge] know *1735–42.*
[2] deserves] has desert enough *1735–42.*
[3] to conquer another] to conquer or oppress another *1735–42.*
[4] I am certain . . . loved One?] I am certain that whoever wants these, can never have a *Publick-spirit*; for (as a friend of mine says) how is it possible for that man to love twenty thousand people, who never loved one? *1735–42.*
[5] I do . . . ought.)] I do, and one always thinks that to be just as it ought. *1735–42.*
[6] Sort] kind *1735–42.*
[7] as . . . Prophaness] as it would be prophane *1735–42.*
[8] Buckingham . . . praises] B—m is sometimes the High Priest of your praises *1735–42.*
[9] Men who . . . sincerely do.] Men that are not sorry at your departure, as Women that are; *1735–42.*
[10] For . . . Generosity] for you know most of your Sex want good sense, and therefore must want generosity: *1735–42.*
[11] you have enough . . . despise.] You have so much of both, that I am sure you pardon them; for one cannot but forgive whatever one despises. *1735–42.*

Truth, | Madam | Your most faithfull & | most obliged humble Servant⌝.[1]

⌜This letter is written on the 20th of August tho it will scarce reach you in a month, at my Lord James Hay's Arrival at Leghorne.[2] I shall then be in a particular manner sollicitous for you, on your going again by Sea; and therfore beg the earliest notice of your safe Landing, on the other side.⌝

SWIFT *to* POPE — 30 *August* 1716

1740

Aug. 30, 1716

I had the favour of yours by Mr. F.[3] of whom, before any other question relating to your health, or fortunes, or success as a poet, I enquired your principles in the common form, "Is he a Whig or a Tory?"[4] I am sorry to find they are not so well tally'd to the present juncture as I could wish. I always thought the terms of *Facto* and *Jure* had been introduced by the Poets, and that Possession of any sort in Kings was held an unexceptionable title in the courts of Parnassus. If you do not grow a perfect good subject in all its present latitudes, I shall conclude you are become rich, and able to live without dedications to men in power, whereby one great inconvenience will follow, that you and the world and posterity will be utterly ignorant of their virtues. For, either your brethren have miserably deceiv'd us these hundred years past, or Power confers virtue, as naturally as five of your Popish sacraments do Grace.[5]—You sleep less and drink more.—But your master Horace was *Vini somnique benignus*:[6] and as I take it, both are proper for your trade. As to mine, there are a thousand poetical texts to confirm the one; and as to the other, I know it was anciently the custom to sleep in temples for those who would consult the Oracles, "Who dictates to me slumbring", &c.[7]

You are an ill Catholick, or a worse Geographer, for I can assure you, Ireland is not Paradise, and I appeal even to any Spanish divine, whether addresses were ever made to a friend in Hell, or Purgatory. And who are all these enemies you hint at? I can only think of Curl, Gildon, Squire Burnet, Blackmore, and a few others whose fame I

[1] The holograph letter is unsigned, and in Pope's texts the postscript is omitted.

[2] Mr. Wortley Montagu originally intended to proceed to Constantinople by sea from Leghorn.—Moy Thomas.

[3] Charles Ford.

[4] In *Gulliver's Travels*, the second voyage, chapter iii, Gulliver records that the King of Brobdingnag, 'taking me up in his right hand, and stroking me gently with the other, after an hearty fit of laughing, asked me, whether I were a Whig or a Tory'.

[5] The five sacraments not recognized as such by Protestants are confirmation, penance, extreme unction, holy orders, and matrimony.—Elwin.

[6] Horace, *Satires*, II. iii. 3. Indulgent to himself in Sleep and Wine.—Faulkner, 1741. Much given to Wine as well as Sleep.—Curll. 1741.

[7] *Paradise Lost*, ix. 23.

have forgot: Tools[1] in my opinion as[2] necessary for a good writer, as pen, ink, and paper. And besides, I would fain know whether every Draper does[3] not shew you three or four damned pieces of stuff to set off his good one? however, I will grant, that one thorough bookselling Rogue is better qualified to vex an author, than all his cotemporary scriblers in Critick or Satire, not only by stolen Copies[4] of what was incorrect or unfit for the publick, but by downright laying other mens dulness at your door. I had a long design upon the ears of that Curl, when I was in credit, but the rogue would never allow me a fair stroke at them, though my penknife was ready and sharp.[5] I can hardly believe the relation of his being poisoned, though the Historian pretends to have been an eye-witness:[6] But I beg pardon, Sack might do it, though[7] Rats-bane would not. I never saw the thing you mention as falsely imputed to you; but I think the frolicks of merry hours, even when we are guilty, should not be left to the mercy of our best friends, till[8] Curl and his resemblers are hanged.

With submission to the better judgment of you and your friends, I take your project of an employment under Langallerie[9] to be idle and unnecessary. Have a little patience and you will find more merit and encouragement at home by the same methods. You are ungrateful to your country; quit but your own Religion, and ridicule ours, and that will allow you a free choice for any other, or for none at all, and pay you well into the bargain. Therefore pray do not run and disgrace us among the Turks by telling them you were forc'd to leave your native home because we would oblige you to be a Christian; whereas we will make it appear to all the world, that we only compelled you to be a Whig.

There is a young ingenious Quaker[10] in this town who writes

[1] All editors read *Tools* except Elwin. His emendation to *Fools* makes obvious sense, but since Pope for the London editions inserted *are* (Tools in my opinion are . . .) without changing the word, one must have doubts. Without *are*, *Tools* makes good sense.

[2] opinion as] opinion are as *1741 Lab.*

[3] does] doth *1741 Dab; Lab.* (This small word adds evidence that in his quarto and folio (1741 Lab) Pope reprinted, with revision, Faulkner's Dublin text for the first five letters, and not his own clandestine volume: *doth* is typical of the Dublin texts; *does* is used by the London printers.)

[4] This is notoriously False, Mr. *Pope*'s being handed to the Press by a Gift of his Friend, Henry Cromwell, Esq; to Mrs. Thomas, as is now well known.—Curll (1741Lc).

[5] ready and sharp] ready drawn and sharp *1741–2Labc.*
What gave this Edge to the *Dean*'s Penknife, was, *A Key to the Tale of a Tub.* By Ralph Noden, Esq; Printed for Mr. *Curll.*—Curll (1741 Lc).

[6] The Historian was Pope himself. For his *Full and True Account of a Horrid and Barbarous Revenge by Poison* see Elwin and Courthope, x. 462–8.

[7] The clandestine text here three times in two sentences uses *though*, and is followed in the use by the Dublin texts of Faulkner. The London texts in all three cases use *although.*

[8] All Pope's octavos read *till*; other texts read *until.*

[9] Langallerie] the Turks *1741Lab; 1742Lc.*

[10] George Rook, an eminent linen draper.—Faulkner (1741 Db). Rook was possibly related to Swift. See his *Correspondence*, ed. Ball, i. 367–8.

verses to his mistress, not very correct, but in a strain purely what a poetical Quaker should do, commending her look and habit, &c. It gave me a hint that a sett of Quaker-pastorals might succeed, if our friend Gay could fancy it, and I think it a fruitful subject; pray hear what he says. I believe further, the Pastoral[1] ridicule is not exhausted; and that a porter, foot-man, or chair-man's pastoral might do well.[2] Or what think you of a Newgate pastoral, among the whores and thieves there?

Lastly, and[3] to conclude, I love you never the worse for seldom writing to you. I am in an obscure scene, where you know neither thing nor person. I can only answer yours, which I promise to do after a sort whenever you think fit to employ me. But I can assure you the scene and the times have depressed me wonderfully, for I will impute no defect to those two paltry years which have slipt by since I had the happiness to see you. I am with the truest esteem, | Yours, &c.

†JAMES CRAGGS *to* POPE[4] — 2 *September* 1716

1735

Paris, Sept. 2, 1716.

Last post brought me the favour of your letter of the 10th *Aug. O.S.* It would be taking too much upon me to decide, that 'twas a Witty one; I never pretend to more judgment than to know what pleases me, and can assure you, it was a very Agreeable one. The proof I can give you of my sincerity in this Opinion, is, that I hope and desire you would not stop at this, but continue more of them.

I am in a place where Pleasure is continually flowing. The Princes set the Example, and the Subjects follow at a distance. The Ladies are of all parties, by which means the conversation of the Men is very much softened and fashioned from those blunt disputes on Politicks, and rough Jests, we are so guilty of, while the Freedom of the Women takes away all Formality and Constraint. I must own, at the same time, these Beauties are a little too artificial for my Taste; you have seen a *French* Picture, the Original is more painted, and such a crust of Powder and essence in their Hair, that you can see no difference between black and red. By disusing Stays, and indulging themselves at Table, they are run out of all Shape; but as to that, they may give

[1] Pastoral] personal *1741 Lab; 1742 L; 1742 Da.*

[2] Gay's 'Espousal' (1720) was perhaps due to this suggestion. Swift himself wrote realistic and burlesque pastorals. Possibly *The Beggar's Opera* owes something to this mention of Newgate.

[3] Lastly, and to] Lastly, to *London texts of 1741–2.*

[4] This letter was printed in all Pope's editions except 1735 a2 and the quarto and folios of 1737. The date quite possibly may be New Style, and in the English style mean 22 Aug. Pope's letter of the 10th is unknown.

a good reason, they prefer Conveniency to Parade, and are by this means as ready, as they are generally willing to be Charitable.

I am surpriz'd to find I have wrote so much Scandal; I fancy I am either setting up for a Wit, or imagine I must write in this Style to a Wit; I hope you'll prove a good natured one, and not only let me hear from you sometimes, but forgive the small Encouragement you meet with. ⌜If you'll compleat your favours, pray give my humble Services to Lords *W—ck*, *St—*, and *H—y*. I have had my hopes and fears they would have abused me before this Time; I am sure it is not my business to meddle with a nest of Bees (I speak only of the Honey.)⌝[1] I won't trouble my self to finish finely, a true Compliment is better than a good one, and I can assure you without any, that I am very sincerely, | Sir, Yours, &c.

LADY MARY WORTLEY MONTAGU *to* POPE[2]

14 *September* [1716]

1763

Vienna, Sept. 14, O.S.

Perhaps you'll laugh at me, for thanking you very gravely for all the obliging concern you express for me. 'Tis certain that I may, if I please, take the fine things you say to me for wit and raillery, and, it may be, it would be taking them right. But I never, in my life, was half so well disposed to take you in earnest, as I am at present, and that distance which makes the continuation of your friendship improbable, has very much encreased my faith in it. I find that I have (as well as the rest of my sex) whatever face I set on't, a strong disposition to believe in miracles. Don't fancy, however, that I am infected by the air of these popish countries; I have, indeed, so far wandered from the discipline of the church of England, as to have been last Sunday at the opera, which was performed in the garden of the *Favorita*, and I was so much pleased with it, I have not yet repented my seeing it. Nothing of that kind ever was more magnificent; and I can easily believe, what I am told, that the decorations and habits cost the Emperor thirty thousand pounds sterling. The stage was built over a very large canal, and at the beginning of the second act, divided into two parts, discovering the water, on which there immediately came, from different parts, two fleets of little gilded vessels, that gave the representation of a naval fight. It is not easy to imagine the beauty of this scene, which I took particular notice of. But all the rest were

[1] This sentence was omitted in the Roberts octavo of 1737 and thereafter. The three lords were the Earl of Warwick, Philip Dormer Stanhope (Lord Stanhope until 1726 when he succeeded as 4th Earl of Chesterfield), and Carr, Lord Hervey, whose younger brother John later became Pope's enemy.

[2] Published in the *Letters* of Lady Mary (1763), i. 34–39, as 'To Mr. P—'.

perfectly fine in their kind. The story of the Opera is the Enchantment of *Alcina*, which gives opportunities for great variety of machines and changes of the scenes, which are performed with a surprizing swiftness. The theatre is so large that 'tis hard to carry the eye to the end of it, and the habits in the utmost magnificence to the number of one hundred and eight. No house could hold such large decorations; but the ladies all sitting in the open air, exposes them to great inconveniences; for there is but one canopy for the imperial family; and the first night it was represented, a shower of rain happening, the opera was broke off, and the company crouded away in such confusion, that I was almost squeezed to death.—But if their operas are thus delightful, their comedies are, in as high a degree, ridiculous. They have but one play-house, where I had the curiosity to go to a German comedy, and was very glad it happened to be the story of Amphitrion. As that subject has been already handled by a Latin, French and English poet, I was curious to see what an Austrian author would make of it. I understand enough of that language to comprehend the greatest part of it, and besides I took with me a lady that had the goodness to explain to me every word. The way is to take a box, which holds four, for yourself and company. The fixed price is a gold ducat. I thought the house very low and dark; but I confess the comedy admirably recompensed that defect. I never laughed so much in my life. It begun with *Jupiter*'s falling in love out of a peep-hole in the clouds, and ended with the birth of *Hercules*. But what was most pleasant was the use Jupiter made of his metamorphosis, for you no sooner saw him under the figure of *Amphitrion*, but instead of flying to *Alcmena*, with the raptures Mr. *Dryden* puts into his mouth, he sends for Amphitrion's taylor, and cheats him of a laced coat, and his banker of a bag of money, a Jew of a diamond ring, and bespeaks a great supper in his name; and the greatest part of the comedy turns upon poor Amphitrion's being tormented by these people for their debts. *Mercury* uses *Sosia* in the same manner. But I could not easily pardon the liberty the poet has taken of larding his play with, not only indecent expressions, but such gross words as I don't think our mob would suffer from a mountebank. Besides, the two Sosia's very fairly let down their breeches in the direct view of the boxes, which were full of people of the first rank that seemed very well pleased with their entertainment, and assured me this was a celebrated piece. I shall conclude my letter with this remarkable relation, very well worthy the serious consideration of Mr. Collier.[1] I won't trouble you with farewell compliments, which I think generally as impertinent, as curtisies at leaving the room when the visit has been too long already.

[1] Jeremy Collier, author of *A Short View of the Immorality and Profaneness of the English Stage* (1698).

POPE *to* LADY MARY WORTLEY MONTAGU[1]

The Pierpont Morgan Library [*October* 1716]

Madam,—After having dream'd of you severall nights, besides a hundred Rêveries by day, I find it necessary to relieve myself by writing: tho this is the fourth letter I have sent, two by Mr Methuen, and one by Lord James Hay, who was to be Your Convoy from Leghorne. In all I can say, I only make you a present in many words of what can do you no manner of good, but only raises my own opinion of my self; All the good wishes and hearty dispositions I am capable of forming or feeling for a deserving object. But mine are indeed so warm, that I fear they can proceed from nothing but what I can't very decently own to you, much less to any other; yet what if a man has, he can't help it.

For God's sake Madam, let not my correspondence be like a Traffic with the Grave, from whence there is no Return. Unless you write to me, my wishes must be but like a poor Papists Devotions to seperate Spirits; who, for all they know or hear from them, either may or may not be sensible of their Addresses. None but your Guardian Angels can have you more constantly in mind, than I; and if they have, it is only because they can see you always. If ever you think of those fine young Beaus of Heaven, I beg you to reflect that you have just as much Consolation from them, as I at present have from you.

While all people here are exercising their speculations upon the Affairs of the Turks, I am only considering them as they may concern a particular person, and instead of forming prospects of the general Tranquility of Europe am hoping for some effect that may contribute to your greater Ease. Above all, I would fain indulge an imagination, that the nearer View of the unquiet Scene you are approaching to, may put a stop to your farther Progress. I can hardly yet relinquish a faint hope I have ever had, that Providence will take some uncommon care of one who so generously gives herself up to it, and I can't imagine God almighty so like some of his Vice-gerents, as absolutely to neglect those who surrender to his mercy.

May I thus tell you the truth of my heart; or must I put on a more unconcerned Person, and tell you gayly, that there is some difference between the Court of Vienna and the Camps in Hungary; That scarce a Basha living is so inoffensive a creature as Count Volkra; that the Wives of Ambassadours are as subject to human accidents, & as tender as their Shins, that it is not more natural for Glass to cutt, than for Turks and Tartars to plunder, (not to mention ravishing,

[1] The date can be only approximate. The first leaf of this letter has the upper right-hand corner (including a date?) torn away.

against which I am told Beauty is no defence in those parts) That you are strangely in the wrong to forsake a Nation that but last year toasted Mrs Walpole, for one that has no taste of Beauty after twenty, and where the finest Woman in England will be almost Superannuated. Would to God, Madam, all this might move either Mr Wortley or you; and that I may soon apply to you both, what I have read in one of Harlequin's Comedies: He sees Constantinople in a Raree Show, vows it is the finest thing upon earth, and protests it is prodigiously Like. Ay Sir, says the Man of the Show, you have been at Constantinople I perceive—No indeed, (says Harlequin) I was never there myself, but I had a Brother I lov'd dearly, who had the greatest mind in the world to have gone thither.

This is what I really wish from my Soul, tho it would ruin the best project I ever lay'd, that of obtaining, thro' your means, my fair Circassian Slave. She, whom my Imagination had drawn more amiable than Angels, as beautiful as the Lady who was to chuse her by a resemblance to so divine a face; she, whom my hopes had already transported over so many Seas and Lands, & whom my eager wishes had already lodg'd in my arms & heart; She, I say, upon this condition, may remain under the Cedars of Asia; and weave a garland of Palmes for the brows of a Turkish Tyrant, with those hands, which I had destined for the soft Offices of love, or at worst for transcribing Amorous Madrigals! Let that Breast, I say, be now joind to some Savage Heart, that never beat but with Lust or Rage; that Breast inhabited by far more truth, fidelity, and innocence, than those that heave with Pride and glitter with Diamonds; that Breast whose very Conscience would have been Love, where Duty and Rapture made but one thought, & Honour must have been the same with Pleasure!

I can't go on in this style: I am not able to think of you without the utmost Seriousness, and if I did not take a particular care to disguise it, my Letters would be the most melancholy things in the world. I believe you see my Concern thro' all this Affectation of gayety, which is but like a Fitt of Laughing in the deepest Spleen or Vapours. I am just alarmd with a piece of news, that Mr Wortley thinks of passing thro' Hungary notwithstanding the War there: If ever any man loved his Wife, or any Mother her Child, this offers you the strongest Reason imaginable for staying at Vienna, at least this winter. For God's sake, value Yourself a little more, and don't give us cause to imagine that such extravagant Virtue can exist any where else than in a Romance. I tremble for you the more, because (whether you'll believe it or not) I am capable myself of following one I lov'd, not only to Constantinople, but to those parts of India, where they tell us the Women best like the Ugliest fellows, as the most admirable productions of nature, and look upon Deformities as the Signatures of divine

Favour. But (so romantic as I am) I shoud scarce take these Rambles, without greater encouragement, than I fancy any one who has been long married can expect. You see what danger I shall be in, if ever I find a Fair one born under the same Planet with Astolfo's Wife? If, instead of Hungary, you past thro' Italy, and I had any hopes That Lady's Climate might give a Turn to your inclinations, it is but your sending me the least notice, and I'll certainly meet you in Lombardy, the Scene of those celebrated Amours between the fair Princess and her Dwarf.[1] From thence, how far you might Draw me, and I might run after you, I no more know than the Spouse in the Song of Solomon: This I know, that I could be so very glad of being with you in any pleasure, that I could be content to be with you in any danger. Since I am not to partake either, Adieu! But may God, by hearing my prayers, and Preserving you, make me a better Christian than any modern Poet is at present. I am | Madam, most faithfully Yours. | A. Pope.

Endorsement: Letters | from Mr Pope | 3 [Mr. Wortley's hand]

LADY MARY WORTLEY MONTAGU *to* POPE[2]

10 *October* 1716

1763

Vienna, Oct. 10, O.S. 1716.

I deserve not all the reproaches you make me. If I have been some time without answering your letter, it is not, that I don't know how many thanks are due to you for it; or that I am stupid enough to prefer any amusements, to the pleasure of hearing from you; but after the professions of esteem you have so obligingly made me, I cannot help delaying, as long as I can, shewing you, that you are mistaken. If you are sincere, when you say, you expect to be extremely entertained by my letters, I ought to be mortified at the disappointment that I am sure you will receive, when you hear from me; tho' I have done my best endeavours to find out something worth writing to you. I have seen every thing that was to be seen with a very diligent curiosity. Here are some fine villa's, particularly, the late Prince of Lichtenstein's; but the statues are all modern, and the pictures not of the first hands. 'Tis true, the Emperor has some of great value. I was yesterday to see the repository, which they call his *Treasure*, where they seem to have been more diligent in amassing a great quantity of things, than in the choice of them. I spent above five hours there, and yet there were very few things that stopped me long to consider them. But the

[1] This story forms the subject of a tale in verse entitled 'Woman', published in 1709 in Jacob Tonson's Miscellany, to which Pope contributed some of his early poems.—Thomas–Elwin.

[2] The text comes from Lady Mary's *Letters* (1763), i. 74–78. It is printed simply as 'To Mr. —' and may not be to Pope at all.

number is prodigious, being a very long gallery filled, on both sides, and five large rooms. There is a vast quantity of paintings, amongst which are many fine miniatures, but the most valuable pictures are a few of *Corregio*, those of *Titian* being at the *Favorita*.

The cabinet of jewels did not appear to me so rich as I expected to see it. They shewed me there a cup, about the size of a tea dish, of one entire *emerald*, which they had so particular a respect for, that only the Emperor has the liberty of touching it. There is a large cabinet full of curiosities of clock-work, only one of which I thought worth observing, that was a craw fish with all the motions so natural, that it was hard to distinguish it from the life.

The next cabinet was a large collection of *Agates*, some of them extremely beautiful and of an uncommon size, and several vases of *Lapis Lazuli*. I was surprized to see the cabinet of medals so poorly furnished; I did not remark one of any value, and they are kept in a most ridiculous disorder. As to the *Antiques*, very few of them deserve that name. Upon my saying they were modern, I could not forbear laughing at the answer of the profound antiquary that shewed them, that *they were ancient enough, for to his knowledge they had been there these forty years*; but the next cabinet diverted me yet better, being nothing else but a parcel of wax babies, and toys in ivory, very well worthy to be presented to children of five years old. Two of the rooms were wholly filled with these trifles of all kinds, set in jewels, amongst which I was desired to observe a crucifix, that they assured me had spoke very wisely to the Emperor *Leopold*. I won't trouble you with a catalogue of the rest of the lumber, but I must not forget to mention, a small piece of loadstone that held up an anchor of steel too heavy for me to lift. This is what I thought most curious in the whole treasure. There are some few heads of ancient statues; but several of them are defaced by modern additions. I foresee that you will be very little satisfied with this letter, and I dare hardly ask you, to be good-natured enough to charge the dulness of it, on the barrenness of the subject, and to overlook the stupidity of | Your, &c. &c.

*POPE *to* RICHARD GRAHAM[1] [2 *November* 1716]

Arthur A. Houghton, Jr.

2d Novr 1716

Sir,—I am obliged to go into the City at the hour you mention to morrow, & from thence to Chiswick, but the inclosed Directions will

[1] The date and the endorsements are presumably in the hand of Graham; they are not in Pope's hand. Possibly Graham should have dated the letter 1715 when Gribelin might have been working on the frontispiece that he did for Graham's edition of Du Fresnoy, in which Pope was concerned. But in Nov. 1715 Pope was not living at Chiswick (though he might have visited Burlington there), and the date 1716 may stand on the ground that Graham may then have been engaged on another project.

be sufficient for Mr Gribelin to proceed upon for a beginning. I am, with my thanks for this trouble, with all sincerity | Your most affect: | humble Servant | A. Pope.

Address: For Mr Graham
Endorsements (twice): 2d Novr 1716 | Mr Pope

||POPE *to* LADY MARY WORTLEY MONTAGU[1]

10 *November* [1716]

The Pierpont Morgan Library

The more I examine my own mind, the more Romantick I find myself: Methinks it is a noble Spirit of Contradiction to fate and fortune, not to give up those that are snatchd from us, but follow them with warmer Zeal, the farther they are removd from the sence of it. Sure Flattery never traveld so far as three thousand miles; it is now only for Truth, which overtakes all things, to reach you at this distance. Tis a generous Piece of Popery that pursues even those who are to be Eternally absent into another world; let it be right or wrong, the very Extravagance ⌜is⌝ a sort of Piety: I cannot be satisfied with strowing flowers over you, & barely honoring you as a thing lost; but must consider you as a glorious, tho' remote Being, & be sending Addresses ⌜and prayers⌝ after you. You have carryed away so much of my Esteem, that what remains ⌜of it⌝ is daily languishing and dying over my Acquaintance here; and I believe, in three or four months more, I shall think Aurat-Basar as good a place as Coventgarden. You may imagine this but Raillery, but I am really so far gone, as to take pleasure in Reveries of this kind. Let them say I am Romantick, so is every one said to be that either admires a fine thing, or praises one: ⌜'Tis no wonder such people are thought mad, for they are as much out of the way of common Understanding as if they were mad, because they are in the Right.⌝ On my conscience as the world goes, tis never worth any bodys while to do a Noble thing for the honour of it; Glory, the only Pay of generous actions, is now as ill pay'd as other just Debts ⌜are⌝; and neither Mrs Macfarland[2] for immolating her Lover, nor Lady Mary for sacrificing herself, must hope to be ever compared with[3] Lucretia or Portia.

[1] Pope printed a text of this letter in his octavos of 1737–42. The letter did not appear in the editions of 1735, nor is it in his quarto and folio of 1737. Warton seems to have been the first to print the letter as it was actually sent to Lady Mary (Pope's *Works* [1797], viii. 382–7), and in so doing the date 10 Nov. was carelessly omitted. That date, from the holograph letter, is here first printed. Pope's omissions from the original letter are placed in half-brackets. A few significant verbal changes are here noted.

[2] Mrs. Macfarland shot Captain Cayley for an attempt upon her chastity at Edinburgh, 2nd Oct. 1716, as appears by the narrative published in *The Weekly Journal* of Oct. 13.—Moy Thomas and Elwin.

[3] nor Lady Mary . . . compared with] nor you, for constancy to your Lord, must ever

I write this in some anger; for having frequented those people most since you went, who seemd most in your favor, I heard nothing that concern'd you talkd of so often, as that you went away in a black Full-bottome, which I did but assert to be a Bob, and was answer'd, Love is blind. I am persuaded your Wig had never sufferd this Criticisme but on the score of your head, and the two ⌜fine⌝ Eyes that are in it.

For Gods sake Madam, when[1] you write to me, talk of your self, there is nothing I so much desire to hear of: talk a great deal of yourself, that She who I always thought talk'd best, may speak upon the best subject. The Shrines and Reliques you tell me of, no way engage my curiosity. I had ten times rather go on Pilgrimage to see your Face, than St. John Baptist's Head; I wish you had not only all those fine Statues you talk of, but even the Golden Image which Nebuchadnezzar sett up, provided you were to travel no further than you could carry it.

The Court of Vienna is really very edifying: The Ladies with respect to their Husbands seem to understand that Text ⌜very⌝ literally, that commands ⌜us⌝ to *Bear one another's Burthens*: But I fancy many a man there is like Issachar, *an Ass between two Burthens.* I shall look upon you no longer as a Christian, when you pass from that charitable Court to the Land of Jealousy⌜, where the unhappy Women converse with none but Eunuchs, and where the very Cucumbers are brought to them Cutt⌝. I expect to hear an exact account, how, and at what places, you leave one Article of Faith after another as you approach nearer to Turkey.[2] Pray how far are you gone already? Amidst the charms of High Mass and the Ravishing Trills of a Sunday-Opera, what think you of the Doctrine and Discipline of the Church of England? have you from your heart a reverence for Sternhold & Hopkins? How do your Christian Virtues hold out in so long a Voyage? You have already (without passing the bounds of Christendom) outtraveld the Sin of Fornication⌜, and are happily arrived at the free Region of Adultery⌝: In a little time you'l look upon some other Sins, with more Impartiality[3] than the Ladies here are capable of. I reckon you'll time it so well, as to make your Faith serve out just to the last Verge[4] of Christendom; that you may discharge your Chaplain (as humanity requires) in a place where he may find some business⌜, and not be out of the way of all Trade⌝.

hope to be compared to *1737–42*. (Had Pope edited this letter from the original after 1730, when he hated Lady Mary, he might aptly have left in this phrase as uncomplimentary to Lady Mary's reputation.)

[1] For . . . when] Pray when *1737–42*.

[2] one Article . . . Turkey.] one of the thirty-nine articles after another, as you approach to the lands of infidelity. *1737–42*.

[3] Impartiality] patience *1737–42*.

[4] your Faith . . . Verge] your religion last to the verge *1737–42*.

I doubt not but I shall be told, (when I come to follow you thro' those Countries) in how pretty a manner you accomodated yourself to the Customes of the True-Believers. At this Town, they will say, She practised to sit on the Sofa; at that village, she learnt to fold the Turbant; here she was bathd and anointed; & there she parted with her black Full-bottome. ⌜At every Christian Virtue you lost, and at every Christian Habit you quitted, it will be decent for me to fetch a holy Sigh, but still I shall proceed to follow you.⌝ How happy will it be, for a gay young Woman, to live in a Country where it is a part of Religious worship to be giddy-headed? I shall hear at Belgrade, how the good Basha receivd the fair Convert with tears of joy, how he was charm'd with her pretty manner of pronouncing the words Allah, and Muhammed, and how earnestly you joind with him in exhorting Mr Wortley to be circumcised.[1] But he satisfies you by demonstrating, how in that condition, he could[2] not properly represent his Brittannick Majesty. Lastly I shall hear how the very first Night you lay at Pera, you had a Vision of Mahomet's Paradise, and happily awaked without a Soul. From which blessed instant the beautiful Body was left at full liberty to perform all the agreeable functions it was made for.

⌜But if my Fate be such, that this Body of mine (which is as ill-matchd to my Mind as any wife to her husband) be left behind in the journey, let the Epitaph of Tibullus be set over it.

> ⌜Hic jacet immiti consumptus morte Tibullus,
>   Messalam, terra, dum sequiturque, mari.[3]
>
> Here stopt by hasty Death, Alexis lies,
> Who crost half Europe, led by Wortley's eyes![4]

⌜I shall at least be sure to meet you in the next world, if there be any truth in Our new Doctrine of the Day of judgment. Since your Body is so full of fire, and capable of such Solar motions as your Letter describes, your Soul can never be long going to the Fixed Stars (where I intend to settle) Or Else you may find me in the milky way, because Fontanelle assures us, the Stars are so crowded there that a man may stand upon one, and talk to his friend on another. From thence, with a good Telescope, what do you think one should take such a place as this world for? I fancy for the Devil's Rookery, where the Inhabitants are ready to deafen and destroy one another with eternal Noise and Hunger.⌝

I see I have done in this letter as I have often done in your Conversation, talk'd myself into a good humour tho' I begun in an ill one.

[1] Mr Wortley . . . circumcised] your friend to embrace that religion *1737–42*.

[2] But . . . he could] But I think his objection was a just one, that it was attended with some circumstances under which he could *1737–42*.

[3] *Elegies*, I. iii. 55–56.

[4] The appeal of Lady Mary's eyes is mentioned in other letters and in Gay's 'Mr. Pope's Welcome from Greece' (l. 58) and Pope's 'Epistle to Jervas' (l. 60 of the first edition).

The meer pleasure of addressing to you makes me run on, and it is in your own power to shorten this letter by giving over where you please, so I'll make it no longer by Apologies.

⌜The rapidity of your Journies is what I have been imitating, tho' in a less Sphere: I have been at York,[1] & at Bath, in less than a fortnight. All that time, your Letter (for which you have a thousand thanks from me) lay in London. I had just before sent one by Mr Stanyan, giving another for lost that went by Lord James Hay to Leghorne, where you was then expected—Mr Congreve had written some time before, as I acquainted you in that, who (I assure you) no way deserves to be thought forgetful of you—I obey your Orders in sending inclosed two little pieces,[2] the printed one has made much noise, and done some good at Court: I am wrongfully suspected to be author of it—They talk of some Alterations there, which little affect a man who never ask'd for any thing but your Pastoralls—Lady Rich is brought to bed—I can only add my desire of being always thought yours, & of being told I am thought so by yourself, whenever you would make me as happy as I can be at this distance. | Madam Your most Faithfull | humble Servant | A. Pope

⌜Novr the 10th O.S.⌝

⌜Mr Craggs is very much yours.⌝

⌜I am just now told you are to go by way of Italy. I hope to God this is true, and that you will stay this winter to refresh yourself for new Travels, at Vienna. The Seas will show no respect to Merit or Beauty, in the winter-season. To give you a convincing proof how Romantic I am, if you pass thro Italy next Spring, & will give me timely notice & direction, It is very possible I may meet you there, & attend you till you take Sea again, for Constantinople.⌝

†POPE *to* JERVAS[3] 14 *November* 1716

1735

Nov. 14, 1716.

If I had not done my utmost to lead my Life so pleasantly as to forget all Misfortunes, I should tell you I reckoned your Absence no small

[1] With the Earl of Burlington. See Pope to Teresa Blount, 7 Aug. 1716.

[2] The enclosures are unidentifiable. The 'printed one' might be 'God's Revenge against Punning'. The comment about its effect at Court is jocose, though it mentions various placemen. The 'Pastoralls', mentioned below, are her court-eclogues.

[3] Under this date Pope printed this letter in 1735 a1, but it is lacking in 1735 a2 and 1737 b. It appears in all octavos, 1737–42. The date has been suspected, chiefly because of the apologetic first sentence (for not writing) in Pope's next letter to Jervas (29 Nov.). It must postdate early March of this year when, in his *Essays*, Blackmore attacked Swift, and thus provoked Gay's courageous reply. Gay's retort can hardly be identified. Possibly there was an unknown publication of his *Verses to be placed under the Picture of England's Arch-poet*, which attacked Blackmore. These lines were published later in a revised (the only known)

one; but I hope you have also had many good and pleasant Reasons to forget your Friends on this side the World. If a wish could transport me to you, and your present Companions, I could do the same. Dr. *Swift*, I believe, is a very good Landlord, and a chearful Host at his own Table; I suppose he has perfectly learnt himself, what he has taught so many others, *Rupta non insanire lagena*.[1] Else he would not make a proper Host for your humble Servant, who (you know) tho' he drinks a Glass as seldom as any Man, contrives to break one as often. But 'tis a Consolation to me, that I can do this, and many other Enormities, under my own Roof.

But that you and I are upon equal terms of all friendly Laziness, and have taken an inviolable Oath to each other, always to do what we will; I should reproach you for so long a silence. The best amends you can make for saying nothing to me, is by saying all the good you can of me, which is that I heartily love and esteem the Dean, and Dr. *Parnelle*.

Gay is yours and theirs. His Spirit is awakened very much in the Cause of the Dean, which has broke forth in a courageous Couplet or two upon Sir *Richard Bl—*[2] He has printed it with his Name to it, and bravely assigns no other Reason, than that the said Sir *Richard* has abused Dr. *Swift*. I have also suffered in the like Cause, and shall suffer more; unless *Parnelle* sends me his *Zoilus* and *Bookworm* (which the Bishop of *Clogher*, I hear greatly extols) it will be shortly, *Concurrere Bellum atque Virum*.[3]—I love you all, as much as I despise most Wits in this dull Country. *Ireland* has turned the tables upon *England*; and if I have no Poetical Friend in my own Nation, I'll be as proud as *Scipio*, and say (since I am reduced to Skin and Bone) *Ingrata patria, ne* ossa *quidem habeas*.[4]

†POPE *to* THE EARL OF BURLINGTON[5] [*November* 1716]

1735

My Lord,—If your Mare could speak, she would give you an account of the extraordinary company she had on the road; which since she cannot do, I will.

form. Gay's *Epistle to the Earl of Burlington*, which has been thought to contain the courageous couplets, first appeared in Feb. 1717. Gay's name was affixed to the retort, whatever the retort was.

[1] Horace, *Epistles*, II. ii. 134 (adapted).

[2] *Bl—*] Blackmore *1737–42*.

[3] Lucan, *Pharsalia*, vi. 191–2.

[4] This classic remark may be found in the *Memorabilia* of Valerius Maximus, Book V, chap. iii, as well as in Livy and other authors.

[5] This letter is one of Pope's most finished performances, and it was doubtless subjected to much revision before printing. Most of Lintot's profanity was modified in the quarto and folio of 1737. The letter must have been written while Lord Lansdowne was in the Tower (26 Sept. 1715 to 8 Feb. 1716/17). Borrowing a horse of Lord Burlington suggests a date later than Apr. 1716 when the Popes 'fixed at Chiswick under the wing of my Lord Burlington'. Pope's letter to Jervas, 29 Nov. 1716, indicates that Pope has recently returned from Oxford.

It was the enterprizing Mr. *Lintott*, the redoutable rival of Mr. *Tonson*, who mounted on a stonehorse, (no disagreeable companion to your Lordships mare) overtook me in *Windsor-forest*. He said, he heard I design'd for *Oxford*, the seat of the muses, and would, as my bookseller, by all means, accompany me thither.

I asked him where he got his horse? He answer'd, he got it of his publisher: "For that rogue, my printer, (said he) disappointed me: I hoped to put him in a good humour by a treat at the tavern, of a brown fricassee of rabbits which cost two shillings, with two quarts of wine, besides my conversation. I thought my self cocksure of his horse, which he readily promis'd me, but said, that Mr. *Tonson* had just such another design of going to *Cambridge*, expecting there the copy of *a Comment upon the Revelations*;[1] and if Mr. *Tonson* went, he was preingaged to attend him, being to have the printing of the said copy."

"So in short, I borrow'd this stonehorse of my publisher, which he had of Mr. *Oldmixon* for a debt; he lent me too the pretty boy you see after me; he was a smutty dog yesterday, and cost me near two hours to wash the ink off his face: but the Devil is a fair-condition'd Devil, and very forward in his catechise:[2] if you have any more baggs, he shall carry them."

I thought Mr. *Lintott*'s civility not to be neglected, so gave the boy a small bagg, containing three shirts and an Elzevir *Virgil*; and mounting in an instant proceeded on the road, with my man before, my courteous stationer beside, and the aforesaid Devil behind.

Mr. *Lintott* began in this manner. "Now damn them! what if they should put it into the news-paper, how you and I went together to *Oxford*? why what would I care? If I should go down into *Sussex*, they would say I was gone to the Speaker.[3] But what of that? if my son were but big enough to go on with the business, by G—d I would keep as good company as old *Jacob*."

Hereupon I enquir'd of his son. "The lad (says he) has fine parts, but is somewhat sickly, *much as you are*—I spare for nothing in his education at *Westminster*. Pray don't you think *Westminster* to be the best school in *England*? most of the late *Ministry* came out of it, so did many of *this Ministry*; I hope the boy will make his fortune."

Don't you design to let him pass a year at *Oxford*? "To what pur-

[1] The *Comment* is unidentified; in the text of 1737–42 it becomes 'the Copy of a new kind of Horace from Dr. ——'. This second reading is presumably a jibe at Bentley's famous edition of 1711.

[2] catechise] catechism *1742*. (Probably a printer's 'correction'.)

[3] Lintot's place, whether at Wadhurst or Horsham, was not too suspiciously near Eastbourne where the Speaker (Sir Spencer Compton) lived. Henry Lintot (1703–58) was his father's partner after 1730.

pose? (said he) the Universities do but make Pedants, and I intend to breed him a man of Business."

As Mr. *Lintott* was talking, I observ'd he sate uneasy on his saddle, for which I express'd some sollicitude: Nothing says he, I can bear it well enough; but since we have the day before us, methinks it would be very pleasant for you to rest a-while under the Woods. When [we][1] were alighted, "See here, what a mighty pretty *Horace* I have in my pocket? what if you amus'd your self in turning an Ode, till we mount again? Lord![2] if you pleas'd, what a clever *Miscellany* might you make at leisure hours." Perhaps I may, said I, if we ride on; the motion is an aid to my fancy; a round trott very much awakens my spirits. Then jog on apace, and I'll think as hard as I can.

Silence ensu'd for a full hour; after which Mr. *Lintott* lug'd the reins, stopt short, and broke out, "Well, Sir, how far have you gone?" I answer'd seven miles. "Z—ds,[3] Sir, said *Lintott*, I thought you had done seven stanza's. *Oldsworth* in a ramble round *Wimbleton-hill*, would translate a whole Ode in half this time. I'll say that for *Oldsworth*, (tho' I lost by his *Timothy*'s)[4] he translates an Ode of *Horace* the *quickest* of any man in *England*. I remember Dr. King[5] would write verses in a tavern three hours after he couldn't speak: and there's Sir *Richard*[6] in that rumbling old Chariot of his, between *Fleet-ditch* and *St. Giles*'s pound shall make you half a *Job*."

Pray Mr. *Lintott* (said I) now you talk of Translators, what is your method of managing them? "Sir (reply'd he) those are the saddest pack of rogues in the world: In a hungry fit, they'll swear they understand all the languages in the universe: I have known one of them take down a *Greek* book upon my counter and cry, Ay this is *Hebrew*, I must read it from the latter end. By G—d[7] I can never be sure in these fellows, for I neither understand *Greek*, *Latin*, *French*, nor *Italian* my self. But this is my way: I agree with them for ten shillings *per* sheet, with a proviso, that I will have their doings corrected by whom I please; so by one or other they are led at last to the true sense

[1] *we* is inserted in the texts of 1735 e and thereafter.

[2] Omitted in the quarto and folio of 1737.

[3] Z—ds] Lord *1737 b*.

[4] William Oldsworth (1680–1734) wrote *A Dialogue between Timothy and Philatheus*, which appeared in successive parts forming finally three volumes (1709–11). It is said (*DNB*) that he received £75 for the work. He also did a version of Horace with translations of Bentley's notes included (3 vols., 1712–13), which conceivably may have been in Pope's mind. See *supra*, p. 372, n 1.

[5] Dr. William King (1663–1712).

[6] Sir Richard Blackmore, author of *A Paraphrase on the Book of Job*, apologized for the deficiencies of his *Prince Arthur* in his Preface to *King Arthur* (1697) on the ground that 'the greatest part of that *Poem* was written in Coffee-houses, and in passing up and down the Streets'. Dryden as well as Pope (here and elsewhere) satirizes Blackmore's rumbling, jolting verse. In 1716 Blackmore was offensive to Pope because of his *Essays*. See Pope to Jervas, 14 Nov. 1716.

[7] By G—d] By the Lord *1737 b*.

of an author; my judgment giving the negative to all my Translators." But how are you secure that those correctors may not impose upon you? "Why I get any civil gentleman, (especially any *Scotchman*) that comes into my shop, to read the original to me in *English*; by this I know whether my first Translator be deficient, and whether my Corrector merits his money or no?

"I'll tell you what happen'd to me last month: I bargain'd with *S*—[1] for a new version of *Lucretius* to publish against *Tonson*'s; agreeing to pay the author so many shillings at his producing so many lines. He made a great progress in a very short time, and I gave it to the corrector to compare with the *Latin*; but he went directly to *Creech*'s translation, and found it the same word for word, all but the first page. Now, what d'ye think I did? I arrested the *Translator* for a cheat; nay, and I stopt the *Corrector's pay* too, upon this proof that he had made use of *Creech* instead of the original."

Pray tell me next how you deal with the Critics? "Sir (said he) nothing more easy. I can silence the most formidable of them; the rich one's for a sheet apiece of the blotted manuscript, which costs me nothing. They'll go about with it to their acquaintance, and pretend they had it from the author, who submitted to their correction: this has given some of them such an air, that in time they come to be consulted with, and dedicated to, as the top critics of the town.—As for the poor Critics, I'll give you one instance of my management, by which you may guess at the rest. A lean man that look'd like a very good scholar came to me t'other day; he turn'd over *Homer*, shook his head, shrug'd up his shoulders, and pish'd at every line of it; *One would wonder* (says he) *at the strange presumption of men*; Homer *is no such easy task*, *that* every *Stripling*, every *Versifier*—he was going on when my Wife call'd to dinner: Sir, said I, will you please to eat a *piece of beef* with me? Mr. *Lintott*, said he, *I am sorry you should be at the expence of this great Book*, *I am really concern'd on your account*—Sir I am oblig'd to you: if you can dine upon a piece of beef, together with a slice of pudding—*Mr.* Lintott, *I do not say but Mr.* Pope, *if he would condescend to advise with men of learning*—Sir, the *pudding* is upon the table, if you please to go in—My critic complies, he comes to a taste of your poetry, and tells me in the same breath, that the *Book* is commendable, and the *Pudding* excellent."

Now Sir (concluded Mr. *Lintott*) in return to the frankness I have shewn, pray tell me, "Is it the opinion of your friends at Court that my Lord L—[2] will be brought to the Bar or not?" I told him I heard *not*,

[1] S— was first glossed by Courthope as George Sewell. Courthope adds: 'In Lintot's Account Book is the following entry:—"10th March 1714. Pd. Dr. Sewell for translating pt. of Q. Curtius and pt. of Lucretius, and writing observations on ye Tragedy of Jane Shore, £6 19*s*. 9*d*."' (EC x. 208 n.)

[2] L—] Lansdown *1737–42*.

and I hop'd it, my Lord being one I had particular obligations to. "That may be (reply'd Mr. *Lintott*) but by G—d[1] if he is not, I shall lose the printing of a very good Trial."

These my Lord are a few traits by which you may discern the genius of my friend[2] Mr. *Lintott*, which I have chosen for the subject of a letter. I dropt him as soon as I got to *Oxford*, and paid a visit to my Lord *Carlton*[3] at *Middleton*.

The conversations I enjoy here are not to be prejudic'd by my pen, and the pleasures from them only to be equal'd when I meet your Lordship. I hope in a few days to cast my self from your horse at your feet. | I am, &c.

POPE *to* MARTHA BLOUNT [*November* 1716]

Mapledurham

Madam,—It is usual with unfortunate Young Women to betake themselves to Romances, and therby feed & indulge that melancholy which is occasioned by the Want of a Lover: As the Want of Money is generally attended with the Want I have mentioned, I presume it may be so far your present case, as to render the five Volumes of the Grand Cyrus[4] no unseasonable Present to you. My dear Mandana, if you are disposed to wander upon adventures, suffer the unhappy Artamenes to be your Companion! Great as he afterwards was, he would rather have chose to rule your heart than the Empires of Persia & Media. Let your faithless Sister triumph in her ill-gotten Treasures; let her put on New Gowns to be the Gaze of Fools, and Pageant of a Birth-night! While you with all your innocence enjoy a Shadey Grove without any leaves on, & dwell with a virtuous Aunt in a Country Paradise.

Tell that abandon'd Creature who is unworthy to be called your Relation, and who has so lately Prostituted herself to a man in a Sheet of paper,[5] that her money like her self, shall be put out to Use to such

[1] but by G—d if] but if *1737 b.*

[2] of my friend Mr. *Lintott*] of Mr. *Lintott* *1737–42.*

[3] Lord Carlton, who had recently built the original Carlton House in London, was the uncle of the Earl of Burlington.

[4] *The Grand Cyrus* ties this letter to the next one to Miss Blount, written a week or so later and about four or five weeks before *Three Hours* was staged. The present letter was written in late autumn, as the mention of the 'shadey grove with no leaves on' might indicate, as does also the fact that Teresa has been in town for the birth-night celebration of the Prince of Wales, which fell on 30 Oct. (See *The Weekly Packet*, 3 Nov. 1716.) In October Pope and Lord Burlington had made flying visits to both York and Bath (see *The Weekly Journal*, 27 Oct. 1716, and Pope to Lady Mary, 10 Nov. 1716). During the first half of November he was possibly at Chiswick 'besieged with fifty Greek books'.

The letter is here printed entire. Carruthers and Elwin printed a curiously abbreviated text of it.

[5] i.e. Teresa has sent Pope ('a man') money to invest. See his December letter to Martha Blount.

people as will give most for it, tho' it be to a whole Company. I have been an entire week at home besieged with fifty Greek books, which have been all written to explain a Story of a fine Lady that was Ravishd. As soon as I am able to take my thoughts from so high a Theme as a Rape, to attend to the things of this world, I'll consult the Elders of the City concerning her Profits in the Mammon of Iniquity, and I will then write to her upon that groveling subject.

You who are truly virtuous, I know detest all manner of Vices, whereof Punning is not the least, and therfore I send you this Paper.[1] I would write more but my Head akes enough to be brought to bed of some dead-born Poem. | Madam, I am in all & every part | Yours.

The romance will come to Reading by the Coach, as soon as this Letter can reach you. My faithful Service to Mrs Blount.

The Romances were sent two days since by the Reding Coach, directed to Mr Dean the apothecary.

Address: To Mrs. Martha Blount.

†POPE *to* JERVAS[2] — 29 *November* 1716

1735

Nov. 29, 1716.

That you have not heard from me of late, ascribe not to the usual laziness of your Correspondent, but to a ramble to *Oxford*, where your name is mentioned with honour, even in a land flowing with Tories. I had the good fortune there to be often in the conversation of Doctor *Clarke*:[3] He entertained me with several Drawings, and particularly with the original designs of *Inigo Jones's Whitehall.* I there saw and reverenced some of your first Pieces; which future Painters are to look upon as we Poets do on the *Culex* of *Virgil*, and *Batrachom.* of *Homer*.

Having named this latter piece, give me leave to ask what is become of Dr. *Parnelle* and his Frogs? *Oblitusque meorum, obliviscendus &* *illis*, might be *Horace*'s wish, but will never be mine, while I have such *meorums* as Dr. *Parnelle* and Dr. *Swift*. I hope the spring will

[1] The paper about punning is perhaps *God's Revenge against Punning*, the date of which is undetermined, though it postdates 7 Aug. when Pope reports to the Misses Blount Gay's fall from his horse (also reported in the paper) and antedates *An Heroi-Comical Epistle . . . in Defense of . . . Punning*, advertised on 27 Nov. It may possibly be this last item that Pope sends to Martha now.

[2] This letter is omitted from 1735 a2 and 1737 b. In other editions verbal changes are negligible. The date and the first sentence of this letter combine to discredit the date of the preceding letter to Jervas (10 Nov.). There seems to be less chance of the date of this letter being wrong than that of the preceding one. Inconsistent as they may seem, there is no way of surely rearranging them under other dates.

[3] Dr. George Clarke (1661–1736), Fellow of All Souls and benefactor of Worcester College, had been an early patron of Jervas. He had a great reputation as a man of taste and as a collector. See *DNB*.

restore you to us, and with you all the beauties and colours of nature. Not but I congratulate you on the pleasure you must take in being admired in your own Country, which so seldom happens to Prophets and Poets. But in this you have the Advantage of Poets; you are Master of an Art that must prosper and grow rich, as long as people love, or are proud of themselves, or their own persons. However, you have stay'd long enough, methinks, to have painted all the numberless Histories of old *Ogygia.* If you have begun to be Historical, I recommend to your hand the story which every pious *Irishman* ought to begin with, that of St. *Patrick*: To the end you may be obliged (as Dr. *P.* was, when he translated the *Batrachomuomachia*) to come into *England* to copy the Frogs, and such other Vermine as were never seen in that land since the time of that Confessor.

I long to see you a History Painter. You have already done enough for the Private, do something for the Publick; and be not confined, like the rest, to draw only such silly stories as our own faces tell of us. The Ancients too expect you should do them right; those Statues from which you learned your beautiful and noble Ideas, demand it as a piece of Gratitude from you, to make them truly known to all nations, in the account you intend to write of their *Characters.* I hope you think more warmly than ever of that noble design.

As to your enquiry about your House, when I come within the walls, they put me in mind of those of *Carthage* where your Friend, like the wandring *Trojan*,

Animum Pictura pascit inani.[1]

For the spacious Mansion, like a *Turkish* Caravanserah, entertains the Vagabond with only bare Lodging. I rule the Family very ill, keep bad Hours, and lend out your Pictures about the Town. See what it is to have a Poet in your House! *Frank* indeed does all he can in such a Circumstance, for considering he has a wild Beast in it, he constantly keeps the Door chain'd. Every time it is open'd, the Links rattle, the rusty Hinges roar, the House seems so sensible that you are its support, that it is ready to drop in your absence; but I still trust my self under its Roof, as depending that Providence will preserve so many *Raphaels*, *Titian's* and *Guido's*, as are lodg'd in your Cabinet. Surely the Sins of one Poet can hardly be so heavy, as to bring an old House over the Heads of so many Painters. In a word, your House is falling, but what of that? I am only a Lodger.[2]

[1] *Aeneid*, i. 464.

[2] Jervas is here reminded of the story about the Irishman who was only a lodger. See Pope to Caryll, 21 Dec. 1712.

‖ ATTERBURY *to* POPE[1] [*December* 1716]

Longleat Portland Papers, xiii (Harleian transcripts)

Sir,—I return the Preface[2] which I have read twice with Pleasure. The Modesty, and good Sense there is in it, must please every One that reads it, And since there is ⌜as I said,⌝ nothing that can Offend, I see not, why you should ballance a Moment about Printing it always provided that there is nothing said there, which you have Occasion to unsay here after: of which you your self are the best and the only Judge. This is my Sincere Opinion, which I give because you ask it; and which I would not give, tho' Ask'd, but to a Man I value as much as I do You, being Sensible how Improper it is on many Accounts for me to Interpose in things of this Nature which I never understood well, and now understand somewhat less than ever I did. But I can deny you nothing; especially since you have had the Goodness often and patiently to hear what I have said against Rhime, and in behalf of blank Verse with little Discretion perhaps, but I am sure without the least Prejudice, being my self equally incapable of writing well in either of those ways; and leaning therefore to neither Side of the Question, but as the appearance of Reason inclines me. Forgive me this Error, if it be one, an Error of above 30 years Standing, and which therefore I shall be very loth to part with: In other matters, which relate to polite Writing, I shall seldome differ from you: or if I do, shall, I hope have the Prudence to conceal my Opinion: I am as much as I ought to be, that is as much as any Man can be | Sir | Your Affectionate humble Servant | F: R.

Dec. 1716[3]

Tuesday Morn[4]

I am still a Prisoner, but hope to be abroad to morrow unless the Severity of weather hinders me. That too must be my Excuse for not transcribing this Letter, which I find upon folding up, to be too much blotted to be sent to any one who has less good nature than you have.

[1] First printed in 1737 a and reprinted in all later editions. The printed texts differ from the Harleian transcript verbally only in the first two sentences. There 'the Preface' becomes 'your Preface' and 'as I said' is omitted. The only verbal change in Pope's printed texts occurs in 1742 Le, which ineptly inserts in the third sentence the word *you*: 'I would not give you, tho' ask'd.' This is the first letter from Atterbury; signed F[rancis] R[offensis].

[2] A marginal note in the Harleian transcript reads: 'Preface to Mr Pope's Miscellaneous Poems.' Pope's own note, as printed, reads: 'The General Preface to Mr. Pope's Poems, first printed in 1717, the year after the date of this letter.' The Preface is perhaps Pope's most polished piece of prose, and it is interesting that it is by Dec. of 1716 above criticism by Atterbury.

[3] The date in the transcript is added in Lord Oxford's hand. Pope printed the same date.

[4] This postscript, found in the transcript, seems not to have been printed hitherto. The bishop is made a 'prisoner' by the gout.

POPE *to* MARTHA BLOUNT[1] [*December* 1716]

Mapledurham

Madam,—This is purely to give you the Satisfaction of knowing that I have not been unmindful of your Affairs, & that I shall omit no Occasion of doing what you order me. I find, from those whose judgment I myself most depend upon, that it is thought the South Sea will rather fall than rise toward the sitting of the Parliament, and upon this belief I have myself kept a thousand five hundred pounds lying by me, to buy at such a juncture. The general Opinion is that the Parliament will tax the funds; & if so; one may certainly make advantages of mony then in one's hands, which will more than answer its lying dead these two months.

However I have given orders to buy 500ll for myself as soon as South Sea falls to 103: which you shall have if you have a mind to it. It will amount so to near 6 per cent: And my Broker tells me he thinks it will fall to that.

But if you order me to do otherwise, with part, or all of the Sum, I have of yours, I will obey you: Hitherto I have only acted in your affair as I have done in my owne.

I hope you had the Grand Cyrus by Reding Coach above a week ago—I am in London almost constantly,[2] & every hour in Company, have renewed all my idle, and evil Haunts; am not very well, sit up very late, &c. I have lately been told my Person is in some danger, and (in any such case) the sum of 1121ll will be left for you in Mr Gay's hands: I have made that matter secure against Accidents—

Gay is well at Court and more in the way of being served than ever. However, not to trust too much to Hopes, he will have a Play acted in 4 or 5 weeks, which we have driven a bargain for.[3]

I long to see you both; and love you so very well, that I wish I were the handsomest fellow in England for your sakes. I dined yesterday with Jacky Campbell[4] at the D. of Argyle's. Gay dines daily with the Maids of honour. Adieu—I am Melancholy—and Drunk—

Tuesday night.

[1] The date here suggested depends on two factors: (1) In the autumn of 1716 South Sea stock rose to above 103 by the middle of October. Very briefly, on 24 and 26 Nov. it fell just below 103, and throughout the latter half of December it registered approximately 103. (2) If written four or five weeks before Gay's play *Three Hours after Marriage* was acted (16 Jan. 1717), the letter would date near the beginning of December.

[2] Pope is in London, and the Blount sisters are elsewhere. The girls at least seem to have been at Whiteknights in August (see Pope to Teresa, 7 Aug.), and in November Pope speaks of Martha as living 'with a virtuous aunt in a country paradise'.

[3] It is possible that this undescribed 'bargain' had something to do with the evident cabal formed to 'damn' Gay's play. See *Modern Philology*, xxiv (1926), 91–109 for an account of the reception of the play.

[4] Lieut.-Col. John Campbell (*c.* 1693–1770) was the nephew of the 2nd Duke of Argyle, whose son he succeeded as 4th Duke in 1761. In 1720 Col. Campbell married Pope's friend Mary Bellenden, Maid of Honour to the Princess of Wales. She died in 1736.

†POPE *to* MRS. ——[1] [1716]

1737

You have put me into so much gayety of temper, that there will not be a serious word in this day's letter. No more you'll say there wou'd, if I told you the whole serious business of the town. All last night I continu'd with you, tho' your unreasonable regularity drove me out of your doors at three a clock. I dream'd all over the evening's conversation, and saw the little bed in spite of you. In the morning I wak'd very angry at your phantom for leaving me so abruptly.—I know you delight in my mortification. I din'd with an old Beauty; she appear'd at the table like a Death's head enamell'd. The Egyptians, you know, had such things at their entertainments; but do you think they painted and patch'd them? However the last of these objections was soon remov'd; for the lady had so violent an appetite for a salmon, that she quickly eat all the patches off her face. She divided the fish into three parts; not equal, God knows; for she help'd Gay to the head, me to the middle, and making the rest much the largest part took it herself and cry'd very naive-ly, I'll be content with my own tail.

My supper was as singular as my dinner. It was with a great Poet and Ode-maker (that is, a great poet out of his wits, or out of his way.) He came to me very hungry; not for want of a dinner, (for that I shou'd make no jest of) but having forgot to dine. He fell most furiously on the broil'd relicks of a shoulder of mutton, commonly call'd a blade-bone: he profess'd he never tasted so exquisite a thing! beg'd me to tell him what joint it was? wonder'd he had never hear'd the name of this joint, or seen it at other tables? and desir'd to know how he might direct his butcher to cut the same for the future? And yet this man so ignorant in modern butchery, has cut up half a hundred heroes, and quarter'd five or six miserable lovers in every tragedy he has written. I have nothing more to tell you to day.

†MRS. —— *to* POPE[2] [1716]

1737

The Answer

You should have my Day too, Sir, but indeed I slept it out, and so I'll give you all that was left, my last Night's entertainment. You know

[1] In octavo editions of 1737–42 this letter, and the following as its answer, were printed together without textual revision. Written apparently in the days when Pope and Gay were favourites with the Maids of Honour, it can otherwise only vaguely be dated. The 'old beauty' has (rather improbably) been thought to be Gay's former employer, the Duchess of Monmouth, and the hungry poet to be Edward Young. Neither identification should be taken too seriously.

[2] See the note on the immediately preceding letter. This answer is obviously written (or supposed to be written) by a Maid of Honour, and pictures behaviour 'offstage' at Court.

the company. I went in late, in order to be better receiv'd; but unluckily came in, as Deuce-ace was flinging (Lord H.[1] would say I came in the Nick.) The Lady colour'd, and the men took the name of the Lord in vain: No body spoke to me, and I sat down disappointed; then affecting a careless air, gap'd, and cry'd seven or eight times, *D'ye win or lose?* I cou'd safely say at that moment I had no temptation to any one of the seven, lively sins; and in the innocent way I was, happy had it been for me if I had died! Moralizing sat I by the hazard table; I looked upon the uncertainty of riches, the decay of beauty, and the crash of worlds with as much contempt as ever Plato did. But ah! the frailty of human nature! some ridiculous thought came into my head, waken'd my passions, which burst forth into a violent laughter: I rose from my seat, and not considering the just resentments of the losing gamesters, hurl'd a ball of paper cross the table, which stop'd the dice, and turn'd up seven instead of five: Curs'd on all sides, and not knowing where to fly, I threw my self into a chair, which I demolish'd and never spoke a word after. We went to supper, and a lady said, Miss G.[2] *looks prodigiously like a Tree*; every body agreed to it, and I had not curiosity to ask the meaning of that sprightly fancy: Find it out, and let me know. Adieu, 'tis time to dress, and begin the business of the day.

†POPE *to* ——[3] [1716]

1737

In the Style of a Lady

Pray what is your opinion of *Fate*? for I must confess I am one of those that believe in Fate and Predestination.—No, I can't go so far as that, but I own I am of opinion one's stars may incline, tho' not compell one; and that is a sort of free will; for we may be able to resist inclination, but not compulsion.

Don't you think they have got into the most preposterous fashion this winter that ever was, of flouncing the petticoat so very deep, that it looks like an entire coat of lutestring?

It is a little cool indeed for this time of year, but then, my dear, you'll allow it has an extream clean pretty look.

Ay, so has my muslin apron; but I would not chuse to make it a winter suit of cloaths.

[1] Hervey? (Not John but his more amiable brother, Carr.)

[2] Miss Griffin or Griffith?

[3] This is one of Pope's *jeux d'esprit* in letter form. It fits the period of great intimacy with the young ladies of the Court, and is placed, where Pope (1737–42 octavos) placed it—just after the two facetious letters here immediately preceding. It is satire in the light, if also frivolous, vein of *The Spectator*. The Elwin–Courthope placing makes this the letter to which 'The Answer' was written—an accidental misplacing probably.

Well now I'll swear, child, you have put me in mind of a very pretty dress; let me die if I. don't think a muslin flounce, made very full, would give one a very agreeable *Flirtation*-air.

Well I swear it would be charming! and I shou'd like it of all things—Do you think there are any such things as *Spirits*?

Do you believe there is any such place as the Elysian Fields? O Gad, that would be charming! I wish I were to go to the Elysian Fields when I die, and then I should not care if I were to leave the world to-morrow; But is one to meet there with what one has lov'd most in this world?

Now you must tell me this positively. To be sure you can, or what do I correspond with you for, if you won't tell me all? you know I abominate Reserve.

||POPE *to* LADY MARY WORTLEY MONTAGU[1]

[1716–17]

The Pierpont Morgan Library

Madam,—I no more think I can have too many of your letters,[2] ⌜than that I could have too many Writings to entitle me to the greatest estate in the world; which I think so valuable a friendship as yours is equal to.⌝ I am angry at every Scrap of paper lost, ⌜as at something that interrupts the history of my title;⌝[3] and tho' it is but an odd Compliment to compare a fine Lady to Sybill, your leaves methinks, like hers, are too good to be committed to the winds; tho I have no other way of receiving them but by those unfaithful Messengers. I have had but three,[4] & I reckon in that short one from D⌜ort⌝, which was rather a dying Ejaculation than a letter. ⌜But I have so great an opinion of your goodness, that had I receivd none, I should not have accused you of neglect or insensibility. I am not so wrong-headed as to quarrel with my friends the minute they don't write; I'd as soon quarrel at the Sun the minute he did not shine, which he is hindred from by accidental causes, & is in reality all that time performing the same course and doing the same good offices as ever.⌝

[1] Other editors seem to have placed this letter somewhat too early. In his letter of 10 Nov. Pope imagined Lady Mary progressing into Turkey; he had not then heard of the detour to Hanover. He seems to have learned of it possibly from *The London Gazette* of 8 Dec., which reported that on 13 Nov. O.S. Mr. Wortley Montagu left Vienna for Hanover, 'designing to return in a short time'.

Pope published the letter, with large omissions (here placed in half-brackets), in his editions of 1737–42, without indication as to the addressee. Various editors have divided it into two letters, but since Pope published it as one, and since the manuscript leaves might or might not form parts of a single letter, they are here placed together with space between the two parts.

[2] I no more . . . letters] I can never have too many of your letters *1737–42*.

[3] Pope's omissions here excise reflections that concern the difficulties over estate papers that Catholics might be having because of the registration act.

[4] The three letters of which we have knowledge would be the one from Dort (now lost),

You have contrived to say in your last, the two most pleasing things to me in nature;[1] the first is, that whatever be the fate of your letters, you will continue to write in the discharge of your Conscience. ⌜This is generous to the last degree, and a Virtue you ought to enjoy: be assured in return, my Heart shall be as ready to think you have done every good thing, as yours can be to do it. So that you shall never be able to favour your absent friend, before he has thought himself obliged to you for the very favor you are then conferring.⌝

The other is the justice you do me, in taking what I writ to you in the serious manner it was meant. It is the Point upon which I can bear no suspicion, & in which above all I desire to be thought serious. It would be the most vexatious of all Tyranny, if you should pretend to take for Raillery,[2] what is the meer disguise of a discontented heart that is unwilling to make you as melancholy as itself; and for Wit, what is really only the natural Overflowing ⌜and Warmth⌝ of the same Heart, as it is improved & awakend by an Esteem for you.[3] But Since you tell me you believe me, I fancy my expressions have not ⌜at least⌝ been entirely unfaithful to those[4] thoughts⌜, to which I am sure they can never be equal⌝. May God increase your faith[5] in all Truths that are as great as this, and depend upon it, to whatever degree your Belief may extend, you can never be a Bigot.

If you could see the heart I talk of, you would really think it a foolish, good kind of thing, with some qualities as well deserving to be half-laughd at and half-esteemd, as any in the world.[6] Its grand Foible in regard to you, is the most like Reason of any Foible in nature. Upon my faith,[7] this heart is not like a great Ware-house stored only with my own Goods, with vast empty spaces to be supplyd as fast as Interest or Ambition can fill them up; but it is every inch of it let out into Lodgings for its friends, and shall never want a Corner at your service: where I dare affirm Madam, your Idea lyes as warm, and as close, as any Idea in Christendom.

⌜If I don't take care, I shall write my self all out to you; and if this correspondence continues on both sides at the free rate I would have it, we shall have very little Curiosity to encourage our meeting at the

that of 14 Sept., and that of 10 Oct. During her absence Lady Mary seems to have written to Pope perhaps a dozen letters. He evidently had news of her through letters to her other friends.

[1] the two . . . the first] the two things most pleasing to me: The first *1737–42*.

[2] This passage seems a comment on parts of Lady Mary's letter of 14 Sept.

[3] It would be . . . for you.] It would be vexatious indeed, if you should pretend to take that for wit, which is no more than the natural overflowing of a heart improv'd by an esteem for you: *1737–42*.

[4] unfaithful . . . thoughts,] unfaithful to my thoughts. *1737–42*.

[5] May . . . faith] May your faith be encreased *1737–42*. (In Pope's texts this sentence becomes a paragraph by itself.)

[6] as any in the world] as most hearts in the world *1737–42*.

[7] faith] word *1737–42*.

Day of Judgment. I foresee that the further you go from me, the more freely I shall write, & if (as I earnestly wish) you would do the same, I can't guess where it will end? Let us be like modest people, who when they are close together keep all decorums, but if they step a little aside, or get to the other end of a room, can untye garters or take off Shifts without scruple.⌉

If this Distance (as you are so kind as to say) enlarges your belief of my friendship;[1] I assure you it has so extended my notion of your Value, that I begin to be impious on your account, and to wish that even Slaughter Ruin and Desolation might interpose between you and Turkey: I wish you restored[2] to us at the expence of a whole People. ⌈I barely hope you will forgive me for saying this, but I fear God will scarce forgive me for desiring it.

Make me less wicked then;⌉ is there no other expedient to return you and your Infant in peace to the bosome of your Country? I hear you are going to Hanover;[3] ⌈can there be no favorable planet at this conjuncture? or⌉ do you only come back so far, to Dye twice? Is Eurydice once more snatch'd to the Shades? If ever mortal had reason to hate the King, it is I. For it is my particular misfortune, to be almost the Only Innocent man whom he has made to suffer, both by his Government at home, and his Negotiations abroad.[4]

If you must go from us, I wish at least you might pass to your banishment by the most pleasant way; Might all your road be roses and myrtles, and a thousand objects rise round you, agreable enough to make England less desireable to you. I am glad, Madam, your native Country uses you so well as to justify your regret for it: It is not for me to talk of it with tears in my eyes; I can never think[5] that Place my Country, where I can't call a foot of paternal Earth my owne. Indeed it may seem some alleviation, that when the wisest thing I can do is to leave my country, that which was most agreable in it should be taken from thence beforehand.[6] I could overtake you with pleasure in Italy,[7] (if you took that way) & make that Tour in your company. Every reasonable Entertainment, and beautiful View, would be doubly

[1] Here we have another reference to Lady Mary's letter of 14 Sept.

[2] and Turkey . . . restored] and the place you design for; and that you were restored *1737–42*.

[3] The King with his Secretary of State was in Hanover at this time, and Mr. Wortley Montagu was evidently summoned for an unexpected audience.

[4] At home Pope is double-taxed; negotiations abroad have deprived him of Lady Mary. With this sentence the letter possibly ended. What follows is on a separate sheet and has at times been printed as a separate letter. Pope printed the two sections as parts of one letter.

[5] It is not . . . think] It is not now my interest to wish England agreeable: It is highly probable it may use me ill enough to drive me from it. Can I think *1737–42*.

[6] that which . . . beforehand] what was most agreeable in it should first be snatch'd away from it *1737–42*.

[7] in Italy] in ——. *1737–42*. (In Pope's texts a new paragraph begins with this sentence.)

engaging when you partook of it, and doubly instructive when you talkd of it. I should at least attend you to the Sea-Coast, & cast a last look after the Sails that transported you⌜; if I liked Italy enough to reside in it⌝. But I believe, I should be as uneasy in a Country[1] where I saw Others persecuted, by the Rogues of my own Religion, as where I was so myself by those of yours. And it is not impossible ⌜but⌝ I might run into Turkey in search of Liberty; for who would not rather live a free man among a nation of Slaves, than a Slave among a nation of free men?

In good earnest, if I knew your motions toward Italy (on the supposition you go that course) and your exact time, I verily think I should be once more happy in a sight of you, next Spring. ⌜I'll conclude with a wish, God send you with us, or me with you!⌝

⌜By what I have seen of Mons. Rousseau's Works,[2] I should envy you his conversation. But I am sure I envy him yours.⌝

⌜Mr Addison has not had One Epithalamium[3] that I can hear of, and must e'en be reduced, like a poorer & a better Poet, Spencer, to make his owne.⌝

⌜Mr Congreve is entirely yours, & has writ twice to You. He is not in town, but well. I am in great health, & sit up all night; a just Reward for a Fevor I just come out of, that kept me in bed seven days.⌝

⌜How may I send a large Bundle to you?⌝[4]

⌜I beg you will put dates to your letters—They are not long enough—⌝

[1] But . . . Country] But perhaps I might care as little to stay behind you; and be full as uneasy to live in a country *1737–42*.

[2] Jean-Baptiste Rousseau (1670–1741) was living in exile and in 1716 in Vienna, where he was a protégé of Prince Eugene.

[3] Addison had married the Countess of Warwick on 9 Aug., and Pope is somewhat pleased apparently over public neglect of the event. See *Notes & Queries*, VII. xii (1891), 96.

[4] See i. 407.

1717

This year sees the poet busy with Homer and yet finding time in June to publish, besides the third volume of that translation, his collected *Works*, containing new poems (notably *Eloisa* and the *Unfortunate Lady*), and to bring out for Lintot the miscellany called *Poems on Several Occasions*. Early in the year he had been much abused for his share in *Three Hours after Marriage*. At this time also Dennis published his *Remarks* on Pope's Homer, and Pope retaliated presently with Parnell's *Homer's Battle of the Frogs and Mice with the Remarks of Zoilus*. His letters reflect his increasing preoccupation with titled personages, the Duchess of Hamilton, the Duke of Buckingham, and Dr. Atterbury, Bishop of Rochester, among others. His chief correspondents seem to be Caryll, Lady Mary Wortley Montagu, and the Blount sisters. Late in November Mr. Wortley was recalled from Constantinople. In September Pope made one of his best-recorded 'rambles'—to Hampton Court, to Hallgrove (his sister's), to Oxford, Cockthorpe (Lord Harcourt), Blenheim, and home again. With the Blount sisters, now settled in London, particularly with Teresa, he had some difficulties, not too serious apparently. In the night of 23 October his father suddenly died, and the decease changed Pope's life greatly, since thereafter it became increasingly desirable for him not to be long or far distant from his aged mother.

---

*THE DUKE OF BUCKINGHAM *to* POPE[1] [1717?]

The Pierpont Morgan Library

Reading agen that trifle which nothing but your reccomendation could have made me think worth it, I think I have altered it to be less faulty by changing the word Lust: for however fancy overrules me, it has alwayes been my opinion that no word should be in Poetry, especially in this little kind, which a woman cannot decently pronounce.

The other changes I referr intirely to you, not only as my freind but the best iudg I know, and am | Your very humble servant | Buckingham

Address: For Mr Pope

THE DUKE OF BUCKINGHAM *to* POPE[2] [1717?]

Sotheby Sale of 10 June 1869

EXCERPT

When I saw you I never recollected that I had written two Chorus's already such as they are for . . . Brutus.

[1] In July 1717 Pope published through Lintot a miscellany, *Poems on Several Occasions*, which printed for the first time no less than seventeen 'trifles' by His Grace. Some of these might naturally have used the offensive word that has been expunged. Of course we cannot date the revision, but one assumes that it may be for the miscellany of 1717.

[2] Included simply for the record, this sentence seems to refer to two choruses, 'Written

*THE DUKE OF BUCKINGHAM *to* POPE[1] [1717?]

Hartlebury Castle

Monday morning

Hearing nothing about Wensday I am now ingaged that day, and all this week except Fryday; so if you are like to be then in town, I shall be glad of our meeting with the Doctour, and shall also get the Bishop to meet us there. But use me as freely in your turn, and do not think it worth coming to London on purpose, tho nobody can desire it more than | Your humble servant | Buckingham

Pray bring with you both those imperfect copyes of the Essay,[2] which is indeed at best but too imperfect.

Address: To Mr. Pope the Younger | at his house in Chiswick | near Branford.

LADY MARY WORTLEY MONTAGU *to* POPE

16 *January* 1716/17

1763

Vienna, Jan. 16, O.S. 1717.

I have not time to answer your letter, being in all the hurry of preparing for my journey;[3] but, I think, I ought to bid adieu to my friends with the same solemnity, as if I was going to mount a breach, at least, if I am to believe the information of the people here, who denounce all sort of terrors to me; and, indeed, the weather is at present such, as very few ever set out in. I am threatned, at the same time, with being frozen to death, buried in the snow, and taken by the Tartars, who ravage that part of Hungary I am to pass. 'Tis true, we shall have a considerable *escorte*, so that, possibly, I may be diverted with a new scene, by finding myself in the midst of a battle. How my adventures will conclude, I leave entirely to providence; if comically, you shall hear of them.—Pray be so good as to tell Mr. ——[4] I have received his letter. Make him my *adieus*; if I live, I will answer it. The same compliment to my Lady R—.[5]

. . . in the Year 1708', that Pope included in the miscellany *Poems on Several Occasions*, published in July of this year. Other choruses included were written in 1692, so the Contents tells us. The verses had also been included in Lintot's *Miscellaneous Poems and Translations* (1712). For an additional letter of this group see among the Additional Letters, vol. v, p. 5.

[1] The letter must date after the settlement of the Popes at Chiswick (Apr. 1716) and before the death of the elder Pope in Oct. 1717.

[2] The Duke's *Essay on Poetry* had been frequently reprinted, and since it was reprinted in collections in 1716 and 1717, mention of it does not help date the letter.

[3] It appears from *The London Gazette*, 2 and 5 Feb. 1716/17 that Lady Mary and her husband left Vienna this day, N.S., Jan. 27th.—Elwin. Writing to her sister the Countess of Mar on the 16th O.S., Lady Mary speaks of 'designing tomorrow to begin my journey'. Which of Pope's letters she has just received is not apparent. The mails were slow.

[4] Mr. —— becomes in some editions Mr. Congreve.

[5] Lady R— becomes in some editions Lady Rich.

GAY *to* POPE[1] [? *January* 1717]

1745

Dear Pope,—Too late I see, and confess myself mistaken, in Relation to the Comedy, yet I do not think had I follow'd your Advice, and only introduc'd the *Mummy*, that the Absence of the *Crocodile* had sav'd it. I can't help laughing myself, (though the Vulgar do not consider that it was design'd to look very ridiculous) to think how the poor Monster and Mummy were dash'd at their Reception, and when the Cry was loudest, thought that if the Thing had been wrote by another, I should have deem'd the Town in some Measure mistaken, and as to your Apprehension that this may do us future Injury, do not think it; the Doctor has a more valuable Name than can be hurt by any Thing of this Nature, and yours is doubly safe; I will (if any Shame there be) take it all to myself, as indeed I ought, the Motion being first mine, and never heartily approv'd of by you: As to what your early Enemy said at the Duke of *Dorset*'s and Mr. *Pulteney*'s, you will live to prove him a false Prophet, as you have already a Liar, and a Flatterer, and Poet in Spight of Nature; whether I shall do so or no, you can best tell, for with the Continuance of your dear Friendship and Assistance, never yet withheld from me, I dare promise as much.

I beg of you not to suffer this, or any Thing else, to hurt your Health. As I have publickly said,[2] that I was assisted by two Friends, I shall still continue in the same Story, professing obstinate Silence about Dr. *Arbuthnot* and yourself. I am going Tomorrow to *Hampton Court* for a Week, notwithstanding the Badness of the Weather, where, tho' I am to mix with Quality, I shall see nothing half so engaging as you my dear Friend.

I am (not at all cast down) | Your sincere Friend, | John Gay.

POPE *to* LADY MARY WORTLEY MONTAGU

3 *February* [1716/17]

The Pierpont Morgan Library

Febr. 3d

Madam,—I wish I could write any thing to divert you, but it is impossible in the unquiet state I am put into by your letter.[3] It has

[1] This letter seems to have been written shortly after the publication (21 Jan. 1716/17) of the play *Three Hours after Marriage*. The play was written in collaboration by Gay, Pope, and Arbuthnot, and was presented 16–23 Jan. before full but riotous houses. For a detailed account of its welcome see *Modern Philology*, xxiv (1926), 91–109. How the letter happens to be preserved only in William Ayre's *Life of Pope* (ii. 102) is a mystery, but the letter may well be genuine. It contains little that Pope did not know before it was received.

[2] In the Advertisement, signed by Gay, he remarks, 'I must farther own the Assistance I have receiv'd in this Piece from two of my Friends.' Gay preserved their anonymity, but the public in general knew their identities.

[3] It is doubtful if this letter answers that of Lady Mary written from Vienna 16 Jan. Probably it is an answer to an earlier lost letter. The remark 'I hear you have left Vienna'

grievously afflicted me, without affectation; and I think you would hardly have writ it in so strong terms, had you known to what a degree I feel the loss of those I value: (It is only decency that hinders me from saying, of her I value). From this instant you are doubly dead to me, and all the Vexation & concern I endured at your parting from England, was nothing to what I suffer the moment I hear you have left Vienna. Till now, I had some small Hopes in God, and in fortune; I waited for accidents, and had at least the faint comfort of a wish, when I thought of you. I am now—I can't tell what—I won't tell what, for it would grieve you—This letter is a piece of madness, that throws me after you in a distracted manner. I don't know which way to write, which way to send it, or if ever it will reach your hands. If it does, what can you inferr from it, but what I am half afraid, & half willing, you should know; how very much I was yours, how unfortunately well I knew you, and with what a miserable constancy I shall ever remember you?

If this falls into any other hands, It will say nothing I shall be ashamed to own, when either Distance, or Death (for ought I can tell) shall have removed you for ever from the scandal of so mean an admirer.

What you say of your illness frightens me with a prospect I can never so much as dream of without horrour. Tho I am never to see you again, may you live to please Other eyes, and improve other minds than mine; may you appear to distant Worlds like a Sun that is sunk out of the sight of our Hemisphere, to gladden the other. It is no figure of speech when I tell you, that those Mountains of Snow, and Woods layd in ashes you describe, are what I could wish to traverse with you. I find I flatterd myself, when I thought Italy had pleasures that could allure me to have met you there; I see it was only the view of meeting you that made that Country appear charming to me; and I now envy the deserts and devastations of Hungary, more than any parts of the polite world. It is seriously true, that I have not, since your last letter, the least inclination to see Italy; tho' before I receivd it, I long'd for your Summons thither—But it is foolish to tell you this—did I say, foolish? it is a thousand times worse, it is in vain!——

You touch me very sensibly, in saying you think so well of my *friendship*: In that, you do me too much *honour*—Would to god you would (even at this distance) allow me to correct this period, and change these phrases according to the real truth of my heart—I am foolish again, and methinks I am imitating in my ravings the dreams

might well refer to the announcement of her departure printed in the *Gazette* on 2 Feb. In the letter of 16 Jan. Lady Mary does not mention illness, and there is no description of 'woods layd in ashes'. This letter of 3 Feb. Lady Mary did not receive until the middle of June (see Lady Mary to Pope, 17 June 1717).

of Spleenatic Enthusiasts and Solitaires, who fall in love with Saints, and fancy themselves in the favour of Angels, and Spirits, whom they can never see, or touch. I hope indeed that you, like one of those better beings, have a Benevolence towards me; and I (on my part) really look up to you with zeal and fervour; not without some faint Expectation of meeting hereafter, which is something betwixt Piety and madness.

Madam, I beg you to be so just to my impatience and anxiety for your sake, as to give me the first notice possible of your health, and progress. This letter takes its chance from Mr Stanhope's office, tho' you direct me to the Merchants Ships bound for Constantinople. I could not stay so long as till one of those sets out. Whether you receive letters from me or not, you may depend upon my having writ, as the consequence of my thinking so often and so warmly of you. May Providence overshadow you, and that virtue and Spirit which exposes you to dangers, protect you from them! I am the most earnest of your Well-wishers, and I was going to say your most faithful Servant, but am angry at the weakness of all the terms I can use to express myself Yours.

LADY MARY WORTLEY MONTAGU *to* POPE[1]

12 *February* 1716/17

1763

Belgrade, Feb. 12, O.S. 1717.

I did verily intend to write you a long letter from Peterwaradin, where I expected to stay three or four days, but the Bassa here was in such haste to see us, that he dispatched the courier back (which Mr. W— had sent to know the time he would send the convoy to meet us) without suffering him to pull off his boots. My letters were not thought important enough to stop our journey, and we left Peterwaradin the next day, being waited on by the chief officers of the garrison, and a considerable convoy of Germans and Rascians. The Emperor has several regiments of these people; but, to say the truth, they are rather plunderers than soldiers; having no pay, and being obliged to furnish their own arms and horses; they rather look like vagabond gypsies, or stout beggars, than regular troops. I cannot forbear speaking a word of this race of creatures, who are very numerous all over Hungary. They have a patriarch of their own at Grand Cairo, and are really of the Greek church, but their extreme ignorance gives their priests occasion to impose several new notions upon them. These fellows letting their hair and beard grow inviolate, make exactly the figure of the Indian Bramins. They are heirs-general to all the money

[1] This is one of Lady Mary's best letters. She had evidently written to Pope from Peterwaradin (see his letter to her [June 1717]), but not a *long* letter.

of the laiety; for which, in return, they give them formal passports signed and sealed for Heaven; and the wives and children only inherit the house and cattle. In most other points they follow the Greek church.—This little digression has interrupted my telling you we passed over the fields of *Carlowitz*, where the last great victory was obtained by Prince Eugene over the Turks. The marks of that glorious bloody day are yet recent, the field being yet strewed with the skulls and carcasses of unburied men, horses and camels. I could not look, without horror, on such numbers of mangled human bodies, nor without reflecting on the injustice of war, that makes murther, not only necessary, but meritorious. Nothing seems to be a plainer proof of the *irrationality* of mankind (whatever fine claims we pretend to reason) than the rage with which they contest for a small spot of ground, when such vast parts of fruitful earth lie quite uninhabited. 'Tis true, custom has now made it unavoidable; but can there be a greater demonstration of want of reason, than a custom being firmly established, so plainly contrary to the interest of man in general? I am a good deal inclined to believe Mr. *Hobbs*, that the *state of nature*, is a *state of war*; but thence I conclude human nature not rational, if the word reason means common sense, as I suppose it does. I have a great many admirable arguments to support this reflexion; I won't however trouble you with them, but return, in a plain stile, to the history of my travels.

We were met at Betsko (a village in the midway between Belgrade and Peterwaradin) by an Aga of the Janizaries, with a body of Turks, exceeding the Germans by one hundred men, though the Bassa had engaged to send exactly the same number. You may judge by this of their fears. I am really persuaded, that they hardly thought the odds of one hundred men set them even with the Germans; however, I was very uneasy till they were parted, fearing some quarrel might arise notwithstanding the *parole* given. We came late to Belgrade, the deep snows making the ascent to it very difficult. It seems a strong city, fortified, on the east side, by the Danube; and on the south, by the river *Save*, and was formerly the barrier of Hungary. It was first taken by Solyman the Magnificent; and since, by the Emperor's forces, led by the Elector of Bavaria. The Emperor held it only two years, it being retaken by the Grand Vizier. It is now fortified with the utmost care and skill the Turks are capable of, and strengthened by a very numerous garrison, of their bravest Janizaries, commanded by a Bassa *Seraskier* (*i.e.* General;) though this last expression is not very just; for to say truth, the Seraskier is commanded by the Janizaries. These troops have an absolute authority here, and their conduct carries much more the aspect of rebellion, than the appearance of subordination. You may judge of this by the following story, which at the same time, will give you an idea of the *admirable* intelligence of the Governor of Peterwaradin, though so few hours distant. We were told by him at Peterwaradin, that the garrison and inhabitants of Belgrade were so weary of the war, they had killed their Bassa about two months ago, in a mutiny, because he had suffered himself to be prevailed upon, by a bribe of five purses (five hundred pound sterling) to give permission to the Tartars to ravage the German frontiers. We were very well pleased to hear of such favourable dispositions in the people; but when we came hither, we found the governor had been ill informed, and the real truth of the story to be this. The late Bassa fell under the displeasure of his soldiers, for no other reason, but restraining their incursions on the Germans. They took it into their heads from that mildness, that he had intelligence with the enemy, and sent such information to the Grand Signior at Adrianople; but, redress not coming quick enough from thence, they assembled themselves in a tumultuous manner, and by force dragged their Bassa before the Cadi and Mufti, and there demanded justice in a mutinous way; one crying out, Why he protected the Infidels? Another, Why he squeezed them of their money? The Bassa, easily guessing their purpose, calmly replied to them, that they asked him too many questions, and that he had but one life, which must answer for all. They then immediately fell upon him with their scymitars, (without waiting the sentence of their heads of the law) and in a few moments cut him in pieces. The present Bassa has not dared to punish the murder; on the contrary, he affected to applaud the actors of it, as brave fellows, that knew how to do themselves justice. He takes all pretences of throwing money amongst the garrison, and suffers them to make little excursions into Hungary, where they burn some poor Rascian houses.

You may imagine, I cannot be very easy in a town which is really under the government of an insolent soldiery.—We expected to be immediately dismissed, after a night's lodging here; but the Bassa detains us till he receives orders from Adrianople, which may, possibly, be a month a coming. In the mean time, we are lodged in one of the best houses, belonging to a very considerable man amongst them, and have a whole chamber of Janizaries to guard us. My only diversion is the conversation of our host *Achmet-beg*, a title something like that of Count in Germany. His father was a great Bassa, and he has been educated in the most polite Eastern learning, being perfectly skilled in the Arabic and Persian languages, and an extraordinary scribe, which they call *Effendi.* This accomplishment makes way to the greatest preferments; but he has had the good sense to prefer an easy, quiet secure life, to all the dangerous honours of the Porte. He sups with us every night, and drinks wine very freely. You cannot imagine how much he is delighted with the liberty of conversing with me. He has explained to me many pieces of Arabian poetry, which, I observe, are in numbers, not unlike ours, generally of an alternate verse, and of a very musical sound. Their expressions of love are very passionate and lively. I am so much pleased with them, I really believe I should learn to read Arabic, if I was to stay here a few months. He has a very good library of their books of all kinds; and, as he tells me, spends the greatest part of his life there. I pass for a great scholar with him, by relating to him some of the Persian tales, which I find are genuine.[1] At first, he believed I understood Persian. I have frequent disputes with him, concerning the difference of our customs, particularly the confinement of women. He assures me, there is nothing at all in it; only, says he, we have the advantage, that when our wives cheat us, no body knows it. He has wit, and is more polite than many Christian men of quality. I am very much entertained with him.—He has had the curiosity to make one of our servants set him an alphabet of our letters, and can already write a good roman hand. But these amusements do not hinder my wishing heartily to be out of this place; though the weather is colder than I believe it ever was, any where, but in Greenland.—We have a very large stove constantly kept hot, and yet the windows of the room are frozen on the inside.—God knows when I may have an opportunity of sending this letter; but I have written it, for the discharge of my own conscience; and you cannot now reproach me, that one of yours makes ten of mine. Adieu.

*POPE *to* THOMAS DANCASTLE 18 *February* [1716/17]

The Huntington Library

Feb. 18th

I had not deferrd paying you *a thousand thanks* (which tho' it makes a great sound, generally signifies no great matter) but for a very severe Fit of Illness that confind me a fortnight. Your Transcription[2] arrived very seasonably, just as I had done the rest, and is now in a fair way of being blotted. I hope you are arisen from the Gout with which I hear you were laid up, & that your Brother is also well. The Memory of our old neighbors yet lives in me; I often give a Range to my Imagination, & goe a strolling with one or other of you, up & down Binfield Wood, or over Bagshot Heath. I wish you all health, not you only, but your Horse, your Dog Lilly, &c. May your gun never fail, and your aim never miss. May your Pouch come swagging home, laden with woodcocks, and may those woodcocks be so fatt & good as to please Mr Philips.[3]

[1] The Persian tales appeared first in Europe as a translation by Monsieur Petit de la Croix; and what are called 'The Arabian Nights', in a similar manner, by Monsieur Galland.—Dallaway, 1803.

[2] Of part of vol. iii of the *Iliad.*

[3] Dancastle's chaplain.

I can only add the old, impertinent Repetition, that I am truly & constantly | Dear Sir | Yours. | A. Pope

Address: To | Mr Thomas Dancastle, at | Binfield near Ockingham, | Berks. Bagshot Bag.
Postmark: 18/FE
Endorsement (modern): from A. Pope—

POPE *to* BROOME[1] [1717?]

Elwin–Courthope, viii. 38

I desire, for fear of mistakes, that you will cause the space for the initial letter to the Dedication to the Rape of the Lock to be made of the size of those in Trapp's Prælectiones. Only a small ornament at the top of that leaf, not so large as four lines breadth. The rest as I told you before.

I hope they will not neglect to add at the bottom of the page in the Essay on Criticism, where are the lines "Such was the Muse whose rules," &c., a note thus: "Essay on Poetry, by the present Duke of Buckingham," and to print the line "Nature's chief masterpiece" in italic. Be pleased also to let the second verse of the Rape of the Lock be thus,

What mighty contests rise from trivial things.

Excuse all this trouble from an impertinent brother author who has not a moment's time from the company he is engaged in, but just to tell you I am yours.

Pray put the enclosed immediately into the penny post.

POPE *to* HIS FATHER[2] [*March* 1717]

Homer MSS. Add. 4807

I have recoverd t[he] ten guineas at Sir Rich Hoare['s].[3] Dr Arbuthnot says, since my Moth[er] is better, to cure the bitterness s[he] com-

[1] In Mar. 1717 Lintot was advertising (e.g. *Daily Courant*, 20 Mar. 1717) that 'in a few days' Mr. Pope's *Works* would be published. It is this optimism that places the present letter early in the year. The letter is printed as Elwin gave it. Clearly only the last two sentences are addressed to Broome. The rest is the enclosure that he is to forward to the printer.

[2] The date is chiefly based on the assumption that it is South Sea stock that Pope has sold. In Dec. 1716 he spoke to Martha Blount about investing £500 in such stock at 103. The first half of Mar. 1717 saw the stock declining below 100. After the 1st of April it never in 1717 fell below 101. Pope might have sold on Saturday 16 Mar. at 100, and on Monday the 18th it was back at 101$\frac{5}{8}$. The neighbouring letters in the Homer MSS. all come from the second half of 1717; but the stock was notably stronger in those months.

[3] Sir Richard Hoare, banker and Lord Mayor of London, died in Jan. 1718.

plains of she shoud chaw Rhub[arb] root about half a dram each morn-[ing] for 2 or 3 days, instead of a [vomit.] But if she will venture a vomit, Carduus Tea[1] can do no harm even if [she] shoud not vomit.

I have sold 500ll at 100ll which [is bad] luck, since It might have been so[ld yes-]terday & to day at 101 & a ha[lf.] I hope soon to see you, but desire s[oon] an account how my Mother does. I [am] hers & Your most obedient & affectionate | Son. | A. [Pope.]

Postmark: PENY POST PAYD T/TU

POPE *to* PARNELL[2] [1717]

1770 (Goldsmith, *Life of Parnell*)

I write to you with the same warmth, the same zeal of good will and friendship with which I used to converse with you two years ago, and can't think myself absent, when I feel you so much at my heart; the picture of you, which Jervas brought me over, is infinitely less lively a representation, than that I carry about with me, and which rises to my mind whenever I think of you; I have many an agreeable reverie, through those woods and downs, where we once rambled together; my head is sometimes at the Bath, and sometimes at Letcomb, where the Dean makes a great part of my imaginary entertainment, this being the cheapest way of treating me; I hope he will not be displeased, at this manner of paying my respects to him, instead of following my friend Jarvas's example, which to say the truth, I have as much inclination to do as I want ability. I have been ever since December last in greater variety of business than any such men as you (that is, divines and philosophers,) can possibly imagine a reasonable creature capable of. Gay's play, among the rest, has cost much time and long suffering, to stem a tide of malice and party, that certain authors have raised against it; the best revenge upon such fellows, is now in my hands, I mean your *Zoilus*, which really transcends the expectation I had conceived of it. I have put it into the press, beginning with the poem *Batrachom:* for you seem by the first paragraph of the dedication to it, to design to prefix the name of some particular person.[3] I beg therefore to know for whom you intend it, that the publication may

[1] Maidservants in Shakespeare's time (*Much Ado*, III. iv. 73) thought 'distilled Carduus Benedictus' was 'the only thing for a qualm'.

[2] This letter is dated vaguely by the mention of the 'tide of malice and party' evoked by Gay's play (*Three Hours*), which puts the letter later than Jan., and by the fact that Parnell's *Batrachomuomachia* has been 'put into the press'. Parnell's pamphlet was published in May. Gay received the copy money (£16. 2*s.* 6*d.*) on 4 May from Lintot (Nichols, *Lit. Anec.* viii. 296). Since Pope expected to hear from Parnell again before publication, the letter should fall in March or April.

[3] *The Battle of the Frogs and Mice*, as the work was called, has no dedication, but the first paragraph of the Preface bears out Pope's notion that it was addressed to a particular person—to a presumptive translator.

not be delayed on this account, and this as soon as is possible. Inform me also upon what terms I am to deal with the bookseller, and whether you design the copy-money for Gay, as you formerly talk'd, what number of books you would have yourself, &c. I scarce see any thing to be altered in this whole piece; in the poems you sent I will take the liberty you allow me; the story of Pandora, and the Eclogue upon Health, are two of the most beautiful things I ever read. I don't say this to the prejudice of the rest, but as I have read these oftener. Let me know how far my commission is to extend, and be confident of my punctual performance of whatever you enjoin. I must add a paragraph on this occasion, in regard to Mr. Ward,[1] whose verses have been a great pleasure to me; I will contrive they shall be so to the world, whenever I can find a proper opportunity of publishing them.

I shall very soon print an entire collection of my own madrigals, which I look upon as making my last will and testament, since in it I shall give all I ever intend to give, (which I'll beg your's and the Dean's acceptance of) you must look on me no more a poet, but a plain commoner, who lives upon his own, and fears and flatters no man. I hope before I die to discharge the debt I owe to Homer, and get upon the whole just fame enough to serve for an annuity for my own time, though I leave nothing to posterity.

I beg our correspondence may be more frequent than it has been of late. I am sure my esteem and love for you never more deserved it from you, or more prompted it from you. I desired our friend Jervas, (in the greatest hurry of my business) to say a great deal in my name, both to yourself and the Dean, and must once more repeat the assurances to you both, of an unchangeing friendship and unalterable esteem. I am, dear Sir, most entirely, | Your affectionate, | Faithful, obliged friend and servant, | A. Pope.

LADY MARY WORTLEY MONTAGU *to* POPE[2]

1 *April* [1717]

1763

Adrianople, April 1. O.S.

I dare say you expect, at least, something very new in this letter, after I have gone a journey, not undertaken, by any Christian, for some hundred years. The most remarkable accident that happened to me, was my being very near overturned into the Hebrus; and, if I had much regard for the glories that one's name enjoys after death, I should certainly be sorry for having missed the romantic conclusion of

[1] A number of poems by the Rev. James Ward are printed in *Poems on Several Occasions*, 'Pope's Own Miscellany' as Norman Ault called it, published by Pope in July 1717.

[2] On 1 Apr. 1717, if one may believe the printed datings, Lady Mary wrote thirteen letters, which fill ninety small octavo pages of print.

swimming down the same river in which the musical head of *Orpheus* repeated verses, so many ages since:

> Caput a cervice revulsum,
> Gurgite cum medio, portans Oeagrius Hebrus
> Volveret, Euridicen vox ipsa, et frigida lingua
> Ah! miseram Euridicen! anima fugiente vocabat,
> Euridicen toto referebant flumine ripæ.[1]

Who knows but some of your bright wits, might have found it a subject affording many poetical turns, and have told the world, in an heroic Elegy, that,

> As equal were our souls, so equal were our fates.

I despair of ever hearing so many fine things said of me, as so extraordinary a death would have given occasion for.

I am at this present moment writing in a house situated on the banks of the Hebrus, which runs under my chamber window. My garden is full of tall cypress trees, upon the branches of which, several couple of true turtles are saying soft things to one another from morning till night. How naturally do *boughs* and *vows* come into my mind, at this minute? And must not you confess, to my praise, that 'tis more than an ordinary discretion, that can resist the wicked suggestions of poetry, in a place where truth, for once, furnishes all the ideas of pastoral. The summer is already far advanced, in this part of the world; and for some miles round Adrianople, the whole ground is laid out in gardens, and the banks of the rivers are set with rows of fruit trees, under which all the most considerable Turks divert themselves every evening, not with walking, that is not one of their pleasures; but a set party of them choose out a green spot, where the shade is very thick, and there they spread a carpet, on which they sit drinking their coffee, and are generally attended by some slave with a fine voice, or that plays on some instrument. Every twenty paces you may see one of these little companies, listening to the dashing of the river; and this taste is so universal, that the very gardeners are not without it. I have often seen them and their children sitting on the banks of the river, and playing on a rural instrument, perfectly answering the description of the ancient *Fistula*, being composed of unequal reeds, with a simple but agreeable softness in the sound.

Mr. *Addison* might here make the experiment he speaks of in his travels;[2] there not being one instrument of music among the Greek or Roman Statues, that is not to be found in the hands of the people of this country. The young lads generally divert themselves with making garlands for their favourite lambs, which I have often seen

[1] Virgil, *Georgics*, iv. 523–7.

[2] Addison's 'Remarks on Italy' (s.v. Rome).

painted and adorned with flowers, lying at their feet, while they sung or played. It is not that they ever read Romances. But these are the ancient amusements here, and as natural to them as cudgel-playing and foot-ball to our British swains; the softness and warmth of the climate forbidding all rough exercises, which were never so much as heard of amongst them, and naturally inspiring a laziness and aversion to labour, which the great plenty indulges. These gardeners are the only happy race of country people in Turkey. They furnish all the city with fruits and herbs, and seem to live very easily. They are most of them Greeks, and have little houses in the midst of their gardens, where their wives and daughters take a liberty, not permitted in the town, I mean to go unveiled. These wenches are very neat and handsome, and pass their time at their looms under the shade of the trees.

I no longer look upon *Theocritus* as a romantic writer; he has only given a plain image of the way of life amongst the peasants of his country; who, before oppression had reduced them to want, were, I suppose, all employed as the better sort of them are now. I don't doubt, had he been born a Briton, but his *Idylliums* had been filled with descriptions of thrashing and churning, both which are unknown here, the corn being all trod out by oxen; and butter (I speak it with sorrow) unheard of.

I read over your *Homer* here, with an infinite pleasure, and find several little passages explained, that I did not before entirely comprehend the beauty of: Many of the customs, and much of the dress then in fashion, being yet retained. I don't wonder to find more remains here, of an age so distant, than is to be found in any other country, the Turks not taking that pains to introduce their own manners, as has been generally practised by other nations, that imagine themselves more polite. It would be too tedious to you to point out all the passages that relate to present customs. But I can assure you, that the Princesses and great ladies pass their time at their looms, embroidering veils and robes, surrounded by their maids, which are always very numerous, in the same manner as we find *Andromache* and *Helen* described. The description of the belt of *Menelaus* exactly resembles those that are now worn by the great men, fastened before with broad golden clasps, and embroidered round with rich work. The snowy veil, that *Helen* throws over her face, is still fashionable; and I never see half a dozen of old Bashaws (as I do very often) with their reverend beards, sitting basking in the sun, but I recollect good King *Priam* and his counsellors. Their manner of dancing is certainly the same that *Diana* is *sung* to have danced on the banks of *Eurotas*. The great lady still leads the dance, and is followed by a troop of young girls, who imitate her steps, and, if she sings, make up the chorus. The tunes are extremely gay and lively, yet with something in them wonderfully soft. The steps are varied according to the pleasure of her that leads the dance, but always in exact time, and infinitely more agreeable than any of our dances, at least in my opinion. I sometimes make one in the train, but am not skilful enough to lead; these are the Grecian dances, the Turkish being very different.

I should have told you, in the first place, that the Eastern manners give a great light into many Scripture-passages, that appear odd to us, their phrases being commonly what we should call Scripture language. The vulgar Turk is very different from what is spoke at court, or amongst the people of figure; who always mix so much Arabic and Persian in their discourse, that it may very well be called another language. And 'tis as ridiculous to make use of the expressions commonly used, in speaking to a great man or lady, as it would be to speak broad Yorkshire, or Somersetshire, in the drawing room. Besides this distinction, they have what they call, the *sublime*, that is, a stile proper for poetry, and which is the exact Scripture stile. I believe you would be pleased to see a genuine example of this; and I am very glad I have it in my power to satisfy your curiosity, by sending you a faithful copy of the verses that *Ibrahim Bassa*, the reigning favourite, has made for the young Princess, his contracted wife, whom he is not yet permitted to visit without witnesses, though she is gone home to his house. He is a man of wit and learning; and whether or no he is capable of writing good verse, you may be sure that, on such an occasion, he would not want the assistance of the best poets in the Empire. Thus the verses may be looked upon as a sample of their finest poetry, and I don't doubt you'll be of my mind, that it is most wonderfully resembling the *Song of Solomon*, which also was addressed to a Royal Bride.

TURKISH VERSES addressed to the *Sultana*, eldest daughter of SULTAN ACHMET III.

STANZA I.

Ver. 1. The Nightingale now wanders in the vines;
Her passion is to seek roses.

2. I went down to admire the beauty of the vines;
The sweetness of your charms has ravished my soul.

3. Your eyes are black and lovely
But wild and disdainful as those of a stag;

STANZA II.

1. The wished possession is delayed from day to day,
The cruel Sultan ACHMET will not permit me
To see those cheeks, more vermillion than roses.

2. I dare not snatch one of your kisses,
The sweetness of your charms has ravish'd my soul.

3. Your eyes are black and lovely,
But wild and disdainful as those of a stag.

STANZA III.

1. The wretched IBRAHIM sighs in these verses,
One dart from your eyes has pierc'd thro' my heart.

2. Ah! when will the hour of possession arrive?
Must I yet wait a long time?
The sweetness of your charms has ravish'd my soul.

3. Ah! SULTANA! stag-ey'd—an angel amongst angels!
I desire,—*and*, my desire remains unsatisfied.
Can you take delight to prey upon my heart?

STANZA IV.

1. My cries pierce the heavens!
My eyes are without sleep!
Turn to me, SULTANA—let me gaze on thy beauty.

2. Adieu—I go down to the grave.
If you call me—— I return.
My heart is—hot as sulphur;—sigh and it will flame.

3. Crown of my life, fair light of my eyes!
My SULTANA! my Princess!
I rub my face against the earth;—I am drown'd in scalding tears—I rave!
Have you no compassion? will you not turn to look upon me.

I have taken abundance of pains to get these verses in a literal translation; and if you were acquainted with my interpreters, I might spare myself the trouble of assuring you, that they have received no poetical touches from their hands. In my opinion, (allowing for the inevitable faults of a prose translation into a language so very different) there is a good deal of beauty in them. The epithet of *stag-ey'd* (though the sound is not very agreeable in English) pleases me extremely; and I think it a very lively image of the fire and indifference in his mistresses eyes—Monsieur *Boileau* has very justly observed, that we are never to judge of the elevation of an expression in an antient author, by the sound it carries with us; since it may be extremely fine with them, when, at the same time, it appears low or uncouth to us. You are so well acquainted with *Homer*, you cannot but have observed the same thing, and you must have the same indulgence for all oriental poetry. The repetitions at the end of the two first Stanza's are meant for a sort of *Chorus*, and are agreeable to the antient manner of writing. The music of the verses apparently changes in the third Stanza, where the burden is altered; and I think he very artfully seems more passionate at the conclusion, as 'tis natural for people to warm themselves by their own discourse, especially on a subject in which one is deeply concerned; 'tis certainly far more touching, than our modern custom of concluding a song of passion, with a turn which is inconsistent with it. The first verse is a description of the season of the year; all the country now being full of Nightingales, whose amours with roses, is an Arabian fable, as well known here, as any part of *Ovid* amongst us, and is much the same as if an English poem should begin, by saying,—'*Now Philomela sings.*' Or what if I turned the whole into the stile of English poetry, to see how it would look?

STANZA I.

Now Philomel renews her tender strain,
  Indulging all the night her pleasing pain;

I sought the groves to hear the wanton sing,
  There saw a face more beauteous than the spring.

Your large stag-eyes where thousand glories play,
As bright, as lively, but as wild as they.

STANZA II.

In vain I'm promis'd such a heavenly prize.
Ah, cruel Sultan! who delay'st my joys!

While piercing charms transfix my amorous heart,
I dare not snatch one kiss, to ease the smart.
Those eyes like, &c.

STANZA III.

Your wretched lover in these lines complains;
From those dear beauties rise his killing pains.

When will the hour of wish'd-for bliss arrive?
Must I wait longer?—Can I wait and live?

Ah! bright Sultana! Maid divinely fair!
Can you, unpitying, see the pains I bear?

STANZA IV.

The Heavens relenting hear my piercing cries,
I loath the light, and sleep forsakes my eyes,
Turn thee, Sultana, ere thy lover dies;

Sinking to earth, I sigh the last adieu,
Call me, my Goddess, and my life renew.

My Queen! my angel! my fond heart's desire!
I rave—my bosom burns with heavenly fire!
Pity that passion which thy charms inspire.

I have taken the liberty in the second verse, of following what I suppose the true sense of the author, though not literally expressed. By his saying *he went down to admire the beauty of the Vines, and her charms ravished his soul*; I understand a poetical fiction, of having first seen her in a garden, where he was admiring the beauty of the spring. But I could not forbear retaining the comparison of her eyes with those of a stag, though perhaps the novelty of it may give it a burlesque sound in our language. I cannot determine, upon the whole, how well I have succeeded in the translation, neither do I think our English proper to express such violence of passion, which is very seldom felt amongst us. We want, also, those compound words which are very frequent and strong in the Turkish language.

You see I am pretty far gone in Oriental learning, and to say truth, I study very hard. I wish my studies may give me an occasion of entertaining your curiosity, which will be the utmost advantage hoped for from them, by | Yours, &c:

POPE *to* FENTON — 5 *May* 1717

[See 5 May [1720].]

POPE *to* HIS FATHER[1] — [1717]

Homer MSS. Add. 4807

This is to beg you would enquire of Mrs Clark if she will board a family for the Summer in her house, & at what rate? Be pleasd also to ask at the house over against ours, Mr Gascoins Sister, if she will board, &c & how many Beds there are to be lett there, & the lowest rate? And send word by the first post you can to me. I am very well, and beg you both to believe me most affectionatly | Your most dutifull | & obedient Son, | A. Pope.

[1] On this letter was translated some of the latter part of *Iliad* xiii in the summer of 1717; hence one assumes that the summer of 1717 was the period for which Pope's friends might have lodged with Mr. Gascoign's sister.

*POPE *to* JOHN DANCASTLE 30 *May* 1717

The Huntington Library

May the 30, 1717

Not only the many various businesses & amusements, serious and comical, which have employd me of late; but also the Expectation of seeing you on this side the world, have hindred my writing to you thus long. I am very sure myself, and therefore think you do not doubt, how truly and mindfully I preserve that friendship which you have allowed me to profess to you. I encounterd Father Philips[1] the other day, on the high way of Salvation of Souls, and I believe suspended a Confession, or reprieved a Penance, during the time we drank a Dish of Coffee. He gave me some view of your coming to London pretty soon; however I resolvd no longer to defer the pleasure of writing, as I hope it will bring me at least that of hearing from you.

My Father just now told me of a thing that may give this letter the air of a letter of business. For I am sensible, few people that have any thing to do in the Country, care much for any other sort of letters. Dr Irish writ to him about buying the Palfrey that has lived upon you so long. I am ashamd of his Impudence (for I would not call it my own) in staying as unmercifully at his friend's charges, as if he had been a younger Brother. I hope you always use him as your own, but if you would now put it beyond dispute that he is not so, I desire you'll drive a bargain for him with Mr Irish. Sell him for what you think fitting, but take the money, which else I shall not know how to come at, and I hate to quarrel with a Physician—My journey to Mr Caryl's is become so uncertain in point of time, that I cannot say when I could hope to call at Binfield in order to it. But when I have had the pleasure of seeing you at Chiswick (where I shall now be pretty constantly) It will go hard with me if I don't either take a ramble with you, or go home with you.

I shall send you by the Ockingham Coach in about a week, a small present of all I am worth, my whole Works, better printed than written: which I desire you to lay up somewhere with Nicholas de Lyra, and others my dead and forgotten Brethren.

I beg my faithful Service to your Brother, & to Mr Angels family. You will not forget my kind love to all at Hall-grove. I am with all sincerity | Dear Sir | Your most obliged & affec-|tionate humble Servant | A. Pope:

My father & mother are heartily yours.

Address: To Mr Jno Dancastle | in | Binfeild, | neer | Ockingham
Endorsed [in a much later hand]: from A. Pope— | 1717 | the Superscription [i.e. address] | is probably his Father's—
Added [on the flap of the outside in a contemporary hand]: Dear Sir [and in another part:] for Mr Pope | I am yours for | ever and for aye a

[1] Mentioned as a gourmet in Pope to Dancastle, 18 Feb. 1717.

JOHN DANCASTLE *to* POPE[1] [*Summer of* 1717]

Homer MSS. Add. 4807

Sun[day in heast]

I had writ to you before to have a[cquain]ted you that Mr Raquett haveing told me of an oppor[tunity] he had of selling your Palfrey, accordingly I let him have him who sold him for 5 guineas I told him that was the lowest price he was to sell him for) Mr Raquett acquainted me of the selling of him as likewise that he had sent you word of it and told me that you had promised to be a[t] his house in 3 or 4 days which rejoiced me very much[.] I was in hopes every day of seeing you I beg of you tho you have delay'd your comeing you will make us so happy at last. I beg the favour of your Father Mr Pope to please to come with you I will make him my head Gardener and that he will think a very great preferment. I wish Mrs Pope would come too, then we should be entirely happy I wish her conveniency may permit. I would write much more to you but haveing this day more company then Usualy I will only say which I can with much truth that I am sincerely | Your very affectionate | oblig'd humble servant | Jo: Dancastle.

My Brother desiers me to give his humble service to you and Mr Pope and your good Mother.

G. MADDISON *to* POPE[2] [*June* 1717?]

Homer MSS. Add. 4808

Sir,—My Lady Dutchess being dru*nk at this present* &[3] not able to write her self has c*ommanded me to* acquaint you that there is to b*e musick on the* water on Thursday next; *th*erefore desi*res You* to be that

[1] On the back of this letter Pope translated a part of *Iliad* XIV, almost certainly during the summer of 1717, before he started his rambles of September. Dancastle may have written the letter any time after 30 May 1717, when Pope advised selling the palfrey to Dr. Irish, and before Pope's visit to Binfield in September. On 18 Oct. Pope wrote to Dancastle that he had completed Book XV. More precise dating is impossible. Pope's visit to the Racketts in September would hardly fit a promise to be at Hallgrove 'three or four days' after the Sunday when (8 Sept.) he was at Staines. This letter evidently records a promised arrival that was deferred.

When printed in the *Additions* to Pope's *Works* in 1776, the edge of the leaf evidently was less worn, and we have the superscription reading 'Sunday in heast'.

[2] From its place in the Homer MSS. as part of Book XXII one might place this letter as late as 1718 or 1719; but in Oct. 1717 Pope wrote to Her Grace of Hamilton 'the writer drunk', and one assumes that his drunkenness is a jocose reply to hers, which he had learned of earlier. For a few days in early June Pope was at Jervas's to oversee the publication of the third volume of Homer and also of his *Works*. If the Duchess caught him on short notice, it was probably then (4 June was Tuesday). Handel's famous Water Music was first performed on 17 July 1717, and one would like to imagine Pope as listening to it in the Hamilton barge: but that date seems improbable for him.

[3] Parts of the letter printed in italic type are overwritten in the original, but are still legible.

evening at her house in Bond *Street* by Six a Clock at furthest & Her [G]*race wi*ll call of you *ther*e to take you to her *barge* which she has order'd to be ready at *that time* at white Hall with Provisions & sha*ll land* you on the wish'd for Shoare. I am | S[ir] | Your Most hu*mble Servant* | G. Ma*ddison*

East Acton | Tuesday night

[In another hand:] out of the abundance *of the heart* the mouth speaketh *Pope is the Word* a disappointment is [not to] be *endured.*

Address: To | Alexr Pope Esqr at Mr | Jarvis's House in Cleaveland | Court

POPE *to* LADY MARY WORTLEY MONTAGU

[*June* 1717]

The Pierpont Morgan Library

Lon[don][1]

Madam,—If to live in the memory of others have any thing desireable in it, 'tis what you possess with regard to me, in the highest sense of the words. There is not a day in which your Figure does not appear before me, your Conversations return to my thought, and every Scene, place, or occasion where I have enjoyd them are as livelily painted, as an Imagination equally warm & tender can be capable to represent them. Yet how little accrues to You from all this, when not only my wishes, but the very expressions of them, can hardly ever arrive to be known to you? I can't tell whether you have seen half the letters I have writ, but if you had, I have not said in 'em half of what I desired to say; & you can have seen but a faint slight, timorous Eschantillon of what my Spirit suggests, & my hand follows slowly, & imperfectly, indeed unjustly, because discreetly & reservedly. When you told me there was no way left for our correspondence but by the Merchant-Ships, I watchd ever since for any that set out, & this is the first I yet could learn of. I owe the knowledge of it to Mr Congreve, (whose Letters, with my Lady Rich's accompany this) However I was impatient enough to venture two from Mr Methuen's office;[2] if they have miscarryd, you have lost nothing but such words, & wishes, as I repeat every day in your memory, and for your welfare. I have had thoughts of causing what I write for the future to be transcribed, & to send copies by more ways than one, that one at least might have a chance to reach You. The letters themselves would be artless & natural enough to prove there could be no vanity in this practise, & to show it proceeded from the belief of their being welcome to you, not as they came from me, but from England. My Eye-sight is grown so bad, that I have left off all correspondence except with

[1] Half of Pope's superscribed 'London' is torn away, and the whole word is written below the extant half in a modern hand. [2] Methuen in April ceased to be Secretary of State.

yourself: in which methinks I am like those people who abandon and abstract themselves from all that are about them, (with whom they might have business and intercourse) to employ their addresses only to Invisible & distant Beings, whose good offices and favours cannot reach 'em in a long time, if at all. If I hear from you, I look upon it as little less than a miracle, or extraordinary Visitation from another world; Tis a sort of Dream of an agreable thing, which subsists no more to me, but however 'tis such a Dream as exceeds most of the Dull Realities of my Life. Indeed, what with ill health & ill fortune, I am grown so stupidly philosophical as to have no thought about me that deserves the name of warm or lively, but that which sometimes awakens me into an Imagination that I may yet see you again. Compassionate a Poet, and (which is more) a Young Poet, who has lost all manner of Romantick Ideas; except a few that hover about the Bosphorus & Hellespont, not so much for the fine Sound of their names, as to raise up images of Leander, who was drownd in crossing the Sea to kiss the hand of fair Hero. This were a destiny less to be lamented, than what we are here told of the poor Jew, one of your Interpreters, who was beheaded at Belgrade as a Spy. I confess such a death would have been a great disappointment to me; and I believe Jacob Tonson will hardly venture to visit you, after this news.

You tell me, the pleasure of being nearer the Sun has a great effect upon your health and Spirits. You have turnd my affections so far East-ward, that I could almost be one of his worshippers: For I think the Sun has more reason to be proud of raising your Spirits, than of raising all the Plants, & ripening all the minerals in the earth. It is my opinion, a reasonable man might gladly travel three or four thousand leagues, to see Your Nature, and Your Wit, in their full Perfection. What may'nt we expect from a creature that went out the most perfect of this part of the world, and is every day improving by the Sun in the other? If you don't now write and speak the finest things imaginable, you must be content to be involvd in the same imputation with the rest of the East, and be concluded to have abandond your self to extreme Effeminacy, Laziness, & Lewdness of life.

I make not the least question but you could give me great Eclaircissements upon many passages in Homer, since you have been enlightend by the same Sun that inspired the Father of Poetry. You are now glowing under the Climate that animated him; you may see his Images rising more boldly about you, in the very Scenes of his story and action; you may lay the immortal work on some broken column of a Hero's Sepulcher, and read the Fall of Troy in the Shade of a Trojan Ruin. But if, to visit the Tomb of so many Heroes, you have not the heart to pass over that Sea where once a Lover perishd; you may at least, at ease, in your own Window, contemplate the Fields of

Asia, in such a dim & remote prospect, as you have of Homer in my Translation.

I send you therfore with this, the third volume of the Iliad,[1] and as many other things as fill a wooden box directed to Mr Wortley. Among the rest, you have all I am worth, that is, my Workes: There are few things in them but what you have already seen, except the Epistle of Eloisa to Abelard; in which you will find one passage, that I can't tell whether to wish you should understand, or not?

For the news of London, I'll summ it up in short. We have Masquerades at the Theatre in the Haymarket of Mr Heideker's institution; they are very frequent, yet the Adventures are not so numerous but that of my Lady Mohun still makes the chief figure. Her Marriage to young Mordant, & all its circumstances, I suppose you'll have from Lady Rich or Miss Griffith.[2] The Political State is under great divisions, the Parties of Walpole and Stanhope as violent as Whig and Tory. The K. and P.[3] continue Two Names: there is nothing like a Coalition, but at the Masquerade; however the Princess is a Dissenter from it, and has a very small party in so unmodish a Seperation.

The last I receivd from your hands was from Peterwaradin:[4] It gave me the joy of thinking you in good health and humour: One or two expressions in it are too generous ever to be forgotten by me. I writ a very melancholy one just before, which was sent to Mr Stanyan[5] to be forwarded thro' Hungary. It would have informd you how meanly I thought of the pleasure of Italy, without the qualification of your Company: and that Meer Statues & pictures are not more cold to me, than I to them. I have had but four of your letters; I have sent several, & wish I knew how many you have receiv'd. For God's sake Madam, send to me as often as you can; in the dependance that there is no man breathing more constantly, or more anxiously, mindful of you. Tell me that you are well, tell me that your little Son is well, tell me that your very Dog (if you have one) is well. Defraud me of no one thing that pleases You: for whatever that is, it will please me better than any thing else can do—

I am always Yours.

[1] The *Iliad*, vol. iii, was published 3 June, and since Pope in his letter of [October?] asks if she got the box of books sent by merchant ship 'last June', this letter would seem surely to be written in June.

[2] Lady Rich and Miss [Anne?] Griffith were daughters of Lady Mohun by her first husband, Col. Edward Griffith. In a letter written a year later to Lady Mary, Pope spells the name Griffin. See i. 470.

[3] The King and the Prince of Wales, who were not at this time friendly.

[4] See Lady Mary's letter from Belgrade, 12 Feb. 1716/17. It is not necessary to assume that she did not write from Peterwaradin: she did not write a *long* letter.

[5] Abraham Stanyan (1669?–1732) was envoy extraordinary to the Emperor. To forward a letter through him from Vienna would mean passing it through lines of battle.

†POPE *to* ROBERT DIGBY[1] 2 *June* 1717

1735

Chiswick, Jan. 2, 1717.

I had pleas'd myself sooner in writing to you, but that I have been your Successor in a Fit of Sickness, and am not yet so much recovered, but that I have thoughts of using your [2]Physicians They are as grave Persons as any of the Faculty, and (like the Antients) carry their own Medicaments about with them. But indeed the Moderns are such Lovers of Raillery, that nothing is grave enough to escape them. Let 'em laugh, but People will still have their Opinions: As they think our Doctors Asses to them, we'll think them Asses to our Doctors.

I am glad you are so much in a better State of Health, as to allow me to jest about it. My Concern, when I heard of your Danger, was so very serious, that I almost take it ill Dr. *Evans* should tell you of it, or you mention it. I tell you fairly, if you and a few more such people were to leave the World, I would not give Sixpence to stay in it.

I am not so much concern'd as to the point, whether you are to live fat or lean: Most Men of Wit or Honesty are usually decreed to live very lean; so I am inclined to the opinion that 'tis decreed you shall: However be comforted, and reflect that you'll make the better Busto for it.

'Tis something particular in you, not to be satisfied with sending me your own Books, but to make your Acquaintance continue the Frolick. Mr. *Wharton*[3] forc'd me to take *Gorboduc*, which has since done me great credit with several People, as it has done *Dryden* and *Oldham* some diskindness, in shewing there is as much difference between their *Gorboduc*, and this, as between Queen *Anne*, and King *George*. It is truly a scandal, that Men should write with contempt of a Piece which they never once saw, as those two Poets did, who were ignorant even of the Sex, as well as Sense, of *Gorboduc*.

Adieu! I am going to forget you: This minute you took up all my mind, the next I shall think of nothing but the Terms of *Agamemnon*, and the Recovery of *Briseis*.[4] I shall be *Achilles*'s humble Servant these

[1] In his editions of 1735 Pope dated this letter 'Jan. 2, 1717', but thereafter (1737–42) he dated it 2 June. The later date seems plausible because in the summer of 1717 he was not very well, suffered from trouble with his eyes, and drank asses' milk. See the letters to Caryll and to Lady Mary Wortley Montagu. Letters completely dated in superscription are so rare from Pope's pen that one may even be suspicious of the year. The recovery of Briseis (*Iliad* xix) concerned Pope in 1718 more probably than in 1717.

[2] Asses.—Pope, 1735–42 n.

[3] The passage seems to indicate that young Digby had brought Pope and the elder Thomas Warton (1688?–1745) acquainted. Digby probably knew Warton at Magdalen College where Digby had been a student. The idea that Warton first brought Milton's early poems to Pope's attention is controverted by Pope's letter to Sir William Trumbull, 19 Oct. 1705. On *Gorboduc* see Pope to Atterbury, 18 Feb. [1718?].

[4] This must be a general sort of remark: Pope had not, one may be sure, reached *Iliad* XIX, in which Briseis is recovered.

two Months (with the good Leave of all my Friends.) I have no Ambition so strong at present, as that noble One of Sir *Salathiel Lovel*,[1] Recorder of *London*, to furnish out a decent and plentiful Execution, of *Greeks* and *Trojans*—It is not to be exprest how heartily I wish the Death of *Homer*'s Heroes, one after another. The Lord preserve me in the Day of Battle, which is just approaching! Dear Sir, join in your prayers for me, and know me to be always (whether I live, die, or am damn'd as a Poet) | Yours most faithfully.

POPE *to* TERESA *and* MARTHA BLOUNT[2] [*June* 1717]

Mapledurham

If my memory has not deceivd me this was the Volume of Clarendon which you commanded. It is accompanyd with a Book which I think a very pretty one, & I believe you have never read. I can't express the Desire I have of being Happy with you a few days (or nights, if you would give me leave) at Mapledurham; where I dare say, you relish the Delights of Solitude and Shades, much better than I can be able to do till I see you. For in very deed Ladies, I love you both, very sincerely and passionately, tho not so romantically (perhaps) as such as you may expect who have been us'd to receive more Complimental Letters and High flights from your own Sex, than ever I am like to reach to. In earnest, I know no Two Things I would change you for, this hot Weather, except Two good Melons.

I have hitherto been detaind here by a Doctor of Divinity, whom I am laboring to convert from the Protestant Religion, and in 2 days I must be at Hampton Court, & (for all I know) at London. Upon my Return Mr Harcourt has promised me to be here, after which I will try if you will admit me. I am without any more Nonsense than I was born to, that is to say without any Ceremony; I am (I say) before the Lord | Ladies | Your most faithfull in-|significant humble | Servant | A. Pope.

Address: A Mademoiselles, Therese, | & Marth: Blount. | Pres:

[1] This picturesque person, whose lack of memory led him to be called the 'Obliviscor of London', died in 1713 at the age of 94.

[2] The dating is guess-work. If, as Elwin thought, the 'pretty book' was Pope's *Works*, published 3 June, the letter would certainly date within the month. The King was briefly at Hampton Court on 16 and 17 June, and Pope may have had an engagement with his friends the Maids of Honour for either Hampton Court or London. In his letter to Caryll, 7 June 1717, Pope expects Mr. Harcourt that day.

POPE *to* JERVAS[1] [*June–July* 1717]

Homer MSS. Add. 4807

I am much rejoyced at Your safe Arrival at Dublin, the news of which I had from Frank last post. I am obligd to you for the care which I doubt not you'll take of the Books I troubled you with. Dr Ellwood has writ for several 3rd volumes for the Subscribers he collected. They amount to twelve with Elwoods own for which he has sent the Mony to me. I therfore desire you to give to Ellwood 11 third vols of comon paper out of your Parcell, to the following Gentlemen & one of best paper for himself.

Mr Rob. Howard
Geo. Rockford Esq
Mr Ludlow
Mr Synge
Dr Gilbert
Mr Hill
Mr Morton
Mr Singleton
Mr Tucker
Dr Walmsley
Mrs Ford—best paper
Lord Massarine

POPE *to* CARYLL[2] 7 *June* 1717

Add. 28618

Chiswick. June 7th 1717.

Tho' I heard nothing from you, since my last, I conclude you may be as busy as I, and then, I can assure you, you are sufficiently employed. I left the town for ease and study in the country (if I may be allowed to call Chiswick so), and have not yet been able to read three hours or think one. The company that find me out here, and the various employments[3] Mr Lintot engages me in of correcting the press, overlooking verses, and managing with my subscribers, have robbed me of all pretence to quiet and philosophy. At length my *Works* are out, of which I will not say a word to you (tho' an author may reasonably be allowed to be at least as full of his *Works*, when they come out in

[1] Jervas has evidently taken over to Ireland copies of the *Iliad*, vol. iii, which was published on 3 June. From his parcel he is to give Dr. Elwood twelve copies of the book. Either Jervas had arrived in Dublin before 6 July or else he took over to Parnell Pope's letter of that date. The text is from the revised draft, which remained in Pope's possession. The original as sent is not known to exist.

[2] From June 1716 to June 1717 we have no letters between Pope and Caryll, though this letter says nothing of a lapse in the correspondence. Evidently not all the letters were preserved.

[3] In May Pope had published Parnell's *Battle of the Frogs and Mice*; early in June his *Works* in quarto and folio appeared; and at the same time he was distributing vol. iii of his *Iliad*. Less known is another volume, *Poems on Several Occasions*, a miscellany which Lintot published in July, and for which Pope was evidently now 'correcting the press'. For Pope's part in this last volume see the edition of it prepared by Norman Ault, *Pope's Own Miscellany* (1935).

a new Edition as a lady of a new suit of clothes). The Preface will tell you everything to a tittle that I think of 'em. The third volume of Homer too is published, but I can't tell certainly how to send you either till I receive your directions. If you [will name] any person, or place, to whom or where the books may be delivered (as well as those which were subscribed for by your interest), you shall be carefully obeyed by Mr Lintot or myself. Be pleased to direct to Mr Jervas's.

I may now think of seing Ladyholt, tho' not a line of my next year's task is writ. As to Gay, he is just upon the wing for Aix la Chapelle with Mr Pulteney the late Secretary.[1] Mrs Patty Blount talked some time since of paying her duty to her godmother,[2] but neither she nor any body else can be more desirous of seing you all than myself. I just heard Lady Mary Caryll was in town, when I was obliged to go to Chiswick; and have since been never able to stay above a few hours in London. I am really in St Paul's condition, distracted with many businesses. I expect this instant Mr Harcourt, who is to pass some days with me. Mr Edw. Blount and Sir H. Bedingfield follow next: I am engaged to Mr Stoner's afterwards (there you have all my Catholics at once, except Mrs Blounts[3] who have me always). Then my Lord Burlington and Duchess Hamilton upon ten or 20 parties. I had made one with Lord Jersey last week to have run away to see the Ile of Wight and Stanted.[4] He thought it a mere ramble, but my design lay deeper, to have got to you. But the late setting of the Parliament hindered this project. In short, if I stay at home, I shall do nothing; I must go abroad to follow my business; and if Ladyholt shades afford me protection, it is there Homer's battles must be fought.

O quis me in vallibus Æmi
Sistat, et ingenti ramorum protegat umbra![5]

I see I am out running my paper, and must beg you to continue the belief of a thing as true as any article of faith, that I am with the truest sincerity and friendship most affectionately | Yours | A: P:

LADY MARY WORTLEY MONTAGU *to* POPE

17 *June* [1717]

1763

Belgrade-Village, June 17, O.S.

I hope, before this time, you have received two or three of my letters. I had yours but yesterday, though dated the third of February, in

[1] Gay and William Pulteney seem not to have left England until July. Pulteney (cr. Earl of Bath in 1742) had resigned in April as Secretary at War. See *DNB*.

[2] Mrs. Caryll was her godmother.

[3] *We* might say 'except the Mrs. Blounts'. Pope habitually leaves out the article in this expression.

[4] Stanted, for *Stanstead*.

[5] Virgil, *Georgics*, ii. 488–9. (Pope misquotes somewhat.)

which you suppose me to be dead and buried. I have already let you know that I am still alive; but to say truth, I look upon my present circumstances to be exactly the same with those of departed spirits. The heats of Constantinople have driven me to this place, which perfectly answers the description of the Elysian fields. I am in the middle of a wood, consisting chiefly of fruit trees, watered by a vast number of fountains, famous for the excellency of their water, and divided into many shady walks, upon short grass, that seems to me artificial; but, I am assured, is the pure work of nature—within view of the Black-sea, from whence we perpetually enjoy the refreshment of cool breezes, that make us insensible of the heat of the summer. The village is only inhabited by the richest amongst the Christians, who meet every night at a fountain, forty paces from my house, to sing and dance. The beauty and dress of the women, exactly resemble the ideas of the antient nymphs, as they are given us by the representations of the poets and painters. But what persuades me more fully of my decease, is the situation of my own mind, the profound ignorance I am in, of what passes among the living (which only comes to me by chance) and the great calmness with which I receive it. Yet I have still a hankering after my friends and acquaintances left in the world, according to the authority of that admirable author,

> That spirits departed are wonderous kind
> To friends and relations left behind,
> Which no body can deny.

Of which solemn truth I am a *dead* instance. I think *Virgil* is of the same opinion, that in human souls there will still be some remains of human passions:

> Curæ non ipsa in morte relinquunt.[1]

And 'tis very necessary to make a perfect Elysium, that there should be a river *Lethe*, which I am not so happy as to find. To say truth, I am sometimes very weary of the singing and dancing, and sunshine, and wish for the smoke and impertinencies in which you toil; though I endeavour to persuade myself that I live in a more agreeable variety than you do; and that *Monday*, setting of partridges; *Tuesday*, reading English; *Wednesday*, studying in the Turkish language, (in which, by the way, I am already very learned;) *Thursday*, classical authors; *Friday*, spent in writing; *Saturday*, at my needle, and *Sunday*, admitting of visits and hearing of music, is a better way of disposing of the week, than, *Monday* at the drawing-room; *Tuesday*, Lady Mohun's; *Wednesday*, at the opera; *Thursday*, the play; *Friday*, Mrs. Chetwynd's, &c. a perpetual round of hearing the same scandal, and seeing

[1] *Aeneid*, vi. 444.

the same follies acted over and over, which here affect me no more than they do other dead people. I can now hear of displeasing things with pity and without indignation. The reflection on the great gulph between you and me, cools all news that come hither. I can neither be sensibly touched with joy or grief, when I consider that, possibly, the cause of either is removed, before the letter comes to my hands. But (as I said before) this indolence does not extend to my few friendships; I am still warmly sensible of yours and Mr. *Congreve*'s, and desire to live in your remembrance, though dead to all the world beside. | I am, &c. &c.

*POPE *to* ——[1] [*June* 1717]

Homer MSS. Add. 4807

Sunday

Sir,—I ought to beg your pardon for my negligence yesterday, in omitting to leave with you a Bill for Lintot: And I beg you will allow me to make use of this opportunity to thank you for the Trouble I have occasiond you. I am, with a true respect, | Sir, | Your most obedient and | most humble Servant | A. Pope.

My most humble Service attends my Lord Percivall & the whole family.

POPE *to* CARYLL[2] [30 *June* 1717?]

Add. 28618

July 30th

That one of us disappointed the other is evident; and which of us it was, the shades of Ladyholt can witness, which saw you there and not me. Gay is to be excused on account of strange desire to see foreign lands, but I—*Habes confitentem reum*, as the lover says in Petronius,[3] and I ask only as he did to be permitted to try again and repair my omission. You may be confident, if I do not in any thing gratify you, it is downright impotence and not coldness.

Having got rid of many businesses, Homer yet lies so heavy upon my hands, that 'tis an ill sign he may do so on Lintott's; for (as somebody has observed) people will seldom read in a good humour, what a man writ in an ill one.

I discharged as punctually as I could all your commissions touching

[1] The letter is obviously addressed to an unknown agent of Lord Perceval, who was among the subscribers to the *Iliad*. The position of the letter in the Homer MSS. indicates that it falls after, and not long after, the publication of vol. iii in June 1717.

[2] The July date found in the transcript is clearly wrong, since Caryll answers this letter in his of 16 July. The June date, suggested by Elwin, seems to be what Caryll's scribe should have written.

[3] Petronius, *Satyricon*, 130.

the books: but could not find Lady Mary during the few days I was in town. Tempest[1] had 3 of the 3rd vols the 4th Lintott told me Lady Mary had sent for before. I also sent thither the *Works* in best paper, and if I have mistaken one in the account thro' the hurry I was in, be pleased to acquaint me, for I would rather send it you my self than have it ordered from Lintott.

I beg my most faithful service may be made acceptable to the worthy gentleman your son, whom I have not seen this age. We were young people when we parted last, and I wish we may meet again, but as much wiser as we are older. But to say truth I despair of it on my own part, unless I have your help and advice, which I observe has always made any one who would take it the better for it. However, if I should (like most of my poetical fraternity) prove incorrigible, I shall at least be sure of one thing which poets love, pleasure, which I could not miss at Grinsted, nor in Brentford highway, no nor in Nova Zembla, if you were there. You must be prepared one time or other this summer to send your chariot, for this unworthy charge, to Epsom. Mrs Patty Blount has seemed for some months past, to have what we call a hankering after her godfather; and whether it be that she has a mind to see what effect the example of a whole Christian family can have upon me? or to have some rakish example from my behaviour among you, to countenance her own irregularity? which of these reasons it be, I cannot tell; but she advises me to delay my visit till she can make hers. And this if she does not do soon, I shall think she puts a feint upon me; for Mrs Blount goes this next week to settle in her new house at London,[2] a place in my opinion not very proper at this season for the young lady I speak of, whose health is by no means yet confirmed. In short whatever she does, I will see you, and that pretty soon, if you continue to give me that encouragement which I have hitherto deserved so little.

You will the more take notice of the length of this epistle when you know that I have been this month under the directions and operations of an eye doctor, who drops nine drops a day into each eye. I also drink asses' milk, upon which I will make no jokes tho' it be a fertile subject. I eat like a horse, that is to say, abundance of sallet and herbs. In all things else I am as I was, *videlicet*—a poor papist and | Your most faithful affectionate | Friend and servant. | A: P:

[1] Tempest must have been either a friend or landlord of Caryll's, who would forward parcels to Ladyholt. Lady Mary Caryll should have aided, but Pope failed to find her. Tempest is mentioned again in the letter of 18 Oct. [1718].

[2] Mrs. Blount and her daughters lived in Bolton Street for twenty years after this date. Then they removed to Welbeck Street. Pope seems to have visited someone in Charles Street both before and after Lady Mary left there in 1716. Possibly the Blount ladies were there: we do not know where they lived after their departure from Mapledurham in 1715 or 1716. See Pope to Martha Blount [Mar. 1716], i. 338, n. 3, and to Lady Mary, 18 Aug. 1716, where Pope passes her house—which is vacated.

I should take it as a particular kindness if you know anyone who cares to sell an annuity for life of 1000ll which I am inclined to purchase: such an information [if it] falls in your way, will be very obliging.

POPE *to* PARNELL[1] 6 *July* [1717]

Elwin–Courthope, vii. 465

July 6.

I write to you as a friend, without apology or study, without intending to appear anything but what I am, and without so much as thinking I stand in need of any excuses or ceremonies for doing so. If it were otherwise, how many pretty things might be said for my silence, and what ingenious turns might be given to yours,—that as soon as you have obliged a man you quite forget it, and that I know nothing is so ungrateful to you as thanks. To tell you that your translation of the Batrachomuomachia is an excellent piece is no more than everybody now knows, and to say that I like it still the better, and am more in your debt than the rest of the world, because it was done at my desire, is no more than you know already; and to acquaint you that there is not one man of any taste who does not approve the whole, verse and prose, is (after all that modesty may fancy it thinks) no more than what you must needs give a good guess at.

The other pieces you entrusted to my care lie preserved with the same veneration as relics, but I look upon them with greater pleasure when I reflect that the owner of them is yet living, though indeed you live to me, but as a saint or separated spirit whose sight I must never enjoy,[2] though I am always sure of his good offices. It is through your mediation that Homer is to be saved,—I mean my Homer, and if you could yet throw some hours away, rather upon me than him, in suggesting some remarks upon his 13th, 14th, 15th, and 16th books, it would be charitable beyond expression; for I am very backward in this year's task, through the interruption of many different cares and distractions, to which none but as intimate and tender a friend as you ought to be privy. I could unload upon you with much comfort and confidence, but the very things I complain of prevent my seeing you in Ireland, which else I had done this summer.

I have, before I was aware, run into my own affairs too far when I only meant to have told you the reason that your poems are not

[1] Elwin printed this letter from the original then in the possession of his publisher, John Murray. The holograph seems to have disappeared.

[2] i.e. whom I never see. Parnell came over to England during the summer of 1718. He joined in sending a 'poetic' invitation to Lord Oxford to receive the Scriblerus group on 8 July 1718, and on 11 Sept. he saw Pope at Jervas's house. On his way back to Ireland in Oct. he died (aged 39) at Chester. This is the last letter in the Pope–Parnell correspondence that has come to light.

published.[1] The present violent bent to politics and earnest animosities of parties, which grow within one another so fast, that one would think even every single heart was breeding a worm to destroy itself,—these have left no room for any thought but those of mischief to one another. The muses are all run mad and turned bacchanals, and a poet now may be like Amphion and sing with the stones about his ears. This is my case whose works my bookseller would publish at such a juncture that I take it to be tempting Providence. I send them you all, and I think them but a poor return for those fine lines you allowed me to print in the front of them.[2]

I must never forget my obligations to the Dean of St. Patrick's, and I hope you never omit to acquaint him with all that esteem, affection, and remembrance, which there is no putting upon paper, and which can only be felt in the heart. You will also put Dr. Ellwood and Mr. Ward in mind of me, each of whom I have desired by Mr. Jervas to accept of all I am worth—that is to say my poems.

Gay is going for France next week in company with the late Secretary Pulteney. I remain within four miles of London,[3] a man of business and poetry, from both which I pray to be delivered. I am always the same in one respect—that is, always yours most sincerely.

CARYLL *to* POPE[4] — 16 *July* 1717

Homer MSS. Add. 4807

I have not had a word from your Holynesse since my last to you, nor any account of the receipt of some Pictures that I desir'd you to gett fram'd and scour'd. This and the earnest Desire I have of kissing your Toe att Grinsted, or rather a pritty Lady's cheek (whom you talked of as a companion in your Journey) occasions you the trouble of this to know the Reason why you flagg in your good Resolutions, or rather in the Execution of them Butt I enjoy you in spirit tho' I cannot in person for your Workes are my dayly Lectures and with what Satisfaction [I] need not repeat to you. Butt pray in your next tell me who was the Unfortunate Lady you addresse a Copy of Verses to. I think you once gave me her history, butt tis now quite outt of my head. Butt now I have named such a person Mrs Cope[5] occurs to my mind.

[1] Pope may here allude to poems sent by Parnell for inclusion in a miscellany—perhaps for Pope's miscellany *Poems on Several Occasions*, which he was to publish in another week now. Pope brought out Parnell's *Poems* in a posthumous edition dated 1722, but published in Dec. 1721.

[2] Among the commendatory verses prefixed to Pope's *Works* just published at this time were ninety lines by Parnell, 'To Mr. Pope'.

[3] At Chiswick.

[4] This letter seems clearly an answer to that misdated by Caryll's scribe 30 July and here placed as 30 June.

[5] Mrs. Cope is mentioned as *an* unfortunate lady, not as *the* unfortunate of Pope's poem. She was Caryll's first cousin, unhappily married, and supported in France by the generosity

I have comply'd with her Desires, tho' I thinke a Second Voyage to such a Rascall is the most preposterous thing imaginable butt *mulierem fortem quis inveniet*! tis harder to find than the Man Diogenes lookt for with a Candle and Lantern att noon Day. Adieu I am most abruptly butt most sincerely | Yours | J: Caryll

W: Grinsted. 16 July 1717.

LADY MARY WORTLEY MONTAGU *to* POPE

1 *August* 1717

[Among the letters listed by Lady Mary in her 'Heads' as printed in the Memoir of Mr. Moy Thomas is found a notation that a letter of this date to Pope was 'Copied at length' (Wharncliffe and Thomas, i. 19). No such letter is known.]

POPE *to* CARYLL

[6 *August* 1717][1]

Add. 28618

What has till now delayed my answering your obliging letter of July 16th was my intention of doing it personally at Grinsted, and the natural prospect of that pleasure which the hopes of a young lady's company gave me. I don't find myself yet totally deprived of them, and I flatter myself that her letter to Mrs Caryll may have appointed the time when I may attain so desirable an end, by so agreeable means. But, at worst, see you I will, this summer; tho' friends and enemies oppose, and tho' pleasure and business intervene; Homer with all his gods has not the force to control me.

That you may see I have no common obstacles hitherto (beside the neighbourhood of your fair cosens) I have been indispensably obliged to pass some days at almost every house along the Thames; half my acquaintance being upon the breaking up of the Parliament become my neighbours.[2] After some attendance on my Lord Burlington, I have been at the Duke of Shrewsbury's, Duke of Argyle's, Lady Rochester's, Lord Percival's, Mr Stonor's,[3] Lord Winchelsea's, Sir Godfrey Kneller's (who has made me a fine present of a picture) and Dutchess Hamilton's. All these have indispensable claims to me, under

of Caryll and Pope. See Pope to Caryll, 19 July 1711, and, for a full account of the lady, *The Athenaeum*, 22 July 1854.

[1] In replying to this letter on 18 Aug., Caryll speaks of it as 'yours of the 6th instant', and thus fixes its date—or perhaps the date of its arrival.

[2] Parliament was prorogued on 15 July.

[3] Thomas Stonor, Esq., had a house at Twickenham as well as another, Stonor Park, in Oxfordshire, which latter Pope passed on his journey to Oxford in September. See Pope to Martha Blount [Sept. 1717]. *The British Journal*, 11 Jan. 1723/4, announces the marriage of Stonor's daughter at Twickenham, and speaks of Stonor as of 'Wattleton-Park' in Oxfordshire.

penalty of the imputation of direct rudeness, living within 2 hours sail of Chiswick. Then am I obliged to pass some days between my Lord Bathurst's, and three or four more on Windsor side. Thence to Mr Dancastle, and my relations on Bagshot Heath.[1] I am also promised three months ago to the Bishop of Rochester for 3 days on the other side of the water.[2] Besides all this, two of my friends have engaged to be here a week; and into this computation I don't reckon Dr Arbuthnot and others in town, who have an immediate jurisdiction over me. In a word, the minute I can get to you, I will, tho' Lintott's accounts are yet to settle, and three parts of my year's task to do. Your pictures I received, and it is not my fault the frames have not been finished before, Mr Jervas being in Ireland, and none but a servant (none of the wisest neither which that nation has produced) left to take care of pictures, sculptures, and their appurtenances. If you please now to acquaint me whither to direct and send them, it shall be done without delay.

Mr Edward Blount charged me with his respects to you when I writ next, and it is some merit that I remember them, when he has been absent from England this fortnight and better.

Dr Garth has published a translation of Ovid's *Metamorphoses* by several hands,[3] with a preface and dedication of a new fashion. Folio. Price 20*s*. I advertise you to borrow it.

Your whole family must always think me the greatest rogue in the world or their most humble servant.

I had forgot to tell you in my list of rambles (which if it goes on at this rate will shortly exceed in dimension the map of the children of Israel) that I must necessarily go some time this season to my Lord Harcourt's in Oxfordshire: but that I'll postpone till I have seen you. I am with more truth and zeal than can be expressed, | Dear sir | your most affectionate and obliged humble | Servant. | A. P.

CARYLL *to* POPE — 18 *August* 1717

Homer MSS. Add. 4807

18 Aug. 1717.

When yours of the 6th Instant arrived here, I was gott into the East, not among the wyse Men of that corner butt amidst the fools of Tunbridge. my stay with them was butt of two Dayes, butt I had spent the three preceeding ones, I think in worse Company, the knaves of the Law att our County Assizes att Lewes. A cause call'd me thither which tho' I gain'd, I may brag off Like my Brother Teague that it was just nothing att all, nor had I gott that neither had not I bestirr'd my Stumps.

[1] The Racketts. [2] At Bromley.

[3] The volume included Pope's version of the fable of Dryope in Book IX.

When my Pictures are don be pleased to order them down to Ladyholt, by the Stansted Carrier, who Inns in Gerrard Street. You answer not my question, who the Unfortunate Lady was that you inscribe a copy of Verses to in your Book. I long to be retould her Story, for I beleeve you allreddy tould me formerly, butt I shall referr that and a thousand other things more to chatt over att our next Meeting which I hope draws neer, presume my wife has fixd on a time with my Dear Patty, to whom I pray my humble Service as also to her fair Sister. adieu I am in more haste or rather hurry than usuall, butt not lesse | Sir— | Your freind and Servant | J. Caryll

Address: To | Mr Alex. Pope. To be left | with Mr B. Lintot Bookseller | neer Temple Barr | London

Postmark: 19/AV

POPE *to* CARYLL 22 *August* 1717

Add. 28618

London. 22. Aug. 1717.

I had heard of your rambling from your lady (as it is most natural a husband's rambles should be complained of by his lady) in hers to Mrs Patty. She says that you shall not be long absent from Ladyholt, to which place you very well know I have long had a partiality, and therefore shall endeavour to make it my retirement this autumn. After the list of visits which I gave you in my last, you may reasonably conclude I am neither fond of rambling itself, nor of rambling to any place which is not in a particular manner agreeable to me. The greatest solitude at present is London, where scarce a wheel of a coach is to be heard, or a hawker of news. Guess from thence how dead a scene this is, where the busy and the inquisitive are not to be found.

I send this day your pictures by the Stansted carrier, as your direction implies: I've put them in such frames as are modish yet cheap. They come to 8*s*. a piece. As I have discharged this small office for you, I beg you to do me a familiar or rather domestic piece of service; it is, when a hogshead of good French wine falls into your hands (whether out of the skies, or whatever element that pays no customes) that you'd favour me with about 12 dozen of it at the price you give; the bottling I must defray over and above to you. But that you may not think me grown an exorbitant toper, from so large a demand, know that half of the quantity is for your good goddaughter, who scorns to [be] behind hand with me in any vicious appetite I can pretend to—and yet (God knows, for your ghostly comfort) may be a saint for all that.

The question I lately begged you to ask concerning any person who would be willing to take a thousand paid to give an annuity for life, is what I may extend farther to 2000ll in proportion, and what I shall look upon as a most particular favour. It is possible some that would not care to take up a smaller sum might engage for a more considerable one, so that I could undertake for either one, two, or between two and three thousand paid as they might have inclination. ⌜I know you'll take part in rejoicing for the victory of Prince Eugene over the Turks,[1] in the zeal you bear to the Christian interest, tho' your cousin of Oxford (with whom I dined yesterday) says, there is no other difference in the Christians beating the Turks, or the Turks beating the Christians; than whether the Emperor shall first declare war against Spain, or Spain declare it against the Emperor?⌝[2]

I must not end without making my services and heartiest wishes attend on your whole family, and entreating you always to continue the belief of a truth so invariable, as that I am sincerely | Dear sir | Your most faithful and most obliged | Freind and humble servant | A: P:

POPE *to* ——[3] [*Summer*, 1717]

Homer MSS. Add. 4807

Sir,—I have deferrd to give you [t]his trouble, to the very [l]ast settling of my accounts. I have a demand [u]pon me for first volumes of Homer which are wanted for some [n]ew Subscribers, no more having been printed than were Subscribd for at first. You will therfore oblige me equally, and it will be equally to my interest, either to order the payment of Mr Legrands & Mr Buckingham's Subscriptions, or to return me the books again. I beg the favor of a Line on this subject, & at the same time the pleasure of knowing that Yourself & family are in all that health & happiness which I heartily wish them. I am with all affection | Dear Sir | Your

DR. ABEL EVANS *to* POPE[4] [*August* 1717]

Homer MSS. Add. 4808

FRAGMENT

I rec'd some time since ten Homers third Volumes Half of which I have deliverd & the rest will be dispos'd of this Week & I have taken

[1] In a brilliant and surprising action Prince Eugene caused Belgrade to capitulate on the 19th. Preliminary victories are reported in *The Evening Post* in its issue of 22 Aug., and other papers (*The Weekly Packet*, 24 Aug., for example) detail the capitulation. The speed of the reports is to be explained on the assumption that the date of the 19th is New Style (i.e. properly 8 Aug. O.S.).

[2] The matter placed in half-brackets was inserted as the greater part of a postscript in the letter Pope printed as to Edward Blount, 8 Sept. 1717.

[3] The placing of the letter in the summer of 1717 is due to the fact that adjacent letters in the Homer MSS. date from that period. Pope is asking the friend who secured the subscriptions of Owen Buckingham and William Lewis Le Grand to the *Iliad* to persuade these delinquent subscribers to return their first volumes to Lintot via the Reading coach.

[4] This fragment must date after 26 July 1717 when the will of Dr. Robert Adderley,

up the guineas, which when I have em all I will pay to your order at sight. those I have rec'd are Trinity, Baliol, New Colledge, All souls, Queens. there remains Pembroke. Magdalen, Corpus Christi, Merton have rec'd theirs but Dr adderlys Executour will take that who is dead. & the tenth I suppose is for the university for I had no letter of directions sent me in the Parcel.[1] I find People have been somewhat disobleidgd in being made stay so long which I suppose is owing to Lintot's ill manners or Covetousness or both no matter.

LADY MARY WORTLEY MONTAGU *to* POPE[2]

1 September 1717

1767

Sept. 1, 1717.

When I wrote to you last, Belgrade was in the hands of the Turks; but, at this present moment, it has changed masters, and is in the hands of the Imperialists. A Janissary who in nine days, and yet without any wings but what a pannick terror seems to have furnished, arrived at Constantinople from the army of the Turks before Belgrade, brought Mr. W— the news of a compleat victory obtained by the Imperialists, commanded by Prince Eugene, over the Ottoman troops. It is said, the Prince has discovered great conduct and valour in this action, and I am particularly glad that the voice of glory and duty has call'd him from the * * *[3] Two days after the battle the town surrendered. The consternation, which this defeat has occasioned here, is inexpressible; and the Sultan apprehending a revolution from the resentment and indignation of the people, fomented by certain leaders, has begun his precautions, after the goodly fashion of this blessed government, by

late Fellow of All Souls, was proved, and before 6 Sept., when Pope left home on his ramble to Oxford. Since the subscribers were annoyed at having to wait for their books, late Aug. seems probable.

[1] The ten copies present problems, especially since sent without directions for distribution. Ten colleges subscribed to the *Iliad*, but there were at least half a dozen individual subscribers in Oxford, among them the deceased Adderley and Evans himself. From Evans's letter postmarked 16 Oct. it is evident that further copies were then still overdue in Oxford. From Pope's letter to Joseph Bowles, Bodley's librarian, 25 Sept. 1721, it is apparent that Pope sent volumes to Bodley as they appeared. One finds in W. D. Macray's *Annals of the Bodleian Library* (1890), p. 204, that Pope presented both the *Iliad* and the *Odyssey* in 1725. Obviously the *Iliad* was there at an earlier date.

[2] This letter comes from *An Additional Volume to the Letters of Lady M—y W—y M—e* (1767), pp. 24–36. Letters in that volume have been suspected as spurious. The letter was not printed by Dallaway in 1803, a fact which indicates that (unlike other letters by Lady Mary) the original was not then extant in the archives of the Marquess of Bute. From internal evidence one is not led to suspect the authenticity of the letter, except by the fatal mention of Twickenham in the third paragraph, to which place Pope had not yet removed. It is possible, of course, that an editor in 1767 might change *Chiswick* to *Twickenham.*

[3] At this point the editor of the 1767 volume inserts in the text '(*here several words of the manuscript are effaced*)'. The parenthesis might, at face value, seem to authenticate the letter; to a suspicious mind it would be a device to make the letter *seem* authentic. No other remark about MSS. has been noted in the volume.

ordering several persons to be strangled who were the objects of his royal suspicion. He has also ordered his Treasurer to advance some months pay to the Janissaries, which seems the less necessary, as their conduct has been bad in this campaign, and their licentious ferocity seems pretty well tamed by the publick contempt. Such of them as return in straggling and fugitive parties to the metropolis, have not spirit nor credit enough to defend themselves from the insults of the mob; the very children taunt them, and the populace spit in their faces as they pass. They refused during the battle to lend their assistance to save the baggage and the military chest, which however were defended by the Bashaws and their retinue, while the Janissaries and Spahis were nobly employed in plundering their own camp.

You see here I give you a very *handsome* return for your obliging letter. You entertain me with a most agreeable account of your amiable connexions with men of letters and taste, and of the delicious moments you pass in their society under the rural shade; and I exhibit to you in return, the barbarous spectacle of Turks and Germans cutting one another's throats. But what can you expect from such a country as this, from which the muses have fled, from which letters seem eternally banished, and in which you see, in private scenes, nothing pursued as happiness but the refinements of an indolent voluptuousness, and where those who act upon the publick theatre live in uncertainty, suspicion, and terror. Here pleasure, to which I am no enemy when it is properly seasoned and of a good composition, is surely of the cloying kind. Veins of wit, elegant conversation, easy commerce, are unknown among the Turks; and yet they seem capable of all these, if the vile spirit of their government did not stifle genius, damp curiosity, and suppress an hundred passions, that embellish and render life agreeable. The luscious passion of the Seraglio is the only one almost that is gratified here to the full, but it is blended so with the surly spirit of despotism in one of the parties, and with the dejection and anxiety which this spirit produces in the other, that to one of my way of thinking it cannot appear otherwise than as a very mixed kind of enjoyment. The women here are not, indeed, so closely confined as many have related; they enjoy a high degree of liberty even in the bosom of servitude, and they have methods of evasion and disguise that are very favourable to gallantry; but after all, they are still under uneasy apprehensions of being discovered; and a discovery exposes them to the most merciless rage of jealousy, which is here a monster that cannot be satiated but with blood. The magnificence and riches that reign in the apartments of the ladies of fashion here, seem to be one of their chief pleasures, joined with their retinue of female slaves, whose music, dancing and dress amuse them highly; but there is such an air of form and stiffness amidst this grandeur, as hinders it from pleasing me at long run, however I was dazzled with it at first sight. This stiffness and formality of manners are peculiar to the Turkish ladies; for the Grecian belles are of quite another character and complexion; with them pleasure appears in more engaging forms, and their persons, manners, conversation and amusements are very far from being destitute of elegance and ease.—

I received the news of Mr. Addison's being declared Secretary of State[1] with the less surprize, in that I know that post was almost offered to him before. At that time he declined it, and [I] really believe that he would have done well to have declined it now. Such a post as that, and such a Wife as the Countess, do not seem to be, in prudence, eligible for a man that is asthmatick; and we may see the day when he will be heartily glad to resign them both. It is well that he laid aside the thoughts of the voluminous dictionary, of which I have heard you or somebody else frequently make mention. But no more on that subject; I would not have said so much, were I not assured that this letter will come safe and unopened to hand. I long much to tread upon English ground, that I may see you and Mr. Congreve, who render that ground *classick ground*; nor will you refuse our present Secretary a part of that merit, whatever reasons you may have to be dissatisfied with him in other respects. You are the three happiest poets I ever heard of; one a secretary of state, the other enjoying leisure with dignity in two lucrative employments; and you, tho' your religious profession is an obstacle to court promotion, and disqualifies you from filling civil employments, have found the *Philosophers stone*, since by making the Iliad pass through your poetical crucible into an English form without losing aught of its original beauty, you have drawn the golden current of Pactolus to Twickenham.[2] I call this finding the Philosophers stone, since you alone found out the secret, and nobody else has got into it. A—n and T—l[3] tried it, but their experiments failed; and they lost, if not their money, at least a certain portion of their fame in the trial—while you touched the mantle of the divine Bard, and imbibed his spirit. I hope we shall have the Odyssey soon from your happy hand, and I think I shall follow with singular pleasure the traveller Ulysses, who was an observer of men and manners, when he travels in your harmonious numbers. I love him much better than the hot-headed son of Peleus, who bullied his general, cried for his mistress, and so on. It is true, the excellence of the Iliad does not depend upon his merit or dignity, but I wish nevertheless that

[1] Addison became Secretary in Apr. 1717.

[2] Pope had not moved to Twickenham in 1717.

[3] The mention of Addison and Tickell has been regarded as strange coming from a friendly Whig quarter. On the other hand, the fact that Addison and Mr. Wortley had been close friends does not mean that Lady Mary would value the new Secretary of State, and one can hardly imagine that she would be keenly appreciative of Addison's fine quality.

Homer had chosen a hero somewhat less pettish and less fantastick: a perfect hero is chimerical and unnatural, and consequently uninstructive; but it is also true that while the epic hero ought to be drawn with the infirmities that are the lot of humanity, he ought never to be represented as extremely absurd. But it becomes me ill to play the critick; so I take my leave of you for this time, and desire you will believe me, with the highest esteem, | Yours, &c.

POPE *to* CHARLES RACKETT[1] [7 *September* 1717]

Homer MSS. Add. 4807

Saturday.

Dear Brother,—I hope to be with you on Munday next: If you don't see me that night, I desire you to send a Man & Horse (such an one as I may ride safely) on Tuesday mornin[g] to the Toy by Hampton Court Gate, by te[n] a clock, and I will not fail to wait upon you. Which being all the business of this letter, I shall add no more than that I am my Sister's, and | Yours, most affectionately | A. Pope.

‡POPE *to* EDWARD BLOUNT[2] 8 *September* 1717

1735

Sept. 8. 1717.

I think your leaving *England*[3] was like a good Man's leaving the World, with the blessed Conscience of having acted well in it: And I hope you have received your Reward, in being happy where you are. I believe, in the Religious Country you now inhabit, you'll be better pleas'd to find I consider you in this light, than if I compared you to those *Greeks* and *Romans*, whose Constancy in suffering Pain, and whose Resolution in pursuit of a generous End, you would rather imitate than boast of.

But I had a melancholy hint the other day, as if you were yet a Martyr to the fatigue your Virtue made you undergo on this side the Water. I beg if your health be restor'd to you, not to deny me the Joy of knowing it: Your endeavours of Service and good Advices to the poor Papists, put me in mind of *Noah's* preaching forty years to those folks

[1] Pope must have written this letter before 8 a.m. when he left Hampton Court for Staines. See Pope to the Misses Blount, 13 Sept. 1717.

[2] Practically all the correspondence with Edward Blount is suspiciously doctored. The present letter would seem quite plausibly authentic if it were not for two things: (1) The postscript is borrowed from a Caryll letter—a fact that need not undermine the letter as a whole perhaps. (2) The date falls on the day when (Pope to the Misses Blount, 13 Sept.) the poet was at Staines keeping Miss Griffin from church all day. If he had been writing letters, surely she might have gone to church.

[3] Blount had returned from the Continent in the spring of this year, but went abroad again in July.—Elwin (vi. 373 n.).

that were to be drowned at last. At the worst I heartily wish your Ark may find an *Ararat*, and the Wife and Family, (the hopes of the good Patriarch) land safely after the Deluge upon the Shore of *Totness.*[1]

If I durst mix prophane with sacred history, I would chear you with the old Tale of *Brutus* the wandering *Trojan*, who found on that very Coast the happy End of his Peregrinations and Adventures.

I have very lately read *Jeffery* of *Monmouth* (to whom your *Cornwall* is not a little beholden) in the Translation of a Clergyman in my neighbourhood.[2] The poor Man is highly concerned to vindicate *Jeffery*'s veracity as an Historian; and told me he was perfectly astonished, we of the *Roman* Communion could doubt of the Legends of his Giants, while we believ'd those of our Saints? I am forced to make a fair Composition with him; and, by crediting some of the Wonders of *Corinæus* and *Gogmagog*, have brought him so far already, that he speaks respectfully of St. *Christopher*'s carrying Christ, and the Resuscitation of St. *Nicholas Tolentine*'s Chickens. Thus we proceed apace in converting each other from all manner of Infidelity.

Ajax and *Hector* are no more, compared to *Corinæus* and *Arthur*, than the *Guelphs* and *Ghibellines* were to the *Mohocks* of ever-dreadful memory. This amazing Writer has made me lay aside *Homer* for a Week, and when I take him up again, I shall be very well prepared to translate with belief and reverence the Speech of *Achilles*'s Horse.[3]

You'll excuse all this trifling, or any thing else which prevents a Sheet full of Compliment: And believe there is nothing more true (even more true than any thing in *Jeffery* is false) than that I have a constant Affection for you, and am, &c.

[1] Totnes, where the mythical Brutus, founder of Britain, had landed, was not far from Blagdon, Blount's estate.

[2] In Apr. 1718 the Rev. Aaron Thompson, 'late of Queen's College, Oxon.', as the title-page said, published the first English translation of Geoffrey of Monmouth, *The British History*, &c. Pope's help, as here detailed, led to an interest that eventuated in his design for an epic on the subject of Brutus. See Edward D. Snyder, 'Pope's Blank Verse Epic', *The Journal of Eng. and Germ. Philology*, xviii (1919), 580–3. Judging from the list of subscribers to *The British History* the Burlingtons were among Thompson's chief patrons.

In his official text of 1737 (quarto and folio) Pope at this point (after *neighbourhood*) inserted the following: 'He wanted my help to versify the prayer of Brutus, made when he was much in our circumstances, enquiring in what land to set up his seat, and worship like his fathers?

> 'Goddess of Woods, tremendous in the chace,
> To Mountain-wolves and all the Savage race,
> Wide o'er th' aerial Vault extends thy sway,
> And o'er th' infernal Regions void of day,
> On thy third Reign look down; disclose our Fate,
> In what new Nation shall we fix our Seat?
> When shall we next thy hallow'd Altars raise,
> And Quires of Virgins celebrate thy praise?'

The passage did not appear in other editions by Pope.

[3] The speech comes at the very end of Book XIX. At the time of writing this letter Pope seems not to have finished Book XVI, which had to be available for the volume of 1718.

P.S.[1] I know you will take part in rejoycing for the Victory of Prince *Eugene* over the *Turks*, in the Zeal you bear to the Christian Interest, tho' your Cousin of *Oxford* (with whom I dined yesterday) says, there is no other difference in the Christians beating the *Turks*, or the *Turks* beating the Christians, than whether the Emperor shall first declare War against *Spain*, or *Spain* declare it against the Emperor. I must add another Apothegm of the same noble Earl; it was the Saying of a Politick Prince, "Time and he would get the better of any two others." To which Lord *Oxford* made this Answer,

Time and I 'gainst any two?
Chance and I 'gainst *Time* and *you.*

JOHN WESTON *to* CHARLES RACKETT[2] 9 *September* 1717

Homer MSS. Add. 4807

Sep the 9th 1717

Sir,—Our Ladys doe Designe to waight on you and Mrs Raket to morrow att Dinner, if not Inconvenient to you, we all Desier that you would make noe Strangers of us, In which you will Adde much to the Obligations of | Your Reall freind | John Weston

Pray All our Respects | to Mrs Raket and my | Cosin Manuke.[3]

Address: To | Mr Rakett These Present

||POPE *to* TERESA *and* MARTHA BLOUNT[4] 13 *September* 1717

Mapledurham

⌜Sept. 13th 1717.⌝

⌜Dear Ladies,⌝—You can't be surprized to find him a dull Correspondent, whom you have known so long for a dull Companion. And tho I am pretty sensible, that if I have any wit I may as well write to show it, as not; ⌜because any Lady that has once seen me will naturally ask, what I can show that is better?⌝[5] Yet I'll content myself with

[1] Pope evidently borrowed this postscript—except the last two sentences—from his letter to Caryll, 22 Aug. 1717. After 1735 the last two sentences were omitted in all Pope's texts. Lord Oxford is not known to have been an actual cousin of either Caryll or Blount. *The Evening Post*, 31 Aug. 1717, reports that Lord Oxford left London on the 25th of that month—a fact which somewhat undermines Pope's date of 8 Sept.

[2] This letter relates neatly to that of 13 Sept. Pope had arrived at Hallgrove on Sunday night from Staines, and when this letter announced Weston as a guest for dinner on Tuesday, Pope fled to the Dancastles, apparently taking the letter along with him.

[3] 'Cosin Manuke' is probably the Rev. William Mannock, the Racketts' chaplain. Father Mannock was a source for some of Spence's *Anecdotes*.

[4] Printed by Pope in 1735 as Letter X among his 'Letters to Several Ladies'. Normally his text has been reprinted by editors—by Elwin, for example. Here the text is that of the original letter still at Mapledurham. Pope's omissions (numerous) are placed in half-brackets. The letter was probably written at Oxford.

[5] The words in half-brackets are omitted after 1735.

giving you as plain a History of my Pilgrimage as Mr Purchas himself, or as John Bunyan could do, of his Walking thro' the Wilderness of this world, &c.

First then I went by water to Hampton Court, unattended by all but my own Virtues, which were not of so modest a nature as to keep themselves, or me, conceald from the Courtiers. For I met the Prince with all his Ladies ⌜(tho few or none of his Lords)⌝ on horseback coming from Hunting. Mrs B⌜ellendine⌝ & Mrs L⌜epell⌝ took me into protection (contrary to the Laws against harbouring Papists), & gave me a Dinner, with something I liked better, an opportunity of conversation with Mrs H⌜oward⌝. We all agreed that the life of a Maid of Honor[1] was of all things the most miserable; & wished that every Woman who envyd it had a Specimen of it. To eat Westphalia Ham in a morning, ride over Hedges & ditches on borrowed Hacks, come home in the heat of the day with a Feavor, & what is worse a hundred times, a red Mark in the forehead with a Beaver hatt[2]; all this may qualify them to make excellent Wives for Fox-hunters, & bear abundance of ruddy-complexion'd Children. As soon as they can wipe off the Sweat of the day, they must simper an hour, & catch cold, in the Princesses apartment; from thence[3] *To Dinner*, *with what appetite they may*—And after that, till midnight, walk, work, or think, which they please? I can easily believe, no lone House in Wales, with a Mountain & a Rookery, is more contemplative than this Court; and as a proof of it I need only tell you Mrs L⌜epell⌝ walk'd all alone with[4] me three or 4 hours, by moonlight; and we mett no Creature of any quality, but the King, who gave audience all alone to the Vice-chamberlen, under the Garden-wall.[5]

In short, I heard of no Ball, Assembly, Basset-Table, or any place where two or three were gatherd together, except Mad. Kilmanzech's,[6] to which I had the honour to be invited, & the grace to stay away.

I was heartily tired;[7] ⌜& glad to be gone by 8 aclock next morning;

[1] On the three Maids of Honour here named see Norman Ault's *New Light*, chapters x and xvii. Pope in his printings left most personal names either blank or mere initials.

[2] times, . . . hatt] times, with a red mark in the forehead from an uneasy hat *1735–42*.

[3] thence *To Dinner*] thence (as *Shakespear* has it) *To Dinner* *1735–42*.

[4] walk'd all alone with] walk'd with *1737–42*.

[5] Pope liked this picture of the unfrequented Court so well that he echoed it months later in a letter to Lady Mary. See i. 470.

[6] The Baroness von Kielmansegge, mistress of George I, came over to England in 1714. Her husband died 15 Nov. 1717; she was created Countess of Darlington in 1722. Her chief German rival, Mme von Schulemberg, was called 'the Maypole', whereas the figure of Mme von Kielmansegge made it pleasant to call her 'the Elephant and Castle'.

[7] In printing his text Pope here omitted sentences and jumped from Hampton Court to (unidentified) B— Park, as follows: 'I was heartily tired and posted to B— Park; there we had an excellent Discourse of Quackery; Dr. Shadwell was mentioned with honour. . . .' After 1735 Pope deleted the *B* of 'B— Park'; Dr. Shadwell became Dr. S* and Lady A. became Lady ——. In no printed text did Pope mention Staines or Miss Griffin. Presumably B— Park was near Staines, and there Pope met Lady Arran and her relative (?) Col. Butler.

hir'd two damnd Horses, gallopd to Staines, lost leather, kept Miss Griffin from Church all the Sunday, & lay at my Brothers near Bagshot that night.

⌜Col. Butler (who is as well known by the name of Fair Butler, as ever Fair Helen was) came to complain of me to my Lady Arran. That Gentleman chanc'd to keep his word in calling at Hampton Court, but I was too quick by an hour or two. I met him here, and there ensued an excellent discourse of Quackery;⌝ Dr Shadwell[1] was mentiond with honour⌜; & we had a word or two in private concerning the secret disease, not altogether Impertinent.⌝ Lady A⌜rran⌝ walked a whole hour abroad, without dying after it, at least in the time I stayd there; tho' she seem'd to be fainting, and to have convulsive motions in her head several times.[2]

This day, my Father took a great deal of care to send after me a Letter, which containd certain Advices from my friend —— where ——[3] were to be met with in a civil house at Oxford.

⌜I defy them and all their [works,] for I love no meat but Ortolans, and no women but you. Tho indeed that's no proper comparison but for fatt Dutchesses; For to love you, is as if one should wish to Eat Angels, or drink Cherubim-Broath.⌝

I arrived at Mr Dancastles on Tuesday-noon[4], having fled from the face (I wish I could say from the horned face) of Mr Weston,[5] who dined that day at my Brother's. ⌜I have seen my Farmer, yea and the Gold-ring which I forgot, on his finger.⌝ I ⌜have sent to Sir W. Compton,[6] &⌝ past the rest of the day in those Woods where I have so often enjoyd—an Author & a Book;[7] ⌜and begot such Sons upon the Muses, as I hope will live to see their father what he never was yet, an old and a good Man.⌝ I made a Hymn as I past thro' ⌜these Groves;⌝ it ended with a deep Sigh, which I will not tell you the meaning of.[8]

[1] Sir John Shadwell (1671–1747) was physician in ordinary to both Queen Anne and George I (*DNB*).

[2] Lady Arran achieved her 77th year, dying in 1756.

[3] The blanks represent illegible words overscored in the original. In the text of 1735 the sentence reads: 'This day I receiv'd a Letter with certain advices where women were to be met with at *Oxford*.' After 1735 the sentence was omitted, as was the following short paragraph.

[4] I arrived . . . Tuesday-noon] I arrived in the forest by *Tuesday* noon *1735–42*.

[5] For John Weston's letter to Mr. Rackett see here under date of 9 Sept. 1717. Concerning Weston's treatment of his wife Pope had been furious since 1711. See *The Athenaeum*, 15 July 1854, pp. 876–9. In the original letter *Weston* though overscored is legible. In 1735 Pope printed instead of *Weston* 'Moses B—'. In 1737–42 he printed only 'Moses'.

[6] Sir William Compton, Bt., lived at Hurst near Ockingham.

[7] an Author & a Book] a Book and a Friend *1735–42*.

[8] From this point Pope's printed text omitted the rest of the letter and ineptly substituted a paragraph from his letter to Martha Blount (still preserved at Mapledurham) sent about the end of Nov. 1714. Dr. Radcliffe had died 1 Nov. 1714, but this mention of him as recently dead might have been thought strange only if Pope had printed a date for this letter. In 1735 in Pope's text *Shadwell* is *Sh*—. Thereafter in his texts the name is merely *S*—. In 1735 the paragraph read: 'Your Doctor is gone the way of all his patients, and was hard put to it

⌜All hail! once pleasing, once inspiring Shade,
Scene of my youthful Loves, and happier hours!
Where the kind Muses met me as I stray'd,
And gently pressd my hand, and said, Be Ours.

⌜Take all thou e're shalt have, a constant Muse:
At Court thou may'st be lik'd, but nothing gain;
Stocks thou may'st buy & sell, but always lose;
And love the brightest eyes, but love in vain!

⌜On Thursday I went to Stonor, which I have long had a mind to see since the romantic description you gave me of it. The Melancholy which my Wood, and this Place,[1] have spread over me, will go near to cast a cloud upon the rest of my letter, if I don't make haste to conclude it here. I know you wish my happiness so much, that I would not have you think I have any other reason to be melancholy: And after all, He must be a beast[2] that is so, with two such fine women for his friends. Tis enough to make any creature easy, even such an one as | Your humble Servant.⌝

||POPE *to* TERESA *and* MARTHA BLOUNT[3]

[September 1717]

Mapledurham

Ladies,—⌜I came from Stonor (its Master not being at home) to Oxford the same night.⌝ Nothing could have more of that Melancholy which once us'd to please me, than that days[4] journey: For after having passd thro' my favorite Woods in the forest, with a thousand Reveries of past pleasures; I rid over hanging hills, whose tops were edgd with Groves, & whose feet water'd with winding rivers, listening to the

how to dispose of an estate miserably unweildy, and splendidly unuseful to him. Sir *Samuel Garth* says, that for *Ratcliffe* to leave a Library, was as if a Eunuch should found a Seraglio. Dr. *Sh*— lately told a Lady he wonder'd she cou'd be alive after him: she made answer She wonder'd at it for two reasons, because Dr. *Ratcliffe* was dead and because Dr. *Sh*— was living. I am | *Your*, &c.'

[1] Presumably the 'ancient dusky part of the University' of Oxford, from which he was writing.

[2] Towards the end of a later letter to Lady Mary Wortley Montagu Pope recalled this phrase (which he could hardly have had by him as he wrote?) and said: 'and after all he must be a beast that can be melancholy with such a fine woman as you to his friend.' See i. 471.

[3] This undated letter seems to fit into the ramble of Sept. 1717. Pope left the Dancastles (or the Racketts) on Thursday, 12 Sept.; he had hoped to spend the night at Stonor with Caryll's friend Thomas Stonor, Esq.; but the absence of a host forced him to continue to Oxford, where he arrived about midnight. On the 17th he wrote to his father that he had reached Oxford on Friday, and possibly it was after midnight of Thursday when he arrived. One should note the care exercised by Pope in rhythm and phrasing—seen even in his minute revisions or omissions made when he printed in 1735. The text of the original letter is here given, with changes (including a 'new' final paragraph) duly noted.

[4] than that days] than my last days *1735–42*.

falls of Cataracts below, & the murmuring of Winds above. The gloomy Verdure of Stonor succeeded to these, & then the Shades of the Evening overtook me, the Moon rose in the clearest Sky I ever saw, by whose solemn light I pac'd on slowly, without company, or any interruption to the range of my thoughts. About a mile before I reachd Oxford, all the ⌜Night⌝ bells toll'd, in different notes; the Clocks of every College answerd one another; & told me, some in a deeper, some in a softer voice, that it was eleven a clock.[1]

All this was no ill preparation to the life I have led since; among those old walls, venerable Galleries, Stone Portico's, studious walks & solitary Scenes of the University. I wanted nothing but a black Gown and a Salary, to be as meer a Bookworm as any there. I conform'd myself to the College hours, was rolld up in books ⌜& wrapt in meditation,⌝ lay in one of the most ancient, dusky parts of the University,[2] and was as dead to the world as any Hermite of the desart. If any thing was awake or alive in me, it was a little Vanity, such as even those good men used to entertain when the Monks of their own Order extolld their Piety & Abstractedness.[3] For I found my self receivd with a sort of respect, which this idle part of mankind, the Learned, pay to their own Species; who are as considerable here, as the Busy the Gay and the Ambitious are in your World. Indeed I was so treated,[4] that I could not but sometimes ask myself in my mind, what College I was founder of,[5] or what Library I had built? Methinks I do very ill, to return to the world again, to leave the only place where I make a ⌜good⌝ figure, and from seeing myself seated with dignity on the most conspicuous Shelves of a Library, go to contemplate this wretched person in the abject condition[6] of lying at a Lady's feet in Bolton street.[7]

I will not deny, but that like Alexander, in the midst of my Glory, I am wounded, & find myself a meer man. To tell you from whence the Dart comes, is to no purpose, since neither of you will take the tender care to draw it out of my heart, & suck the poison with your lips⌜; or are in any disposition to take in a part of the venome yourselves, to ease me⌝. Here, at my Lord H⌜arcourt⌝'s, I see a Creature nearer an Angel than a Woman, (tho a Woman be very near as good as an Angel) I think you have formerly heard me mention Mrs

[1] a clock] at night *1735–42*.

[2] The letter to his father (17 Sept.) leads one to think Pope the guest of Dr. Abel Evans, chaplain of St. John's College.

[3] Abstractedness] abstraction *1735–42*.

[4] so treated] treated in such a manner *1735–42*.

[5] Is it over-subtle to imagine that Pope had in mind the fact that Sir Thomas Pope (not a relative, alas!) had founded Trinity College and that the Radcliffe Camera was a library, the building of which must have been under discussion?

[6] go . . . condition] put myself into the abject posture *1735–42*.

[7] Bolton street] St. *James*'s Square *1735–42*. (The Blount ladies had by 1717 established themselves in Bolton Street, and the name was changed to avoid identification.)

Jennings[1] as a Credit to the Maker of Angels. She is a relation of his Lordships, and he gravely proposd her to me for a Wife, being tender of her interests & knowing (what is a Shame to Providence) that she is less indebted to Fortune than I. I told him his Lordship could never have thought of such a thing but for his misfortune of being blind, and that I never cou'd till I was so:[2] ⌜But that, as matters now were, I did not care to force so fine a woman to give the finishing stroke to all my deformities, by the last mark of a Beast, horns.

⌜Now I am talking of Beauty, I shall see my Lady Jane Hyde[3] to morrow, at Cornbury. I shall pass a day and night at Blenheim-park, & will then hasten home, (taking Reding[4] in my way) I have every where made enquiry if it be possible to get any Annuities on sound Security: It would really be an inexpressible joy to me if I could serve you, and I will always do my utmost to give myself pleasure.

⌜I beg you both to think as well of me, that is to think me as much yours, as any one else. What degree of friendship and tenderness I feel for you, I must be content with being sure of myself; but I shall be glad if you believe it in any degree. Allow me as much as you can: and think as well as you are able of one whose imperfections are so manifest, and who thinks so little of himself, as to think ten times more of either of you.⌝[5]

†POPE *to* MRS. ——[6] [*September* 1717?]

1735

I will not describe *Bl*— in particular, not to forestall your expectations before you see it: Only take a short account, which I will hazard my

[1] Mrs. Jennings] Mrs. T— *1735*. (This entire sentence was omitted in the texts of 1737–42.)

[2] told his Lordship . . . was so] told him 'twas what he could never have thought of, if it had not been his misfortune to be blind, and what I never could think of, while I had eyes to see both her and my self. *1735–42*. (From this point Pope omitted in his printings the rest of the original letter.)

[3] Lady Jane and her sister the Duchess of Queensberry were regarded as about the most beautiful women of their day—but less beautiful than their mother, Jane, Countess of Clarendon. Lady Jane married a year later than this William Capell, Earl of Essex. Pope was evidently planning to visit her brother Viscount Cornbury.

[4] Reading he would pass through, but Mapledurham had no appeal now that the girls no longer lived there.

[5] Having omitted the last part of the original letter in his printings, Pope substituted what seems obviously a decorous rewriting of parts about annuities. He may, however, have borrowed the paragraph from an unknown letter. It read: 'I must not conclude without telling you, that I will do the utmost in the affair you desire. It would be an inexpressible joy to me if I could serve you, and I will always do all I can to give my self pleasure. I wish as well for you as for my self; I am in love with you both much as I am with my self, for I find my self most so with all three, when I least suspect it. | I am, &c.' In texts of 1737–42 he changed *all three* in the last sentence to *either*; and *both much as I am* became *both as much as I am*.

[6] This letter might describe Blenheim as seen in any of several visits to its neighbourhood. But since in Sept. 1717 Pope was in a descriptive mood, as his letters to Martha Blount

little credit is no unjust one. I never saw so great a thing with so much littleness in it: I think the Architect built it entirely in compliance to the taste of its Owners: for it is the most inhospitable thing imaginable, and the most selfish: it has, like their own hearts, no room for strangers, and no reception for any person of superior quality to themselves. There are but just two Apartments, for the Master and Mistress, below; and but two apartments above, (very much inferior to them) in the whole House. When you look upon the Outside, you'd think it large enough for a Prince; when you see the Inside, it is too little for a Subject; and has not conveniency to lodge a common family. It is a house of Entries and Passages; among which there are three Vista's through the whole, very uselessly handsome. There is what might have been a fine Gallery, but spoil'd by two Arches towards the End of it, which take away the sight of several of the windows. There are two ordinary stair-cases instead of one great one. The best things within the house, are the Hall, which is indeed noble and well-proportion'd; and the cellars and offices under-ground, which are the most commodious, and the best contrived, of the whole. At the top of the building are several Cupola's and little Turrets that have but an ill effect, and make the building look at once finical and heavy. What seems of the best taste, is that Front towards the gardens, which is not yet loaded with these turrets. The two Sides of the building are intirely spoil'd by two monstrous bow-windows which stand just in the middle, instead of doors: And as if it were fatal that some trifling littleness should every where destroy the grandeur, there are in the chief front two semicircles of a lower structure than the rest, that cut off the angles, and look as if they were purposely design'd to hide a loftier and nobler piece of building, the top of which appears above them. In a word, the whole is a most expensive absurdity; and the Duke of *Shrewsbury* gave a true character of it, when he said, it was a great *Quarry of Stones above ground.*

We paid a visit to the spring where *Rosamond* bathed her self, on a hill where remains only a piece of a wall of the old Palace of *Henry* the Second. We toasted her shade in the cold water, not without a thought or two, scarce so cold as the liquor we drank it in. I dare not tell you what they were, and so hasten to conclude, | Your, &c.

show, it is placed there—with no real assurance that it was written then. It seems to some degree inspired by the same epigram of Martial (xii. 50. 7–8) that inspired the lines (EC iv. 451) 'Upon the Duke of Marlborough's House at Woodstock', which were published in 1714. The letter has been regarded as addressed to Martha Blount, and it may well be so; but there is no evidence at all as to the addressee.

POPE *to* HIS FATHER[1] 17 *September* [1717]

Homer MSS. Add. 4808

Sept. 17th

FRAGMENT

I came to Oxford on Friday last, & shall continue here and at my Lord Harcourt's about a week, after which I hope to return to you, calling at Reding & at Halgrove as I return. My Journey into Herefordshire I have, upon second thoughts, put off, the season being so far advanced. all your acquaintance were well, where I pass'd; and I have been so, ever since my coming out. I beg to have a line of your healths, directed to Dr Evans's in St. John's College Oxon, which will reach me in a day or two where-ever I am. I writ to you from Henley, a week agoe, and to Mr Rollinson.[2] I live here very regularly in College hours, & have

POPE *to* HIS FATHER[3] 25 [*September* 1717]

Homer MSS. Add. 4807

Wensday, the 25th

I design to see you to morrow, or on Friday: And shall now only add that I am my dear Mothers and Your most dutiful Son | A. Pope

Address: For | Mr Pope, at Mawson's Buildings. | Chiswick | With speed.

*—— *to* POPE[4] [*October* 1717]

Homer MSS. Add. 4808

FRAGMENT

I am desired by my Aunt Mace to acquaint you with her reception of your kind Letter, and that it came safe to her hands, she takes the

[1] The year of this fragment is partly determined by its position among the Homer MSS. and partly by its congruity with neighbouring letters. What he wrote from Henley a week ago, perhaps having no blank spaces for use in translation, was not preserved.

[2] William Rollinson, who had hoped to be at Oxford with Pope in 1714.

[3] During the period of the residence of Pope's father at Chiswick (to which place this letter is addressed), the 25th fell on a Wednesday only three times: 25 April and 25 July in 1716 and 25 Sept. 1717. Letters to Caryll and Dancastle indicate that both father and son were moving into their new home about 25 Apr. 1716. In July he writes to Parnell from home, apparently, complaining of ill health. The date 25 Sept. 1717 fits neighbouring letters perfectly, and seems sure. It also fits the general location of the letter in the Homer MSS.

[4] The position of this fragment in the Homer MSS. indicates that it is probably of 1717. Pope returned from his 'long journeys' about 27 Sept., and the letter should date between that time and the death of his father on 23 Oct. 'Aunt Mace' is presumably also Pope's aunt, since one of Mrs. Pope's sisters (more than one of whom lived to extreme age) had married the Rev. Charles Mace of York, who died about 1711 while in the pulpit preaching in York Castle to the prisoners. Which of the other numerous sisters of Mrs. Pope had survived to this time is unknown. See Robert Davies, *Pope's Maternal Ancestry* (1858), p. 50.

same as a very great favour from you, and now returnes you her hearty thankes, she alsoe is glad you are safely return'd from your long Journeys, and wishes you all the happynesses the world affords—The death of her sister makes a great Impression upon her, but the extraordinary manner you have represented it to her does much conduce to the mitigation of that affliction—she is alsoe mightily concernd for your Mothers Indisposition and prayes she may have a speedy recovery —what I am further to add is that her hearty wishes upon all attends your ffather Mother and your selfe, and what else can be thought on is not wanting in her—my Cousen Mace

JAMES CRAGGS *to* POPE[1] [1717?]

Homer MSS. Add. 4808

Sir,—I have business which will not permit me to have the pleasure of your good company to morrow at dinner, but if you'l doe me that favour on Sunday next, & that it is not too early for you to drink Chocolate with me to morrow morning at 8 a clock You'l very much oblige | Your most humble | servant | J Craggs

Friday night

Address [on a separate folio]: [To Alexa]nder Pope Esqr | [at Mawson]'s Buildings | [in Chiswic]k | with Care

POPE *to* TERESA BLOUNT[2] [1717?]

Mapledurham

Dear Madam,—I am going to Kensington, which makes me desire you'l let George secure a Coach & 4 of your neighbor Angell against to morrow. I must tell you in fulness of heart, I am with much gratitude | Yours.

pray Let me know to night, your Hour.

I'll try for Mrs Glanvil to night: I can't avoid going out of town to day

put a wafer into the Inclosd & return it to the bearer

Address: Mrs Teresa Blount

[1] This letter from the younger Craggs, at this time Secretary at War, can be chronologically placed only from its position in the Homer MSS. It is a part of Book XVI, and its neighbouring letters date, or seem to date, from the autumn of 1717.

[2] In placing this letter chronologically—it cannot be surely dated—one is influenced by the fact that the Blounts are now established and have neighbours, and by the fact that Pope is still friendly with Teresa.

POPE *to* TERESA *and* MARTHA BLOUNT[1] [?1717]

Mapledurham

Dear Ladies,—If you'll take an Airing this fine morning in Kensington Gardens, I'll carry you thither at eleven a clock: By which time my visit to the D. of B. will be perform'd. I have sent the Bearer for the Haunch of Venison, so you may spare George's Gravity that trouble. | I am faithfully | Yours, | A. [Pope.]

TERESA BLOUNT *to* POPE[2] [*Autumn* 1717]

Homer MSS. Add. 4808

Wensday

This is only to let you Know We expect you Either tomorrow or friday, & we have told Mrs Scoop that we Should be at her house one of those Evenings; let me Know if it Cannot be; I hope you are all well | Teresa

Mrs Scroop expects [*cætera desunt*]

Address: To | Mr Pope at his house | in the New Buildings at | Chiswick

POPE *to* TERESA *and* MARTHA BLOUNT[3] [?1717]

Mapledurham

Ladies,—I have repented, & can't find in my heart to go, if you care to let me see you again today—whatever company you thought of having, I shall be glad to make one, provided you'l promise not to be confined from any on my account. If Mrs Scrope be to come, pray give me a word's notice, & I'll call first at her door, to pay her a visit. —I'll write to night by Candlelight what I should have writ to morrow morning, & finish it to morrow night at Chiswick.

From Dr Arbuthnot's.

[1] No dating is possible for this letter. One guesses that the Blount ladies were now established in London. Pope from 1716 or thereabouts was friendly with the Duke of Buckingham, whose levee he evidently plans to attend.

[2] Since part of *Iliad* XVI was translated on the verso of this note, it must have been written not later than 1717, and it seems to postdate the time when the Blounts were established in Bolton Street. Pope had returned to Chiswick from Oxford about Friday 27 Sept., and the social tone of the letter would seem to place it on a Wednesday before the 23rd (2, 9, or 16 Oct.), the day when the poet's father died. But it might possibly postdate that event.

[3] This is another letter impossible for sure dating. Some phrases suggest that it was written after the death of the poet's father, and the mention of Mrs. Scrope possibly ties it in with Teresa's 'Wensday' letter to Pope.

*POPE *to* LADY ——[1] [*October* 1717?]

(Drafted for Francis Bourne)

Homer MSS. Add. 4808

Please your Ladiship,—I do humbly crave your good Honourable Ladiships pardon to your poor alms woman Francis Bourne who has been supported (with my Mother) from your good Ladyships house for these thirty years: for which I shall be ever bound to pray for your honour, and honorable family

Being this twelvemonth kept out from the door, & not receiving the Weekly Bread I always had, or any other Charity which your Good Honour always allowd me with the rest of your Ladiships poor Parish Women. My condition is very deplorably sad, and if my good Lady would order me to be let work or wash in the house, or continue Your Honourable charity to me by your Ladishipps Ourder, I shall be ever praying for your honors & all yours health & happiness. But whether your Ladishipp dos or not, continue, I shall daily pray for as I always do.

By | Your Good honors poor Alms woman | Francis Bourne

POPE *to* THE DUCHESS OF HAMILTON[2] *October* [1717]

The New York Public Library (Berg)

London, October the — Between day and night —
The writer drunk—

Madam,—Mrs Whitworth, (who, as her Epitaph on Twitnam High-way assures us, had attaind to as much perfection & purity as any since the Apostles)[3] is now deposited according to her own order

[1] This letter, in Pope's hand, is a typical charitable act on his part. Apparently Bourne cannot write, and Pope here writes at her dictation or pretended dictation. He evidently tries to make the letter sound like the almswoman and even corrupts his spelling consciously. It is a literary as well as a charitable act. The chronology of the letter is conditioned by its place in the Homer MSS., and is unsure.

[2] First printed in *The Universal Museum*; rptd. in *Lloyd's Evening Post*, 5 Dec. 1764; also in *The Annual Register* (1764), pp. 222–3. The year of the letter is determined by the fact that John Gay and William Pulteney are together in Blois.

[3] Since Pope was not yet an inhabitant of 'Twitnam High-way' there is a chance that he knew this epitaph from the source that has longest preserved it, *The Censor*, No. 27 (10 June 1715). *The Censor* says: 'I cannot dismiss this Subject without taking Notice of a Monument, which has more Ostentation in it than is decent on these Occasions. It is erected on the side of a Garden-Wall on the Entrance to the Town of *Twickenham*, under which are laid the Ashes of Mrs. *Whitrow* a *Quaker*, and over which this Inscription is ingrav'd on a Stone. | Nosce Teipsum [in black letter]. | *Here, at her Desire,* | *are deposited in a Vault the* | *Remains of Mrs.* Joane Whitrow; | *whose Soul on the 8th of* Septem. 1707. | *left this World, and ascended* | *into the glorious Joys of the Just,* | *having liv'd about 76 Years.* | *She was Eminent for her* | *Great ABSTINENCE;* | *Her Charity was universal;* | *She lov'd all good Persons* | *without Regard to Party.* | *She was favour'd by Heaven* | *with Uncommon*

between a Fig-tree and a Vine, there to be found out at the last Resurrection.

I am just come from seeing your Grace in much the like Situation, between a Hony-suckle and a Rose-bush; where you are to continue as long as Canvas can last: I suppose the Painter by those Emblems intended to intimate, on the one hand, your Grace's sweet Disposition to your friends;[1] & on the other, to show you are near enough related to the Thistle of Scotland to deserve the same Motto with regard to your Enemies. *Nemo me impune lacessit.*[2]

The two foregoing Periods, methinks, are so mystical, learned & perplext, that if you have any Statesmen or Divines about you, they can't chuse but be pleased with them. One Divine you cannot be without, as a good Christian; & a Statesman you have lately had, for I hear my Lord Selkirk has been with you.[3] But (that I may not be unintelligible quite to the bottome of this page) I must tell Your Grace in english, that I have made a Painter bestow the foresaid Ornaments round about You (for upon you there needs none) & am, upon the whole, pleasd with my Picture beyond expression.

I may now say of your Picture, it is the thing in the world the likest you, except yourself; as a Cautious person once said of an Elephant, It was the biggest in the world, Except itself.

You see Madam it is not impossible for you to be compared to an Elephant: and you must give me leave to shew you one may carry on the Simile.

An Elephant never bends his knees; & I am told Your Grace says no Prayers. An Elephant has a most remarkable command of his Snout, & so has your Grace when you imitate my Lady O—y.[4] An

Gifts. | *She wrot several pious Books,* | *She was an extraordinary Person,* | *and came as near Perfection,* | *as the brightest Saints* | *that Ever adorn'd the Church* | *since the Apostolick Age.* | *Examine your selves* | 2 Cor. 13. 5. | *Death and Judgment* | *will come.*'

It will be noted that *The Censor* gives the name as Whitrow, and Joan Whitrow wrote 'pious books'. Possibly Pope erred accidentally, but the name Whitworth might arouse the Duchess, since the Duke of Hamilton's reflections in 1712 on Richard Whitworth (Lord Mohun's witness in their lawsuit) led to the duel that ended the Duke's life. The point of the mention of the tombstone is that it is placed 'between a fig-tree and a vine', and Pope has had the Duchess somewhat similarly surrounded in a portrait he has commissioned.

[1] Pope's phrasing reminds one of Swift (To Stella, 16 Nov. 1712), who said of the Duchess: 'She has abundance of wit and spirit; . . . and seldom spared any body that gave her the least provocation; by which she had many envyers, and few friends.'

[2] In the margin opposite this Latin Pope writes: 'Lord William will conster this Latine if you send it to Thistleworth.' Lord William, second son of the Duchess, was still a schoolboy.

[3] Charles, Earl of Selkirk, was brother-in-law to the Duchess. Pope early acquired the 'strange spleen to Selkirk' (from the Duchess?) that he was to express as late as his 'Epilogue to the Satires'.

[4] The wife of the 1st Earl of Orkney was sister-in-law to the Duchess. Of the two ladies Swift told Stella (17 Nov. 1712): 'They hate one another.' Swift preferred the countess. Pope wrote O—y, but when the letter was printed in *Lloyd's Evening Post* the name was given, doubtless rightly, in full.

Elephant is a great Lover of Men, & so is your Grace for all I know, tho from your Partiality to myself I shoud rather think you lovd little Children.

I beg you not to be discouraged in this point. Remember the Text which I'll preach upon, the first day I am a Parson. Suffer little children to come to me—And—Despise not one of these Little ones.

No Madam—despise Great Beasts, such as Gay; who now goes by the dredful name of, *The Beast of Blois*, where Mr Pulteney & he are settled, & where he shews Tricks Gratis, to all the Beasts of his own Country, (for Strangers do not yet understand the Voice of the Beast.) I have heard from him but once, Lord Warwick twice, Mrs Lepell thrice; If there be any that has heard from him four-times, I suppose it is you.

I beg Mr Blondel may know, Dr Logg[1] has receivd Ordination, & enters upon his Function this winter at Mrs Blount's. They have chosen this innocent Man for their Confessor; and I believe most Roman Catholick Ladies, that have any Sins, will follow their example. This good Priest will be of the Order of Melchisedeck, a Priest for ever, & serve a Family from generation to generation. He'll stand in a corner as quietly as a Clock, & being wound up once a week strike up a loud Alarum to S[in] on a Sunday morning. Nay, if the Christian Religion should be abolishd (as indeed there is great reason to expect it from the Wisdom of the Legislature) He might at worst make an excellent Bonefire, which is all that (upon a change of Religion) can be desired from a Heretique. I do not hope Your Grace should be converted, but however, I wish you would call at Mrs Bs out of curiosity. To meet people one likes, is thought by some the best reason of going to Church, & I dare promise you'll like one another. They are extreamly your Servants, or else I shoud not think them my friends.

I ought to keep up the custom, & ask you to send me Something. Therefore pray, Madam, send me Yourself, that is a Letter; & pray make haste to bring up your self, that is all I value, to Towne. I am with the truest respect, the least ceremony, & the most Zeal, Madam, | Your Graces most obedient, faithfull | & most humble Servant. | A. Pope.

Mr. Hamilton, I am Yours. There is a short Letter for you.

Endorsement (in an old hand, on a separate sheet): Mr Popes Letter to the Dutchesse of Hamilton.

[1] Probably Pope wrote or intended to write *Legg*. See the reply of the Duchess immediately following this letter.

THE DUCHESS OF HAMILTON *to* POPE[1] [*October* 1717]

Homer MSS. Add. 4808

I have obey'd your orders & was in so great hast to do it that I did not stay to Walk down stairs but came tumbling to you in the utmost hurry & attend you in St Albans street where I hope you'l not keep me long under the impatience of wanting to see you father Leggs friend who is come on purpose to be one of his flock greets you as do's mr Hamilton & mounsier.[2] don't think that I'm any thing short of the above mention'd in being Your sincere servant.

fryday

My snout has been exercis'd since my arrivall.

Address (on the same folio in a different hand): To | Alexr Pope Esqr

POPE *to* LADY MARY WORTLEY MONTAGU[3]

[*Autumn* 1717]

The Pierpont Morgan Library

Madam,—I could quarrel with you quite thro' this paper, upon a period in yours, which bids me Remember you if possibly I can. You would have shown more knowledge both of yourself and of me, had you bid me Forget you if possibly I could. When I do, may this hand (as the Scripture says) forget its cunning, and this heart its—Folly, I was going to say, but I mean its Reason, & the most rational Sensation it ever had, that of your merit.

The poetical manner in which you paint some of the Scenes about you, makes me despise my native country and sets me on fire to fall into the Dance about your Fountain in Belgrade-village. I fancy myself, in my romantic thoughts & distant admiration of you, not unlike the man in the Alchymist that has a passion for the Queen of the Faeries. I lye dreaming of you in Moonshiny Nights exactly in the posture of Endymion gaping for Cynthia in a Picture. And with just such a Surprise and rapture should I awake, if after your long revolutions were accomplishd, you should at last come rolling back again, smiling with all that gentleness and serenity (peculiar to the Moon and

[1] The dating is mere guess-work, but this seems to follow shortly after the letter immediately preceding. Pope might say, as did Swift (To Stella, 27 Jan. 1711/12), 'Ladies always visit me in third places.' At whose house in St. Albans Street Pope was keeping the Duchess waiting is not known.

[2] Heretofore printed 'mumper', but it is probably 'mounsier', possibly referring to Mr. Blondel mentioned in the preceding letter to the Duchess.

[3] It is impossible to date this letter precisely, but in his next letter to Lady Mary (of [June 1718?]) Pope remarks that his father's death 'happened within a few days after I had writ to you inviting myself to meet you in your journey homewards'. Consequently the letter dates vaguely 'a few days' before 23 Oct.

you) and gilding the same Mountains from which you first set out on your solemn, melancholy journey. I am told that Fortune (more just to us than your virtue) will restore the most precious thing it ever robbd us of.[1] Some think it will be the only Equivalent the world affords for Pits's Diamond, so lately sent out of our Country, which after you was gone, was accounted the most valuable thing here. Adieu to that Toy! let the costly Bawble be hung about the neck of the Baby King it belongs to! So England does but recover that Jewel which was the wish of all her sensible hearts, & the joy of all her discerning eyes. I can keep no measures in speaking of this subject. I see you already coming, I feel you as you draw nearer, My heart leaps at your arrival: Let us have You from the East, and the Sun is at her service.

I write as if I were drunk, the pleasure I take in thinking of your return transports me beyond the bounds of common Sence and decency. Yet believe me, Madam, if there be any Circumstance of Chagrin in the occasion of your return, if there be any publick or private ill fortune that may give you a displeasure, I must still be ready to feel a part of it, notwithstanding the Joy I now express.

I have been mad enough to make all the enquiry I could at what time you sett out, & what Route you were to take? If Italy run yet in your thoughts, I hope you'll see it in your return. If I but knew you intended it, I'd meet you there and travel back with you. I would fain behold the best and brightest thing I know, in the Scene of ancient Virtue and Glory. I would fain see how you look, on the very Spot where Curtius sacrificd himself for his Country? and observe what difference there would be in your Eyes, when you ogled the Statue of a Julius Caesar, and a Marcus Aurelius? Allow me but to sneak after you in your train, to fill my pockets with Coins, or to lug an old Busto behind you, & I shall be proud beyond expression. Let people think if they will, that I did all this for the pleasure of treading on Classic Ground: I would whisper other reasons in your ear. The joy of following your Footsteps would as soon carry me to Mecca, as to Rome; and let me tell you as a friend, if you are really disposed to embrace the Mahometan religion, I'll fly on Pilgrimage with you thither, with as good a heart and as sound devotion, as ever Jeffery Rudel the Provençall Poet, went after the fine Countess of Tripoly to Jerusalem. If you never heard of this Jeffery, I'll assure you he deserves your acquaintance: He livd in our Richard the first's time, put on a Pilgrims weed, took his voyage, and when he got ashore, was just upon the point of expiring. The Countess of Tripoly came to the Ship, took him by the

[1] Addison's letter to Mr. Wortley Montagu announcing his recall is dated 28 Sept. 1717. When Pope learned of the move is uncertain. Newspapers (e.g. *The Weekly Packet*) as early as 21 Sept. announced that Sir Robert Sutton was being returned to Turkey to negotiate a peace; and such announcements obviously implied recall for Mr. Wortley Montagu. Abraham Stanyan succeeded him as ambassador.

hand: He lifted up his eyes, said, that having been blest with a sight of her, he was satisfied; and so departed this life. What did the Countess of Tripoly upon this? She made him a Splendid funeral, built him a Tomb of Porphyry, put his Epitaph upon it in Arabic verse, had his Sonnets curiously copied out and illumind with letters of gold, was taken with Melancholy, and turnd Nun. All this Madam you may depend upon for a truth and I send it you in the very words of my Author.[1]

I don't expect all this should be punctually copyd on either side, but methinks something like it is done already. The letters of Gold, and the curious Illumining of the Sonnets, was not a greater token of respect than what I have paid to your Eclogues: They lie inclosd in a Monument of Red Turkey, written in my fairest hand; the gilded Leaves are opend with no less veneration than the Pages of the Sybils; like them, lockd up & conceald from all prophane eyes: None but my own have beheld these sacred Remains of yourself, and I should think it as great a wickedness to divulge them, as to Scatter abroad the Ashes of my Ancestors.[2] As for the rest, if I have not followed you to the ends of the earth, 'tis not my fault; if I had, I might possibly have dyd as gloriously as Jeffery Rudel; and if I had so dyed, you might probably have done ev'ry thing for me, that the Countess of Tripoly did, except turning Nun.

But since our Romance is like to have a more fortunat Conclusion, I desire you to take another course to express your Favor towards me. I mean by bringing over the fair Circassian we us'd to talk of. I was Serious in that request, & will prove it by paying for her, if you will but lay out my money so well for me. The thing shall be as secret as you please, & the Lady made an Other Half of me, that is both my Mistress and my Servant, as I am both my own Servant & my own Master. But I beg you to look oftener than you use to do, in your Glass, in order to chuse me one I may like. If you have any regard to my happiness, let there be something as near as possible to that face, but if you please, the colours a little less vivid, the eyes a little less bright (such as a Reflexion will show 'em) in short, let her be such an one as you seem in your own eyes, that is a good deal less amiable than you are; Take care of this, if you have any regard to my Quiet; for otherwise instead of being her Master, I must be only her Slave.

I cannot end this letter without asking, if you receivd a Box of

[1] Pope's 'author' was probably the learned Thomas Rymer. See Rymer's *Short View of Tragedy* (1693), pp. 70–72. Rymer follows Johan de Nostradamus, *Les Vies des plus célèbres et anciens poètes provensaux* (1575).

[2] This comment concerns the fair copy Pope himself made of Lady Mary's *Court Poems* ('eclogues') in his most elegant hand. As he says, he had them bound in red morocco, the paper gilded. The volume still exists, and is now in the Arents Collection in the New York Public Library.

Books, together with Letters from Mr Congreve and myself. It was directed to Mr Wortley at Constantinople by a Merchant Ship that set sail last June. Mr Congreve, in fitts of the Gout, remembers you. Dr Garth makes Epigrams in prose when he speaks of you. Sir Robert Rich's Lady loves you, tho' Sir Robert admires you. Mr Crags commemorates you with honour; the Duke of Buckingham with Praise: I myself with something more; when people speak most highly of you, I think them spareing; when I try myself to speak of you, I think I am cold and Stupid. I think my letters have nothing in 'em, but I am sure my heart has so much, that I am vexd to find no better name for your Friend & Admirer, than your Friend & Admirer, | A. Pope.

POPE *to* CARYLL — 6 *October* 1717

Add. 28618

London Oct. 6. 1717.

I have gone through all my variety of rambles; and am at length, where I would always be, at your service: having accomplished every lesser duty first, that I might with the more leisure attend to the greater; like men that first make their wills, leave legacies of spoons, baubles and rings, and then prepare to die. I don't know how I shall carry on this metaphor but by saying I am heartily weary of this world, here about town, and willing to go to a much better at Ladyholt. I only wait your call, with some assurance that you are there; with all the happy people about you, into whose blessed society I hope to arrive. Faith will not do in this case, without an actual revelation that I may be sure of enjoying it.

It was keeping ill company (that common complaint)[1] which hindered me 'till now from doing my duty: And as the Allurements and false promises of women usually attend the other, so your goddaughter must be contented to bear a part of the blame.[2] It is but justice in you to allow me the merit of an extraordinary conversion, when (as you will shortly see) I part with almost all that is dear to sinfull men, and leave the strongest of earthly temptations behind me to fly to you.

I ought not to pass in silence those paragraphs of your letter, where you are so good as to promise your endeavours to oblige me in those articles of money[3] and wine. I can say no more than that if charity is to be measured by the want of those who ask it, yours will be very signal upon both those heads.

If you chance to be upon coming to London; I would chuse to travel with you down again; otherwise I will take whatever method

[1] Here Elwin unhappily erred in printing, without parentheses, 'that caused a complaint'.

[2] This seems a jocose way of saying that Martha had falsely promised to accompany him to Ladyholt—and now has decided not to do so.

[3] The money may be an annuity or the small matter of interest that Caryll owed the Popes.

you think the most practicable for my journey at this wintry season. I have nothing to add but the assurance of a constant esteem to all your good family and that inviolable one of my being at all times | Dear Sir | Your most obliged most | affectionate friend and servant | A: P:

Your pictures are very pretty copies from Bassano.[1]

*J. *and* T. DANCASTLE *to* POPE'S FATHER

7 *October* 1717

Homer MSS. Add. 4807

Octo: the 7th 1717

Sir,—I have enquired of Mr Tanner for some white strabery plants who told me he has now planted his so that he has none to spear and mine are now planted so that I could not send you any this day as I promised. I will endeaver to send you some by the Coach on this day sennight I am in hopes to have some from Mr Nevill's garden. My Brother and Mr Philips joine with me in our service to you Mrs Pope and Mr Alexander Pope I am | Sir | Your most affectionate | humble servant | John Dancastle

Pray acquaint my great Master his Book is ready I shall wait his orders how to send it him— Our River Dry looks frightful, is fordable in no place, I beleive the very sight of it would deter the young Gentleman from the thoughts of a Winter Journey | Your most obedient | T: Dan

McKRIE *to* POPE[2]

10 *October* 1717

Homer MSS. Add. 4807

10th of October 1717.

Sir,—I have been this evening with Mr Chetwynd who was willing to do what you desired in favour of Mr Boden; but as he assured me, that, because of the great number of those who have already the King's letter, the Board of Admirality has made an Order lately, that they will grant no more, till some of the others shal be provided for or promoted; that 'tis in vain to hope for any such Letter, and the rather that at this season they are paying off the ships, as fast as they return from abroad; but that you may not think this a groundless pretext, he is pleasd to warrant my promising you his best offices in that matter, & that if

[1] Possibly Jacopo da Ponte of Venice (1515?–92).

[2] Printed in the Warton–Roscoe *Supplemental Volume to the Works of Pope* (1825), pp. 118–19, where the signature is printed as 'Mckzie' and expanded in the heading to Mackenzie. The letter shows how early Pope was officious in attempting kind offices to others. McKrie and Boden are unknown; Mr. Chetwynd is probably William Richard, later 3rd Viscount Chetwynd, who at this time was a junior lord of the admiralty. Mackenzie is a possibility.

there should not happen to be any room for that Young Man's geting a letter before the next Spring, that then Mr Chtd will get him recommended to a Captn of one of the King's ships, which, I'm made believe, will be no less effectual than his Mty's letter. | I am allwayes | Sir | Your most Obedient | & | Most humble Servant | McKrie

*JOHN BARBER *to* POPE — 16 *October* 1717

Homer MSS. Add. 4808

Oct. 16th 1717.

Sir,—I am commanded by Lady Bolingbroke[1] to wait on you, to know whether her Ladyship is entitled to the 3rd Vol of Homer by any Payment of my Lord's: You will please to let me know by a Letter on Sight of this; for if she is not, I must buy One, and Send without delay. I am | Sir | Your most Obedient Servant | Jno Barber | on Lambeth Hill | near Doctors Commons

Address: To Mr Pope | at Mawson's Buildings | in Chiswick

Postmark: PENNY POST PAYD

DR. ABEL EVANS *to* POPE[2] — [*October* 1717]

Homer MSS. Add. 4808

FRAGMENT

Yours I rec'd dated oct 11th & I had writ to you if I had not heard from you about the middle of this Month. & now I find you are got safe to Chiswick I may perhaps be more frequent & more impertinent in my Epistolary Visits than you may well approve of. I will take due care about the binding of your Books which Lintot has not yet sent who is a very careless Fellow & somewhat ill mannerd or he woud take care to obleidge the Colledges who are publick societies & send em their Books I am persuaded his Mony woud be very safe. I will now out of hand acquaint those Colledges which have not sent for their Books. as for my Milton You shall receive it by the first opportunity & to your care I commend it. I lent and

Postmark: 16/OC

[1] Bolingbroke, now in exile, had long neglected his wife, and had doubtless not paid for his or her *Iliad*. The first Lady Bolingbroke died in Oct. 1718.

[2] Pope used the verso of this fragment of Evans's letter for a part of *Iliad* XVI, which was published in June 1718. Hence 1717 is the latest October possible, and it seems to fit, since we know that Evans tried to help distribute the *Iliad*, vol. iii, among the Oxford colleges—as Edward Young had helped with vol. i. Evans's letter here placed in Aug. 1717 indicates that he had received ten books from Lintot (i.e. vol. iii of the *Iliad*), but ten would not supply all Oxford subscribers, and he is evidently impatient for more.

POPE *to* THOMAS DANCASTLE 18 *October* [1717]

The Gentleman's Magazine, ci[2] (1831), 292

Chichester[1] Oct. 18.

I deferr'd to trouble you with any of my impertinent Commissions or Exhortations to a Winter Journey when I heard you had a great Cold, an Obstacle which I hope may by this time be removed. The weather is very inviting, and I wait only for notice by a Letter from Ladyholt, to sally forth on that expedition. But I dont intend to tye you to an old promise, which I take to be the worst sort of Tye in the world, except one (which you may probably guess at). Therefore, as I can contrive matters pretty easily to myself as to this Journey, so I beg you to use me, in regard to it, with all the freedom of a Friend, and a due regard to your own ease.

I entreat the favour of you to send the 14th Book, as you have done me the pleasure to copy it fair, by the Ockingham Coach next Monday, when I shall send to meet it. But be pleased to keep by you the Original, for fear of any accident.

I have just ended the 15th, which must wayt a better Opportunity, and may perhaps by that delay grow the more correct. If it travels too young, it may come again like most young travellers, very unfinished and unentertaining.

I have no more to add, but my hearty services to yourself and Brother, our thanks for his last Visit, our hopes of another either from him or you, our acknowledgments for the Strawberry[2] plants, *cum multis aliis*. And (what I shall never neglect either to profess myself, or to be with all sincerity), Dear Sir, your most affectionate Friend and Servant, | A. Pope.

I beg our kind loves to Hallgrove, and a line from you of your health.

Address: To Mr. Tho. Dancastle.

†THE REV. GEORGE BERKELEY *to* POPE[3]

2 *November* O.S. 1717

1735

Naples, Oct. 22, N.S. 1717.

I have long had it in my thoughts to trouble you with a Letter, but was discouraged for want of something that I could think worth

[1] The year is determined by the books of the *Iliad* mentioned. They appeared in vol. iv in June 1718. The superscription Chichester is an obvious mis-transcription for Chiswick.

[2] On the strawberry plants see Dancastle's letter to Pope's father, 7 Oct. 1717.

[3] Printed in all Pope's editions except 1735 a2, and reprinted by him with negligible changes in text. To Berkeley's name in the heading Pope appended the following footnote: 'Afterwards Bishop of *Cloyne* in *Ireland*, a celebrated Metaphysician, Author of the Dialogues of *Hylas* and *Philonous*, the *Minute Philosopher*, &c.' In 1737–42 Pope corrected the 1735 misspelling *Philonouses*.

sending fifteen hundred Miles. *Italy* is such an exhausted Subject, that, I dare say, you'd easily forgive my saying nothing of it; and the imagination of a Poet is a thing so nice and delicate, that it is no easy matter to find out Images capable of giving Pleasure to one of the few, who (in any Age) have come up to that Character. I am nevertheless lately returned from an Island, where I passed three or four Months, which, were it set out in its true Colours, might methinks amuse you agreeably enough for a minute or two. The Island *Inarime* is an Epitome of the whole Earth, containing within the compass of eighteen Miles, a wonderful variety of Hills, Vales; ragged Rocks, fruitful Plains, and barren Mountains, all thrown together in a most romantic Confusion. The Air is in the hottest Season constantly refreshed by cool breezes from the Sea. The Vales produce excellent Wheat and *Indian* Corn, but are mostly covered with Vineyards, intermixt with Fruit-trees. Besides the common kinds, as Cherries, Apricots, Peaches, &c. they produce Oranges, Limes, Almonds, Pomegranates, Figs, Water Melons, and many other Fruits unknown to our Climates, which lie every where open to the Passenger. The Hills are the greater part covered to the top with Vines, some with Chestnut Groves, and others with thickets of Myrtle and Lentiscus. The Fields on the Northern side are divided by hedge-rows of Myrtle. Several Fountains and Rivulets add to the Beauty of this Landscape, which is likewise set off by the variety of some barren Spots, and naked Rocks. But that which crowns the Scene, is a large Mountain, rising out of the middle of the Island (once a terrible *Volcano*, by the Ancients called *Mons Epomeus*) its lower parts are adorned with Vines and other Fruits, the middle affords Pasture to flocks of Goats and Sheep, and the top is a sandy pointed Rock, from which you have the finest Prospect in the World, surveying at one view, besides several pleasant Islands lying at your Feet, a tract of *Italy* about three hundred Miles in length, from the Promontory of *Antium*, to the Cape of *Palinurus*. The greater part of which hath been sung by *Homer* and *Virgil*, as making a considerable part of the Travels and Adventures of their two Heroes. The Islands *Caprea*, *Prochyta*, and *Parthenope*, together with *Cajeta*, *Cumæ*, *Monte Miseno*, the Habitations of *Circe*, the *Syrens*, and the *Lestrigones*, the Bay of *Naples*, the Promontory of *Minerva*, and the whole *Campagnia felice*, make but a part of this noble Landscape; which would demand an Imagination as warm, and numbers as flowing as your own, to describe it. The Inhabitants of this delicious Isle, as they are without Riches and Honours, so are they without the Vices and Follies that attend them; and were they but as much strangers to Revenge, as they are to Avarice or Ambition, they might in fact answer the poetical Notions of the Golden Age. But they have got, as an alloy to their Happiness, an ill habit of murdering one another on slight Offences. We had an Instance of this the second Night after our Arrival; a Youth of eighteen, being shot dead by our Door: And yet by the sole secret of minding our own business, we found a means of living securely among these dangerous People. Would you know how we pass the time at *Naples*? Our chief Entertainment is the Devotion of our Neighbours. Besides the gayety of their Churches (where Folks go to see what they call *una Bella Devotione* (i.e.) a sort of Religious Opera) they make Fireworks almost every Week out of Devotion; the Streets are often hung with Arras, out of Devotion; and (what is still more strange) the Ladies invite Gentlemen to their Houses, and treat them with Musick and Sweetmeats, out of Devotion; in a word, were it not for this Devotion of its inhabitants, *Naples* would have little else to recommend it, beside the Air and Situation. Learning is in no very thriving state here, as indeed no where else in *Italy*. However, among many pretenders, some Men of taste are to be met with. A Friend of mine told me not long since, that being to visit *Salvini*[1] at *Florence*, he found him reading your *Homer*. He liked the Notes extreamly, and could find no other fault with the Version, but that he thought it approached too near a Paraphrase; which shews him not to be sufficiently acquainted with our Language. I wish you Health to go on with that noble Work, and when you have that, I need not wish you Success. You will do me the Justice to believe, that whatever relates to your Welfare, is sincerely wished, by | Yours, &c.

*POPE *to* THE EARL OF BURLINGTON[2]

[23 *October* 1717]

Chatsworth

Chiswick: December 23.

I beg the favor of your Lordship to lend me a Servant of yours to send into the Country to a Relation of mine, with the ill news of my poor Fathers death—Your Lordship will believe I can never forget the obligations I owe You, when I remember them at this moment.

I am always My Lord, | Entirely Yours | A. Pope.

I beg a few Hartshorn drops | of my Lady, for my Mother.

POPE *to* THE MRS. BLOUNTS [24 *October* 1717]

Professor C. B. Tinker

My poor Father dyed last night. Believe, since I don't forget you this moment, I never shall. | A. Pope

Address: To | Mrs Blounts.

[1] Antonio Maria Salvini (1653–1729) translated into Italian several works, including the *Iliad* (1723) and Addison's *Cato* (1715).

[2] Since the December date is in Pope's hand, one can only explain it as written in haste and emotional unbalance. There is no doubt that his father died in the night of 23 Oct.

POPE *to* CARYLL[1] [?28 *October* 1717]

Add. 28618

You have humanity enough to believe I can be in no disposition to write to anybody, or have one thought that can be entertaining, when I acquaint you that I lost my father five days ago. My poor mother is so afflicted that it would be barbarity to leave this winter, which is the only and the true reason, that I am not now at Ladyholt.

His death was the happiest to himself,[2] imaginable; but I have lost one whom I was even more obliged to as a friend, than as a father. You who have sentiments of this, and of every virtuous and tender kind, will be convinced that to remember any other friend at this time, as I do you, is a proof of my being very greatly yours: A: P:

I beg your prayers on this occasion.

DR. ABEL EVANS *to* POPE [? *November* 1717]

Homer MSS. Add. 4808

FRAGMENT

Yours I rec'd by chance dated October but my Boy had put the letter in a strange place so that I did not light of it till it had been in my chamber a fortnight. however all things go on very well & Mr Peachy[3] gives his service to you & He will have finishd what he promisd you & will send it to you about the Middle of December. you must consider Him a little for he is really but in low circumstances but is a very Learned & ingenious Man if you approve of what He shall send you He will then proceed to look into Philostratus's Heroicks. I have dispos'd of all your Books & have in my custody nine guinneas which I will contrive to return you with all speed & convenience or other wise that you

POPE *to* CARYLL 6 *November* 1717

Add. 28618

No: 6th 1717.

I was not surprised at your speedy condolence of my father's death,[4] tho' it looked as if you had received advertisement of it by some angel.

[1] Pope writes to explain that he cannot come to Ladyholt and leave his mother alone. As frequently, he may not be carefully precise in saying his father died 'five days ago'. Caryll had already heard of the death of Pope's father and had written before receiving this letter. See Pope to Caryll, 6 Nov. 1717.

[2] Compare l. 403 of the *Epistle to Dr. Arbuthnot*:

His Death was instant, and without a groan.

[3] Pope, well behind in his vol. iv of the *Iliad*, had met Mr. Peachy at Oxford and employed him, presumably on notes for *Iliad*, vol. iv. The learned and ingenious scholar was probably William Peche, Fellow of St. John's College, 1704–28.

[4] Evidently Caryll had heard of the elder Pope's death before the son's letter of [28 Oct.], and had sent a note of condolence.

I know the first minute any man is afflicted, you are likeliest to know it, and[1] to prove you do so by doing or tendering good offices. I heartily acknowledge your charity to me on this occasion, and the comfort you endeavour to give me for the suddenness of his death. I will say no more on that head, than that I heartily beg of God to give me just such a death, on condition he will in his mercy allow me just such a life.

I am extremely obliged to you for your friendly wishes in regard to myself. As to my present circumstances, they'll make me less a poet than I have been, but I think not much more a gentleman. I therefore continue the request I made you, in case you could procure such an annuity as I wrote about. You may be assured nothing could make me trouble you with my affairs, but the certainty of a friendship which I have now a habit of experimenting[2] from you. As a farther proof of this frankness, I will so far embrace the kind offer you make, of doing me any service at this juncture, as to desire a bill for the small sum that is between us due on the 200ll, this unhappy accident having put us upon some unforeseen expences, that may disorder the accounts of one so little used to keep any as my self.

Dear sir, I can't tell what farther to say to you, unless I repeat eternally my sense of your goodness and favours, which is all summed up in one word, when I give myself so true, and so deserv'd a title as that of | Your most obliged and most affectionate | Friend and servant. A: P:

My mother is extremely yours; and I at all times your whole family's hearty servant. Be pleased to direct to me at Mr Jervas's in Cleveland Court St James's.

†POPE *to* GAY 8 *November* [1717]

1735

London, Nov. 8, 1718.[3]

I am extremely glad to find by a Letter of yours to Mr. *Fortescue*, that you have receiv'd one from me; and I beg you to keep, as the greatest of Curiosities, that Letter of mine which you receiv'd and I never writ.

But the Truth is, that we were made here to expect you in a short time, that I was upon the Ramble most part of the Summer, and have concluded the Season in Grief, for the death of my poor father.

I shall not enter into a detail of my Concerns and Troubles, for two

[1] After *and* the transcript has illegible strokes resembling *do do.*

[2] experimenting] experiencing *Elwin.*

[3] In his text of 1735 Pope printed '1718'; in all later texts he corrected this to '1717'.

reasons; because I am really afflicted and need no Airs of grief, and because they are not the concerns and troubles of any but my self. But I think you (without too great a compliment) enough my friend, to be pleas'd to know he died easily, without a groan, or the sickness of two minutes; in a word, as silently and peacefully as he lived.

Sic mihi contingat vivere, sicque mori![1]

I am not in the humour to say gay things, nor in the affectation of avoiding them. I can't pretend to entertain either Mr. *Pulteney* or you, as you have done both my Lord *Burlington* and me, by your letter to Mr. *Lowndes.*[2] I am only sorry you have no greater quarrel to Mr. *Lowndes*, and wish you paid some hundreds a year to the Landtax. That Gentleman is lately become an inoffensive person to me too; so that we may join heartily in our addresses to him, and (like true Patriots) rejoice in all that Good done to the Nation and Government, to which we contribute nothing our selves.

I should not forget to acknowledge your letter sent from *Aix*;[3] you told me then that writing was not good with the Waters, and I find since you are of my opinion, that 'tis as bad without the Waters. But I fancy, it is not writing but thinking, that is so bad with the Waters; and then you might write without any manner of prejudice, if you writ like our Brother-poets of these days.

[4]⌜I have no story to tell that is worth your hearing; you know I am no man of Intrigue; but the Duchess of *Hamilton* has one which she says is worth my hearing, that relates to Mr. *Pulteney* and your self; and which she promises, if you won't tell me, she will. Her Grace has won in a Raffle a very fine Tweezercase; at the sight of which, my Tweezercase, and all other Tweezercases on the globe, *Hide*[5] *their diminish'd Heads.*⌝

That Dutchess, Lord *Warwick*, Lord *Stanhope*, Mrs. *Bellenden*, Mrs. *Lepell*,[6] and I can't tell who else, had your letters: Dr. *Arbuthnot* and I expect to be treated like Friends. I would send my services to Mr. *Pulteney*, but that he is out of favour at Court; and make some

[1] Either the source or a translation of lines 17, 18 of Pope's 'Ode on Solitude'. Cf. also l. 404 of the 'Epistle to Dr. Arbuthnot'.

[2] The 'letter' was in verse, published in 1720 in Gay's *Poems*, as 'To my ingenious and worthy Friend W[illiam] L[owndes] Esq; *Author of that celebrated treatise in folio*, called the Land-Tax Bill'. Pope, since the place at Binfield was sold, paid no land-tax; hence Lowndes had 'lately become inoffensive' to him.

[3] Apparently the Pulteneys and Gay had gone first to Aix and later to Blois.

[4] This paragraph appears only in the text of 1735; it is omitted in all texts 1737–42.

[5] *Paradise Lost*, iv. 35.

[6] The ladies mentioned are maids of honour to the Princess. Lord Warwick is Addison's graceless stepson; Lord Stanhope was later the 4th Earl of Chesterfield, author of the famous letters, and from this time on a friend of Pope's. In his text for genteel consumption (the quarto and folio of 1737) this sentence began (omitting all names): 'All your Correspondents have receiv'd your letters.'

compliment to Mrs. *Pulteney*,[1] if she were not a Whig. My Lord *Burlington* tells me she has as much outshin'd all the *French* Ladies, as she did the English before: I am sorry for it, because it will be detrimental to our holy Religion, if heretical Women should eclypse those Nuns and orthodox Beauties, in whose eyes alone lie all the hopes we can have, of gaining such fine Gentlemen as you to our Church. | Your, &c.

I wish you joy of the birth of the young Prince,[2] because he is the only Prince we have, from whom you have had no Expectations and no Disappointments.

||ATTERBURY *to* POPE[3] 8 *November* 1717.

Longleat Portland Papers, xiii (Harleian transcripts)

Bromly, Novr 8, 1717.

Sir,—⌜I hop'd to have wayted on you, when I was last in Town, and sent (whither I now send this letter) to Mr Jervisses for that purpose: but you were abroad; and the multiplicity of my own little Affairs would not permit me afterwards to renew my intended Visit. But I shall fix at the Deanery for this Winter, about Ten days hence; and then I promise my self, I shall have sure and frequent Opportunitys of seeing you.⌝

I have nothing to say to you on that Melancholly Subject, with an account of which the printed Papers have furnish'd me, but what you have already said to your self. When you have paid the Debt of Tenderness you owe to the Memory of a Father, I doubt not, but you will turn your Thoughts towards improving that Accident to your Own ease and Happiness. You have it now in your Power to pursue that Method of Thinking and Living which you like best. Give me leave, if I am not too early in my Applications of this hand,[4] to Congratulate you upon it, and to assure you, that there is no man living, who wishes you better, &[5] would be more pleas'd to contribute any ways to your Satisfaction, or Service.

[1] Mrs. *Pulteney*] Mrs.—— *1737 b*. Mrs. Pulteney was the daughter of a rich manufacturer named Gumley. She was one of the most celebrated beauties of her day.

[2] Prince George William was born 3 Nov. 1717. He died in Feb. 1718.

[3] Pope printed this letter in his editions 1737–42 but omitted the first paragraph and diverged in small phrases from the Harleian transcript. Oxford's scribe combined in one paragraph the remarks on the death of Pope's father and those about Milton. Since all Pope's texts make two paragraphs of this matter, his separation is here followed. After the word *Service* (end of the second paragraph) Pope printed five asterisks as if he had omitted some of Atterbury's remarks on changing his religion. No such lacuna is indicated in the Harleian transcript.

Possibly the cover of this letter became a part of the Homer MSS. On Add. 4808, f. 14*v* appears the address: To | Mr Pope, at Mr | Jerves's, in Cleveland Court, | near St James's | Westminster. The frank is Fr. Roffen, and the postmark 9/NO.

[4] hand] kind *1737–42* (doubtless a scribal error).

[5] &] or *1737–42 and all later texts.*

I return you your Milton, which, upon Collating I find, to be both *Revised*, and *Augmented* in several places, as the Title page of my third Edition pretends to be. When I see you next, I will shew you the several Passages alter'd, and added by the Author, beside that you mention'd to me. I protest to you, this last Perusal of him has given me such new degrees (I will not say, of Pleasure, but) admiration and Astonishment, that I look upon the Sublimity of Homer, and the Majesty of Virgil, with some what less reverence than I used to doe. I challenge you with all your Partiality, to shew me in the first of these, any thing Equal to the Allegory of Sin, and Death, either as to the Greatness, and Justness of the Invention, or the Height and Beauty of the Colouring. What I look'd upon as a Rant of Dr Barrows,[1] I now begin to think a Serious Truth, & could almost venture to set my hand to it.

Haec quicunq leget,[2] tantum cecinisse putabit
Mæonidem Ranas, Virgilium Culices.[3]

But more of this, when we meet. When I left the Town the D. of Buckingham continued so ill, as to receive no Messages. If this finds you at Mr Jervises, oblige me so far, as to let me know how he does. At the same time, I shall know how yours does,[4] and that will be a double Satisfaction to | Your ever faithful Servant | Fr. Roffen.

⌜I miss of the Opportunity I propos'd to my self of sending the Book, and therefore I send the letter without it.⌝

MARTHA BLOUNT *to* POPE [*c.* 10 *November* 1717]

Homer MSS. Add. 4808

Sir,—My sister and I shall be at home all day: if any company comes that you dont like;[5] I'll go up in to my room with you; I hope we shall see you | Yours | M.

sunday morning

Address: To Mr Pope at Mr | Jervasses in cleevland Court

[1] Rant of Dr. Barrows] rant of Barrow's *1737–42*.
[2] leget] legit *1737–42 and all printed texts*.
[3] The last two lines of the verses prefixed to the second edition of *Paradise Lost*, published 1674. The writer was Samuel Barrow, M.D.—Elwin.
[4] how yours does] how you do *1737–42*.
[5] Upon the assumption that this is written shortly after the death of Pope's father, when the poet might not like to meet miscellaneous company, the date might well be a Sunday in November—such as the 10th. We know from other letters that Pope was in London on the 6th and 8th. The letter cannot from its position in the Homer MSS. fall later than 1717.

†POPE *to* ATTERBURY[1] 20 *November* 1717

1737

Nov. 20, 1717.

My Lord,—I am truly oblig'd by your kind condoleance on my Father's death, and the desire you express that I should improve this incident to my advantage. I know your Lordship's friendship to me is so extensive, that you include in that wish both my spiritual and my temporal advantage; and it is what I owe to that friendship, to open my mind unreservedly to you on this head. It is true, I have lost a parent for whom no gains I could make would be any equivalent. But that was not my only tye: I thank God another still remains (and long may it remain) of the same tender nature: *Genitrix est mihi*—and excuse me if I say with Euryalus,

—nequeam lacrymas perferre parentis.[2]

A rigid divine may call it a carnal tye, but sure it is a virtuous one: at least I am more certain that it is a duty of nature to preserve a good parent's life and happiness, than I am of any speculative point whatever.

—Ignaram hujus quodcunque pericli
Hanc ego, nunc, linquam?[2]

For she, my Lord, would think this separation more grievous than any other, and I, for my part, know as little as poor Euryalus did, of the success of such an adventure, (for an Adventure it is, and no small one, in spite of the most positive divinity.) Whether the change would be to my spiritual advantage, God only knows: this I know, that I mean as well in the religion I now profess, as I can possibly ever do in another. Can a man who thinks so, justify a change, even if he thought both equally good? To such an one, the part of *Joyning* with any one body of Christians might perhaps be easy, but I think it would not be so to *Renounce* the other.

Your Lordship has formerly advis'd me to read the best controversies between the Churches. Shall I tell you a secret? I did so at fourteen years old, (for I loved reading, and my father had no other books)[3] there was a collection of all that had been written on both sides in the reign of King James the second: I warm'd my head with them, and the consequence was, that I found my self a Papist and a Protestant by

[1] First printed in the editions of 1737–42, this letter follows that to Pope from Atterbury, 8 Nov., and has the heading, 'The Answer'.

[2] *Aeneid*, ix. 284–5, 289, and 287 (adapted in paraphrase). The appeal to a Virgilian episode on such an occasion bespeaks much concerning the status of the Ancients!

[3] The sentence structure, faulty through bad punctuation, is improved in the quarto and folio texts of 1737—a fact that makes the Roberts octavo (here reprinted) seem earlier than the larger formats. The quarto discards parentheses, and begins a new sentence with 'There was a collection . . .'.

turns, according to the last book I read. I am afraid most Seekers are in the same case, and when they stop, they are not so properly converted, as out-witted. You see how little glory you would gain by my conversion. And after all, I verily believe your Lordship and I are both of the same religion, if we were thoroughly understood by one another; and that all honest and reasonable christians would be so, if they did but talk enough together every day; and had nothing to do together, but to serve God and live in peace with their neighbour.

As to the *temporal* side of the question, I can have no dispute with you. It is certain, all the beneficial circumstances of life, and all the shining ones, lie on the part you would invite me to. But if I could bring myself to fancy, what I think you do but fancy, that I have any talents for active life, I want health for it; and besides it is a real truth, I have less Inclination (if possible) than Ability. Contemplative life is not only my scene, but it is my habit too. I begun my life where most people end theirs, with a dis-relish of all that the world calls Ambition: I don't know why 'tis call'd so, for to me it always seem'd to be rather *stooping* than *climbing*. I'll tell you my politick and religious sentiments in a few words. In my politicks, I think no further than how to preserve the peace of my life, in any government under which I live; nor in my religion, than to preserve the peace of my conscience in any Church with which I communicate. I hope all churches and all governments are so far of God, as they are rightly understood, and rightly administred: and where they are, or may be wrong, I leave it to God alone to mend or reform them; which whenever he does, it must be by greater instruments than I am. I am not a Papist, for I renounce the temporal invasions of the Papal power, and detest their arrogated authority over Princes, and States. I am a Catholick, in the strictest sense of the word. If I was born under an absolute Prince, I would be a quiet subject; but I thank God I was not. I have a due sense of the excellence of the British constitution. In a word, the things I have always wished to see are not a Roman Catholick, or a French Catholick, or a Spanish Catholick, but a true Catholick: and not a King of Whigs, or a King of Tories, but a King of England. Which God of his mercy grant his present Majesty may be, and all future Majesties! You see, my Lord, I end like a preacher: but this is *Sermo ad Clerum*, not *ad Populum*. Believe me, with infinite obligation and sincere thanks, ever | Your, &c.

†POPE *to* EDWARD BLOUNT — 27 *November* 1717

1735

Nov. 27. 1717.

The Question you proposed to me is what at present I am the most unfit Man in the world to answer, by my Loss of one of the best of Fathers.

He had liv'd in such a Course of Temperance as was enough to make the longest Life agreeable to him, and in such a Course of Piety as suffic'd to make the most sudden Death so also. Sudden indeed it was: However, I heartily beg of God to give me such an one, provided I can lead such a Life. I leave him to the Mercy of God, and to the Piety of a Religion that extends beyond the Grave: *Si qua est ea cura*, &c.

He has left me to the ticklish Management of a narrow Fortune, where every false Step is dangerous. My Mother is in that dispirited State of Resignation, which is the effect of long Life, and the Loss of what is dear to us. We are really each of us in want of a Friend, of such an humane Turn as yourself, to make almost any thing desirable to us. I feel your Absence more than ever, at the same time I can less express my Regards to you than ever; and shall make this, which is the most sincere Letter I ever writ to you, the shortest and faintest perhaps of any you have receiv'd. 'Tis enough if you reflect, that barely to remember any Person, when one's Mind is taken up with a sensible Sorrow, is a great degree of Friendship. I can say no more but that I love you, and all that are yours; and that I wish it may be very long before any of yours shall feel for you what I now feel for my Father. Adieu.

POPE *to* TERESA *and* MARTHA BLOUNT[1] [*Late* 1717?]

Mapledurham

Dear Ladies,—I think myself obligd to desire, you would not put off any Diversion you may find, in the prospect of seeing me on Saturday, which is very uncertain. I Take this occasion to tell you once for all, that I design no longer to be a constant Companion when I have ceas'd to be an agreable one. You only have had, as my friends, the priviledge of knowing my Unhappiness; and are therefore the only people whom my Company must necessarily make melancholy. I will not bring myself to you at all hours, like a Skeleton, to come across your diversions, and dash your pleasures: Nothing can be more shocking than to be perpetually meeting the Ghost of an old acquaintance, which is all you can ever see of me.

You must not imagine this to proceed from any Coldness, or the least decrease of Friendship to you. If You had any Love for me, I should be always glad to gratify you with an Object that you thought agreable. But as your regard is Friendship & Esteem; those are things that are as well, perhaps better, preservd Absent than Present. A Man that you love is a joy to your eyes at all times; a Man that you Esteem

[1] The chronological place of this letter has to be guessed at. Pope has been melancholy over his especial 'unhappiness'—which may be the death of his father. The young ladies are living in Bolton Street and the winter is coming on.

is a solemn kind of thing, like a Priest, only wanted at a certain hour to do his Office: Tis like Oyl in a Sallet, necessary, but of no manner of Taste. And you may depend upon it, I will wait upon you on every real occasion, at the first summons, as long as I live.

Let me open my whole heart to you: I have some times found myself inclined to be in love with you: and as I have reason to know from your Temper & Conduct how miserably I should be used in that circumstance, it is worth my while to avoid it: It is enough to be Disagreable, without adding Fool to it, by constant Slavery. I have heard indeed of Women that have had a kindness for Men of my Make; but it has been after Enjoyment, never before; and I know to my Cost you have had no Taste of that Talent in me, which most Ladies would not only Like better, but Understand better, than any other I have.

I love you so well that I tell you the truth, & that has made me write this Letter. I will see you less frequently this winter, as you'll less want company: When the Gay Part of the world is gone, I'll be ready to stop the Gap of a vacant hour whenever you please. Till then I'll converse with those who are more Indifferent to me, as You will with those who are more Entertaining. I wish you every pleasure God and Man can pour upon ye; and I faithfully promise you all the good I can do you, which is, the Service of a Friend, who will ever be | Ladies, Entirely Yours.

Address: To | The two Young Ladies. | Bolton street.

POPE *to* TERESA BLOUNT[1] [1717?]

Mapledurham

Madam,—I ought to acknowledge so much Civility, when my Sincerity so little deserves it. My Mother has been in racking pains of the Rheumatism, has had no rest but by Laudanum, & no Spirits but by drops and Hartshorn these 5 days. This is the first morning we have thought her better.

If your Eccho be like other Ecchos, Words without meaning, I need not take notice of it.

If it be otherwise, We are Both in the right: and I hope you will continue so, in regard to | Madam | Your humble Servant.

Pray tell your Sister how much You think me her Servant.

Address: To Mrs Teresa Blount | at Mrs Blount's in Bolton | street, Piccadilly. | London

Postmark: PENY POST PAYD

[1] This letter cannot be surely dated. It may represent a part of the slight misunderstanding evident in the letter immediately preceding. Mrs. Pope's health is so frequently bad that it affords no clue as to a date.

||POPE *to* CARYLL[1] 28 *December* [1717]

Add. 28618

London December 28

⸢The hopes I have of seeing you shortly here, can't hinder me from the impulse I have to write to you, and the pleasure I take in obeying it.⸣ 'Tis the season ⸢of the year⸣ to wish you a good end of one and a happy begining of another; but both these you know how to make yourself, by only continuing such a life as you have been long accustomed to lead⸢, a life of resignation and innocence.⸣ As for good works they are things I dare not name, either to those that do them, or to those that do not. The first are too modest, and the latter too selfish, to bear the mention of things which are become either too old fashioned, or too private, to constitute any part of the vanity or reputation of the present age. However, it were to be wished people would now and then look upon good works, as they do upon old wardrobes, merely in case any of them should come[2] into use again. ⸢Perhaps, the very finest new fashions fall as short of them,⸣ as the modern hooped petticoats do of ancient fardingales,[3] which may be properly compar'd to charities as they cover a multitude of sins.

I am strongly inclined[4] to think there are at this very day at Grinsted, certain antique charities and obsolete devotions yet in being: that a thing call'd Christian cheerfullness, (incompatible[5] with Christmass pies and plum-broth) whereof frequent is the mention in old sermons and almanacs, is really kept alive and in practice ⸢at the said place:⸣ That feeding the hungry, and giving alms to the poor, do yet make a part of good housekeeping in a latitude not more remote from London than forty[6] miles; and lastly that prayers and roast beef, do actually make some folks as happy, as a whore and a bottle. [7]Secondly, this season puts me in mind of evening my accounts, with heaven and earth. I ought to be as punctual in discharging what I owe to him to whom we owe all things as in expecting an exact payment of what others owe me. A man that goes to bed on a quarter-day without saying his prayers, if justice were done upon him from above, has nothing due to him here below.

[1] Pope printed much of this letter (1735–42), with changes here (a few) noted, as if sent to the Hon. Robert Digby under date of 28 Dec. 1724. His omissions are indicated by half-brackets.

[2] should come] should by chance come *1735–42*.

[3] as the modern . . . fardingales] as ancient Fardingales revive in modern Hoop'd Petticoats *1735–42*.

[4] I am strongly . . . certain antique] They tell me that at —— certain antiquated *1735–42*. In texts of 1737–42 the blank (originally *Grinstead*) of 1735 became *Coleshill*, a Digby house.

[5] Elwin silently emends the text by adding *not*: *not incompatible* makes obvious sense. Pope also added the negative in printing the passage in the 'Digby' version.

[6] forty] fourscore *1735–42*.

[7] Beginning with 'Secondly' the Digby letter parts company with this and uses that to Caryll of 29 Mar. [1718].

When Socrates lay a-dying, one of his last words was, that he owed about ninepence to his friend Esculapius. Now (to compare myself in the only instance I can to that just man) I owe you for seven dozen of wine and bottles, which when I have accounted for, I may rest in peace, as to all my debts on this side of the poles.

I beg you not to forget this material point when you come next to town. Adieu—at Chiswick nothing is talked of but Homer and you—at Bolton Street[1] you are prayed for in the mornings, commemorated at noons, talked of at Nights. Your cardinal's coat is arrived. It blushes like the rosy morn, or your god-daughter's cheek. All happiness to you all. | A. P.

POPE *to* TERESA BLOUNT — 31 *December* [1717][2]

Mapledurham

Chiswick, 4 aclock | Tuesday Decr 31st

Dear Madam,—'Tis really a great Concern to me that you mistook me so much this morning. I have sincerely an extreme Esteem for you; & as you know, I am distracted in one respect, for God's sake do'nt judge and try me, by the methods of reasonable people. Upon the faith of a Man who thinks himself not dishonest, I meant no disrespect to you; I have been ever since so troubled at it, that I could not help writing the minuit I got home. Believe me, much more than I am my own, | Yours, | A. Pope.

Address: To Mrs Teresa Blount, | at Mrs Blount's in Bolton street, | Piccadilly | London

Postmark: PENY POST PAYD

[1] The Blount ladies were having their first Christmas in Bolton Street.

[2] The dating from Chiswick and the fact that in 1717 the 31st fell on a Tuesday make the year absolutely certain. This letter confirms the dating of preceding letters to Teresa in which a misunderstanding is evident.

1718

The chief correspondents for 1718 were Caryll, the Misses Blount, and Lady Mary Wortley Montagu. Notable is Pope's tendency to send similar, almost duplicate letters to different correspondents, and to echo phrases in letters written months apart. Volume iv of the *Iliad* was the only important new publication for the year. It appeared in June. At the beginning of the year the poet was ill, seriously so, if we may believe a letter to Lady Mary. In the spring he was either in London or at home in Chiswick. In May or June he returned from an early (brief?) visit to Cirencester, and after spending much of July in London returned to Stanton Harcourt with his mother. He more or less concealed himself there, so as to expedite work on Homer. Near the beginning of August he witnessed the funeral of the rustic lovers of Stanton Harcourt, and wrote epitaphs for them. About the middle of that month he and Gay went to Cirencester, whence he frequently journeyed to Stanton Harcourt to see his mother, and once or twice to London (briefly) on business. He and his mother returned to Chiswick about the middle of October. During the summer he continued to plan to build a house in London; for evidently after the death of his father Chiswick was less agreeable. During the year his officious relations with the Misses Blount, uneasy at the start, definitely improved. He was annoyed by the failure of Caryll to invite these young ladies to spend the summer at Grinstead.

ATTERBURY *to* POPE — 1 *January* 1717/18

[Under this date Folkstone Williams in his *Memoirs and Correspondence of Francis Atterbury*, 1869, i. 264–5, printed as if addressed to Pope a letter that seems not to be connected with Pope. It sends the addressee two poems, thought to be Prior's *Alma* and *Solomon*, and these would almost certainly be familiar to Pope already. The letter speaks also of the addressee's deafness, and Pope was not, so far as is known, troubled with that ailment.]

POPE *to* TERESA BLOUNT — [1718?]

Mapledurham

Madam,—I wonder you should imagine I thought You had done any thing amiss; when the letter I sent you last, so fully explained all my meaning. I think that shows you, it is unreasonable I shoud trouble you so frequently; & I can't think you so much a Woman, as to expect I shoud continue to act unreasonably, only because I have done so too long alredy.

I will wait upon you before noon, and am very truly and honestly what I profess myself | Madam | Your most faithful Friend | & sincere humble Servant.

POPE *to* TERESA *and* MARTHA BLOUNT[1] [1718?]

Mapledurham

Thursday morn.

Ladies,—Pray think me sensible of your Civility & good meaning in asking me to come to you.

You will please to consider that my Coming or not is a thing Indifferent to both of you. But God knows, it is far otherwise to me, with respect to One of you.

I scarce ever come but one of two things happens, which equally afflicts me to the Soul. Either I make her Uneasy, or I see her Unkind.

If She has any Tenderness, I can only give her every day Trouble and melancholy. If she has none, the daily sight of so undeserved a coldness must wound me to death.

It is forcing one of us, to do a very Hard and very unjust thing, to the other.

My continuing to see you, will, by turns, teize all of us. My Staying away can at worst be of ill consequence only to myself.

And if One of us is to be sacrific'd, I believe, we are all three agreed, Who shall be the person.

POPE *to* TERESA BLOUNT [1718?]

Mapledurham

Two a clock.

Dear Madam,—I am glad my righteous Labors at last prove effectual: The Lady will be to night at the Play. I'll not fail at noon to mention your Confinement by a Town-Cold. I hope for my Reward about seven in the Evening, in finding you at home. I am very honestly | Dear Madam | Ever Yours. | A. Pope.

Address: To Mrs Teresa Blount | at Mrs Blount's in | Bolton street | Piccadilly

LADY MARY WORTLEY MONTAGU *to* POPE

8 *January* 1717/18

(Letter unpreserved?)

[Mr. Moy Thomas in his Memoir of Lady Mary, published in his editions of her *Letters*, prints the 'Heads of L.M.'s Letters from Turkey' (ed. 1861, i. 17–19). In the list of letters she includes under the date 8 January 1717/18 a letter to Congreve described as 'Why he lets P. [Pope] make lampoons. Bps. [Bishops?] facetious'. She also includes mention of an unknown letter to Pope of the same date: 'Thanks for his works. Reception of my last letter.']

[1] A spate of quarrelling between Pope and the sisters came early in this year; but one must realize that young people are likely to have slight disagreements more than once. The dating here is highly hypothetical.

*POPE *to* THE EARL OF BURLINGTON[1]

14 *January* 1717/18

Chatsworth

Jan: 14. 1717.

My Lord,—The natural Love all Poets and Fame-Hunters bear to their Name, occasions your Lordship this trouble: For the Fellow that brings this is called Pope, & will not let me alone, without recommending him to you in the Quality of your Water-man, when that important Place becomes vacant by the decease of the Old Gentleman who serves you at present. I know the man to be honest enough, by Land at least, for he has a good Character at Chiswick: And upon the water he pretends to be accounted a Triton of no small ability. I wish you would accept of him, that so my Glory may be great upon the River & all the Banks thereof, when it shall be proclaimed that Your Lordships Waterman was Elected by my Interest.

I beg to know when you next come to Chiswick, that I may not live another week without seeing you. I am with all Truth & respect | My Lord | Your most obliged, most | faithful humble Servant. | A. Pope.

Address: To the Right Honble. the Earl | of Burlington: | Present.

POPE *to* CARYLL[2]

18 *January* 1717/18

Add. 28618

Chiswick Jan. 18th 1718–19.

Since my last to you I have been much indisposed, and not without some fear that you might be so, from having heard nothing concerning the method of disposing the wine you bought at my request. I writ several posts since to desire your notice two posts before the day it was to come to Wandsworth, at what place, time, &c., I should send to meet it. But I will say no more on that subject, only that I hope it was no indisposition of yours, or any cross accident, but a prudent consideration (a thing I may expect from you at all times, and upon all occasions) that the coldness of the season might prejudice it in the carriage.

I have passed almost all my time here of late being pretty much sick of the vanities of the town which agree as little with my constitution as the madness and political fur[y] does with my judgement. I took

[1] Pope is not entirely consistent in dating letters as if the year began in March, but that is his normal procedure. This seems to belong in 1718.

[2] It is probable that Caryll or his scribe added the year date, which is pretty certainly wrong. In Jan. 1719 Pope still lived at Chiswick, but the mention of masquerades (new in 1717), of the Bangorian controversy, and the '4th year of King George' make 1718 practically certain. The mention of wine in the first sentence refers back to the letters to Caryll of 1717.

my last leave of impertinence at a masquerade some time ago, the true[1] epitome of all absurdities; and of all shows to no purpose, the greatest show to the least purpose. I was led thither, as one is to all foolish things, by keeping foolish company; after saying which, it would be unmannerly to add, it was that of a great person.

But of late the great have been the shining examples of folly, public and private; and the best translation at this time of *O Tempora! O Mores!* would be

O Kings! O Princes![2]

[3]I am now immersed in books, and preparing to tire others as much with my own volumes, as I have been tired with those of others. Innocent amusement after all! I charitably take pains for others' ease, and wake to make you sleep![4] When I think of the unrighteous labours of wrangling statesmen, and the quarrelsome ones of uncharitable divines, I honour and worship the memory of old Ogleby. So may posterity be just to me and mine; and say, that in the 4th year of K. George, and in the days of the Bishop of Bangor,[5] Pope writ and caused no disturbance but to Lintot.

I beg your whole family's acceptance of my most constant services, and from you, dear sir, I only beg the continuance of so just an opinion of me as that of my being with the utmost sincerity | Your most obliged and most affectionat servant | A: P:

POPE *to* CARYLL — 25 *January* 1717/18

Add. 28618

January 25. 1717.

I trouble you with this to acquaint you of the safe receipt of the hamper, which I was under no small apprehensions for, on account of the frost it came in, together with other Anxieties. For fear of the like hazard in the rest, I beg you to defer sending it till some time hence. I must now return you a part of my thousand thanks; the remainder you shall have hereafter. I mean not only the remainder of my thanks but my debts which are yet wholly unpaid. The kind offer you make

[1] Elwin emended *time* (the MS. reading) to *true*—rightly, one guesses.

[2] The scandalous estrangement of the King and the Prince of Wales was notorious at the end of 1717 and in the early months of 1718.

[3] This paragraph, with several minor changes, became in Pope's texts of 1735–42 the last paragraph of a synthetic letter addressed to Atterbury under the date 3 Sept. 1718.

[4] Cf. *Dunciad*, i. 93–94:

> While pensive poets painful vigils keep,
> Sleepless themselves, to give their readers sleep.

[5] The controversy between the low-church Bishop Hoadly and his high-church opponents (Snape, Hare, Sherlock, *et al.*) raged throughout the years 1717–20, and was disgracefully vituperative.

me of the choice of another sort in case this does not fully content me is very obliging and (tho' I think this very good) one may be tempted to (the natural passion of mankind) variety. As for myself I am, however, quite satisfied with this, but having promised a friend a part of it, will consult his taste just for as much as concerns him. The hamper was not corded, but very close stitched, and I believe the whole cargo in it, tho' I've not taken out the bottles this cold weather to count them, and tho' I find there was room in it for near a dozen more. I therefore beg the favour that you'll let me know when the cargoes come, what quantity is in each.

I can tell you no news of the world, for I generally live out of it in this deep desert solitude four miles from London.[1] It is seriously true, that sometimes for a week together I see no company but our own family, and hear not a syllable of what is done so near me. If I did not think my self obliged to be with my poor mother (whose health is so excessively precarious that my life with her is like watching the rising and falling of a taper on its last socket), I should at this time I faithfully assure [you] be at Ladyholt, a place I remember with tenderness as I do every branch of it with gratitude and respect. I shall ever be, dear sir, with the sincerest affection | Your's | A. P.

POPE *to* CARYLL 4 *February* [1717/18]

Add. 28618

Feb: 4th

I have been overjoyed with a report here of your designing[2] very soon to come to town, which I can't tell you how very much I wish for. The immoderate hurry I have long been in is near over, and I might hope again to possess my soul in peace, and to possess what is next to one's own soul, a friend in peace. In the meantime I must give you the disturbance of one more letter, rather of business than friendship; tho' in truth it be a proof of my friendship when I trouble any man with my business.

The wine you sent deserves the approbation of all who have a good taste, if I have any myself; and as it has strength and body, will grow better yet like ancient wit, which was made to keep long. I am pretty well convinced that if I have any of either, it must be owing to my friends in as great measure, as this wine is owing to you. I beg you to take the opportunity of this open weather to send the rest. And (merely for variety) be pleased to let 2 or 3 dozen be of the other sort you mentioned, distinguished by some mark from the rest. There came in this Hamper 3 dozen and a half.

I find, upon stating the final account of the last volume of Homer,

[1] i.e. at Chiswick.

[2] designing] intention *Elwin* (wrongly).

that not above ten persons of all the living subscribers, have refused to continue and send for their third volumes; (a thing which I'm sure you'll be pleased to hear), of which number Sir Harry Tichbourn is one and Will. Plowden Esqr. another.[1] I beg when you see 'em you would propose to repay 'em the subscription money, and take back their first volume, which may be sent me in one of the hampers. I have taken that course with the rest of my deserters, and may do it with evident profit, having a demand for more entire new sets than I can furnish any other way. I also find the two Lady Petres[2] have not yet had the third, but am pretty confident it proceeds only from their not knowing where to send for 'em, and therefore wish you could be at the trouble of directing how they may have 'em. Pray pardon this, which I believe will be the last imposition of the kind that I shall charge you with. My poetical affairs drawing toward a fair period, I hope the day will shortly come when I may honestly say

> Nunc versus et cætera ludicra pono,
> Quid *verum* atque *decens*, curo et rogo et omnis in hoc sum.[3]

That *cætera ludicra* is very comprehensive: it includes visiting, masquerading, play-hanting, sauntering, and indeed almost includes all that the world calls living. I hope, in one word, to become a companion more worthy of such as you, more fit to live at Ladyholt, and (to comprehend all) more deserving the two titles I ought to desire in preference to all others,—those of a reasonable man and of | Dear sir | Your most faithful real friend and | Servant | A: P.

POPE *to* CARYLL — 18 *February* 1717/18

Add. 28618

Feb. 18. 1717/18

The event has surpassed my hopes, the wine I gave for lost is arrived. The next return of the carrier fully paid for all the disappointments of the last day. To which may be properly applied that of the Poet—

> —Quod optanti divum promittere nemo
> Auderat, volvenda dies, en! attulit ultro.[4]

But now I am singing Io Pæans, I ought to confess a horrible omission in not having said or sung something upon Lady Mary's performance, or at least part of the performance in the *Double Discovery*[5] lately

[1] These were subscribers secured, evidently, by Caryll.

[2] Caryll had served as guardian for the 7th Lord Petre, who married in 1712, shortly after being celebrated for cutting off the famous lock of Miss Fermor's (Belinda's) hair.

[3] Horace, *Epistles*, I. i. 10–11.

[4] *Aeneid*, ix. 6–7.

[5] Lady Mary Caryll was delivered of twins on the 21st of January.—Elwin.

exhibited at your house. But you are sensible 'tis not the task of an Heroic Poet like myself, to sing, at marriages, burials, and Christenings: Besides that every song relating to christenings[1] may be thought satirical in this age. Therefore in plain prose I wish the fruit may grow ripe and crown the proudest expectations of [the] planter and that the fair tree may burgeon, bud, blossom, and bring forth *in sæcula sæculorum.*

I am lately fallen acquainted with Mr Hatton, it may callen a seasonable acquaintance since he is the greatest manager of time in the universe. This measurer of moments, to whom hours is literally precious because they get him money, is not only the most ingenious, but also the most civil person I ever met with.[2]

> Scilicet ingenuas didicisse fideliter artes,
> Emollit mores, nec sinit esse feros.[3]

I believe his very clocks speak in a softer tone than those of others; to say they strike is too boisterous a word. No—

> From hour to hour melodiously they chime
> With silver sounds, and sweetly tune out time.

He is likewise curious in microscopes and showed my mother some of the *semen masculinum*, with animascula[4] in it. He married the daughter of Peter My, or Mee (for historians spell it variously), keeper of the beautiful park of Ladyholt, and flourished the beginning of the eighteenth century in Duke Street near Lincoln's Inn Fields.

There is perhaps nothing that more conduces to the honor of eminent persons, whether in arms or arts, than the intimacies and friendships which we trace them to have contracted with the most estimable men of their time. It is for this cause, and to reflect a like honour upon myself, that I transmit to you so studiously this happy incident of my life, in my correspondence and familiarity with Mr Hatton of Duke Street.

But indeed I should also add that this artist's having mentioned your name with esteem, and allowing me to acquaint you how much he is your servant, was not the least reason, that made me write even a single line of him. If after his name, I may insert one so inferior, be pleased to accept in like manner the faithful respects of | Dear Sir | Your most affectionate and obedient servant | A: P:

This last hamper was so out of repair, that some of the bottles are broke.

[1] Alluding to the indecorums at the christening of Prince George William.

[2] The language of the MS. in this paragraph is eclectically preserved on the theory that it may represent the speech of the clock-maker himself.

[3] Ovid, *Ex Ponto*, II. ix. 47–48.

[4] The scribe's word for *animalcula*.

POPE *to* SIR GODFREY KNELLER[1] 18 *February* 1717/18

Yale University

Febr. 18th 1717/18

Sir,—It was not the least of my misfortunes (and Poets, you know, generally think they have many) that I mist of seeing you so often. My Stars were to blame, & if it were true, that *A wise Man can govern his Stars*, Indeed I would teach them better manners. But I can scarce repent my loss of your Company, when it was the occasion of the pleasure of your letter, which convinces me that whatever another wise man can be, a wise & great Painter at least can be above the Stars, when he pleases. The Elevation of Such a Genius is not to be measurd by the Object it flies at, it soars far higher than its Aim, & carries up the Subject along with it. Like the Arrow in Virgil, that intending only to hit a common Mark, kindled in its flight and blaz'd into a Comet. Such is your praise of so unworthy a Subject as I, when you raise me to such a degree, that (like most other pitiful Fellows of my Race) I think myself *paulò minus ab Angelis.*[2] But this is no more than you daily do upon Canvass; I thought, to Complement upon Paper had been left to Poets & Lovers. Dryden says he has seen a Fool Think, in your picture of him: And I have reason to say I have seen the least of mankind appear one of the greatest under your hands. I really believe (from the conviction I have how much better you make things than Nature herself,) that even a Man in love woud think his Mistress improved by you. For You are the only one in the world, whom the most jealous Lover would beg to Touch his Mistress. For my part, when I am in Love I will desire you only to assist me as a Friend, or as a [Chris]tian; for if She encourages my passion, y[ou could] Reward her by painting her, & give As much beauty [to her] as she bates in me: If she rejects me, you can [paint] for me a finer creature in her owne kind, that would put her out of countenance.

You will perceive Sir, that I am as much at [a loss] how to Express myself, as you pretend to be. [But] a Genius like yours never fails to Express it[self well] to all the world. And in the warmth with which [it is] agitated, let it but throw the Pen or [Pen]cil with never so careless a dash, all peop[le would] see 'tis a noble Frenzy, a Vaghezza, like the *Foam* of a Great Master. I am | Sir | Your most obedient obligd / Servant / A. Pope.

Address: For Sir Godfrey Kneller | Bart at Whitton, near | Brentford | Middlesex

Postmark: 18/ [ ]

[1] One margin of the letter has been mended and the words here placed in brackets are supplied in a later hand, not Pope's.

[2] Psalm viii. 6.

†ATTERBURY *to* POPE[1] 18 *February* 1717/18

1737

Feb. 18, 1717.

I hop'd to find you last night at Lord Bathurst's, and came but a few minutes after you had left him. I brought *Gorboduc*[2] with me; and Dr. Arbuthnot telling me he should see you, I deposited the book in his hands: out of which, I think my Lord Bathurst got it before we parted, and from him therefore you are to claim it. If Gorboduc should still miss his way to you, others are to answer for it; I have deliver'd up my trust. I am not sorry your Alcander[3] is burnt; but had I known your intentions, I would have interceded for the first page and put it with your leave among my curiosities. In truth, it is the only instance of that kind I ever met with, from a person good for any thing else, nay for every thing else to which he is pleas'd to turn himself.

Depend upon it, I shall see you with great pleasure at Bromley; and there is no request you can make to me, that I shall not most readily comply with. I wish you health and happiness of all sorts, and would be glad to be instrumental in any degree towards helping you to the least share of either. I am always, every where, most affectionately and faithfully | Yours, &c.

POPE *to* TERESA *and* MARTHA BLOUNT[4] [1718?]

Mapledurham

Dear Ladies,— If you are inclind to go to morrow to Sir Richard Child's, I shall be very glad to attend you. Otherwise I would take Mr Fenton with me to Chiswick very early. To day I have been in

[1] Pope was in town in Feb. 1718, though not continuously. He was ill in Feb. 1717 (see Pope to Dancastle, 18 Feb. 1716/17), and if he had been absent from Lord Bathurst's because of illness, Atterbury would here condole with him. The letter was first printed in the octavos of Pope, 1737–42. It was omitted from the quarto and folio of 1737.

[2] A Tragedy, written in the Reign of Edward the sixth (and much the best performance of that Age) by Sackvil afterwards Earl of Dorset, and Lord Treasurer to Queen Elizabeth. It was then very scarce, but lately reprinted by R. Dodsley in Pall-mall.—Pope, 1737–42. Dodsley's edition (1736) has a dedicatory 'Account of the Lord Buckhurst' by Joseph Spence, addressed to the Earl of Middlesex (to whom in 1732 Savage—or Pope?—had dedicated the *Collection of Pieces in Verse and Prose, which have been publish'd on Occasion of the Dunciad*). Spence's 'Account' states that the Dodsley reprint was due to Pope's activity. The rare edition of *Gorboduc* had been lent to Pope by Thomas Warton the elder in the summer of 1717 (Pope to Digby, 2 June 1717), and Pope had apparently lent it to Atterbury.

[3] An Heroic Poem writ at 15 years old.—Pope, 1737–42. (For further details about Alcander see Spence, pp. 24, 276, 279.)

[4] The mention of Chiswick and an architect places the letter in 1718. Since Sir Richard Child was created Viscount Castlemain on 24 Apr., the letter should antedate that event. It was only after the death of his father that the poet considered building in town. Sir Richard was a banker, and the postscript (heretofore unprinted) places the letter in the undefined period when Pope was perhaps somewhat officiously attempting to improve the financial status of the Blount sisters.

the utmost Engagements of business and as soon as I can get from Mr Dormer's where I dine at 3, must be with my Architect.

If you send a note to night to my lodging, I'll take all other necessary cares upon me. I hope you are both well. I am sincerely | Yours | A P.

[Ter]esa, give the bearer the Lottery Order.

POPE *to* TERESA BLOUNT[1] 21 *February* [1717/18]

Mapledurham

Feb. 21st

Madam,—I am too much out of order to trouble you with a long letter. But I desire to know what is your meaning to resent my complying with your request, & endeavoring to serve you in the way you proposd, as if I have done you some great injury? You told me if such a thing was the Secret of my heart, you shoud entirely forgive and think well of me. I told it, & find the contrary—You pretended so much generosity, as to offer your Services in my behalf: the minute after, you did me as ill an office as you could, in telling the party concern'd, it was all but an Amusement occasiond by my Loss of another Lady.

You exprest your self desirous of increasing your present income upon Life: I proposed the only method I then could find, & you encoragd me to proceed in it—when it was done, you received it as if it were an Affront.—Since when, I find the very thing, in the very manner you wishd, & mention it to you; You don't think it worth an answer.

If your meaning be, that the very things you ask, and wish, become Odious to you, when it is I that comply with 'em, or bring 'em about; pray own it, & deceive me no longer with any thought, but that you Hate me. My Friendship is too warm & sincere to be triffled with; therfore if you have any meaning, tell it me, or you must allow me to take away That which perhaps you don't care to keep. | Your humble Servant. | A. P.

I shall speedily obey you in sending the Papers you order'd; which when I do, Be pleasd to sign the inclosd receit, & return it by the bearer of 'em.

Address: For Mrs Teresa Blount, | at Mrs Blount's in | Bolton street | Piccadilly | London.

Postmark: PENY POST PAYD

[1] This letter seems to relate to the misunderstanding with Teresa evident in recent letters and here tending to an acute stage. Apparently peace prevailed, for on 10 Mar. 1717[18], according to Carruthers (p. 76), 'Pope executed a deed by which he settled upon Teresa an annuity of forty pounds a year for six years, on condition that she should not be married during that term.' These curious conditions may have seemed offensive to Teresa. The circumstances are inexplicable.

LADY MARY WORTLEY MONTAGU *to* POPE

1 *March* 1717/18

[Mr. Moy Thomas in his 'Heads of L.M.'s Letters from Turkey' printed in his editions of her *Letters* (i [1861], 19) lists a letter—otherwise totally unknown—under the date 1 March with the description: 'The world here romantic. Women differ from ours. Unaffected. Lazy life.' Parts of the letter that she arranged for publication under the date 1 April 1717 might fit such a description, but there may well have been another letter emphasizing the traits indicated.]

POPE *to* LADY MARY WORTLEY MONTAGU[1] [1718]

The Pierpont Morgan Library

I write this after a very severe Illness, that had like to have cost you a Friend: and in writing, I rebell against a Despotic Doctor, whose Tyranny the greatest here obey, and from the same servile Principle that most men obey Tyrants, the Fear of Death. He says, I must think but slightly of anything: Now I am practising if I can think so of You, which if I can, I shall be above regarding any thing in nature for the future: I may then look upon the Sun as a Spangle & the World as a Hazel-nut. But in earnest, you should be pleas'd at my recovery, as it is a thing you'll get something by: Heaven has renew'd a Lease to you of a sincere Servant; Abundance of good wishes & grateful thanks will be added to those you have had from me already; and Lady Mary will be spoken of with respect and tenderness some years longer.

This last winter has seen great revolutions in my little affairs. My Sickness was preceded by the death of my Father, which happend within a few days after I had writ to you, inviting myself to meet you in your journy homewards.[2] I have yet a Mother of great age & infirmitys, whose last precarious days of life I am now attending, with such a solemn pious kind of officiousness, as a melancholy Recluse watches the last risings & fallings of a dying Taper. My natural temper is pretty much broke, & I live half a Hermite within five miles of London. A Letter from you sooths me in my Reveries; 'tis like a Conversation with some Spirit of the other world the least Glympse of whose Favour setts one above all taste of the Things of this. Indeed there is little or nothing Angelical left behind you. The Women here are—Women. I can't express how I long to see you, face to face, If ever you come again I shall never be able to behave with decency, I shall walk, look, & talk at such a rate that all the Town must know

[1] Perhaps Pope exaggerates his ill health, which is less featured in other letters of this year. The return of Lady Mary and the phrases 'this last winter' suggest placing the letter in the spring of 1718. There is in the original no superscription.

[2] See Pope to Lady Mary, Oct. 1717, here i. 400.

I have seen something more than human—Come for God's sake, come Lady Mary, come quickly!

I extreamly regret the loss of your Oriental Learning, for that letter I never had, but am heartily glad you kept a Copy. I believe one of mine had the same fate, wherein I beggd a Circassian Woman of you, the likest yourself that could be purchased. Don't think to put me off with a little Likeness of You; The Girl which I hear you have, some way or other, procured, & are bringing with you, is not fitt for me—Whatever you may fancy, Molineux is marryd,[1] and I am past a Boy.

I must tell you a Story of Molineux. The other day at the Princes Levee, he took Mr Edgecomb[2] aside, and askd with an Air of Seriousness, What did the Czar of Muscovy, when he disinherited his Son, do with his Secretary? To which Edgecomb answerd, He was sow'd up in a Football, and tost over the water.

Now I am got among your Acquaintance, you must be content to hear how often I talk of you with Mr Craggs, Mr Methuen, Mr Congreve, D. of Buckingham, Sir R. Rich, Miss Griffin, &c. I am almost angry to go into any body's company where I ever saw you. I partly enjoy and partly regrett it. It is not without vexation that I roam on the Thames in a fine Evening, or walk by moonlight in St. James' park. I can scarce allow that any thing should be calm, or any thing should be sweet without you. Give me leave at this distance to say, that I am something so much between a Philosopher and a Lover, that I am continually angry at Fortune for letting me enjoy those amusements which I fancy you want, and I seldom receive any pleasure but it is got into my head, Why has not She a Share in it? This is really true, and yet you are not so prodigiously obligd to me neither; because I wish almost every body, not only every Sensible Pleasure, but almost every Vanity that can delight them.

Our Gallantry and Gayety have been great Sufferers by the rupture of the two Courts here. Scarce any Ball, Assembly, Basset table, or any place where two or three are gathered together. No lone house in Wales with a Rookery, is more contemplative than Hampton Court; I walk'd there the other day by the Moon, and met no creature of any quality but the King, who was giving Audience, all alone, to the Birds under the Garden-Wall.[3]

How many hundred things have I to say to you, not ten of which

[1] Samuel Molyneux, secretary to the Prince of Wales (later George II), had married Lady Elizabeth Capell on 5 Apr. 1717.

[2] Very likely Richard, later Baron Edgecumbe, and in 1716 one of the lords of the treasury.

[3] This passage echoes a part of Pope's account of life at Court sent to Martha Blount [13 Sept. 1717]. The original letters both still exist, and give striking evidence of Pope's habit of echoing himself in phrase in two letters written months apart. This sort of echoing is not infrequent in the letters to Lady Mary and Martha Blount of this period.

perhaps I shall remember when we meet? I have seen many fine things, many vile things, & many ridiculous things, all which are an amusement to those who can think: the one naturally emulates the first sort, is hurt by the second, and vex'd at the third. If one laughs at the world, they'l say he is proud, if one rails at it, they'l say he is ill-natured; and yet one or other of these one must do. Upon the whole I am melancholy, which (to say truth) is all one gets by pleasures themselves. But I should not tell you this, if I did not think you of opinion that Melancholy does me as little hurt as any man. And after all, he must be a Beast, that can be melancholy with such a fine Woman as you to his friend. Adieu. Were I your Guardian Spirit, your Happiness would be my whole Care, as I am, a poor mortal, it is one of my most earnest Wishes. | Dear Madam, Yours.

I beg you, write to me soon; you are now come into the region of Posts, and under the Care of Secretaries; the whole Succession of whom are your Servants, and give me more than pensions and places when they give me your letters.

POPE *to* CARYLL — 29 *March* [1718]

Add. 28618

London. March 29.

The last important cargo arrived as safely as the rest, and I am now to return you not only all thanks for the trouble, but all due praise for the care and circumspection employed about this affair. I take this (as times go) for a very proper topic of Panegyric; since to cheat the publick, or the prince, seems the grand end of all great Genius's in politics, &c. But as wine may be reckoned a part of that by which we live, so the necessity under which all polite people lie, of drinking, and of drinking only French wine, must render us blameless in the conscientious point, tho' criminal in the letter of the law.

If I knew how to entertain you thro' the rest of this paper, it should be spotted and diversified with conceits on every side. But I have experimentally found that men of late are as little affected by writing, as by preaching, and that 'tis as possible to nod over a dull letter as a dull sermon. The complimental part of a letter, like that of a sermon is generally what pleases most, and there too you cut me out, by a certain old-fashioned virtue (and you know virtues that are old-fashioned are vices, in the same manner as the richest old wardrobes are the most awkward and ridiculous of dressing to us moderns),—I mean a virtue, once so reputed, called humility. This hinders at least the half of a well bred epistle from shining and pleasing. Much good may that virtue do you; [1]but here in town, men, women, and children have done with it;[2] ⌜and the rest of the obsolete train are going after it.⌝ Charity not only begins, ⌜now a days,⌝ but ends at home. ⌜Ask Esquire Blount else. And⌝ the four cardinal virtues being abrogated as popish, the four princely ones succeed, cunning, rapine, time-serving, and luxury.[3] Whatever you may fancy at Ladyholt,[4] where you live in a state of ignorance, and see nothing but ⌜innocence,⌝ quiet, religion and good humour, the case is [as] I tell you ⌜in London, and every where else,⌝ where people understand the [world], and know how to live with credit and glory. I wish that Heaven, would open the eyes of men, and make 'em sensible which of these is the right? whether upon a due conviction, we are to quit factions and high feeding, and gaming,[5] and whoring, and take to your country way? or you to leave prayers ⌜and fasting,⌝ and almsgiving, and reading, and exercise, and come into our measures? I wish (I say) that God would direct us all; and am with much veracity | Dear Sir | your affectionate[6] ⌜obliged servant | A: P:⌝

⌜I was to wait upon you, and Mr Caryll, the day you left the town, about 2 hours too late. Your picture requires directions how to be sent, unless you'd have it stay till I see you in May. Mrs Patty Blount is picking up a large collection of libels[7] to send you: we are here of opinion, that scandal is the only vice, of which those of Ladyholt have any taste left.⌝

†POPE *to* ROBERT DIGBY[8] 31 *March* 1718

1735

London, March 31, 1718.

To convince you how little pain I give myself, in corresponding with Men of good Nature, and good Understanding, you see I omit to answer your Letters till a time, when another man would be ashamed to own he had received them. If therefore you are ever moved on my

[1] Beginning with 'but here in town' Pope used the rest of this letter (except the postscript) as the last part of a letter printed as to Digby, 28 Dec. 1724. His changes are noted below, with his omissions placed in half-brackets.

[2] it] these things *1735–42*.

[3] Ask . . . luxury] Instead of the four Cardinal Virtues, now reign four Princely ones: We have Cunning for Prudence, Rapine for Justice, Time-serving for Fortitude, and Luxury for Temperance. *1735–42*. (Apart from rhetorical improvement Pope had to omit reference to Michael Blount and wished to soften 'abrogated as popish'.)

[4] at Ladyholt] where you live *1735–42* (a necessary adaptation).

[5] factions . . . gaming] Faction, and Gaming, and High-feeding *1735–42*.

[6] that God . . . your affectionate] that this Matter were as clear to all Men, as it is to | Your affectionate *1735–42*.

[7] The large collection of libels, if it included anything by Pope, probably included his attack on Cibber's anti-Catholic play, *The Non-Juror*. Pope's effort was probably *A Clue to the Non-Juror*, published 15 Feb. and republished shortly as *The Plot Discover'd: or a Clue to the Non-Juror*.

[8] Printed by Pope in all his editions except the 'afternoon' edition of 12 May 1735, with a few quite negligible revisions in various printings.

Account by that Spirit, which I take to be as familiar to you as a Quotidian Ague, I mean the Spirit of Goodness, pray never stint it, in any fear of obliging me to a Civility beyond my natural Inclination: I dare trust you, Sir, not only with my Folly when I write, but with my Negligence when I do not; and expect equally your Pardon for either.

[1]If I knew how to entertain you thro' the rest of this Paper, it should be spotted and diversified with Conceits all over; you should be put out of Breath with Laughter at each Sentence, and pause at each Period, to look back over how much Wit you had pass'd. But I have found by Experience, that People now-adays regard Writing as little as they do Preaching: The most we can hope is to be heard, just with Decency and Patience, once a Week, by Folks in the Country: Here in Town we hum over a Piece of fine Writing, and we whistle at a Sermon. The Stage is the only place we seem alive at; there indeed we stare, and roar, and clap Hands for K. *George* and the Government.[2] As for all other Virtues but this Loyalty, they are an obsolete Train, so ill-dress'd, that Men, Women, and Children hiss 'em out of all good Company. Humility knocks so sneakingly at the Door, that every Footman out-raps it, and makes it give way to the free Entrance of Pride, Prodigality, and Vain-glory.

My Lady *Scudamore*,[3] from having rusticated in your Company too long, really behaves herself scandalously among us: She pretends to open her eyes for the sake of seeing the Sun, and to sleep because it is Night; drinks Tea at nine in the Morning, and is thought to have said her Prayers before; talks without any manner of shame of good Books, and has not seen *Cibber*'s Play of the *Non-juror*. I rejoyced the other day to see a Libel on her Toilette, which gives me some hope that you have at least a Taste of Scandal left you, in defect of all other Vices.

Upon the whole matter, I heartily wish you well; but as I cannot entirely desire the ruin of all the Joys of this City, so all that remains is to wish you wou'd keep your Happiness to yourselves, that the happiest here may not die with Envy at a Bliss which they cannot attain to. | I am, &c.

†ROBERT DIGBY *to* POPE[4] 17 *April* 1718

1737

Coleshill, Apr. 17, 1718.

I have read your letter over and over with delight. By your description

[1] The first part of this paragraph should be compared with the preceding letter to Caryll, 29 Mar. 1718, which it closely follows.

[2] Cibber, in his *Letter from Mr. Cibber to Mr. Pope* (1742), p. 28, regarded—plausibly enough—this remark as a slap at *The Non-Juror* and in retort remarked, 'You think the Town as ridiculous to roar and clap at it' (inasmuch as it is loyal to King George and his government).

[3] Viscountess Scudamore was young Digby's cousin.

[4] Printed by Pope in all editions from 1737 to 1742, unrevised.

of the town, I imagine it to lie under some great enchantment, and am very much concerned for you and all my friends in it. I am the more afraid, imagining since you do not fly those horrible monsters, rapine, dissimulation and luxury, that a magick circle is drawn about you, and you cannot escape. We are here in the country in quite another world, surrounded with blessings and pleasures, without any occasion of exercising our irascible facultys; indeed we cannot boast of good-breeding and the art of life, but yet we don't live unpleasantly in primitive simplicity and good humour. The fashions of the town affect us but just like a raree-show, we have a curiosity to peep at 'em and nothing more. What you call pride, prodigality, and vain-glory, we cannot find in pomp and splendour at this distance; it appears to us a fine glittering scene, which if we don't envy you, we think you happier than we are in your enjoying it. Whatever you may think to persuade us of the humility of virtue, and her appearing in rags amongst you, we can never believe: our uninform'd minds represent her so noble to us, that we necessarily annex splendour to her; and we could as soon imagine the order of things inverted, and there is no man in the moon, as believe the contrary. I can't forbear telling you we indeed read the spoils of Rapine as boys do the English rogue,[1] and hug our selves full as much over it; yet our roses are not without thorns. Pray give me the pleasure of hearing (when you are at leisure) how soon I may expect to see the next volume of Homer. I am, &c.

POPE *to* CARYLL[2]

1 *May* [1718]

Add. 28618

Chiswick. May 1.

'Tis impossible for me to say any thing to you, which your own sense and your own religious thoughts have not already suggested in your comfort. Those are the strong supports that still must maintain you, that you have ever been a good man and a resigned Christian. I can only very truly assure you that I bear a tender part in all things that afflict you but hope at the same time nothing can afflict you beyond the limits of so well grounded a virtue as your whole life has manifested. In one word I am most unfeignedly sorry you feel the misfortunes of a man, but am heartily glad you possess the constancy of a Christian, who can cheerfully Say *Deus dedit, Deus abstulit.* Dear sir, I am sincerely and tenderly | Yours. A. Pope.

[1] It is interesting that this work—*The English Rogue Described in the Life of Meriton Latroon* (1665–71), by Richard Head and Francis Kirkman—should be regarded as a 'juvenile'.

[2] This is a letter of condolence on the death of Mr. John Caryll. The event is thus recorded in his father's diary: 'April 6, being Palm Sunday, my dear son, never to be forgotten, died of the small-pox. Sweet Jesus, grant me resignation, and to him eternal rest.'—Elwin.

POPE *to* CARYLL *June* 1718

Add. 28618

June 1718.

I received not your kind letter, which gave me notice of your coach, till it was too late to make use of it by several days: having been at Cirencester and Oxford for some time. Just then, upon the publication of my Homer, that affair and many others since (of which building a house in town[1] is not the greatest), have made me stay here of absolute necessity, and will require a farther care from time to time. Notwithstanding which I am bound to go thro' my year's labours in poetry, with a hundred distractions, that render me as unfit for conversation as writing. I should be ashamed to be absent[2] in the company of such a friend as you; for 'till I am perfectly my own master, I am really unworthy to be called your servant. The ladies who bring you this letter[3] can vouch for the truth of what I say; who I am sure will not scruple to tell you, I never was so ill company in my life.

The consciousness of this has made me resolve to be alone for some months. As I can't be so at Chiswick, nor long absent from my mother, and necessarily engaged to study, I am going near Oxford[4], the seat of the muses, and at this time of vacation solitary enough. A line from you will find me, directed to Mr Jevas's[5] as usual, whose people will carefully send it after me. Pray write to me, and, if you can, persuade [the] Mrs Blounts to do the same. Dear sir, I truly wish you all happiness, or in default of all happiness, all resignation.' Tis the best amends we can make ourselves for any misfortune here and the surest means to obtain felicity hereafter. I have loved you long, esteem you still, and wish I could imitate your virtue when I may have occasion to resign anything that is dear to me; which will happen, one time or other, to every honest heart in the world.

To say truth, I think, except for one or two such examples as yours, all family virtues, or regard for those which were once thought tender and obliging ties, of relations, friendship or affinity,—all these (I say) seem lost and ridiculed. A family nowadays is a little Commonwealth of malignants, where each has a paltry, separate interest from the other. The son wishes the death of the father, the younger brother of the elder, the elder grudges the portions of the sisters; and when any of them marry, then rise new interests and new divisions *in sæcula sæculorum.* It would be no ill praise of your family to say it is the most

[1] Pope thought of building in London at this time. Lord Bathurst discouraged him (14 Aug. 1718) and Pope gave up his option on a site in a letter to Lord Burlington, 2 Feb. 1718/19.

[2] That is, absent-minded or inattentive.

[3] Evidently this letter was to be taken to Caryll by Teresa and Martha Blount, but the visit was deferred.

[4] To Stanton Harcourt.

[5] An obvious careless miswriting for *Jervas's*.

unlike a family in the world. And one might justly allow Esquire Blount to be the truest son, and the truest brother in the nation.

I hope to see you unfashionably good this long time, which is only wishing you long life in other Words. I am always Dear sir | Your faithful and affectionat | Servant | A: P:

*M. VYNER *to* POPE[1] — 7 *June* [1718]

Homer MSS. Add. 4808

Sir,—Mr Vyner being rid out makes Me give you this troble to let you Know how glad he will be of the Honour you desine him as will also Mrs Marryot & your Most | Humble Servant | M Vyner

Swakeley | June the 7

Address: To Mr Pope

*R. VYNER *to* POPE[2] — [8 *June* 1718]

Homer MSS. Add. 4808

Swakley Sunday morning

Sir,—I was in hopes my being gone out to take the Air, would not have prevented our seeing you here last night, I am so sorry it did that I shall stay from Church in expectation of you this morning, We have no body with us but Mrs Marriot, and if you do not know the Way pray detain the Messenger who will conduct you to | Sir | Your Most Oblig'd | Hum: Servant | R Vyner

Address: To | Mr Pope | These.

POPE *to* LORD BATHURST — 5 *July* [1718]

The Boston (Mass.) Public Library

London, July 5th

My Lord,—To say a word in praise either of your Wood or You, would be alike impertinent, each being, in its kind, the finest thing I know, & the most agreeable. I can only tell you very honestly, (without a word of the high Timber of the one, or the high Qualities of the other) that I thought it the best company I ever knew, & the best Place to enjoy it in.

[1] This and the following letter concern an attempt of Pope to call on Miss Marriott, who was apparently staying with the Vyners at Swakeley, near Uxbridge. One imagines that Pope had written to say that he would call on Saturday or Sunday, and here Mrs. Vyner replies for her husband who has 'rid out'. The next morning Mr. Vyner sends a messenger with the second note. One assumes that 'M. Vyner' is Mrs. Vyner.

[2] R. Vyner is Robert Vyner, named after his great-uncle, Sir Robert, who was Lord Mayor of London as well as a difficult bankrupt. See Charles J. Vyner, *Vyner, A Family History*, 1885, and *Vyner, A Family History, Supplement*, 1885.

I came hither but this day,[1] where I find as much Business, as I left Pleasure: I wish it would last as short a time, that I might return to you before you quit Cirencester, but I really see no prospect of ending what I must necessarily do, in less than a Fortnight. Mr Gay is as zealously carry'd to the Bower by the force of Imagination as ever Don Quixote was to an Enchanted Castle. The Wood is to him the Cave of Montesinos: He has already planted it with Myrtles, & peopled it with Nymphs. The old Woman of the Pheasantry appears alredy an Urganda;[2] & there wants nothing but a Christal Rivulet to purl thro the Shades, which might be large enough to allay Mr Lewis's[3] great Thirst after water.

But my Lord, I beg you to be comforted. Gay promises, that whatever may be said by the Prose-men, of this age, Posterity shall believe there was water in Okely wood; And (to speak boldly) wood also:

A Wood? quoth Lewis: and with that,
He laughd, and shook his Sides so fat:
His tongue (with Eye that markd his cunning)
Thus fell a reas'ning, not a running.
Woods are (not to be too prolix)
Collective Bodies of strait Sticks
It is, my Lord, a meer Conundrum
To call things woods, for what grows und'r 'em
For Shrubs, when nothing else at top is,
Can only constitute a Coppice.
But if you will not take my word,
See Anno quart. of Edward, third.
And that they're Coppice calld, when dock'd,
Witness Ann. prim. of Henry Oct.
If this a Wood you will mantain
Meerly because it is no Plain;
Holland (for all that I can see)
Might e'en as well be termd the Sea;
And C—by[4] be fair harangu'd
An honest man, because not hang'd.

The rest of Mr Lewis's Arguments I have forgotten, for as I am determin'd to live in the Wood, I am likewise resolvd to hear no reasons

[1] Pope has been at Cirencester and doubtless at Lord Harcourt's seat near Oxford. He has arrived in London 'this day' probably to settle accounts with Lintot, and consult about building in town. He already plans to take his mother to Stanton Harcourt where he can frequently see her while he is in Lord Bathurst's 'bower'. Apparently Pope spent most of July in London, since he arrived (he tells us later) at Stanton Harcourt on the evening when John Hewet and Sarah Drew were being buried. (Possibly he arrived from Cirencester?)

[2] In *Amadis de Gaul.*

[3] Erasmus Lewis.

[4] Thomas Coningsby, a violent opponent in Parliament of Lord Oxford. His haranguing is satirized by Pope in the Epistle to Lord Bathurst (Moral Essay III), l. 397.

against it. I have made a Coup de Maitre upon my mother, in persuading her to pass a month or two at Stanton Harcourt, in order to facilitate my Journies to her from Cicester. And I will not fail to be with you, whatever time you shall pass there in August.[1] I beg to be informed when your Lordship comes to Richkins, by the first message you send to London, directed to Jervas's. I have only to add, my most faithful Services to the Ladies;[2] to desire Mr Lewis to think as well of me as he can, of a man that writes Verses half the year; and to beg your Lordship to believe I love you so very well, as to be ashamd to find no better Expression for myself, than that of | My Lord, your most obedient & | most humble Servant, | A. Pope.

*SCRIBLERUS *to* ROBERT, EARL OF OXFORD[3]

8 *July* 1718

Longleat Portland Papers, xiii

To the Right Honourable
The Earl of Oxford.

Tuesday, 5 a clock

One* that should be a Saint, *Parnell
and one* that's a Sinner *Gay
And one* that pays reckning *Pope
but ne'er eats a Dinner,
In short Pope and Gay (as
you'l see in the margin)
Who saw you in Tower, and since
your enlarging,
And Parnell who saw you not since
You did treat him,
Will venture it now—You have
no Stick to beat him—
Since these for your Jury, good
and true men, vous-avez;
Pray grant Us Admittance,
and Shut out Miles Davies.[4]

[1] Apparently his lordship found it impossible to be at Cirencester before the autumn.

[2] Lady Bathurst and her daughters.

[3] These lines indicate an attempt to revive the spirit and custom of 1714—with Swift and Dr. Arbuthnot missing. It is not clear when Parnell had arrived in London, where he remained until Sept. The lines show that Gay had accompanied Pope to town. The lines themselves and the marginal identifications are all in Pope's hand. Another copy of the lines in the same volume of MSS. is said to be in Pope's autograph, but that seems improbable.

[4] The account of Miles Davies in *DNB* suggests that this antiquarian author died in 1715, but these lines indicate that he was possibly in the employ or was soliciting patronage of Lord Oxford as late as 1718. In 1716 he was himself selling his learned and fantastic *Athenae Britannicae*, which pays compliments to Pope in a somewhat daft style.

ROBERT, EARL OF OXFORD *to* SCRIBLERUS[1]

Longleat Portland Papers, xiii

July 8: 1718

To my old friends
In Paper course
This kindly comes to Greet you.
Let Parnel pray—
a Beau be Gay—
And Pope come heer to meet you.
'Til hower Eight
I Heer shal wait
But after Davies take you—

In Answer to a Letter in verse sent from the Ship Taverne[2] & receivd at the end of Dinner | Answerd while the company was buy. Note) their Letter was wrote by them in Gilt paper.

Superscribed Qui potest capere capiat.

Address: Qui potest capere | Capiat.

POPE *to* [MARTHA] BLOUNT[3] 6–9 *August* 1718

Mapledurham

August 6. 1718.

Dear Madam,— The only news you can expect to have from us here, must be News from heaven, for we are seperated from the earth, & there's scarce any thing can reach us except the noise of Thunder; which you have heard too, for no body in Christendome has a quicker

[1] This letter (on ff. 76–78) exists in the fair copy sent in reply to the verses from Parnell, Gay, and Pope, and exists also in a draft. Both forms are in Lord Oxford's hand, but the fair copy is signed, in another hand, possibly Pope's, 'E. of Oxford'. It was presumably returned after Pope's death to the Duchess of Portland with other letters to Pope from the 2nd Earl. The text here printed is that of the draft, identical with the fair copy so far as the verses go. The address is from the fair copy (f. 77); the rest of the prose is from f. 78.

[2] The Ship Tavern, long established at Charing Cross, was evidently the sort of house where one might have gilt paper.

[3] This is possibly Pope's earliest *extant* account of the deaths of the two lovers at Stanton Harcourt, which gave rise to more than one epistolary version of the event. Since this letter is written in a clear, steady hand, it may be regarded as almost a 'fair copy' or adaptation of another version—perhaps the 'melancholy novel . . . of the two unhappy lovers' mentioned by Lord Bathurst in his letter to Pope of 14 Aug. as sent to him as a joint effort of Pope and Gay. This present letter begins with the plural 'we' and presently adopts the more personal 'I'. Pope retold the story in his letter to Lady Mary, 1 Sept., and mentions it at least in letters to Caryll (3 Sept.) and to Atterbury (8 Sept.). The only version that he printed was that from Gay to Mr. F—, 9 Aug., which is here given as an example of adaptation. James Thomson used the episode in *Summer* some years before Pope's (or Gay's) account of the story was in print. Brief mentions of the case appeared in newspapers (e.g. Mist's *Weekly Journal*, 18 Aug. 1718); and *The Weekly Packet*, 11 Oct. 1718, printed Pope's later epitaph (in ten lines) for the lovers. See the letter immediately following this.

Ear for thunder than your self. We have read in old books, how Thunder levels high Towers, while the humble Vally escapes; & how proud Oaks are blasted, while the lowly Shrub remains unsindg'd: They say, the only thing that scapes it is the Lawrel, which yet we take not to be a Sufficient Security to the brains of modern Poets. But to let you see that the contrary to this often happens, I must acquaint you that here in our neighborhood, Blenheim, the most proud & extravagant Heap of Towers in the nation, stands untouchd; while a Cock of Corn in the next field is miserably reduced to ashes.

Would to God, that Cock of Corn had been all that sufferd! for unhappily beneath that little Shelter sate Two Lovers, no way yielding to those you so often find in a Romance under a Beechen Shade. The name of the one was John Hewet, of the other Sarah Drew. John was black, of about five & twenty; Sarah was of a comely brown, near the same age. John had for several months born the Sweat of the day & divided the labour of the harvest with Sarah: he took a particular delight to do her all the little offices that might please her: it was but last Fair he brought her a present of Green Silk to line her Strawhatt, and that too he had bought for her but the Market day before. Whenever she milkd, it was his care to bring the Cows to her Pail, and after to attend her with them to the field upon pretence of helping to drive 'em. In short, their Love was the Talk but not the scandal of the whole Neighborhood, for all he aimd at was the blameless Possession of her in marriage. It was but this very morning[1] he obtaind the consent of her Parents, and it was but till the next week that they were to wait to be happy. Perhaps this very day, in the intervals of their work, they were talking of their Wedding Cloaths, and John was suiting several sorts of Poppies and Field-flowers to Sarah's complexion, to make her a present of Knots for the day. While they were thus employd (it was on the last of July, between the hours of two and three in the afternoon) the clouds grew black; a terrible Storm of Thunder & Lightning ensued; the Labourers who were in the field, made the best of their way to what Shelter the Hedges or trees afforded. Sarah frighted, & out of breath, sunk down on a heap of Wheatsheaves; & John, who never seperated from her, rak'd two or three heaps together, to protect her, & sate down by her. Immediately there was heard so loud a crack that Heaven seemd burst asunder: every one was sollicitous for the safety of his next neighbor, & called to one another. Those who were nearest our Lovers hearing no Answer, stept to the Sheaves. They first spy'd a little Smoke, and then saw this faithful Pair, John with one Arm about her neck, & the other extended over her face, as to

[1] Pope is being dramatic at the expense of coherence. He dates his letter 6 Aug. (finishing on the 9th); then he says 'this very morning', and goes on in the next sentence but one to date the tragedy on 31 July. *That very morning* would have been clearer.

shield her from the Lightning; both stiff and cold in this tender posture: no mark or blemish on the Bodies; except the left Eyebrow of Sarah a little sing'd, and a small Spot between her breasts.

The Evening I arrived here,[1] I mett the Funeral of this unfortunate Couple. They were both layd in one Grave in the Parish church yard of Stanton-Harcourt. I have prevailed on my Lord Harcourt to erect a little Monument over them, of plain Stone; and have writ the following Epitaph which is to be engravd on it.[2]

When Eastern Lovers feed the fun'ral fire,
On the same Pile the faithful Fair expire;
Here, pitying Heav'n that Virtue mutual found,
And blasted both, that it might neither wound.
Hearts so sincere, th' Almighty saw well-pleas'd,
Sent his own Lightning, and the Victims seiz'd.

After all that we call Unfortunate in this Accident, I cannot but owne, I think next to living so happy as these people might have done, was dying as they did. And did any one love me so well as Sarah did John, I would much rather dye thus with her, than live after her. I could not but tell you this true and tender Story, and should be pleasd to have you as much mov'd by it as I am. I wish you had some Pity, for my sake; and I assure you I shall have for the future more Fear, for yours; since I see by this melancholy example, that Innocence & virtue are no security from what you are so afraid of. May the Hand of God (dear Madam) be seen upon you, in nothing but your Beauties, and his Blessings! I am firmly & affectionately, for ever | Yours.

August 9th

This Letter has been ready three days, but disappointed by the Postboys not calling (for we lie in a Cross Road). Your Sister gave me hopes of a line from you, but I have receiv'd none. I am more vexd at Mrs Caryls than I believe you can be.[3] I'd give the world if you had the courage, both of you, to pass the Fortnight in & about my Wood. I'd secure you of a good house within an hour of it, & a daily Entertainment in it. I go thither very speedily. I am sure of your Sister at least, that she woud do this, or any thing else, if she had a mind to it. Let her take trial of Some of Angels Horses & a Coach, for me. Upon the least hint, I'll send to Prince to conduct them.

[1] The remark helps, perhaps, to date the arrival of Pope (and Gay?) either from London or from Cirencester.

[2] Pope substituted on the 'plain stone' his later epitaph in ten lines, first printed in *The Weekly Packet*; see note 3, p. 479.

[3] Pope is vexed because the Carylls for some reason have not invited Martha and Teresa to Grinstead, as he had expected. His letter to Caryll (June 1718) had been written for them to take to their host. Pope consequently suggests that they come to the neighbourhood of Oakley Wood (Cirencester), where he will find them a house.

My Mother, Gay, & I, will meet you & show you Blenheim by the way, I dare believe Mrs Blount would not stick out at my request. And so Damn Grinsted & all its works. Our roads are very good all September, come, stay, and welcome.

†GAY *to* MR. F—[1] 9 *August* 1718

1737

Stanton Harcourt, Aug. 9, 1718.

The only news you can expect to have from me here, is news from heaven, for I am quite out of the world, and there is scarce any thing can reach me except the noise of thunder, which undoubtedly you have heard too. We have read in old authors, of high towers levell'd by it to the ground, while the humble valleys escap'd: the only thing that is proof against it is the laurell which however I take to be no great security to the brains of modern authors. But to let you see that the contrary to this often happens, I must acquaint you, that the highest and most extravagant heap of towers in the universe, which is in this neighbourhood, stands still undefac'd, while a cock of barley in our next field has been consumed to ashes. Would to God that this heap of barley had been all that had perished! for unhappily beneath this little shelter sate two much more constant Lovers than ever were found in Romance under the shade of a beech-tree. John Hewet was a well-set man of about five and twenty; Sarah Drew might be rather called comely than beautiful, and was about the same age. They had pass'd thro' the various labours of the year together with the greatest satisfaction; if she milk'd, 'twas his morning and evening care to bring the cows to her hand; it was but last fair that he bought her a present of green silk for her straw hat, and the posie on her silver ring was of his choosing. Their love was the talk of the whole neighbourhood; for scandal never affirm'd that they had any other views than the lawful possession of each other in marriage. It was that very morning that he had obtain'd the consent of her parents, and it was but the next week that they were to wait to be happy. Perhaps in the intervals of their work they were now talking of the wedding cloaths, and John was suiting several sorts of poppys and field flowers to her complexion, to chuse her a knot for the wedding-day. While they were thus busied, (it was on the last of July between two or three in the afternoon) the clouds grew black, and such a storm of lightning and thunder ensued, that all the labourers made the best of their way to what shelter the

[1] This letter, which closely follows the text of that to Miss Blount immediately preceding, was printed by Pope in 1737 and thereafter. One may doubt whether he or Gay was the real author of the letter, but Lord Bathurst (14 Aug. to Pope) implies that a similar letter of joint authorship was sent to him. F— might be either Fortescue or Fenton. Ayre in his *Life* of Pope (1745) printed this letter under the date 3 Aug.—probably simply a misprint.

trees and hedges afforded. Sarah was frightned, and fell down in a swoon on a heap of barley. John who never separated from her, sate down by her side, having raked together two or three heaps the better to secure her from the storm. Immediately there was heard so loud a crack, as if heaven had split asunder; every one was now solicitous for the safety of his neighbour, and called to one another throughout the field. No answer being return'd to those who called to our Lovers, they stept to the place where they lay; they perceived the barley all in a smoak, and then spy'd this faithful pair; John with one arm about Sarah's neck, and the other held over her, as to skreen her from the lightning. They were struck dead, and stiffen'd in this tender posture. Sarah's left eye-brow was sing'd, and there appear'd a black spot on her breast; her Lover was all over black, but not the least signs of life were found in either. Attended by their melancholy companions, they were convey'd to the town, and the next day interr'd in Stanton-Harcourt Church-yard. My Lord Harcourt, at Mr. Pope's and my request, has caused a stone to be plac'd over them, upon condition that we furnish'd the Epitaph, which is as follows;

When Eastern lovers feed the funeral fire;
On the same pile the faithful fair expire;
Here pitying heaven that virtue mutual found,
And blasted both, that it might neither wound.
Hearts so sincere th' Almighty saw well pleas'd,
Sent his own lightning, and the Victims seiz'd.

But my Lord is apprehensive the country people will not understand this, and Mr Pope says he'll make one with something of scripture in it,[1] and with as little of poetry as Hopkins and Sternhold. | Your, &c.

POPE *to* CARYLL 11 *August* 1718

Add. 28618

Oxford, August 11th 1718.

I can hardly tell you how uneasy your letter has made me. You write to me in a style that indeed was never properly used to me, that wherein we upbraid forgetful friends. I am sorry you can think my friendship depends upon so trivial [a circumstance] as that of writing every two months. 'Tis what a lame arm, or a strained thumb may hinder the best friend in England from doing. If I should tell you I have had both these misfortunes, it might pass for an apology, and yet in effect be worse since they happened both on my left arm. Or if I should say, that I was prevented by two or three fits (and pretty long

[1] For both epitaphs see Pope to Lady Mary, 1 Sept. 1718.

ones) of illness, 2 or 3 journeys, many and continual interruptions of business and company, much application to Homer, and what not? tho' all this be really true, yet the very best and very truest reason I can give for not writing so long is, that I trusted so much to the certainty you have of my friendship by a prior right, and a longer possession than all my other friends, that I thought you of all others, the safest man to be negligent to.

But now I reflect, I have not been so negligent as I thought. For above a month ago, I writ you a long epistle, which is yet in the hands of [the] Mrs Blounts upon the belief that they were just going to Grinsted.[1] I presume their constant expectation from day to day of a summons from your family, made the letter (together with two books which you sent for, and your female black's picture)[2] lie so long unknown to you.

I was necessitated to come hither to continue my translation of Homer, for at my own house I have no peace from visitants, and appointments of continual parties of pleasure: things very unseasonable to a man who has such a cruel, unproportionable task on his hands.

There will be no stirring for me from the country hereabouts, till I have done this whole volume.[3] For here except this day that I spend at Oxford, I am quite in a desert incognito from my very neighbours, by the help of a noble lord who has consigned a lone house to me for this very purpose. I could not lie at his own, for the same reason I don't go to Grinsted, because I love his company too well, to mind any thing else, when it is in my way to enjoy that.

I can't tell whether [the] Mrs Blounts will venture upon a Sussex road so late in the year; but if they do, I really think you ought to pay them with as many entertainments as you have given this whole season (according to the method of the husbandman in the Scripture), since, tho' they came latest; yet they have, on your account, born all the sweat and fatigue of the summer, in London. I can't say I shall envy them the venison they shall eat with you, but I shall the partridges; for, being here in the finest setting country in England, we can no where procure a dog to help us to any.[4] I beg your whole family to know me for their servant, and you to repent your rashness and still believe | your faithfull affectionate friend | A: P:

[1] See the letter of June 1718 to Caryll, here on p. 475.

[2] This may have been the portrait of an old domestic, who is always called 'Black Phil' in Caryll's accounts.—Elwin.

[3] Carruthers, p. 186, records that 'on a pane of red stained glass, in his lofty chamber at Stanton Harcourt' Pope inscribed the fact that 'In the year 1718 Alexander Pope finished here the Fifth Volume of Homer'. In his letter to Caryll, 18 Oct., Pope notified his friend that he had 'in a manner' finished the volume.

[4] Gay was the hunter; Pope the gourmet. Later (Gay to Swift, 8 Nov. 1730) Gay boasted his record for the season at Amesbury was 'five brace of partridges and four brace and a half of quails'.

THE DUKE OF BUCKINGHAM *to* POPE[1] [*August* 1718]

1723

You desire my opinion as to the late dispute in *France* concerning *Homer*: And I think it excusable (at an age alas of not much pleasure) to amuse my self a little in taking notice of a controversy, than which nothing is at present more remarkable (even in a nation who value themselves so much upon the *Belles Lettres*) both on account of the illustrious subject of it, and of the two persons ingaged in the quarrel.

The one, is extraordinary in all the lyrick-kind of Poetry even in the opinion of his very adversary. The other, a Lady (and of more value for being so) not only of great Learning, but with a Genius admirably turn'd to that sort of it which most becomes her Sex, for softness, genteelness, and promoting of vertue: and such as (one would think) is not so liable as other parts of scholarship, to rough disputes, or violent animosity.

Yet it has so happen'd that no writers, even about Divinity itself, have been more outragious or uncharitable than these two polite authors; by suffering their judgments to be a little warped (if I may use that expression) by the heat of their eager inclinations, to attack or defend so great an Author under debate: I wish, for the sake of the publick which is now so well entertain'd by their quarrel, it may not end at last in their agreeing to blame equally a third man, who is so presumptuous as to censure both, if they should chance to hear of it.

To begin with matter of fact. M. *D'Acier* has well judg'd, that the best of all poets certainly deserv'd a better translation, at least into *French* prose, because to see it done in verse was despair'd of: I believe indeed from a defect in that language, incapable of mounting to any degree of excellence suitable to so very great an undertaking.

She has not only perform'd this task as well as prose can do it, (which is indeed but as the wrong side of tapestry is able to represent the right) she has added to it also many learned and useful annotations. With all which she most obligingly delighted not only her own sex, but most of ours, ignorant of the *Greek*, and consequently her adversary himself, who frankly acknowledges that ignorance.

'Tis no wonder therefore if in doing this, she is grown so inamour'd of that unspeakably-charming Author, as to have a kind of horror at the least mention of a man bold enough to blame him.

[1] The dating is based on the fact that Pope published his reply to this letter as of 1 Sept. 1718. The quarrel discussed is not that between Pope and Mme Dacier, but that between her and Houdart de la Motte. Her 'reflections' on parts of Pope's Preface to the *Iliad* appeared at the end of vol. iii of the second edition of her *Iliad* in 1719. See Pope to Buckley, 12 Feb. 1722/3. The lady's attack on Pope was briefly mentioned in *St. James's Journal*, 3 May 1722, in an obituary of Mme Dacier.

The letter was first printed in Pope's edition of the Duke's *Works* (1723), ii. 288–95.

Now as to M. *de la Motte*, he being already deservedly famous for all sorts of Lyrick poetry, was so far introduc'd by her into those beauties of the Epick kind, (though but in that way of translation) as not to resist the pleasure and hope of reputation by attempting that in verse, which had been applauded so much for the difficulty of doing even in prose; knowing how this, well executed, must extreamly transcend the other.

But, as great Poets are a little apt to think they have an ancient right of being excus'd for vanity on all occasions; he was not content to out-do M. *D'Acier*, but endeavour'd to out-do *Homer* himself, and all that ever in any age or nation went before him in the same enterprize; by leaving out, altering, or adding whatever he thought best.

Against this presumptuous attempt, *Homer* has been in all times so well defended, as not to need my small assistance; yet I must needs say his excellencies are such, that for their sakes, he deserves a much gentler touch for his few seeming errors. These if M. *de la Motte* had translated as well as the rest, with an apology for having retain'd 'em only out of meer veneration; his judgment in my opinion would have appear'd much greater than by the best of his alterations, though I admit them to be written very finely.

I join with M. *de la Motte* in wondering at some odd things in *Homer*, but 'tis chiefly because of his sublime ones, I was about to say his divine ones, which almost surprize me at finding him any where in the fallible condition of humane nature.

And now we are wond'ring, I am in a difficulty to guess, what can be the reason of all these exceptions against *Homer*, from one who has himself translated him, contrary to the general custom of translators. Is there not a little of that in it? I mean the desire to be singular in getting above the title of a translator, though sufficiently honourable in this case. For such an ambition no body has less occasion, than one who is so fine a poet in other kinds; and who must have too much wit to believe, any alterations of another can intitle him to the denomination of an *Epick Poet* himself: though no man in this age seems more capable of being a good one, if the *French* tongue would bear it. Yet in his translation he has done too well, to leave any doubt (with all his faults) that her's can be ever parallel'd with it.

Besides he could not be ignorant, that finding faults is the most easy and vulgar part of a critick; whereas nothing shews so much skill and taste both, as the being thoroughly sensible of the sublimest excellencies.

What can we say in excuse of all this, but *Humanum est errare*? Since as good a Poet as I believe the *French* language is capable of and as sharp a Critick as any nation can produce, has by too much censuring *Homer*, subjected a translation to censure, that would have otherwise stood the test of the severest adversary.

But since he would needs chuse that wrong way of criticism, I wonder he miss'd a stone so ready to be thrown against *Homer*, for his filling the Iliad not only with so much slaughter, (for that is to be excused, since a War is not capable of being described without it) but with so many various particulars of wounds and horror, as shew the writer I am afraid so delighted that way himself, as not the least to doubt his reader being so also. Like *Spanioletta*, whose dismal pictures are the more disagreeable for being always so very movingly painted. Even *Hector*'s last parting from his son and *Andromache*, hardly makes us amends for his body's being dragg'd thrice round the town. M. *de la Motte* in his strongest objection about that dismal combat, has sufficient cause to blame his inrag'd adversary, who here gives an instance that it is impossible to be violent without committing some mistake; her passion for *Homer* blinding her too much to perceive the very grossest of his failings. By which warning I am become a little more capable of impartiality, though in a dispute about that very poet for whom I have the greatest veneration.

M. *D'Acier* might have considered a little, that whatever were the motives of M. *de la Motte* to so bold a proceeding, it could not darken that fame which I am sure she thinks shines securely even after the vain attempts of *Plato* himself against it: caus'd only perhaps by a like reason with that of Madam *D'Acier*'s anger against M. *de la Motte*, namely, the finding that in prose his genius (great as it was) could not be capable of the sublime heights of poetry, which therefore he banish'd out of his common-wealth.

Nor were these objections to *Homer* any more lessening of her merit in translating him as well as that way is capable of, *viz.* fully, plainly, and elegantly, than the most admirable verses can be any disparagement to as excellent prose.

The best excuse for all this violence is, its being in a cause which gives a kind of reputation even to suffering, by never so ill a management of it.

The worst of defending even *Homer* in such a passionate manner, is its being more a proof of her weakness, than of his being liable to none. For what is it can excuse *Homer* any more than *Hector*, for flying at the first sight of *Achilles*? whose terrible aspect sure needed not such an inexcusable fright to set it off; and methinks all that account of *Minerva*'s restoring his dart to *Achilles*, comes a little too late, for excusing *Hector*'s so terrible apprehension at the very first.

LORD BATHURST *to* POPE[1]

14 *August* 1718

Elwin–Courthope, viii. 324–6

Aug. 14, 1718

I hope my last came to your hands in which I advised you to take the opportunity of this warm weather to inhabit the silvan seat I mentioned to you, at the same time that I could not have the happiness of meeting you in the country till towards Michaelmas. You may then be assured that it can be no manner of inconvenience to me to have my house at Cirencester made use of.[2] On the contrary it affords me a real satisfaction that any thing of mine can be of service to you, but it will destroy the pleasure if I perceive that you are not as free with it as if it were entirely your own. You know there is nothing in it can be spoilt, and I trust to you to give an account how it comes to be so oddly bad. I must now return my thanks to Mr. Gay and you for your melancholy novel[3] you sent me of the two unhappy lovers; but why unhappy after all? A great deal may be said to prove the contrary, but for fear of ill constructions (I being in the bonds of matrimony, and you two loose,) I will only say that their names would never have been recorded to posterity but for this accident, and therefore I may conclude them *fortunati ambo si quid carmina possunt*.[4] We have had nothing of this kind in our neighbourhood. I have only been disturbed with the noise of saws and hammers, which has no other ill effect whatsoever attending it but only that it is apt to melt money sometimes. It may be proper for you to consider of the phenomenon against you begin to employ those engines about your *palazzotto* at London.[5] Neither Aristotle nor Descartes can find a method to hinder the noise from having that effect, and though the one should tell you that there was an occult quality[6] in those machines which operated in that manner upon gold and silver, and the other should say that there were certain atoms which flow from them adapted to the pores of those metals, it would be of no manner of use to you towards preserving the coin; but

[1] The original has not been seen. Elwin announces, obscurely, that the text is 'From the Oxford Papers'.

[2] The house, Pope's 'bower' in Oakley Wood, had been offered to Gay and Pope, evidently, for the summer.

[3] This lost narrative seems to be the first version of the accounts given to Miss Blount (6 Aug.) and to F— (9 Aug.).

[4] *Aeneid*, ix. 446.

[5] Dissatisfied with Chiswick Pope was considering the project of a house in town, in Burlington Gardens. In letters to Caryll (June 1718) and to Lord Burlington (2 Feb. 1718/19) he speaks of the project, as he does in an undated letter to the Misses Blount, here placed in the middle of February of this year. It is possible that roughly drawn plans in the Homer MSS. (Add. 4808, f. 30) concern the *palazzotto*. The project was in 1719 abandoned in favour of the villa at Twickenham.

[6] 'The Aristotelians', says Sir Isaac Newton, 'gave the name of occult qualities, not to manifest qualities, but to such qualities only as they supposed to lie hid in bodies, and to be the unknown causes of manifest effects. Such occult qualities put a stop to the improvement of natural philosophy, and therefore of late years have been rejected.'—Elwin, viii. 325.

we that lay out our money in the country have the sanction of Horace upon our prudence who says,

> Vos sapere et solos aio bene vivere, quorum
> Conspicitur nitidis fundata pecunia villis.[1]

I have consulted Dr. Bentley and I find that he is of opinion that *fundata pecunia* means money which was in the funds. But now since I am got into Horace give me leave to tell you that I am just going to dinner, and

> Excepto quod non simul esses, cætera lætus.[2]

[3]*Address*: To | Mr Pope att the Right | Honourable the Lord Harcourts att | Cockthorpe near | Witney | Oxfordshire.

Frank: Bathurst

Postmark: 16/AV

POPE *to* LORD BATHURST (draft)[4] [1718]

Homer MSS. Add. 4808

My Lord,—I had the (best kind of Honour) the Pleasure, of both your letters. I never was more earnest for any innocent thing than to enjoy the Silvan Bower this season. One desire only overcame it, which was that of having you a witness of the pleasure I should take in it: the moment I find my self disapointed of the hope, I fly thither: Accordingly we lye there to night

I cant tell you in what a manner I am affected by every thing you say to me. I begin to wish I desired more things to give you the pleasure of gratifying me in em. The Ladies[5] I talkd of have disappointed me, (that is disapointed You) in taking away my Expectation of seeing them. I'll not say a word now, for fear of writing like those that mean nothing that is, writing in all the Terms of respect & gratitude. For the Rogues (as Montaign says)[6] have got all those in their possession, & have left no honest man wherewithal to speak his mind unsuspectedly. I'd rather send you any thing else as you'll see by the pains I have prevaild upon Mr Gay to take in the Inclosed. Who is (as I am) with the truest Esteem | Yours

[1] *Epistles*, I. xv. 45–46. Bentley has no note on the passage.

[2] Ibid., x. 50.

[3] The address, frank, and postmark come from the Homer MSS. (Add. 4808, f. 69*v*), where they seem to have been preserved apart from the rest of the letter. (It seems obvious that they must belong to this letter.)

[4] This rough draft is obviously a reply to Lord Bathurst's letter of 14 Aug., addressed to Cockthorpe. One assumes that Gay and Pope were still at Stanton Harcourt.

[5] The ladies of the Blount family. See Pope to Martha Blount, 6–9 Aug.

[6] The allusion is possibly to the *Essays*, bk. i, ch. 39.

POPE *to* TERESA *and* MARTHA BLOUNT [*August* 1718]

Mapledurham

Dear Ladies,—The minute I find there's no hopes of you, I fly to the Wood.[1] It is as fit for me to leave the World, as for you to stay in it; & to prefer a Wood to any Acquaintance or company, as for you to prefer any Cosen, even the gravest relation you have, to a Wood. Perhaps you may think your Visit as melancholy as my Retirement: if you have not as much time to think as I shall have, you will have more to pray, which some think as melancholy. What I shall gather from thence I know not, except Nutts; which I believe Gay & I shall oft'ner crack, than Jokes. But you shall hear more of our life there, when we have experienced it longer.

I send this letter to answer a few friendly questions you have made. My Mother is, & has been, in as good health as I have known her these many years. She is mighty well acquainted with all Lord Harcourt's family, children & all. I shall not leave her seven days together, whatever Excursions I make. I have felt my arm more within these 3 days than I did when I left you. I have gone a good way in Homer ev'ry day I was at Stanton Harcourt: I'll shortly send you a particular description of that place.[2] It was no small grief to me that the fine Nectarines there were not ripe enough by a fortnight to send you. Shou'd any thing keep you longer in town than a week, or bring you back in three, I could accomodate you with very good ones upon the least Hint. I have not forgot the strong beer. I writ to Mr Caryl some posts agoe, & told him he ought to treat you like the Husbandman in the Scripture: Give you as much as those who came earliest, since you had born the Sweat & labour of the whole Summer for his sake.— I write very dully. I must send a better letter next, but I snatch a quarter of an hour for this, just while our Horses bait before our journey. Twas time for me to get away a while, for all Oxford was coming upon me with Duke Hamilton at the head of 'em. I had done a whole Book of Homer before any creature knew I was here.

I once more thank you both for your Letters: Pray continue to

[1] This letter must date after the middle of August, at a time when Pope had begun to 'commute' between Stanton Harcourt (where his mother was) and Cirencester, to which he went intermittently, so as to avoid social incursions (the Duke of Hamilton *et al.*) from Oxford. On 16 Aug. the Hon. Mrs. Simon Harcourt wrote to her mother (Mrs. John Evelyn) from Cockthorpe: 'Mr. Gay has left us; Mr. Pope and his mother being come to Stanton Harcourt; she is a very good sort of woman, and will make a very good neighbour whilst she stays, which I believe will be about a month or six weeks longer, by that time I sopose they will be weary of theyr solitude' (*Harcourt Papers*, ii. 184). The lady goes on to the story of John Hewet and Sarah Drew, and remarks: 'My Father tells Mr Pope and Mr Gay, that he thinks they ought to make an Epitaph upon them.' The first epitaph was sent to Martha Blount 6 Aug., and the second to Lady Mary on 1 Sept.

[2] We have no such description written to Miss Blount, but presently he sent such accounts of the place to Lady Mary and the Duke of Buckingham.

oblige me as often as ever you can. Those I send shall come free to London, but mayn't I as well send sometimes directly to Grinstead with Franks? Yours, if given by George to Jervas, can't fail of being sent right. Mr Gay is much yours, I always so.

God bless you, or I must be an ill Christian.

THE HON. SIMON HARCOURT *to* MRS. POPE[1]

[*August* 1718]

Homer MSS. Add. 4808

Madam,—I send you a Letter your Son Left for you, the charriot will be with you to morrow about eleven in which you must remember to bring my friend nurse. | I am Madam | Your Very humble servant | S Harcourt[2]

Address: To Mrs Pope

*THE EARL OF BURLINGTON *to* POPE[3]

26 *August* [1718?]

Chatsworth

My dear Pope,—I was agreably surprised last post with your letter, I need not tell you that it is always the greatest pleasure in the world to me to hear from one that I love so well and whose Epistles are something more entertaining than those, that one receives from the rest of mankind. you can expect no return, to your news paper from this remote quarter, but however to let you see that we are not quite void of curiosity I send you a weekly paper from Yorke I am my dear Pope your most affectionate humble servant | Burlington

Londesbrough aug 26

Pray my sincere respects to Gay

[1] Probably written in Aug. 1718 when Pope and Gay were at Cirencester and Mrs. Pope was at Stanton Harcourt. The chariot (one surmises) was to take Pope's mother and his nurse Mercy Beach to Cockthorpe for a day with the Harcourts. On the back of the note Pope translated a bit of Book XX of the *Iliad*—a fact that places the letter with probability in the summer of 1718.

[2] The signature indicates that the letter is by Lord Harcourt's son. Lady Harcourt's name was Elizabeth. Elwin thought her the writer of the note.

[3] The dating of this letter, so far as the year goes, is almost completely guess-work. In 1718 Pope and Gay were at Cirencester (or Stanton Harcourt) together, and Pope might be sending his lordship one of the newspaper accounts of the two lovers struck by lightning. The other most probable year seems to be 1728 when Pope and Gay may have been at Bath together. Lord Burlington was frequently in Yorkshire, but whether he was there in either of these Augusts is uncertain.

†POPE *to* THE DUKE OF BUCKINGHAM[1]

1737

Sept. 1. 1718.

I am much honour'd by your Grace's compliance with my request, in giving me your opinion of the French dispute concerning Homer. And I shall keep my word, in fairly telling wherein I disagree from you. It is but in two or three very small points, not so much of the dispute, as of the parties concern'd in it. I cannot think quite so highly of the Lady's learning, tho' I respect it very much. It is great complaisance in that polite nation, to allow her to be a Critic of equal rank with her husband. To instance no further, his remarks on Horace shew more good Sense, Penetration, and a better Taste of his author, and those upon Aristotle's art of poetry more Skill and Science, than any of hers on any author whatever. In truth, they are much more slight, dwell more in generals, and are besides for the most part less her own; of which her remarks upon Homer are an example, where Eustathius is transcribed ten times for once that he is quoted. Nor is there at all more depth or learning in those upon Terence, Plautus, (or where they were most wanted) upon Aristophanes, only the Greek scholia upon the latter are some of the best extant.

Your Grace will believe me, that I did not search to find defects in a Lady; my employment upon the Iliad forc'd me to see them: yet I have had so much of the French complaisance as to conceal her thefts; for wherever I have found her notes to be wholly anothers, (which is the case in some hundreds) I have barely quoted the true Proprietor without observing upon it. If Madam Dacier has ever seen my observations, she will be sensible of this conduct, but what effect it may have upon a Lady, I will not answer for.

In the next place, as to Mr. de la Motte, I think your Grace hardly does him right, in supposing he could have no idea of the beauties of Homer's Epic Poetry but what he learn'd from Madam Dacier's Prose-translation. There had been a very elegant Prose-translation before, that by Monsieur de la Valterie, so elegant, that the style of it was evidently the original and model of the famous Telamaque. Your Grace very justly animadverts against the too great disposition of finding faults, in the one, and of confessing none, in the other: But doubtless, as to Violence, the Lady has infinitely the better of the Gentleman. Nothing can be more polite, dispassionate or sensible, than Mr. de la Motte's manner of managing the dispute: and so much as I see your Grace admires the beauty of his verse (in which you have the suffrage too of the Archbishop of Cambray) I will venture to say, his prose is full as good. I think therefore when you say,

[1] This letter was published in all Pope's editions beginning in 1737, with only very slight changes in the text.

no disputants ev'n in Divinity cou'd be more outragious and uncharitable than these two authors, you are a little too hard upon M. de la Motte. Not but that (with your Grace) I doubt as little of the zeal of Commentators as of the zeal of Divines, and am as ready to believe of the passions and pride of mankind in general, that (did but the same interests go along with them) they wou'd carry the learned world to as violent extremes, animosities, and even persecutions, about variety of opinions in Criticism, as ever they did about Religion: and that in defect of Scripture to quarrel upon, we shou'd have French, Italian, and Dutch Commentators ready to burn one another about Homer, Virgil, Terence and Horace.

I do not wonder your Grace is shock'd at the flight of Hector upon the first appearance of Achilles in the twenty-second Iliad. However (to shew my self a true Commentator, if not a true Critick) I will endeavour to excuse, if not to defend it, in my notes on that Book. And to save my self what trouble I can, instead of doing it in this letter, I will draw up the substance of what I have to say for it in a separate paper which I'll shew your Grace when next we meet. I will only desire you to allow me, that Hector was in an absolute certainty of death, and depress'd over and above with the conscience of being in an ill cause. If your heart be so great, as not to grant the first of these will sink the spirit of a Hero, you'll at least be so good, as to allow the second may: But I can tell your Grace, no less a Hero than my Lord Peterborow, when a person complimented him for never being afraid, made this answer; "Sir, shew me a danger that I think an imminent and real one, and I promise you I'll be as much afraid as any of you." I am your Grace's, &c.

POPE *to* LADY MARY WORTLEY MONTAGU

1 *September* [1718]

The Pierpont Morgan Library

Sept. 1st

Madam,—I have been (what I never was till now) in debt to you for a letter some weeks. I was informd you were at Sea, & that 'twas to no purpose to write, till some news had been heard of your arriving somewhere or other. Besides, I have had a second dangerous Illness, from which I was more diligent to be recovered than from the first, having now some hopes of seeing you again. If you make any Tour in Italy, I shall not easily forgive you for not acquainting me soon enough to have mett you there: I am very certain I can never be Polite, unless I travel with you. And it is never to be repaird, the loss that Homer has sustained, for want of my translating him in Asia. You will come hither full of criticismes against a man, who wanted nothing to be in the right but to have kept you company. You have no way of making me amends, but by continuing an Asiatic when you return, to me, whatever English Airs you may put on to other people. I prodigiously long for your Sonnets, your remarks, your oriental learning; but I long for nothing so much as your Oriental Self. You must of necessity be *advanced* so far *Back* into true nature & simplicity of manners, by these 3 years residence in the East, that I shall look upon you as so many years Younger than you was, so much nearer Innocence (that is, Truth) & Infancy (that is Openness.) I expect to see your Soul as much thinner dressd as your Body; and that you have left off, as unwieldy & cumbersome, a great many damn'd Europœan Habits. Without offence to your modesty be it spoken, I have a burning desire to see your Soul stark naked, for I am confident 'tis the prettiest kind of white Soul, in the universe—But I forget whom I am talking to, you may possibly by this time Believe according to the Prophet, that you have none. If so, show me That which comes next to a Soul; you may easily put it upon a poor ignorant Christian for a Soul, & please him as well with it: I mean your Heart: Mahomet I think allows you Hearts: which (together with fine eyes & other agreeable equivalents) are worth all the Souls on this side the world. But if I must be content with seeing your body only, God send it to come quickly: I honor it more than the Diamond-Casket that held Homer's Iliads. For in the very twinkle of one eye of it, there is more Wit; and in the very dimple of one cheek of it, there is more Meaning, than in all the Souls that ever were casually put into Women since Men had the making them.

I have a mind to fill the rest of this paper with an accident that happen'd just under my eyes, and has made a great Impression upon me. I have past part of this Summer at an old romantic Seat of my Lord Harcourt's which he lent me; It overlooks a Common-field, where under the Shade of a Hay cock sate two Lovers, as constant as ever were found in Romance, beneath a spreading Beech. The name of the one (let it sound as it will) was John Hewet, of the other Sarah Drew. John was a wellset man about five and twenty, Sarah a brown woman of about eighteen. John had for several months born the labour of the day in the same field with Sarah; When she milk'd, it was his morning & evening charge to bring the Cows to her pail: Their Love was the Talk, but not the Scandal, of the whole neighbourhood, for all they aimd at was the blameless possession of each other in marriage. It was but this very morning[1] that he had obtain'd her Parents consent, and it was but till next week that they were to wait to be happy. Perhaps, this very day in the intervals of their work, they were talking

[1] Pope writing a month after the event can speak of what happened to the lovers 'this very morning' and afternoon, and in a following sentence tell us they were killed 'on the last of July'. The moral-emotional effect of the episode was all that concerned him.

of their wedding clothes, and John was now matching several kinds of poppies and field-flowers to her Complexion, to make her a Present of Knots for the day. While they were thus employd (it was on the last of July) a terrible Storm of Thunder and Lightning arose, that drove the Labourers to what Shelter the Trees or hedges afforded. Sarah frighted, and out of breath, sunk down on a Haycock, & John (who never seperated from her) sate by her side, having rak'd two or three heaps together to secure her. Immediately there was heard so loud a Crack as if Heaven had burst asunder: the Labourers, all sollicitous for each other's safety, calld to one another: those that were nearest our Lovers, hearing no answer, stept to the place where they lay; they first saw a little Smoke, & after, this faithful Pair. John with one arm about his Sarah's neck, and the other held over her face as if to screen her from the Lightning. They were struck dead, & already grown stiff and cold in this tender posture. There was no mark or discolouring on their bodies, only that Sarah's eyebrow was a little sindg'd, and a small Spot appeard between her breasts. They were buried the next day in one grave, in the Parish of Stanton-Harcourt in Oxfordshire; where my Lord Harcourt, at my request, has erected a monument over them. Of the following Epitaphs which I made, the Criticks have chosen the godly one: I like neither, but wish you had been in England to have done this office better; I think 'twas what you could not have refused me on so moving an occasion.

When Eastern Lovers feed the fun'ral fire,
On the same Pile their faithful Fair expire;
Here pitying Heav'n that virtue mutual found,
And blasted both, that it might neither wound.
Hearts so sincere, th' Almighty saw well-pleas'd,
Sent his own Lightning, & the Victims seiz'd.

1.

Think not, by rig'rous Judgment seiz'd,
  A Pair so faithful could expire;
Victims so pure Heav'n saw well-pleas'd,
  And snatchd them in celestial fire.

2.

Live well, & fear no sudden fate:
  When God calls Virtue to the grave,
Alike 'tis Justice, soon, or late,
  Mercy alike, to kill, or save.
Virtue unmov'd, can hear the Call,
And face the Flash that melts the Ball.

Upon the whole, I can't think these people unhappy: The greatest happiness, next to living as they would have done, was to dye as they did. The greatest honour people of this low degree could have was to be remembered on a little monument; unless you will give them another, that of being honourd with a Tear from the finest eyes in the world. I know you have Tenderness; you must have it: It is the very Emanation of Good Sense & virtue: The finest minds like the finest metals, dissolve the easiest.

But when you are reflecting upon Objects of pity, pray do not forget one, who had no sooner found out an Object of the highest Esteem, than he was seperated from it: And who is so very unhappy as not to be susceptible of Consolation from others, by being so miserably in the right as to think other women what they really are. Such an one can't but be desperately fond of any creature that is quite different from these. If the Circassian be utterly void of such Honour as these have, and such virtue as these boast of, I am content. I have detested the Sound of *honest Woman*, & *loving Spouse* ever since I heard the pretty name of Odaliche. Dear Madam I am for ever Yours, and your Slave's, Slave, & Servant.

My most humble Services to Mr Wortly.
Pray let me hear from you soon:
Tho' I shall very soon write again.
I am confident half our letters have been lost.

FENTON *to* POPE[1] [*September* 1718]

Homer MSS. Add. 4808

I have received a Specimen of the Extracts from Eustathius but this Week; the first Gentleman who undertook the affair grew weary, &

[1] The letter is placed chronologically through its concern with work done on Book XVII. This was the first of the books included in vol. v of Pope's *Iliad*, and vol. v was 'in a manner finished' in Oct. of this year. The undergraduate who helped Pope was John Jortin (1698–1770), later a considerable scholar. His own account of his work for Pope, given in Nichols's *Lit. Anec.* ii. 556–7, is worth quoting: 'When I was a soph at Cambridge, Pope was about his translation of Homer's Ilias, and had published part of it. He employed some person (I know not who he was) to make extracts for him from Eustathius. . . . The person employed by Mr. Pope was not at leisure to go on with the work; and Mr. Pope (by his bookseller I suppose) sent to Jefferies, a bookseller at Cambridge, to find out a student who would undertake the task. Jefferies applied to Dr. Thirlby, who was my tutor, and who pitched upon me. . . . I cannot recollect what Mr. Pope allowed for each book of Homer; I have a notion that it was three or four guineas. . . . When I had gone through some books (I forget how many) Mr. Jefferies let us know that Mr. Pope had a friend to do the rest, and that we might give over. . . . As I was not directly employed by him [Pope], but by a bookseller, I did not inform him who I was, or set my name to my papers. When that part of Pope's Homer came out in which I had been concerned, I was eager, as it may be supposed, to see how things stood, and much pleased to find that he had not only used almost all my notes, but had hardly made any alteration in the expressions. I observed also, that in a subsequent

now Mr Thirlby of Jesus has recommended another to me with a very great Character: I think indeed at first sight that his performance is commendable enough; & have sent word for him to finish the 17th B. & to send it with his Demands for his trouble: He engageth to complete a Book every Month 'till Christmass; & the remaining Books in a Month more, if you require them. The last time I saw Mr Lintot he told me that Mr Brome had offer'd his Service again to You; if you accept it, it wou'd be proper for him to let you know what Books he will undertake that the Cambridge Gentleman may proceed to the rest. I am ever Dear Sir | Your most obliged and | most Obedient Servant. | E. Fenton.

I have here inclos'd the Specimen; if the rest come before you return I will keep 'em 'till I receive your Orders.—I have desir'd the Gent. to write the rest in Folio, with half the page left blank.

POPE *to* CARYLL[1] 3 *September* 1718

Add. 28618

Sept. 3d (1718)

⌜You shall be convinced it was mere stress of business that so long interrupted my correspondence with you; for the moment that I get a little leisure, my letters return thick upon you.⌝[2] What gives me the subject of this, is a reflection I have had occasion to make here, on the common superstitious turn of mankind. A young man and Woman were lately destroyed here by lightning, and the country people are hardly in charity with their minister for allowing them Christian burial. They can't get it out of their heads but it was a judgment of God. It is odd enough to consider, how people who fancy themselves good Christians are so absurd as to think, the same misfortunes, when they happen to others, are a punishment of vice, and when they happen to themselves an exercise of virtue. On the contrary, true piety would make us know that all misfortunes, may as well be blessings, and even sudden death itself only[3] a timely and speedy reward of good life. I

edition, he corrected the place to which I had made objections. I was in hopes in those days (for I was young) that Mr. Pope would make inquiry about his *coadjutor*, and take some civil notice of him; but he did not, and I had no notion of obtruding myself upon him; I never saw his face.'

Pope's first help on Eustathius came from Parnell and Broome. Briefly in 1717 Mr. Peachy (or Peche) was secured at Oxford as helper. Jortin evidently did not work long, for in December of this year Pope is thanking Broome for notes received from him.

[1] The letter is dated in the transcript with the year placed in parentheses. With some revisions and conflations from another letter this was transcribed and placed among the letters of Pope to Atterbury in the Harleian transcripts (Portland Papers, xiii, f. 232). Collations with that text are here given. Pope did not print the letter in either form.

[2] The Harleian transcript omits the first sentence.

[3] even Sudden death itself only] even Sudden death only *Harl.*

therefore hope I have done some service, in procuring the following epitaph to be set[1] over the two people[2] I mentioned.

Think not, by rigorous judgment seiz'd,
Two hearts like these could e're expire;[3]
Victims so pure Heav'n saw well-pleas'd,
And snatched them in celestial fire.
Their souls on wings of lightning fly,
So Soar'd Elijah to the sky.

Live well, and fear no sudden fate.
When God calls virtue to the grave,
Alike 'tis justice, soon, or late,
Mercy alike, to kill or save:
Virtue unmov'd can hear the call;
And face the flash that melts the ball.

On the contrary the superstitious man looks on the great Father of all as a tyrant; and in how miserable a state is he, who lies under perpetual apprehensions of such a power, from whom no might can protect, no flight can save, and neither time, nor death itself can deliver him! Accordingly he serves his Maker but as slaves do their tyrants, with a gloomy, savage zeal against his fellow creatures; whom he insults and persecutes[4] with all barbarity, whenever they seem never so little deficient in their duty; tho' at the same time he trembles with the dread of being ill used himself, notwithstanding all his endeavours of service to their common Lord.[5] Plutarch[6] has set both the vice and folly of superstitions in the best light I have seen. He observes that these wretches are more impious than atheists, since 'tis worse to conceive an unworthy opinion of God, than not to believe there is one. As I would rather (says he) it were said there was no such as Plutarch, than that he was passionate, revengeful, and implacable. The superstitious man fears most, where others are most secure; he is afraid of Heav'n; and yet flies to it for succour. The atheist when he falls under misfortunes, adversity, or sickness, complains only of fortune, or accuses the temper of the air, or his own irregularities. But the superstitious accounts every unhappiness an immediate stroke of heaven: nay, thinks it is criminal even to avoid it. In a word, such a wretch must of necessity at once fear God and hate him.

[1] in procuring the following Epitaph to be set] in persuading my Lord Harcourt to set *Harl.*
[2] two people] two poor people *Harl.*
[3] Two hearts . . . expire] A Pair so faithful could expire *Harl.*
[4] Caryll's scribe wrote *prosecute*, here emended.
[5] of Service . . . Lord] to Gratify their common Lord. *Harl.* After this phrase the Caryll letter and the composite in the Atterbury (Harleian) transcripts part company.
[6] Plutarch, *Moralia*, 164–71.

I believe there is not in the whole course of the Scripture any precept so often and so strongly inculcated, as the trust and eternal dependance, we ought to repose in that Supreme Being who is [our] constant preserver and benefactor. I know no man who practises this in a more exemplary manner than yourself, and therefore cannot conclude this letter better, than by desiring you to pray for the same grace for one who has already begun, and doubtless in the course of his life will continue, to want it. I mean | Dear sir | Your affectionate friend and servant | A: P:

Pray let your own family and Mrs Blounts, know, that I scorn to use such a phrase, as making compliments to them—I hope you will make your neighbour Mr Fuller (if he is in your parts) a better neighbour to them in London. I hear very good things of him as to the Catholic interest.

POPE *to* ATTERBURY — 3 *September* 1718

Longleat Portland Papers, xiii, 232 (Harleian transcripts)

[Under this date Pope fabricated, but did not print, a letter to Atterbury made from two letters to Caryll (3 September and 18 January 1717/18). He probably decided to print Gay's version of the deaths of John Hewet and Sarah Drew in preference to this version. From the letter of 18 January Pope took only the next to the last paragraph for the letter to Atterbury. This fabrication of 3 September is not to be confused with the letter to Atterbury (printed first by Nichols in 1783) dated 8 September, which included the epitaph on the rural lovers.]

POPE *to* ATTERBURY[1] — 8 *September* 1718

1783

[Stanton Harcourt,] Sept. 8, 1718.

My Lord,—I have long had a desire to write to your Lordship, though I cannot imagine to what end; since it is not any thing I can say upon paper that can give you any title to me which you have not already, or (I hope) tell you any part of my respect or esteem which you know not already. But I have got a sort of a subject for blotting this, by means of an accident which has happened here: a young man and woman were destroyed by one stroke of lightning, who were contracted in marriage some days before. They were people of a very good character; yet the country here are ready to rise against their minister for allowing them Christian burial. They cannot get it out of their heads but so remarkable a death was a judgement from God. It is pleasant enough to consider, that people who fancy themselves good

[1] The text is from Atterbury's *Correspondence*, ed. J. Nichols, 1783, ii. 63.

Christians should be so absurd as to think the same misfortunes, when they befall others, a punishment of vice; and, when they happen to themselves, an exercise of virtue. I would try to do some service in procuring the following epitaph to be set over them, or something to this purpose. I send it to your Lordship for your opinion, both as to the doctrine and the poetry; as I am very certain, nothing is either fit for the church or the publick which is not agreeable to your sentiments.[1]

I beg you, my Lord, not to spare me one word that is put in for the sake of rhime. I know you will be so gentle to the modern Goths and Vandals, as to allow them to put a few rhimes upon tombs, or over doors, where they have not room to write much, and may have hopes to make rhime live by the material it is graved upon. In return, I promise your Lordship, as soon as Homer is translated, to allow it unfit for long works; but to say so at present would be what your second thoughts could never approve of; because it would be a profusion [profession?] of repentance and conviction, and yet a perseverance in the sin.

I have lived where I have done nothing but sinned, that is, rhimed, these six weeks.[2] I dare not approach you till the fit is over. I thank God, I find the symptoms almost gone, and may therefore soon expect to pass my time much more agreably in London or at Bromley. I beg you to think me, what I am most proud and pleased to be thought, my Lord, your most obliged, and most faithful humble servant, | A. Pope.

*CHARLES CHEVALLIER *to* POPE[3] [*c.* 11 *September* 1718]

Homer MSS. Add. 4808

Sir,—Yesterday I received a Letter from Mr Wortley Dated 20th past O.S. from Genoa where he arriv'd the 14th: he & my Lady Designed to Set out for paris in a Weeks time I am now writing to him thither | I am | [Sir] | Your most humble Servant | Cha. Chevallier

[1] Nichols does not print the epitaph as a part of the letter, but refers his reader to a footnote preceding. The text given in his footnote is identical with that given in the second (ten-line) epitaph sent to Lady Mary under date of 1 Sept.

[2] Duration and its simple modes was easier for my Uncle Toby to grasp than for Mr. Pope to put in writing. For something less than six weeks he had been alternately at Stanton Harcourt and Oakley Wood. Since, however, his mail came to Cockthorpe normally, one may assume that he regarded Stanton Harcourt as his summer base. Preserved in the Homer MSS. (Add. 4808, f. 102*v*) is the cover of a letter addressed to Pope at Cockthorpe and franked by Alex. Urquhart, with the postmark 6/SE. There are similar addresses during the course of the summer.

[3] This letter occurs on two leaves of the Homer MSS. (Add. 4808, ff. 105–6). The two were formerly one. Chevallier, employed in the Foreign Office, sent this brief and hasty note to Jervas's house, where Jervas's servant Francis Waters received it and forwarded it to Pope, with the next letter (which gives the date for this one) written below Chevallier's signature. On the dating of Lady Mary's return see vol. v, pp. 1–2.

*FRANCIS WATERS *to* POPE[1] 11 *September* 1718

Homer MSS. Add. 4808

September the 11: 1718

To Mr. Pope.

Sir,—Yesterday I receiv'd yours, then I carri'd the Inclos'd to Westminster & I Left it at the Porters Lodge, the Porter will send it to the Bishop to Bromley in Kent. the other Letter I put into the Post. Doctor Parnell Call'd to wait of you to Day. | I am Sir Your Obedient Servant | Francis Waters

||ATTERBURY *to* POPE[2] 12 *September* 1718

Longleat Portland Papers, xiii (Harleian transcripts)

Bromly Septr 12. 1718.

Sir,—I received here this Morning a *Letter* from you without any Account of the Place from whence it was written. I suppose you thought this a Notable Contrivance to escape an Answer. I have ill nature enough to take a Pleasure in defeating that Design and will therefore guess, as well as I can, where you are, and venture a Letter at randome, which I hope through my Lord Harcourts Cover, may possibly reach[3] You. If it dos, I have my Revenge; a Principle, which, on this particular Occasion, I am not asham'd to own!

In good earnest, Sir, I was pleas'd to see a Letter from You, and pleas'd with the Subject of that Letter. Christianity is the best natur'd Institution in the World; and is so far from allowing such harsh Censures that it has directly forbidden them, and expresly decided against them. You know the Passage—"Suppose ye that these Galileans were Sinners above all the Galileans, because they suffer'd such things? I tell you, Nay: but except ye repent, ye shall all likewise perish."[4] What think you of Letting the Minister of the Parish contribute this as his Share, towards the Inscription on the Grave Stone? and as a proper

[1] Pope has sent a letter to 'Frank' or Francis Waters and enclosed, evidently, his own letter to Atterbury of 8 Sept. This Frank has forwarded, via the deanery, to Bromley (see Atterbury's letter to Pope, 12 Sept.). He now, below the signature of Chevallier on the letter immediately preceding this, writes to tell Pope what he has done and to forward the news of Lady Mary's arrival in Genoa. The note is the last news we have of Parnell before his departure and death.

[2] This text from Longleat differs somewhat from that printed in 1783 by Nichols (ii. 71–78). Apart from several minor textual variants that might derive from polishing, the materials of the latter part of the Nichols text are rearranged. After what is here the fifth paragraph (ending 'Pergite Pierides') the Nichols text places the paragraphs beginning 'In the first stanza' and 'Your second stanza'; which are succeeded by that beginning 'Virtue unmov'd'. This is followed by Atterbury's Latin verses, after which come the paragraphs beginning 'You see, Sir, I have obey'd', and 'I say nothing to you about Rhime'. The Nichols text is more logically arranged, but the arrangement seems to be the result of editorial care rather than the first spontaneous writing. Either Pope or Morice (Atterbury's son-in-law) may have done the rearranging, or possibly Atterbury himself.

[3] which I hope . . . reach] but I hope . . . it may reach *Nichols*.

[4] Luke xiii. 2, 3.

Rebuke[1] to his Censorious Neighbours? How far this Prose and your Poetry, a Verse of Scripture and the Stanzas you sent me, are fitt Company for each other, I pretend not to say: but sure I am, the Words are weighty and worthy of being inscrib'd, not on such a Monument onely, but on the Heart of every one that owns himself a Christian!

You are too good to me, to think that my Relish of such Performances is nice enough to make me Capable of advising you. Or If I were, yet my Partiality in behalf of what ever you write would steal away my Judgment. However since You are so Civil, and seem so Sincere, I will try, for once, to divest myself of my Prejudices, and will venture to tell you my Mind on a Subject you understand so much[2] better than I do. If I shew my unskillfulness, I shall yet give you a proof of my Friendship, and an Instance of the Power you have over me. Perhaps, there is no one but you that could so easily have led me into so great a mistake. Use your Influence gently, if you intend to increase, or preserve it.

I like the Lines well: they are Yours, and they are Good, & on both accounts, very welcome to me. You know my Opinion, That Poetry without a Moral is a Body without a Soul. Let the Lines be never so finely turn'd, if they do not point at some Useful Truth, if there be no degree of Instruction[3] at the bottom of them, they can give no true delight to a Reasonable mind; they are *versus inopes rerum, nugæq; canoræ*;[4] and as such they may tinkle prettily in the Ear, but will never reach the Heart, or leave a durable Impression behind them. No body that reads your Verses, will blame you on this account for they are all over Morality, from the beginning to the End of them.[5] And it pleases me the better, because I fancy it drawn from Horace's Fountain,[6] for I cannot help thinking, that his *Si fractus illabatur Orbis—Impavidum ferient ruinæ*[7] was, whether you attended to it or no, the Original, from whence your two last Verses were Copy'd. I wish, you had prepar'd the way for the latter of them, as he has done, for the Idea given us by *fractus illabatur Orbis*,[8] is strong enough to support that which follows, *Impavidum ferient ruinæ*, whereas you

[1] The Nichols text has here been revised to give the praise not to Pope but to the Scripture. It reads: 'a proper rebuke to his censuring neighbours, worthy of being inscribed, not on such a monument only, but on the heart of every one that owns himself a Christian? How far this prose and your poetry . . . are fit to keep company with each other, I pretend not to say; but sure I am that the words are weighty.'

[2] Mind . . . so much] mind of what you know so much *Nichols.*

[3] if there be . . . Instruction] if there is not instruction *Nichols.*

[4] Horace, *De Arte Poetica*, l. 322.

[5] Nichols reads: 'No body that reads what you have written, will blame you in this respect; for it is all over Morality, from the beginning to the end of it.'

[6] from Horace's Fountain] from the sources of Horace *Nichols.*

[7] *Carmina*, III. iii. 7, 8. (Oxford's scribe wrote *Orbes* for *orbis.*)

[8] *Orbis*, is] *orbis*, which is *Nichols.*

melt the Ball at once, without giving us any warning, and are led, on the sudden, from a particular Accident to the General Conflagration; & That too is to be effected by a *Flash*, a word, me thinks, not equal to the work on which you have employ'd it.[1] Pardon this freedom! but my Old Master, Roscommon, has an Expression, which I always look'd upon as very happy and Significant (He that[2] *proportion'd wonders* can disclose) without that just Proportion, nothing is truly admirable! Will you forgive me, if I add, that *melting the Ball*, without that Preparation of the Reader I mention'd, is too apt to lead us into the Image of a Snow Ball. Waller, I am perswaded, for the sake of the Fs and Bs, of which he was remarkably fond, would have rather chosen[3] to say, and face the Flash, that Burns the Ball. I am far from proposing this, as an Improvement. I do not think it such: or if I did, yet I would[4] not offer it; for, where the Images themselves are not well suited, 'tis in vain to alter a particular Expression.

I know not, Whither I am going in this Tract[5] of Criticism, to which I have been long a Stranger. But since I am in for it, Pergite Pierides[6]—

Virtue unmov'd should you not rather say *Goodness*, than repeat the word, Virtue, which you had us'd three Lines before? So you had *Call*, also: but that Repetition is graceful; the Verb being chang'd into a Substantive, and becoming by that means a new word which echoes to the former and yet differs from it. *Aliudq; et idem nascitur*,[7] says he, who says every thing better than anyone[8] but Virgil.

Your Second Stanza is full of good Sense shortly express'd. But, methinks, there is some Obscurity in it *quo vitio minime teneri soles*, as Suetonius says of Horace.[9] For, when God calls the Virtuous to his Grave, tho' he be alike just, whether he calls him soon or late, yet it should not be said, that he is alike merciful, whether he kills or saves him: for, if he saves him, the very Supposition of his being call'd to the Grave, is destroy'd. Nor am I perfectly satisfy'd with that Phrase (when God calls Virtue to the Grave): tho' if the Connexion of it with the 4th Line were exact in point of Sense, the Expression it self would not shock me.

[1] a word . . . employ'd it] a word not equal to the work on which it is employed. *Nichols.*

[2] that] who *Nichols.* (Prefixed to Roscommon's translation of Horace's *Art of Poetry* in 1717 appeared 'Of this Translation, and of the Use of Poetry, by Edmund Waller, Esq.', containing the lines:

> He that proportion'd Wonders can disclose,
> At once his Fancy and his Judgment shows.)

[3] have rather chosen] have chosen *Nichols.*

[4] or if I did, yet I would] or, if it were, I would *Nichols.*

[5] Tract] track *Nichols.*

[6] At this point the Nichols text begins shuffling the paragraphs. See the first note to this letter. The bishop quotes Virgil's *Eclogues*, vi. 13.

[7] Horace, *Carmen Saec.*, ll. 10, 11 (adapted).

[8] anyone] any body *Nichols.*

[9] In his Life of Horace: *quo vitio minime tenebatur.*

In the first Stanza I must take the Liberty to Object against *so faithful*, and *so pure*, because they are *so near* to one another, and yet belong to different Sentences. Nor can I approve that confusion of Ideas, which seems to be in the two last Lines. Elijah indeed was *snatch'd* up in a Chariot of Fire: but pure Victims, consum'd *by* fire from heaven, cannot be said to be snatch'd up *in* it. Has the word Celestial, in the 4th Line any force? If Heaven snatches them in fire, that fire must needs be Celestial, i.e. heavenly.

You see Sir I have obey'd your Commands, because they were Yours, with a frankness, which I should like in another man, and do therefore[1] hope, that you will not dislike in me, I have ventur'd to Object to what I could not have written, and cannot mend. I was pleas'd with the thought[2] of writing to you, tho' upon a Subject that did not altogether please me; for Experience has taught me, That 'tis a wiser and better Entertainment,[3] to tast the beautys of good Writers, than to find out their faults; especially, since it is great Odds, but that, when we are playing Critics,[4] we commit more real mistakes, than we pretend to find. That, I doubt not is my Case; but[5] jacta est alea.—

I say nothing to you about Rhime, because 'tis a Subject upon which I have so much to say. Why should you forego an Advantage; which you enjoy in perfection? and own that way of writing not to be the best in which you write better than any Man? I am not so unreasonable as to expect it. But I know I have the Testimony of your Poetical Conscience on my side, tho' you are wise enough not to own so unpopular and unproffitable a Truth. When I see you here, as you seem to promise, ⌜I shall, these matters will make one Part of our Conversation, and I rely so much on your good Sense and Fairness, that I will be your Convert, unless I can make you mine. Till then adieu, and believe me, Sir at what distance soever I am⌝[6] | Your very affectionate | and faithful Servant | Fr. Roffen.

Hæc ego dictabam, Sylvas Saltusq; peragrans
Bromlejos—[, urbes urbanaque gaudia vitans,][7]
Excepto quod non simul esses, cætera lætus
Hæ Latebræ dulces, etiam si credis amœnæ
Incolumen tibi me Præstant Septembribus horis.

[1] in another man, and do therefore] in another, and therefore *Nichols.*
[2] thought] thoughts *Nichols.*
[3] Entertainment] pleasure *Nichols.*
[4] playing Critics] playing the critick *Nichols.*
[5] but] however *Nichols.*
[6] promise . . . I am / Your] promise, more of these matters. In the mean time, I am, Sir, yours, &c. *Nichols* (briefer ending).
[7] The Harleian scribe omitted the second half of this second line, presumably as illegible. It is here supplied in brackets from Nichols's text.

POPE *to* LADY MARY WORTLEY MONTAGU[1] [1718]

The Pierpont Morgan Library

Dear Madam,—'Tis not possible to express the least part of the Joy, your Return gives me. Time only, and Experience, will convince you how very sincere it is—I excessively long to meet you; to say so much, so very much to you, that I believe I shall say nothing—I have given orders to be sent for the first minute of your arrival, (which I beg you'l let them know at Mr Jervas's.) I am fourscore miles from London, a short journey, compared to that I so often Thought at least of undertaking, rather than dye without seeing you again. Tho' the place I am in is such as I would not quit for the Town, if I did not value you more than any, nay every, body else, there. And you'l be convinc'd, how little the Town has engagd my affection in your Absence from it, when You know what a place this is, which I prefer to it. I shall therefore describe it to you at large, as the true picture of a genuine Ancient Country Seat.

You must expect nothing regular in my description of a House that seems to be built before Rules were in fashion. The whole is so disjointed, & the parts so detachd from each other, and yet so joining again one can't tell how; that in a poetical Fitt you'd imagine it had been a Village in Amphions time, where twenty Cottages had taken a dance together, were all Out, and stood still in amazement ever since. A Stranger would be grievously disappointed, who should ever think to get into this house the right way. One would expect, after entring thro the Porch, to be let into the Hall: Alas nothing less—you find yourself in a Brewhouse. From the Parlor you think to step into the Drawing room, but upon opening the iron-nail'd door, you are convinced by a flight of birds about your ears & a cloud of dust in your eyes, that tis the Pigeon-house. One each side our Porch are two chimnies, that wear their Greens on the outside, which wou'd do as well within, for whenever we make a Fire we let the Smoke out of the windows. Over the Parlor window hangs a Sloping Balcony, which Time has turned to a very convenient Penthouse. The top is crown'd with a very venerable Tower, so like that of the Church just by, that the Jackdaws build in it as if it were the true Steeple.

The great Hall is high & spatious, flankd with long tables (images of ancient hospitality) ornamented with monstrous horns, about 20 broken Pikes, & a match-lock Musquet or two, which they say were used in the Civil Wars. Here is one vast archd Window, beautifully

[1] This letter seems perhaps to have been written about the middle of Sept., since Pope has heard of her near approach and has 'given orders' to Jervas's man, doubtless, to notify him of her arrival. Lady Mary seems to have received the letter only on reaching Dover. The letter closely resembles that sent (?) about the same time to the Duke of Buckingham, which immediately follows this.

darken'd with divers Scutcheons of painted Glass. There seems to be great propriety in this old manner of Blazoning upon Glass, Ancient Families being like ancient Windows, in the course of generations seldome free from Cracks. One shining Pane bears date 1286: There the Face of Dame Elinor owes more to this single piece, than to all the Glasses she ever consulted in her life. Who can say after this, that Glass is frail, when it is not half so perishable as human Beauty, or Glory? For in another Pane you see the memory of a Knight preserved, whose marble Nose is molderd from his monument in the church adjoining. And yet, must not one sigh to reflect, that the most authentic record of so ancient a family should lye at the mercy of ev'ry Boy that throws a stone? In this Hall, in former days have dined Garterd Knights & Courtly Dames, with Ushers, Sewers, and Seneshalls; And yet it was but tother night that an Owl flew in hither, and mistook it for a Barn.

This Hall lets you Up, (and Down) over a very high Threshold into the Parlor. It is furnishd with Historical Tapistry, whose marginal Fringes do confess the moisture of the air. The other contents of this room are a broken-belly'd Virginal, a couple of crippled Velvet chairs, with two or three mildewd Pictures of mouldy Ancestors who look as dismally as if they came fresh from Hell with all their Brim-Stone about 'em. These are carefully set at the further corner; for the windows being every where broken, make it so convenient a place to dry Poppies and Mustard seed in, that the room is appropriated to that use.

Next this parlor lies (as I said before) the Pigeon house: by the side of which runs an Entry that leads on one hand and t'other, into a Bedchamber, a Buttery, and small Hole called the Chaplain's Study. Then follow a Brewhouse, a little green-and-gilt Parlor, and the great Stairs, under which is the Dairy. A little further on the right, the Servants hall, and by the side of it up six steps, the old Lady's Closet, which has a Lettice into the side hall, that while she said her prayers, she might cast an eye on the men and maids. There are upon this Ground-floor in all 24 apartments, hard to be distinguished by particular names, among which I must not forget a Chamber, that has in it a large Antiquity of Timber, which seems to have been either a Bedstead, or a Cyderpress.

Our best Room above, is very long & low; of the exact Proportion of a Bandbox. It has Hangings of the finest work in the world, those I mean which Arachne spins out of her own bowells. Indeed the roof is so decayd, that after a favourable Shower of rain we may (with God's blessing) expect a crop of Mushromes between the chinks of the floors.

All this upper Story has for many years had no other Inhabitants than certain Rats, whose very Age renders them worthy of this venerable mansion, for the very Rats of this ancient Seat are gray. Since these have not yet quitted it, we hope at least this House may stand during the small remainder of days these poor animals have to live, who are now too infirm to remove to another. They have still a small Subsistance left them, in the few remaining Books of the Library.

I had never seen half what I have described, but for an old Starched grey headed Steward, who is as much an Antiquity as any in the place, and looks like an old Family picture walkd out of its Frame. He faild not as we past from room to room to relate several memoirs of the Family, but his observations were particularly curious in the Cellar. He showd where stood the triple rows of Butts of Sack, & where were rang'd the bottles of Tent for Toasts in the morning. He pointed to the Stands that supported the Iron-hoop'd Hogsheads of strong Beer. Then stepping to a corner, he lugg'd out the tatterd fragment of an unframed Picture—This says he, with tears in his eyes, was poor Sir Thomas! once Master of all the Drink I told you of! He had two Sons, (poor young Masters) that never arrivd to the Age of his Beer! They both fell ill in this very Cellar, and never went out upon their own legs. He could not pass by a broken bottle, without taking it up to show us the Arms of the Family on it. He then led me up the Tower, by dark winding Stone steps, which landed us into several littl[e] rooms one above another. One of these was nailed up, and my Guide whisperd to me the occasion of it. It seems, the Course of this noble blood was interrupted about two Centuries ago, by a Freak of the Lady Frances, who was here taken with a neighboring Prior: ever since which, the Room has been made up, & branded with the name of the Adultery-chamber. The Ghost of Lady Frances is supposed to walk here; some prying Maids of the family formerly reported that they saw a Lady in a fardingale thro' the keyhole; but this matter was hushd up, & the Servants forbid to talk of it.

I must needs have tired you with this long letter: but what ingagd me in the description was a generous principle to preserve the memory of a thing that must itself soon fall to ruin, nay perhaps, some part of it before this reaches your hands. Indeed I owe this old house the same sort of gratitude that we do to an old friend, that harbors us in his declining condition, nay even in his last extremities. I have found this an excellent place for Retirement and Study, where no one who passes by can dream there is an Inhabitant, and even any body that would visit me, dares not venture under my roof. You will not wonder I have translated a great deal of Homer in this Retreat; Any one that sees it will own, I could not have chosen a fitter or more likely place to converse with the Dead. As soon as I return to the Living, it shall be to converse with the best of them. I hope therfore very speedily to tell you in person how sincerely and unalterably I am | Madam | Your most faithfull, obliged | & obedient Servant, | A. Pope.

I beg Mr. Wortley to believe me his most humble Servant.

Address: To the Right Honourable, the | Lady Mary Wortley. | These

†POPE *to* THE DUKE OF BUCKINGHAM[1] [1718?]

1737

Pliny was one of those few authors who had a warm house over his head, nay two houses, as appears by two of his epistles. I believe if any of his contemporary authors durst have inform'd the publick where they lodg'd, we should have found the garrets of Rome as well inhabited as those of Fleet-street; but 'tis dangerous to let creditors into such a secret, therefore we may presume that then as well as now-a-days, no body knew where they lived but their Booksellers.

It seems, that when Virgil came to Rome, he had no lodgings at all: he first introduc'd himself to Augustus by an epigram, beginning *Nocte pluit tota*[2]—an observation which probably he had not made, unless he had lain all night in the street.

Where Juvenal lived we cannot affirm, but in one of his satyrs, he complains of the excessive price of lodgings; neither do I think he would have talk'd so feelingly of Codrus's bed, if there had been room for a bedfellow in it.

I believe, with all the ostentation of Pliny, he would have been glad to have chang'd both his houses for your Grace's one; which is a country-house in the summer,[3] and a town-house in the winter; and must be owned to be the properest habitation for a wise man, who sees all the world change every season without ever changing himself.

I have been reading the description of Pliny's house with an eye to yours, but finding they will bear no comparison, will try if it can be matched by the large country seat I inhabit at present, and see what figure it may make, by the help of a florid description.

[4]You must expect nothing regular in my description, any more than

[1] Printed by Pope in his editions of 1737–42. It appeared in 1737 under the heading '[In answer to a Letter, to which he inclosed the Description of Buckingham-house written by him to the D. of Sh.]'. The 'Letter to the D. of Sh.' (very likely the Duke of Shrewsbury) was published by Pope in Buckingham's *Works*, ii. (1723), 275–87. At what time in the summer of 1718 Pope wrote this fanciful description of Stanton Harcourt it is impossible to determine. Pope made verbal changes in his text only in the quarto and folio editions of 1737—all in the nature of polishing of style.

[2] *Vitae Virgilianae* (ed. Jacob Brummer, Leipzig, 1933), p. 31.

[3] This may conceivably allude to the inscription over the four central pilasters in the garden front of Buckingham House: RUS IN URBE. Over the court front appeared the Duke's name and SIC SITI LAETANTUR LARES. See his *Works* (1723), ii. 274, 275 for small engravings.

[4] Pope's letter to Lady Mary (which immediately precedes this) has from this point on so much in common with the present letter that this has been thought merely a revision of

in the house; the whole vast edifice is so disjointed, and the several parts of it so detach'd one from the other, and yet so joining again, one cannot tell how, that, in one of my poetical fits I imagined it had been a village in Amphion's time, where the cottages having taken a country dance together, had been all out, and stood stone-still with amazement ever since.

You must excuse me if I say nothing of the Front, indeed I don't know which it is. A stranger would be grievously disappointed who endeavour'd to get into this house the right way. One would reasonably expect, after the entry through the Porch, to be let into the Hall; alas nothing less! you find your self in the house of office. From the parlour you think to step into the drawing-room, but upon opening the iron-nail'd door, you are convinc'd by a flight of birds about your ears and a cloud of dust in your eyes, that it is the Pigeon-house. If you come into the chappel, you find its altars like those of the Ancients, continually smoaking, but it is with the steams of the adjoining kitchin.

The great hall within is high and spacious, flank'd on one side with a very long table, a true image of ancient hospitality: the walls are all over ornamented with monstrous horns of animals, about twenty broken pikes, ten or a dozen blunderbusses, and a rusty matchlock musquet or two, which we were inform'd had serv'd in the civil wars. Here is one vast arch'd window beautifully darken'd with divers scutcheons of painted glass: one shining pane in particular bears date 1286, which alone preserves the memory of a Knight whose iron armour is long since perish'd with rust, and whose alabaster nose is moulder'd from his monument. The face of dame Eleanor in another piece owes more to that single pane than to all the glasses she ever consulted in her life. After this, who can say that glass is frail, when it is not half so frail as human beauty, or glory! and yet I can't but sigh to think, that the most authentick record of so ancient a family should lie at the mercy of every infant who flings a stone. In former days, there have dined in this hall garter'd Knights, and courtly Dames, attended by ushers, sewers, and seneschals; and yet it was but last night, that an owl flew hither and mistook it for a barn.

This hall lets you (up and down) over a very high threshold into the great parlour. Its contents are a broken-belly'd virginal, a couple of cripled velvet chairs, with two or three mill-dew'd pictures of mouldy ancestors, who look as dismally, as if they came fresh from hell with all their brimstone about them; these are carefully set at the farther

Lady Mary's letter for purposes of publication. There are, to be sure, divergences—Lady Mary was spared the account of the kitchen—but the text of the one letter must have been composed with the text of the other for 'copy'. But during this summer Pope has been especially ready to send duplicate portions of letters to different correspondents.

corner, for the windows being every where broken make it so convenient a place to dry poppies and mustard seed, that the room is appropriated to that use.

Next this parlour, as I said before, lies the pigeon-house, by the side of which runs an entry, which lets you on one hand and t'other into a bed-chamber, a buttery, and a small hole call'd the chaplain's study; then follow a brewhouse, a little green and gilt parlour, and the great stairs, under which is the dairy; a little farther on the right the servants hall, and by the side of it up six steps, the old lady's closet for her private devotions; which has a lettice into the hall, intended (as we imagine) that at the same time as she pray'd, she might have an eye on the men and maids. There are upon the ground-floor in all twenty-six apartments, among which I must not forget a chamber which has in it a large Antiquity of timber, that seems to have been either a bedstead, or a cyder-press.

The Kitchen is built in form of the Rotunda, being one vast Vault to the Top of the House; where one overture serves to let out the smoak and let in the light. By the blackness of the walls, the circular fires, vast cauldrons, yawning mouths of ovens and furnaces, you would think it either the forge of Vulcan, the cave of Polypheme, or the temple of Moloch. The horror of this place has made such an impression on the country people, that they believe the Witches keep their Sabbath here, and that once a year the Devil treats them with infernal venison, a roasted Tiger stuff'd with ten-penny nails.

Above stairs we have a number of rooms, you never pass out of one into another but by the ascent or descent of two or three stairs. Our best room is very long and low, of the exact proportion of a Band-box. In most of these rooms there are hangings of the finest work in the world, that is to say those which Arachne spins from her own bowels; were it not for this only furniture, the whole would be a miserable scene of naked walls, flaw'd cielings, broken windows, and rusty locks. The roof is so decay'd, that after a favourable shower we may expect a crop of mushrooms between the chinks of our floors. All the doors are as little and low as those to the cabbins of Packet-boats. These rooms have for many years had no other inhabitants than certain rats whose very Age renders them worthy of this Seat, for the very rats of this venerable house are gray: since these have not yet quitted it, we hope at least that this ancient mansion may not fall during the small remnant these poor animals have to live, who are now too infirm to remove to another. There is yet a small subsistance left them in the few remaining books of the Library.

We had never seen half what I had described, but for a starch'd grey-headed Steward, who is as much an antiquity as any in this place, and looks like an old family picture walked out of its frame. He entertain'd us as we pass'd from room to room with several relations of the family; but his observations were particularly curious when we came to the cellar: he informed us where stood the triple rows of buts of sack, and where were ranged the bottles of tent, for toasts in a morning; he pointed to the stands that supported the iron-hoop'd hogsheads of strong beer; then stepping to a corner, he lugg'd out the tatter'd fragments of an unframed picture; "This says he, with tears, was poor Sir Thomas! once master of all this drink! He had two sons, poor young masters! who never arrived to the age of his beer; they both fell ill in this very room, and never went out on their own legs." He could not pass by a heap of broken bottles without taking up a piece, to show us the Arms of the family upon it. He then led us up the Tower by dark winding stone-steps, which landed us into several little rooms one above another. One of these was nail'd up, and our guide whisper'd to us as a secret the occasion of it: It seems the course of this noble blood was a little interrupted about two centuries ago, by a freak of the Lady Frances, who was here taken in the fact with a neighbouring Prior, ever since which the room has been nailed up, and branded with the name of the Adultery-chamber. The[1] ghost of lady Frances is supposed to walk there, and some prying maids of the family report that they have seen a lady in a fardingale through the key-hole; but this matter is husht up, and the servants are forbid to talk of it.

I must needs have tired you by this long description; but what engaged me in it was a generous principle, to preserve the memory of that, which it self must soon fall into dust, nay perhaps part of it before this letter reaches your hands.

Indeed we owe this old house the same kind of gratitude that we do to an old friend, who harbours us in his declining condition, nay even in his last extremities. How fit is this retreat for uninterrupted study, where no one that passes by can dream there is an inhabitant, and even those who would dine with us dare not stay under our roof. Any one that sees it will own I could not have chosen a more likely place to converse with the dead in. I had been mad indeed if I had left your Grace for any one but Homer. But when I return to the living, I shall have the sense to endeavour to converse with the best of 'em, and shall therefore as soon as possible tell you in person how much I am, &c.

[1] This word in the quarto of 1737 was misprinted 'Thr', and the error was corrected before imposition in the folio format. It is minute evidence like this which indicates the slender priority of the quarto over the folio.

POPE *to* MARTHA *and* TERESA BLOUNT[1]

17 *September* [1718]

Bowles (1806), x. 30–32

Sept. 17.

Dear Ladies,—I am in the case which many a man is in with your sex, not knowing where to have you: so I direct this with great respect to the most discreet of servitors, whom I dare hardly call George, even within the folds of this Letter. I hope, if you are in London, that you find company; if you are in the country, that you don't want it. I heartily wish you luck at cards; not only as it is said to be a token of luck in better things, but as it doth really and effectually save money, and sometimes get it. I also wish you good husbands, and think Mr. Caryll, who has the interest of our Catholic religion at heart, ought, if possible, to strengthen it, by allying to some of the supports thereof two such lovely branches as yourselves. Pray tell him so from me, and let me advise you in your ear. 'Tis full as well to marry in the country as in the town, provided you can bring your husbands up with you afterwards, and make them stay as long as you will. These two considerations every wise virgin should have in her head, not forgetting the third, which is,—a separate allowance. O Pin-money! dear, desirable Pin-money! in thee[2] are included all the blessings of woman! In thee are comprised fine clothes, fine lodgings, fine operas, fine masquerades, fine fellows. Foh! says Mrs. Teresa, at this last article—and so I hold my tongue.

Are you really of opinion you are an inconvenient part at present of my friend's family? Do ye fancy the best man in England is so very good, as not to be fond of ye? Why, St. Austin himself would have kissed ye—St. Jerome would have shaved against your coming—St. Peter would have dried his eyes at the sight of you—and St. Thomas would have been for touching and trying you. If you fancy yourselves troublesome at Grinstead, you are too humble indeed; you need not talk of wanting to be humbled. Every place will be proud of you; except Gotham, and the wise men of Gotham. May the Devil take every one that thinks you should be humbled. For me, I sincerely wish to see you exalted, when it shall please heaven, above the cherubims; but first, upon earth, above six horses in a handsome coach.

After all, if it be wholesome for you both to be humbled, Ladies, let me try to do it. I'll freely tell you two or three of your faults.

First, if you are handsome, you know it. This people have unluckily given you to understand, by praising you every day of your

[1] This letter should fall in 1718 rather than in 1716, where it has been placed. Pope rather thinks the young ladies may be visiting Caryll, but addresses them in Bolton Street for George to forward. He sends messages to Caryll in the letter, and mentions Gay as with him 'yesterday'. The situation fits 1718. Bowles (1806, x. 30–32) printed from the original letter, which, like some others that he printed, is no longer at Mapledurham.

[2] Here Bowles misprinted 'these'.

lives. The world has abundance of those indiscreet persons who admire you; and the mischief of it is, you can go no where but you meet with them.

Secondly, you are the greatest self-lovers alive. For ever since you were children, it was preached to you, that you should know yourselves. You have complied with this idle advice, and, upon examining, find a great many qualities, which those who possess cannot but like themselves the better for: and 'tis your misfortune to have them all!

Thirdly, it is insupportable impudence and lying in you, to pretend, as you do, to have no passion or tendency to love and good-nature. For can any thing be so preposterous, as to say you care for nobody, at the same time that you oblige and please every body?

For these, and all other your grievous offences, the Lord afford you his mercy, as I do heartily absolve you. *In nomine*, etc.

Mr. Gay was your servant yesterday: I believe to-day he may be Mrs. Lepell's.

LADY MARY WORTLEY MONTAGU *to* POPE[1]

28 *September* 1718

1763

Lyons, Sept. 28, O.S. 1718.

I received yours here, and should thank you for the pleasure you seem to enjoy from my return; but I can hardly forbear being angry at you, for rejoicing at what displeases me so much. You will think this but an odd compliment on my side. I'll assure you, 'tis not from insensibility of the joy of seeing my friends; but when I consider that I must, at the same time, see and hear a thousand disagreeable impertinents; that I must receive and pay visits, make curtesies, and assist at tea-tables, where I shall be half killed with questions; and, on the other part, that I am a creature, that cannot serve anybody but with insignificant good wishes; and that my presence is not a necessary good to any one member of my native country, I think I might much better have stay'd where ease and quiet made up the happiness of my indolent life.—I should certainly be melancholy, if I pursued this theme one line farther. I will rather fill the remainder of this paper, with the inscriptions on the tables of brass, that are placed on each side of the town-house.

[*Here were inserted three pages of Latin inscriptions, now omitted.*]

I was also shewed, without the gate of St. *Justinus*, some remains of a Roman aquæduct; and behind the monastery of St. *Mary*, there are the ruins of the Imperial palace, where the Emperor CLAUDIUS was born, and where SEVERUS lived. The great cathedral of St. *John* is a

[1] On the date of this letter and those beginning on pp. 519 and 522 see vol. v, p. 1.

good Gothick building, and its clock much admired by the Germans. In one of the most conspicuous parts of the town, is the late king's statue set up, trampling upon mankind. I cannot forbear saying one word here, of the French statues (for I never intend to mention any more of them) with their gilded full-bottomed wigs. If their King had intended to express in one image, *ignorance, ill taste, and vanity*, his sculptors could have made no other figure, so proper for that purpose, as this statue, which represents the odd mixture of an old *beau*, who had a mind to be a *hero*, with a bushel of curl'd hair on his head, and a gilt truncheon in his hand.—The French have been so voluminous on the history of this town, I need say nothing of it. The houses are tolerably well built, and the *Belle cour* well planted, from whence is seen the celebrated joining of the Soane and Rhone.

Ubi Rhodanus ingens amne prærapido fluit
Ararque dubitans quo suos fluctus agat.

I have had time to see every thing with great leisure, having been confin'd several days to this town by a swelling in my throat, the remains of a fever, occasioned by a cold I got in the damps of the Alps. The doctors here threaten me with all sorts of distempers, if I dare to leave them; but I, that know the obstinacy of it, think it just as possible to continue my way to Paris, with it, as to go about the streets of Lyons, and am determin'd to pursue my journey to-morrow, in spite of doctors, apothecaries and sore throats.

When you see Lady R—,[1] tell her I have received her letter, and will answer it from Paris, believing that the place that she would most willingly hear of. | I am, &c. &c.

FENTON *to* POPE

29 *September* 1718

Homer MSS. Add. 4808

September 29th 1718.

Sir,—I have just now receiv'd the inclos'd Papers from Cambridge;[2] be pleas'd to favour me with your Orders about the remaining Books, as they shall be with great pleasure executed by | Sir | Your most humble Servant. | E. Fenton

POPE *to* TERESA AND MARTHA BLOUNT

8 *October* [1718]

Mapledurham

Oakley-Bower, Oct. 8th

Dear Ladies,—Nothing but your having bid me write to you often, could make me do it again without an apology. I don't know where

[1] Doubtless Lady Rich.

[2] Probably Jortin's notes gleaned from Eustathius.

you are, or whether you have receivd my letters, but conclude this can't be disagreable to you unless you have alterd your minds, a thing which in Women I take to be impossible. Twill serve, if for nothing else, to give my Services to Mr Caryl (supposing you with him) if not, keep them yourselves; for Services (you know) are of that nature, that, like certain other common things, they'l fitt every body.

I am with my Lord Bathurst, at my Bower, in whose Groves we had yesterday a dry walk of three hours. It is the place that of all others I fancy, & I am not yet out of humour with it, tho I have had it some months: It does not cease to be agreable to me so late in the Season; the very dying of the leaves adds a variety of colours that is not unpleasant. I look upon it as upon a Beauty I once loved, whom I should preserve a Respect for, in her Decay. And as we should look upon a Friend, with remembrance how he pleas'd us once, tho now declin'd from his former gay and flourishing condition.

I write an hour or two every morning, then ride out a hunting upon the Downes, eat heartily, talk tender sentiments with Lord B. or draw Plans for Houses and Gardens, open Avenues, cut Glades, plant Firrs, contrive waterworks, all very fine and beautiful in our own imagination. At nights we play at Commerce, & play pretty high: I do more, I bett too; for I am really rich, and must throw away my money if no deserving Friend will use it. I like this course of life so well that I am resolvd to stay here, till I hear of some body's being in towne that is worth my coming after.[1]

Since you are so silent in the Country, I can't expect a word from you when you get to London: the first week must needs be wholly employd in making New Gowns, the second in showing them, the third in seeing other peoples, the fourth, fifth, & so on, in Balls, plays, assemblies, Operas, &c. How can a poor Translator and Harehunter hope for a Minute's memory? Yet He comforts himself to reflect that He shall be rememberd when people have forgot what colours you wore, and when those at whom you dress, shall be Dust! This is the Pride of a Poet, let me see if you dare owne what is the Pride of a Woman, perhaps one article of it may be, to despise those who think themselves of some value, and to show your friends you can live without thinking of 'em at all. Do, keep your own secrets, that such fellows as I may laugh at ye in the valley of Jehosaphat, where Cunning will be the foolishest thing in nature, & those white Bums which I dye to see, will be shown to all the world. Now what will it avail, Ladies, if you really should do something to make me wonder at, during the short course of this transitory Life? as long as I shall infallibly

[1] This can hardly refer to Lady Mary, who had arrived in town at least a week earlier. See vol. v, pp. 1–2. Note also Pope's recent visit to London (i. 517).

come to know, in the enlightend state of the next world, what was the real reason why you did not favour me with a line?

But I forget myself, I am talking as to Women, things that walk in the Country when possibly by this time you are got to London and are Goddesses: For how should ye be less when you are in your Heaven? If so, Most adorable Deities, most celestial Beauties, hear the often repeated invocations of a Poet expecting Immortality! So May no Complaints of unhappy mortals ever more disturb your eternal Diversions! But oh dear Angels! do not on any account Scratch your backsides: and oh heavnly Creatures! never leave the company to p—ss. Maintain your dignity blessed Saints! and scorn to reveal yourselves to Fools; (tho it be but fair play, for they reveal themselves to every body.) Goddesses must be all-sufficient, they can neither want a Friend nor a Correspondent: How arrogant a Wretch am I then, who resolve to be one of these (if not both) to you, as long as I have a Day to live? | Dear Ladies | Your most faithful, sincere Servant | A. Pope

*POPE *to* THE EARL OF BURLINGTON[1]

11 *October* [1718]

Chatsworth

Cicester, October the 11th.

My Lord,—I would always have so much regard to the Pleasures of any one I love, as not to trouble him with Business till I needs must. Therfore I never mentioned to your Lordship the Affair of my Building during your Amusements in the Country, designing to speak of it at your return to towne. But I would not longer now defer doing it, that you may not think me so poetical as not to know my own mind & inclination, which I faithfully assure you (my Lord) is to be obliged to you, & to be yours by as many titles as I can. I therfore beg you to know, I have Piqued myself upon being your Tenant in that piece of ground behind Burlington house (which is the Situation I am fond of to the last degree) & that nothing hinderd my building there this Summer, but finding upon the exactest enquiry, the expence Mr Campbell's[2] Proposal would have put me to, to be 200 pound above what I am pretty well assured I can build the same thing for. I promise you, my Lord, to build on the same Plan & Front with Lord Warwick's, so as not to clash with any regular design; & I beg you to believe me always in earnest in whatsoever I speak to your Lordship. I should not

[1] In the Homer MSS. (Add. 4808, f. 111*v*) is preserved the cover of a letter to Pope, postmarked 1/OC, and franked and addressed by Burlington. It is presumably in answer to that letter that Pope now writes.

[2] Colin Campbell, the architect (d. 1729), was a favourite of Lord Burlington. Pope's hesitation in building was in part due to the opinions of Lord Bathurst.

else in the least deserve to call myself (what upon my faith I am much more proud & pleased to call myself, than any thing else) | My Lord, | Your most sincere, most | obliged, & obedient Servant | A. Pope

I went to Town a Fortnight since, in no other view than the hopes to meet you; being miserably chain'd down to finishing Homer just now, which I was never able to do near London. I've almost got over my Task, & hope to wait upon you (I hate so ceremonious a word, I mean, to be perfectly easy in your company) in a Week.

POPE *to* TERESA BLOUNT[1] [*October* 1718]

Mapledurham

Dear Madam,—I send your book & have not forgot to give commission about the Lavender. I find I shall stay a little longer than I intended, my Mother being so much mended by Change of air, both as to her Cough and in Spirits, that she will meet me at Oxford, where she will see the place & return with me.

I could be glad to know certainly whether you will have the Coach I bought, or not? that I may either dispose of it or keep it accordingly. If your Objection be to the Standing, or care of it, this summer you shall not be troubled with any thought of it till Winter. Upon this, & all other such occasions, I can say but just this—Either you would have me your Friend, or you would not. If you would why do you refuse any Service I can do you? If you would not why do you ever receive any?

I have nothing to add but wish you all happiness, & to assure you I am | Dear Madam | Your most faithful | Servant | A. Pope

Address: To Mrs Teresa Blount.

POPE *to* CARYLL[2] 18 *October* 1718

Add. 28618

Oct. 18. (1718

I find by [the] Mrs Blounts, that I am obliged to you for a letter which I assure you has not come to my hands. I look upon it as no little loss when I miss of any expression of a friendship like yours, which extends, I know, far beyond the common ones of the world and is solicitous

[1] One assumes that this is written from Oakley Wood, which Pope is leaving for Oxford, where he will meet his mother (who comes from Stanton Harcourt), show her the place, and return with her to Chiswick. It should date about the middle of Oct. Pope evidently purchased a coach to facilitate his journeys from Stanton Harcourt and Cirencester, &c.

[2] Written apparently from either London or Chiswick. Pope has news of Caryll from the Blounts. The unclosed parenthesis before the year date may mean that Caryll added the year —which is in any case undoubted.

both for the earthly and heavenly felicity of those you love. A man thus befriended, is doubly obliged at once to your moral and Christian virtue, and it would be in such an one the greatest ingratitude to you if he were not in return as well a good man as a good friend. I have always unfeignedly wished for the well-being of your whole family, but I must be allowed to say I wish it still more, since I know how much you have obliged that of [the] Mrs Blounts, to which my best wishes have always been fixed. I thank you for loving them, for it confirms me I have been in the right. And it is a sort of generosity in me, not to envy you the pleasure which I find you have given them.

The interest you take in all that belongs to me will make it agreeable news to you, that I have in a manner finished the fifth volume of Homer. I have the satisfaction of finding that daring work less and less censured, and the last volumes generally allowed to be better done than the former, which yet no way raises my vanity, since it is only allowing [me] not to grow worse and worse.

Before I could see my Lord Burlington (who was as much upon the ramble as myself) I heard Mr Pulteney had agreed for Ladyholt.[1] I writ early to his lordship about it, but had no answer to that particular in his letters. Talking of business puts me in mind of desiring to know of you whether any payment has been made within this year past of the rents of the Hôtel de Ville in Paris? And of putting you in mind how long I have been indebted to [you] for those gifts of Bacchus which I have ungratefully enjoyed without repaying my benefactor, or asking what I owe you for the wines. I beg when you think fit, to deduct that account from the sum there is between us, and to return me only the remainder.

I was but one night in London the last month, when I went to Mr Tempest's,[2] and sent the next morning to inquire if you were returned from Ingatestone[3] (as I doubted), but had the ill luck to miss of you. I very much desire to see you, and if I have any intimation of your being in town nothing shall hinder my meeting you. I am always | Dear sir | yours most faithfully. | A: P:

POPE *to* THOMAS DANCASTLE 25 *October* [1718]

Arthur A. Houghton, Jr.

Chiswick, Oct. 25 [1718]

This last fine Week has made me goe about from Village to Village in my flying chariot, to take my last leave of the Country for this year.

[1] After the death of his son John evidently the father wished to lease Ladyholt.

[2] On Tempest see Pope to Caryll, 30 June 1717, here on p. 414.

[3] Lord Petre lived at Ingatestone, where, so Elwin tells us, Caryll was on 15 Sept. He returned to London on the 25th, and Pope evidently just missed seeing him there on the one night he was in town in September. See To Burlington, 11 Oct. (postscript).

And that hinderd my writing to thank you for the Copies you sent me. I have those of the 17 & 18th, with the odd leaves brought by my Sister, which will be returnd you at her return. In the meantime you'l oblige me by sending the foul papers of the 2 first books by the Ockingham Coach.

As soon as I have acknowledg'd a favor from one of you, I receive one from another. The Grapes from your Brother came safely t'other day, and *Are no more* (to speak poetically, that is, they are eaten: but the Gratitude due for such fine fruit is not departed with them: I most thankfully acknowledge His, and Their, great goodness.

I very much want to see you both, & it was against my conscience I past lately thro' Maidenhead, without deviating into the Forest. But it was in a Stage-coach,[1] wherein no man ought to be accounted a Free Agent.

Here is good Mrs Racket in a melancholy way for want of your good company: she says Chiswick is a very lonely place in comparison of Hallgrove; where, & whereabouts, there are kept above 20 Coaches, besides Stages on the Heath which are without number. This very moment she is in great distress, the Spout of her Tea-pot being stoppd, & she in impatient expectation of that Due Benevolence it ought to dispense for her Breakfast.

You will hereby perceive, that this is written in that Part of the day which the Ancients accounted holy, namely early in the morning: Breakfast (a sacred Rite, & of great antiquity) calls upon me, the Coffee smokes less & less, & tells me it will speedily be cold, unless I conclude this letter; which I obediently do, & in assuring you of a sincere truth, that I am Mr Dancastle's & | Dear Sir | Your most faithfull affectionate Servant | A. Pope

LADY MARY WORTLEY MONTAGU *to* POPE[2]

[*October* 1718]

1767

I have been running about Paris at a strange rate with my sister, and strange sights have we seen. They are, at least, strange sights to me, for after having been accustomed to the gravity of Turks, I can scarce look with an easy and familiar aspect at the levity and agility of the

[1] From this remark one assumes that Teresa did not accept Pope's own coach (see to Miss Blount before 18 Oct.), and that it was perhaps sold in Oxford. Pope's equipage in Twickenham seems to have been a 'chariot' drawn by two horses. See Edward Blount to Pope, 30 Aug. 1719.

[2] This letter was printed in *An Additional Volume to the Letters of . . . Lady M—y W—y M—e* (1767) under the heading 'To Mr. P.' The letters in this volume are said to be of doubtful authenticity, and of course 'Mr. P.' may not have been Mr. Pope; but the letter is here reprinted, as it has been in other editions of modern times. It seems at face value authentic, but on its date see vol. v, pp. 1–2.

airy phantoms that are dancing about me here, and I often think that I am at a puppet-shew amidst the representations of real life. I stare prodigiously, but no body remarks it, for every body stares here; staring is à-la mode—there is a stare of attention and *interêt*, a stare of curiosity, a stare of expectation, a stare of surprize, and it would greatly amuse you to see what trifling objects excite all this staring. This staring would have rather a solemn kind of air, were it not alleviated by grinning, for at the end of a stare there comes always a grin, and very commonly the entrance of a gentleman or lady into a room is accompanied with a grin, which is designed to express complacence and social pleasure, but really shews nothing more than a certain contortion of muscles that must make a stranger laugh really, as they laugh artificially. The French grin is equally remote from the chearful serenity of a smile, and the cordial mirth of an honest English horse-laugh. I shall not perhaps stay here long enough to form a just idea of French manners and characters, tho' this I believe would require but little study, as there is no great depth in either. It appears, on a superficial view, to be a frivolous, restless, agreeable people. The Abbot is my guide, and I could not easily light upon a better; he tells me that here the women form the character of the men, and I am convinced in the persuasion of this by every company into which I enter. There seems here to be no intermediate state between infancy and manhood; for as soon as the boy has quit his leading-strings, he is set agog in the world; the ladies are his tutors, they make the first impressions, which generally remain, and they render the men ridiculous by the imitation of their humours and graces, so that dignity in manners is a rare thing here before the age of sixty. Does not King David say somewhere, that *Man walketh in a vain shew*? I think he does, and I am sure this is peculiarly true of the French man—but he walks merrily and seems to enjoy the vision, and may he not therefore be esteemed more happy than many of our solid thinkers whose brows are furrowed by deep reflexion, and whose wisdom is so often clothed with a misty mantle of spleen and vapours?

What delights me most here is a view of the magnificence often accompanied with taste that reigns in the King's palaces and gardens; for tho' I don't admire much the architecture, in which there is great irregularity and want of proportion, yet the statues, paintings, and other decorations afford me high entertainment. One of the pieces of antiquity that struck me most in the gardens of Versailles was the famous Collossean statue of Jupiter, the workmanship of Myron, which Mark Antony carried away from Samos, and Augustus ordered to be placed in the Capitol. It is of Parian marble, and though it has suffered in the ruin of time, it still preserves striking lines of majesty. But surely, if marble could feel, the God would frown with a generous indignation to see himself transported from the Capitol into a French garden; and after having received the homage of the Roman emperors who laid their laurels at his feet when they returned from their conquests, to behold now nothing but frizzled beaus passing by him with indifference.

I propose setting out soon from this place,[1] so that you are to expect no more letters from this side of the water; besides I am hurried to death, and my head swims with that vast variety of objects which I am obliged to view with such rapidity, the shortness of my time not allowing me to examine them at my leisure. There is here an excessive prodigality of ornaments and decorations, that is just the opposite extreme to what appears in our royal gardens; this prodigality is owing to the levity and inconstancy of the French taste, which always pants after something new, and thus heaps ornament upon ornament without end or measure. It is time, however, that I should put an end to my letter; so I wish you good night, | And am, &c.

*MATTHEW PRIOR *to* POPE[2] [1718?]

Fitzwilliam Museum, Cambridge

Tuesday

If Mr. Pope be not engaged for to Morrow Night He will do me a great favour in meeting Mr Lewis at my house about Seven to confer upon the premises with Jacob Tonson and finish a piece of friendship which Mr Pope has very generously begun to his humble Servant M. Prior

*POPE *to* FORD[3] [1718?]

The Pierpont Morgan Library

I write this to give you timely notice, that the Duke of Buckingham having heard of Mr Priors & Our Meeting, desires it may be at his Grace's house, next Munday at Six in the Evening (the Time appointed by you) I beg you to pre-ingage Mr Gay. As for my own part, I shall goe to London on purpose that day. In the meantime

[1] The Wortley Montagus arrived in London not later than 2 Oct. 1718. See vol. v, pp. 1–2.

[2] This letter dates after 12 Jan. 1716/17 when Erasmus Lewis wrote to Swift reporting the decision of himself and guests (Pope, Gay, and Prior) to aid Prior in bringing out a subscription edition of his poems. It dates before the publication of the *Poems* in Mar. 1718/19. The word *finish* suggests late 1718, but is slender evidence.

[3] This undatable letter falls in the period during which Prior's friends were advising about his folio *Poems*, i.e. about the year 1718. It may refer to the same meeting as that projected in the letter immediately preceding or to some unknown meeting. It may possibly be the *convivium poeticum* mentioned by Prior in his letter to Lord Harley, 16 June 1720 (*Hist. MSS. Comm.*, *Bath MSS.* iii (1908), 482); but that was a dinner-party, and in Pope's day one did not dine as late as 6 p.m.

believe me | Dear Sir | Your most faithful, | most obedient Servant, | A. Pope.

Twick'nham, | Wensday.

Address: To Charles Ford, Esqr at | Mr Hoyes's, at the blew Periwig | Pall-Mall.

Endorsement: A. Pope

POPE *to* CARYLL[1] [*November* 1718?]

Add. 28618

Meeting with the gentleman who has been to wait on you in relation to Mrs Cope's affair, I find that her husband is very suddenly to go back to his command, and that her relief will be almost impracticable if not attempted before. The Board of Officers will not meddle in a family concern, and people of skill in these matters assure me that the only method is to procure a writ from the chancery *Ne exeat regno*, which may be had for a trifle, and will so far distress him as to oblige him to find bail, and bring him to some composition, not to be hindered from going abroad. If once he is over, you'll be obliged to a prosecution of more trouble and time; or he will not allow her a groat (as he has declared). I cannot but lay before you this case which is of the last importance to the poor lady, and indeed must affect any charitable man. The gentleman[2] (who desires to see you tonight at nine at your lodgings) is acted purely by that humanity which is inherent to his family. And I doubt not the same humanity will prompt you to assist so melancholy a circumstance, as it has been ever the distinguishing character of your self in particular. I beg you to believe I am at all hours | Dear sir | Your most faithful and most | Affectionate humble Servant | A.P.

Wednesday morning.

LADY MARY WORTLEY MONTAGU *to* POPE[3] [*September*] 1718

1763

Dover, Novr. 1, O.S. 1718.

I have this minute received a letter of yours sent me from Paris. I

[1] Elwin dated this letter [November 1718], without giving his reasons. Since he may have had evidence not known to the present editor the date is allowed to stand—but with strong reservations. It seems to be written at a time when Caryll was in London, but Pope's letter of 18 Oct. to Caryll indicates that Caryll had been in London late in September and had left. Is there evidence that he was back again in November? Dilke in *The Athenaeum*, 22 July 1854 (reprinted in *Papers of a Critic*, i. 142), conjectured the date as 1715 or 1716.

[2] Possibly Mrs. Cope's brother.

[3] In answer to Pope's letter of 1 Sept., but her date is evidently wrong. See vol. v, pp. 1–2. If amidst confused attempts 'to regulate our march to London, bag and baggage' Lady Mary fails to show the tearful tenderness that Pope's letter had ascribed to her, one may excuse her callousness by her preoccupied situation.

believe and hope I shall very soon see both you and Mr. *Congreve*; but as I am here in an inn, where we stay to regulate our march to London, bag and baggage, I shall employ some of my leisure time in answering that part of yours that seems to require an answer.

I must applaud your good nature in supposing that your pastoral lovers, (vulgarly called Haymakers) would have lived in everlasting joy and harmony, if the lightning had not interrupted their scheme of happiness. I see no reason to imagine that *John Hughes* and *Sarah Drew* were either wiser or more virtuous than their neighbours. That a well-set man of twenty-five should have a fancy to marry a brown woman of eighteen, is nothing marvellous; and I cannot help thinking that had they married, their lives would have passed in the common track with their fellow-parishioners. His endeavouring to shield her from a storm was a natural action, and what he would have certainly done for his horse, if he had been in the same situation. Neither am I of opinion that their sudden death was a reward of their mutual virtue. You know the Jews were reprov'd for thinking a village destroyed by fire, more wicked than those that had escaped the thunder. Time and chance happen to all men. Since you desire me to try my skill in an *epitaph*, I think the following lines perhaps more just, tho' not so poetical as yours.

Here lies John Hughes and Sarah Drew;
Perhaps you'll say, What's that to you?
Believe me, friend, much may be said
On that poor couple that are dead.
On Sunday next they should have married;
But see how oddly things are carried!
On Thursday last it rain'd and lighten'd,
These tender lovers sadly frighten'd,
Shelter'd beneath the cocking hay
In hopes to pass the time away.
But the BOLD THUNDER found them out
(Commission'd for that end no doubt)
And seizing on their trembling breath,
Consign'd them to the shades of death.
Who knows if 'twas not kindly done?
For had they seen the next year's sun,
A beaten wife and cuckold swain
Had jointly curs'd the marriage chain;
Now they are happy in their doom,
FOR POPE HAS WROTE UPON THEIR TOMB.

I confess these sentiments are not altogether so heroic as yours; but I hope you will forgive them in favour of the two last lines. You see how much I esteem the honour you have done them; tho' I am not very impatient to have the same, and had rather continue to be your stupid, *living*, humble servant, than be *celebrated* by all the pens in Europe.

I would write to Mr. C—; but suppose you will read this to him if he enquires after me.

*POPE *to* THOMAS DANCASTLE 16 *December* 1718

Arthur A. Houghton, Jr.

Chiswick Decr 16. 1718

I am afraid, by what you say in yours, that you never receivd a letter of mine sent about 3 weeks since to thank you for your kind trouble on my account this year. I have been out of town some days, which has yet hindred my seeing your good Brother. And am still so taken up in scribbling notes, that I can hardly pay common Civilityes to any of my friends.

Nurse is not a little concernd that the Parish officers can question whether any of her Rent was received before? The last Overseers never paid her; Taylor & Osborn promisd it, but never payd. So that forty shillings is due to her from the Parish this Christmass, of which she hopes, by your assistance, not to be defrauded. She had nothing the last Easter.

I am dull enough (after a whole days fatigue) to have nothing to say except to wish you a merry Christmass. But I am not so totally dead to all past obligations, as not yet to remember how many woodcocks you have indulgd me in about this Season, when we drank metheglin & chatted together. I really wish myself a few frosty days in the forest. I shall always be (I assure you) with Ancient fidelity and affection | Dear Sir | Your ever obliged | & faithful Friend | & Servant | A. Pope.

My Mother is most heartily yours:
Service to all at Halgrove, with decent thanks for certain Puddings.

Address: To Mr Thomas Dancastle | at Binfield near | Ockingham | Berks. Carriage paid.

Endorsement: from A. Pope. | 1718.